Lecture Notes in Computer Science　　　10717

Commenced Publication in 1973
Founding and Former Series Editors:
Gerhard Goos, Juris Hartmanis, and Jan van Leeuwen

Editorial Board

More information about this series at http://www.springer.com/series/7410

Rudrapatna K. Shyamasundar · Virendra Singh
Jaideep Vaidya (Eds.)

Information Systems Security

13th International Conference, ICISS 2017
Mumbai, India, December 16–20, 2017
Proceedings

 Springer

Editors
Rudrapatna K. Shyamasundar
Indian Institute of Technology Bombay
Mumbai
India

Jaideep Vaidya
Rutgers University
Newark, NJ
USA

Virendra Singh
Indian Institute of Technology Bombay
Mumbai
India

ISSN 0302-9743   ISSN 1611-3349   (electronic)
Lecture Notes in Computer Science
ISBN 978-3-319-72597-0   ISBN 978-3-319-72598-7   (eBook)
https://doi.org/10.1007/978-3-319-72598-7

Library of Congress Control Number: 2017961798

LNCS Sublibrary: SL4 – Security and Cryptology

Printed on acid-free paper

This Springer imprint is published by Springer Nature
The registered company is Springer International Publishing AG
The registered company address is: Gewerbestrasse 11, 6330 Cham, Switzerland

Preface

This volume contains the papers selected for presentation at the 13th International Conference on Information Systems Security (ICISS 2017), held in Mumbai, Maharashtra, India, during December 16–20, 2017. In response to the call for papers of this edition, 73 submissions were received, and all submissions were evaluated on the basis of their significance, novelty, and technical quality. After an initial technical screening for relevance, 64 of the papers were reviewed by the Program Committee. The Program Committee, which comprised 52 members, performed an excellent task and with the help of additional reviewers all submissions went through a careful anonymous review process. Each paper was reviewed by three or more reviewers, and then discussed. The entire process was carried out electronically, and after intensive discussions, 16 full papers and seven short papers were selected for presentation at the conference, covering a range of topics including privacy, network security, systems security, security analysis, identity management, and access control, among others.

We were fortunate to have four eminent speakers delivering keynote presentations at the conference: Sushil Jajodia (George Mason University), Stefano Zatti (European Space Agency), Prof. Luigi Vincenzo Mancini (University of Rome), and Gulshan Rai (National Cyber Security Coordinator, India). It is indeed our pleasure to formally express our gratitude to these speakers who came from far off places under a tight schedule. We also thank Dr. Stefano Zatti (Head, of the ESA Security Office) and Prof. Luigi Mancini, who also contributed to the proceedings.

The success of ICISS 2017 depended on the volunteering effort of many individuals, and there is a long list of people who deserve special thanks. We would like to thank all the members of the Program Committee and all the external reviewers, for all their hard work in evaluating the papers and for their active participation in the discussion and selection process. We are very grateful to everyone who gave their assistance and ensured a smooth organization process, in particular the Steering Committee and Prof. Sushil Jajodia for his guidance and support as well as Yuan Hong (Publicity Chair) for helping with publicity. Special thanks go to the keynote speakers, who accepted our invitation to deliver keynote talks at the conference.

There were several tutorials and preconference workshops. This year there was the Second Workshop on Blockchain Technology: Platforms, Applications and Challenges on December 17, as well as several tutorials on topics such as access control, using mathematics for security, and AI and security.

It is a pleasure to thank the support from DST (JC Bose Fellowship to R. K. Shyamasundar) and the support of MEITY for the ISRDC center at IIT Bombay. We are thankful for the institutional support provided by IIT Bombay, in particular the support of the staff, faculty, and student volunteers of the Department of Computer Science and Engineering and the Department of Electrical Engineering. We appreciate the support of Springer, in particular Alfred Hofmann, in publishing the proceedings as well as monetarily supporting the best paper award for the conference. We would also like to acknowledge EasyChair for their conference management system, which was freely used to manage the process of paper submissions and reviews. Last but certainly not least, we would like to thank all the authors who submitted papers and all the conference attendees. We hope you find the proceedings of ICISS 2017 interesting, stimulating, and inspiring for your future research.

November 2017   Rudrapatna K. Shyamasundar
                                                        Virendra Singh
                                                        Jaideep Vaidya

Organization

Program Committee

Claudio Ardagna	Università degli Studi di Milano, Italy
Vijay Atluri	Rutgers University, USA
Aditya Bagchi	Ramakrishna Mission Vivekananda University, India
Anirban Basu	KDDI Research, Inc., Japan
Bogdan Carbunar	Florida International University, USA
Rajat Subhra Chakraborty	IIT Kharagpur, India
Sanjit Chatterjee	Indian Institute of Science, India
Mauro Conti	University of Padua, Italy
Frédéric Cuppens	Telecom Bretagne, Institut Mines-Telecom, France
Nora Cuppens	Telecom Bretagne, Institut Mines-Telecom, France
Manik Lal Das	DA-IICT, India
Sabrina De Capitani di Vimercati	Università degli Studi di Milano, Italy
Mohan Dhawan	IBM, India
Changyu Dong	Newcastle University, UK
Wenliang Du	Syracuse University, USA
Sara Foresti	Università degli Studi di Milano, Italy
Manoj Gaur	IIT Jammu, India
Vikram Goyal	IIIT-Delhi, India
Yuan Hong	Illinois Institute of Technology, USA
Sushil Jajodia	George Mason University, USA
Wei Jiang	Missouri University of Science and Technology, USA
Murat Kantarcioglu	University of Texas at Dallas, USA
Aniket Kate	Purdue University
Ram Krishnan	University of Texas at San Antonio, USA
Ashish Kundu	IBM Research, USA
Peng Liu	The Pennsylvania State University, USA
Haibing Lu	Santa Clara University, USA
Chandan Mazumdar	Jadavpur University, India
Barsha Mitra	BITS Pilani Hyderabad Campus, India
Prateek Mittal	Princeton University, USA
Samrat Mondal	Indian Institute of Technology Patna, India
Sukumar Nandi	Indian Institute of Technology Guwahati, India
Eiji Okamoto	University of Tsukuba, Japan
Atul Prakash	University of Michigan, USA
R. Ramanujam	Institute of Mathematical Sciences, Chennai, India
Kai Rannenberg	Goethe University Frankfurt, Germany
Chester Rebeiro	IIT Madras, India

Bharath Kumar Samanthula	Montclair State University, USA
Pierangela Samarati	Università degli Studi di Milano, Italy
Somitra Sanadhya	IIT Ropar, India
Anirban Sengupta	CDC-JU, India
Edoardo Serra	Boise State University, USA
Basit Shafiq	Lahore University of Management Sciences, Pakistan
Sandeep Shukla	Indian Institute of Technology Kanpur (IIT Kanpur), India
Rudrapatna Shyamasundar	IIT Bombay, India
Virendra Singh	Indian Institute of Technology (IIT) Bombay, India
Anoop Singhal	NIST, USA
Scott D. Stoller	Stony Brook University, USA
Shamik Sural	IIT Kharagpur, India
Mahesh Tripunitara	University of Waterloo
Jaideep Vaidya	Rutgers University, USA
Cong Wang	City University of Hong Kong, Hong Kong, SAR China
Lingyu Wang	Concordia University, Canada
Wendy Hui Wang	Stevens Institute of Technology, USA
Meng Yu	University of Texas at San Antonio, USA
Ting Yu	Qatar Computing Research Institute, Qatar

Additional Reviewers

Ahlawat, Amit	Li, Yanying
Akowuah, Francis	Mukherjee, Sayantan
Baskar, A.	S, Venkatesan
Bhandari, Shweta	Shafiq, Basit
Biondo, Andrea	Srivastava, Shubham Sahai
Cao, Chen	Sun, Haipei
Dong, Boxiang	Sundararajan, Vaishnavi
Gajrani, Jyoti	Vairam, Prasanna Karthik
Gangwal, Ankit	Veseli, Fatbardh
Guo, Pinyao	Wijesekera, Duminda
Hamm, Peter	Yesuf, Ahmed Seid
Krishnakumar, Gnanambikai	Ying, Kailiang
Kumar, Shravan	Zhang, Bo

Contents

Network Security

Invited Papers

The Protection of Space Missions: Threats and Cyber Threats

Stefano Zatti[(✉)]

European Space Agency Security Office, 00044 Frascati, Italy
Stefano.Zatti@esa.int

Abstract. Space-based systems play an important role in our daily life and business. The trend is likely to rely on the use of space based systems in a growing number of services or applications that can be either safety-of-life critical or business and mission-critical. The security measures implemented in space-based systems may turn out to be insufficient to guarantee the information assurance properties, in particular confidentiality (if required by the data policy), availability and integrity of these services/applications. The various and possible cyber-attacks on space segments, ground stations and its control segments are meanwhile well known and experienced in many cases.

This paper will first introduce ESA and its constituency, then address the security specific aspects of its space missions. Threats specific to them from the cyberspace will be introduced, and the possible countermeasures briefly addressed. A categorization of the different types of space missions will then lead to the creation of the different protections profiles to be implemented respectively for the different categories.

Keywords: Space missions · Threats · Countermeasures

1 Introduction: The European Space Agency and Its Missions

The European Space Agency, ESA, was founded in 1975 by merging two existing launch and space research organization, with the aim expressed in article 2 of the ESA Convention "To provide for and promote, for exclusively peaceful purposes, cooperation among European states in space research and technology and their space applications." Composed of 22 Member States, with eight sites/facilities in Europe, about 2200 staff, ESA has in the course of its lifetime designed, tested and operated in flight over 80 satellites.

2 A Security-Flavoured Space

Although they are designed and for peaceful purposes, the space missions of ESA can indeed present security aspects and address security elements.

Such critical elements of space missions can influence the level of sensitivity and consequently the level of threats, each on of those space missions have to face. In

© Springer International Publishing AG 2017
R. K. Shyamasundar et al. (Eds.): ICISS 2017, LNCS 10717, pp. 3–8, 2017.
https://doi.org/10.1007/978-3-319-72598-7_1

particular, the following aspects of "security from space" have been highlighted by the ESA Council as critical for the benefit of European Citizens, leading to the development of specific missions to address them:

Security on Earth

- Critical Infrastructures Protection
- Maritime surveillance
- Land surveillance
- Humanitarian crisis support and rescue tasks
- Public Safety (incl. Civil Protection)
- Other Emergent security threats (e.g., climate change)

Security in Space

- Space situational awareness, i.e., real time information of the status of specific objects in space
  - Near-Earth Objects: asteroids, meteorites, in the vicinity of our planet.
  - Space weather: phenomena out ide the atmosphere that can affect the Earth, like solar wind.
  - Satellite tracking: knowledge of position and trajectory and speed of the man-made objects, active and inactive, circling around our planet.

3 Hacking in Space: Astro-Hackers?

In the past, in order to reach a satellite in orbit to threaten its function, it would have been necessary for the adversary to build or possess an infrastructure to send tele-commands, an expensive and massively complex endeavour. Nowadays, via the omni-pervasive access networks all connected to the Internet, it is sufficient for a hacker to tamper with and bypass the existing protection measures … And this is not just science fiction, cases exist and are documented.

Some unclassified examples from open literature include:

- In 1998, the German-US ROSAT space telescope inexplicably turned towards the Sun, irreversibly damaging a critical optical sensor, following a cyber-intrusion at the Goddard Space Flight Center of NASA in the US.
- On October 20, 2007, Landsat 7 experienced 12 or more minutes of interference. Again, on July 23, 2008, it experienced other 12 min of interference. The responsible party did not achieve all steps required to command the satellite, but the service was disturbed.
- In 2008, NASA EOS AM–1 satellite experienced two events of disrupted control: in both cases, the attacker achieved all steps required to command the satellite, but did not issue commands.

These cases made the news, as shown in Fig. 1.

Fig. 1. A news post on Mail Online of 2011, reporting on hacking of US government satellites in 2008

Some more cases are documented in the following figures, that are grouped by the categories of the missions that were affected (Figs. 2, 3 and 4).

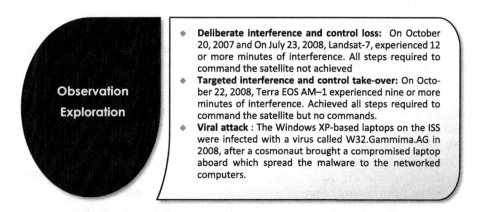

Fig. 2. Cyber attacks on missions of Observation and Exploration

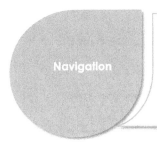

    ◆ **Denial of service** : On January 2010, a software update of the GPS Ground Segment caused a denial of service. Impact observed on 8,000 to 10,000 military receivers during several days

    ◆ **Spoofing:** In 2009, a group of students at the University of Texas at Austin successfully tested a GPS spoofing device to remotely redirect an $80 million yacht

Fig. 3. Cyber attacks on missions of Navigation.

    ◆ **Deliberate Jamming** : ARABSAT "Deliberate jamming incidents have dramatically increased in 2012 which indeed put a threat on services over Satellites"

    ◆ **Unauthorized access** : The conjunction of open standard and cheap DVB cards for computer made possible the rise of Open Source Software dealing with the automated capture of image flow or data flow, for Private Person As a consequence, a "radio ham" captured the pictures/video of the NATO surveillance flights, during the Balkan War, as they were using an insecure satellite link.

Fig. 4. Cyber attacks on missions of Telecommunications.

4   Threats and Countermeasures

The infrastructures supporting space missions can be characterized by a *Ground Segment, a Space Segment, and a Control Segment.* The control segment is used by the mission controllers, who issue Telecommands (TC) that via the ground segment can be uploaded all the way up to the space segment, a set of spacecraft that circles in space at possibly different altitudes, depending on the mission type. In the other direction, the spacecraft send back to Earth Housekeeping Telemetry (HKTM) to indicate the status of the various instruments and on-board parameters, and the Payload, that is the *raison d'etre* of the mission.

The threats that can face a spacecraft in orbit can be characterised by the different ways that adversaries can use to tamper with the Telecommands that are normally sent from the on-Earth control centre to the spacecraft to perform specific mission related actions, and with the data that returns to Earth, be it either payload related to the mission or house-keeping telemetry that informs ground control of the status of the instruments on board.

5   End-to-End Cybersecurity

In order to ensure the proper protection of all the assets related to a space missions, the segments described above, material and human, as well the mission data, it is necessary to tackle the various aspects of security as a process that spans end-to-end.

This implies the consideration of the security pillars and the respective counter-measures, as follows.

- Physical: zoning, access control for data centers, perimeter and internal fencing
- Personnel: vetting, clearances, trust, peer control
- Information protection: classified vs unclassified data and parameters
- Information assurance (IA) properties:
  - Confidentiality - encryption
  - Integrity - MAC
  - Availability - redundancy
  - Authenticity - identity management, cross check, access control, signature of data
  - Non-repudiation - notarization, certificates

It is essential, in order to be able to apply security measures on the ground-to-orbit link, that a set of cryptographic functionalities is installed on board, what normally goes simply under the term "Crypto-chip", before the launch. This function is able to perform on the Telecommands and on the Telemetry all the functions necessary to implement the Information Assurance properties, as required by the mission designers on the basis of the risk assessment specific to that mission (see next section).

In addition, some missions may require that also the payload should be protected (property of Confidentiality). This implies the encryption of the whole payload, with the consequent need to renew the keys used for the encryption on a periodic basis, determined by the amount of the data to be transmitted.

6 Mission Categories and Security Protection Profiles

There is a difference in the threats that different categories of mission can be subject to. Different mission types have actually different security requirements based on the need to protect one or more of the five property of Information Assurance, plus and with priority the well-being of humans (Safety of life applications and manned spaceflight).

Missions categorized by different categories of risks, with increasing depth and level of concerns:

- Scientific
- Earth Observation
- Navigation
- Communications
- Space Situational Awareness
- Manned spaceflight and exploration

In order to approach the cyber-security of missions in a systematic way leading to a streamlined engineering, five different protection profiles of Tele-commands and Telemetry have been developed, to be applied to the different mission categories (from 0 to 4).

Profile 0: No specific security
   No TC authentication and encryption
   No House-Keeping Telemetry or science data encryption
   Standard terrestrial links security (firewalls, IDP, SIEM etc.…)
   Implemented in ERS/ENVISAT and Earth Explorers
Profile 1: Static Tele Command protection
   TC authentication and anti-replay
   Authentication key pre-loaded on board
   TC authentication can be enabled/disabled automatically or by ground
   Currently implemented on MetOp and ATV
Profile 2: Dynamic TC protection
   TC authentication and anti-replay
   Authentication keys are loaded by ground using preinstalled Master Keys for the
   encryption of the related TCs
   TC authentication can be enabled/disabled automatically or by ground
   Implemented in the Sentinels of the Copernicus programme.
Profile 3: Dynamic TC + payload data protection
   Payload data is encrypted
   4 types of keys: Master key, TC authentication key, payload data encryption
   key, TC encryption key
   Payload data encryption can be enabled/disabled automatically or by ground
Profile 4: Dynamic TC + payload + HKTM data protection
   HKTM data is also encrypted
   5 types of keys: Master key, TC authentication key, data encryption key, HKTM
   data encryption key, TC encryption key
   HKTM data encryption can be enabled/disabled automatically or by ground

7 Conclusions: New Space – New Cyber Threats!

- The cybersecurity of space missions is a matter of competiveness for the European space industry, and, at the same time, is a vital subject for the European Union, as owner of the Copernicus and Galileo programmes.
- The need to guarantee high production rates (e.g. 4 satellites per day in the case of the densest constellations) requires the system integrators to stretch globally the existing supply chain, and to include new components providers.
- The globalization of manufacturing capabilities and the increased reliance upon commodity software and hardware for space and ground segments has expanded the opportunities for malicious modification in a manner that could compromise critical functionality. This is introducing additional risks.

SOF on Trial. The Technical and Legal Value of Battlefield Digital Forensics in Court

Luigi V. Mancini[✉], Andrea Monti, and Agostino Panico

Dipartimento di Informatica, Sapienza University Roma, 00198 Rome, Italy
mancini@di.uniroma1.it

Abstract. The transition from "ordinary" or "civil" digital forensics to battle-field digital forensics is characterized by the inclusion of the "time" variable into the equation that describes the process of finding, selecting and securing information gathered during forensics activities. While in some cases (such as the post-factum investigation of the Military Police) there may indeed be time to follow usual standard forensics methods, as soon as the scenario turns into an emergency response or a Special Operations Forces (SOF) intervention, it may be difficult to do so. Therefore, the digital forensics best practices developed for the ordinary civil and criminal proceedings as well as its legal value must be re-thought and adapted to the different scenarios of deployment.

But does this latter statement mean that the technical standards should be less stringent and that Battlefield Digital Forensics has a lesser or no legal status when its outcomes will be judged in Court?

The aim of this paper is to try to answer these questions, challenging first the common assumption that there is only "one" way to define the robustness of digital forensics outcomes. Furthermore, the paper advocates that the value of these outcomes should be assessed on a relative, comparative way, setting the level of acceptance per actual operating scenario.

In other words: it is desirable that laboratory-performed digital forensics should match very strict technical procedures to be accepted as a scientific method in Court. But when evidence is gathered under duress and/or with limited technological support, the technical level of the digital forensics techniques and procedures should be adapted accordingly, while preserving its full legal value in a trial.

To draw in the clearest possible way all these distinctions and provide technical advice to the operators in the field, this paper starts with a classification of the kind of operations performed in a battlefield theatre, making a distinction among military operations, MP investigations, and International Criminal Court (ICC) trials. Then, it moves to a taxonomy of the rules of evidence set forth by the ICC and advocates that the technical standards that should be acceptable as evidence-supporting could be less stringent than those usually required in ordinary trials.

The second part of the paper describes the technical implications of the above-mentioned conclusion, by providing both a framework and technical suggestion to be implemented in battlefield operation.

Keywords: Digital forensics · Battlefield digital forensics
Special Operations Forces

© Springer International Publishing AG 2017
R. K. Shyamasundar et al. (Eds.): ICISS 2017, LNCS 10717, pp. 9–26, 2017.
https://doi.org/10.1007/978-3-319-72598-7_2

1 Introduction

While "Computer Forensics" may be defined in several ways, for the purposes of this paper, we will use a functional approach that defines it as a system of processes, methods and tools able to guarantee the integrity and inalterability of the data held in (either volatile or nonvolatile) storage.

Of course, there are other activities belonging to the realm of Computer Forensics such as (just to name a few) data recovery, log analysis and incident handling and response. Nonetheless, since we are only discussing the legal status of the evidence acquired from storage, it is safe to adopt a rather narrow definition.

Also, this paper focuses on purely military operations that either directly target digital information or acquire digital information as a byproduct of a "traditional" action. The complexity of the geopolitical evolution, and in particular the fact that even political leaders sometimes may arrested and tried within their own country or by the International Criminal Court lead to the direct involvement of the military as a supporting force in those places where the local authorities are not able to secure the wanted men to the Justice. On the other hand, military-peacekeeping operations can lead to the discovery of crimes against humanity or other forms of criminal actions that are of interest of local or international prosecutors.

While the Computer Forensics techniques can be employed in several tactical scenarios, this paper examines a specific subsection of military-based Computer Forensics (from now on, "Battlefield Digital Forensics" or "BDF"), that is: the activities of Special Operations Forces, Tier 1 forces. The reason of this choice is that Tier1 forces represent the worst-case scenario in terms of resource constraints and the time duration of the operation, hence the legal-technical solutions identified for BDF of Tier 1 could be applied to Tier2 and 3, possibly relaxing and simplifying some of the steps identified. Note that Tier2 and Tier3 forces are often deployed in scenarios where time constraint is not a relevant variable and their target is not necessarily "critical" in terms of evidence gathering. In other words, Tier 1 operators act in a very selective way, against targets whose apprehension can lead to evidence gathering to be assessed by the intelligence circles. This is true, too, when Tier 1 operators are deployed as possible support for the activities of the International Criminal Court like in the case of Slobodan Milosevic apprehension in June 2001.

As will be apparent in the next Sections the bare minimum that should be granted, as a Best Practice for BDF, is the indisputable attribution of the digital evidence collected by SOF or other military operators to the defendant. However, the battle-related chain of data custody, that is one of the means that allows the attribution of the evidence, should still be granted but, clearly, under a less strict standard because of the operating conditions of SOF operations. In other words, the impossibility of follow each and every step set forth by the best practice for the secure collection of evidence might be caused by the harshness of the operating conditions, that don't put the operators at liberty of using - for instance - fast blocks to avoid accidental data writing or complex hash-generating tools to protect the data from possible tampering.

The main contributions of this paper are summarized as follows:

- to investigate whether the best practices of lab-based computer forensics are still valid when information have to be collected in an emergency situation;
- to advocate that computer-forensics best practices in military-gathered information should be adapted to the peculiar condition of the operation, while preserving full value in Court;
- to assess whether there is legal ground to give civil Criminal trial evidentiary status to digital information gathered with a less strict computer forensics best practices.

The remainder of this paper is organized as follows: Sect. 2 provides an overview of the issues - as handled by Court and Legislators - related to the legal value of computer-forensics gathered digital evidence in civil Criminal Trials. Section 3 describes the legal issues involved by the transition of SOF-gathered digital information toward a civil Criminal Trial, while Sect. 4 - through information available only from open source - dissects a case of cooperation between the Italian Military Air Force and the "Arma dei Carabinieri" in a drug-related investigation. As said, the case is relevant because involves both the use of classified digital reconnaissance technologies that are at risk of being disclosed in Court unless the classified information is erased from the imagery given back to the investigators, and the risks coming from the lack of a proper method to "sanitize" these classified files while keeping the chain of custody strong enough to resist to the defense counsel cross examination. Sections 5 and 6 describe the technical implications by providing both a framework and technical suggestions to be implemented in battlefield operation. Section 7 concludes.

2   The Legal Value of Computer Forensics-Gathered Information

There is a widely-spread belief, among the Computer Forensics experts, that if the data acquisition process has not been handled following a strict procedure, the results cannot be granted full evidential value. Therefore, they advocate the necessity of employing strict technical measures to obtain a sound result that will stand up against the cross-examination by a lawyer. If evidence gathering is compromised in some way, a forensic investigator may consider the data discovered – for example the content of a USB dongle or hard disk - to have no evidential value.

This is an application of the legal doctrine known as "poisoned fruit" that can be summarized like this: *does the lack of forensic soundness render evidence inadmissible, and poison all subsequent evidence gathered by law enforcement as a result?* [1].

This question has been asked many times in both side of the Ocean and got a disturbingly standard answer over the time: the lack of compliance with forensics best practice doesn't affect - per se - the evidence gathered by the investigators.

Just to name a few cases, in 1994, *United States v. Harrington* affirmed that *Merely raising the possibility of tampering is not sufficient to render evidence inadmissible; the possibility of a break in the chain of custody of evidence goes to the weight of the evidence, not its admissibility* [2]. In 1997 - *United States v. Allen* [3] - the US Court of Appeal for the 6th Circuit, criticizing the defense tactic of challenging the "process" before challenging the "results", held that merely raising the possibility of tampering is insufficient to render evidence inadmissible [1].

About ten year after, in 2005 the Criminal Court of Bologna, Italy, spoke the very same language in the decision that indicted the first Italian virus writer ever tried: *it must be stressed-out that the defense is limited to claim that the methods adopted, by not being compliant with the (alleged) scientific best practice, lead to results that ab origine cannot be held as reliable without - by the way - claiming that in the actual case some form of alteration has been or would have been done, and providing no source, way of doing and course of action* [4].

A "dissenting opinion" came in 2012 from another Italian Supreme Court decision [5] where the judges acknowledged the necessity to follow a technically correct digital evidence gathering method to give it full status in Court.

Another decision that counterbalances the legal doctrine of the limited relevance in Court of digital forensics best practice has been released on January, 10 2017 by the First Branch of the Criminal Court of Rome. The decision 148/17 exonerated the defendant, charged of having hacked a computer connected to the network of an Italian critical infrastructure. The exoneration has been based upon the fact that Police-manned digital forensics was not been able to positively tell which one, among the accounts found on the computer allegedly used to launch the attack, belonged to the defendant.

As this quick recollection of the court decisions shows the debate about the weight and the quality standard of digital forensics in Court is still open.

So, coming back to the original question: is it true that only by following the computer forensics' best practices, gathered-data have an evidentiary value in Court?

This article argues that it is not necessary so, because - as said - the match between the technical requirements of an investigation and its role in a trial must be done taking into account the actual conditions of where the activities have been carried out.

So, to put it short, the Computer Forensics experts need to develop a specific best practice for emergency-based forensics.

To support this conclusion, let's start from scratch and go back to the claim of those who support a "black-or-white" position (no best practices standard forensics, no evidence). Their syllogism major premise is: "if the data acquisition process hasn't been handled following a strict procedure, the results cannot be granted full evidential value."

But this major premise is flawed by the meaning itself of the words "granted" and "full evidential value".

From a technical standpoint, it is fair to assume that if during an investigation, data found on a crime scene and duplicated on-the-fly are handled without proper care, nobody can "swear" that the copy is an exact clone of the original. But, on the other hand, it doesn't mean that only by using sophisticated Computer Forensics tools in the peace of a laboratory, one can be 100% sure that the cloned copy is unaltered.

Let's look at those options from the Court perspective.

Affirming the right to be defended is of the utmost importance in a criminal trial, because is the only way to pronounce a decision "beyond reasonable doubt" and to prevent a mistrial.

When digital evidence started finding its way into the criminal legal system, lawyers, prosecutors and justices had to rely upon the "geeks" to assess its value, who had little experience of handling evidence, gathering and presenting the information. It became a common experience to hear defense counsels to ask for the dismissal of digital evidence solely because of the lack of care in its gathering, and - as seen early in this paper - it was frequent to hear Courts dismissing the objection on equally "blinded" basis.

As time goes by, the courts of several countries, included the International Criminal Court, have established a set of legal principles in relationship with the evidence value of information. The key points of this jurisprudence (that is valid for digital information too) are:

− *illegally obtained evidence may be admitted in court as soon as it has been corroborated by independent evidence* [6] *or it is "sound enough"* [3];
− *if the (digital) information has been obtained by way of official channels, it doesn't matter that the party providing the evidence obtained it in a non-legal way* [7, 8];
− *the burden of proving the alteration of a digital evidence because of a poorly executed technical operation rests on the defense's shoulders. This means that unless the challenging party succeeds in providing positive evidence of an error, the (sloppily acquired) digital evidence may be admitted into the courtroom* [3].

Under these principles, it might looks like Computer Forensics has a very limited citizenship in the legal world.

But this is a false impression, because while the Courts have often decided against the absolute value and the role of forensics' best practice, new legislations have positively given Computer Forensics a full seat on the right side of the judicial bench.

Since 2001 the Budapest Convention on Cybercrime set forth specific, computer forensics-oriented rules of evidence.

Article 19 of the Budapest Convention, which deals with "Search and seizure of stored computer data", grants the prosecutors the power to:

a. *seize or similarly secure a computer system or part of it or a computer-data storage medium;*
b. *make and retain a copy of those computer data;*
c. *maintain the integrity of the relevant stored computer data;*
d. *render inaccessible or remove those computer data in the accessed computer system.*

The subsequent Articles 20 that deals with "real-time collection of traffic data" (i.e.: information about the source, destination and volume of transmitted information), and 21 (that regulates wiretapping activities), grants the "competent authorities" the power to:

a. *collect or record through the application of technical means on the territory of that Party, and*
b. *compel a service provider, within its existing technical capability:*
    i. *to collect or record through the application of technical means on the territory of that Party; or*
    ii. *to co-operate and assist the competent authorities in the collection or recording of traffic data, in real-time, associated with specified communications in its territory transmitted by means of a computer system.*

To put it short, the Budapest Convention:

– *allows network (i.e. remotely operated) forensics, that includes hacking into a system,*
– *makes it mandatory for the prosecution services to guarantee that the digital data gathered during an investigation is integral (i.e. collected in a manner that ensures that no tampering occurred),*
– *authorizes the prosecution service to perform "man-in-the-middle" attacks, to hack into other computer systems suspected of containing relevant evidence.*

Of course, the Budapest Convention doesn't cover the whole cyber warfare domain and is of little value in those operations that either target "information" as such or have information gathering as a by-product of a conventional strike.

Nevertheless, it cannot be excluded from the realm of possibility that the outcomes of a cyber-military operation could become part of legal proceedings. Thus, while obviously aimed at governing "ordinary" criminal proceedings, the Budapest Convention offers guidance to other kind of jurisdictions such as the ICC, Special Criminal Courts, and military trials in war and peacetime. Furthermore, the Budapest Convention can become a leading legislation to be taken into account when and if legislators will decide to regulate the evidence status of battlefield-gathered digital evidences.

3   SOF Deployment and Legal Scenarios

As the work in [6] has pointed out:

When operators are confronted with digital equipment during an operation that is not intended to collect evidence for future criminal proceedings, the focus might be on collecting information for intelligence.

This is because a soldier (deployed abroad) has no law enforcement status so he is not bound to follow the rule of evidence provisions during a mission. This is true, too, for exceptions like the Italian "Arma dei Carabinieri" and "Corpo della Guardia di Finanza", whose enlisted men have both military and law enforcement status (but the latter, only within the Italian jurisdiction).

If the digital information rescued by SOF stays within the military/intelligence circle the only actual computer forensics issues to care about are those related:

– *to defeat the anti-forensics ("digital booby traps" or "digital IED") measures,*
– *to locate, identify and exfiltrate as quickly as possible the greatest possible quantity of information.*

Once collected and quarantined, it will be the intelligence analyst's duty to make sense of the information that was gathered in the field.

But if the outcome of a SOF mission lands on a civil public prosecutor desk, the legal value of the digital evidence should be carefully assessed in terms of compliance with the rules of evidence and, more important, in terms of impact on the disclosure of SOF operating protocols and operators' identity.

Whatever evidence is entered a Court docket, it allows the defense counsel to ask for a direct examination of all the possible witnesses involved and to analyze all the actions that led to the evidence being admitted.

Thus, if the prosecution fails to "sanitize" its docket or is not aware of the consequences of releasing information to the defense counsel, critical - but not necessarily classified - information may fall into public domain.

While the problem of the admissibility of illegally obtained, digital evidence has been already dealt with by the courts, the issue of the disclosure of unnecessary information is more and more relevant with the growth in number and importance of SOF missions.

In 1994 the Italian Guardia di Finanza led one of the biggest-ever online copyright piracy investigations. In the final report for the public prosecutor, the commanding officer included details of the Telemonitor TM40, a device that was proved to be capable of wire-tapping computer-to-computer communications [9]. This report was included within the prosecutor's docket and finally made available to the defense counsels and their clients. Thank to this careless handling of sensitive information the hacking community of the era - that had only suspected the existence of such a device - could obtain a positive "proof of life" and modify its "behaviors" accordingly to the new intelligence.

A grey area where the BDF might play a relevant role is the support given by SOF either to Military Police (MP) investigations or to the enforcement of international arrest warrant. At least in theory, in these cases the specific duties of both SOF and MP could be clearly distinct. The SOF should oversee handling the break-in and securing the perimeter, while the actual arrest and the evidence collection should be performed by the MP or by the concerned local authority. By enforcing a clear separation of the operational roles, the DBF issues are no more relevant to SOF activities, thus reducing the possibility of having to expose in court confidential information and the personal identity of the SOF operatives.

4 Case Study: The Quinzano Investigation

At least in Italy, there are no known (non-military) court cases where the public prosecutor presented in court a digital evidence gathered on his behalf by a SOF operator. It is, then, necessary to look at similar cases involving different military operations that might provide support to the ideas presented in this paper.

While not related to a SOF activity, a useful example revealing the kind of legal and technical issues involved in the military and law enforcement path's crossing is the deployment of Predators and Tornados by the Italian Air Force in a Carabinieri-handled drug-related investigation happened in 2016.

This case study shows that the technical standards of the digital evidence gathered during a military operation could be less stringent than those usually required in ordinary trials. For example, in the Quinzano investigation, the video files gathered by the deployment of Predators and Tornados were purged by the Italian Air Force of all classified information before the delivery to the investigators.

On November 26 2014 the Italian Air Force, the "Carabinieri" and "Polizia di Stato" signed an agreement to use the Air Force UAVs (namely, a Predator) belonging to the 32th Wing, in aerial reconnaissance activities to become part of the investigation.

On October 27 2016 Air Force Tornados belonging to the Sixth Wing based in Ghedi (IT) have been tasked by the Carabinieri to photograph a weed cultivation in Quinzano (a small town in the Northern Italy) [1].

Speaking in general terms, without entering the intricacies of the Italian Rules of Evidence and investigation, there is a common ground to (almost) all the democratic countries:

– *a criminal investigation is exclusive jurisdiction of the Prosecution Service that can investigate on its own and/or with the help of a law enforcement agency (LEA),*
– *a LEA can act only under the Prosecutor's direction - and in some cases under a Court-issued warrant,*
– *the Prosecution must disclose to and make available to the defense counselor all the evidences that support the charges,*
– *the defendant has the right to verify in Court all the activities performed during the investigation by the LEA and the other bodies that provided support.*

So, in the weed's aerial photography case, the evidence gathering process looks like this: the Prosecutor orders the investigating LEA (Carabinieri, in this case) to do a reconnaissance activity; under the Air Force-Carabinieri-Polizia agreement, the LEA asks for the support of the Air Force to perform the field activity, the Air Force - acting as a "simple" executor of a technical operation gives Carabinieri back the videos or the pictures taken during the flight.

This process is straightforward, but - as the devil is in the details - reality tells another story.

Inside the cockpit of a Tornado there is only room for two pilots: one handles the aircraft, the other mans the video equipment. In other words, no investigator is on board to first-person witness what happens during the flight. Neither could be possible to ground the second pilot and have a Carabiniere manning the video equipment, since to sit into a military plane and handle its commands it is necessary a specific training and certification.

So, the only option for the investigators is to wait for the videos and pictures be transmitted to the control center and get a copy of the recording; but this means that the only thing that the investigators can tell about the aerial recording is that somebody gave them a file "allegedly" containing the results of the imagery manned by the Air Force pilot. The situation is made more complicated by the fact that the file given to the investigators is a "stripped down" version, purged by all the technical information related to the flight and the plane that usually are embedded in such files. In other words: the raw digital aerial-recording never leaves the Air Force premises.

If the Public Prosecutor, instead of looking for independent confirmation, put these aerial recording into its docket, the defense counsel become aware of the existence of the recordings.

While it shouldn't be a problem, legally speaking, that the video and the pictures come from a non-LEA autonomous activity (as in the case of obtaining a copy of private CCTV streams or TV broadcasts), the situation becomes tricky as soon as the defense counsel asks to know who, how, where and when did the recording, with what kind of equipment, how is it possible to be sure that the recordings are genuine and so on. To put it short: the defense counsel is given the power to sneak into the Air Force organization and protocols, thus throwing sensitive/classified information into public domain.

Of course, the Air Force can refuse to disclose this information but - side-putting the risk of a contempt of court charge - this would make the recording useless as evidence because of the infringement of the right of the defendant to review in court every evidence gathered against him.

In a real-life scenario, especially if the recordings are the only evidence offered by the Prosecution Service, the Court might reject the request of the defense, at the price of creating ground for the appeal of the conviction based (solely) on this evidence.

The Quinzano's case is still in its early stage so there are neither further hint about the actual challenging of the Air Force involvement evidentiary value by the defense counsel, nor about a decision issued by the court on the topic. Nevertheless, this case shows that the involvement of military personnel and information in any criminal investigation is an actual possibility whose legal and technical implications are still widely ignored or downplayed.

A new legislation (or a Court decision) dealing with the partnership between the military and law enforcement domains to collect legally sound evidence should address also the need of protecting the classified information that can be extracted or derived from the military activities.

At the very same time, it should be affirmed that if digital forensics best practices must be followed in combat or other emergency situations, the level of these best practices might be lower, while still acceptable in Court, of those designed for civil criminal investigation.

Finally, and where possible, some sort of chain of custody should be granted in BDF, so that the defense counsel cannot challenge the legal value of a "skimmed" evidence.

If all this is relatively easy to do when the military-law enforcement cooperation is not pressed by time, it becomes fairly a hard task when the object of the digital evidence gathering activity is hidden behind a rain of flying pieces of lead.

5 Overview of the Actual Technological and Methodological Solutions for Battlefield Digital Forensics

Plenty of information may be gathered on the battlefield from digital devices. Often this information is used for intelligence, but some issues, both technical and juridical, make it difficult to use the acquired information as evidence in Court. The reason is not given by the information itself, but by the way in which this information is collected and cataloged, as we have discussed in the previous case study. Some typical battlefield situation and the reluctance of the operators to step into the digital forensic technicalities, remaining focused only on the primary objective, often lead to the impossibility to categorize such information as evidence.

This section describes additional constraints and limitations that the operators have to face during SOF operations, and evaluates what is offered by the technological and procedural point of view to allow field operators to acquire forensic evidences, considering also their battlefield limitations.

The limitations to be considered for such information acquisition include:

- *Weight of the forensic equipment;*
- *Fragility of the forensic equipment;*
- *Tight time constraints to conduct the operation;*
- *External agents, enemy, etc.*

The above limitations define a specific contest in which the information acquisition will be carried out by the SOF operators. Indeed, the techniques and procedures for such information acquisition have to be reconsider in order to have a legal status when its outcome are taken in Court, and at the same time to be complete within the constrained context of the operation.

Below, we examine some of the current proposed procedures for the acquisition by field operators.

Considering the challenges and limitations posed by the battlefield crime scene, Pearson [10] defined the so-called Digital Triage Forensics (DTF) process, a methodology tailored for terroristic attacks, or post-blast investigations which allows the collection of intelligence and potential evidence in the battlefield. The Digital Triage Forensics model differs from the CFFTPM (Computer Forensics Field Triage Process Model) [11] in that triage processing is done at the Forward Operating Base (FOB), before in-depth analysis, rather than on the crime scene. The forensic team, who is tasked of collecting evidence in the battlefield, must always operate in a timely manner and under safe conditions. It is noteworthy to mention that both Rogers and Pearson focused their attention on the crime scene rather than the DFLs (Digital Forensics Laboratories).

There have also been proposals to automate the process of triage of digital devices on the crime scene. The pioneering Five Minutes Forensics (5MF) [12] opened the field of Machine Learning-based Digital Triage with the aim to categorize computer users, and to establish an effective priority schedule based on extracted data. Marturana [13] proposes the definition of a partially automated Digital Triage process model. In such work, authors introduce the concept of automated categorization templates which would help identifying relevant devices in each digital media category.

Today, no specific technology implemented and used in SOF operations is currently public, also because the main focus of such operations is not forensic data acquisition but rather kinetic attacks on certain enemy sites. Probably, the field operators use, in special cases, the same tools used by the law enforcement counterparts. The only source currently available to analyze the initial concept of triaging and forensic data acquisition in the battlefield is the course conducted at NSHQ (NATO Special Operation Headquarters) under the title "Technical Exploitation Operation", whose content appears to be mainly oriented towards familiarization by operators with certain basic forensic tools for data acquisition.

The state of the art described above highlights the need for a new methodology and new technology support to successfully complete the battlefield digital acquisition process so that it can acquire information that can be used both as intelligence but also, if required, as evidence supporting legal activity. An example of such use of battlefield information could arise in the case of war crimes investigations by the International Criminal Court.

6   A Family of Digital Forensics Tools and Techniques Developed for Battlefield Digital Forensics

As introduced in the previous section, two different main aspects need to be developed in order to try to solve the problems in conducting forensic analysis on the battlefield, namely: the procedural and technological aspects. The methodological and procedural part needs to be revised and streamlined in the light of the typical limitations of a forensic analysis on the battlefield. The second aspect concerns the development of a technological support infrastructure that allows the operator to perform the assigned task without requiring mastery of sophisticated and advanced forensics skills and techniques.

In order to better evaluate possible solutions, we must first understand the implications of one of the tightest constraints of those indicated in the previous section, namely the tight time constraints to conduct the operation.

This constraint makes it vital for the operator to select and prioritize the different sources of digital information available on the operation site. In particular, the field operator is forced to make the decisions on site applying a triaging process. In other words, the operator needs to define a priority in the acquisition of the various digital devices so that, by performing a probabilistic prediction, to select and to acquire those devices that are more likely to contain important information. This process must be based on the information that the operator is able to locate, and must be as fast as possible.

In order to achieve this goal, the following part of this paper covers the statistical analysis of the information present on different kind of devices. It should be underlined that the approach is based on empirical data mixed with a statistical overview, and the results might change if correlated with information-gathering about the target.

When collecting evidence, it is recommended to proceed from the volatile to the less volatile. This is an example of order of volatility for a typical system:

- *registers, cache;*
- *routing table, address resolution protocol (ARP) cache; process table, kernel statistics, memory;*
- *temporary file systems;*
- *disk;*
- *remote logging and monitoring data relevant to the system in acquisition;*
- *physical configuration, network topology;*
- *archival media.*

The goal in this approach is to assure that the gathered information is the most comprehensive possible. To reach this goal, a formal model to assist in determining the best choice of information gathering is necessary. In order to carry out the statistical analysis, the following information is needed:

- *Effectiveness: this parameter considers how effective an acquisition of a specific type of device can be, e.g. based on the operator experience and familiarity with the tools required. This parameter can assume a value based on the ability to retrieve information from a particular device, usually a positive value less than 1.*
- *Acquisition time of the dataset: this parameter expressed in minutes consider the data acquisition time for each specific device. It is important to evaluate the amount of data that can be acquired in the mission amount of time;*
- *Additional Efforts expressed in minutes consider the unexpected. For example, this parameter should cover the additional troubleshooting time needed in case of a failure of an acquisition tool.*
- *Power Status: this parameter should cover the power status of the device to be acquired. Usually, this parameter assumes a positive value less than 1. The value equal 1, if the device is switched on and fully charged, and a smaller value if the device is off and completely discharge,*
- *Connectivity Status: this parameter should cover the connectivity status of the device. Usually, this parameter assumes a positive value less than 1. The value equal 1, if the device is connected and has access to the internet, and a smaller value if the device is isolated.*
- *Anti-forensics measures: this parameter should consider the statistical degradation of information acquired, if an anti-forensics measure is in place. Usually, this parameter assumes a positive value less than 1. The value is equal 1, if there are no anti-forensics measures, and a smaller value according to the level of sophistication of the advanced anti-force measures in place.*

The following function acquire(Xi) considers all the above parameters and returns a number that indicates the acquisition priority of a specific device. This concept has been preliminarily introduced in [6]. We propose below an updated and more comprehensive model:

$$
\begin{aligned}
acquire(X) = Log[&(1/(Effectiveness) * (OperatorTimeFrame \\
&- AcquisitionTime - AdditionalEffort) * (PowerStatus) \\
&* (ConnectivityStatus) * (1/AntiForensics)]
\end{aligned}
$$

In particular, given a set of digital device X1, ..., Xn on the site, first the operator should acquire the device Xi with the greater acquire(Xi) value. Note that if the log parameter of acquire(X) is negative, then the device X cannot be acquired. In fact, the operation-time-frame is not enough for the acquisition of the digital information stored in X.

Statistical Identification Equation

So, starting from this formal setting, the acquisition triaging should be defined as follows:

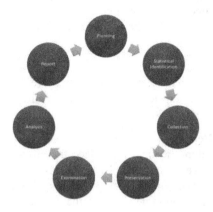

6.1   Cycle *Acquisition Process*

Planning

The first step of any process must be based on a detailed planning, such step must be supported by all the available information, both online and offline, by specialized engineers (intelligence team) in collaboration with SOF operators, in this way they may possibly guide the collection of information based on operational needs.

This phase is crucial to allow operators to have a first evaluation of the possible information to look for and where is possible find them. For example, the activity at the CCDCOE (Cooperative Cyber Defense Centre of Excellence), done during the Crossed Sword exercise [14] has tested, among other, this aspect of the procedure, in particular performing the OSINT (Open Source Intelligence Analysis) research, the operators have found some comments on social media, and some photos that could afford them the a priori identification of some of the equipment that the target in question was using. This phase allow the SOF team to optimize the gear and the tools to use, other than test the procedure and reduce the *AdditionalEffort* parameter as close to zero as possible.

Statistical Identification

Downstream of the planning process you make a rough estimation of those that might be the acquisition methodologies to be used in kinetic action, if the previous analysis was carried out in a comprehensive manner, the operators will have at their disposal a handbook, or a guide digital or hardcopy, in which shows the step by step procedures to be followed and targeted for the devices that need to be identified, and an evaluation, calculated on site, that consider the statistical amount of information that can be gathered. In this way, operators need to identify devices as a priority and subsequently acquire them, in order, starting from the one with higher outcome of the acquire(d) formula.

Collection
Following the statistical identification, operators process may proceed to the acquisition with tools and techniques given in the Handbook, and tested previously. This activity will use technological supports which will be described in the next section, which will have the characteristic to ensure that the acquisition takes place as much as possible in line with the forensic standard.

Preservation
After the acquisition phase operators will have to preserve the result of the acquisition carried out, using the supporting technology infrastructure and other techniques that will be described in the next section.

Examination\Analysis\Report
These parts of the procedure are held at a place that does not have the limitations mentioned above, and, above all, it is done by technicians who carry out the analysis of the information acquired according forensic standards. These processes can be completed at the time of the final report delivered to the competent authorities, or it can be the input for a new phase of planning for later kinetic operation, cyclically. These processes have been described in great detail in the literature as it falls in the standard forensic cases.

In the first part of this chapter we defined the procedure to identify and acquire the information in a battlefield. Now we describe the technological part to be used in support of the acquisition triaging procedure.

The technological solutions proposed, some available and other to be developed, would allow the SOF operators to acquire on-site in a way that is accepted in the ordinary courts.

For simplicity we will analyze only the steps in the procedure involving operators of the special forces, that are the one that perform the triage, and are the one that start the Chain of Custody [15], so Statistical Identification, Collection and Preservation.

Statistical Identification
This step of the procedure requires a technological support that contains the following information:

- *Numerical evaluation of the average bitrate available to capture data from each possible devices and device technology;*
- *Standard procedures of a Hard Disk dismantling;*
- *The system of recognition of certain preset objects (i.e. laptop, usb, servers, storage);*
- *Recognition system of physical techniques of anti-forensics.*

In order to support the operator in the forensic analysis and acquisition process, because of the constraints on the size and the weight placed by the equipment, we need a portable device that is not excessively uncomfortable for the operators. Using as a starting point the equipment described in [16], whose graphic representation is shown in the figure below, a technological solution could be based on the use of augmented reality smart googles. Using the same format, it is possible to hypothesize the use of such googles that with their computing capabilities can support the identification and calculation of the statistical identification of the devices to be captured, and thus can free the operator of these charges simplifying and speeding up the data acquisition process.

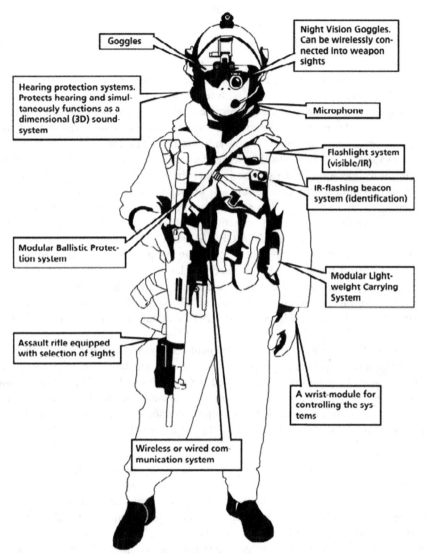

The system should dynamically recalculate the percentage of acquirable evidence from each device, to help the operator in the next step and at the same time not load it in performing statistical evaluations. This system must also be able to take photographs at the time of each identification, and these photographs must be accompanied by a timestamp per a certified time synchronization at the beginning of the mission by the entire team.

Although at present these devices are produced, no one complies with all specifications set natively, so will be part of next development phase, design a deep learning algorithm, trained with the necessary dataset, to perform the environment analysis. This option however, based on the qualitative representation of some of the parameters will not be as precise as wished, but should be continuously trained. This kind of result can be achieved using some experience that comes from the literature.

Collection

About collection, the operator must follow several techniques known in the literature. To make the collection in accordance with best practices, the operator should carry a tool for copying the storage devices in forensic way, and a portable storage medium of suitable size for the mission. The storage size we need to have available for data capture can be dimensioned based on the mission time duration.

As an example, for data acquisition, assume a total time window of about 15 min for the entire SOF operation, and hypothesize that the time that can be devoted to data acquisition is 3 min, in this case 3 min will be the value to use as parameter operationtimewindow in the formula above. At this point, we can also dimension the storage we need to have available for the acquisition. For example, with only 3 min, a fast acquisition storage can be about 12/16 GB SSD size.

Due to the tight timing of the data, it is not always possible to acquire all the data that is available on the device but a selective data acquisition must be made. For example, when you acquire a PC disk, you can only acquire data that was created by the user, and do not capture known or standard files: some kernel components, which are static and known, or files listed in the NIST National Software Reference Library (NSRL) could be ignored by the acquisition process.

This type of approach implies less stringent requirements than regular forensics, limiting the search for particular artifact or particular information within the storage. To achieve this goal, a system that can be used is OSForensics [17]. This system allows selective acquisition in compliance with forensic standards. Hence, despite not having a complete data acquisition of the disk, this approach allows a detailed reconstruction of the components in the file system, making the acquisition legally acceptable.

Preservation

Finally, the part of preservation. This part appears to be the real critical point of the whole process.

Indeed preserve data means that these are secured and manipulated later without losing the chain of custody. To this end, operators must be equipped with a series of Faraday Bag [18], already serialized, and easily sealable. These containers already used in regular investigation, allowing to eliminate possible external interference, and thus preserve the evidence. At the end of the preservation process such containers are to be photographed with the equipment supplied, the preceding paragraphs, revealing the serial number of containers, and seal.

This system allows to preserve the chain of custody of the test and then make it usable both as intelligence in the planning of a subsequent mission but also during an ordinary process.

7 Concluding Remarks

There is an increasing trend showing the cooperation between the Military domain and the non-military (here called also "civil") Criminal Justice system. Enforcing international arrest warrants often needs that law enforcement investigators be assisted by SOF military operators. Peacekeeping or other international missions lead to the discovery of "ordinary" crimes. Special Operations Forces might be targeted at gathering information possibly relevant to a civil criminal trial or obtain such information as a by-product of their operations. Law enforcement agencies might rely upon the Military's technical infrastructure to obtain imagery or other information that they couldn't otherwise have access to.

When information stay inside the intelligence circle, rule of evidence and other similar concerns are not relevant, since there is no Court that must assess the evidentiary status of these data. But when there is a transition from the Military world to the Judicial domain, then rules of evidence - digital evidence included - must be abided to.

While there is plenty of Court decision and legislations that regulate the evidence status of digital information collected by the Prosecution Services and/or the Law Enforcement Agencies in the civil Criminal Trials, the impact of Military-collected evidences to be used in a civil Criminal Trial is still widely unassessed. In the absence of civil Criminal Court decision and specific legislation, this paper tried to point out some of the legal and technical issues related to military-to-law-enforcement digital evidence transition and provided hints for a future legislation or Court decisions. The conclusion are based upon a known case, related to a criminal investigation run by the Prosecutor of Brescia (IT), whose investigators tasked the Italian Military Air Force to acquire digital imagery of a drug-cultivated farmland.

While marginal at first sight, this case is relevant because exemplifies the main issues relevant for the paper: Military-acquired digital imagery carries classified information about the technologies involved, and let this imagery slip out of the military inner circles means that it must first cleared from what cannot be made public. But - and here comes the question - what about the chain of custody? Who can guarantee that digital files haven't been corrupted or altered in the process?

This is a common question in the civil Criminal Trials when assessing the results of an investigation carried out by a Prosecutor, that got mixed answers, but at least it has been answered. Not the same can be told for the hypothesis of this paper.

Civil Criminal Forensics heavily relies upon the strict following of procedures and best practice as a condition to admit digital information as evidence in a trial or to weight its value. But in a military operation, this very same best practice can't work. So here come the questions: is computer forensics' best practice used in the laboratory still valid when information has to be collected in an emergency situation?

Is there any legal ground to give civil Criminal trial evidentiary status to digital information gathered with a less strict computer forensics best practice?

Again, with the idea in mind to provide guidance for future Court decisions and legislation, we chose to study a sub-set of military operations, those ran by SOF, because of its peculiarity: the very short time-frame in which such activities are usually carried out and the high probability that digital information are a collateral outcome.

In conclusion, the acquisition of evidence during the SOF activities seems possible. The main problem encountered is the technical and legal management of acquired evidence that may not necessarily correspond, for various reasons, to the complete digital information acquired on the site of the operation. The reasons for this difference may be caused by the confidentiality of a part of the information acquired, but also by temporal impediments that do not allow the complete acquisition and transmission of the data in the device to the Court of justice. Despite this, having a process of identifying and capturing evidence on the battlefield appears possible, and requires significant support from SOF so that the identification and acquisition of data can be accepted in the legal field without the need for the first operators, to come to the scene, to be specialized technicians of the police.

References

1. Monti, A., Kennealy, E.: Case study: a failure success clothing. Digit. Invest. **2**, 247–253 (2005)
2. United States v. Harrington, 923 F.2d 1371 (1994)
3. United States Supreme Court - Utah vs. Strieff - Certiorari to the Supreme Court of Utah No. 14–1373. Argued 22 February 2016—Decided 20 June 2016
4. Criminal Court of Bologna, Decision n. 1823/05 (2017)
5. Criminal Court, Decision n. 44851 (2012)
6. Braccini, C., Vaisanen, T., Sadlon, M. et. al.: Battlefield Digital Forensics Digital Intelligence and Evidence, pp. 1–69 (2016)
7. Corte di cassazione (Italian Supreme Court) Orders nn. 8605 and 8606 (2015)
8. Corte di cassazione (Italian Supreme Court) Orders n. 9760 (2015)
9. Chiccarelli, S., Monti, A.: Spaghetti Hacker. Pescara: s.n., p. 187 (2011)
10. Pearson, S., Watson, R.: Digital Triage Forensics. s.l.: Syngress (2010)
11. Rogers, M.K., et al.: Computer forensics field triage process model. J. Digit. Forensics Secur. Law **1**, 19–38 (2006)
12. Grillo, A., et al.: Fast user classifying to establish forensic analysis priorities. In: Fifth International Conference on IT Security Incident Management and IT Forensics (2009)
13. Marturana, F., Tacconi, S.: A Machine Learning-based Triage methodology for automated categorization of digital media. Digit. Invest. **10**, 193–204 (2013)
14. NATO CCDCOE. Crossed Sword Exercise. Tallinn: s.n. (2017)
15. Giannelli, P.C.: Chain of Custody and Identification of Real Evidence. s.l.: Case Western Reserve University (1983)
16. Saaralein, T.: Optimizing the performance of a dismounted future force warrior by means of improved situational awareness. Int. J. Adv. Telecommun. **5**, 42–54 (2012)
17. OSForensics [Online] (2017). [Cited: 22 May 2017]. http://www.osforensics.com
18. Mohseni, H.: Faraday Cage. University of Tehran High Voltage Lab, Tehran (2006)
19. Bussoletti, F.: Analisi Difesa [Online], 27 October 2016. [Cited: 22 May 2017]. http://www.analisidifesa.it/2016/10/tornado-anti-droga/

Privacy/Cryptography

A Secure Anonymous E-Voting System Using Identity-Based Blind Signature Scheme

Mahender Kumar$^{(\boxtimes)}$, C. P. Katti, and P. C. Saxena

School of Computer and Systems Sciences,
Jawaharlal Nehru University, New Delhi, India
mahendjnu1989@gmail.com,
{cpkatti,pcsaxena}@mail.jnu.ac.in

Abstract. Electronic voting is an alternative mechanism of ballot based voting which empowers voters to cast their secret and secure vote electronically over a public channel. Many onward-thinking countries are adopting the electronic voting system to upgrade their election process. E-voting system is more complicated to construct. Thus it expects more security as compared to the postal voting system. The objective of the paper is twofold. Firstly, we proposed an efficient blind signature scheme using the identity-based cryptosystem in the random oracle model. The proposed scheme uses the combination of Boldyreva's blind signature scheme and Choon-Cheon's Identity-based signature. Additionally, we reduce its security to the Gap Diffie-Hellman Complexity (GDH). Under the adaptive chosen message and ID attacks it is secure against existential forgery attack. We show our proposed system performed better as compared to existing systems. Secondly, we construct an E-voting system based on our ID-based blind signature and Boneh's short signature scheme (EVS-ID-BS) that fulfills the E-voting security requirements. To the best of our knowledge, EVS-ID-BS is the first practical implementation of E-voting system based on ID-BS Scheme which is constructed in the random oracle model. Proposed EVS-ID-BS scheme provides batch verifiability for a significantly large number of voters, needs less bandwidth cost and require less interaction with election authority.

Keywords: E-voting system · ID-based blind signature
Elliptic curve cryptosystem · Bilinear pairing · Blind signature

1 Introduction

Electronic voting is a way to augment and enhance the democratic system of balloting in forward-thinking countries. Several modern emerging information societies are adopting the electronic voting system to improve further and automate the voting system. Naturally, an electronic-voting system empowers voters to cast their secret and secure vote electronically over an unsecured channel. However, the ballot based voting system is simple, portable and affordable, but it has many disadvantages, e.g., the low participation rate, time-consuming, booth capturing and low tally speed. As the rapid growth of internet technology, E-voting system considered as an interesting way to overcome the weaknesses of ballot based voting system.

© Springer International Publishing AG 2017
R. K. Shyamasundar et al. (Eds.): ICISS 2017, LNCS 10717, pp. 29–49, 2017.
https://doi.org/10.1007/978-3-319-72598-7_3

In general, an E-voting system will be ideally acceptable, if the system must ensure the following constitutional and legal requirements [1, 2]:

- *Voter Anonymity*: Difficult for an eavesdropper to make the relationship between a voter and a vote before and after the election has done.
- *Coercion-Resistant*: Difficult for an eavesdropper to find whether a coerced voter complies with the demands.
- *Authentication*: It ensures that only authenticate/eligible voter can cast a vote at the time of the election.
- *Integrity*: Ensures that only valid votes enumerated at the end tally process. That means Votes cannot alter from the voter to the vote counting entity.
- *Verifiability*: Ensures that voter can verify their enumeration at the end tally process and anyone can check the performance of election after the election has done.
- *Uniqueness*: Ensures that one voter can only cast one vote.

According to experts, E-voting system based on the cryptographic technique categorized into three classes: mix-net [3], homomorphic encryption [4], and blind signature [5]. The mix-net cryptographic method [3] allows the number of machines to mix-up the encrypted votes and hides the relationship between the voters and votes by performing various mathematical operations. Another technique is, homomorphic encryption method allows the election commission to count votes without decrypting them. Based on homomorphic function, some E-voting schemes are proposed by [4, 6, 7]. The third is, the blind signature is [5] another tool for implement a practical E-voting system that allows the election commission to get votes without identifying the identity of the voter. Some blind signature based e-voting scheme are proposed by [5, 8–11].

In 1983, David Chaum gave the novel idea of the blind signature scheme [12, 13]. The blind signature scheme provides the two significant properties: (1) blindness says signer issued sign on given message without knowing the content, and other is (2) untraceability says signer cannot trace the original signature from signature which he signed in. Due to these two essential properties of the blind signature scheme, it plays a significant role in those applications where user anonymity is the key concern, for example, E-voting system, E-cash payment system and E-commerce [9, 14, 15]. With the benefits of the blind signature scheme, in 1992, Fujiokta et al. [16] introduced the first secret E-voting mechanism based on the blind signature scheme which ensures the privacy and provides fairness. Since then, several blind signatures based E-voting systems have been proposed [5, 8–11]. These schemes are based on traditional public key cryptosystem which requires a significant computational cost for certificate management and public keys.

Shamir's primary idea of Identity-based cryptosystem (IBC) [17] is to simplify the certificate management and public key revocation problem. IBC maps the user's identity ID with the public key that means the public key directly determined from the user's unique identity. Later several cryptographic primitives such as Boneh's and others' identity-based encryption (IBE) [18, 19] and Choon-Cheon's identity-based signature (IBS) [20] has been introduced. Using the notion of IBC, Zhang et al. [21] proposed the identity-based blind signature (ID-BS) scheme. Later, several blind signature schemes using IBC is given by Huang et al. [22], Zhang et al. [23, 24], and

Kumar et al. [25]. Ribarski et al. in [26] studies and examines the existing ID-BS schemes for E-voting system, but they could not implement.

Our contribution. E-voting system is vulnerable to security attacks, and their construction is very complicated as compared to ballot based voting system, so it requires more security with an efficient tool to implement. The goal of this article is twofold. Firstly,

- We proposed an efficient blind signature scheme using identity-based cryptosystem (ID-BS) in the random oracle model which is inspired from Bolyreva et al.'s blind signature scheme [27] and Choon-Cheon et al.'s IBS scheme [20].
- We reduce the ID-BS security to Gap Diffie-Hellman complexity and secure against existential forgery attack under the adaptive chosen message and ID attacks.
- The proposed model provides better performance in terms of communication cost and computation cost, as compares with related existing schemes.
- Furthermore, our proposed scheme provides more security attributes such as the user anonymity, privacy, integrity, coercion-resistant, uniqueness, individual and batch verifiability. Thus we show our ID-BS scheme is more suitable for implementing E-voting system.

Secondly,

- We defined an E-voting system based on our ID-BS scheme and BLS's short signature scheme (EVS-ID-BS) [28] that fulfills the E-voting security requirements as mentioned above. To the best of our knowledge, proposed EVS-ID-BS is the first practical implementation of E-voting system based on ID-BS Scheme which is constructed in the random oracle model.
- Our proposed EVS-ID-BS scheme is the identity-based version of Garcia's E-voting system. As compared to the Garcia et al. scheme [5], for a large number of the voter, proposed EVS-ID-BS requires less pairing operations and support batch verifiability which save up to $2(n-1)$ and $2n$ pairing operations in vote counting and voter authentication phase.
- For implementation purposes, we use type A pairing of Lynn's PBC library [29] with $|P| = 512$ bits and $q = 160$ bits which built on the curve $y^2 = x^3 + x$ over the finite field F_q. Both groups G_1 and G_2 are the groups of points $E(F_q)$, so the pairing is symmetric with embedding degree $k = 2$. It if found that the authentication phase, vote casting phase and verification of our proposed EVS-ID-BS schemes takes ~ 6.28 ms and ~ 10.39 ms and ~ 2.46 ms respectively, running on 3.4 GHz Intel Core i7 system

The arrangement of paper is as follows: Sect. 2 gives the preliminaries about the elliptic curve, bilinear pairing, mathematical assumption and required security constraints. An overview of our ID-BS system and security definition presented in Sect. 3. Section 4 gives the construction of our ID-BS scheme. The security analysis and computational comparison provided in Sect. 5. Section 6 presents the E-voting system based on our proposed ID-blind signature system; finally, the conclusion shown in Sect. 7.

2 Preliminaries

2.1 Elliptic Curve Cryptosystem

Suppose the elliptic curve equation $y^2 = (x^3 + mx + n) \bmod p$, where x, y $\in F_p$ and $4m^3 + 27n^2 \bmod p \neq 0$. Formally, the Elliptic Curve is a set of points (x, y) which satisfies the above equation and an additive abelian group with point 0 (identity element). The condition $4m^3 + 27n^2 \bmod p \neq 0$ tells that $y^2 = (x^3 + mx + n) \bmod p$ has a finite abelian group that can be defined based on the set of points $E_p(m,n)$ on the elliptic curve. Consider points $A = (x_A, y_A)$ and $B = (x_B, y_B)$ over $E_p(m, n)$, the addition operation of elliptic curve is represented as $A + B = C = (x_C, y_C)$, defined as following: $x_C = (\mu^2 - x_A - x_B) \bmod p$ and $y_C = (\mu(x_A - x_C) - y_A) \bmod p$, where μ is given in Eq. (1).
   Where,

$$\mu = \begin{cases} \left(\frac{y_B - y_A}{x_B - x_A}\right) modp, & \text{if } A \neq B \\ \left(\frac{3x_A^2 + m}{2y_A}\right) modp, & \text{if } A = B \end{cases} \tag{1}$$

Based on the elliptic curve, Victor Miller [30] and Neal Koblitz [31] introduced elliptic curve cryptosystem. Let O denotes the point at infinity that is a point which is not on the curve and X be points on E with prime order q then a cyclic subgroup of E generated by X is represented in Eq. (2).

$$<X> = \{O, [1]X, [2]X, [3]X \ldots [q-1]X\} \tag{2}$$

From Eqs. (1) and (2), it derives that for an integer n $\in Z_q$ and point X and Y in the group, such that $Y = nX$, where nX is n times operation of adding the point X using group's addition law. It is noted that addition operation and multiplication operation in ECC is equivalent to modular multiplication and modular exponentiations in RSA respectively.

2.2 Bilinear Pairing

Suppose two cyclic groups have same order q are G_1 and G_2 and generator of G_1 be P. A map, e: $G_1 \times G_1 \rightarrow G_2$ is a bilinear map if it fulfills the following three properties:

1. *Bilinearity*: For every X, Y $\in G_1$, and x, y $\in Z_q$

$$e(xX, yY) = e(X, Y)^{xy} = e(xyX, Y) \tag{3}$$

2. *Non-Degeneracy*: If X is a generator of G_1 then $e(X, X)$ is a generator of G_2 that means if there exist X $\in G_1$ such that $e(X, X) \neq 1$, where 1 is the identity element of G_2.
3. *Computability*: There must exist an algorithm that can efficiently compute $e(X, Y)$ for every X, Y $\in G_1$.

2.3   Mathematical Assumption

- *Discrete logarithm problem on Elliptic Curve (ECDLP).* Consider $Y = xX$ where $X, Y \in E_p(a, b)$, and $x \in Z_q$, it is computationally easy to compute Y from X and x but difficult to compute x from Y and X.
- *Decision Diffie-Hellman problem (DDH).* Given $x, y, z \in Z_q$, $X \in G_1$ and $<X, xX, yX, zX>$ check if $z = xy \bmod q$.
- *Computational Diffie-Hellman Problem (CDH).* Given $x, y \in Z_q$, $X \in G_1$ and $<X, xX, yX>$, compute xyX.
- *Gap Diffie-Hellman problem (GDH).* Group of problems where DDHP is easy while CDHP is hard.

3   Our Identity Based-Blind Signature Scheme

3.1   Overview

Recall to the blind signature scheme based on the traditional certificate-based public key cryptosystem. This system restricts the signer that he signs on user's requested message without seeing the information. However, this setting preserves the unblinding and untraceability property, but the cost of signer's public key management suffers from certificate management and key revocation problem. The IBC is an interesting approach to mitigate the management cost. Here, we take the combined advantage of blind signature and IBS. Thus, our ID-BS scheme uses blind signature scheme of Bolyreva et al. and IBS scheme of Cha-Choon et al.

Boldyreva's blind signature. Boldyreva's [27] blind signature is based on the bilinear pairing. For signature, it needs the additive group on an elliptic curve, and for verification, it requires the multiplicative group. That means, scalar multiplication of points on an elliptic curve is the primary cryptographic operation for blinding the message, signing the blinded message and unblinding the blinded signature, and the bilinear property of pairing based cryptography to compute the DDHP is the cryptographic operation to verify the signature. Assuming the random oracle model, the security proof is somewhat identical to BLS' short Signature scheme. This scheme is secure against the one-more forgeable attack, under the chosen message attack, hardness of CDHP and the collision resistant behavior of hash function.

Choon-Cheon's Identity-Based Signature. Assuming the hardness of solving GDH problem, Choon-Cheon [20] presented an Identity based signature scheme. This system exploits the use of Boneh-Franklin IBE scheme [18] and is equally efficient. Choon-Cheon in [20] proved that if group G is such that if CDHP is difficult and DDHP is easy, then this scheme is secure against existential forgery attack under chosen message attack for ID–based scheme.

3.2 Definition

Definition 1 (Identity-Based Blind Signature). Our ID-BS protocol consists of Four Probabilistic Polynomial-Time (PPT) algorithms, namely, *Setup, Extract, BlindSig,* and *Verifying,* run among four entities, namely, *Private Key Generator (PKG), Signer, Requester,* and *Verifier,* where

1. *Setup*: On some security parameter k, PKG computes the system parameter (PARAM) and master secret key s. PARAM includes the public parameter which is published publically and s is known to PKG only.
2. *Extract*: On given inputs PARAM, master key s, and signer's Identity ID_S, PKG computes the private key S_{IDS} and S_{IDU} corresponding to identity signer's and user's identities.
3. *BlindSig:* This algorithm consists of four sub-algorithms, runs between the user and the signer.
   a. *Commitment:* Signer computes public parameters k against random integer, delivers it to the user as commitment.
   b. *Authenticating & Blinding:* Upon receiving the public parameter k, user authenticate by computing K using his private key S_{IDU}. Then user blinds the given with his random chosen integer, and sends blinded message b_M to the signer.
   c. *Signing:* On given blinded Message b_M, Signer blindly computes the signature S using his private key S_{IDS} and delivers the blind signature S to the user.
   d. *Stripping:* Upon receiving the Blinded Signature S, user strips it against his secret key to outputs the original Signature S'. Finally, the user published the message-signature pair (M, S) for verification.
4. *Verifying*: With user's ID_U and message-signature pair (M, S), verifier verifies the Signature.

3.3 Security Threat

ID-based blind signature scheme achieves the property of blindness and, under parallel chosen message and ID attacks, the proposal is secure against non-forgeability of additional signature. The reader may refer [32] for more details. An ID-BS scheme considered as safe and secure if it fulfills the following two properties:

Definition 2 (Blindness). Blindness property defined against the following game playing between the challenger *C* and PPT adversary A is as follows:

– *Setup*: The challenger *C* chooses a security parameter k and executes the *Setup* algorithm to compute the published parameter PARAM and master key s. Challenger C sends PARAM to A.
– *Phase1*: A selects two distinct message M_0 and M_1 and an ID_i, and sends to C.
– *Challenge*: C uniformly chooses a random bit b $\in$ {0, 1} and ask A for signature on M_b and M_{1-b}. Finally, C strips both the Signatures and gives the original signatures (σ_b, σ_{1-b}) to A.

- *Response*: A guesses bit $b' \in \{0, 1\}$ on tuple $(M_0, M_1, \sigma_b, \sigma_{1-b})$. A wins the game if $b = b'$ holds with probability $[b = b'] > 1/2 + k^{-n}$.

Definition 3 (Non-forgeability). An ID-BS scheme is broken by an Adversary A (t, q_E, q_B, k^{-n}), if A runs no more than t, A make Extract query no more than q_E and runs BlindSig phase no more than q_B, with an advantage more than equal to k^{-n}. Under the adaptive chosen message and ID attacks, our ID-BS scheme is said to secure against one-more forgery, if no adversary A (t, q_E, q_B, k^{-n})-breaks the scheme.

To define the Non-forgeability, let us introduce the following game playing between the Adversaries A who serve as the user and the Challenger C who serve as the honest signer.

- *Setup*: On random Security parameter k, the challenger C executes the *Setup* algorithm and computes the parameter *PARAM* and master key s. Challenger C sends *PARAM* to A.
- *Queries*: Adversary A can perform numbers of queries as follows:
  - *Hash function queries*: For requested input, challenger C computes the hash function values and sends it to the attacker A.
  - *Extract queries*: A selects an Identity ID and ask for S_{ID} to A.
  - *BlindSig queries*: A selects an *ID* and Message *M* blindly requested the Signature from *C.C* compute signature on Message M for identity ID.
- *Forgery*: Game is in favor of A, if against identity ID*, A response with n valid Message-Signature $(M_1, \sigma_1 = (S_1, R_1, r_1)), (M_2, \sigma_2 = (S_2, R_2, r_2))\ldots\ldots (M_n, \sigma_n = (S_n, R_n, r_n))$ such that
  - Each message M_i is distinct from other Message M_j in given Message-Signature $(M_1, \sigma_1 = (S_1, R_1, r_1)), (M_2, \sigma_2 = (S_2, R_2, r_2))\ldots\ldots (M_n, \sigma_n = (S_n, R_n, r_n))$ set.
  - Adversary A is restricted to ask an extract query on Identity ID*.
  - n bounds execution of BlindSig algorithm

4   Construction: Identity-Based Blind Signature Scheme

In this section, we construct an ID-BS scheme which is based on the GDH problem group as shown in Fig. 1.

4.1   ID-Based Blind Signature Scheme

Suppose P be the generator of group G_1 of prime order q. Bilinear map e: G_1 X $G_1 \rightarrow G_2$. Let the three pre-image resistant cryptographic hash function are H_1: $\{0, 1\}^* \rightarrow G_1$, H_2: $\{0, 1\}^* \rightarrow Z_q$, and H_3: $\{0, 1\}^* X G_1 \rightarrow Z_q$. Let the private key of the signer, and the user is denoted as S_{IDS} and S_{IDU}, respectively. Let t indicates the timestamp. The proposed ID-BS scheme consists of four algorithms run between the user and the signer defined as follows:

User		Signer
$K = e(S_{IDU}, R) \in Z_q$ Pick $a \in Z_q$ $A = a^{-1}.R \in G_1$ $h = H_3(m, A) \in Z_q$ $b_M = a.h \in Z_q$ $X = H_3(b_M, K) \in Z_q$	$\xleftarrow{\{R\}}$	Pick $r \in Z_q$. $k = e(S_{IDS}, rH_2(t)Q_{IDU}) \in Z_q$ $R = rH_2(t)Q_{IDS} \in G_1$
	$\xrightarrow{\{X, b_M\}}$	$X' = H_3(b_M, k) \in Z_q$ Check $X' ?= X$
	$\xleftarrow{\{S\}}$	$S = (rH_2(t) + b_M)S_{IDS} \in G_1$
$S' = a^{-1}S \in G_1$ Publish $\{S', m, A\}$		

Fig. 1. BlindSig phase of proposed ID-BS scheme

Setup: PKG selects randomly $s \in Z_q$ and computes public key $P_{Pub} = sP$. Publishes PARAM = $\{G_1, q, e, P, P_{Pub}, H_1, H_2, H_3\}$, and keep secret key s secretly.

Extract: PKG computes $S_{IDS} = sQ_{IDS}$, and $S_{IDU} = sQ_{IDU}$, where $Q_{IDS} = H_1(ID_S)$ and $Q_{IDU} = H_1(ID_U)$, and sends S_{IDS} and S_{IDU} to the signer and the user respectively.

BlindSig: Suppose a user wants to sign on message m, four sub-algorithms (Commitment, Authenticating & Blinding, Signing, Unblinding) must runs between the signer and the user as follows:

Commitment: On random chosen integer $r \in Z_q$, the signer computes $k = e(S_{IDS}, rH_2(t)Q_{IDU})$ and $R = rH_2(t)Q_{IDS}$, and passes R as a commitment to the user.

Authenticating & Blinding: Using his private key, the user computes $K = e(S_{IDU}, R)$. If $k \neq K$, the user picks a random number $a \in Z_q$ as a blinding factor, computes $A = a^{-1}R$, $h = H_3(m, A)$, $b_M = ah$ and $X = H_3(b_M, K)$, and sends (b_M, X) to the signer.

Signing: The signer computes $X' = H_3(b_M, k)$ and check if $X' == X$ holds. For valid justification, the signer produces a signature with his private key as $S = (rH_2(t) + b_M)S_{IDS}$, and sends it back to the user.

Unblinding: The user unblinds the blinded signature S with blinding factor a as $S' = a^{-1}S$, and publishes signature $\{S', A, m\}$ on the message m.

Verify: On given (S', A, m), verify that $(S', P, A + H_3(m, A)Q_{IDS}, P_{pub})$ is a valid Gap-Diffie-Hellman tuple, i.e., if DDHP is easy to solve while CDHP is hard, the signature is valid. Using pairing mapping function, verifier accept the signature if and only if

$$e(S', P) ?= e(A + H_3(m, A)Q_{IDS}, P_{pub}) \tag{4}$$

5 Analysis of Our Proposed Scheme

This section gives the analysis of our proposed ID-BS scheme regarding security and computational efficiency.

5.1   Security Analysis

Theorem 1 (Completeness). The proposed ID-BS scheme is proven to be completeness.

Proof. Since $S' = a^{-1}S$ and $h = H_3(m, A)$, the following equations verifies the correctness of our scheme.

$$e(S', P) = e(a^{-1}S, P) = e(a^{-1}(rH_2(t) + b_M)S_{IDS}, P) = e(a^{-1}r \, H_2(t)Q_{IDS}, + a^{-1}b_M Q_{IDS} \, sP)$$
$$= e(A + hQ_{IDS}, P_{Pub}) = e(A + H_3(m, A)Q_{IDS}, P_{Pub})$$

$$(5)$$

Hence, this confirmed the correctness of our ID-BS scheme. Similarly, the correctness of our ID-BS scheme can be proved for batch verification.

Theorem 2 (Blindness). The proposed ID-BS scheme is blind.

Proof. Suppose (m, S', A) be the message-signature pair and data exchange between the user and signer be (R, b_M, S). Let these data are given to adversary A. To prove the blindness property we show that given valid signature and data exchange during one signature generation, there exists a unique blind factor integer $a \in Z_q$ that maps (R, b_M, S) to (m, S', A). In authenticating and blinding algorithm, the user computes $A = a^{-1}R$ with the random chosen blind factor a. So, to find the message m from the given blinded message $b_M = aH_3(m, A)$, the signer must first locate the value of a and then get the pre-image of hash function H_3. Since H_3 is pre-image resistant and ECDLP is hard to solve in G_1, the proposal satisfies the blindness property. Therefore, even an infinitely powerful A outputs a correct value b' with probability exactly ½. So the scheme is unconditional blind.

Theorem 3 (Non-forgeability). The proposed ID-BS scheme is secure against forgeable attack.

Proof. Suppose an adversary A wants to forge a valid message-signature pair of the signer. Upon request to the challenger C for public parameter PARAM = $\{G_1, G_2, P, e, q, P_{Pub}, H_1, H_2, H_3\}$, C runs the setup algorithm and sends to A. To extract the private key corresponds to the signer identity ID_S, A performs the number of queries as follows:

- *Hash function queries*: For given input ID_i, C computes the hash function values Q_{IDi} and send them to A.
- *Extract queries*: A selects an Identity ID and ask for private key S_{ID} corresponds to ID from C. A runs Extract queries q_E times ($q_E > 0$ and is limited by the polynomial in k) using (PARAM, ID_i) and get the corresponding S_{IDi} where $1 < i < q_E$.
- *BlindSig queries*: A selects an ID_i and Message M, blindly requested the Signature from the C. C compute signature on Message M for identity ID_S.

From hash queries, if A obtains the pair (ID_i, S_{IDSi}) such that $H_1(ID_i) = H_1(ID_S)$, then the A can easily forge the valid signature on message m. Since the hash function is the random oracle, i.e., it uniformly generates the output, he/she cannot get any hint from queries output and could not forge the signature, shown in the followings equation:

$$e(S', P) = e(aS_f, P) = e(a(rH_2(t) + b_M)S_{IDf}, P) = e(ar\, H_2(t)Q_{IDf}, + ab_M Q_{IDf}, sP)$$
$$= e(A_f + hQ_{IDf}, P_{Pub}) = e(A_f + H_3(m, A_f)Q_{IDf}, P_{Pub}) \neq e(A + H_3(m, A)Q_{IDS}, P_{Pub}) \quad (6)$$

The above inequality shows that proposed ID-BS approach is secure against the non-forgeable attack. Now, let (R, b_M, S) be the parameter known to A and suppose he/she had known with signer ID_S. To find the value of S_{IDS} from S, A must know the value of r which was chosen randomly by the signer. To find r from R, it is similar to solve the DLP in G1. Under the assumption of the hardness of ECDLP in G_1, A could not get any handy data in Signature issuing phase.

Upon given R, A could not compute the correct value of k. Consider an Adversary A supposed to forge the signature; he could not get the proper value of k because the private key is known to the signer only. With his own chosen variables, say S_{IDf}, and r_f, Adversary computes shared information.

$$k_f = e(S_{IDf}, r_f.H_2(c)Q_{IDU}), A_f = a_f R, h_f = H_3(m, A_f), b_{Mf} = a_f h,$$
$$S_f = (rH_2(t) + b_M)S_{IDf} \text{ and } S'_f = a_f S_f \quad (7)$$

To forge the signature, an adversary must know S_{IDS}, r_A and x_A. Otherwise, the adversary could not forge the blinded signature on M.

The proposed signature and verification equation is similar to the Boneh's short signature scheme. A can forge the signature if, for given message m, A can compute the value of S' and b_M, such that $e(S', P)? = e(A + H3(m, A)Q_{IDS}, P_{pub})$. As similar to Choon-Cheon's scheme, under the assumption of random oracle model and difficulty to compute CDHP, our system is proven to be secure against the existential forgery attack.

Additionally, to get the original signature, an adversary could not forge the user. Suppose he wants to replace the original message M with forged message M', so he must reproduce the value of k, which is equivalent to solve the GDP problem. Because of the inconsistency of received parameters A_A, b_{MA} and X_A, a signer will refuse to sign on forged blinded signature b_{MA}.

Theorem 4 (Replay attack). The proposed scheme is proven to be secure against the replay attack.

Proof. During commitment and authenticating and blinding phase in our scheme, from following equations:

$$k = e(S_{IDS}, rH_2(t)Q_{IDU}), R = rH_2(t)Q_{IDS}, \text{ and } K = e(S_{IDU}, R) \quad (8)$$

Assuming the use of collision resistant hash function H_2, time stamp t and the hardness to solve the ECDLP, we claim that proposed ID-BS scheme prevents the replay attack.

Theorem 5 (Non-Repudiation). The proposed ID-BS scheme is proven to be non-repudiation.

Proof. In signing phase, the signer computes the signature $S = (rH_2(t) + b_M)S_{IDS}$ with his private key S_{IDS} on any blinded message b_M and pre-computed information k is required to obtain the blinded signature in *BlindSig* algorithm. The pre-computed information k is either calculated with the private key S_{IDS} and randomly chosen value r, at the signer side or the private key S_{IDU} and receiving parameter R, at the user side. Since the signer ID_S is required for the verification, so he/she could not refuse the signature on message m. Therefore, the proposed scheme is proven to secure against the non-repudiation attack.

5.2 Performance Comparison

This section compares our scheme with three existing ID-BS schemes [21, 22, 24]. Table 1 shows the comparison of our scheme with existing scheme regarding operations performed by the user, the signer, and the verifier. Here, the notation of used keywords are given as; P: pairing operation, M: multiplication operation of scalar and element on G_1, A: addition operation of two elements on G_1, H: hash function H: $\{0,1\}$ $* \rightarrow G_1$, M_S: two scalar multiplication, I_S: scalar inversion, C_S: comparison of two scalar, H_S: hash function H_S: $\{0,1\}^{*}$x $G_2 \rightarrow Z_q$, E_P: exponentiation of pairing, M_P: multiplication operation on two pairing, C_P: two pairing elements comparison. Concerning the bandwidth cost, Table 2 shows the comparison of our scheme with three existing ID-BS schemes [21, 22, 24].

Assuming the pairing operation on elliptic curve is very time taken operation, Table 1 shows that our scheme needs $2P + 6 M + 1M_S + 1I_S + 1C_P$ operations and is much efficient than [21, 22, 24] schemes, while scheme in [21] needs $3P + 6 M + 4 A + 1A_S + 1I_S + 2H_S + 1E_P + 1M_P$ operations, the scheme in [22] needs $6P + 2$

Table 1. Computational cost comparison of our scheme with existing schemes

Schemes	Entities	P	M	A	H	M_S	A_S	I_S	C_S	H_S	E_P	M_P	C_P
[21] 2002	Signer		3	1									
	User	1	3	3			1			1			
	Verifier	2						1		1	1	1	
	Total	**3**	**6**	**4**			**1**	**1**		**2**	**1**	**1**	
[22] 2005	Signer	1	1		1					1			
	User	3	1	1	1	2				2	2		
	Verifier	2						1		1	1		1
	Total	**6**	**2**	**1**	**2**	**2**		**1**		**4**	**3**		**1**
[24] 2003	Signer		2				1						
	User		3	1		2	1	1		1			
	Verifier	2	1	1						1			1
	Total	**2**	**6**	**2**		**2**	**2**	**1**		**2**			**1**
Our	Signer		2			1		1	1	2			
	User		2			1				2			
	Verifier	2	1	1						1			1
	Total	**2**	**5**	**1**		**2**	**1**	**1**	**1**	**5**			**1**

M + 2H + 1A + 1A$_S$ + 2M$_S$ + 1I$_S$ +4E$_P$ + 3M$_P$ + 1C$_P$ operations and the scheme in [24] needs 2P + 6 M + 2M$_S$ + 2A + 1A$_S$ + 1I$_S$ +2H$_S$ + 1C$_P$ operations. As compared to scheme [24], proposed scheme is fast which takes one less pairing operation. While our scheme takes less than two-third runtime of [21] scheme and one-third runtime of [22] scheme.

To calculate the cost of all arithmetic operations, we use the panda project [33]. To calculate bandwidth cost in Table 2, we use the results of pairing-friendly elliptic curve introduced by Barretto-Naehrig [34], where the size of points in G$_1$ is 32 bytes, the scalar element is 32 bytes, and pairing points in G$_2$ is 384 bytes. From Table 2, the reader can see that total bandwidth of proposed scheme is 160 bytes equivalent to schemes [21, 24]. But significantly very less bandwidth as compared to scheme in [22] which needs 864 bytes. From Tables 1 and 2, authors say that the proposed model provides better performance in terms of communication cost and computation cost, as compares with related existing schemes.

Table 2. Comparison of Bandwidth cost of our scheme with existing scheme.

Schemes	Communication	G$_1$	G$_2$	S	Cost (in Bytes)
[21]	Signer → User	1			32
	User → Signer			1	32
	Signer → User	1			32
	User → All	1		1	64
	Total	**3**		**2**	**160**
[22]	Signer → User		1		384
	User → Signer			1	32
	Signer → User	1			32
	User → All	1	1		416
	Total	**2**	**2**	**1**	**864**
[24]	Signer → User	1			32
	User → Signer			1	32
	Signer → User			1	32
	User → All	2			64
	Total	**3**		**2**	**160**
Our	Signer → User	1			32
	User → Signer			1	32
	Signer → User	1			32
	User → All	1		1	64
	Total	**3**		**2**	**160**

5.3 Comparison with Zhang's Scheme

Zhang's scheme [24] is the blind version of Choon-Cheon' IBS scheme [20]. To blinding the message, this setting needs two blind factor. Our proposed ID-BS scheme uses the combination of the blind signature scheme suggested by Boldyreva [27] and the IBS scheme proposed by Choon-Cheon [20]. As compared to Zhang's scheme, our scheme requires only one blind factor. Assuming that hash function takes negligible time, our scheme saves $1 M + 1A + 1A_s$ operations with the same size of bandwidth cost of 160 bytes as seen in Tables 1 and 2.

5.4   Optimization for Batch Verification

For a significantly large number of voters' verification, it is required to optimize the verification algorithm of our proposed IDBS scheme. Suppose n users request the signer to make a signature on their message m_1, m_2,.... m_n. Let the signatures are (m_1, R_1, S'_1, A_1), (m_2, R_2, S'_2, A_2),.... (m_n, R_n, S'_n, A_n) on messages m_1, m_2, ... m_n. The batch verification is accepted if and only if the following equations satisfied:

$$e\left(\sum_{i=0}^{n} S'_i, p\right)? = e\left(\sum_{i=0}^{n} A + \sum_{i=0}^{n} H_3(m_i, A_i)Q_{IDS}, P_{Pub}\right) \qquad (9)$$

Verifier needs $2nP + nM$ operations, if he/she verify one by one. In batch verification, verifier needs only $2P + M + 2(n-1)A$. Thus, we claim that our scheme is efficient for batch verification. Our batch verification is comfortable for that environment where the number of verification is huge. For example, in e-voting system, authentication party issues a large number of ballots for voters and send them to the voting party. The voting party can easily verify the correctness of large ballots with above batch verification.

6   A Secure Anonymous Electronic-Voting System

In this section, recall to our ID-BS scheme has been presented in Sect. 4, we proposed an Electronic-voting system. We start with the formal definition of the draft E-voting system.

6.1   Design a Framework

The proposed EVS-ID-BS system consists of five algorithms, namely, Registration, Authentication, Vote casting, and Vote Counting run among the following five parties, namely, Voter, Authentication party (AP), the Vote casting party (VCP), Vote Tallying party (VTP) and Trusted third party (TTP). The voter must have a valid Identity ID, e.g., voters ID, license, passport etc., which is uniquely identified by anyone, TTP is responsible for computing and securely sending the private key for AP, VCP, and VTP with corresponding ID's. AP is in charge of authenticating the legal voters with their valid Identities, VCP is responsible for successful receiving, casting and validating the vote, and VTP is responsible for correctly counting the valid votes.

Short signature scheme. Consider the GDH problem assumption, Boneh-Lynn-Shacham [28] proposed the short signature scheme. As compared to the RSA and DSA, this scheme produce the smaller signature with the same level of security. For example, RSA and DSA generate the signature of 3072 bits and 512 bits respectively for a 128 bits level of security, while this scheme produces a signature of just 257 bits. Under the chosen message attack, hardness of CDHP, and the collision-resistant property of hash function H_1, security proof of short signature is based on the random oracle model.

Definition 4 (E-Voting System). The proposed E-voting system consists of four algorithms among the Voter, AP, VCP, VTP, and TTP, and is defined as follows:

Registration. Similar to setup algorithm of our ID-BS scheme, TTP computes the public parameter with his master and computes the private key for AP, VCP, and VTP with his master key by using Extract algorithm of our scheme. Additionally, Voter and nominal candidate pre-registered himself as a valid voter. Electoral entity prepares a simple list contains the registered voters with their identities.

Authentication. In authentication stage, as shown in Fig. 2, voters' blind the digital message with random blind factor and requests a blank digital ballot to the AP. To generate the blind signature on a blank digital ballot, the AP must first authenticate the voter, and check whether the voter is legal that means voter's name is present in the list and check whether the ballot is unique that does not present previously generated. Then, the AP generates and releases a blank digital ballot to the voter using the *BlindSig* algorithm of our proposed ID-BS technique. The voter gets the blind signature, unblind it and produces the signature.

Vote casting. The voter produces a signature on his given vote with a randomly chosen integer. An electronic ballot is generated which includes the blind signature, signature on the vote, vote and A. The electronic ballot is sent to the VCP. On receiving the ballot, the VCP checks the authenticity of A using the verification of our proposed scheme, which means, whether AP signs A. Then, VCP checks the validity of authenticity of vote using Boneh's Short signature scheme. Upon successful verification of both conditions, VCP produces the hash of the concatenation of electronic ballot and a randomly chosen integer, signs it using his/her private key and sends the electronic ballot to the voter and cache for checking the vote duplicity in future. Then Voter checks his vote by verifying the authenticity of the signature on the hash.

Vote counting. The VTP makes sure that there are no invalid or duplicate electronic ballots. The signature on A and vote are generated using the randomly chosen integer a so the signatures must be unique. The VTP filters the invalid voter by comparing the two ballots with their signature. If two signature in the stored list of electronic ballots is same, one vote considered as invalid, and other is valid. The VTP considered the first ballot as valid and invalidate the election. To count the valid votes, the VTP maintains the valid ballots with the receipt Rcpt in the first list and other list contained the all invalid ballots with their receipts Rcpt and published the two lists.

6.2   Construction of Proposed E-Voting System

Recall to our proposed ID-BS scheme; we offered an E-voting (EVS-ID-BS) system consists of four algorithms as:

Registration: TTP selects random integer $s \in Z_q$ and computes public key $P_{Pub} = sP$. TTP publishes PARAM = $\{G, q, P, P_{Pub}, H_1, H_2, H_3\}$, and keep secret key s secretly. AP and voter registered themselves against their Identity ID_A and ID_V respectively. Using his master key s, TTP computes private keys $S_{IDA} = sQ_{IDA}$ and $S_{IDV} = sQ_{IDV}$ where $Q_{IDA} = H_1(ID_A)$ and $Q_{IDV} = H_1(ID_v)$, and sends S_{IDA} and S_{IDV} to the AP and the voter respectively.

Voter		Authentication Party
		Pick $r \in Z_q$.
$K = e(S_{IDV}, R) \in Z_q$	$\{R\}$	$k = e(S_{IDA}, rH_2(t)Q_{IDV}) \in Z_q$
Pick $a \in Z_q$	$\longleftarrow$	$R = rH_2(t)Q_{IDA} \in G_1$
$A = a^{-1}.R \in G_1$		
$h = H_3(A) \in Z_q$	$\{X, b_M\}$	
$b_M = a.h \in Z_q$	$\longrightarrow$	
$X = H_3(b_M, K) \in Z_q$		$X' = H_3(b_M, k) \in Z_q$
		Check $X' ?= X$
	$\{S\}$	$S = (rH_2(t) + b_M)S_{IDA} \in G_1$
$S' = a^{-1}S \in G_1$	$\longleftarrow$	
Publish (S', A)		

Fig. 2. Authentication phase of EVS-ID-BS system

Voter		Vote Casting Party
Pick vote $\in Z_q$		
$V = aH_1(vote)$	$\{Ballot\}$	
Ballot = $\{S', A, R, vote, V\}$	$\longrightarrow$	
		$e(S', P) ?= e(A + H_3(A)Q_{IDA}, P_{pub})$
		$e(V, A) ?= e(H_1(vote), R)$
		Pick $x \in Z_q$
	$\{Rcpt, S_{Rcpt}\}$	Rcpt = $H_2(Ballot|x)$
	$\longleftarrow$	$S_{Rcpt} = Rcpt.S_{IDC}$
$e(S_{Rcpt}, Q_{IDV}) ?= e(RcptQ_{IDC}, S_{IDV})$		

Fig. 3. Vote Casting stage of EVS-ID-BS system

Authentication: Identical to *BlindSig* algorithm of our ID-BS scheme, this algorithm is run as follows:

- *(Commitment).* The AP chooses a secret random integer $r \in Z_q$, computes k and R where, $k = e(S_{IDA}, rH_2(t)Q_{IDV})$ and $R = rH_2(t)Q_{IDA}$, and delivers R to the voter.
- *(Blind).* Using private key S_{IDV}, the voter computes $K = e(S_{IDV}, R)$. If any forger wants to compute k with his private key S_{IDf}, he couldn't compute next step correctly because of $k \neq K$. Only an authenticate voter can proceed. Now, Voter chooses a random number $a \in Z_q$ as blinding factor, computes $A = a^{-1}R$, h, b_M and X, where, $h = H_3(m, A)$, $b_M = ah$ and $X = H_3(b_M, K)$. Now, voter sends b_M and X to the AP.

- *(Sign)*. On given blinded message (b_M, X), AP computes $X' = H_3(b_M, k)$. AP sign the blinded message with his private key as $S' = b_M S_{IDS}$ if and only if X' and X are equals.
- *(Unblind)*. On receiving the blinded signature S from AP, the voter strips it to computes the actual signature as $S' = a^{-1}S$.

Vote casting: As shown in Fig. 3, Voter computes $V = aH_1(vote)$, where vote $\in \{0, 1\}^*$ and electronic ballot B and send to VCU, where $B = \{S', A, R, vote, V\}$. Then, VCP checks two phase verification as

$$e(S', P) ? = e(hQ_{IDA}, P_{pub}) \tag{10}$$

$$e(V, A) ? = e(H_1(vote), R) \tag{11}$$

Identical to verify algorithm of ID-BS scheme, for every valid verification the VCP keeps it as a valid ballot, otherwise, leave as an invalid. Now, VCP selects a random $x \in Z_q$ and generates a receipt Rcpt and signature on receipt S_{Rcpt} with his private key S_{IDC} to prevent vote coercion, where

$$Rcpt = H_1(B||x) \tag{12}$$

$$S_{Rcpt} = H_2(Rcpt)S_{IDC} \tag{13}$$

VCP sends the receipt and signature (Rcpt, S_{Rcpt}) to the voter. The voter checks $\{S_{Rcpt}, Q_{IDV}, RcptQ_{IDC}, S_{IDV}\}$ is the valid tuple of GDP and verifies if the following equation holds.

$$e(S_{Rcpt}, Q_{IDV}) ? = e(RcptQ_{IDC}, S_{IDV}) \tag{14}$$

Vote counting: After voting, VTP completes the vote counting and then filters identical or electronic fraud ballots. Suppose $B_i = \{S'_i, A_i, R_i, vote_i, V_i\}$ and $B_{i+1} = \{S'_{i+1}, A_{i+1}, R_{i+1}, vote_{i+1}, V_{i+1}\}$ are two ballots in electronic ballot list. The signatures S_i' on A_i and Signature V_i and on $vote_i$ are generated using the two different randomly chosen integer a_i so the signatures must be unique. The VTP filters the invalid voter by comparing the two ballots with their signature. If $S'_i == S'_{i+1}$ and $V_i == V_{i+1}$ in the stored list of electronic ballots are same, the one ballot is considered as invalid and other is valid. The VTP considered the first ballot as valid and invalidate the vote. To count the valid votes, the VTP maintains the two lists: the first list contains the valid ballots with their corresponding receipt Rcpt and other list included the all invalid ballots with their receipts Rcpt and published the two lists.

6.3   Security Analysis

Voter anonymity: Voters hide their identity with randomly chosen integer a, serving as the private key and public key is $A = a^{-1}R$. The pair of private and public key for voter be (a, A) also called Pseudonym private and Pseudonym public key. For any given pseudonym public key A, it is hard to identify the voter identity as there is no mapping between the Voter identity and the pair of keys. To limit the voter that he could not generates more than one pseudonym, the voter restricted to blinds its alias public key A as $b_M = ah$ where $h = H_3(A)$, with their private key a and pass the AP. So we can say that voter's alias public key A blinded with his secret random info a and signed just once by the AP. For any given R and A, find the value of a, is identical to break the proposed ID-BS scheme as proved in Theorem 2. Therefore, it is claimed that proposed EVS-ID-BS scheme provides the voter anonymity.

Coercion-resistant: The property of coercion-resistant is provided by the use of random number x which gives the randomness in Rcpt. In order to generate the duplicate acknowledgment, the voter must choose the exact value of x. Since hash function, H_3 is pre-image resistant, so it is infeasible to compute the value of x from given required parameters. Rcpt ensures the voter that without compromising the value of the vote, the ballot is successfully given by VCP. Thus, our proposed EVS-ID-BS scheme is free from the coercion attack.

Authentication: In authentication phase, AP authenticates the voter, signs on the blinded ballot and sends blindly signed ballot to the voter. The voter will be considered as eligible if AP authenticate the voter and verifies the pre-computed information. Since randomly chosen $r \in Zq$, AP's private key SIDA and voter's public key QIDV, the following equations justify the verification as:

$$k = e(S_{IDA}, rH_2(t)Q_{IDV}) = e(rH_2(t)Q_{IDA}, sQ_{IDV}) = e(R, S_{IDV}) = K \qquad (15)$$

Since the private key S_{IDV} correspond to the identity ID_V is only accessible by the voter who claims his identity ID_V. The value of K computed either by AP or by the voter. Therefore, the EVS-ID-BS scheme ensures the voter's eligibility.

Integrity: In vote casting phase, the voter signs the vote with his random chosen number a, i.e., $V = aH_1(vote)$. If any entity wants to alter the value of a vote, he must have to guess the exact value of a, which is equivalent to solve the ECDLP problem and break our proposed ID-based signature scheme which is negligible to break proved in Theorem 1. Therefore, proposed EVS-ID-BS system guarantees the vote integrity.

Uniqueness: After generating the blind signature for each voter, VCP verifies the ballot. On valid verification, the vote is considered as valid and stored in the list, otherwise invalid. In voting stage, each voter has the same vote, but two signatures distinguished by their random number a, which guarantees that each voter creates the different signature for their vote.

Verifiability: After vote counting stage, VTP published two lists containing the name of valid and invalid voters with their Rcpt. To check the voter participation, each voter can verify the equation $e(S_{Rcpt}, Q_{IDV})$? $= e(RcptQ_{IDC}, S_{IDV})$ using Rcpt obtaining from the valid list, the public key of VCP and sign on receipt. If the verification is valid, voter confirms that his vote is counted otherwise not counted.

Batch verifiability: Identical to the batch verification in our proposed scheme, the VCP can verify a large number of ballots in a single unit of time as:

$$e\left(\sum_{i=0}^{n} S_i', p\right)? = e\left(\sum_{i=0}^{n} A + \sum_{i=0}^{n} H_3(m_i, A_i) Q_{IDS}, P_{Pub}\right) \qquad (16)$$

For n number of ballots proposed system can save the computational cost around 2 $(n-1)$ pairing operations.

6.4   Comparison with Garcia et al.'s E-Voting Scheme

The E-voting system proposed by Garcia et al. [5] is based on certificate-based cryptography and uses the advantage of Boneh's short signature scheme [28] and Boldyreva's blind signature scheme [27]. To Excel the overhead of managing certificates and public key, our proposed EVS-ID-BS system uses the advantage of Boneh' short signature [28], Boldyreva's blind signature scheme [27] and the Choon-Cheon's IBS scheme [20]. Our EVS-ID-BS system needs only one hash operation for verifying the user authenticity while Garcia's system needs two pairing operations. Additionally, proposed system is more suitable for verifying a large number of voters as seen in Sect. 6.3.

6.5   Implementation

Our scheme assumes the pairing type A of [29] with $|P| = 512$ bits and $q = 160$ bits with $k = 2$, where, $|p|$ is the length of P, q is the order of group G and k is embedding a degree of elliptic curve. All results run by gcc compiler of version 4:4.8.2-1ubuntu6 on Ubuntu 14.04 operating system with 4 GB RAM and Intel(R) Core(TM)2 Duo CPU E8400 @ 3.00 GHz processor. The implementation of our scheme written in C/C+ + based on PBC library of Version 0.5.14 and GMP library version 6.1.0 that computes the authentication phase, vote casting phase and verification in ~ 6.28 ms, ~ 10.39 ms and ~ 2.46 ms respectively, as given in Table 3.

Table 3. Computation cost (in msec) of our proposed EVS-ID-BS scheme

Phases	Cost (in msec)
Voter's authentication	~ 6.28 ms
Vote casting	~ 10.39 ms
Vote verification	~ 2.46 ms

7   Conclusion

In this paper, first, we proposed an efficient ID-BS Scheme which simplifies the certificate management and public key revocation problem. The proposed ID-BS scheme uses the combined advantage of Bolyreva et al.'s blind signature scheme and Choon-Cheon et al.'s IBS Scheme. The security of our proposed system is based on the hardness of GDH problem and secure against existential forgery attack under the adaptive chosen message and ID attacks. As compared to the existing scheme, ID-BS scheme performs better as it takes consumes less pairing operation. Further, it provides the user anonymity, privacy, integrity, coercion-resistant, uniqueness, individual and batch verifiability. Secondly, we construct a practical implemented E-voting system based on our ID-BS scheme and BLS's short signature scheme (EVS-ID-BS) that fulfills the needed security requirements of the E-voting system. EVS-ID-BS scheme provides batch verifiability for a significantly large number of voters, requires less bandwidth cost and require less interaction with election authority.

Acknowledgement. This research work has been partially supported by the Council of Scientific and Industrial Research, a research and development organization in India, with sanctioned no. 09/263(1052)/2015 EMR-I and the UPE-II grant received from JNU. Additionally, the author would like to sincere thanks to the anonymous reviewers for their fruitful comments.

References

1. Awad, M., Leiss, E.L.: The evolution of voting: analysis of conventional and electronic voting systems. Int. J. Appl. Eng. Res. **11**(12), 7888–7896 (2016)
2. Cetinkaya, O., Analysis of security requirements for cryptographic voting protocols. In: Third International Conference on Availability, Reliability and Security, ARES 2008, pp. 1451–1456 (2008)
3. Chaum, D.L.: Untraceable electronic mail, return addresses, and digital pseudonyms. Commun. ACM **24**(2), 84–90 (1981)
4. Benaloh, J.D.C.: Verifiable secret-ballot elections. Yale University. Department of Computer Science (1987)
5. López-García, L., Perez, L.J.D., Rodríguez-Henríquez, F.: A pairing-based blind signature e-voting scheme. Comput. J. **57**, 1460–1471 (2013). bxt069
6. Peng, K., Bao, F.: A design of secure preferential E-voting. In: Ryan, P.Y.A., Schoenmakers, B. (eds.) Vote-ID 2009. LNCS, vol. 5767, pp. 141–156. Springer, Heidelberg (2009). https://doi.org/10.1007/978-3-642-04135-8_9
7. Porkodi, C., Arumuganathan, R., Vidya, K.: Multi-authority electronic voting scheme based on elliptic curves. IJ Netw. Secur. **12**(2), 84–91 (2011)
8. Gupta, N., Kumar, P., Chokar, S.: A secure blind signature application in E-voting. In: Proceedings of the 5th National Conference, Computing for National Development, pp. 1–4 (2011)
9. Zhang, H., You, Q., Zhang, J.: A lightweight electronic voting scheme based on blind signature and Kerberos mechanism. In: 2015 5th International Conference on Electronics Information and Emergency Communication (ICEIEC), pp. 210–214 (2015)
10. Zhang, L., Hu, Y., Tian, X., Yang, Y.: Novel identity-based blind signature for electronic voting system. In: 2010 Second International Workshop on Education Technology and Computer Science (ETCS), vol. 2, pp. 122–125 (2010)
11. Kharchineh, B., Ettelaee, M.: A new electronic voting protocol using a new blind signature scheme. In: Second International Conference on Future Networks, ICFN 2010, pp. 190–194 (2010)

12. Chaum, D.: Blind signatures for untraceable payments. In: Chaum, D., Rivest, R.L., Sherman, A.T. (eds.) Advances in cryptology, pp. 199–203. Springer, Boston (1983). https://doi.org/10.1007/978-1-4757-0602-4_18

13. Chaum, D., Fiat, A., Naor, M.: Untraceable electronic cash. In: Goldwasser, S. (ed.) CRYPTO 1988. LNCS, vol. 403, pp. 319–327. Springer, New York (1990). https://doi.org/10.1007/0-387-34799-2_25

14. Kumar, M., Katti, C.P.: An efficient ID-based partially blind signature scheme and application in electronic-cash payment system (2017)

15. Kumar, M., Katti, C.P., Saxena, P.C.: An untraceable identity-based blind signature scheme without pairing for e-cash payment system. In: International Conference on Ubiquitous Communication and Network Computing (2017)

16. Fujioka, A., Okamoto, T., Ohta, K.: A practical secret voting scheme for large scale elections. In: Seberry, J., Zheng, Y. (eds.) AUSCRYPT 1992. LNCS, vol. 718, pp. 244–251. Springer, Heidelberg (1993). https://doi.org/10.1007/3-540-57220-1_66

17. Shamir, A.: Identity-based cryptosystems and signature schemes. In: Blakley, G.R., Chaum, D. (eds.) CRYPTO 1984. LNCS, vol. 196, pp. 47–53. Springer, Heidelberg (1985). https://doi.org/10.1007/3-540-39568-7_5

18. Boneh, D., Franklin, M.: Identity-based encryption from the weil pairing. In: Kilian, J. (ed.) CRYPTO 2001. LNCS, vol. 2139, pp. 213–229. Springer, Heidelberg (2001). https://doi.org/10.1007/3-540-44647-8_13

19. Boldyreva, A., Goyal, V., Kumar, V.: Identity-based encryption with efficient revocation. In: Proceedings of the 15th ACM conference on Computer and Communications Security, pp. 417–426 (2008)

20. Choon, J.C., Hee Cheon, J.: An identity-based signature from gap Diffie-Hellman groups. In: Desmedt, Y.G. (ed.) PKC 2003. LNCS, vol. 2567, pp. 18–30. Springer, Heidelberg (2003). https://doi.org/10.1007/3-540-36288-6_2

21. Zhang, F., Kim, K.: ID-based blind signature and ring signature from pairings. In: Zheng, Y. (ed.) ASIACRYPT 2002. LNCS, vol. 2501, pp. 533–547. Springer, Heidelberg (2002). https://doi.org/10.1007/3-540-36178-2_33

22. Huang, Z., Chen, K., Wang, Y.: Efficient identity-based signatures and blind signatures. In: Desmedt, Y.G., Wang, H., Mu, Y., Li, Y. (eds.) CANS 2005. LNCS, vol. 3810, pp. 120–133. Springer, Heidelberg (2005). https://doi.org/10.1007/11599371_11

23. He, D., Chen, J., Zhang, R.: An efficient identity-based blind signature scheme without bilinear pairings. Comput. Electr. Eng. **37**(4), 444–450 (2011)

24. Zhang, F., Kim, K.: Efficient ID-based blind signature and proxy signature from bilinear pairings. In: Safavi-Naini, R., Seberry, J. (eds.) ACISP 2003. LNCS, vol. 2727, pp. 312–323. Springer, Heidelberg (2003). https://doi.org/10.1007/3-540-45067-X_27

25. Kumar, M., Katti, C.P., Saxena, P.C.: A new blind signature scheme using identity-based technique. Int. J. Control Theory Appl. **10**(15), 36–42 (2017)

26. Ribarski, P., Antovski, L.: Comparison of ID-based blind signatures from pairings for e-voting protocols. In: 2014 37th International Convention on Information and Communication Technology, Electronics and Microelectronics (MIPRO), pp. 1394–1399 (2014)

27. Boldyreva, A.: Threshold signatures, multisignatures and blind signatures based on the gap-Diffie-Hellman-group signature scheme. In: Desmedt, Y.G. (ed.) PKC 2003. LNCS, vol. 2567, pp. 31–46. Springer, Heidelberg (2003). https://doi.org/10.1007/3-540-36288-6_3

28. Boneh, D., Lynn, B., Shacham, H.: Short signatures from the weil pairing. In: Boyd, C. (ed.) ASIACRYPT 2001. LNCS, vol. 2248, pp. 514–532. Springer, Heidelberg (2001). https://doi.org/10.1007/3-540-45682-1_30

29. Lynn, B.: The pairing-based cryptography (PBC) library (2010)

30. Miller, V.S.: Use of elliptic curves in cryptography. In: Williams, H.C. (ed.) CRYPTO 1985. LNCS, vol. 218, pp. 417–426. Springer, Heidelberg (1986). https://doi.org/10.1007/3-540-39799-X_31

31. Koblitz, N.: Elliptic curve cryptosystems. Math. Comput. **48**(177), 203–209 (1987)

32. Pointcheval, D., Stern, J.: Security arguments for digital signatures and blind signatures. J. Cryptol. **13**(3), 361–396 (2000)

33. Chuengsatiansup, C., Naehrig, M., Ribarski, P., Schwabe, P.: PandA: pairings and arithmetic. In: Cao, Z., Zhang, F. (eds.) Pairing 2013. LNCS, vol. 8365, pp. 229–250. Springer, Cham (2014). https://doi.org/10.1007/978-3-319-04873-4_14

34. Barreto, P.S.L.M., Naehrig, M.: Pairing-friendly elliptic curves of prime order. In: Preneel, B., Tavares, S. (eds.) SAC 2005. LNCS, vol. 3897, pp. 319–331. Springer, Heidelberg (2006). https://doi.org/10.1007/11693383_22

SEMFS: Secure and Efficient Multi-keyword Fuzzy Search for Cloud Storage

Sanjeet Kumar Nayak$^{(\boxtimes)}$ and Somanath Tripathy

Department of Computer Science and Engineering,
Indian Institute of Technology Patna, Patna, India
{sanjeet.pcs13,som}@iitp.ac.in

Abstract. Cloud computing has become a popular technology for outsourcing data and providing reliable data services. Encryption is essential to preserve privacy of the outsourced sensitive data. Keyword search over encrypted data would enhance the effective utilization of outsourced storage. In this work, we propose an efficient Searchable Symmetric Encryption (SSE) scheme called SEMFS (Secure & Efficient Multi-keyword Fuzzy Search Scheme) to allow the cloud to search over outsourced encrypted data. SEMFS uses quotient filter for efficient indexing and faster searching. The most attractive feature of this scheme is to allow update the entries of index file dynamically (to achieve better performance) preserving data privacy. Experimental analysis shows that SEMFS achieves higher throughput than the bloom filter based scheme, when implemented. Security of SEMFS has been analyzed against known ciphertext and known plaintext attack models.

Keywords: Cloud storage · Searchable symmetric encryption
Multi-keyword search · Quotient filter · Fuzzy search

1 Introduction

With the advancement of cloud computing, data outsourcing has become a major motive of several individuals and enterprises. But simply outsourcing the sensitive data like personal, financial, medical, etc., in plaintext format would lead to security risk. In addition to this, there could be risks from cloud storage server, as both data owner (DO) and cloud server (CS) are not in the same trusted domain [24]. This issue would be addressed if encrypted data is uploaded on CS. As DO outsources data in encryption format, it creates difficulty for the data users (DUs) to search a data file using keywords. Therefore, there is a call for some mechanisms to facilitate data users to search directly over the encrypted data.

Searchable encryption (SE) facilitates DU to securely search a file from encrypted files, using certain specific keywords without decrypting. Hence, SE is a widely adopted solution that helps DU to search over a vast collection of

© Springer International Publishing AG 2017
R. K. Shyamasundar et al. (Eds.): ICISS 2017, LNCS 10717, pp. 50–67, 2017.
https://doi.org/10.1007/978-3-319-72598-7_4

outsourced data. There are two kinds of SE schemes, namely, searchable symmetric encryption (SSE) and searchable public-key encryption (SPE). The inherent cryptographic techniques used by the SSE and SPE schemes are symmetric key cryptography and asymmetric key cryptography respectively. SSE schemes are more efficient and easier to implement as compared to SPE based schemes.

Song et al. [27] presented a searchable encryption which searches the entire document sequentially, so consumes more time. Subsequently, many works including [6,11,13] have been proposed to address this issue, using index based matching of keywords. But, unfortunately, all these schemes facilitate single keyword search over encrypted data. For enriching the search functionality, several schemes like [7,14,16] proposed multiple keyword search over encrypted data. However, these schemes only support exact keyword search. But, in practical scenario user searching behavior would lead to minor typing mistakes and format inconsistencies. Data users may not input exactly the same pre-set keyword due to some typos, inconsistencies in the representation of the word or due to lack of exact knowledge. Recently, few works [10,17,19,20] extended the search functionality to address this issue supporting user searching behavior (known as fuzzy search). Wang et al. [29] proposed an efficient multi-keyword fuzzy search over the encrypted data. They used bloom filter for efficient search algorithm.

In this paper, we propose an efficient multi-keyword fuzzy search technique for cloud storage named SEMFS. It preserves privacy of the index file, search query and documents without needing predefined dictionary for dynamic data operation. We use quotient filter for the first time to enable searching over encrypted data; as a result, SEMFS achieves efficient indexing and faster searching as compared to bloom filter based scheme. This scheme allows the data owners to directly update the secure index file present in the cloud server if the corresponding files are modified. The effectiveness and efficiency of the scheme is evaluated using experimental evaluation. Along with this, we analyze the security of the proposed scheme against known ciphertext and known plaintext attack models.

The rest of the paper is organized as follows. Section 2 discusses the related works in this area. Section 3 describes the system model and threat model. In Sect. 4, we introduce details of our proposed scheme. We describe the security analysis of the proposed scheme in Sect. 5. Section 6 provides some discussions on the proposed scheme along with performance analysis. Finally, the concluding remarks are provided in Sect. 7.

2   Related Work

Searchable encryption (SE) was first proposed by Song et al. [27]. The motive behind their proposal is to enable searching on encrypted data without leaking any information to the untrusted server. Their scheme is a symmetric key based proposal. Here, data user has to go through the entire document to search a particular keyword in a document. So searching overhead is linear in terms of length of the document. In [13], the author has developed a secure index per file to reduce the searching overhead. A data user can query for a keyword using the trapdoor which is a function of keyword and secret key. Bloom filter [5], a space efficient data structure, is used as a per document index to track words in each document. Thus, searching overhead is reduced. The authors in [9] proposed a keyword index which associates each word with its corresponding file. Data owner uses pseudo random bits to mask the dictionary based keyword index for each file and sends it to the cloud server. Later the data user recovers the index. Curtmola et al. [11] proposed an inverted index based searchable symmetric encryption scheme which indexes per-keyword. A single encrypted hash table is built for the entire file collection. Here, each entry consists of a keyword trapdoor corresponding to the encrypted form of those file identifiers contain that keyword. The searching scheme proposed in [28] reduces the search time to logarithm order. It ensures the privacy of searched keywords. First public key encryption with keyword search (PKES) scheme is given by Boneh et al. [6]. Functionality of this scheme is quite similar to that of the Song et al. [27]. But, only the authorized data users can search with the corresponding private key. This scheme uses an adversary model similar to Goh et al.'s scheme [13], but requires the use of computationally intensive pairing operations [21]. All above works support single keyword search over the outsourced encrypted data.

As multiple keyword search has become a necessary functionality of SE schemes, many techniques try to incorporate this. Among these works, conjunctive keyword search schemes [14–16] return the list of documents that contain all the keywords while disjunctive keyword search schemes [7,33] return list of documents that contain a subset of query words. However, these multi-keyword search schemes do not provide ranking of the search result, which helps in retrieving most relevant files containing the keywords. Cao et al. [8] proposes a privacy preserving multi-keyword ranked search scheme over encrypted data.

A fuzzy keyword search algorithm proposed by Li et al. [19]. This is a wild card based scheme and facilitates the data users to search the desired file with minor typing errors and even if the format is inconsistent. Liu et al. [20] improves this scheme by reducing the index size. Chuah et al. [10] proposed a privacy preserving tree based fuzzy searching algorithm. All these schemes support single keyword based fuzzy search. Later Wang et al. [29] proposes a multi-keyword based fuzzy search using bloom filter. It uses locality sensitive hashing in place of wild cards to enhance the efficiency of fuzzy search. Along with this, it eliminates the need of a predefined dictionary for dynamic data updation.

3   Problem Formulation

3.1   System Model

A typical system model for secure search over encrypted data is as shown in Fig. 1. It consists of three entities, namely, data owner (DO), cloud server (CS) and data user (DU). DO outsources the data files (documents) to an untrusted cloud server. Each document contains a set of words referred as "keywords", through which the document can uniquely be identified. Keywords can

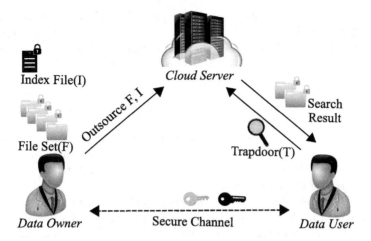

Fig. 1. Cloud data storage architecture for secure search over encrypted data. (Color figure online)

be extracted by analyzing the entire document either manually or through an automated procedure or more sophisticated text mining algorithms like multi purpose automatic topic indexing (Maui) [22] and rapid automatic keyword extraction (RAKE) [25]. DU submits a set of keywords as a query to CS. CS returns the corresponding files by searching those keywords in the index file. Let $F = \{f_1, f_2, f_3, ..., f_n\}$ denotes the set of files that DO wants to outsource. To protect the confidentiality, these files could be encrypted using symmetric encryption like advanced encryption standards (AES) [12].

To facilitate searching over encrypted files in efficient manner, DO creates a quotient filter based secure searchable index file (QF_i) using a secret key (K_{sec}). QF_i is formed using a collection of distinct keywords $W = \{w_1, w_2, w_3, ..., w_m\}$ of the file f_i. Finally, data owner outsources both F and QF_i to CS. Cloud server stores F and QF_i in its data storage to enable data searching mechanism for DU. When DU sends a trapdoor $(T_{kw'})$ of a keyword kw' to CS, it checks for the same in QF_i. It sends the corresponding collection of files. In addition to this necessary operations, DO sometimes update a file and corresponding QF_i and informs regarding the same to the cloud server.

Initially, data owner shares the symmetric encryption key (K_{sym}) and secret key (K_{sec}) to all authorized DUs. Using K_{sec}, DU generates the trapdoor $(T_{kw'})$ of a keyword kw' and sends it to CS. Cloud server searches for the corresponding trapdoor in the index file and returns the encrypted data files to DU. DU can decrypt those files using K_{sym}.

3.2 Threat Model

Cloud server is considered to be an "honest-but-curious." This signifies that CS executes secure searching over outsourced data honestly, at the same time it is curious to derive the information regarding queried word [18,30]. However, data owner and data user are assumed to act honestly and trust each other. The focus of this work is mainly over confidentiality rather than availability. Distribution of the secret informations (K_{sym}, K_{sec}) are being performed via a secure channel, and such key distribution mechanisms are studied separately in [2,23].

Based on the information available to CS, we consider the following two threat models.

- **Known Ciphertext Model:** In this model, the cloud server has access to the collection of encrypted files F, secure index file I (outsourced by DO) and trapdoor of the keyword $T_{kw'}$ (submitted by DU). Further, CS can have a collection of previously submitted trapdoors.
- **Known Plaintext Model:** This model is more stronger than the previous model. Here, the cloud server has some extra background knowledge including the information of the known ciphertext model. Background information includes statistical information that can be generated using a similar kind of data set as that data owner used. They can use the known index/trapdoor generation mechanism using frequency of words. This information can help them to find some private information of the data owner.

In both these models, target of CS is to derive exact keywords that DU searches. It will also try to find the content of the encrypted files which can leak privacy of the keywords.

3.3 Design Goals

To enable secure searching over encrypted data with the above system and threat model the following design goals are desired.

- **Multi-keyword Fuzzy Search:** This feature allows to search multiple keywords using logical connectives like "AND", "OR", etc. This scheme should allow fuzzy search so that minor typos and format inconsistencies will not disappoint the user searching experience. For example, files containing keyword "international football match" should be returned as a search result for the mis-typed word "international football <u>mach</u>" or "<u>internasional</u> football match."
- **Dynamic Update:** DO sometimes update a file and corresponding QF_i stored in the cloud server has to be updated. So, scheme should be designed to provide dynamic data operation (insertion/deletion/modification) over the secure index file in an efficient manner.
- **Ranking of Search Result:** Scheme should rank the relevance of files in response to a given search query for the convenience of the data user.
- **No Predefined Dictionary:** Use of a predefined dictionary for the search operations leads to difficulty during dynamic update of index file. Schemes without predefined dictionary can update index file comfortably.
- **Confidentiality of Document, Privacy of Index File and Trapdoor:** The keywords stored in the index file as well as the search query (or trapdoor)

should not reveal any information to the cloud server regarding the searched keywords (w_i). As the outsourced documents are present in the CS, they have to be encrypted to preserve the confidentiality of the documents. Therefore, if any one of the three is not encrypted, then the privacy of the searched keyword may leak.

4   SEMFS: The Proposed Scheme

4.1   Basic Idea

SEMFS creates a per file quotient filter (QF_i) which contains an index information of all the keywords present in file f_i. To enable multi-keyword search, we convert each keyword into a trigram set and use a modified quotienting function to insert the trigram set into QF_i. Quotient filter and trigram set are precisely discussed as under.

Quotient Filter: Quotient filter (QF) has been introduced by Bender et al. in [4]. It is a time-efficient data structure for representing a set, to support membership queries. QF returns no to the membership query assures that the queried element is definitely not present in the set. Otherwise, the element is said to be probably present. Thus, quotient filter never returns false negative.

QF stores a m bit hash value (known as fingerprint (FP)) of an element $\mathbb{E}$ as follows. This m bit value is split into two parts as remainder (FP_r) and quotient (FP_q). The least significant r bit constitute remainder and the most significant $q = m - r$ bit constitute quotient (FP_q). This is known as quotienting technique. FP_q is used as an index to find the corresponding slot (or bucket) for FP in the QF and the slot is filled with FP_r. Inserting a fingerprint in QF may encounter a soft collision when only FP_q of two or more fingerprints are same. The canonical slot is the bucket in which a fingerprint's remainder (FP_r) would be stored in the absence of a collision. All remainders of fingerprints with the same quotient are stored contiguously, and known as run for the corresponding quotient. Hence, a run constitutes of all the slots that contain remainders with the same quotient. But, a cluster is a greater sequence of occupied slots whose first element is the only element stored in its canonical slot. One or more runs may present in a cluster.

To search a stored fingerprint within a cluster, each bucket contains additional three bits known as *is_occupied*, *is_continuation*, *is_shifted*. All these are initialized to 0 at the beginning. *is_occupied* bit of bucket i is set when the bucket i is the canonical slot ($FP_q = i$) for some fingerprint FP which is stored somewhere in QF. *is_continuation* bit is set to 0 indicates the start of a run. *is_shifted* bit is set to 0 indicates start of a cluster. Algorithms 1 and 2 describe the searching and insertion procedure of a fingerprint FP in the QF respectively [3].

A schematic diagram of a QF is shown in Fig. 2. This example considers $FP_q = \lfloor \frac{FP}{2^8} \rfloor$ and $FP_r = FP \mod 2^8$. This QF contains fingerprint values 258,

---

Algorithm 1. To search an element $\mathbb{E}$ in QF

Input: QF, $\mathbb{E}$
Output: Probably present/Definitely not present
 1: Find fingerprint (FP) of $\mathbb{E}$.
 2: Find quotient (FP_q) and remainder (FP_r) for FP.
 3: Set $running\_count \leftarrow 0$.
 4: **if** $\neg(is\_occupied$ QF$[FP_q] = 0)$ **then**   ▷ bucket FP_q is empty
 5:     FP is not present in the filter.
 6: **else**
 7:     **repeat**
 8:         Scan left from bucket FP_q
 9:         **if** $is\_occupied = 1$ **then**
10:             $running\_count$ ++;
11:         **end if**
12:     **until** find a bucket with $is\_shifted = 0$
13:     **repeat**
14:         Scan right from current bucket
15:         **if** $is\_continuation = 0$ **then**
16:             $running\_count$ −−;
17:         **end if**
18:     **until** $running\_count = 0$
19:     Compare the stored remainder in each bucket in the quotient's run with FP_r.
20:     **if** found **then**
21:         Element is in the filter (probably).
22:     **else**
23:         Element is not in the filter (definitely).
24:     **end if**
25: **end if**

Algorithm 2. To insert an element $\mathbb{E}$ in QF

Input: QF, $\mathbb{E}$
Output: QF with $\mathbb{E}$ inserted
 1: Find fingerprint (FP) of $\mathbb{E}$.
 2: Find quotient (FP_q) and remainder (FP_r) for FP.
 3: Proceed as Algorithm 1 till FP is definitely not in QF.
 4: Choose a bucket in the current run by keeping the order sorted.
 5: Insert FP_r and (set $is\_occupied$ bit).
 6: Shift forward all remainders at or after the chosen bucket. Update the buckets'
    bits.

369, 124, 66, 469, 58 and 364. Figure 2 (a) presents the quotient, remainder pair for each fingerprint. Using these quotients and remainders, we inserted corresponding fingerprints using Algorithm 2 in the QF. At last, the contents of QF is shown in Fig. 2 (b). Here, remainders are stored in the corresponding bucket (quotient represents the bucket number) in the filter. Each bucket of QF contains three bits known as $is\_occupied$, $is\_continuation$, $is\_shifted$ (meta data) and the remainder. Here, fingerprints 124, 66, and 58 have the same quotient

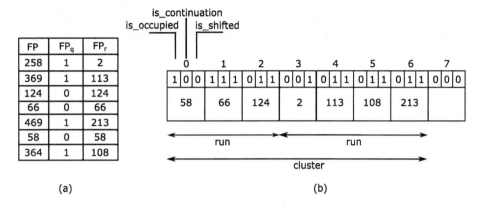

Fig. 2. An example of quotient filter

and constitute a run. Even though 258 could be placed in slot 1, but as run of 0 occupies 3 slots, it is shifted from its canonical slot. Fingerprints 258, 369, 469, and 364 constitute run of quotient 1. Fingerprints 258, 369, 124, 66, 469, 58 and 364 constitute a cluster.

Trigram Set Construction from Keyword: Each keyword of the corresponding file is transformed into a trigram set (TS). A trigram set contains all the contiguous three letters appeared in the keyword (considering circular way). For example, the trigram set of a keyword "relativity" is {rel, ela, lat, ati, tiv, ivi, vit, ity, tyr, yre}. Here, we assume that keywords $\in \{a, b, ..., z\}^{+}$.

Each different trigram element (of alphabet set) is enumerated to a unique decimal number using a function $\mathbb{F}$ which works as follows. Letters $[a \cdots z]$ are mapped to $[0 \cdots 25]$. The equivalent decimal representation of the trigram entry can be obtained using Eq. 1.

$$\mho_i = \mathbb{F}(TS_i) = (TS_i[0] * 26^2 + TS_i[1] * 26^1 + TS_i[2] * 26^0) \qquad (1)$$

For example,

$$\begin{aligned}\mathbb{F}(rel) &= (r * 26^2 + e * 26^1 + l * 26^0) \\ &= (17 * 26^2 + 4 * 26^1 + 11 * 26^0) \\ &= (11492 + 104 + 11) = 11607\end{aligned}$$

Now, the modified representation of TS (i.e. $\mho_i, \forall i \in TS$) contains equivalent decimal representations of a trigram.

Inserting Trigrams into Quotient Filter: At first, $\mho_i$ is divided into two parts ($\mho_{iq}$ and $\mho_{ir}$) as

$$\mho_{iq} = \left\lfloor \frac{\mho_i}{\beta} \right\rfloor \qquad (2)$$

$$\mho_{ir} = \mho_i \mod \beta \qquad (3)$$

Here, β is a user defined parameter.[1] $\mho_{iq}$ is used as an index in QF and $\mho_{ir}$ is stored in the corresponding slot. Insertion is carried out as per Algorithm 2.

4.2 Operational Details of SEMFS

SEMFS consists of following four phases as depicted in Fig. 3 and discussed below.

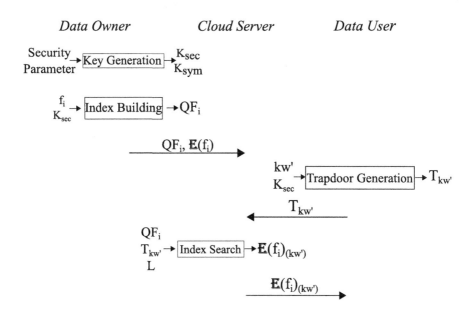

Fig. 3. Schematic diagram of proposed SEMFS.

1. **Key generation phase:** DO generates a secret key (K_{sec}) and a symmetric key (K_{sym}) to be shared with the DUs. It declares a secure hash function ($\mathbb{H}$) like SHA 2 [1] and symmetric encryption algorithm like advanced encryption standard (AES) [12]. In addition, data owner declares a system wide parameter L which indicates the level of fuzziness. Level of fuzziness would be defined as the ability of the technique to support at most L number of typing mistake or format inconsistencies. For example, if $L = 1$, then SEMFS should return the files indexed by keywords "Tom and Jane", when a data user submits query for the keywords "Tom a<u>md</u> Jane."

2. **Index building phase:** In this phase, DO constructs a QF using Algorithm 3 with the input as keywords (kw_j) of the corresponding file.

---

[1] Let, $\alpha \times \beta = \gamma$ where α is the total number of slots in QF and β is the total number of different values that can be stored in each slot.

A delimiter (like ",") may be placed at the end of each keyword as the terminating character. Then, a trigram set (TS) is constructed for each keyword. Each entry of TS is represented in equivalent decimal form. Hash digest of the equivalent decimal form of trigram entry and K_{sec} (secret key) is computed. Then, the digest is divided by β, results into quotient and remainder which would be inserted into QF_i accordingly using Algorithm 2. Finally, this algorithm results in a secure index (QF_i) of the corresponding file f_i. QF_i is treated as secure index of the file f_i as CS does not know K_{sec}.

Now DO encrypts file (f_i) using AES with key K_{sym} and uploads the encrypted file $(\mathscr{E}(f_i))$ with the corresponding secure index file QF_i to the CS.

Algorithm 3. BuildIndex

Input: f_i, kw_j, $\mathbb{H}$, K_{sec}, γ
Output: QF_i
1: **for** $j = 1$ to m **do**   ▷ for each keyword $\{kw_1, ..., kw_m\}$ in f_i
2:     Construct trigram set $TS_j = \{t_1, ..., t_p\}$.
3:     **for** $k = 1$ to p **do**
4:         Find decimal representation of $t_k(\mho_k)$.
5:         Find $\mathscr{C}_k = \mathbb{H}(\mho_k \| K_{sec})$.
6:         Find $\mathbb{C}_k = \mathscr{C}_k \bmod \gamma$ ▷ $\gamma = \alpha \times \beta$
7:         Find $\mathbb{C}_{kq} = \left\lfloor \frac{\mathbb{C}_k}{\beta} \right\rfloor$ and $\mathbb{C}_{kr} = \mathbb{C}_k \bmod \beta$
8:         Using $\mathbb{C}_{kr}$ and $\mathbb{C}_{kq}$ insert $\mathbb{C}_k$ in the QF_i.
9:     **end for**
10: **end for**

---

3. **Trapdoor generation phase:** In this phase, DU builds trapdoors for each keyword (to be searched) using Algorithm 4. Then, a trigram set TS' is constructed for each keyword (after placing the same delimiter used during *index building phase*) to be searched. Each entry of TS' is represented in equivalent decimal form. Hash of the equivalent decimal form of trigram entry and K_{sec} is computed. This digest value is inserted into the trapdoor set $(T_{kw'})$. Then, DU sends $(T_{kw'})$ to the CS.

4. **Searching phase:** Here, CS executes Algorithm 5 to get the list of corresponding encrypted files $\mathscr{E}(f_i)$ containing the keywords present kw'. Algorithm 5 searches for each element of $T_{kw'}$ (i.e. $\mathbb{C}_j'$) in each QF_i using Algorithm 1 and remembers the number of matching found. As proposed scheme SEMFS converts all the keywords (either to insert in QF_i or to search in QF_i) into trigram format, then, three trigrams will be affected if one letter is mismatched. As L defines the permissible number of typing mistakes or format inconsistencies that will be relaxed to find the corresponding file that contains the keywords, we say if number of matching is $\geq 3L$, the corresponding file is returned by this algorithm. At last, a collection of all such files is sent back to the DU. Upon receiving the encrypted files, DU will decrypt the files using symmetric encryption key K_{sym}.

Algorithm 4. BuildTrapdoor

Input: kw', $\mathbb{H}$, K_{sec}, γ
Output: $T_{kw'}$

1: **for** $j = 1$ to q **do**   ▷ for each keyword to be searched $kw' = \{kw_1', ..., kw_q'\}$
2:     Construct trigram set $TS_j' = \{t_1', ..., t_r'\}$.
3:     **for** $k = 1$ to r **do**
4:         Find decimal representation of t_k' $(\mho_k')$.
5:         Find $\mathscr{C}_k' = \mathbb{H}(\mho_k'||K_{sec})$.
6:         Find $\mathbb{C}_k' = \mathscr{C}_k' \bmod \gamma$
7:         Insert $\mathbb{C}_k'$ into trapdoor set $(T_{kw'})$.
8:     **end for**
9: **end for**

Algorithm 5. IndexSearch

Input: $T_{kw'}$, L
Output: f_i

1: count $\leftarrow 0$
2: **for** $i = 1$ to n **do**
3:     **for** $j = 1$ to ψ **do**   ▷ $|T_{kw'}| = \psi$
4:         **if** $\mathbb{C}_j' \in \mathrm{QF}_i$ **then**
5:             count $\leftarrow$ count $+ 1$
6:         **end if**
7:     **end for**
8:     **if** count $\geq (\psi - 3L)$ **then**
9:         return f_i
10:     **end if**
11: **end for**

---

5   Security Analysis

In this section, we analyze the security of SEMFS under two different kinds of security attack models, namely, known ciphertext model and known plaintext model.

5.1   Confidentiality of Files

In SEMFS, the outsourced files ($\mathscr{E}(f_i)$) are encrypted using a standard symmetric encryption algorithm AES [12]. In addition to this, DO sends K_{sym} (used to encrypt/ decrypt the files) through a secure channel to the authorized DUs. Without this key, CS can not decrypt the files as AES encryption scheme is secure. So, confidentiality of the files can be achieved.

5.2   Privacy Protection of Index Files

In case of known ciphertext model, CS has only the following information. It has access to the quotient filter (QF_i), encrypted files ($\mathscr{E}(f_i)$) and trapdoor set

$T_{kw'}$. To break the security of SEMFS under known ciphertext model, CS could try to guess the content of QF_i to find exact keywords of f_i. But, due to the following reasons, CS fails to guess the content of QF_i correctly.

In index building phase, DO inserts $\mathbb{C}_k$'s ($= \mathscr{C}_k$ mod γ) in quotient filter QF_i, where $\mathscr{C}_k = \mathbb{H}(\mathfrak{V}_k \| K_{sec})$. $\mathscr{C}_k$'s are computed using a secret key K_{sec}. As DO sends K_{sec} through a secure channel to the authorized DUs, CS cannot know K_{sec}. In addition to this, it is computationally difficult for the CS to find $\mathscr{C}_k$ and K_{sec}, only by knowing the digest of secure hash function ($\mathbb{H}$) as it is a one-way hash function. Hence, the content of the index file QF_i is well protected from CS in SEMFS.

In case of known plaintext model, including the information regarding quotient filter, encrypted files and trapdoor set, CS has extra information regarding plaintext of some documents. It is computationally difficult for the CS to generate a correct index file (same as that of the DO) of the files using the known information regarding plaintext of some documents due to the following reason. As K_{sec} is used to generate $\mathscr{C}_k$ and only DO and authorized DUs know K_{sec}, CS cannot generate correct $\mathscr{C}_k$. Also, CS cannot find K_{sec} by knowing a pair of trigram $\mathfrak{V}_k$ and corresponding encrypted trigram $\mathscr{C}_k$ due to the one way property of hash function. Hence, the index file generated by the CS will be different from the original one. Thus, content of the index file QF_i is well protected from CS in SEMFS under known plaintext model.

5.3   Privacy Protection of Search Query

In case of known ciphertext model, CS has only the following information. It has access to the trapdoor set $T_{kw'}$, quotient filter (QF_i) and encrypted files ($\mathscr{E}(f_i)$). It has access to the trigram set $T_{kw'}$. To break the security of SEMFS under known ciphertext model, CS could try to guess the content of trapdoor set $T_{kw'}$ to know exact keywords that DU wants to search. But, due to the following reasons, CS fails to guess the content of $T_{kw'}$ correctly.

In the trapdoor building phase, DU constructs the trapdoor set $T_{kw'}$ which contains $\mathbb{C}_k'$ ($= \mathscr{C}_k'$ mod γ, where $\mathscr{C}_k' = \mathbb{H}(\mathfrak{V}_k' \| K_{sec})$). $\mathscr{C}_k'$'s are computed using a secret key K_{sec}. As DO sends K_{sec} through a secure channel to the authorized DUs, CS cannot know K_{sec}. In addition to this, it is computationally difficult for the CS to find $\mathscr{C}_k'$ and K_{sec}, only by knowing the digest of secure hash function ($\mathbb{H}$) as it is a one-way hash function. Hence, the privacy of the trapdoor set $T_{kw'}$ is protected from CS in SEMFS.

In case of known plaintext model, including the information regarding quotient filter, encrypted files and trapdoor set, CS has extra information regarding plaintext of some documents. It is computationally difficult for the CS to generate a correct trapdoor set (same as that of the DU) using the known information regarding plaintext of some documents due to the following reason. As K_{sec} is used to generate $\mathscr{C}_k'$ and only DO and authorized DUs know K_{sec}, CS cannot generate correct $\mathscr{C}_k'$. Also, CS cannot find K_{sec} by knowing a pair of trigram $\mathfrak{V}_k'$ and corresponding encrypted trigram $\mathscr{C}_k'$ due to the one way property of hash function. Hence, the index file generated by the CS will be different from the original one. Thus, privacy of the trapdoor set is preserved in SEMFS under known plaintext model.

6   Discussion

6.1   Choice of Trigrams

Trigram set would be the best alternative as unigram and bigram set of a keyword would be identical for those words with anagram. As an example, the unigram set of "cat" and "act" is identical ($\{c, a, t\}$). Similarly, the bigram set of the keywords "deeded" and "deed" are identical ($\{de, ee, ed\}$). Trigram set of these two keywords are different ($\{dee, eed, ede, ded\}$ and $\{dee, eed\}$ respectively). This kind of two meaningful words with same trigram set we could not find from English dictionary and therefore conjectured to be least probable. Therefore, we choose to represent keywords using a trigram set.

CS returns all the files correspond to the set of trapdoors, if the number of matching trigrams $\leq 3L$ which is used in Algorithm 5. SEMFS converts all the keywords into circular trigram format to ensure each letter is present in three trigrams (otherwise, first and last letter will be present in only one trigram). This ensures that exactly $3L$ numbers of trigrams mismatched between trigrams present in trapdoor and trigrams present in QF_i.

6.2   Efficient Index File Updation in SEMFS

After updating a document, DO needs update the corresponding index file also. A straight forward way of updating (inserting/deleting/modifying) the index file is to download it from the CS, update it and resend the updated index file to CS, which is generally considered in bloom filter based searching schemes like Wang et al. [29]. This method increases the I/O operation and file transfer cost in the network. SEMFS supports direct updation of index file without downloading them as quotient filter supports addition and deletion of elements. In SEMFS, the update on the index file is carried out by the CS when it receives a tuple of 3 values $\langle \mathbb{C}_k, \mathrm{QF}_i, \mathrm{UpdateType} \rangle$ from the DO (Here, UpdateType $\in$ {Insert, Delete}). CS insert/delete/modify $\mathbb{C}_k$ in QF_i using similar procedure as Algorithm 2. Here, CS cannot learn anything about the keyword as $\mathbb{C}_k$ is generated using K_{sec} and $\mathbb{H}$. Insertion or deletion of a whole document is also possible in SEMFS.

6.3   Ranking the Search Result

Ranking of the search result immensely enhances schemes usability by returning the matching files in a ranked order. SEMFS supports ranking of search results. For this CS has to do some additional work during the searching phase. It maintains a list containing name of the file and number of matching trigrams. This list is sorted in ascending order the number of matching trigrams. Now, top-k most relevant files corresponding to DU's interested keyword are sent to the DU.

Keyword's frequency can also be considered as a tool to find the relevance between the files and keywords which can help in ranking the search result. Relevance score of a keyword for a file is more if the frequency of the keyword is more in the document. A scoring technique is widely used in plaintext information retrieval [26]. It helps in choosing most relevant document containing a set of keywords when we find more than one documents containing the same set of keywords.

6.4 Performance Analysis

Search functionalities like single keyword search, multiple keyword search, fuzzy keyword search, ranked keyword search, requirement of index file, requirement of predefined dictionary, confidentiality of files, preserving privacy of index file and preserving privacy of trapdoor are the important features need to be considered for designing an efficient SSE scheme in cloud storage. Table 1 summarizes the comparison of said features for different existing schemes with SEMFS. [9, 27] and [13] schemes do not support multiple keyword search, while [11, 15, 30–32] and [18] do not support fuzzy keyword search. However, Li et al.'s scheme [19] enables fuzzy search but suitable for a single keyword searching. Later on Wang et al. [29] proposed an SSE scheme based on Bloom filter that enables fuzzy multi-keyword search. It can be observed that, SEMFS supports all the search functionalities mentioned earlier. Along with these functionalities, SEMFS performs dynamic update of index files efficiently.

To verify the efficiency of SEMFS, we implemented both bloom filter and quotient filter on a PC equipped with Intel Core i5 processor at 3.2 GHz and 4 GB RAM. An introduction to bloom filter is provided in Appendix A. Figure 4 shows that the time consumed by quotient filter during insertion and searching process is less than bloom filter as the number of elements increases. It can be observed from the result that with the increase in number of elements the speedup of quotient filter increases as compared to bloom filter as only a single hash function is required in case of quotient filter. We implemented Wang et al.'s scheme [29] and SEMFS and the result is shown in Fig. 5. This result is obtained for a single file with gradually increasing the number of keywords. Index generation time and trapdoor generation time of the respective schemes are very close as algorithms for index file generation and trapdoor generation are identical. Index file generation time and trapdoor generation time in Wang et al's scheme is more as compared to SEMFS in both Fig. 5 (a) and (b) respectively due to the following reason. Wang et al's scheme is a bloom filter based scheme and contain extra matrix multiplications than SEMFS. Therefore, we assure that the SEMFS is efficient as compared to Wang et al.'s scheme [29] with the application of QF for searchable symmetric encryption.

Table 1. Comparison of SSE schemes in cloud storage

Schemes	SKWS	MKWS	FKWS	RKWS	IF	PD	PP	CD
Song et al. [27]	Y	**N**	**N**	**N**	**N**	N	**N**	Y
Chang et al. [9]	Y	**N**	**N**	**N**	Y	**Y**	**N**	Y
Goh et al. [13]	Y	**N**	**N**	**N**	Y	N	Y	Y
Curtomola et al. [11]	Y	Y	N	**N**	Y	**Y**	Y	Y
Wang et al. [30]	Y	Y	**N**	Y	Y	N	Y	Y
Wang et al. [31]	Y	Y	**N**	Y	Y	N	Y	Y
Yu et al. [32]	Y	Y	**N**	Y	Y	**Y**	Y	Y
Li et al. [18]	Y	Y	**N**	Y	Y	**Y**	Y	Y
Li et al. [19]	Y	**N**	Y	**N**	Y	N	Y	Y
Wang et al. [29]	Y	Y	Y	**N**	Y	N	Y	Y
Hong et al. [15]	Y	Y	**N**	**N**	Y	N	Y	Y
SEMFS	Y	Y	Y	Y	Y	N	Y	Y

SKWS: Single Keyword Search, MKWS: Multiple Keyword Search, FKWS: Fuzzy Keyword Search, RKWS: Ranked Keyword Search, IF: Requirement of Index File, PD: Requirement of Predefined Dictionary, PP: Privacy Preserving, CD: Confidentiality of Document

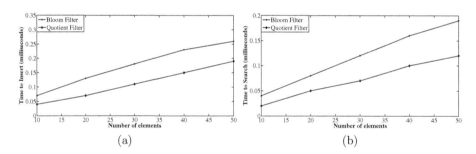

(a)   (b)

Fig. 4. Insertion and searching time comparison between bloom filter and quotient filter

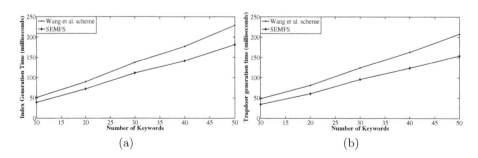

(a)   (b)

Fig. 5. Index generation and trapdoor generation time comparison between Wang et al.'s scheme [29] and SEMFS

7   Conclusion

Sensitive data are encrypted (to preserve privacy) before storing remotely, so achieving effective utilization of stored data in cloud has become challenging. This work proposed an efficient Searchable Symmetric Encryption (SSE) scheme called SEMFS which facilitates the data owner to outsource the encrypted data allowing a user to search the file using trapdoor (of keyword) without giving a clue to others (including CS) about the keyword. SEMFS uses quotient filter for efficient indexing and faster searching. Most appealing feature of the proposed scheme is to support dynamic updation of index file. Experimental analysis showed that SEMFS had higher throughput than the bloom filter based scheme, when implemented.

Appendix A   Bloom Filter

Bloom filter is a space-efficient data structure for representing a set in order to support membership queries [5]. A bloom filter for representing a set S containing n number of elements is described by an array of m bits size. All these m bits are initialized to 0. It uses k independent hash functions defined as $\mathcal{H} = \{h_i | h_i : S \rightarrow [1, m], 1 \leq i \leq k\}$. To insert an element $s \in S$ into the bloom filter, all the $h_i(s)$-th position are set to 1 in the m bit array. To search an element $q \in S$, first we find k number of array positions using $h_i(q), 1 \leq i \leq k$. Then, we check if the corresponding bit of any of the k position is 0, then q is definitely not present in the set S. Otherwise, q probably present in the set S. Consider the following example. Figure 6 shows an example of bloom filter with m = 10 and k = 3. Here, the filter represents the set $S = \{A, B\}$. Black colored arrow shows the corresponding positions of the bloom filter that each element of set S is mapped to. Now if we will search for an element D, then we can observe from the figure that at least one position to which D is mapped contains 0 (shown in red colored lines). So D is definitely not present in the set. If we will search for an element C, then we can observe from the figure that all the positions to which C is mapped contain 1. Hence, C is probably present in the set.

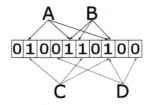

Fig. 6. An example of boolean filter (Color figure online)

References

1. Secure Hash Algorithm 2. http://csrc.nist.gov/publications/fips/fips180-2/fips180-2withchangenotice.pdf
2. Adusumilli, P., Zou, X., Ramamurthy, B.: DGKD: distributed group key distribution with authentication capability. In: Proceedings of the Sixth Annual IEEE SMC Information Assurance Workshop, pp. 286–293. IEEE (2005)
3. Bender, M.A., Farach-Colton, M., Johnson, R., Kraner, R., Kuszmaul, B.C., Medjedovic, D., Montes, P., Shetty, P., Spillane, R.P., Zadok, E.: Don't thrash: how to cache your hash on flash. Proc. VLDB Endow. **5**(11), 1627–1637 (2012)
4. Bender, M.A., Farach-Colton, M., Johnson, R., Kuszmaul, B.C., Medjedovic, D., Montes, P., Shetty, P., Spillane, R.P., Zadok, E.: Don't thrash: how to cache your hash on flash. In: Proceedings of the 3rd USENIX Conference on Hot Topics in Storage and File Systems, p. 1 (2011)
5. Bloom, B.H.: Space/time trade-offs in hash coding with allowable errors. Commun. ACM **13**(7), 422–426 (1970)
6. Boneh, D., Di Crescenzo, G., Ostrovsky, R., Persiano, G.: Public key encryption with keyword search. In: Cachin, C., Camenisch, J.L. (eds.) EUROCRYPT 2004. LNCS, vol. 3027, pp. 506–522. Springer, Heidelberg (2004). https://doi.org/10.1007/978-3-540-24676-3_30
7. Boneh, D., Waters, B.: Conjunctive, subset, and range queries on encrypted data. In: Vadhan, S.P. (ed.) TCC 2007. LNCS, vol. 4392, pp. 535–554. Springer, Heidelberg (2007). https://doi.org/10.1007/978-3-540-70936-7_29
8. Cao, N., Wang, C., Li, M., Ren, K., Lou, W.: Privacy-preserving multi-keyword ranked search over encrypted cloud data. In: Proceedings of the IEEE INFOCOM 2011, pp. 829–837. IEEE (2011)
9. Chang, Y.-C., Mitzenmacher, M.: Privacy preserving keyword searches on remote encrypted data. In: Ioannidis, J., Keromytis, A., Yung, M. (eds.) ACNS 2005. LNCS, vol. 3531, pp. 442–455. Springer, Heidelberg (2005). https://doi.org/10.1007/11496137_30
10. Chuah, M., Hu, W.: Privacy-aware bedtree based solution for fuzzy multi-keyword search over encrypted data. In: Proceedings of the 31st IEEE International Conference on Distributed Computing Systems Workshops (ICDCSW) 2011, pp. 273–281. IEEE (2011)
11. Curtmola, R., Garay, J., Kamara, S., Ostrovsky, R.: Searchable symmetric encryption: improved definitions and efficient constructions. In: Proceedings of the 13th ACM Conference on Computer and Communications Security, pp. 79–88. ACM (2006)
12. Daemen, J., Rijmen, V.: The Design of Rijndael: AES-The Advanced Encryption Standard. Springer, Heidelberg (2013). https://doi.org/10.1007/978-3-662-04722-4
13. Goh, E.J.: Secure indexes. Technical report 2003/216, IACR Cryptology ePrint Archive (2003)
14. Golle, P., Staddon, J., Waters, B.: Secure conjunctive keyword search over encrypted data. In: Jakobsson, M., Yung, M., Zhou, J. (eds.) ACNS 2004. LNCS, vol. 3089, pp. 31–45. Springer, Heidelberg (2004). https://doi.org/10.1007/978-3-540-24852-1_3
15. Hong, C., Li, Y., Zhang, M., Feng, D.: Fast multi-keywords search over encrypted cloud data. In: Cellary, W., Mokbel, M.F., Wang, J., Wang, H., Zhou, R., Zhang, Y. (eds.) WISE 2016. LNCS, vol. 10041, pp. 433–446. Springer, Cham (2016). https://doi.org/10.1007/978-3-319-48740-3_32

16. Hwang, Y.H., Lee, P.J.: Public key encryption with conjunctive keyword search and its extension to a multi-user system. In: Takagi, T., Okamoto, T., Okamoto, E., Okamoto, T. (eds.) Pairing 2007. LNCS, vol. 4575, pp. 2–22. Springer, Heidelberg (2007). https://doi.org/10.1007/978-3-540-73489-5_2

17. Kuzu, M., Islam, M.S., Kantarcioglu, M.: Efficient similarity search over encrypted data. In: Proceedings of the IEEE 28th International Conference on Data Engineering (ICDE), pp. 1156–1167. IEEE (2012)

18. Li, H., Yang, Y., Luan, T.H., Liang, X., Zhou, L., Shen, X.S.: Enabling fine-grained multi-keyword search supporting classified sub-dictionaries over encrypted cloud data. IEEE Trans. Dependable Secure Comput. **13**(3), 312–325 (2016)

19. Li, J., Wang, Q., Wang, C., Cao, N., Ren, K., Lou, W.: Fuzzy keyword search over encrypted data in cloud computing. In: Proceedings of the IEEE INFOCOM 2010, pp. 1–5. IEEE (2010)

20. Liu, C., Zhu, L., Li, L., Tan, Y.: Fuzzy keyword search on encrypted cloud storage data with small index. In: Proceedings of the IEEE International Conference on Cloud Computing and Intelligence Systems (CCIS) 2011, pp. 269–273. IEEE (2011)

21. Lynn, B.: The pairing-based cryptography library (2006). https://crypto.stanford.edu/pbc/. Accessed 27 Mar 2013

22. Medelyan, O.: Human-competitive automatic topic indexing. Ph.D. thesis, The University of Waikato (2009)

23. Nabeel, M., Yoosuf, M., Bertino, E.: Attribute based group key management. In: Proceedings of the 14th ACM Symposium on Access Control Models and Technologies, pp. 115–124. ACM (2014)

24. Nayak, S.K., Tripathy, S.: Privacy preserving provable data possession for cloud based electronic health record system. In: Proceedings of the IEEE Trustcom/BigDataSE/ISPA, pp. 860–867. IEEE (2016)

25. Rose, S., Engel, D., Cramer, N., Cowley, W.: Automatic keyword extraction from individual documents. In: Text Mining: Applications and Theory, pp. 1–20. John Wiley & Sons (2010)

26. Singhal, A.: Modern information retrieval: a brief overview. IEEE Data Eng. Bull. **24**(4), 35–43 (2001)

27. Song, D.X., Wagner, D., Perrig, A.: Practical techniques for searches on encrypted data. In: Proceedings of the IEEE Symposium on Security and Privacy, pp. 44–55. IEEE (2000)

28. van Liesdonk, P., Sedghi, S., Doumen, J., Hartel, P., Jonker, W.: Computationally Efficient searchable symmetric encryption. In: Jonker, W., Petković, M. (eds.) SDM 2010. LNCS, vol. 6358, pp. 87–100. Springer, Heidelberg (2010). https://doi.org/10.1007/978-3-642-15546-8_7

29. Wang, B., Yu, S., Lou, W., Hou, Y.T.: Privacy-preserving multi-keyword fuzzy search over encrypted data in the cloud. In: Proceedings of the IEEE INFOCOM 2014, pp. 2112–2120. IEEE (2014)

30. Wang, C., Cao, N., Li, J., Ren, K., Lou, W.: Secure ranked keyword search over encrypted cloud data. In: Proceedings of the 30th International Conference Distributed Computing Systems (ICDCS), pp. 253–262. IEEE (2010)

31. Wang, C., Cao, N., Ren, K., Lou, W.: Enabling secure and efficient ranked keyword search over outsourced cloud data. IEEE Trans. Parallel Distrib. Syst. **23**(8), 1467–1479 (2012). IEEE

32. Yu, J., Lu, P., Zhu, Y., Xue, G., Li, M.: Toward secure multikeyword top-k retrieval over encrypted cloud data. IEEE Trans. Dependable Secure Comput. **10**(4), 239–250 (2013)

33. Zhang, B., Zhang, F.: An efficient public key encryption with conjunctive-subset keywords search. J. Netw. Comput. Appl. **34**(1), 262–267 (2011)

Towards Generalization of Privacy Policy Specification and Property-Based Information Leakage

Dileep Kumar Koshley[(✉)], Sapana Rani, and Raju Halder

Indian Institute of Technology Patna, Patna, India
{dileep.pcs15,sapana.pcs13,halder}@iitp.ac.in

Abstract. In spite of deep and intensive research, the existing data privacy preserving approaches primarily suffer from the lack of generality. Some solutions deal with direct information leakage, whereas others deal with indirect information leakage which occurs due to the presence of data or functional dependencies. Moreover, privacy policy specification supported by individual method has limited expressibility, which allows to express very specific forms of privacy concerns. In this paper, we formalize a privacy-preserving policy specification language which is highly expressive to adapt a wide range of constraints in various forms, fitting suitably to the real world scenarios. Furthermore, we introduce a new form of dependency, known as *Property-based Dependency*, which may also cause an indirect information leakage. Finally, we propose a preventive solution, on top of the existing ones, for privacy policies expressed in our proposed language.

Keywords: Data privacy · Information leakage
Privacy Policy Specification Language · Abstraction

1 Introduction

Privacy of sensitive database information in any information system has always been a prime concern to the scientific community over the past several decades. In the modern age of information, when amount and variety of data is increasing at an unprecedented rate, the evolution of technological solutions to meet various demands on data, *e.g.* publishing, sharing, storing into external disk-space, *etc.*, give rise to many research challenges on its privacy in relational databases [1,2]. A widely accepted solution to this problem is to disclose sensitive information in such a way that illegitimate users can not infer anything about sensitive information in an exact way. A number of methods providing solutions to fulfill this objective are proposed. They include k-anonymity [3], l-diversity [4], t-closeness [5], *etc.* Their intent is to release sensitive information in an anonymized form. In k-anonymized dataset, each record is made identical to at least k - 1 other records with respect to those attributes acting as quasi-identifiers [3]. The principle of

R. K. Shyamasundar et al. (Eds.): ICISS 2017, LNCS 10717, pp. 68–87, 2017.
https://doi.org/10.1007/978-3-319-72598-7_5

l-diversity ensures the presence of at least l distinct values for the sensitive field in each equivalence class [4]. The t-closeness model [5] extends the l-diversity model by treating values of an attribute distinctly taking into account the data distribution for that attribute.

In addition to the privacy need of the sensitive data, Vimercati et al. [6] in their notable work first considered the visibility requirement as well. The sensitive information after fragmentation is released as "loose associations" in order to guarantee a specified degree of privacy. Later, they described how the publication of multiple loose associations between different pairs of fragments expose sensitive associations [7,8].

Beside direct information leakage as addressed by the above techniques, there is a possibility of indirect information leakage due to the presence of non-sensitive information in public domain. Interestingly, Sweeney [3] showed that combinations of few characteristics, $e.g.$ 5-digit ZIP, gender, date of birth, likely made 87% of US population unique. She combined the medical data with voter list and was able to identify the information leakage. There exists a series of works [9–11] addressing indirect information leakage which occurs due to the presence of functional dependencies (FD) and data dependencies (DD). Authors in [9] studied the privacy threat resulting from the full functional dependency as part of adversary knowledge, and they defined a privacy model, called (d, ℓ)-inference, as a way of prevention. [10] suggested the encryption of a small amount of non-sensitive data to defend FD-attack. The authors in [11] proposed fragmentation as a solution to prevent information leakage from data dependency.

Unfortunately, despite of many proposals in the literature as briefed above, this is observed that none of them is able to address different possible way of information leakage in a unified way. Some deal with direct information leakage, whereas others deal with indirect information leakage. Moreover, privacy policy specifications supported by individual method has limited expressibility. This allows only to express very specific privacy concerns which do not often fit to the real world scenarios. For example, [12] expresses the confidential information at cell level, whereas [8,10] express the confidentiality in the form of selection-projection and attribute-association respectively. Consequently, this gives rise to the scalability problem, resulting into a failure of adapting one solution to address the other. Observe, for example, that the solutions in [3–5] are not scalable enough to adapt as a solution to the visibility constraints. Furthermore, our observation revealed that the absence of data and functional dependencies may not always guarantee the absence of sensitive data leakage in database systems. This is due to the fact that, in reality, properties (instead of values) of some attributes may often depend on the properties or values of other attributes. This may lead to a partial inference about sensitive data. For example, an attacker who is able to observe the properties "Age Group" and "Deficiency" from the values of the attributes "Age" and "Food Habit" respectively, may guess some symptoms about patient's disease.

Addressing these concerns, we propose in this paper a privacy preserving scheme for sensitive information in relational databases, considering more generic scenarios where multiple form of privacy constraints exist. Furthermore, we introduce a new kind of dependency – *property-based dependency* (PD) – that may lead, in addition to FD- and DD-dependences, a leakage of sensitive information. To summarize, our main contributions in this paper are:

- Formalization of privacy policy specification language which is highly expressive so as to adapt a wide range of privacy concerns.
- To propose a solution, on top of the existing ones, that respects the privacy concerns expressed in our policy specification language.
- Identification of a new kind of dependency, named *property-based dependency* (PD), and to propose a solution to this implicit leakage using ordered binary decision diagram (OBDD).

The structure of the paper is as follows: Sect. 2 describes briefly the existing privacy preservation techniques in the literature. In Sect. 3, we introduce a generic form of privacy-policy specification language for relational databases in Back-us Naur form. In Sect. 4, we discuss how to remove redundancy from a set of privacy policies specified in our specification language by naive users. In Sect. 5, we propose a solution, on top of the existing ones, to prevent explicit information leakage from relational databases. Section 6 elaborates how information may implicitly be leaked due to dependencies. Section 7 introduces *property-based dependency*. In Sect. 8, we propose a unified solution for implicit leakage covering all three dependencies. We compare our proposals *w.r.t.* the literature in Sect. 9. Finally, we conclude our work in Sect. 10.

2   Related Works

Releasing non-sensitive information while maintaining confidentiality of the sensitive one is becoming extremely challenging due to the exponential growth in the number and variety of data collections. Broadly to prevent unauthorized information leakage there is a need to disclose sensitive information in such a way that illegitimate users can not infer anything about sensitive information in an exact way.

A wide range of privacy preserving solutions [3–5,8–12] is proposed in the literature. Each of these proposals refer to very specific form of constraints. The authors in [3] identified some set of attributes as quasi-identifiers and then ensure that each sequence of values for these quasi-identifiers appears with at least k-occurrences. In [4], the equivalence classes are having at least l distinct values for the sensitive attribute. In order to overcome the limitations in [4], the authors in [5] proposed a solution which requires that the distribution of a sensitive attribute in any equivalence class should be close to the distribution of the attribute in the overall table. The solutions proposed in [3–5] consider only the confidentiality constraints: they considered neither visibility constraint nor any dependency-based leakage. In [8], the authors partitioned the database relation and published universal association at group level to increase the probability of anonymity. Authors in [10] proposed a solution based on the encryption of evidence records which may facilitate an information leakage about sensitive records. In a different research line, to address implicit leakage, the authors in [9,10] addressed the functional dependency, whereas [11] dealt with only data dependency. In particular, [11] proposed graph based fragmentation of database relations. The authors in [10] expressed confidentiality constraints in selection-projection form only. The cell level confidential constraints were addressed in [12] by masking the sensitive cells with a specific type of variables. The authors in [13] proposed the concept of δ-dependency in order to deal with hierarchical sensitive data taken from a hierarchical tree structure where data values become more specific as we move down the tree. The authors in [14] surveyed data inference problems resulted from indirect accesses to sensitive data through inferences.

This is worthwhile to mention here that our current policy language doesn't cover any access control policy as proposed in [15,16]. Although in this work we refrain ourselves from considering access control policy specifications, however in future we plan to extend our work to include this part as well.

3 Privacy Policy Specifications

In this section, we formalize a privacy-preserving policy specification language which is highly expressive so as to cover a wide range of constraints defined on relational databases, considering the real-world situations.

We use Back-us Naur Form of Context-free Grammars [17] to express our specification language. This allows us to define two kind of policy specifications: *explicit/direct* and *implicit/indirect*. Explicit or direct policy specification refers to the part of data which are sensitive and prone to direct leakage. Indirect or implicit policy specification expresses some dependency information which may lead to an indirect information leakage. Observe that database owners are responsible to specify only explicit policy specification, whereas database designers are responsible for implicit policy specification.

3.1 Explicit/Direct Policy Specification

Explicit policy specification can be formalized in two forms: confidentiality and visibility constraints. Let DB be a relational database consisting of relations $T_1, T_2, ..., T_n$. Let $A_i = \texttt{attribute}(T_i)$ be the set of attributes of T_i and $A_{DB} = \bigcup_{i \in 1,...,n} A_i$. The confidentiality and visibility constraints are formalized as follows:

Confidentiality Constraints: We consider various possible forms of constraints to include in our specification language as confidential constraints. They include *attribute-association, selection-projection, cell-level*, and their combinations. The confidentiality constraints P_c is formalized below:

$$P_c ::= \ g \mid \pi_g \sigma_\phi \mid [\![g]\!]_{\texttt{Val(PK(g))}} \mid P_c \wedge P_c.$$

where $g \in \wp(A_{DB})$ is a subset of A_{DB} which represents that all attributes in g *must not be contained* in the same relation. Confidential policy $\pi_g \sigma_\phi$ in terms of selection-projection operation represents that data for attributes g satisfying condition ϕ are *confidential*. $[\![g]\!]_{\text{Val}(PK(g))}$ specifies a fine-grained *confidential* constraint in terms of sensitive data cells. The data cells are uniquely represented by the attributes g and the tuple's primary key values $\text{Val}(PK(g))$, where $PK(g)$ denotes primary key (computed as $PK(g) = \text{Primary\_Key}(\bowtie_i T_i)$ applying natural join $\bowtie$ on all T_i such that $\exists\, a \in g.\ a \in \text{atribute}(T_i)$) and $\text{Val}(PK(g))$ denotes the set of primary key values corresponding to $PK(g)$.

Visibility constraints: We formalize the visibility constraints P_v as:

$$P_v ::= g \mid \pi_g \sigma_\phi \mid [\![g]\!]_{\text{Val}(PK(g))} \mid P_v \wedge P_v \mid P_v \vee P_v.$$

where $g \in \wp(A_{DB})$ is a subset of A_{DB} which represents that all attributes in g *must be present* in at least one of the relations. Visibility policy $\pi_g \sigma_\phi$ in terms of selection-projection operation represents that data for attributes in g satisfying condition ϕ must be *visible*. The fine grain visibility constraint $[\![g]\!]_{\text{Val}(PK(g))}$ specifies that data in cells uniquely identified by g and its corresponding primary key values $\text{Val}(PK(g))$ are *visible*. Observe that, unlike confidential constraints, the policy language allows visibility constraints to express in the form of OR ($\vee$). For example, the visibility constraint *Phone_No* $\vee$ *Email_ID* specifies that either phone number or email ID or both must be present in one of the database relations.

Example 1. Consider the relation *"Patients"* shown in Table 1. Consider a composite confidentiality constraint $P_c = \{Name, Disease\} \wedge \{SSN\} \wedge \{Age, ZIP, Gender\} \wedge \pi_{Disease}\sigma_{Gender=F} \wedge [\![Disease]\!]_{(104)}$ and visibility constraint $P_v = \{Name, Age\} \wedge \pi_{Age}\sigma_{Gender=M} \wedge [\![Disease]\!]_{(101)}$. Let us now illustrate different forms of explicit constraints using P_c and P_v.

Table 1. *"Patients"*

SSN	Name	Age	Gender	ZIP	Food_Habit	Disease
101	Alice	4	M	100025	cereals, carrot, fish oil, yoghurt	Kwashiorkor
102	Bob	26	F	110091	cereals, fish, yoghurts	Night Blindness
103	Carol	39	M	100025	pulses, yellow fruits, cranberries	Osteomalacia
104	David	3	F	123001	pulses, yellow fruits, cranberries	Rickets
105	Ela	22	M	110091	pulses, yellow fruits, cranberries	Ostemalacia
106	Frudo	5	M	110091	pulses, milk, yellow fruits	Goiter
107	Gram	45	F	123001	cereals, fish, yoghurts	Cataract

Attribute-association: {*Name, Disease*} is an example of confidentiality constraint in the form of attribute association. This specifies that the combination of name and disease information is confidential and must not be present together when releasing. Similarly, a visibility constraint {*Name, Age*} represents that these two attributes in combination must be released together in the same database relation.

Selection-projection: The confidentiality constraint $\pi_{Disease}\sigma_{Gender=F}$ represents that disease of all female must be confidential. Similarly, the visibility constraint $\pi_{Age}\sigma_{Gender=M}$ states that age of all male must be visible to public.

Cell-level: Cell level confidential constraint $[\![Disease]\!]_{(104)}$ represents that disease of patient having SSN (which is primary key) equal to 104 is confidential. Similarly, the visibility constraint $[\![Disease]\!]_{(101)}$ states that disease of patient having SSN equal to 101 must be publicly visible.

3.2   Implicit/Indirect Policy Specification

Implicit policy specification represents those which may lead to indirect information leakage. Various kind of dependencies (for example, data-dependency and functional dependency) may implicitly or indirectly leak sensitive-information. These are completely specific to the design of databases and their implementation. We use the notation [ ] and ⟨ ⟩ to represent data dependency and functional dependency respectively. Let R be the database relation where $X, Y \in \wp(\texttt{attribute}(R))$ and $X \cap Y = \phi$.

Data Dependency (DD): We denote data dependency by P_{DD}: $[X \xrightarrow{DD} Y]$. This represents that for each tuple $t \in R$, $t(X)$ determines $t(Y)$, where $t(X)$ and $t(Y)$ are the values of X and Y in tuple t.

Functional Dependency (FD): Functional dependency is denoted by P_{FD}: $\langle X \xrightarrow{FD} Y \rangle$ which represents that for tuples $t_i, t_j \in R$, if $t_i(X) = t_j(X)$ then $t_i(Y) = t_j(Y)$.

The information leakage due to FD and DD are exemplified in Sect. 6. This is worthwhile to mention our observation that the absence of FD- and DD-based leakage does not always guarantee the preservation of privacy concerns, and in this context we introduce a new kind of dependency, named *property-based dependency*, which we will include in the specification later on.

4   Redundancy Removal from Explicit Policy Specification

The explicit policy specification provided by naive users may contain redundancy and inconsistency. In this section, we introduce an algorithm to remove the redundant explicit policy expressions, yielding a minimal form of policy specification.

Let us describe various cases where redundancy removal may take place:
Case-1: Consider a database relation R. Let $P_c = g_0 \wedge g_1 \wedge \cdots \wedge g_n$ be a composite confidential constraint composed of a set of atomic constraints g_0, g_1, $\ldots$, $g_n \in \texttt{attribute}(R)$ each in attribute-association form. Let us suppose that g_0 is covered by the least upper bound of $S \subseteq \{g_1, g_2, \ldots, g_n\}$. In this case, g_0 is redundant as constraints in S are enough to express g_0. Let us illustrate this with a simple example: suppose $\texttt{attribute}(R) = \{w, x, y, z, u, v\}$ and $P_c = g_0 \wedge g_1 \wedge g_2 \wedge g_3$ where $g_0 = \{w, x, y\}$, $g_1 = \{w, y\}$, $g_2 = \{x, y, z\}$, $g_3 = \{u, z, v\}$. This is depicted using Venn diagram in Fig. 1(a). This is clear from the diagram that the constraint g_0 is a subset of the least upper bound of g_1 and g_2, and therefore it is redundant in P_c. **Case-2:** Given two confidentiality constraints $c_i = \pi_{g_i}\sigma_{\phi_i}$ and $c_j = \pi_{g_j}\sigma_{\phi_j}$ in P_c. If $\phi_i \equiv \phi_j$, we can combine them into $\pi_{g_i \sqcup g_j}\sigma_{\phi_i}$. Similarly, if $g_i = g_j$, we can combine them into $\pi_{g_i}\sigma_{\phi_i \vee \phi_j}$. This is depicted in Fig. 1(b). **Case-3:** Given a composite confidentiality constraint $P_c = \pi_{g_0}\sigma_{\phi_0} \wedge \pi_{g_1}\sigma_{\phi_1} \cdots \wedge \pi_{g_n}\sigma_{\phi_n}$ which is composed of a set of atomic constraints each in selection-projection form. Let $S \subseteq \{\pi_{g_i}\sigma_{\phi_i} \mid i = 1, \ldots, n\}$ such that g_0 is the least upper bound of $\{g_k \mid \pi_{g_k}\sigma_{\phi_k} \in S\}$ and ϕ_0 implies $\vee\{\phi_k \mid \pi_{g_k}\sigma_{\phi_k} \in S\}$. Then we can say that $\pi_{g_0}\sigma_{\phi_0}$ is subset of the union of S and hence it is redundant. An example of this considering three atomic constraints is depicted in Fig. 1(c). **Case-4:** Given two cell-level confidential constraints $[\![g_i]\!]_{\texttt{Val}(\texttt{PK}(g_i))}$ and $[\![g_j]\!]_{\texttt{Val}(\texttt{PK}(g_j))}$ in P_c, if $\texttt{Val}(\texttt{PK}(g_i)) = \texttt{Val}(\texttt{PK}(g_j))$ then we can combine them into $[\![g_i \sqcup g_j]\!]_{\texttt{Val}(\texttt{PK}(g_i))}$.

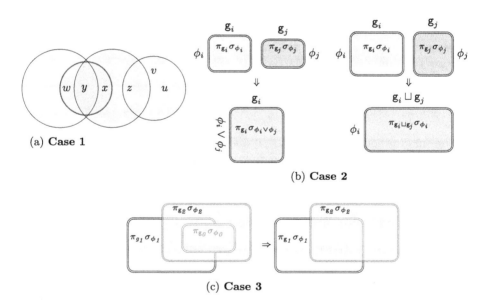

(a) **Case 1**

(b) **Case 2**

(c) **Case 3**

Fig. 1. Various cases of confidentiality constraints reduction

Case-5: If $P_c = P_{c_1} \wedge P_{c_2}$ such that P_{c_1} and P_{c_2} are in different form then the redundancy can be removed based on the equivalence between them. For example, $P_{c_1} = \pi_g \sigma_\phi$ and $P_{c_2} = g$ are equivalent if ϕ is a tautology. In this case we can replace P_c by one of these equivalent constraints. **Case-6:** In case when a visibility constraint is contained within a confidentiality constraint, we always prioritize the confidentiality constraint considering the visibility constraint as redundant. For example, let $P_c = g_0$ where $g_0 = \{x, y\}$ and $P_v = g_1$ where $g_1 = \{x, y\} \vee \{w, z\}$ then we can remove $\{x, y\}$ from P_v.

A formal algorithm addressing above cases is depicted in Algorithm 1. Observe that similar algorithm to remove redundant visibility constraints considering these cases can easily be formalized this way. We skip it for space constraint.

Algorithm 1. SPEC_REDUCTION

Input: Explicit confidentiality constraint P_c which may contain redundancy
Output: Non-redundant confidentiality constraint

1: $S := $**extractAtomicAA**$(P_c)$;   ▷ *Extracting all atomic constraints in attribute-association form.*
2: **for all** $g \in S$ **do**
3:   **if** g is least upper bound (lub) of $T \subseteq (S - \{g\})$ **then**
4:     $P_c = P_c \downarrow \{g\}$ ▷ *Dropping g from P_c*
5: $S := $**extractAtomicSP**$(P_c)$;   ▷ *Extracting all atomic constraints in projection-selection form.*
6: **for all** $\pi_{g_i}\sigma_{\phi_i}, \pi_{g_j}\sigma_{\phi_j} \in S$ **do**
7:   **if** $\phi_i \equiv \phi_j$ **then**
8:     $P_c = (P_c \downarrow \{\pi_{g_i}\sigma_{\phi_i}, \pi_{g_j}\sigma_{\phi_j}\}) \Uparrow \pi_{g_i \sqcup g_j}\sigma_{\phi_i}$ ▷ *Dropping $\{\pi_{g_i}\sigma_{\phi_i}, \pi_{g_j}\sigma_{\phi_j}\}$ and then adding $\pi_{g_i \sqcup g_j}\sigma_{\phi_i}$ to P_c*
9:   **else if** $g_i = g_j$ **then**
10:     $P_c = (P_c \downarrow \{\pi_{g_i}\sigma_{\phi_i}, \pi_{g_j}\sigma_{\phi_j}\}) \Uparrow \pi_{g_i}\sigma_{\phi_i \vee \phi_j}$
11: $S := $**extractAtomicSP**$(P_c)$;
12: **for all** $\pi_{g_i}\sigma_{\phi_i} \in S$ **do**
13:   **if** $\exists\, T \subseteq (S - \{\pi_{g_i}\sigma_{\phi_i}\})$ such that g_i is lub of $\{g_k \mid \pi_{g_k}\sigma_{\phi_k} \in T\}$ & ϕ_i implies $\vee\{\phi_k \mid \pi_{g_k}\sigma_{\phi_k} \in T\}$ **then**
14:     $P_c = P_c \downarrow \{\pi_{g_i}\sigma_{\phi_i}\}$ ▷ *Dropping $\pi_{g_i}\sigma_{\phi_i}$ from P_c.*
15: $S := $**extractAtomicCL**$(P_c)$; ▷ *Extracting all atomic constraints in cell-level form.*
16: **for all** $[\![g_i]\!]_{\text{Val}(\text{PK}(g_i))}, [\![g_j]\!]_{\text{Val}(\text{PK}(g_j))} \in P_c$ **do**
17:   **if** $\text{Val}(\text{PK}(g_i)) = \text{Val}(\text{PK}(g_j))$ **then**
18:     $P_c = (P_c \downarrow \{[\![g_i]\!]_{\text{Val}(\text{PK}(g_i))}, [\![g_j]\!]_{\text{Val}(\text{PK}(g_j))}\}) \Uparrow [\![g_i \sqcup g_j]\!]_{\text{Val}(\text{PK}(g_i))}$
19: Apply equivalences between various forms of constraints to remove redundancy.

Example 2. Consider the relation *"Patients"* in our running Example 1. Consider the confidentiality constraint P_c and the visibility constraint P_v defined as: $P_c = \{SSN\} \wedge \{Name, Age\} \wedge \{Age, Disease\} \wedge \{Name, Disease\} \wedge \{Name, Age, Disease\} \wedge \pi_{ZIP}\sigma_{Age \geq 10} \wedge \pi_{Name, ZIP}\sigma_{Age \geq 5}$ and $P_v = \{Name\} \vee \{SSN\}$. Observe that the atomic confidentiality constraint $\{Name, Age, Disease\}$ is redundant since it is covered by least upper bound of the constraints $\{Name, Age\}$, $\{Age, Disease\}$ and $\{Name, Disease\}$. Similarly, the constraint $\pi_{ZIP}\sigma_{Age \geq 10}$ is redundant because $\{ZIP\} \subseteq \{Name, ZIP\}$ and $(Age \geq$

10) *implies* $(Age \geq 5)$. The visibility constraint on "*SSN*" is filtered from the specification as it contradicts the confidentiality constraint on itself specified in P_c. Therefore, the reduced form of confidentiality and visibility constraints are: $\mathrm{P}'_c = \{SSN\} \wedge \{Name, Age\} \wedge \{Age, Disease\} \wedge \{Name, Disease\} \wedge \pi_{Name,ZIP}\sigma_{Age \geq 5}$ and $\mathrm{P}'_v = \{Name\}$.

In the rest of the paper, we use the term "policy specification" which refers only the reduced form of policy specification.

5   Proposed Solution to Prevent Explicit Leakage

We are now in a position to propose solution to preserve privacy policies defined in our specification language. It is clear from the specification language that the proposed solution should aim to address any explicit constraints of the form *attribute-association, selection-projection, cell level* or their combination. We propose a simple way of solving this generalized form of privacy-preservation concern by adapting a combination of existing approaches proposed so far. To be more specific, our solution combines three existing solutions from [10, 12] and [6] respectively.

Before describing the algorithm, let us recall from [12] the notions of *Type-1* and *Type-2* variables:

Definition 1 Type-1 *Variable* [12]. *A* Type-1 *variable is a symbol in some alphabet. Given two different* Type-1 *variables* v_1, v_2, "$v_1 = v_1$" *is true, while* "$v_1 = v_2$" *and* "$v_1 = c$" *are unknown, where* c *is a constant value.*

Definition 2 Type-2 *Variable* [12]. *A* Type-2 *variable is given as* $\langle \alpha, d \rangle$, *where* α *and* d *are called the name and the domain of the variable, respectively. Given* α, β, d_1, d_2, "$\langle \alpha, d_1 \rangle = \langle \alpha, d_1 \rangle$" *and* "$\langle \alpha, d_1 \rangle \neq \langle \beta, d_1 \rangle$" *are true, while whether* "$\langle \alpha, d_1 \rangle = \langle \alpha, d_2 \rangle$", "$\langle \alpha, d_1 \rangle = \langle \beta, d_2 \rangle$", "$\langle \alpha, d_1 \rangle = v$" *or* "$\langle \alpha, d_1 \rangle = c$" *are unknown, where* v *is a* Type-1 *variable and* c *is constant value.*

Observe that *Type-2* Variables are used to mask sensitive cells while at the same time are also used to maintain a secure linking among various relational tables, whereas *Type-1* is used to mask only sensitive cells in a relation.

The overall algorithmic steps are depicted in Algorithm 2. In Step 1, we apply the reduction Algorithm 1 in order to obtain a minimal form of policy specification. In Step 2(a), cell level constraints are first addressed by replacing sensitive cells with their corresponding *Type-1* or *Type-2* variables, ensuring the non-disclosure of their exact values and at the same time maintaining the secure referential linking among various tables in the database [12]. Similarly, in Step 2(b), database-parts referred by selection-projection constraints are replaced by *Type-1* or *Type-2* variables with the similar aim. Lastly, in Step 3, the algorithm deals with attribute-association constraints by performing fragmentation and then publishing the loose-association at group level [6]. It is noteworthy to mention that the order of these steps are very crucial. For example, if any privacy

---

Algorithm 2. Preventing Explicit Information Leakage

Input: Relation R, Privacy Policy Specification P in the form of *attribute-association* **g** , *selection-projection* $\pi_g\sigma_\phi$ and *cell level* $[\![g]\!]_{\text{Val(PK(g))}}$
Output: Relations satisfying P

1: Apply reduction algorithm in **Algorithm 1** and compute minimal form of policy specification.
2: For all X $\in$ P, perform the following steps to obtain relation R':
   2(a): *If* X *is in the form of* $[\![g]\!]_{\text{Val(PK(g))}}$:
   If X acts as referential key linking other relation, then corresponding cell will be masked by *Type-2*. Otherwise, the value will be masked by *Type-1*.
   2(b): *If* X *is in the form of* $\pi_g\sigma_\phi$:
   If any cell in X is involved in any referential integrity, then corresponding cell will be masked by *Type-2*. Otherwise, the value will be masked by *Type-1*.
3: For all **g** $\in$ P, apply Fragmentation Algorithm in [6] on the relation R' which is obtained in step 2.

---

constraint in the form of attribute-association is addressed first, then it may be impossible to respect any cell-level or selection-projection constraints on the same database. This is because when sensitive cells or sensitive database-parts are divided into different fragments, their corresponding cell-level or selection-projection constraint-expressions defined on previous relation may not be valid anymore.

Example 3. Consider the relation *"Patients"* in the running Example 1. Consider the policy specification consisting of confidentiality and visibility constraints P_c and P_v on *"Patients"* defined in Example 1. The resulting database after applying Algorithm 2 is depicted in Table 2.

Table 2. Fragments and group association applying Algorithm 2 on *"Patients"*

(a) *"F_1"*

Name	ZIP	Age	Food_Habit	GID
Alice	100025	4	cereals, carrot, fish oil, yoghurt	g_1
Bob	110091	26	cereals, fish, yoghurts	g_2
Carol	100025	39	pulses, yellow fruits, cranberries	g_1
David	123001	3	pulses, yellow fruits, cranberries	g_3
Ela	110091	22	pulses, yellow fruits, cranberries	g_2
Frudo	110091	5	pulses, milk, yellow fruits	g_2
Gram	123001	45	cereals, fish, yoghurts	g_3

(b) $A_{F_1 F_2}$

GID_{F_1}	GID_{F_2}
g_1	h_1
g_2	h_1
g_2	h_2
g_3	h_1
g_3	h_2

(c) *"F_2"*

GID	Disease	Gender
h_1	Kwashiorkor	M
h_2	α	F
h_1	Osteomalacia	M
h_1	$\top$	M
h_2	β	F
h_1	Goiter	M
h_2	γ	F

Observe that Step 2(a) masks the sensitive cell represented by $[\![Disease]\!]_{(104)}$ with *Type-1* variable $\top$. Similarly, Step 2(b) masks the database part represented by selection-projection confidentiality constraint $\pi_{Disease}\sigma_{Gender=F}$ by other *Type-1* variables α, β, and γ.

In the third step, in order to preserve the constraints expressed in attribute-association form, the relation obtained in Step 2 is fragmented and all the fragments ("F_1" and "F_2") along with their group association ($A_{F_1 F_2}$) are released, as shown in Table 2. Observe, as an instance, that Alice belongs to the group g_1 after fragmentation. It is clear from the group association Table 2(b) that g_1 is associated with the group h_1 which contains four possible diseases, i.e. Kwashiorkor, Osteomalacia, Goiter and $\top$. This produces anonymized result when attackers try to infer the exact value of disease for Alice. For example, although attacker can infer that Alice may suffer from Kwashiorkor, Osteomalacia, Goiter or any of these diseases, but she will be unable to get exact value of the disease.

6   Functional and Data Dependency: A Gateway to Implicit Information Leakage

The purpose of this section is just to briefly recall the privacy concerns in presence of functional dependency (FD) and data dependency (DD). The authors in [10] and [11] explored the information leakage due to FD and DD respectively. In particular, as preventive measures, [10] proposed encryption of a small amount of non-sensitive data in order to nullify the effect of FD on the relation, whereas [11] applied fragmentation as a way to prevent leakage due to DD.

Examples 4 and 5 show how functional dependency (FD) and data dependency (DD), formalized in Sect. 3.2, can serve as adversary knowledge and may cause privacy violation.

Example 4. Consider a hospital relation that stores its patients' details as given in Table 3(a). Suppose, Alice and Carol do not want to disclose their disease information, however Bob is ready to disclose his disease information. Suppose Table 3(b) is the resultant relation, after applying Algorithm 2, preserving these explicit privacy constraints.

Table 3. Leakage in PD' due to $\langle\{Disease\_Code\} \xrightarrow{FD} \{Disease\}\rangle$

(a) Original relation PD

Name	Disease_Code	Disease
Alice	HI15	HIV
Bob	CC22	Cancer
Carol	CC22	Cancer

(b) Masked relation PD'

Name	Disease_Code	Disease
Alice	HI15	α
Bob	CC22	Cancer
Carol	CC22	β

Assume that the following functional dependency $F = \langle\{Disease\_Code\} \xrightarrow{FD} \{Disease\}\rangle$ exists. With the knowledge of F, an attacker can easily derive Carol's disease from Bob's record, as Bob and Carol have same disease-code resulting into same disease for both.

Example 5. Consider a relation "R" as depicted in Table 4(a) with confidential constraint $P_c = \{Name, Disease\}$ and data dependency D: $[\{Birth, ZIP\} \xrightarrow{DD} \{Name\}]$. By following Algorithm 2, the resulting fragments satisfying P_c is shown in Table 4(b). Due to the presence of data dependency D, for each tuple an attacker can easily get the values of "$Name$" attribute if she knows the values of "$Birth$" and "ZIP" and hence the constraint P_c is violated.

Table 4. Leakage in R due to $[\{Birth, ZIP\} \xrightarrow{DD} \{Name\}]$

(a) Database Relation R

Name	Birth	ZIP	Disease	Drug	Dosage
Alice	11/01/2014	1111	soar throat	Diphen	6mg
Bob	12/11/1990	2222	sneezing	Beadryl1	20mg

(b) Correct fragmentation of R

Name	Birth	ZIP	Disease
Alice	11/01/2014	1111	soar throat
Bob	12/11/1990	2222	sneezing

Drug	Dosage
Diphen	6mg
Benadryl	20mg

7   Property-Based Dependency: A New Adversarial Knowledge

In this section, we introduce a new kind of dependency which may also trigger implicit data leakage even though DD- and FD-based leakages are absent. We name this new kind of dependency as *property-based dependency*(PD). Let us start this section with the following research question:

"Does the absence of functional dependency and data dependency guarantee the absence of implicit information leakage?"

This can be understood by a simple example, illustrated below in Example 6, which shows a possible information leakage even in absence of DD- and FD-based leakages.

Example 6 Consider the relation in Table 5(a). Suppose that an attacker is able to observe the properties *Age_Group* and *Deficiency* from the attributes "Age" and "$Food\_Habit$" according to following definitions:

$$Age\_Group(Age) = \begin{cases} child, & if\ Age \in [0\text{--}15] \\ adult, & if\ Age \in [15\text{--}40] \\ old, & otherwise. \end{cases}$$

$Deficiency(Food\_Habit) =$

$$\begin{cases} Vitamin\ A, & if\ (cord\ liver\ oil \vee yellow\ fruits) \notin Food\ Habit \\[1em] Vitamin\ D, & if\ (milk \vee fish\ oil) \notin Food\ Habit \\[1em] Iodine, & if\ (sea\ food \vee organic\ yoghurts \vee cranberries) \notin Food\ Habit \\[1em] Protein, & if\ (pulses \vee fish) \notin Food\ Habit \end{cases}$$

Observe that there is no leakage of concrete database values due to FD or DD present in the system. In spite of that, an attacker may carefully observe the properties *Age_Group* and *Deficiency* of a person looking his or her *Age* and *Food_Habit* and may infer the property of disease by which he or she gets affected. This is due to the observational power of attackers [18] at property-level on the dependencies exhibited in the concrete level. This is depicted in Table 5(b).

Table 5. Leakage based on property observation

(a) Relation *"Patient_diet"*

Name	ZIP	Age	Food_Habit	Disease
Alice	100025	4	cereals, carrot, fish oil, yoghurt	Kwashiorkar
Bob	110091	26	cereals, fish, yoghurts	Night Blindness
Carol	100025	39	pulses, yellow fruits, cranberries	Osteomalacia
David	123001	3	pulses, yellow fruits, cranberries	Rickets
Ela	110091	22	pulses, yellow fruits, cranberries	Osteomalacia
Frudo	110091	5	pulses, milk, yellow fruits	Goiter
Gram	123001	45	cereals, fish, yoghurts	Cataract

(b) Property-based Abstraction of *"Patient_diet"*

Name	ZIP	Age_Group	Deficiency	Disease_Effects
Alice	100025	Child	Protein	Distended abdomen
Bob	110091	Adult	Vitamin A	Vision problem in darkness
Carol	100025	Adult	Vitamin D	Joint pain, stiffness
David	123001	Child	Vitamin D	Stunted growth
Ela	110091	Adult	Vitamin D	Joint pain, stiffness
Frudo	110091	Child	Iodine	Swollen neck
Gram	123001	Old	Vitamin A	Complete loss of vision

Let us now formally define the *property-based dependency* (PD) and propose a preventive measure for this.

The formal definition is based on upper closure operator of Abstract Interpretation [19]. Abstract domains can be equivalently formulated either in terms of Galois Connections or Closure Operators. As usual, in Abstract Interpretation, a property is an upper closure operator on the concrete domain of computation.

Definition 3 Upper Closure Operator [19]: *An upper closure operator $\rho : S \rightarrow S$ on a poset S is (i) Monotone: $\forall x_1, x_2 \in S. \; x_1 \leq_S x_2 \Rightarrow \rho(x_1) \leq_S \rho(x_2)$. (ii) Idempotent: $\forall x \in S. \; \rho^2(x) = \rho(x)$. (iii) Extensive: $\forall x \in S. \; x \leq_S \rho(x)$.*

The set of all closure operators on S is denoted by $uco(S)$. If $\langle H, \leq, \sqcup, \sqcap, \bot, \top \rangle$ is a complete lattice, then $uco(H)$ is isomorphic to lattice of abstract interpretation of H. For example, the SIGN and PARITY properties [19] as represented in Fig. 2 may act as the upper closure operators of the lattice H of integers.

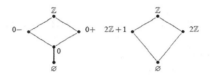

Fig. 2. SIGN and PARITY domain

Definition 4 Property-based dependency (PD): *Let a and b be two attributes of a relation R. Let C_a and C_b be the domains of a and b respectively, such that $r \subseteq C_a \times C_b$. Given $\rho \in uco(C_a)$ and $\eta \in uco(C_b)$, we say that there exists (ρ, η) - property-based dependency if either (1) $\forall \; t_i \in R : \; \rho(t_i(a))$ determines $\eta(t_i(b))$ or (2) $\forall t_i, t_j \in R: \; if(\rho(t_i(a)) = \rho(t_j(a)))$ then $(\eta(t_i(b)) = \eta(t_j(b)))$, where $t_i(a)$ denotes the value of attribute a in tuple t_i.*

In general, we denote PD dependency by the notation P_{PD}: $\langle\!\langle \rho(X) \xrightarrow{PD} \eta(Y) \rangle\!\rangle$ where $X, Y \in \wp(\texttt{attribute(DB)})$ and ρ and η are the respective closure operators. For example, in Example 6 the PD is represented as $\langle\!\langle Age\_Group(Age), Deficiency(Food\_Habit) \xrightarrow{PD} Disease\_Effects(Disease) \rangle\!\rangle$. This is worthwhile to mention here that the relation r on C_a and C_b represents either DD- or FD-dependency on the concrete relation R.

The above definitions can be extended for any number of attributes and the definition of the generalized form of PD-dependencies is given below:

Definition 5 Generalized Property-based Dependency: *The above definition can be generalized to $(\langle \rho_1, \rho_2, \ldots, \rho_k \rangle, \langle \eta_1, \eta_2, \ldots, \eta_k \rangle)$-property-based dependency if $\exists \; a_m, \; \ldots, \; a_n, \; b_u, \ldots, b_v \in \texttt{attribute}(R)$: (1) $\forall \; t_i \in R : \rho_1(t_i[a_m]) \wedge \cdots \wedge \rho_k(t_i[a_n])$ determines $\eta_1(t_i[b_u]) \wedge \cdots \wedge \eta_k(t_i[b_v])$ or (2) $\forall \; t_i, t_j \in R : if \; \rho_1(t_i[a_m]) = \rho_1(t_j[a_m]) \wedge \ldots \wedge \rho_k(t_i[a_n]) = \rho_k(t_j[a_n])$ then $\eta_1(t_i[b_u]) = \eta_1(t_j[b_u]) \wedge \cdots \wedge \eta_k(t_i[b_v]) = \eta_k(t_j[b_v])$.*

The existence of PD allows attackers to infer some partial information representing property of data, instead of their actual values. We can restrict the attacker to observe properties at a higher level of abstraction only, *e.g.* "Vitamins deficiency" instead of "Vitamin A" or "Vitamin D" deficiency so that the property based dependency $\langle\!\langle (Age\_Group(Age), Deficiency(Food\_Habit)) \xrightarrow{PD} Disease\_Effects(Disease) \rangle\!\rangle$ is broken.

Considering all these three dependency-based information leakage, lets rewrite our formal policy specification language for implicit leakage below:

$$P_{IM} ::= P_{DD} \mid P_{FD} \mid P_{PD} \mid P_{IM}, P_{IM}$$

where P_{DD}: $[X \xrightarrow{DD} Y]$ is data dependency, P_{FD}: $\langle X \xrightarrow{FD} Y \rangle$ is functional dependency, and P_{PD}: $\langle\langle \rho(X) \xrightarrow{PD} \eta(Y) \rangle\rangle$ is *property-based dependency*, where $X, Y \in \wp(\texttt{attribute(R)})$ and $X \cap Y = \phi$ and ρ, η are the respective closure operators.

8 Proposed Solution to Prevent Implicit Leakage

Although DD- and FD-dependences information are specified by the database designers, however the presence of possible *property based dependences* can be identified based on the database abstractions w.r.t. attackers observational power in abstract domains [18]. Due to space restriction, we do not detail this here.

In this section, we provide a unified solution framework to prevent implicit leakage in presence of all three dependences (i.e., DD, FD and PD). To this objective, we extend the Ordered Binary Decision Diagram (OBDD)-based approach which was primarily proposed in [20] to address explicit constraints in attribute-association form only. The idea behind this is to enable the approach to nullify the effect of dependencies.

Our solution consists of following phases: (*a*) *representation of constraints in boolean logic*, (*b*) *computing correct truth assignment of the OBDD of boolean formula*, (*c*) *computing minimal correct truth assignments of the OBDDs*.

Representation of constraints in boolean logic. Let $\bar{x} \in$ Bvar be a boolean formula corresponding to x where Bvar is the set of boolean variables. Given a relation R, any data dependency of the form $[X \xrightarrow{DD} Y]$ is represented as $(\bar{x}_1 \wedge \cdots \wedge \bar{x}_k) \xrightarrow{DD} (\bar{y}_1 \wedge \cdots \wedge \bar{y}_l)$ for all $x_i \in X$ and $y_i \in Y$. Similarly functional dependency of form $\langle X \xrightarrow{FD} Y \rangle$ is represented as $\wedge x_i \xrightarrow{FD} \wedge y_i$ where $x_i \in X$, $y_i \in Y$ the PD of the form $\langle\langle \rho(X) \xrightarrow{PD} \eta(Y) \rangle\rangle$ is represented as $\rho(\wedge x_i) \xrightarrow{PD} \eta(\wedge y_i)$.

Computing correct truth assignment of the OBDD of boolean formula. Once we get the boolean representation, we compute the correct truth assignment of the boolean formula. Let us consider a DD $[X \xrightarrow{DD} Y]$ and its corresponding boolean formula $(\bar{x}_1 \wedge \cdots \wedge \bar{x}_k) \xrightarrow{DD} (\bar{y}_1 \wedge \cdots \wedge \bar{y}_l)$. If all the attributes in X belong to a single fragment then it may lead to implicit information leakage. Therefore, one-paths of the OBDD of the boolean formula $\neg(\bar{x}_1 \wedge \cdots \wedge \bar{x}_k)$ represent the truth assignment that breaks the dependency. The same holds true for FD and PD.

The formal definition of the correct truth assignment by considering both explicit and implicit policies is as follows:

Definition 6 *Correct truth assignments. Given a relation R, let there exist a DD: $(\bar{x}_1 \wedge \cdots \wedge \bar{x}_k) \xrightarrow{DD} (\bar{y}_1 \wedge \cdots \wedge \bar{y}_l)$, a FD: $(\bar{w}_1 \wedge \cdots \wedge \bar{w}_m) \xrightarrow{FD} (\bar{z}_1 \wedge \cdots \wedge \bar{z}_n)$ and a PD: $\rho(\bar{q}_1 \wedge \cdots \wedge \bar{q}_i) \xrightarrow{PD} \eta(\bar{r}_1 \wedge \cdots \wedge \bar{r}_j)$. The one-paths of the OBDDs of boolean formulas $\neg(\bar{x}_1 \wedge \cdots \wedge \bar{x}_k), \neg(\bar{w}_1 \wedge \cdots \wedge \bar{w}_m), \neg(\bar{q}_1 \wedge \cdots \wedge \bar{q}_i)$ represent the truth assignments that break the dependencies.*

Example 7. Consider the relation *"Patients"* in our running example depicted in Example 1. Suppose, there exists a data dependency D: $[\{Gender, ZIP\} \xrightarrow{DD} \{Age\}]$, a functional dependency F : $\langle\{Age, Gender, ZIP\} \xrightarrow{FD} \{Name\}\rangle$ and a property-based dependency P: $\langle\langle\{Age\_Group(Age), Deficiency(FoodHabit)\} \xrightarrow{PD} \{Disease\_Effects(Disease)\}\rangle\rangle$. The corresponding representation in boolean formula for these constraints are as follows: $\bar{D}D$: $(\overline{Gender} \wedge \overline{ZIP}) \to \overline{Age}$, $\bar{F}D$: $(\overline{Age} \wedge \overline{Gender} \wedge \overline{ZIP}) \to \overline{Name}$ and $\bar{P}D$: $(Age\_Group(\overline{Age}) \wedge Deficiency$ $(\overline{Food\_Habit})) \to Disease\_Effects(\overline{Disease})$.

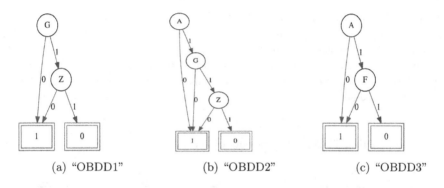

(a) "OBDD1"   (b) "OBDD2"   (c) "OBDD3"

Fig. 3. OBDD for boolean formula of running example

The OBDDs[1] representing the boolean formula $\neg(\overline{Gender} \wedge \overline{ZIP}), \neg(\overline{Age} \wedge \overline{Gender} \wedge \overline{ZIP})$ and $\neg(\overline{Age} \wedge \overline{Food\_Habit}))$ are depicted in Fig. 3(a), (b) and (c) respectively. The nodes in the OBDDs are the attributes of *"Patients"* relation. The one-paths of these OBDDs represent the correct truth assignment that breaks the dependencies. In truth assignments, all variables not appearing in one-paths are considered as don't care variables represented as "-" depicted in Table 6.

Computing minimal correct truth assignments of the OBDDs. After computing OBDDs and correct truth assignments in step (b), the minimal set of truth assignments need to be calculated based the following two properties:

Definition 7 *Link-able truth assignments. Given two assignments I_i and I_j over boolean variables Bvar in an OBDD, we say that I_i and I_j are link-able if and only if $\exists b \in$ Bvar: $I_i(b) = I_j(b) = 1$.*

---

[1] Generated by BDD interface http://formal.cs.utah.edu:8080/pbl/BDD.php.

Table 6. Truth assignments for one-paths

(a) Truth table for OBDD1   (b) Truth table for OBDD2   (c) Truth table for OBDD3

S	N	A	G	Z	F	D
-	-	-	0	-	-	-
-	-	-	1	0	-	-

S	N	A	G	Z	F	D
-	-	0	-	-	-	-
-	-	1	0	-	-	-
-	-	1	1	0	-	-

S	N	A	G	Z	F	D
-	-	0	-	-	-	-
-	-	1	-	-	0	-

Definition 8 _Merge-able truth assignments._ _Given two assignments_ I_i _and_ I_j _over_ Bvar _in an OBDD, we say that_ I_i _and_ I_j _are merge-able if and only if_ $\forall b \in$ Bvar _s.t._ $I_i(b) = 1$, $I_j(b) = 1$ _or_ $I_j(b) = $ - _and vice versa, where "-" denotes_ _"don't care"._

The heuristic algorithm proposed in [20] can easily be extended to compute minimal set of truth assignments for DD, FD and PD. This enables to fragment the relations nullifying the effect of dependencies.

Example 8 Recall the "_Patients_" relation of Example 1. Consider the truth assignments in Table 6. After applying the heuristic algorithm proposed in [20], the minimal set of truth assignments is {[-,-,-,0,-,-,-], [-,-,-,1,0,-,-], [-,-,1,1,0,0,-]}, resulting into a possible fragmentation which is depicted in Table 7. Observe that all the dependencies (_i.e._ DD, FD, PD) are broken and hence there is no implicit information leakage.

Table 7. Correct fragments preserving privacy concerns

(a) "Fragment 1"

Name	Age	Gender
Alice	4	M
Bob	26	F
Carol	39	M
David	3	F
Ela	22	M
Frudo	5	M
Gram	45	F

(b) "Fragment 2"

ZIP	Food_Habit	Disease
100025	cereals, carrot, fish oil, yoghurt	Kwashiorkor
110091	cereals, fish, yoghurts	Night Blindness
100025	pulses, yellow fruits, cranberries	Osteomalacia
123001	pulses, yellow fruits, cranberries	Rickets
110091	pulses, yellow fruits, cranberries	Ostemalacia
110091	pulses, milk, yellow fruits	Goiter
123001	cereals, fish, yoghurts	Cataract

9   Discussions

Although a large number of proposals exist in the literature, none of them is suitable to address privacy concerns expressed as a combination of different possible forms. Authors in [12] consider confidentiality constraints in cell-level form, whereas authors in [10] consider the same in selection-projection form only. In addition to confidentiality constraints, authors in [8] consider both confidentiality and visibility constraints in a different form of attribute association. The solutions proposed in [3–5], similarly, consider only confidentiality constraints but in the form of attribute-association. Unlike explicit information leakage, authors in [9–11] proposed solutions to implicit information leakage occurring due to the presence of various dependencies. Unfortunately, while authors in [9,10] address the leakage due to functional dependency, the proposal in [11] separately deals with the same concern for data dependency only. In a different research direction, although the authors in [21–23] define a number of specification languages with different objectives such as providing user access control or encoding website privacy policies, however in context of relational databases, they can not be adapted.

Due to the lack of expressibility of privacy concerns in a generic way, no proposal in the literature is powerful enough to address different forms of constraints together and therefore does not fit to the real world scenarios. In this paper, we introduced a more generic privacy policy specification language considering a wide range of explicit and implicit privacy constraints. Besides, our proposed solutions aim at addressing the privacy concerns expressed in our specification language. Furthermore, we introduced a new kind of dependency, property-based dependency in our specification language and provided a solution to address this. It is to be noted that the number of constraints affect the number of fragments. As the number of fragments increases, the utility of the data may be compromised.

10   Conclusions

This paper formalized a generic privacy-preserving policy specification language which is highly expressive to adapt a wide range of constraints in various forms, fitting to the real world scenarios. We identified that absence of data dependency and functional dependency does not guarantee the absence of indirect information leakage. In this context, we introduced a new form of dependency, known as *"Property-based Dependency"*. Moreover, we proposed solutions to address privacy concerns expressed in our specification language. Currently, we are in the process of building a prototype based on our proposal.

References

1. Chen, D., Zhao, H.: Data security and privacy protection issues in cloud computing. In: 2012 International Conference on Computer Science and Electronics Engineering (ICCSEE), vol. 1, pp. 647–651. IEEE (2012)
2. Bertino, E., Byun, J.-W., Li, N.: Privacy-preserving database systems. In: Aldini, A., Gorrieri, R., Martinelli, F. (eds.) FOSAD 2004-2005. LNCS, vol. 3655, pp. 178–206. Springer, Heidelberg (2005). https://doi.org/10.1007/11554578_6
3. Sweeney, L.: k-anonymity: a model for protecting privacy. Int. J. Uncertainty Fuzziness Knowl. Based Syst. **10**(05), 557–570 (2002)
4. Machanavajjhala, A., Kifer, D., Gehrke, J., Venkitasubramaniam, M.: l-diversity: privacy beyond k-anonymity. ACM Trans. Knowl. Discov. Data (TKDD) **1**(1), 3 (2007)

5. Li, N., Li, T., Venkatasubramanian, S.: t-Closeness: privacy beyond k-anonymity and l-diversity. In: IEEE 23rd International Conference on Data Engineering, ICDE 2007, pp. 106–115. IEEE (2007)
6. De Capitani di Vimercati, S., Foresti, S., Jajodia, S., Paraboschi, S., Samarati, P.: Fragments and loose associations: respecting privacy in data publishing. Proc. VLDB Endow. **3**(1–2), 1370–1381 (2010)
7. De Capitani di Vimercati, S., Foresti, S., Jajodia, S., Livraga, G., Paraboschi, S., Samarati, P.: Extending loose associations to multiple fragments. In: Wang, L., Shafiq, B. (eds.) DBSec 2013. LNCS, vol. 7964, pp. 1–16. Springer, Heidelberg (2013). https://doi.org/10.1007/978-3-642-39256-6_1
8. De Capitani di Vimercati, S., Foresti, S., Jajodia, S., Livraga, G., Paraboschi, S., Samarati, P.: Loose associations to increase utility in data publishing. J. Comput. Secur. **23**(1), 59–88 (2015)
9. Wang, H.W., Liu, R.: Privacy-preserving publishing data with full functional dependencies. In: Kitagawa, H., Ishikawa, Y., Li, Q., Watanabe, C. (eds.) DASFAA 2010. LNCS, vol. 5982, pp. 176–183. Springer, Heidelberg (2010). https://doi.org/10.1007/978-3-642-12098-5_14
10. Dong, B., Wang, W., Yang, J.: Secure data outsourcing with adversarial data dependency constraints. In: 2016 IEEE 2nd International Conference on Big Data Security on Cloud (BigDataSecurity), IEEE International Conference on High Performance and Smart Computing (HPSC), IEEE International Conference on Intelligent Data and Security (IDS), pp. 73–78. IEEE (2016)
11. De Capitani di Vimercati, S., Foresti, S., Jajodia, S., Livraga, G., Paraboschi, S., Samarati, P.: Fragmentation in presence of data dependencies. IEEE Trans. Dependable Secure Comput. **11**(6), 510–523 (2014)
12. Wang, Q., Yu, T., Li, N., Lobo, J., Bertino, E., Irwin, K., Byun, J.W.: On the correctness criteria of fine-grained access control in relational databases. In: Proceedings of the 33rd International Conference on Very Large Data Bases, VLDB Endowment, pp. 555–566 (2007)
13. Landberg, A.H., Nguyen, K., Pardede, E., Rahayu, J.W.: δ-dependency for privacy-preserving XML data publishing. J. Biomed. Inf. **50**, 77–94 (2014)
14. Farkas, C., Jajodia, S.: The inference problem: a survey. ACM SIGKDD Explor. Newsl. **4**(2), 6–11 (2002)
15. Agrawal, R., Kiernan, J., Srikant, R., Xu, Y.: Hippocratic databases. In: Proceedings of the 28th International Conference on Very Large Data Bases, VLDB Endowment, pp. 143–154 (2002)
16. Paci, F., Zannone, N.: Preventing information inference in access control. In: Proceedings of the 20th ACM Symposium on Access Control Models and Technologies, pp. 87–97. ACM (2015)
17. Earley, J.: An efficient context-free parsing algorithm. Commun. ACM **13**(2), 94–102 (1970)
18. Mastroeni, I.: On the rôle of abstract non-interference in language-based security. In: Yi, K. (ed.) APLAS 2005. LNCS, vol. 3780, pp. 418–433. Springer, Heidelberg (2005). https://doi.org/10.1007/11575467_27
19. Giacobazzi, R., Mastroeni, I.: Abstract non-interference: parameterizing non-interference by abstract interpretation. ACM SIGPLAN Not. **39**(1), 186–197 (2004)
20. Ciriani, V., De Capitani di Vimercati, S., Foresti, S., Livraga, G., Samarati, P.: Enforcing confidentiality and data visibility constraints: an OBDD approach. In: Li, Y. (ed.) DBSec 2011. LNCS, vol. 6818, pp. 44–59. Springer, Heidelberg (2011). https://doi.org/10.1007/978-3-642-22348-8_6

21. Agrawal, R., Bird, P., Grandison, T., Kiernan, J., Logan, S., Rjaibi, W.: Extending relational database systems to automatically enforce privacy policies. In: 21st International Conference on Data Engineering, ICDE 2005, Proceedings, pp. 1013–1022. IEEE (2005)
22. Iyilade, J., Vassileva, J.: P2U: a privacy policy specification language for secondary data sharing and usage. In: 2014 IEEE Security and Privacy Workshops (SPW), pp. 18–22. IEEE (2014)
23. Cranor, L.F.: P3P: making privacy policies more useful. IEEE Secur. Priv. **99**(6), 50–55 (2003)

Privacy-Preserving Proxy Re-encryption with Fine-Grained Access Control

Payal Chaudhari[1,2], Manik Lal Das[2(✉)], and Dipankar Dasgupta[3]

[1] LDRP-ITR, Gandhinagar, India
payal.ldrp@gmail.com
[2] DA-IICT, Gandhinagar, India
maniklal_das@daiict.ac.in
[3] University of Memphis, Memphis, USA
dasgupta@memphis.edu

Abstract. Proxy re-encryption is a useful cryptographic primitive in which a semi-trusted proxy agent is given delegation power to transform a ciphertext for Alice into a ciphertext for Bob without viewing the underlying plaintext. Attribute Based Encryption (ABE) is a promising cryptographic algorithm that provides confidentiality of data along with owner-enforced fine-grained access control. With attribute-based encryption, a data owner can use a set of attribute values (i.e., access policy) for encrypting a message such that only authorized entity who possesses the required set of attribute values can decrypt the ciphertext. In this paper, we propose a proxy re-encryption scheme using the merits of ciphertext-policy anonymous attribute-based encryption. The proposed scheme, termed as PRE-AABE, reduces the computation burden significantly for updating the access policy of a ciphertext to a semi-trusted proxy agent (e.g., cloud server). The proposed PRE-AABE scheme hides the access policy inside the ciphertext, so that parties except the intended receiver will not be able to figure out the purpose of the ciphertext. At the same time, the proxy agent is able to perform the re-encryption successfully without learning anything about the plaintext contents or the access policy. We show that the proposed PRE-AABE scheme is secure in IND-CP-CPA (indistinguishability against ciphertext-policy and chosen-plaintext attack) under the Decisional Bilinear Diffie-Hellman Assumption. We provide the experimental results of the scheme and show that PRE-AABE scheme is efficient and practical.

Keywords: Proxy re-encryption · Access structure
Attribute-based encryption · Anonymity

1 Introduction

The usage of public cloud storage gives the advantages of availability and reliability of data to user without location constraints. However, it also demands some essential security requirements to be satisfied such as fine-grained access

© Springer International Publishing AG 2017
R. K. Shyamasundar et al. (Eds.): ICISS 2017, LNCS 10717, pp. 88–103, 2017.
https://doi.org/10.1007/978-3-319-72598-7_6

control and confidentiality of user's data on cloud server platform. To ensure data confidentiality from third-party server, a working and effective model is to encrypt the data before outsourcing it on the cloud. Symmetric key encryption (e.g. AES) is faster in comparison to public-key cryptography (e.g. RSA) [1], but has limitation of secret key distribution if there is a need to share the encrypted data with other users. Public key cryptographic primitive solves this issue with additional computation cost, but not practical for large size of data encryption. Therefore, a practical approach to encrypt large documents is to first encrypt the document with a symmetric key encryption using a random symmetric key and then encrypting that symmetric key using public key cryptographic algorithm. For controlling the access to user's data, the traditional access control mechanisms require the service provider to enforce the access policy. However, these mechanisms are not well suited for cloud setup, as the cloud server may collude with a revoked user to get access to encrypted data. Attribute Based Encryption (ABE) [2] is a well-accepted public key based primitive, which provides data confidentiality and fine-grained access control together. ABE is appropriate in a system where each user is identified with a set of attribute values. There are two variants of ABE - (i) Key-Policy Attribute Based Encryption (KP-ABE) [3] and (ii) Ciphertext-Policy Attribute Based Encryption (CP-ABE) [4]. In KP-ABE, each ciphertext is labeled by the encryptor with a set of descriptive attributes and the private key of a user is associated with an access structure that specifies which type of ciphertext the user can decrypt. Whereas, in CP-ABE a user is identified by a set of attributes which are included in his private key, and a data owner can decide the access policy for decrypting ciphertext intended to the user. The encrypted message must specify an associated access policy over attributes. A user can only decrypt a ciphertext if the user's attributes pass through the ciphertext's access policy.

Proxy re-encryption is a useful cryptographic primitive in which a semi-trusted proxy agent is allowed to transform a ciphertext designated to Alice into a ciphertext for Bob without viewing the underlying plaintext. Ciphertext-Policy Attribute-Based Proxy Re-encryption (CP-ABPRE) allows a semi-trusted proxy agent such as public cloud server to update the access policy and accordingly ciphertext components of a ciphertext without uncovering the plaintext. Using this technique, a user is able to delegate his access privileges for a ciphertext to the proxy agent. As the access policy attached to a ciphertext in clear form helps the adversary guess the purpose of the ciphertext, it is essential to hide the access policy inside the ciphertext that can preserve the purpose of the ciphertext to intended receiver and also provides the receiver privacy. The need of receiver privacy is also applicable to proxy re-encryption context. To apply the receiver privacy during the proxy re-encryption process, it is required to hide the access policy of ciphertext.

1.1   Related Work

Attribute-Based Proxy Re-encryption (AB-PRE). The concept of proxy re-encryption was introduced by Blaze *et al.* [5]. With proxy re-encryption service, a user provides his delegation key to a proxy agent and wants the proxy agent to perform the re-encryption. For example, Dr. First has received her patient's medical report on public cloud in an encrypted format. She wants to forward this report to Dr. Second for getting a second opinion. To grant the access privileges to Dr. Second, the conventional way for Dr. First is to re-encrypt the report using Second's secret key and then outsourcing again the report on the public cloud server. An alternative and more efficient way to do this is to use the proxy re-encryption technique, in which, Dr. First generates a proxy re-encryption key and sends it to the cloud server. The cloud server, as a proxy agent, is now able to perform the re-encryption on behalf of Dr. First without learning the underlying plaintext. Liang *et al.* [6] have provided the Ciphertext-Policy Attribute-Based Proxy Re-encryption (CP-ABPRE) scheme, that enables the proxy agent to update the access policy associated with a ciphertext. Yu *et al.* [7] proposed a CP-ABPRE scheme that provides proxy re-encryption along with user revocation. Do *et al.* [8] have addressed the issue of security against collusion of revoked user and proxy. The scheme proposed in [9] presents a CP-ABPRE scheme which provides both keyword search and proxy re-encryption functionality. The CP-ABPRE scheme presented in [10] has been proven adaptively secure. Although, there exists some good proposals on proxy re-encryption based on ABE (named as CP-ABPRE) schemes, they did not address an important security concern of receiver privacy.

Anonymous Attribute Based Encryption (AABE). Anonymous Attribute Based Encryption (AABE) scheme uses the features of ABE and hides the access policy inside the ciphertext. This feature helps to cover the identity of receiver, which in turn, preserves privacy of the receiver and protects the data confidentiality to the extend of the purpose of the ciphertext. Kapadia *et al.* [11] proposed a CP-ABE scheme with receiver anonymity. However, the scheme presented in [11] is not collusion-resistant and requires an online semi-trusted server. Boneh *et al.* [12] proposed a scheme based on hidden vector encryption, and another scheme by Katz *et al.* [13] supports inner product predicates. Later, a few AABE schemes [14–16] have been proposed in literature. Zhang *et al.* [17] have proposed an AABE scheme in with an approach of *match-then-decrypt* to reduce the decryption overhead. However, the scheme in [17] found insecure in [18].

Anonymous Attribute Based Proxy Re-encryption (AABPRE). Zhang *et al.* [19] have introduced the concept of anonymous proxy re-encryption. In their scheme the proxy re-encryption task can be transferred to a proxy without compromising the data security. The proxy server will take the approach of *match-then-decrypt*, to avoid the re-encryption overhead for the ciphertext whose access policies cannot be satisfied with user's attributes. However, the scheme has some major limitations. One of the limitations is that the cloud server plays the role of the proxy server. The user has to reveal his attribute information to the proxy server for performing proxy re-encryption. Therefore, the identity of user who has sent the command to perform the proxy re-encryption is known to the proxy server, which in turn, fails to preserve the privacy of receiver and reveals the purpose of the ciphertext.

Our Contributions. We present a proxy re-encryption scheme using ciphertext-policy anonymous attribute-based encryption, termed as PRE-AABE, that allows the cloud server to perform the proxy re-encryption, acting as the proxy agent, without learning the plaintext contents or access policy belongs to it. The proposed PRE-AABE scheme allows multiple level of re-encryption and user's attribute values are kept hidden inside the proxy re-encryption key. The PRE-AABE scheme facilitates re-encryption control, where a data owner or a data user can cease the further re-encryption of a ciphertext. The proposed scheme uses prime-order bilinear pairing operations and is proven secure in IND-CP-CPA (indistinguishability against ciphertext-policy and chosen-plaintext attack) under the Decisional Bilinear Diffie-Hellman Assumption. To reduce the burden of high compute-intensive bilinear pairing operations in decryption algorithm, we make the resource-rich cloud server to perform partial decryption where the user provides his secret key in masked form to cloud server and the cloud server performs the partial decryption of data and then the partially decrypted data is given to the user. After that, the decryption is completed by the user which takes significantly less computational resource. We have implemented the scheme by simulating the proxy re-encryption operation on a google cloud instance to check the practicality of the proposed PRE-AABE scheme and show that the scheme is secure and practical.

Organization of the paper. The remainder of the paper is organized as follows. Section 2 provides some preliminaries for making the paper self-content. Section 3 presents the construction and security model of the proposed PRE-AABE scheme. Section 4 analyzes the proposed scheme. We conclude the paper in Sect. 5.

2 Preliminaries

2.1 Bilinear Mapping

Let G_0 and G_1 be two multiplicative cyclic groups of a large prime order p. Let g be a generator of G_0 and e be a bilinear map, $e : G_0 \times G_0 \to G_1$. The bilinear map e has the following properties:

- Bilinearity: $e(g^a, g^b) = e(g, g)^{ab}$ for all $a, b, \in \mathbb{Z}_p$
- Non-degeneracy: There exists g_1, $g_2 \in G_0$ such that $e(g_1, g_2) \neq 1$.
- Efficiency: There exists an efficient computable algorithm to compute $e(g_1, g_2)$ for all g_1, $g_2 \in G_0$.

We say that G_0 is a bilinear group if it satisfies the above three properties.

2.2 Decisional Bilinear Diffie-Hellman (DBDH) Assumption

Let $a, b, c, z \in \mathbb{Z}_p$ be chosen at random and g be a generator of G_0. The DBDH assumption is that no probabilistic polynomial-time algorithm $\mathcal{P}$ can distinguish the tuple $(A = g^a,\ B = g^b,\ C = g^c,\ e(g,g)^{abc})$ from the tuple $(A = g^a,\ B = g^b,\ C = g^c,\ e(g,g)^z)$ with more than a negligible advantage ϵ.

The advantage of $\mathcal{P}$ is $\Pr[\mathcal{P}(A,\ B,\ C,\ e(g,g)^{abc}) = 0] - \Pr[\mathcal{P}(A,\ B,\ C,\ e(g,g)^z) = 0] = \epsilon$.

2.3 Access Structure

Let there be n attribute in the universe and each attribute i (for all $1 \leq i \leq n$) has value set $V_i = \{v_{i,1}, v_{i,2}, \cdots, v_{i,m_i}\}$. $L = [L_1, L_2, \cdots, L_n]$ is an attribute list, where each L_i represents one value from the value set of attribute i. A ciphertext policy is defined as $T = [T_1, T_2, \cdots, T_n]$, where each T_i represents the set of permissible values of an attribute i in order to decrypt the ciphertext ($T_i \subseteq V_i$). An attribute list L satisfies an access structure T, if $L_i \in T_i$ for all $1 \leq i \leq n$. We assume that the system has n attributes and for each attribute i ($1 \leq i \leq n$) the size of set V_i is m_i.

We define a binary relation $\mathrm{F}(L,\ T)$. $\mathrm{F}(L,\ T) = 1$ if the attributes in L can satisfy the access policy specified in T; else, $\mathrm{F}(L,\ T) = 0$.

3 The Proposed PRE-AABE Scheme

3.1 System Model

The scheme comprises the following entities.

- Attribute Center (AC): Attribute Center (AC) is a trusted third party and is responsible for generating system parameters and issuing keys to users.
- Data Owner: Data owner encrypts and uploads the ciphertext on public cloud storage.
- User: Data users are able to do following tasks:
    1. A data user can issue the re-encryption query to the cloud server, so that cloud server can update the access policy of the ciphertext and the ciphertext becomes accessible to another user whose attributes can satisfy the updated access policy.
    2. A data user can send his masked secret key to the cloud server. The cloud server can perform the partially decryption on the ciphertext and the partially decrypted ciphertext is returned to the user. The final decryption operation is done on user side.
- Cloud Service Provider (CSP): CSP provides storage and computation services to the users of the system. On receiving a re-encryption query from user, CSP performs the re-encryption of the ciphertext. In case of a request for partial decryption, the CSP will do it and returns the partially decrypted ciphertext is returned to the user.

3.2   Design Goals and Assumptions

The scheme aims to achieve the following goals.

Functional Goals. The scheme enables cloud server to perform re-encryption of encrypted data without learning the receiver' attributes. A receiver obtains the ciphertext from the cloud server in partially decrypted form and performs final decryption, which is less compute-intensive.

Security Goals. The ciphertext hides the access policy of the ciphertext. The re-encryption key as well as the partial decryption key hides the user's attribute values. The cloud server is not able to learn the underlined plaintext data or the access policy attached with the ciphertext.

Assumptions. The attribute center (AC) is a trusted party inside the system and it is assumed that AC does not collude with any adversary. The public cloud server is assumed not trusted, who can perform all his tasks efficiently, but curious to learn the information from the data stored by user on the cloud storage. The security of the scheme is relied on the hardness of DBDH assumptions. The hash functions used in the scheme are assumed collision-resistant.

3.3   Definition of the PRE-AABE Scheme

Definition 1. *The PRE-AABE scheme consists of six algorithms - Setup, Key-Gen, Encryption, ReKeyGen, ReEncrypt and Decryption, defined as follows.*

- **Setup**(1^l): The Setup(1^l) is run by Attribute Center. It takes as input parameter a security parameter l and outputs the master private key MK and public parameters PK.
- **KeyGen**(MK,L): The KeyGen(MK, L) algorithm takes as input the master key MK along with user's attribute set L and outputs a secret key SK comprising components for all attributes in L.
- **Encryption**(PK,M,T): The Encryption(PK, M, T) algorithm is used for encrypting user's document M as per the access policy T using the system's public key PK. The algorithm outputs an encrypted document CT which is to be uploaded to the cloud.
- **ReKeyGen**(PK, SK, T'): The algorithm takes as input a user's secret key SK, public key PK and an access policy for re-encrypted ciphertext T'. The algorithm outputs a re-encrypted key RK.
- **ReEncrypt**(RK,CT): It is run by the proxy to generate a re-encrypted ciphertext CT^*. If CT has not gained any re-encryption restriction, then the cloudserver is able to perform re-encryption; else, it aborts.
- **Decryption**(CT(or CT^*), SK): The decryption algorithm is performed in two stages. The first stage of decryption which contains all costly bilinear operations is performed on cloud side and the second stage of decryption which is lightweight, is performed on user side.

3.4 Security Model

We consider indistinguishability against ciphertext-policy and chosen-plaintext attack (IND-CP-CPA) model to analyze the PRE-AABE scheme.

IND-CP-CPA model. The IND-CP-CPA model is defined with the following Challenger($\mathcal{C}$)-Adversary($\mathcal{A}$) game.

Setup: $\mathcal{A}$ gives l as the security parameter to $\mathcal{C}$. $\mathcal{C}$ runs the setup algorithm and returns the public key PK to $\mathcal{A}$.

Phase 1: $\mathcal{A}$ is allowed to issue adaptively generated queries to following oracles (KeyGen and ReKeyGen) as follows.

1. $\mathcal{O}_{KeyGen}$: $\mathcal{A}$ submits a list of attribute values L to the $\mathcal{C}$. $\mathcal{C}$ generates a secret key SK_L for attribute set L and sends that key to $\mathcal{A}$.
2. $\mathcal{O}_{RekeyGen}$: $\mathcal{A}$ submits a list of attribute values L and an access policy T to the $\mathcal{C}$. $\mathcal{C}$ generates a re-encryption key $rk_{L \to T}$ from L and T. The re-encryption key is sent to $\mathcal{A}$.

Challenge: $\mathcal{A}$ submits two pairs (M_0, T_0) and (M_1, T_1). The input submitted by $\mathcal{A}$ must have to satisfy the below mentioned criteria. If either of them fails, then $\mathcal{C}$ aborts.

1. M_0 and M_1 are of equal length.
2. For any set of attribute values L submitted in queries, $F(L,T_0) = F(L,T_1)=0$

The challenger $\mathcal{C}$ randomly chooses $b \in \{0,1\}$, then gets CT_b as output from **Encrypt_Index** algorithm and returns CT_b to $\mathcal{A}$.

Phase 2: Same as in Phase 1. $\mathcal{A}$ issues the adaptively generated queries to the oracles for KeyGen and ReKeyGen without violating the restrictions stated in Challenge phase.

Guess: $\mathcal{A}$ outputs a bit b'. $\mathcal{A}$ wins the game if $b' = b$. The advantage of $\mathcal{A}$ in this game is defined as $\mathrm{Adv}_{\mathcal{A}}(l) = |Pr[b' = b] - 1/2|$.

Definition 2. *The PRE-AABE scheme is secure in IND-CP-CPA, if no polynomially bounded adversary has a non-negligible advantage in the security parameter l with the above game.*

3.5 Detailed Construction of PRE-AABE Scheme

The construction of the PRE-AABE scheme is explained as follows.

Setup(1^l). Attribute Center chooses a security parameter l, which determines the length of key and performs the following steps to generate system keys and public parameters.

- Choose two multiplicative cyclic groups G_0 and G_1 with a prime order p.
- Select g_1, g_2 as two generators of group G_0 and define a bilinear mapping e: $G_0 \times G_0 \rightarrow G_1$ and choose a collision resistant hash function H_0: $\{0,1\}^* \rightarrow \mathbb{Z}_p$.
- Choose $m+3$ random elements $\{\alpha, \beta, \gamma, r_1, r_2, \cdots, r_m\}$ from $\mathbb{Z}_p$. These elements serve as the master key MK of the system.
- Publish the public key PK as $\langle g_1, g_2, e(g_1,g_2)^\alpha, g_2^{\frac{\alpha}{\beta}}, g_2^{\frac{\gamma}{\beta}}, g_1^{\frac{\gamma}{\alpha}}, g_2^{r_1}, g_2^{r_2}, \cdots,$
$g_2^{r_m} \rangle$. We note that $g_2^{\frac{\gamma}{\beta}}, g_1^{\frac{\gamma}{\alpha}}$ will be used for proxy re-encryption purpose.

Key Generation(MK, L). Each user in the system will get a secret key representing the attributes the user possesses. Attribute Center uses the master key MK, attribute set L and chooses a random value r and then generates the user keys as follows.

- $D_0 = g_1^{r\beta}$.
- $\{D_{i1} = g_1^{(H_0(i\|v_{i,j})+r)\frac{\alpha}{r_1}}, D_{i2} = g_1^{(H_0(i\|v_{i,j})^2+r)\frac{\alpha}{r_2}},$
$\cdots, D_{im_i} = g_1^{(H_0(i\|v_{i,j})^{m_i}+r)\frac{\alpha}{r_{m_i}}}\}_{1\leq i\leq n}$ for $v_{i,j} \in L$.

The output of the algorithm is the user's secret key $\langle D_0, \{\{D_{ij}\}_{1\leq j\leq m_i}\}_{1\leq i\leq n}\rangle$.

Encryption(PK, M, T). Let $T = \{T_1, T_2, \cdots, T_n\}$, where T_i $\{1 \leq i \leq n\}$ is the set of values for an attribute i, which are permissible for decryption. When a sender wants to send a document M in encrypted form to a set of users with specific set of attributes, the sender encrypts the document M with the following steps.

- Randomly pick a value K from G_1 which serves as the symmetric key to encrypt the document M using a standard symmetric key encryption (SKE) (e.g. AES [1]) secure against chosen-plaintext attack. We have used two-level of encryption. First the document is encrypted with a randomly chosen symmetric key K and then K is encrypted using the proposed construction of PRE-AABE. This gives an advantage that the encryption of the document using symmetric key encryption will be efficient. Furthermore, the document encryption with a random symmetric key captures the notion of one-time pad symmetric key encryption in the PRE-AABE scheme.
- Compute $C_M \leftarrow SSE(M, K)$.
- Choose a random secret value s from $\mathbb{Z}_p$.
- Randomly pick $s_1, s_2, \cdots, s_{n-1}$ from $\mathbb{Z}_p$ and calculate $s_n = s - \sum_{i=1}^{n-1} s_i$.
- For every attribute field i choose a_i' from $\mathbb{Z}_p$ for $1 \leq i \leq n$ and compute $f(x_i) = a_i'(x_i - H_0(i\|\hat{v}_{i,1}))(x_i - H_0(i\|\hat{v}_{i,2})) \cdots (x_i - H_0(i\|\hat{v}_{i,m_i})) + s_i$, where $\hat{v}_{i,j} = v_{i,j}(j^{th}$ value of attribute $i)$ if $v_{i,j} \in T_i$; else, it will be a random value. The resultant equation is

$$f(x_i) = a_{i0} + a_{i1}x + a_{i2}x^2 + \cdots + a_{im_i}x^{m_i} \tag{1}$$

Summation of all coefficients except a_{i0} from all equations is denoted as A_w $= \sum_{i=1}^{n} \sum_{j=1}^{m_i} a_{ij}$.

– Compute $C_K = K \cdot e(g_1, g_2)^{\alpha(s - \sum_{i=1}^{n} a_{i0})}$

$\hat{C} = g_2^{\frac{A_w \alpha}{\beta}}$, $C' = g_2^{\frac{A_w \gamma}{\beta}}$, $\{C_{i1} = g_2^{a_{i1}r_1}, C_{i2} = g_2^{a_{i2}r_2}, \cdots, C_{im_i} = g_2^{a_{im_i}r_{m_i}}\}$ for $1 \leq i \leq n$.

Here, C' is included in the ciphertext only if the data owner wants to allow the re-encryption of this ciphertext, else it will not be included. The algorithm returns $CT = \langle C_M, C_K, \hat{C}, C' \{\{C_{ij}\}_{1 \leq j \leq m_i}\}_{1 \leq i \leq n} \rangle$ as the output.

ReKeyGen(PK, SK, T'). It is a randomized algorithm and run by a user. The algorithm takes as input the public key PK, a secret key SK and an access policy for re-encryption T'. The output of the algorithm is a rekey rk, which is used by the proxy agent to perform the re-encryption of a ciphertext CT as per new access policy T'. The generation of rk involves the following computation.

– Select a random value K' from group G_1.
– Generate all encryption components $CT_{rk} = \langle C_{K'}, \hat{C}, C', \{\{C_{ij}\}_{1 \leq j \leq m_i}\}_{1 \leq i \leq n} \rangle$ with respect to access policy T' as shown in Encryption algorithm.
– $D'_0 = D_0 \cdot g_1^{\frac{H_0(K')\gamma}{\alpha}} = g_1^{r\beta} \cdot g_1^{\frac{H_0(K')\gamma}{\alpha}}$
– $\{D'_{i1} = D_{i1} \cdot g_1^{H_0(K')} = g_1^{(H_0(i\|v_{i,j})+r)\frac{\alpha}{r_1}} \cdot g_1^{H_0(K')}$

$D'_{i2} = D_{i2} \cdot g_1^{H_0(K')} = g_1^{(H_0(i\|v_{i,j})^2+r)\frac{\alpha}{r_2}} \cdot g_1^{H_0(K')}$

$\cdots D'_{im_i} = D_{im_i} \cdot g_1^{H_0(K')} = g_1^{(H_0(i\|v_{i,j})^{m_i}+r)\frac{\alpha}{r_{m_i}}} \cdot g_1^{H_0(K')}\}_{1 \leq i \leq n}.$

The output of algorithm is $rk = \langle CT_{rk}, D'_0, \{D'_{i1}, D'_{i2}, \cdots, D'_{im_i}\}_{1 \leq i \leq n} \rangle.$

ReEncrypt(rk, CT_M). After receiving a re-encryption key rk, the proxy agent (cloud server) performs the following computation to perform the re-encryption of a ciphertext CT_M.

– $R_{e1} = \prod_{i=1}^{n}(\prod_{j=1}^{m_i} e(C_{ij}, D'_{ij}))$
– $R_{e2} = e(\hat{C}, D'_0) = e(g_1, g_2)^{A_w \alpha r} e(g_1, g_2)^{H_0(K')A_w \frac{\gamma}{\beta}}$
– $C_1 = \frac{C_K \cdot R_{e2}}{R_{e1}} = Ke(A'_w H_0(K') - A_w \frac{\gamma}{\beta} H_0(K'))$
– $C'_1 = \frac{C'}{\prod_{i=1}^{n}(\prod_{j=1}^{m_i} C_{ij})}$ (Here C' is taken from CT_M)

The updated ciphertext CT' now includes C_M (from CT_M), C_1, C'_1 (from computational results) and $C_{K'}, \hat{C}, C', \{\{C_{ij}\}_{1 \leq j \leq m_i}\}_{1 \leq i \leq n}$ from rk. The value of C' from rk should be included only if the data user wants to grant the further re-encryption of this ciphertext, else it will not be included. The output of the algorithm is a re-encrypted ciphertext $CT' = \langle C_M, C_1, C'_1, C_{K'}, \hat{C}, C', \{\{C_{ij}\}_{1 \leq j \leq m_i}\}_{1 \leq i \leq n} \rangle.$

Decrypt(CT(or CT^*), SK). The decryption operation is performed in two phases. In first phase, the user sends his masked secret key SK' to the cloud server and cloud server performs the partial decryption of the ciphertext CT. In second phase, the user performs the final decryption computation.

First Phase: The user generates SK' with his secret key SK and a random value ψ chosen from $\mathbb{Z}_p$ as follows:

- $\hat{D}_0 = D_0^\psi$,
- $\{\hat{D}_{i1} = D_{i1}^\psi, \hat{D}_{i2} = D_{i2}^\psi, \cdots, \hat{D}_{im_i} = D_{im_i}^\psi\}_{1 \leq i \leq n}$

The user submits SK' to cloud. We note that because of the value ψ, SK' can not reveal the user's attribute values. The cloud now performs the following computation to generate the partially decrypted ciphertext $\hat{C}T$

- $R_{d1} = \prod_{i=1}^{n}(\prod_{j=1}^{m_i} e(C_{ij}, \hat{D}_{ij}))=e(g_1, g_2)^{(s-\sum_{i=1}^{n} a_i0)\alpha\psi} \cdot e(g_1, g_2)^{A_w \alpha r \psi}$
- $R_{d2} = e(\hat{C}, D_0) = e(g_1, g_2)^{A_w \alpha r \psi}$
- $R_d = \frac{R_{d2}}{R_{d1}}$

The partially decrypted ciphertext $\hat{C}T$ is returned to the user. If the ciphertext is not re-encrypted, then the cloud server will send $\hat{C}T = \langle\, C_M, C_K, R_d \,\rangle$ to the user. If the ciphertext is re-encrypted, then the cloud server will send $\hat{C}T = \langle\, C_M, C_{K'}, C_1, C_1', R_d \,\rangle$. C_1 and C_1' are included because of proxy re-encryption. With every further re-encryption, these two components will be added.

Second Phase:

- If the ciphertext is not re-encrypted, then user does the following computation to recover the plaintext M.
  - $K = C_K \cdot R_d^{\frac{1}{\psi}}$
  - Decrypt C_M with the symmetric key algorithm used in document Encryption algorithm.
- If the ciphertext is re-encrypted, then the user performs following computation.
  - $K' = C_{K'} \cdot R_d^{\frac{1}{\psi}}$
  - $K = C_1 e(g_1^{H_0(K')}, C_1')$
  - Decrypt C_M with the symmetric key algorithm used in document Encryption algorithm.

The second step of this computation will be repeated as many times a ciphertext is further re-encrypted. This shows that with every new level of re-encryption, one bilinear pairing operation is added on user side. The calculation of R_{e1} and R_{d1} is elaborated below.

$$R_{e1} = \prod_{i=1}^{n}\prod_{j=1}^{m_i} e(g_1^{(H_0(i\|v_i)^j+r)\frac{\alpha}{r_j}} \cdot g_1^{H_0(K')}, g_2^{a'_{ij}r_j})$$

$$= (g_1, g_2)^{(s-\sum_{i=1}^{n} a_{i0})\alpha} \cdot e(g_1, g_2)^{A_w \alpha r \psi} \cdot e(g_1, g_2)^{\sum_{i=1}^{n}\sum_{j=1}^{m_i} a_{ij}r_{ij}H_0(K')}$$

$$= e(g_1, g_2)^{s-\sum_{i=1}^{n} a_{i0}\alpha} \cdot e(g_1, g_2)^{A_w \alpha r} \cdot e(g_1, g_2)^{\sum_{i=1}^{n}\sum_{j=1}^{m_i} A'_w H_0(K')}$$

$$R_{d1} = \prod_{i=1}^{n}\prod_{j=1}^{m_i} e(g_1^{(H_0(i\|v_i)^j+r)\frac{\alpha\psi}{r_j}}, g_2^{a'_{ij}r_j})$$

$$= (g_1, g_2)^{\sum_{i=1}^{n}(s-\sum_{i=1}^{n} a_{i0})\alpha\psi} \cdot e(g_1, g_2)^{A_w \alpha r \psi}$$

$$= e(g_1, g_2)^{s-\sum_{i=1}^{n} a_{i0}\alpha\psi} \cdot e(g_1, g_2)^{A_w \alpha r \psi}$$

4 Analysis of the PRE-ABBE Scheme

4.1 Security Analysis

It is required that the encrypted message does not reveal any information about the ciphertext and underlying access policy to an adversary. We prove this claim by showing the security of PRE-AABE scheme in indistinguishability against ciphertext-policy and chosen plaintext attack (IND-CP-CPA) model. We show that unless a correct secret key is available, the ciphertext is indistinguishable from any other group element.

Theorem 1. *The PRE-AABE scheme is adaptive secure in IND-CP-CPA model under the DBDH assumptions.*

Proof. We prove that without a valid secret key, if the adversary is able to distinguish between the correct ciphertext and a random group element with non-negligible advantage, then we can build a simulator $\mathcal{S}$ that can break the DBDH problem with non-negligible advantage. The DBDH challenger sets the group G_0 and G_1. Then the challenger flips a binary coin μ outside of $\mathcal{S}$ view. If $\mu = 0$ then the challenger sets $(g, A, B, C, Z) = (g, g^a, g^b, g^c, e(g,g)^{abc})$. Else, the challenger sets $(g, A, B, C, Z) = (g, g^a, g^b, g^c, e(g,g)^z)$ for some random value $z \in \mathbb{Z}_p^*$. In the following game $\mathcal{S}$ plays the role of $\mathcal{C}$.

Setup: $\mathcal{S}$ assumes $g_2 = B$ and $g_1 = A$. The remaining components of the masked key are chosen by $\mathcal{S}$ as in the original scheme. $\mathcal{S}$ calculates the PK with these chosen values and submits it to $\mathcal{A}$. A random oracle $\mathcal{O}_H: \{0,1\}^* \rightarrow \mathbb{Z}_p^*$ is defined to simulate the hash function. $\mathcal{O}_H$ maintains a list of (request,response). Let us denote this list as LH. Whenever a query comes to compute $H(S)$ for some string $S \in \{0,1\}^*$, $\mathcal{O}_H$ first makes a search in LH for any pair (S,h). Here, h is a random element chosen from $\mathbb{Z}_p^*$. If any such pair exists in LH, then h is returned as result of $H(S)$, else an element $h \in_R \mathbb{Z}_p^*$ is picked up and send as response of $H(S)$. This newly generated pair $(H(S), h)$ is added in LH.

Phase 1: $\mathcal{A}$ issues adaptively generated queries to following oracles.

1. $\mathcal{O}_{KeyGen}$: $\mathcal{A}$ submits a list of attribute values L to the $\mathcal{C}$. $\mathcal{S}$ performs following computation to derive a secret key SK_L. $\{D_0 = g_1^{r\beta} = A^{r\beta}, \{\{D_{ij} = g_1^{(H_0(i\|v_{i,j})^j + r)\frac{\alpha}{r_j}} = A^{(H_0(i\|v_{i,j})^j + r)\frac{\alpha}{r_j}}\}_{1 \leq j \leq m_i}\}_{1 \leq i \leq n}\}$. At the end $\mathcal{S}$ submits this key SK_L to $\mathcal{A}$.

2. $\mathcal{O}_{RekeyGen}$: $\mathcal{A}$ submits a list of attribute values L and an access policy T to the $\mathcal{C}$. $\mathcal{S}$ first gains a secret key from $\mathcal{O}_{KeyGen}$. Then as in the real scheme he generates the rekey $rk_{L \rightarrow T}$ from L and T. The re-encryption key is submitted to $\mathcal{A}$.

Challenge: $\mathcal{A}$ submits two pairs (M_0, T_0) and (M_1, T_1), where M_0 and M_1 are two equal length messages, and for any set of attribute values L submitted by $\mathcal{A}$ in Phase 1, $F(L, T_0) = F(L, T_1) = 0$. Here, in challenge phase we consider that M_0

and M_1 are elements of group G_1 randomly chosen by $\mathcal{A}$. We do so to reduce the step of encrypting the message with a symmetric key encryption scheme secure against chosen plaintext attack, and then encrypting that symmetric key with our proposed construction. We now prove the security of our proposed construction. Consider c as the secret value used for encryption of keyword. The simulator $\mathcal{S}$ flips a coin $b \in \{0,1\}$. With the outputs obtained from oracles $\mathcal{O}_H$ the simulator $\mathcal{S}$ computes the challenge ciphertext. For $1 \leq i \leq n\text{-}1$ select a_i, s_i and build the equations for each attribute category as follows.

$$f(x_i) = a_i(x - H_0(i\|\hat{v}_{ii})) \cdots (x - H_0(i\|\hat{v}_{im_i})) + s_i \qquad (2)$$
$$f(x_i) = a_{i0} + a_{i1}x + a_{i2}x^2 + \cdots a_{im_i}x^{m_i}$$

where in (2) $\hat{v}_{ij} = v_{ij}$ if $v_{ij} \in T_b$; else, if $v_{ij} \notin T_b$ then $\hat{v}_{ij}$ is some random value chosen from $\mathbb{Z}_p^*$ for $1 \leq j \leq m_i$. $\mathcal{S}$ computes $C_{i1} = B^{a_{i1}r_1} = g_2^{a_{i1}r_1}$, $C_{i2} = B^{a_{i2}r_2}$ $= g_2^{a_{i2}r_2}, \cdots, C_{im_i} = B^{a_{im_i}r_{m_i}} = g_2^{a_{im_i}r_{m_i}}$ for $1 \leq i \leq n\text{-}1$. For the nth attribute category choose a random value $a_n \in \mathbb{Z}_p^*$ and compute the following equation

$$f(x_i) = a_n(x - H_0(\hat{v}_{ni})) \cdots (x - H_0(\hat{v}_{nm_n}))$$
$$= \acute{a}_{n0} + a_{n1}x + a_{n2}x^2 + \cdots a_{nm_n}x^{m_n}$$

We note that $\hat{v}_{nj} = v_{nj}$ if $v_{nj} \in T_b$; else, $\hat{v}_{nj}$ is some random value chosen from $\mathbb{Z}_p^*$ for $1 \leq j \leq m_n$. Now, $\mathcal{S}$ computes $e(g_1, g_2)^{\acute{a}_{n0}\alpha}, C_{n1} = B^{a_{n1}r_1} = g_2^{a_{n1}r_1}$, C_{n2} $= B^{a_{n2}r_2} = g_2^{a_{n2}r_2}, \cdots, C_{nm_n} = B^{a_{nm_n}r_{m_n}} = g_2^{a_{nm_n}r_{m_n}}$. Then, computes $\hat{C} =$ $B^{\frac{A_1\gamma}{\beta}} = g_2^{\frac{A_w\gamma}{\beta}}$, $C' = B^{\frac{A_1\alpha}{\beta}} = g_2^{\frac{A_w\alpha}{\beta}}$, where $A_w = \sum_{i=1}^{n}(\sum_{j=1}^{m_i} a_{ij})$. Compute $C_{M_b} = M_b \cdot \frac{Z^\alpha \cdot e(H_1(w_b), \prod_{i=1}^{n}\prod_{j=1}^{m_i} C_{ij})}{e(A,B)^{\sum a_{i0}\alpha}}$. Now, $\mathcal{S}$ gives ciphertext $CT_b = \langle\, C_{M_b}, \hat{C},$ C', and $\{C_{i1}, C_{i2}, \cdots, C_{im_i}\}$ for $1 \leq i \leq n \,\rangle$.

Phase 2: $\mathcal{A}$ can repeat the queries for keyword w and attribute values L, as it did in Phase 1 with the restrictions that for any input L, $F(L,T_0) = F(L,T_1)$ $= 0$.

Guess: $\mathcal{A}$ outputs a bit b'. If $b' = b$, then $\mathcal{S}$ outputs $\mu = 1$ to indicate that it was given a valid DBDH-tuple; else, it outputs $\mu = 0$ to indicate that the ciphertext is a random element. Therefore, $\mathcal{A}$ gains no information about b, in turn, $Pr[b \neq b'|\mu = 0] = \frac{1}{2}$. As the simulator guesses $\mu' = 0$ when $b \neq b'$, $Pr[\mu = \mu'|\mu = 0] = \frac{1}{2}$. If $\mu = 1$, then the adversary $\mathcal{A}$ is able to view a valid encryption of message with advantage $\epsilon_{dbdh}(l)$, a negligible quantity in security parameter l. Therefore, $Pr[b = b'|\mu = 1] = \frac{1}{2} + \epsilon_{dbdh}(l)$. Similarly, the simulator $\mathcal{S}$ guesses $\mu' = 1$ when $b = b'$, in turn, $Pr[\mu' = \mu|\mu = 1] = \frac{1}{2} + \epsilon_{dbdh}(l)$. The overall advantage of the simulator in DBDH game is $\frac{1}{2} \times Pr[\mu = \mu'|\mu = 0]$ $+\frac{1}{2} \times Pr[\mu = \mu'|\mu = 1] - \frac{1}{2} = \frac{1}{2} \times \frac{1}{2} + \frac{1}{2} \times (\frac{1}{2} + \epsilon_{dbdh}(l)) - \frac{1}{2} = \frac{\epsilon_{dbdh}(l)}{2}$. Therefore, if $\mathcal{A}$ has advantage $\epsilon_{dbdh}(l)$ in the above game instance, then we can build a simulator (S) which can break the DBDH problem with negligible quantity $\frac{\epsilon_{dbdh}(l)}{2}$. $\qquad\square$

Corollary. Theorem 1 proves that the ciphertext of a message does not disclose the message nor the underlying access policy.

4.2 Performance Analysis

We have implemented the PRE-AABE scheme using the PBC library [20] on Linux platform. Bilinear pairings operations are constructed using the curve $y^2 = x^3 + x$ over the field F_q for prime $q = 3 \mod 4$. The order of the groups G_0 and G_1 is a prime of size 160 bits and the length of q is 512 bits. We have evaluated the scheme with varying number of attributes and their various size of valuesets. The user side operations such as Encrypt, RekeyGen and Final Decryption are tested on a machine with 2.30 GHz Intel-i5 Processor configuration. The proxy re-encryption and partial decryption operations are performed by the cloud server. We executed them on a Google cloud computing instance with machine type *n1-standard-1*. The proxy re-encryption time taken by cloud is shown in Fig. 1. The total attribute values is the summation of number of values for each attribute in the system. Unlike the scheme in [19], our scheme involves all ciphertext components in the process of re-encryption and there for our proposed scheme is able to achieve the receiver privacy. With this design criterion, the re-encryption cost increases linearly with the total number of attribute values.

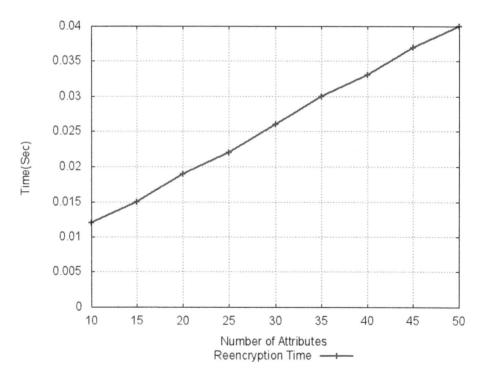

Fig. 1. Re-encryption time by the cloud server

Figure 2 shows the decrease in decryption computation overhead on user side. All the costly bilinear pairing operations are performed on cloud server side during partial decryption operation. To show the difference between computation cost of partial decryption and final decryption, we have plotted the graph shown in Fig. 2 using logarithmic scale. The time complexity of partial decryption increases linearly with the total number of attribute values. However, the compelling computation power of cloud server can bear the computation cost of proxy re-encryption and partial decryption operations. Figure 2 clearly shows that the final decryption done on user side is very efficient.

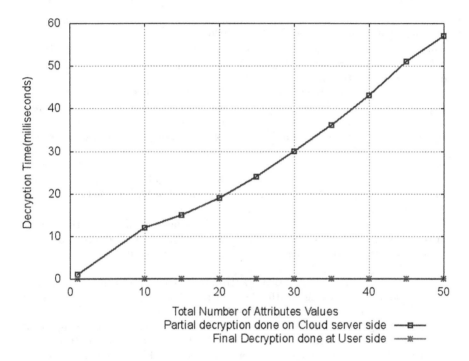

Fig. 2. Comparison of partial decryption time on cloud server and final decryption time on user

5   Conclusions

We have proposed an anonymous attribute based proxy re-encryption scheme (PRE-AABE), that allows a user to delegate the task of updating the access policy of a ciphertext to the cloud server. The cloud server is able to perform the role of proxy agent and performs re-encryption without compromising the data confidentiality or receiver privacy. The proposed PRE-AABE scheme is featured with proxy re-encryption control mechanism, which helps a data owner or data user to prevent the further re-encryption of a ciphertext. To minimize the decryption overhead, the cloud server performs partial decryption of ciphertext on using the server resources, without learning the receiver's attributes. With this partial decryption feature on cloud server, the decryption cost is reduced significantly on user side. The PRE-AABE scheme is proven secure in IND-CP-CPA under BDH assumption. The experimental results show that the CP-ABPRE scheme is efficient and practical.

References

1. Menezes, A.J., van Oorschot, P.C., Vanstone, S.A.: Handbook of Applied Cryptography. CRC Press Inc., Boca Raton (1996)
2. Sahai, A., Waters, B.: Fuzzy identity-based encryption. In: Cramer, R. (ed.) EUROCRYPT 2005. LNCS, vol. 3494, pp. 457–473. Springer, Heidelberg (2005). https://doi.org/10.1007/11426639_27
3. Goyal, V., Pandey, O., Sahai, A., Waters, B.: Attribute-based encryption for fine-grained access control of encrypted data. In: Proceedings of the ACM Conference on Computer and Communications Security, pp. 89–98 (2006)
4. Bethencourt, J., Sahai, A., Waters, B.: Ciphertext-policy attribute-based encryption. In: Proceedings of IEEE Symposium on Security and Privacy, pp. 321–334 (2007)
5. Blaze, M., Bleumer, G., Strauss, M.: Divertible protocols and atomic proxy cryptography. In: Nyberg, K. (ed.) EUROCRYPT 1998. LNCS, vol. 1403, pp. 127–144. Springer, Heidelberg (1998). https://doi.org/10.1007/BFb0054122
6. Liang, K., Fang, L., Susilo, W., Wong, D.S.: A ciphertext-policy attribute-based proxy re-encryption with chosen-ciphertext security. In: Proceedings of the International Conference on Intelligent Networking and Collaborative Systems, pp. 552–559 (2013)
7. Yu, S., Wang, C., Ren, K., Lou, W.: Attribute based data sharing with attribute revocation. In: Proceedings of the ACM Symposium on Information, Computer and Communications Security, pp. 261–270 (2010)
8. Do, J.M., Song, Y.J., Park, N.: Attribute based proxy re-encryption for data confidentiality in cloud computing environments. In: Proceedings of International Conference on Computers, Networks, Systems and Industrial Engineering, pp. 248–251 (2011)
9. Liang, K., Susilo, W.: Searchable attribute-based mechanism with efficient data sharing for secure cloud storage. IEEE Trans. Inf. Forensics Secur. **10**(9), 1981–1992 (2015)
10. Li, H., Pang, L.: Efficient and adaptively secure attribute-based proxy reencryption scheme. Int. J. Distrib. Sensor Netw. **12**(5), 12 (2016). Article No. 5235714
11. Kapadia, A., Tsang, P.P., Smith, S.W.: Attribute-based publishing with hidden credentials and hidden policies. In: Proceedings of Network and Distributed System Security Symposium, pp. 179–192 (2007)
12. Boneh, D., Waters, B.: Conjunctive, subset, and range queries on encrypted data. In: Vadhan, S.P. (ed.) TCC 2007. LNCS, vol. 4392, pp. 535–554. Springer, Heidelberg (2007). https://doi.org/10.1007/978-3-540-70936-7_29
13. Katz, J., Sahai, A., Waters, B.: Predicate encryption supporting disjunctions, polynomial equations, and inner products. J. Cryptol. **26**(2), 191–224 (2008)

14. Yu, S., Ren, K., Lou, W.: Attribute-based content distribution with hidden policy. In: Proceedings of Workshop on Secure Network Protocols, pp. 39–44 (2008)

15. Nishide, T., Yoneyama, K., Ohta, K.: Attribute-based encryption with partially hidden encryptor-specified access structures. In: Bellovin, S.M., Gennaro, R., Keromytis, A., Yung, M. (eds.) ACNS 2008. LNCS, vol. 5037, pp. 111–129. Springer, Heidelberg (2008). https://doi.org/10.1007/978-3-540-68914-0_7

16. Li, J., Ren, K., Zhu, B., Wan, Z.: Privacy-aware attribute-based encryption with user accountability. In: Samarati, P., Yung, M., Martinelli, F., Ardagna, C.A. (eds.) ISC 2009. LNCS, vol. 5735, pp. 347–362. Springer, Heidelberg (2009). https://doi.org/10.1007/978-3-642-04474-8_28

17. Zhang, Y., Chen, X., Li, J., Wong, D.S., Li, H.: Anonymous attribute-based encryption supporting efficient decryption test. In: Proceedings of the ACM SIGSAC Symposium on Information, Computer and Communications Security, pp. 511–516 (2013)

18. Chaudhari, P., Das, M.L., Mathuria, A.: On anonymous attribute based encryption. In: Jajodia, S., Mazumdar, C. (eds.) ICISS 2015. LNCS, vol. 9478, pp. 378–392. Springer, Cham (2015). https://doi.org/10.1007/978-3-319-26961-0_23

19. Zhang, Y., Li, J., Chen, X., Li, H.: Anonymous attribute-based proxy re-encryption for access control in cloud computing. Secur. Commun. Netw. 9(14), 2397–2411 (2016)

20. The pairing-based cryptography library. https://crypto.stanford.edu/pbc/

Systems Security

Hiding Kernel Level Rootkits Using Buffer Overflow and Return Oriented Programming

Amrita Milind Honap$^{(\boxtimes)}$ and Wonjun Lee

Department of Electrical and Computer Engineering,
University of Texas at San Antonio, San Antonio, USA
egn704@my.utsa.edu

Abstract. Kernel Level Rootkits are malwares that can be installed and hidden on a user's computer without revealing their existence. The goal of all rootkits is to carry out malicious execution while being hidden as long as possible on the user's system. We have developed and demonstrated, such a hiding technique for kernel level rootkits from static detection mechanisms. The hiding mechanism uses Return Oriented Programming, which allows the user to execute malicious code in the presence of certain inbuilt security defenses and detection tools. In this technique, an attacker diverts the control flow without injecting any new code in the program overflowing the buffer. We chain together short instruction sequences already present in a program's address space, each of which ends in a "return" instruction. This implemented hiding technique was tested using a custom detection tool which performs static analysis, for specified malicious behavior patterns along with other techniques. We have also examined it with other detection techniques. Experimental results indicate that our prototype was effective in hiding kernel level rootkits.

Keywords: Rootkits · Kernel level rootkits · Hiding · Buffer overflow
Return Oriented Programming

1 Introduction

Malwares are programs that pose a severe threat to the computer system by compromising certain functionalities of the system. Some of the common examples of malwares are virus, trojan, spyware, worms, rootkits, ransomware etc. [1]. They are found in different modified versions, but their final goal is to compromise system security. In this paper, we will be focusing on a special category of malware known as 'rootkits'.

The term rootkit is derived from the combination of words 'root' and 'kit'. Root means highest level of access in Unix-like operating systems and kit is a set of programs designed to exploit a target system [25]. A rootkit is a computer program that is usually designed to maintain root level access or command over a computer without the user knowing about it after the successful breach into the system. Rootkits can provide backdoor capabilities for future attackers as well. It can also access log files and spy on the legitimate computers. Hence it is considered to be very dangerous, as an attacker has unlimited access to the system at any time.

© Springer International Publishing AG 2017
R. K. Shyamasundar et al. (Eds.): ICISS 2017, LNCS 10717, pp. 107–126, 2017.
https://doi.org/10.1007/978-3-319-72598-7_7

Kernel rootkits are able to make detection especially difficult because they operate at the same security level as the operating system itself, and are thus able to intercept or subvert the most trusted operating system operations. The biggest advantage of kernel level rootkits is that, because of their elusive nature, they are hard to detect. Some kernel level rootkits are Adore, Adore-ng, Knark, etc. [29]. They use techniques like system call hooking, function hooking, Direct Kernel Object Manipulation (DKOM) etc. to perform malicious activities. In Unix/Linux systems, kernel level rootkits can be loaded using a Loadable Kernel Modules (LKM). This makes it easy for the attackers to dynamically load and unload the rootkits.

Different methods are adopted to perform malware detection, they are dynamic analysis and static analysis. Dynamic analysis uses integrity checking when the code is executed in the system whereas static analysis observes a malicious behavior before the execution of the code. Our goal is to develop a hiding mechanism to subvert such detection techniques. In this paper we are mainly focusing on subverting static detection. We have developed a hiding mechanism for kernel level rootkits such that it subverts detection from such detection tools. Most tools are built based on the behaviors that are observed by most common type of rootkit attacks.

We have used Return Oriented Programming (ROP) to hide our detectable behaviors. ROP is a technique in which no new code is injected in the targeted system, although we induce certain arbitrary malicious behavior. Our code tries to link short code sequences together which are already present in the memory space [9]. Each of this sequence ends with a 'ret' or return instruction and is called a gadget. Thus different gadgets are linked together to perform the malicious task. Each sequence is an individual instruction or a set of instructions. As a whole when these gadgets are linked, they perform a 'bad' task. But as individuals they are 'good' instructions. Detection tools are built on the concept of finding a sequence of malicious instructions which are newly added to the system. But in our case we use inbuilt instructions. These inbuilt instructions are not even grouped as a whole in the memory from which they are found, but are in a distributed form. Also some instructions are arbitrarily created from the middle of other complete instructions. Thus, the instruction is interpreted as a complete different instruction. We have implemented hiding using these inbuilt instructions and analyzed the result using different detection mechanisms and found that our rootkit code is hidden from most of these techniques. The rest of the paper is organized as follows: Sect. 2 presents some background information. Section 3 gives an overview of the current techniques. Section 4 will give the methodology. Section 5 presents the tools and techniques used for implementing ROP. Section 5 discusses the design and implementation. Section 6 shows the experimental evaluation of results using a detection tool. Conclusions and further work are provided in Sect. 7.

2   Background

We describe a few Kernel attack techniques below. We have implemented our hiding implementation on the system call hooking and inline function hooking techniques.

2.1 Linux Kernel Attack Techniques

Since Linux Operating system is open source, the attack surface of the Linux kernel is quite vast. In this section, we will be discussing about some of the common attacks on Linux kernels.

System Call Hooking. System calls are used to invoke kernel routines from within user applications in order to exploit the special capabilities of the kernel. In system call hooking, the intruders find the location of the system call table using brute force technique and then the address of the particular system call which they want access to. The attackers will now change the jump address of the function pointers in the system call table to redirect the address to our malicious code. Thus our malicious code is executed when normal syscall occurs. So long as the LKM module which is hooked, is loaded into the system, the syscall address will be redirected to the malicious code.

The write protection bit of the cr0 register has to be disabled before performing such a hooking operation. Once the hooking is done, write protection bit of cr0 has to be enabled back, otherwise the kernel will panic and the system will crash.

Function Inline Hooking. Function Inline Hooking is another form of hooking. In function inline hooking, the first few bytes of a function are replaced with an unconditional jump to the malicious function. This is very similar to system call hooking. The difference here is that we jump to the malicious location using a jump instruction whereas in system call hooking, we directly change the address of the jump in the syscall table [30].

The original function is called back after the malicious function execution. This enables the attacker to evade detection. Also, the intruder has to modify the write protection bit of the cr0 register in order to perform the hooking.

Kernel Patching. Kernel patching is almost similar to function inline hooking. In kernel patching, the attacker will search for the CALL instruction in the original function. Once the CALL instruction is found, the malicious code replaces the address location given by the CALL instruction to the address location of the malicious function [8]. Thus, our malicious function is executed first, followed by the original function execution.

The attacker has to modify the write protection bit of the cr0 register to perform kernel patching. Most of the above techniques can be caught by the detection tool, if it runs a check for an instruction setting and resetting of the cr0 register.

2.2 Approaches for Malware Analysis

Malware analysis is a challenging and complicated task. There are mainly two approaches used for malware analysis.

Dynamic Analysis. The process of analyzing a program behavior while it is being executed in a controlled environment is known as dynamic analysis [12]. Dynamic analysis is done when the malware is loaded into the kernel memory. Dynamic analysis takes into account the changes in kernel data structures and can resist obfuscation to an extent. The malware behavior is then extracted by monitoring various malware operations.

Static Analysis. The process of analyzing a program behavior without executing the code is known as static analysis [12]. Static analysis does not require the code to be loaded into the kernel memory. Analysis can be done before loading, so the system remains secure. The malware behavior is then extracted by analyzing the disassembled code or by using control flow graph. The behaviors are then recorded in the form of patterns which is then used in real time scenarios for detection. Also, techniques such as obfuscation and polymorphism makes static analysis a difficult process.

Having such attack and defense techniques current available, we try to develop mechanisms that are in-line with the current attack techniques built and are not detectable.

Our idea is also based on the above attack and defense mechanisms. The hiding technique we use is ROP. We create a buffer overflow to gain access to the return address on the stack frame, we replace this return address with the starting address of our ROP chain. We execute our ROP chain and then restore back the values in the original program as expected and continue execution.

Buffer overflow occurs when a program tries to write to the memory address of the program's stack outside its permissible limits. Buffer overflow is a deliberate attack to gain unauthorized access of the stack. We thus create an attack mechanism that does not directly add malicious code to the system, but uses inbuilt sequences which as individuals are 'good' instructions but together they perform a malicious task.

2.3   Tools Used

We have built our prototype in the Linux environment (Ubuntu 12.04.5 LTS) for x86-32 bit architecture. The function of our hiding techniques on the kernel rootkit code is hooking the write system call with our own malicious write system call, and placing an inline instruction sequence in a function to redirect instruction execution to the malicious code. For hiding we need to replace the write_cr0 instruction with a chain of ROP gadgets. First we need to find the ROP gadgets. We have used 2 tools to find the gadgets. They are as follows:

Ropeme – ROP Exploit Made Easy. Ropeme is a tool for ROP exploit automation on Linux x86 platform. It contains a set of simple Python scripts to search and generate ROP gadgets from binaries and libraries such as libc [26].

In our case, we first try to locate the libc library that is attached to the C code we are currently executing. We set a breakpoint in the main function and start executing the code in the gdb debugger and later we initiate a shell in the debugger. Later, we try to obtain the PID of that process (the newly initiated shell) from which we get the specific library (here, /lib/i386-linux-gnu/libc-2.15.so) attached to it. The base address of this library is noted. As we know the particular library that was attached to the code at run time, we run the Ropeme tool to generate ROP gadgets from the library. Figure 4 is an example of such gadgets. The addresses generated from the ROPs are offset addresses which are added to the base address to get the final address of every ROP gadget.

ROPgadget. This tool lets you search gadgets on the binaries to carry out ROP exploitation. ROPgadget supports ELF format on x86, x64, ARM, ARM64 and MIPS architectures.

Gadgets can be simply extracted from the kernel binary i.e. we need the 'vmlinux' image. We need to decompress the /boot/vmlinuz* (specific to the gcc version) using the extract-vmlinux script. Later, this extracted binary we run the ROPgadget.py python script to generate gadgets (Fig. 1).

```
0xc15aca49 : adc byte ptr [ecx], ch ; ret
0xc15cacea : adc byte ptr [ecx], ch ; ret 0x458b
0xc14ddb93 : adc byte ptr [ecx], ch ; ret 0x5489
0xc11fd2d1 : adc byte ptr [ecx], ch ; ret 0x878b
0xc10e89d9 : adc byte ptr [ecx], ch ; ret 0xc269
0xc122bda3 : adc byte ptr [ecx], ch ; ret 0xd089
0xc12a3501 : adc byte ptr [ecx], ch ; ret 0xea83
0xc15f7cf1 : adc byte ptr [ecx], ch ; ret 0xf089
```

Fig. 1. Gadgets generated after running the ROPgadget.py script.

Nearly 137232 gadgets were generate from the binary. The gadgets consist of a combination of all types of instruction sequences.

For the detection tool, behaviors are collected from the different rootkit samples, which are then fed as rules to a pattern-matching tool, YARA. YARA is a tool aimed at helping malware researchers to identify and classify malware samples. With YARA you can create descriptions of malware families based on textual or binary patterns [29]. One such behavior can be the setting or resetting of the write_cr0 register bits. This tool performs a whole system scan checking for the specified malicious behavior and returns the results if the rules match with any object file on the system.

2.4 Technique to Build a Rop Chain

The figure above describes a ROP chain. The esp points to the first ROP gadget address (0xb88000000) on stack. When the eip pointer points to this address, the code jumps to the address in the memory and executes the pop instruction there. It pops the 0x00000001 value into the eax register. The next instruction to be executed is the return instruction. This instruction causes the eip pointer to point back to the instruction on the stack i.e. instruction at address 0xb8800010. Similarly, the ROP gadgets are executed (Fig. 2).

3   Related Work

The design and detection of rootkits can best be described as an "arms race", with the rootkit developers and the detection community engaging in a constant process of betting one another. All the techniques for attack and detection described in Sect. 2 are kept as a baseline to analyze the different hiding techniques available today.

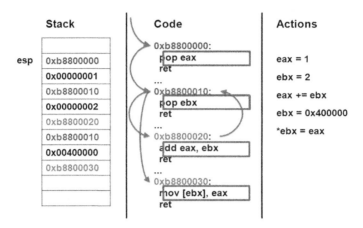

Fig. 2. ROP chain [22]

Today, there are many rootkit hiding techniques that have been proposed like obfuscation, polymorphism, and metamorphism. There are a variety of techniques by which code obfuscation can take place. Like name obfuscation, data obfuscation, control flow obfuscation, watermarking, dead code insertion, subroutine reordering, instruction substitution, and register reassignment. But each one of these techniques is reversible very easily. A detection tool can be trained to optimize itself to remove the dead code. An example would be a compiler which is designed to optimize the code to remove dead code. In static analysis, the behavioral pattern would catch the register reassignment or the subroutine reordering obfuscation techniques.

In Polymorphic techniques, the malicious code can mutate itself every time to keeping the original algorithm intact but just changing the appearance. In this case the semantics of the code do not change and hence when we run a detection tool carrying out semantic analysis it is easy to catch. The metamorphic code is rewritten every time it is replicated. This assures that every time it is rewritten it generates a different instance than the previous one [29]. Hence this tool cannot be caught easily by a signature detection tool. But the drawback in this case is that before the metamorphic code mutates from one form to the other, the viruses themselves need to analyze their code. This makes is pretty hard for the virus itself. Based on the heuristics of the code in static and dynamic time, we can reverse engineer this metamorphic code. We can also design emulators for these patterns found [12].

Encryption techniques and Cryptography is another area of research to hide the malicious part of your code. Till the detection tool does not have the key to decrypt, it is hard to decrypt the data. Even if the malicious part is not decrypted, when a detection tool runs it may observe certain anomaly in its analysis during its search. And when it tries to decode the anomaly, since it does not have the key, it would quarantine the code and label it as malicious even if it may or may not be malicious.

Another approach to hide malicious code was to attack the defense mechanism itself so that we kill the source before it harms the code. But again another detection tool would be built to catch this attack. It is a round-about process.

Analyzing all of these techniques, we finally reached to a solution in Return Oriented Programming to all of these problems above. This technique is a technique in which the attacker executes its code in the presence of security defenses. The attacker obtains control of the stack by different techniques, and then hijacks the control flow to execute specifically chosen assembly instructions. We tried to create a buffer overflow to obtain stack access and put the malicious code in the stack, but the stack protectors and other detection techniques detected the code in the stack. Hence, we found assembly instructions in the memory. These instructions are not direct instructions. These instructions are arbitrarily created instructions from other instructions using the ROPgadget tool. Using ROP gadgets would be a more efficient hiding technique than the remaining techniques. It does not create a lot of overhead either.

Malicious attackers have tried implementing ROP. But ROP was implemented to perform simple tasks as just making a system call. But we have implemented the ROP gadget to work as a part of a rootkit. We did not replace the complete rootkit to be executed by ROP chains but we replaced only the part that was caught by the detection tools i.e. the malicious code. Hence, without that part, the rest of the code is just a good and a normal module.

4   Hiding Model

4.1   Stack Based Buffer Overflow Exploitation

The stack is a contiguous block of memory containing data, which works based on the Last in First out (LIFO) principle. A register ESP points to the top of the stack. The size of the stack is decided dynamically at run time. The stack consists of stack frames that are pushed when a function is called in the program and popped when the function returns. When a function is called, the functions arguments are pushed onto the stack, the EIP (Instruction pointer) is pushed at the end which contains the return address of the function [23].

We create a stack based buffer overflow. A buffer overflow usually occurs when a function tries to copy input data into the buffer without a bounds check i.e. stuffing more data into the buffer than its capacity [23]. Usually buffer overflow attacks occur in programs containing the following functions like strcpy(), memcpy(), gets(), etc.

In our idea, when the buffer overflows we replace the return address stored in the EIP register with our own address which points to the ROP chain that performs malicious activity. The return address stored in the stack is supposed to return to the next address in the code where the stack had left implementation. The figure below shows a diagrammatic representation of the same (Fig. 3).

So now the EIP register is pointing to our required memory location due to buffer overflow. So our required memory location is the starting address of the ROP chain.

4.2   Return Oriented Programming (ROP)

ROP is a technique in which no new code is injected in the targeted system, yet we induce an arbitrary malicious behavior. Our code tries to link together short code

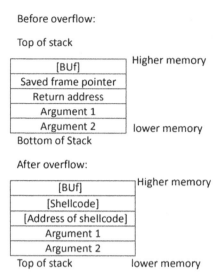

Before overflow:

Top of stack

| [BUf] |
| Saved frame pointer |
| Return address |
| Argument 1 |
| Argument 2 |

Higher memory

lower memory

Bottom of Stack

After overflow:

| [BUf] |
| [Shellcode] |
| [Address of shellcode] |
| Argument 1 |
| Argument 2 |

Higher memory

lower memory

Top of stack

Fig. 3. After buffer overflow the EIP pointer (return address) points to the address of our shell code (ROP chain)

```
0x196b0L: mov [eax] al ; add [eax] al ; add esp 0x8c ;;
0x2e4faL: mov [eax] al ; add [eax] al ; add esp 0x8c ;;
0x2f328L: mov [eax] al ; add [eax] al ; add esp 0x8c ;;
0x14a714L: mov [eax] al ; add [eax] al ; lea eax [ecx+0x4] ;;
0x926a0L: mov [eax] dh ; mov eax [esp+0x8] ; pop esi ;;
0x926b3L: mov [eax] dx ; mov eax [esp+0x8] ; pop esi ;;
0x341ccL: mov [eax] dx ; mov word [eax+0xe] 0x1 ; xor eax eax ;;
0xd905bL: mov [eax] dx ; xor eax eax ;;
0xd908cL: mov [eax] dx ; xor eax eax ;;
0x926e5L: mov [eax] ecx ; mov eax [esp+0x8] ; pop esi ;;
0x2d74fL: mov [eax] ecx ;;
0x2d9b7L: mov [eax] ecx ;;
0x2dd7eL: mov [eax] ecx ;;
0x26efdL: mov [eax] edx ; add esp 0x10 ;;
0x7cfb9L: mov [eax] edx ; add esp 0x18 ; pop ebx ;;
```

Fig. 4. Different ROP gadgets along with their memory locations.

sequences which are already present in the default library address space [9]. Each one of this sequence ends with a 'ret' or return instruction. This allows the attacker who controls the stack (due to overflow) to chain and execute them. Since, this code is in the memory and not in the stack, we can execute it easily because we do not have any protections like NX or ASLR present there.

Every code sequence ending with a 'ret' or return is called as a gadget. It is said to be the organizational unit of a return oriented attack is a gadget [7]. There are various varieties and lengths in which gadgets are present. Gadgets can perform a pop, add, xchg, pop, etc. i.e. a variety of operations can be performed. Below is a snapshot of the different gadgets.

Return-to-libc is a type of ROP attack. In return-to-libc we search for gadgets in the libc library. Here the trick that most users are unaware of is that most of the programs that use functions from a shared library like the "printf" from "libc", will link the entire library into their address space at run time. This means that addresses of all the functions in libc are accessible at runtime. We use the Ropeme tool to generate gadgets for return-to-libc type ROP attack, and the ROPgadget tool for normal ROP attack. The tools would be explained in more details in Sect. 5.

4.3 Chaining of ROP Gadgets

A return-oriented program is made up of a particular layout of the stack segment. Each return-oriented instruction is a word (32-bit) on the stack pointing to an instruction sequence (ordinary programs) somewhere in the exploited program's memory. The stack pointer governs which return-oriented instruction sequence would be fetched next, in the following way. The execution of a ret instruction has two effects: first, the word to which %esp points is read and used as the new value for %eip; and second, %esp is incremented by 4 bytes to point to the next word on the stack. If the instruction sequence now being executed by the processor also ends in a ret, this process will be repeated, again advancing %esp and inducing execution of another instruction [9].

Which instruction sequences are chained together, depending on the type of execution we are trying to do. We first need to know what output is expected, accordingly we will pick from the gadgets found by the tools and create a sequence of ROP gadgets to get the required output. Implemented example codes in Sect. 5.2 will make this concept clear.

4.4 How Hiding Acts Here

We do not include a new code, we use the pieces of code present in the library itself. For code execution we are not required to store the actual instruction in the buffer, we just redirect the control flow of the program to point to such instruction. Even when such instructions are pointed to by the code, the detection tools cannot usually catch them. The reason being, the detection tool again tries to check if the code is present at a location in the library, which is not the case. But individual instructions are accessed from different locations in the memory. The instructions or sequence of instructions also called as gadgets are individually "good" instructions which when executed as a whole do a "bad" task.

ROP gadgets can be formed using complete or partial instructions from the memory. One more important property of ROP is that it may point to the middle of instructions and creates unintended instruction sequences or gadgets.

4.5 Diagrammatic Representation of ROP Working

The figure below shows an overall working of a ROP as explained in background section above (Fig. 5).

The program starts in stage 1 and executes as normal code. Just before we want to execute the ROP chain we create a buffer overflow, by halting the program to wait for

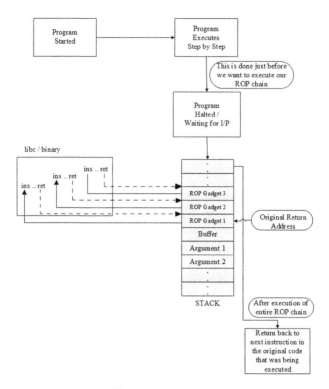

Fig. 5. ROP working

user inputs. Once the user inputs are obtained, a buffer overflow is initiated. The buffer overflow replaces the return address with the starting address of our ROP chain. Now the ROP gadgets start executing one by one obtaining their address from the stack, jumping to that particular location in the memory and returning back to next ROP gadget address on the stack. This process continues till the last gadget on the stack is executed. After the last gadget is executed the execution returns back to next instruction of the original program (where we had left execution). We store this address before jumping to the ROP chain so that we can return back to the original execution sequence. Thus, the original execution is now completed.

5   Design and Implemetation

5.1   Design

Part1
We have first implemented our logic to carry out return-to-libc execution. This is the first step. Ropeme tool is used to find the gadgets from the library that was linked to the main program, when it was compiled. Here we have demonstrated 2 malicious activities using ROP, like starting the "/bin/sh" shell without executing the shell command

and to kill all the processes being executed by the system except the init process. The execution of the last code causes the system to kind off reboot. This indicates we have successfully killed all the PIDs. The system call tables indicate the values that all the registers need to hold for executing the particular system call.

(a) For starting the "/bin/sh" shell i.e. "execve("/bin/sh",0,0)" we follow the following steps. The system call arguments are put into registers ebx, ecx, edx, esi and edi respectively. The function call number is put into the eax register (Fig. 6).

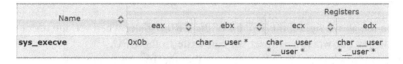

Name		Registers			
		eax	ebx	ecx	edx
sys_execve		0x0b	char __user *	char __user *__user *	char __user *__user *

Fig. 6. System call table reference along with arguments – sys_execve()

1. xor eax eax
2. ecx should hold the NULL value
3. edx should hold the NULL value
4. set ebx to address of "/bin/sh"
5. mov 0xb into eax
6. int 0x80

(b) The following steps are followed to kill all PIDs of a system. This is a generalized working that needs to be done to kill all the processes (except the init process), not the actual ROP gadget (Fig. 7).

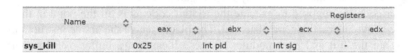

Name		Registers			
		eax	ebx	ecx	edx
sys_kill		0x25	int pid	int sig	-

Fig. 7. System call table reference along with arguments – sys_kill()

1. xor ebx, ebx
2. dec ebx
3. push byte 37
4. pop eax
5. push byte 9
6. pop ecx
7. int 0x80

Part2

We have implemented this complete logic to a rootkit code here. The rootkit code is a generalized rootkit code which contains a system call (syscall) hooking. We have hooked a write system call by our own malicious system call. Detection tools are usually built to detect certain behaviors. In our rootkit code, the particular behavior is the resetting and setting of the cr0 register, so as to change the system call address to point to our rootkit write syscall than the original write system call (Fig. 8).

Bit	Name	Full Name	Description
16	WP	Write protect	When set, the CPU can't write to read-only pages when privilege level is 0

Fig. 8. 16th bit of the CR0 (Control Register)

As seen in the above figure, the 16th bit of the CR0 register when set, the user only has read privileges but when it is reset we can write to the CPU.

In the init_module in Fig. 9, we can see that the 16th bit of the cr0 register is reset, after which we can use write privileges to replace the address of the 'original write system call' with our 'malicious write system call'.

```
static void __exit onunload(void) {
    if (syscall_table != NULL) {
        write_cr0 (read_cr0 () & (~ 0x10000));
        syscall_table[__NR_write] = new_write
        write_cr0 (read_cr0 () | 0x10000);
```

Fig. 9. init_module with the resetting and setting of the 16th bit of the cr0 register.

When this behavior is observed by a detection tool, then the malicious sequence is detected. We replace this behavior by a ROP gadget chain.

So our code is supposed to execute the rootkit code as is till the point in the code where the above instructions are observed. The places where the above instructions are observed are the init and exit module. At these locations, a buffer overflow will be executed causing the control flow to jump to a ROP chain. After the execution of the chain the program will continue its normal execution of the next statement in the rootkit program without any segmentation fault. This process is done twice in the rootkit code (init_function & exit_function)

We have implemented hiding on another rootkit code to perform function inline hooking. We implement the same ROP chain here. The code hides files and directories with a particular name when the module is loaded. Later when the module is unloaded the files and directories are restored back. Instead of just modifying a readdir pointer to point to our own function, we'll hijack the prologue bytes of the VFS readdir function. These bytes will be replaced with a \x68 for push, 4 bytes for the address, and \xc3 for return on x86-32bit. While jacking the code, we need to reset the cr0 register and reset it after the hook is placed [15].

5.2   Implementation

Part1

We have implemented our code on a target system with Intel x86_32 bit processor with a 20 GB RAM, running a Linux 3.13.0.32-generic kernel version. The buffer overflow part of the code will be the same for the codes below. Here the strcpy() function is used, which helps overflow the buffer to change the return address to point to our libc address instruction.

The gadgets are found using Ropeme tool. The library that is linked to the buffer overflow code at run-time is "/lib/i386-linux-gnu/libc-2.15.so" (Fig. 10).

Fig. 10. Buffer overflow code

The /bin/sh shell is called when the following ROP gadget is executed after creating a buffer overflow. In the Figs. 11 and 12 we see the comparison between the expected ROP chain present and the actual ROP chain formed from the available gadgets. Figure 13 shows the output i.e. the /bin/sh shell has started when the ROP chain is actually executed.

1.   xor eax eax
2.   ecx should hold the NULL value
3.   edx should hold the NULL value
4.   set ebx to address of "/bin/sh"
5.   mov 0xb into eax
6.   int 0x80

Fig. 11. Expected ROP chain (/bin/sh)

In the example below all the PIDs or processes are killed (Figs. 14 and 15).

It is not possible to take a screenshot in this case as upon execution all the processes will be killed and the machine will reboot.

Part2

The aim is to avoid the execution of the "write_cr0 (read_cr0 () & (~ 0x10000));" instruction. Since this is one of the behavior fed to the detection tool. The YARA tool is used to create patterns which would execute malicious behaviors and a script is made accordingly. When we run a detection using this script, if we have an executable

1. pop ecx; pop eax; ret
2. "/bin"
3. address of "/bin" in ecx; ret
4. mov [eax], ecx; ret
5. pop ecx; pop eax; ret
6. "//sh"
7. address of "//sh" in eax; ret
8. mov [ecx], eax; ret
9. xor eax, eax; ret
10. pop edx; ret
11. address to write NULL bytes to store in ecx; ret
12. mov [edx+0x18], eax; ret
13. pop ecx, pop edx; ret
14. address of argp to ecx; ret
15. address of envp; ret
16. pop ebx; ret
17. pointer to the string "/bin/sh"
18. add ebx, 0xb; ret
19. call gs: [0x10]

Fig. 12. ROP chain built from the found gadgets (/bin/sh)

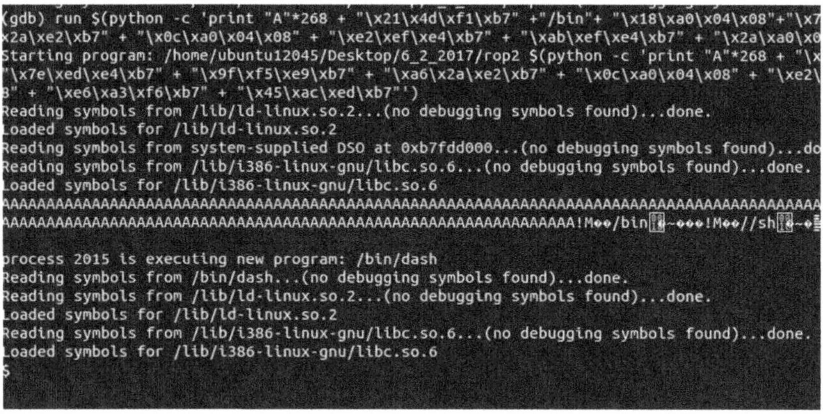

Fig. 13. Output shows shell (/bin/sh) has started

1. xor ebx, ebx
2. dec ebx
3. push byte 37
4. pop eax
5. push byte 9
6. pop ecx
7. int 0x80

Fig. 14. Expected ROP chain (sys_kill)

```
1.  xor edx, edx; ret
2.  mov eax, edx; ret
3.  mov ebx, edx; ret
4.  xor eax, eax; ret
5.  add eax, 0xf; ret
6.  add eax, 0xf; ret
7.  add eax, 0x7; ret
8.  dec ebx; ret
9.  mov ecx, edx; rep stosb; pop edi; ret
10. inc ecx
11. inc ecx
12. inc ecx
13. inc ecx
14. inc ecx
15. inc ecx
16. inc ecx
17. inc ecx
18. inc ecx
19. call gs: [0x10]
```

Fig. 15. ROP chain built from the gadgets (sys_kill)

(binary file) containing this statement, our detection tool catches it. Hence we need to replace this write_cr0 statement with a ROP chain which does a similar task using the arbitrarily found instruction sequences from the memory by the ROPgadget tool.

We have created two ROP chains one for disabling the 16th bit of the cr0 and the other for setting it back. The ROP chain starts execution midway within the rootkit program, hence the ROP gadget is required to do a few other tasks before it resets the cr0 register value. These include restoring the values of ebx, esi, edi and ebp registers. After this, we reset the 16th bit of the cr0 register. We now get back the original return address where the ROP had left execution. We restore this return address along with the esp register. This causes the execution to return correctly without any faults.

Figures below show the screenshots of the outputs from the original rootkit code when loaded and unloaded and output of the changed rootkit code (ROP added).

Canary value is a known value that is placed between the buffer and control data on the stack to monitor buffer overflows. When the buffer overflows, the first data to be corrupted will usually be the canary, and a failed verification of the canary data is therefore an alert of an overflow [12]. We have taken care of this problem by storing the complete stack frame before the buffer overflow changes any values on the stack. Thus when we come back to executing the main code this value is restored. Hence no fault or error is generated for non-matching canary values.

We have implemented our code on 2 types of rootkit attack techniques. The system call hooking and the other is the function inline hooking. Outputs from both the implementations can be seen below.

System call hooking example:
See Figs. 16 and 17.

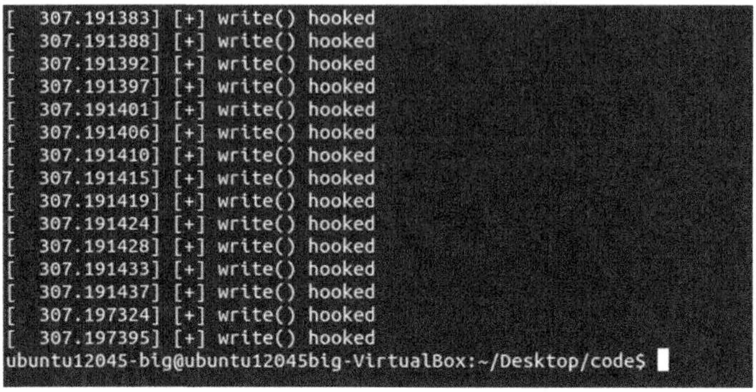

Fig. 16. Program output (dmesg) when rootkit code (original) is loaded

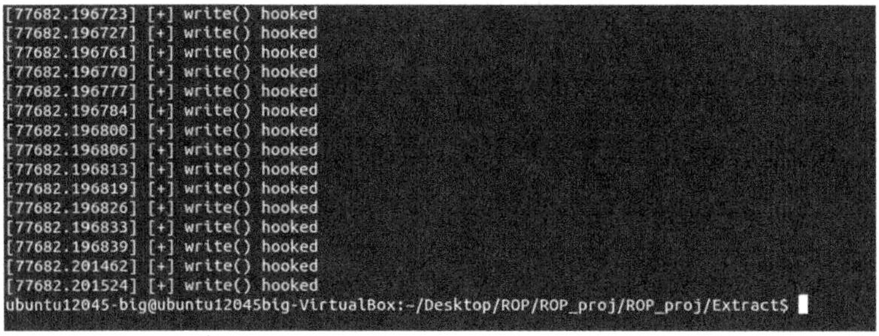

Fig. 17. Program output (dmesg) when rootkit code (malicious) is loaded

Function Inline hooking example:
See Figs. 18 and 19.

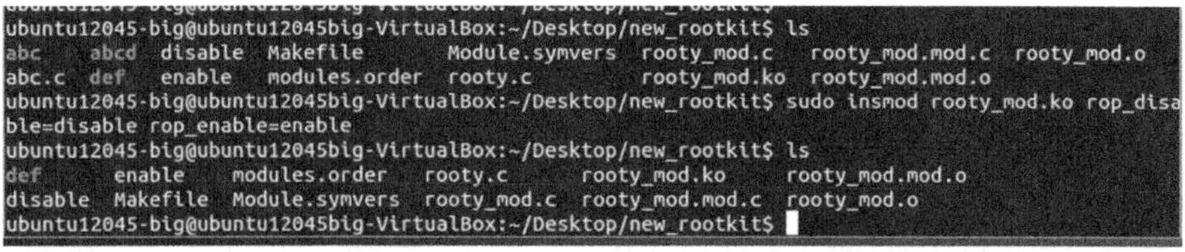

Fig. 18. Program output when 2nd rootkit code (original) is loaded

```
ubuntu12045-big@ubuntu12045big-VirtualBox:~/Desktop/new_rootkit$ ls
abc     abcd    disable  Makefile        Module.symvers  rooty.ko        rooty.mod.c   rooty.o
abc.c   def     enable   modules.order   rooty.c         rooty_mod.c   rooty.mod.o
ubuntu12045-big@ubuntu12045big-VirtualBox:~/Desktop/new_rootkit$ sudo insmod rooty.ko
[sudo] password for ubuntu12045-big:
ubuntu12045-big@ubuntu12045big-VirtualBox:~/Desktop/new_rootkit$ ls
def     enable   modules.order   rooty.c   rooty_mod.c   rooty.mod.o
disable  Makefile  Module.symvers  rooty.ko  rooty.mod.c   rooty.o
ubuntu12045-big@ubuntu12045big-VirtualBox:~/Desktop/new_rootkit$
```

Fig. 19. Program output when 2nd rootkit code (malicious) is loaded

This code can be generalized to apply to all the codes performing hooking of system calls or function hooking inline. Hence all these rootkits types can be hidden using the ROP approach.

6 Detection

This section aims at the detection of malwares or rootkits in the system based on the behaviors observed. The detection mechanism uses a pattern matching tool called YARA for the detection of rootkits. YARA is used for scanning the defined libraries to check any match for behaviors specified in the test rules. The figure below describes the working of the whole detection mechanism Fig. 20.

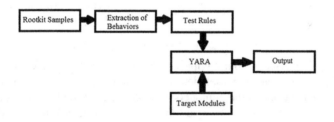

Fig. 20. Overview of detection mechanism [8]

The behavioral Pattern Extraction Process is as follows [8]:

- Analyze the rootkit code
- Disassemble the object file using objdump -d filename.ko
- Extract the malicious behavior from the assembly file
- Write rules from the extracted behavior
- Applying rule created to scan directories using YARA

Hence we have extracted the malicious behavior generated by the new write system call in our rootkit code and added it to the set of rules formed. We checked the system libraries if after adding the ROP gadget the behavior is still observed. It was observed that the ROP gadget was not found by the detection tool i.e. the malicious behavior was not found anywhere in the system. Hence we were successfully able to hide the code from the YARA tool.

Since we use individual instructions from the memory, sometimes we might be able to detect individual instructions, but individual instructions are not "malicious". When a number of "good" instructions are grouped, they do a "bad" task. And when we tried to run the detection on multiple tools we could not detect them.

Now we use the above technique to analyze our modified rootkit code (added the hiding part). We obtain an accuracy of 99.9% nearly. There are a few false positives generated seen in the results below. The tool is run on different locations where the malicious rootkit code is expected to be detected. The detection rules were run in root on the /lib/module directory where the rootkit modules, the home directory, the libraries, and the extracted vmlinux image from where ROP gadgets are developed.

The false positives generated are actually individual instructions (from ROP gadgets) found in the memory when YARA detection tool is run. These individual instructions when analyzed are seen to be 'good' instructions, i.e. a rootkit code be detected by only a single instruction {add eax, 0xf; ret} found in the memory. Since this single instruction is not even malicious.

An overall evaluation of the rootkit analysis gave us the following results (Table 1).

Table 1. Overall evaluation

Module set	Analyzed codes	Detection rate	Error rate
General rootkits	4	100%	0%
Hiding code added Rootkits	2	99.9%	0.1% (false positives which are individually harmless)

The above table describes our complete evaluation and results. We have developed rules to check if the detection tool detects malicious rootkit code (without adding hiding code). Then we added the hiding code in two types of rootkit code and again ran the same detection tool to check the result. In this case our detection succeeded 99.9%. The 0.1% contains a few individual instructions found in the ROP chain. But these can also be passed because as individual instructions, they are good clean instructions.

7   Conclusion and Future Work

Kernel Level rootkits present a serious threat to the operating system. Today a variety of detection tools have been developed to detect different varieties of rootkits. But these techniques are not efficient enough to detect all hidden rootkit approaches.

This work presents a hiding technique that hides kernel level rootkits carrying out system call hooking and inline function hooking. We demonstrated the model which can be used as a baseline to develop more and more hiding techniques. We also checked if this approach was detected by the behaviors developed by YARA but we were able to successfully hide the code. Our hiding technique can be applied to all the rootkits. We try to hide the specific behaviors of the rootkits that are usually a trigger for detection tools. Preliminary data suggests that this rootkit hiding technique can be acceptable.

The detection and hiding will always be a cat and mouse race. Every time a new attack (using hiding) is developed, each time a specific detection tool which catches that attack will be written. In order to improve the hiding tool, we would be developing more such hiding approaches for different types of rootkit attack techniques. In this way we could generalize the approach to different varieties of rootkits.

References

1. Moser, A., Kruegel, C., Kirda, E.: Exploring multiple execution paths for malware analysis. In: IEEE Symposium on Security and Privacy, SP 2007, pp. 231–245 (2007)
2. Rad, B.B., Masrom, M., Ibrahim, S.: Camouflage in Malware: from Encryption to Metamorphism. University Technology Malaysia
3. Kruegel, C., Robertson, W., Vigna, G.: Detecting kernel-level rootkits through binary analysis. In: Proceedings of the 20th Annual Computer Security Applications Conference, ACSAC 2004, Santa Barbara, pp. 91–100 (2004). Technical University Vienna, Reliable Software Group University of California
4. Buchanan, E., Roemer, R., Shacham, H., Savage, S.: When good instructions go bad: generalizing return-oriented programming to RISC (2008). Department of Computer Science and Engineering, University of California, San Diego, California
5. Konstantinou, E.: Metamorphic virus: analysis and detection. Technical report RHUL-MA-2008-02, Department of Mathematics Royal Holloway, University of London Egham, 15 January 2008
6. Sharif, M., Lanzi, A., Giffin, J., Lee, W.: Impeding malware analysis using conditional code Obfuscation, 11 February 2008. School of Computer Science, College of Computing, Georgia Institute of Technology, Dipartimento di Informatica e Comunicazione, Università degli Studi di Milano, Italy
7. Carlini, N., Wagner, D.: ROP is still dangerous: breaking modern defenses. In: Proceedings of the 23rd USENIX Conference on Security Symposium, SEC 2014, pp. 385–399, August 2014. University of California, Berkeley
8. Alexander, N.S.: Behavioral Patterns of Kernel Level Rootkits Attacking Containers in Linux Environment, May 2017. University of Texas, San Antonio
9. Roemer, R., Buchanan, E., Shacham, H., Savage, S.: Return-oriented programming: systems, languages, and applications. ACM Tran. Inf. Syst. Secur. (TISSEC) **15**(1), 2 (2012). Special issue on computer and communications security. University of California, San Diego
10. Arnold, T.M.: A Comparative Analysis of Rootkit Detection Techniques, May 2011. The University of Houston-Clear Lake
11. Mohan, V., Kevin, W.: Frankenstein: stitching malware from benign binaries. Hamlen School of Electrical and Computer Science University of Texas at Dallas
12. Buffer Overflow. https://en.wikipedia.org/wiki/Buffer_overflow_protection, https://www.exploit-db.com/docs/28475.pdf, http://insecure.org/stf/smashstack.html
13. Code Obfuscation. https://www.ncsc.gov.uk/content/files/protected_files/guidance_files/Code-obfuscation.pdf
14. cr0 Register Table. http://wiki.osdev.org/CPU_Registers_x86

15. Hooking Code. https://gitlab.tnichols.org/tyler/syscall_table_hooks/tree/master, http://turbo chaos.blogspot.com/2013/10/writing-linux-rootkits-201-23.html
16. Kernel Debugger. https://www.virtualbox.org/manual/ch12.html#ts_debugger
17. Kill Process. https://www.cyberciti.biz/faq/kill-process-in-linux-or-terminate-a-process-in-unix-or-linux-systems/
18. Linux System Call Table. http://syscalls.kernelgrok.com/
19. Loadable Kernel Module (LKM). https://www.sans.org/reading-room/whitepapers/threats/kernel-rootkits-449
20. Payload Inside. https://media.blackhat.com/bh-us-10/presentations/Le/BlackHat-USA-2010-Le-Paper-Payload-already-inside-data-reuse-for-ROP-exploits-slides.pdf
21. ROP Introduction. http://codearcana.com/posts/2013/05/28/introduction-to-return-oriented-programming-rop.html
22. ROP Chain. http://slideplayer.com/slide/4314077/14/images/6/Return-Oriented+Programming.jpg
23. ROPgadget. https://github.com/JonathanSalwan/ROPgadget
24. ROP v/s ret-to-libc. http://www.cse.psu.edu/~trj1/cse443-s12/slides/cse443-lecture-25-rop.pdf
25. Rootkit Definition. https://en.wikipedia.org/wiki/Rootkit
26. ROPeme. https://github.com/packz/ropeme/
27. Unintended Instruction Formation. https://www.slideshare.net/mwinandy/dynamic-integrity-measurement-and-attestation-towards-defense-against-returnoriented-programming-attacks
28. Vmlinux Script (Extract). https://github.com/torvalds/linux/blob/master/scripts/extract-vmlinux
29. YARA. https://virustotal.github.io/yara/
30. Love, R.: Linux Kernel Development, 3rd edn., 8 September 2010
31. Kong, J.: Designing BSD Rootkits, August 2007

Experimenting Similarity-Based Hijacking Attacks Detection and Response in Android Systems

Anis Bkakria[1], Mariem Graa[1(✉)], Nora Cuppens-Boulahia[1],
Frédéric Cuppens[1], and Jean-Louis Lanet[2]

[1] IMT Atlantique, 2 Rue de la Châtaigneraie, 35576 Cesson Sévigné, France
{anis.bkakria,mariem.graa,nora.cuppens,
frederic.cuppens}@imt-atlantique.fr
[2] Campus de beaulieu, 263 Avenue Général Leclerc, 35042 Rennes, France
jean-louis.lanet@inria.fr

Abstract. Hacker can launch hijacking attacks in Android systems to steal personal information of the targeted user. He/She stealthily injects into the foreground a hijacking Activity indistinguishable from the user interface at the right timing. Hijacking attacks take advantage of the user trust that this interface is real. Therefore, the hacker has chance to acquire user private information. In this paper, we compare user interfaces similarity between victim and hacking activities. Our approach has been proved to be effective in detecting Activity hijacking attacks with reasonable performance overheads and number of false positives. In the worst case, our solution generates 4.2% of false positives and incurs only 0.39% performance overhead on a CPU-bound micro-benchmark.

1 Introduction

Mobile applications are used for performing numerous important life Activities such as communication, shopping, shifting (GPS navigation), banking and web browsing. In May 2016, 65 billion apps had been downloaded from Google Play [2]. Most users are required to communicate sensitive data (passwords, usernames, security codes, and credit card numbers) with these applications. Hacker can launch hijacking attacks in Android smartphones to obtain personal information of the targeted user. Hijacking attacks takes advantage of the user that can not distinguish between the victim and malicious interfaces. For example, Chen et al. [5] stealthily inject into the foreground a hijacking Activity at the right timing and steal sensitive information a user enters. Hijacking attacks [9] use a fake UI indistinguishable from the target user interface to steal a password or payment credentials data.

We implement the Activity hijacking attack proposed in [5] to hijack the credit card payment Activity used by Google Play. Then, we evaluate the attack by asking 50 Android users to use an Android device on which our attack app is installed to buy an item from Google Play without using their real credit card

R. K. Shyamasundar et al. (Eds.): ICISS 2017, LNCS 10717, pp. 127–145, 2017.
https://doi.org/10.1007/978-3-319-72598-7_8

information. All the users who conducted the experiment did not realize that they were under a hijacking attack. Many security techniques [14,17] are used to detect hijacking attacks in Android systems. They are based on analyzing application resource files (XML layout) to detect similarity of UI (fake and target one). However, the layout files can be obfuscated by an attacker without changing UI appearance. In addition, the interface component parameters can be modified in the java application code and the layout files remain unchanged. Thus, attackers can evade this detection mechanisms.

In this paper, we propose an effective approach that compares the similarity between launched Activities in order to detect and react to hijacking attacks. We extract and compare similarity between the UI components visual attributes at application run time by instrumenting the Android operating system code. The outline of our approach can be found in [4]. In the current paper, we demonstrate the effectiveness of our solution by quantifying the number of false positives that can be generated by our system. We observe that, in the worst case, our solution generates 4.2% of false positives and incurs only 0.39% performance overhead on a CPU-bound micro-benchmark.

The rest of this paper is organized as follows: Sect. 2 categorizes application hijacking attacks and analyzes possible countermeasures. We describe Activity display process and Activity transitions in Sect. 3. Section 4 describes the proposed approach. Section 5 provides implementation details. We test the effectiveness of our approach and we study our approach overhead in Sect. 6. Finally, Sect. 7 concludes with an outline of future work.

2   Related Work

The hijacking attacks include similarity and background attacks. Similarity Attack [8,10,18] exploits the similarity between the legitimate and the phishing application to mislead the user. It uses a similar or identical name, icon, and UI. Background attack [3,9] exploits the Android ActivityManager, or a side-channel [13] to detect running of a legitimate application. This attack runs in the background and when a user app is launched, it moves to the foreground and displays a phishing screen. The hijacking attacks [5] include similarity and background attacks. In this class of attacks, a malicious Activity is launched instead of the intended Activity. The hijacker can spoof the victim Activity's UI to steal user sensitive data. As the Android UI does not identify the currently running application, hijacking attacks can be implemented convincingly.

Many works exist in the literature to detect hijacking attacks. Biahchi et al. [3] use static analysis to identify and categorize a variety of attack vectors that allow a malicious app to mimic the GUI of other apps and launch hijacking attacks. Also, they designed and implemented an on-device defense that informs users about the origin of the app with which they are interacting. The Google Bouncer system [11] uses patterns of system calls and permissions to detect hijacking attacks. These signature-based malware detection techniques can not detect hijacking attacks that do not require a specific permission such as the attack considered in this paper. Marforio et al. [15] propose a personalized indicator to mitigate application hijacking attacks in mobile platforms. This approach is based on checking the presence of the correct indicator. At install time, the user attaches an image to the application. At run time, when the user enters his private data, the application shows the image chosen at install time. A hijacking attack is detected if the image is not displayed. Other applications cannot read the indicator since it is stored in application-specific storage. The drawback of this approach is that it requires extra user effort at install time and during application usage. Malisa et al. [14] extract and compare the visual similarity of login interface screenshots. In order to do so, they fix a percentage (deception rate) of users that would confuse the examined screenshot with the reference application. Thus, these users are estimated to consider the hijacking app genuine. Malisa et al. approach incurs a significant runtime overhead. Sun et al. [17] propose the DroidEagle tool that detects similar Android apps by comparing visual characteristics and components in the layout resources. DroidEagle is used to identify repackaged apps and phishing malware. Sun et al. approach cannot detect obfuscation of layout files because UI appearance remains unchanged. Thus, attackers can evade this detection mechanisms. In this paper, we use visual similarity approach to detect hijacking attacks. Our approach extracts UI components parameters at application run time by instrumenting the Android operating system code. Therefore, we can detect obfuscation of layout files.

3 Background

In this section, we present Android Activity display process. Then, we describe Activity transitions phases. we are interested on the use of the shared memory in Activity transition events.

3.1 Activity Display Process

An Activity is an application component that allows the user to interact with application through the UI drawing in the window. As shown in Fig. 1, it is launched by an event that is translated into startActivity() call and transmitted to Activity Manager service through Binder IPC (1).

The Activity Manager controls all aspects of the application lifecycle and Activity stack. It defines different lifecycle methods for different states of Activities. The onCreate(), onRestart(), onStart(), or onResume() methods are called when an Activity gains focus or comes to the foreground (2). When the View System receives the request to create Activity from the Activity Manager (3), it defines a set of views used to create application user interfaces and send them to the WindowManager (4). The Android WindowManager is a system service component responsible for managing the order of appearance and placement of windows which is a container for views in a graphical UI. The WindowManager service sends all of the window metadata to SurfaceFlinger (5) that uses these

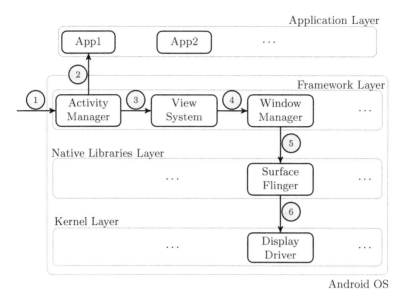

Fig. 1. Android Activity display process

data to define surfaces on the display. The SurfaceFlinger sends the frame buffer (final image) which is displayed on screen via the graphics card's EGL interface (6). Due to security concerns, only the owners or the central Activity manager knows which Activity is currently shown in the foreground.

3.2 Activity Transitions

Most applications consist of multiple Activities. The user will switch back and forth among Activities. The main Activity is presented to the user when launching the application for the first time. It can then start a new Activity. The previous Activity is stopped or paused, but the system preserves it in the Back Stack [1]. A new Activity is pushed onto this stack. The Back Stack supports the "last in, first out" stack mechanism. So, only the top Activity (new Activity) has its window buffer allocated and the other has its buffer deallocated.

Activity transitions can take place when a new Activity is created (create transition), or when an existing Activity resumes (resume transition). Thus, the current foreground Activity is paused and a new one is launched. The create transition calls both onCreate() and onResume() at launch time while the resume transition calls onResume(). Then, performTraversals() is used to browse the Layout tree for drawing Activity. Two pass processes are performed: a measure pass and a layout pass. During the measuring pass (measure()), each View pushes dimension specifications. In the layout pass (layout()), each parent is responsible for positioning all of its children using the sizes computed in the measure pass. Finally, the new Activity is pushed into the Back Stack and the current one is stopped in the create transition, while the current one is popped and destroyed in the resume transition.

3.3   Shared Memory

Shared memory (*shared vm*) is a specific type of memory that may be simultaneously accessed by multiple programs. Shared memory is an efficient means of exchanging data between programs running at the same time without redundant copies. In Android, each application communicates their graphic buffers with the WindowManager through the IPC mechanism using the shared memory.

4   Our Approach

In this section, we describe the threat model we consider and we present our detection and reaction models.

4.1   Threat Model

First, we assume an attacker that controls an application running in the background on the victim device. In addition, we suppose that the attack application can use any existing Android permission to collect information about running applications in order to figure out which Activity is entering the foreground. Second, in order to overcome similarity detection by comparing visual characteristics and components in the layout resources [17], we assume that the attacker can create the hijacking screen dynamically (e.g., by creating UI elements at runtime). Third, in order to avoid the detection of exact similarity between the hijacked and the hijacking Activities, we assume an attacker that can change the visual characteristics (e.g., size, position, colour) of the UI elements in the hijacking Activity by exploiting the properties of human UI interfaces perception. Finally, we assume that the Android OS is not compromised by the attacker.

4.2   Detection Model

By knowing the moment in which a legitimate Activity is launched, the attacker exploits its plotting time to launch a similar Activity. We present the following definitions to compare UIs visual similarity and to detect Activity hijacking attacks.

Definition 1 (*plotting time*). *Given a device D and an Activity A, a plotting time $\mathcal{P}_A^D$ represents the time needed for the device D to plot the Activity A on its screen.*

The previous definition states that a plotting time $\mathcal{P}_A^D$ for a device D represents the elapsed time between an action that triggers the launch of an Activity A and the moment in which A appears on D's screen. The phishing Activity must appear after the launch of the victim activity and before the expiration of its plotting time. Our approach is based on comparing size and content indistinguishability of victim and hacking activities.

Definition 2 (k-size indistinguishability). *Given a device D having a screen size* $s_D = (w_D, h_D)$ *and two Activities* A_1 *and* A_2 *and their respective sizes* $s_{A_1} = (w_{A_1}, h_{A_1})$ *and* $s_{A_2} = (w_{A_2}, h_{A_2})$. A_1 *and* A_2 *are k-size indistinguishable on D iff the following condition holds:*

$$1 - \frac{\|s_{A_1}, s_{A_2}\|}{\sqrt{w_D^2 + h_D^2}} = k$$

where $\|a, b\|$ *denotes the euclidean distance between a and b.*

On the same device, each activity has its own size that cannot be larger than the size of the device screen. Therefore, $k \in [0, 1]$. Actually, in the previous definition, k represents, for an Android user, the difficulty that he/she can distinguish A_1 and A_2 from their sizes. The more k will be close to 1, the more it is difficult to distinguish A_1 and A_2 based on their sizes. In addition, we compare content similarity of the victim and phishing activities. In fact, each Android Activity is composed of different type of user interface elements (e.g., TextView, TextEdit, Button, Spinner, etc.). In the reminder of this paper, we use $E = \{e_1, e_2, \cdots, e_n\}$ to denote all types of user interface elements that can be used in an Android Activity.

Definition 3 (l-content indistinguishability). *Given a device D and two Activities* A_1 *and* A_2. *Let us suppose that the contents of* A_1 *and* A_2 *are represented respectively by* $C_{A_1} = \{e_1^{A_1}, e_2^{A_1}, \cdots, e_n^{A_1}\}$ *and* $C_{A_2} = \{e_1^{A_2}, e_2^{A_2}, \cdots, e_n^{A_2}\}$ *where each* $e_j^{A_i}$ *represents the set of user interface elements of type* e_j *that are contained in* A_i. A_1 *and* A_2 *are l-content indistinguishable on D iff the following condition holds:*

$$\sum_{\substack{i=0 \\ e_i^{A_1} \neq \emptyset}} \left(\frac{\sum\limits_{c \in e_i^{A_1}} \left(\max\limits_{c' \in e_i^{A_2}} indist(c, c', D) \right)}{|e_i^{A_1}| \times \sum\limits_{\substack{i=0 \\ e_i^{A_1} \neq \emptyset}} 1} \right) = l$$

where $|e_i^{A_1}|$ *denotes the cardinality of* $e_i^{A_1}$, $indist(c, c', D) \in [0, 1]$ *represents the level of indistinguishability between c and c' on D, and* $l \in [0, 1]$.

The more l will be close to 1, the more it is difficult to distinguish A_1 and A_2 based on their visual attributes of user interface elements. In fact, to compute the indistinguishability of two user interface elements on a device, for each type of user interface, we use the size, the position and other specific visual attributes (e.g., text, colour, etc.).

Definition 4 (visual attribute). *Given an attribute a of a UI element c, a is a visual attribute of c iff the modification of the value of a implies a modification of the appearance of c on any device screen.*

Definition 5. *Given a device D having a screen size $s_D = (w_D, h_D)$ and two UI elements c_1 and c_2 of the same type e. Indistinguishability is a value between 0 and 1 that has a component involving difference in size, difference in position, and the average similarity of all the components' visual attributes $a_1, \cdots, a_n$. The similarity of c_1 and c_2 in D is computed as following:*

$$indist(c_1, c_2, D) = 1 - \frac{\|s_{c_1}, s_{c_2}\|^* + \|p_{c_1}, p_{c_2}\|^*}{2}$$
$$+ \sum_{i=1}^{n} \frac{sim(a_i^{c_1}, a_i^{c_2})}{n}$$

where:

- $s_{c_1}, s_{c_2}, p_{c_1}, p_{c_2}$ *represent respectively the sizes and the positions of c_1, c_2 on D's screen.*

- $\|a, b\|^* = \begin{cases} 1 & if \quad \frac{\|a,b\|}{\sqrt{w_D^2 + h_D^2}} > 1 \quad (i) \\ \frac{\|a,b\|}{\sqrt{w_D^2 + h_D^2}} & otherwise \end{cases}$

- $sim : \mathcal{D} \to [0, 1]$ *such that :*

$$\forall x_1, x_2 \in \mathcal{D}, \forall y, y' \in [0, 1] :$$
$$(sim(x_1, x_2) = y \land sim(x_1, x_2) = y') \to y = y'$$

In Android Activity, one can use *scrollview* to represent a content that is bigger than the size of the device screen. As a consequence, the euclidean distance between the sizes (resp. positions) of two UI elements can be bigger than the device screen. Therefore we use *(i)* to ensure that if the euclidean distance between the sizes (resp. positions) of two UI elements is bigger than the device screen size, the distinguishably of the two UI elements in terms of size (resp. position) is full.

Definition 6. *Given two Android Activities A_1 and A_2 and an Android user u. A_1 and A_2 are said to be (k,l) indistinguishable to u iff the following conditions hold:*

- A_1 *and A_2 are k-size indistinguishable*
- A_1 *and A_2 are l-content indistinguishable*
- *u cannot distinguish A_1 from A_2.*

We conducted a study to select the Activity indistinguishability threshold for a user (see Sect. 5.4). Based on previous definitions, the detection of an Activity hijacking attack is defined as following.

Definition 7 (Activity hijacking attack). *Given a device D, a user u, two Android Activities A_1 and A_2 launched on D at t_{A_1} and t_{A_2} by two processes p_{A_1} and p_{A_2}. Let us suppose that the plotting time of A_1 is $\mathcal{P}_{A_1}^D$. The Activity A_1 is successfully hijacked by A_2 iff the following conditions hold:*

1. $p_{A_1} \neq p_{A_2}$
2. $t_{A_2} - t_{A_1} < \mathcal{P}_{A_1}^D$
3. $\exists k, l \in [0,1]$ *such that A_1 and A_2 are (k,l) indistinguishable to u*

The hacker must launch hijacking activity before the appearance of the victim activity in the screen (before the expiration of the plotting time $\mathcal{P}_{A_1}^D$ of $A1$). If he/she launchs the activity after, the user can observe the two activities (abnormal behavior).

4.3   Response Model

Our reaction model for Activity hijacking attacks is mainly based on the indistinguishability level between the attack and legitimate Activities. Two cases are considered.

Full Indistinguishability. In our detection model, full indistinguishability between an attack and a legitimate Activities occurs when they are *1-size* and *1-content indistinguishable*. In this case, we react by performing two actions:

– Before entering the foreground, the attack Activity is blocked to prevent its usage by the user.
– The Android user is notified that a hijacking attack was detected and blocked. The notification contains the *pid* and the *name* of the attack application.

The blockage of the attack Activity will not affect the usability of other apps Activities as we experimentally showed (Sect. 6.2) that, in the case of full indistinguishability, we are 99,999% sure that the attack Activity is launched from an attack app.

Partial Indistinguishability. Partial indistinguishability between an attack and a legitimate Activities occurs when there exists $k \in]0,1[$ and $l \in]0,1[$ such that the two Activities are *k-size* and *l-content indistinguishable*. The reaction to this class of hijacking attacks is performed as following:

– In parallel with the entering of the attack Activity to the foreground, we notify the user that he/she is probably under a hijacking attack. We recommend him/her, before entering any input, to check whether a similar Activity (legitimate Activity) exists in the background.
– We associate taint to UI components. Thus, the private data entered by user will be tainted. We track propagation of tainted data in the Android system to detect leakage of these information. A notification appears when the private data are sent to the attacker through the network.

5   Implementation

We have implemented our proposed approach in TaintDroid operating system [7]. To do so, first we instrumented *Window Manager*, *Activity Manager* and *View System* components of the Android os framework layer. Then, we developed and added *Activity Hijacking Protector* – a framework layer system service responsible for detecting and reacting to Activity hijacking attacks. The following sections explain the implementation of the components that are used to detect and react to Activity hijacking attacks.

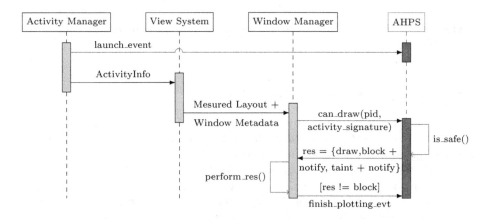

Fig. 2. AHPS interactions during Activity launching process

5.1   Activity Plotting Time

Activity plotting time is a key parameter of our detection model, it depends mainly on the duration of the operations that need to be performed by both *onCreate()* and *onResume()* which, in many cases, depend on unknown parameters. For instance, the contents of some UI elements may have to be retrieved from a server, which makes the plotting time of the Activity depending on the time needed by the server to send those contents.

Consequently, formally identifying the plotting time of an arbitrary Activity before or during its launching is not possible. Actually, our approach can still be valid if we can (1) figure out the launching time of an Activity and (2) at any instant, know whether the plotting of the Activity is finished. To meet (1), we instrumented the *Activity Manager* component by sending a *launch_evt* to the *Activity Hijacking Protector* at the beginning of *handleLaunchActivity()*(ActivityThread.java). To ensure (2), we instrumented the *Window Manager* service by sending, at the end of *finishDrawingWindow()*(WindowManagerService.java), a *finish_plotting_evt* to the *Activity Hijacking Protector*.

```
1  Procedure handle_launch_evt(activity_name)
2  |    pid = Binder.getCallingPid()
3  |    add_to_launched_activity(pid, activity_name)
4  |    return
5  Procedure handle_finish_plotting_evt(activity_pid, activity_name)
6  |    pid = Binder.getCallingPid()
7  |    if pid! = WINDOW_MANAGER_PID then
8  |    |    return
9  |    end
10 |    remove_from_launched_activity(activiy_pid, activity_name)
11 |    return
```

Algorithm 1. Handling *launch_event* and *finish_plotting_evt* events by (AHPS)

5.2 Activity UI Signature Extraction

To get the UI elements features of the Activity to be launched, we instrumented the *View System* component by adding, in each UI element class (e.g., TextView.java, etc.), a function that collects the values of the UI element visual attributes. As presented in Algorithm 1, *AHPS* handles the two events *launch_event* and *finish_plotting_evt* that are sent respectively from the *Activity Manager* component and the *Window Manager* service. Based on those two events, *AHPS* will be able to know, at any instant, (i) if there exists one or more Activities that are launched, but not yet plotted. When a new Activity is going to be plotted by the *Window Manager*, this last queries *AHPS* for the permission to plot the Activity (Algorithm 2 line 3). The permission is computed by the *AHPS*, in Algorithm 3, based on (i), the *pid* that is launching the Activity, the Activity signature, and the user Activity distinguishability threshold (Sect. 5.4). Three permission values can be returned from *AHPS* as a response to the query of the *Window Manager*. The response *"DRAW"* means that the *Window Manager* is authorized to plot the Activity since no attack has been detected from *AHPS*. The response *TAINT* means that the Activity that is going to be launched is probably $(Pr[attack] = 0.94$, See Sect. 6.2) an Activity hijacking attack.

To compute the UI signature of the Activity, we create a function (*contructSignature()*) that traverses the UI layout tree of the Activity, collects all the leaf nodes in the layout tree, and extracts the features that dominate the UI visual appearance. The *contructSignature()* function is called at the beginning of *performDraw()*(ViewRootImpl.java).

5.3 Activity Hijacking Protection Service (AHPS)

AHPS represents the main component in the implementation of our approach. Figure 2 illustrates the sequence of exchanged information and events between *Activity Manager*, *View System*, *Window Manager*, and *AHPS* during the launch

```
1  Procedure can_draw()
2  |   pid = Binder.getCallingPid()
3  |   result = AHPS.is_safe(pid, activity_Signature)
4  |   perform_res(result)
5  |   AHPS.handle_finish_plotting_evt(pid, activity_Signature.get_name())
6  |   return
7  Procedure perform_res(result)
8  |   if result = DRAW then
9  |   |   finishDrawingWindow()
10 |   end
11 |   if result = TAINT then
12 |   |   taint(activity_ui_objects)
13 |   |   notify_user("You are probably under an attack!")
14 |   |   finishDrawingWindow()
15 |   end
16 |   if result = BLOCK then
17 |   |   activity.finish() /* stop the activity thread */
18 |   |   notify_user("An attack from 'pid' is blocked")
19 |   end
20 |   return
```

Algorithm 2. Requesting the permission to draw an activity

of an Activity. The modifications we introduced to the initial process of Activity launching are colored in blue.

In this case, the *Window Manager* taints all the UI objects contained in the Activity, notifies the user about a probable Activity hijacking attack, and plot the Activity (Algorithm 2 lines 12 to 14). Finally, the response *BLOCK* means that *AHPS* is almost sure (99.999%, , See Sect. 6.2) that the Activity that is going to be launched is an Activity hijacking attack. In this case, the *Window Manager* blocks the plotting of the Activity and notifies the user (Algorithm 2 lines 17 and 18).

5.4 Activity Indistinguishability Threshold Selection

It has been demonstrated in [12,16] that user's perception of an interface can be influenced by many factors (e.g., gender, culture, age, etc.). However, the results of those studies are too generic to be used to select an Activity indistinguishability threshold for a user. We conducted a study on the distinguishability perception of mobile app interfaces. The study is performed as an Android app composed of four steps. In the first step, the participant is asked to use a set of Activities belonging to different apps (e.g., Paypal login Activity, Google Play credit card paying Activity, etc.). The purpose of this step is to help the participant to become familiar with the used Activities. Then, for each subsequent step, we change the order in which the Activities is shown to the participant. Moreover, for each Activity, we increasingly modify its appearance (i.e., change

```
1  Procedure is_safe(pid, act_sig)
2  |   k,l = 0, safe = true
3  |   foreach (prev_pid, activity_name) in launched_activity do
4  |   |   if pid != prev_pid then
5  |   |   |   safe = false
6  |   |   |   prev_act_sig = get_signature(prev_pid)
7  |   |   |   (k', l') = compute_similarity(prev_act_sig, act_sig)
8  |   |   |   if k' + l' > k + l then
9  |   |   |   |   (k, l) = (k', l')
10 |   |   |   end
11 |   |   end
12 |   endfch
13 |   if safe then
14 |   |   return DRAW
15 |   end
16 |   if k = 1 and l = 1 then
17 |   |   return BLOCK
18 |   end
19 |   if (k, l) > user_distinguishability_threshold then
20 |   |   return TAINT
21 |   end
22 |   return
```

Algorithm 3. Computing Activity plotting permission

Table 1. Classification of participants that completed our experiment

	Gender		Age						Usage of mobile payment	
	Male	Female	≤ 20	[20–30]	[30–40]	[40–50]	[50–60]	≥ 60	Yes	No
% of participants	60,6%	39,4%	10,1%	23,5%	29,2%	16,8%	14,6%	5,7%	22,4%	77,5%
w_ind_thld	0,48	0,45	0,51	0,55	0,54	0,5	0,48	0,45	0.6	0.45

the size, position, visual attributes of UI elements) compared to the one shown during the first step.

Figure 3 shows, in each step, the appearance of Paypal login Activity shown to the user. The picture (a) of the Fig. 3 represents a slightly different Paypal login activity in which we imperceptibly reduce the size of *EditTexts* compared to the original Paypal login activity. In the picture (b) of Fig. 3, we increase the appearance difference by reducing the size of the Paypal icon used in the activity. In the step 3 in Fig. 3, we remove the *TextView* containing the "forgot?" link and we decrease more the size of the Paypal icon. Finally, in the step 4, we remove the *TextView* containing the "New to PayPal? Sign up" link and we modify "TextEdit"s' hints. The purpose of the developed app is to know in which step the participant will be able to distinguish the modified Activity from the original one (Step 1). This knowledge allows us to select the Activity indistinguishability threshold (*ind_thld*) for the participant as following:

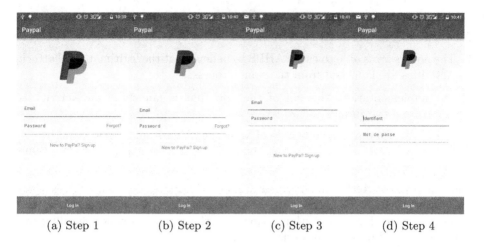

| (a) Step 1 | (b) Step 2 | (c) Step 3 | (d) Step 4 |

Fig. 3. The appearance of Paypal login Activity in the 4 steps of our experiment app

$$ind\_thld = \frac{k+l}{2}$$

where k and l are respectively the size and content indistinguishability between the original Activity and the distinguish one.

Our study was conducted in a public square in Rennes (France). We randomly select 89 participants for our experiment. Table 1 classifies them based on their information (i.e., gender, age, and the usage of mobile payment methods) collected before the usage of our experiment app. In addition, it provides the percentage of participants belonging to each class and shows the worst activity indistinguishability threshold (w_ind_thld) for each class (i.e., the lowest level of distinguishability that allows all members of a class of participants to distinguish two activity based on their appearance on a device screen). The usage of the minimum w_ind_thld as the Activity indistinguishability threshold for Android users allows to reduce to the best the number of false negatives. However, it also increases the number of generated false positives (Sect. 6.2). To overcome this limitation, we classify the user according to their gender, age, and their usage of mobile payment. Then, the user' Activity indistinguishability threshold is computed as the maximum w_ind_thld of the classes in which the user belongs.

6   Evaluation

In this section, we evaluate the security, the effectiveness and the performance of our proposed solution.

6.1   Security Evaluation

In this section, we evaluate the ability of an adversary to prevent AHPS from detecting Activity hijacking attacks. Based on Definition 7, an adversary can successfully perform an undetectable Activity hijacking attack in three cases. For each case, we prove its incorrectness.

1. The adversary is able to cause AHPS to believe that the legitimate and attack Activities are launched from the same process.

In our implementation, the *pid* of the app that is launching an Activity is retrieved from the *Binder* in two levels:

- By the AHPS during the handle of an event (Algorithm 1 lines 2 and 6)
- By the *Window Manager* during the plotting request call (Algorithm 2 line 2)

Since the *Binder*, *AHPS* and *Window Manger* are Android system services, then the adversary needs to compromise the Android OS to modify the *pid* of the app that is launching the Activity. However, this is not possible regarding the adversary model we are considering (Sect. 4.1).

2. The adversary is able to cause *AHPS* to believe that the legitimate Activity is already plotted in the screen.

In our implementation, when the *Window Manager* receives an Activity window to plot, it retrieves the *pid* of the app aiming to plot the Activity window (Algorithm 2 line 2). Later, the retrieved *pid* is used to notify that the Activity launched by *pid* is plotted (resp. blocked) (Algorithm 2 line 5). Based on the fact that *AHPS* accepts only finish plotting events that are sent from *Window Manager* (Algorithm 1 lines 7 to 9), so, in order to achieve 2, the attacker app should either invoke the *Window Manager* using the *pid* of the app launching the legitimate Activity, or invoke AHPS using the *pid* of *Window Manager*. In both cases, it needs to compromise the Android OS which, again, is not possible regarding the adversary model we are considering.

3. The adversary is able to cause *AHPS* to believe that the legitimate Activity and the attack Activity are distinguishable to the user .

Formally speaking, given two *k-size* and *l-content* indistinguishable Activities A_1 and A_2. Case 3 holds *iff* the following conditions hold:

(a) $\exists A_3, k', l'$ such that A_1 and A_3 are *k'-size* and *l'-content* indistinguishable
(b) A_2 and A_3 have exactly the same appearance
(c) $k' < k$ or $l' < l$

We prove by contradiction that conditions (a), (b) and (c) cannot hold together. To do so, let us suppose that A_1, A_2 and A_3 are composed respectively of the sets of visible UI objects $\mathcal{C}_{A_1} = \{e_1^{A_1}, e_2^{A_1}, \cdots, e_n^{A_1}\}$, $\mathcal{C}_{A_2} = \{e_1^{A_2}, e_2^{A_2}, \cdots, e_n^{A_2}\}$ and $\mathcal{C}_{A_3} = \{e_1^{A_3}, e_2^{A_3}, \cdots, e_n^{A_3}\}$ (each $e_j^{A_i}$ represents the set of user interface elements of kind e_j that are contained in A_i) and that their respective sizes are $s_{A_1} = (w_{A_1}, h_{A_1})$, $s_{A_2} = (w_{A_2}, h_{A_2})$ and $s_{A_3} = (w_{A_3}, h_{A_3})$. For each UI object c, we denote its size and position in the screen by s_c and p_c respectively. The set of visual attributes of a UI object type e_i is denoted by $\mathcal{V}_i$ and for each visible attribute a, we denote its value in a UI object c by a^c. Based on (b), we can deduce the following:

(i) $w_{A_1} = w_{A_2}$ and $h_{A_1} = h_{A_2}$

(ii) $\forall i \in [1, n], \forall c \in e_i^{A_2}, \forall a \in \mathcal{V}_i, \exists c' \in e_i^{A_3}$ such that $s_c = s_{c'}$, $p_c = p_{c'}$ and $a^c = a^{c'}$

Since A_1 and A_2 are k-size indistinguishable and A_1 and A_3 are k'-size indistinguishable, then based on Definition 2 we have:

$$1 - \frac{\|s_{A_1}, s_{A_2}\|}{\sqrt{w_D^2 + h_D^2}} = k \quad and \quad 1 - \frac{\|s_{A_1}, s_{A_3}\|}{\sqrt{w_D^2 + h_D^2}} = k' \tag{1a}$$

then, base on (i) we deduce that

$$\|s_{A_1}, s_{A_2}\| = \|s_{A_1}, s_{A_3}\| \tag{2a}$$

then, from (1a) and (2a) we deduce that:

$$k = k' \tag{3a}$$

Now, based on (ii) and Definition 5 we get:

$$\forall i \in [1, n], \forall c \in e_i^{A_1}, \forall c' \in e_i^{A_2}, \exists c'' \in e_i^{A_3} : \tag{4a}$$
$$\sum_{a \in \mathcal{V}_i} \frac{sim(a^c, a^{c'})}{n} = \sum_{a \in \mathcal{V}_i} \frac{sim(a^c, a^{c''})}{n}$$

Then from (ii), Definition 5 and (4a) we deduce that:

$$\forall D, \forall i \in [1, n], \forall c \in e_i^{A_1}, \forall c' \in e_i^{A_2}, \exists c'' \in e_i^{A_3} : \tag{5a}$$
$$indist(c, c', D) = indist(c, c'', D)$$

Where D is a device. Afterwards, from (5a) we deduce that:

$$\forall D, \forall i \in [1, n], \forall c \in e_i^{A_1} : \tag{6a}$$
$$\max_{c' \in e_i^{A_2}} indist(c, c', D) \leq \max_{c'' \in e_i^{A_3}} indist(c, c'', D)$$

Then based on the facts that A_1 and A_2 are l-content indistinguishable, and A_1 and A_3 are l'-content indistinguishable, we use (6a) and Definition 5 to deduce that:

$$l \leq l' \tag{7a}$$

Finally, we deduce that (3a) and (7a) are contradictory with condition (c).

6.2   Effectiveness Evaluation

The activity indistinguishability threshold (ind_thld) is a key parameter to ensure the effectiveness and accuracy of our approach. To evaluate the accuracy of our system under different ind_thld, we quantify the number of false positives that can be generated by our system. To do so, we develop a tool that (1) randomly choose and download a set of Android apps, (2) extract the set of Activities and their corresponding signatures from each app, and (3) for each couple of Activities belonging to two different apps, we compute their size and content indistinguishability levels k and l, finally (4) the tool checks whether or not the simultaneous launching of the two Activities can lead to a false positive (i.e., $(k+l)/2 > ind\_thld$). Our tool downloads 974 apps and checks around 4,138,904 couples of Activities. The distribution of false positives according the value of ind_thld is shown in Fig. 4.

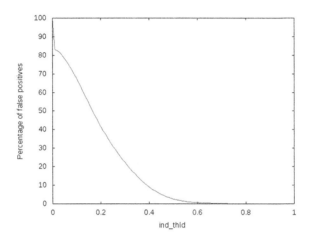

Fig. 4. The distribution of false positives according the value of ind_thld

According to the results, in the case of partial indistinguishability ($k, l \in \,]0, 1[$), our solution can generate in worst case ($ind\_thld = 0.45$, according to Table 1) 4.2 % of false positives. In case of full indistinguishability, our solution can generate $10^{-3}\%$ of false positives. These results support the different reactions we choose in our approach (Sect. 4.3).

Our approach generates false alarms because we associate taint to all UI components. In order to reduce the number of false positives, we can choose to taint only the UI components that allow the user to enter sensitive data. But this, can lead to an under-tainting problem (false negatives) as the attacker can create its own graphical object of which we cannot identify visual attributes.

In addition, our approach can produce false positives because we do not consider only the case of exact similarity where we are sure that it is an attack and we treat other cases of similarity.

We define a minimum rate of similarity ($ind\_thld = 0.45$) to detect Activity hijacking attacks. We observe that our system does not generate false negatives using this rate of similarity. But, we are based on users profiling to fix the minimum rate of similarity. Therefore, our approach can generate false negatives due to this estimated value. To reduce the number of false negatives and to improve the minimum rate of similarity, we can conduct a large-scale user study.

6.3   Performance Evaluation

The main component in our approach is the activity hijacking protection service that compares similarity between the legitimate and the phishing application UIs. In this section, we study our protection service overhead by increasing the number of graphical components. We get up to 30 graphics components.

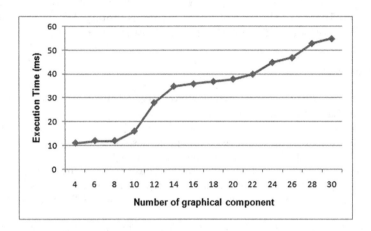

Fig. 5. Activity hijacking protection service overhead

Figure 5 presents the execution time results of our protection service with respect to the number of graphical components. We observe that the number of graphical components is proportional to the execution time. This is because we perform an additional treatment (test of similarity, taint UI components...) when the number of graphical components increased.

Also, we use the CaffeineMark [6] to evaluate the influence of the protection service execution on the system performance. Note that the CaffeineMark scores roughly correlate with the number of Java instructions executed per second and do not depend significantly on the amount of memory in the system or on the speed of a computers disk drives or internet connection. We test our system overhead when the protection service is executed and when it is disabled. We observe that the service generates 0.39% execution time overhead. Thus, it does not really affect the performance of the system.

7   Conclusion

In order to detect and react to hijacking attacks, we have proposed an effective approach based on the indistinguishability level between the attack and legitimate Activities. In this paper, we extract and compare similarity between the

UI components visual attributes at application run time by instrumenting the Android operating system code. We define a reaction mechanism that blocks the attack Activity before entering the foreground to prevent it to be used in the case of full indistinguishability. In the case of partial indistinguishability, we notify Android user and we associate taint to sensitive data to detect leakage of these information through the network. We test security of our approach by evaluating the ability of an adversary to prevent detecting Activity hijacking attacks. We found that an adversary can successfully perform an undetectable Activity hijacking attack in three cases. For each, we prove its incorrectness. Our approach generates 4.2% of false positives in the case of partial indistinguishability and and $10^{-3}\%$ in the case of full indistinguishability. We observe that our approach does not really affect the performance of the system (0.39% overhead).

References

1. Back stack. https://developer.android.com/guide/components/tasks-and-back-stack.html
2. Cumulative number of apps downloaded from the Google play as of May 2016 (in billions). http://www.statista.com/statistics/281106/number-of-android-app-downloads-from-google-play/
3. Bianchi, A., Corbetta, J., Invernizzi, L., Fratantonio, Y., Kruegel, C., Vigna, G.: What the app is that? Deception and countermeasures in the Android user interface. In: 2015 IEEE Symposium on Security and Privacy (SP), pp. 931–948. IEEE (2015)
4. Bkakria, A., Mariem, G., Cuppens-Boulahia, N., Cuppens, F., Lanet, J.L.: Real-time detection and reaction to activity hijacking attacks in Android smartphones. In: 15th International Conference on Privacy, Security and Trust (PST). IEEE, August 2017, to appear
5. Chen, Q.A., Qian, Z., Mao, Z.M.: Peeking into your app without actually seeing it: UI state inference and novel android attacks. In: 23rd USENIX Security Symposium (USENIX Security 14), pp. 1037–1052 (2014)
6. Pendragon Software Corporation: Caffeinemark 3.0 (1997). http://www.benchmarkhq.ru/cm30/
7. Enck, W., Gilbert, P., Han, S., Tendulkar, V., Chun, B.G., Cox, L.P., Jung, J., McDaniel, P., Sheth, A.N.: TaintDroid: an information-flow tracking system for realtime privacy monitoring on smartphones. ACM Trans. Comput. Syst. (TOCS) **32**(2), 5 (2014)
8. F-secure: Warning on possible Android mobile trojans (2010). https://www.f-secure.com/weblog/archives/00001852.html
9. Felt, A.P., Wagner, D.: Phishing on mobile devices (2011)
10. Forbes: Alleged "nazi" Android FBI ransomware mastermind arrested in Russia (2015). http://www.forbes.com/sites/thomasbrewster/2015/04/13/alleged-nazi-android-fbi-ransomware-mastermind-arrested-in-russia/47fd631360a9
11. Google Inc.: Android and security (2012). http://googlemobile.blogspot.fr/2012/02/android-and-security.html
12. Kitayama, S., Duffy, S., Kawamura, T., Larsen, J.T.: Perceiving an object and its context in different cultures a cultural look at new look. Psychol. Sci. **14**(3), 201–206 (2003)

13. Lin, C.C., Li, H., Zhou, X.Y., Wang, X.: Screenmilker: how to milk your Android screen for secrets. In: NDSS (2014)
14. Malisa, L., Kostiainen, K., Capkun, S.: Detecting mobile application spoofing attacks by leveraging user visual similarity perception
15. Marforio, C., Masti, R.J., Soriente, C., Kostiainen, K., Capkun, S.: Personalized security indicators to detect application phishing attacks in mobile platforms. arXiv preprint arXiv:1502.06824 (2015)
16. Simon, S.J.: The impact of culture and gender on web sites: an empirical study. DATA BASE **32**(1), 18–37 (2001). http://doi.acm.org/10.1145/506740.506744 http://doi.acm.org/10.1145/506740.506744
17. Sun, M., Li, M., Lui, J.: DroidEagle: seamless detection of visually similar Android apps. In: Proceedings of the 8th ACM Conference on Security & Privacy in Wireless and Mobile Networks, p. 9. ACM (2015)
18. Trends, D.: Do not use imessage chat for Android, it's not safe (2013). http://www.digitaltrends.com/mobile/imessage-chat-android-security-flaw/

Heavy Log Reader: Learning the Context of Cyber Attacks Automatically with Paragraph Vector

Mamoru Mimura[✉] and Hidema Tanaka

National Defense Academy, 1-10-20 Hashirimizu, Yokosuka, Kanagawa, Japan
`mim@nda.ac.jp`

Abstract. Cyberattack techniques are evolving every second, and detecting unknown malicious communication is a challenging task. Pattern-matching-based techniques and using malicious website blacklists are easily avoided, and not efficient to detect unknown malicious communication. Therefore, many behavior-based detection methods are proposed, which use the characteristic of drive-by-download attacks or C&C traffic. However, many previous methods specialize the attack techniques and the adaptability is limited. Moreover, they have to decide the feature vectors every attack method. This paper proposes a generic detection method, which is independent of attack methods and does not need devising feature vectors. Our method uses Paragraph Vector an unsupervised algorithm that learns fixed-length feature representations from variable-length pieces of texts, such as sentences, paragraphs, and documents, and learns the context in proxy server logs. We conducted cross-validation and timeline analysis with the D3M and the BOS in the MWS datasets. The experimental results show our method can detect unknown malicious communication precisely in proxy server logs. The best F-measure achieves 0.99 in unknown drive-by-download attacks and 0.98 in unknown C&C traffic.

Keywords: Drive by download · C&C · Neural network
Bag of words · Word2vec · Paragraph vector · Doc2vec
Support vector machine · Random forests · Multi-layer perceptron

1 Introduction

Cyber threat is increasing dramatically and the public concern is high. Information and communication technology has been developing rapidly. Because of this, cyberattack techniques are evolving every second. Internet worms such as "Code Red" or "Blaster" used to be a main threat in the early first decade of the 2000s. In recent years, Drive-by Download attack (DbD attack) and Spear Phishing attack are main attack techniques on the Internet. After the initial intrusion, the attacker takes control of the victim's computer over the Internet via a Command and Control (C&C) server. The victim's computer serves

© Springer International Publishing AG 2017
R. K. Shyamasundar et al. (Eds.): ICISS 2017, LNCS 10717, pp. 146–163, 2017.
https://doi.org/10.1007/978-3-319-72598-7_9

as a stepping stone to further deep drilling intrusion. In particular, a set of stealthy and continuous computer hacking processes is called Advanced Persistent Threat (APT). On the other hand, security analysts in Security Operations Center (SOC) attempt to detect cyberattacks and deal with the incidents. They investigate IDS (Intrusion Detection System) alerts or logs recorded in network devices such as a firewall or a proxy server to detect cyberattacks. In general, intrusion detection techniques on a network are classified roughly into methods using pattern matching and methods using blacklists. The methods using pattern matching are effective, if the malicious traffic contains a unique string pattern. IDS uses fixed strings or regular expression to describe the signatures. However, recent malware used in APT attacks communicates via standard http protocol to imitate normal http communication (e.g. Plug X, Emdivi). Therefore, it is difficult to describe the signatures. In this case, an IDS can use the malicious destination server (e.g. Landing site, C&C server) address as the signature. A firewall or a proxy server can also use the malicious destination server address as the blacklist. However, the attacker can change the malicious destination servers easily to evade detection by network devices. In addition, the malicious server address has to be already-known before the cyberattack. Thus, detecting unknown malicious communication is a challenging task.

To tackle the challenging task, many behavior-based detection methods are proposed. These methods capture the characteristics of DbD attacks or C&C traffic, and detect unseen malicious communication. Many previous methods, however, specialize the attack techniques. These methods can detect only DbD attacks or C&C traffic. Because these methods usually use different detection techniques. If attackers change the attack techniques, these previous methods barely detect unseen malicious communication. Besides security researchers have to devise the feature vectors to capture the characteristics. Furthermore, many previous methods require monitoring all network traffic. Many organizations, however, do not keep all network traffic because the size is too huge. Security incidents often occur in the organizations that did not take the countermeasures adequately. In most cases, there are inadequate log files to investigate the incident in the vulnerable organizations. Sometimes we might retrieve only log files on a single proxy server.

This paper focuses on the characteristic that Neural Network (NN) learns feature vector representation automatically. In recent years, NN achieves remarkable results in the fields of image recognition, speech recognition or natural language processing (NLP). In the NLP fields, Word2vec [1] is remarkable. This model takes a large corpus of text and produces a vector space with each unique word in the corpus being assigned a corresponding vector in the space. This model enables not only document classification based on the appearance frequency, but also document classification based on the sense or the context. Furthermore, the same idea was extended to Paragraph Vector an unsupervised algorithm that learns fixed-length feature representations from variable-length pieces of texts, such as sentences, paragraphs, and documents. In this paper, we presume proxy server logs are written in a natural language, and attempt to learn the difference of normal communication and malicious communication automatically with Paragraph Vector. Then we input the extracted feature vectors with the label into supervised learning models to classify normal communication and malicious communication. Our generic detection method does not rely on attack techniques, and does not demand devising feature vectors.

The main contributions of this paper are four-fold: (1) Described how to construct a corpus from proxy server logs and applied Doc2vec. (2) Proposed a generic detection method which did not rely on attack techniques and did not demand devising feature vectors. (3) Verified that our method learned the structure of the URLs automatically, even if a human made no clear indication. (4) Verified that Doc2vec was effective to analyze proxy server logs.

The rest of the paper is organized as follows. Next section discusses related works and makes clear the difference among this method and previous methods. Section 3 describes Natural Language Processing (NLP) techniques. Section 4 proposes a generic detection method, which includes how to use NN and classifiers. Section 5 shows experimental results applying our method to the datasets which contain DbD attacks and C&C traffic. Section 6 evaluates the method in practical perspective and discusses the limitation.

2   Related Work

2.1   Behavior-Based Detection

This paper aims to detect malicious communication, even if both malicious server addresses and the distinctive traffic patterns are unknown. The malicious communication includes DbD attacks and C&C traffic. In general, the main studies of network intrusion detection include signature-based detection and behavior-based detection. Signature-based detection relies on an existing signature database to detect known malicious communication, and barely detects unknown malicious communication. Therefore, many behavior-based detection methods are proposed. For example, some methods focused on the traffic classification from packet traces [2–5]. However, analyzing packets is becoming intractable on broadband networks. The alternative approach is classification based on network logs such as DNS records, NetFlow or proxy server logs. There are several methods which use NetFlow [6–9] or DNS records [10–13]. However, it is unusual to obtain all network traffic or logs in actual incidents. Therefore, we focus on proxy server logs.

2.2   Analyzing Proxy Server Logs

Kruegel et al. [14] categorized URIs by the path, and extracted the parameters from the query strings. Their statistical model learns the features, and detects the statistical outliers as attacks. This method expects detecting direct attacks to web servers such as buffer over flow, directory traversal, cross-site scripting and so on. Our method uses statistical machine learning models for binary classification of malicious communication and benign communication. Our method expects indirect attacks such as DbD attacks or SP attacks too.

Choi et al. [15] extracted feature vectors from the domain, the path and so on included in URLs, and proposed a method using machine learning models to classify malicious URLs and benign URLs. This method uses not only proxy server logs but also the URL popularity, the contents, the DNS traffic or any other traffic. Our method uses only proxy server logs and does not require any other information obtained from the outside. Our method does not even demand devising feature vectors.

Ma et al. [16] extracted feature vectors from the host name, the top level domain name, the path and so on included in URLs, and proposed online learning algorithm to classify malicious URLs and benign URLs. This method divides URLs into tokens by the delimiter such as "dot" (.), "slash" (/), "question mark" (?), "equal" (=), "and" (&) and so on. Our method uses the similar techniques to obtain tokens from URLs. These tokens serve as words to construct a corpus. Their method requires not only proxy server logs but also searching the whois database for IP address and domain name registration information, blacklists, the geographical feature, the bandwidth speed and so on. Our method uses only proxy server logs. Our method does not even demand devising feature vectors.

Huang et al. [17] extracted feature vectors from the structure, the characteristic strings and the brand name included in URLs to detect malicious URLs with machine learning. This method aims to detect phishing URLs. Our method aims to detect DbD attacks and C&C traffic, however, is not limited to these attacks. Our method does not even demand devising feature vectors.

Zhao et al. [18] focused on the cost to force users to analyze and label malicious traffic, and proposed an online active learning framework which updates the classifier to detect malicious URLs. This method uses the whois database for domain name registration information, blacklists and so on. Our method uses only proxy server logs and does not require any other information obtained from the outside.

Invernizzi et al. [19] built a network graph from IP addresses, domain names, FQDNs, URLs, paths, file names and so on. Their method focuses on the correlation among nodes to detect malware distribution. This method uses only the parameters obtained from proxy server logs. However, this method has to cover many range of IP addresses, and performs in large-scale networks such as ISPs. In addition, this method needs the downloaded file types. Our method performs at any scale and does not need the downloaded file types.

Nelms et al. [20] focused on DbD attacks, and extracted the Location field, the Referrer field and so on from http Request messages and Response messages to build a URL transfer graph. They proposed a trace back system which could go back to the source from the URL transfer graph. This method uses hop counts, domain age and common features of the domain names to detect malicious URLs. Our method uses only proxy server logs and does not require any other information obtained from the outside. In addition, our method can detect not only DbD attacks but also any other types of attacks.

Bartos et al. [21] categorized proxy server logs into flows, and extracted many features from the URLs, the paths, the queries, the file names and so on. They proposed how to learn the feature vectors to classify malicious URLs. This method can decide the optimum feature vectors automatically. However, this method demands devising basic features for learning. Our method does not even demand devising basic features.

Mimura et al. [22] categorized proxy server logs by FQDNs to extract feature vectors, and proposed a RAT (Remote Access Trojan or Remote Administration Tool) detection method using machine learning techniques. This method uses the characteristic that RATs continues to access the same path regularly. However, this method performs for only C&C traffic. Our method can detect not only C&C traffic but also any other types of attacks.

Shibahara et al. [23] focus on a sequence of URLs which include malicious artifacts of malicious redirections, and proposed a detection system which uses Convolutional Neural Networks. This method uses a honey client to collect URL sequences and their labels. However, this method performs for DbD attacks. Our method can detect not only DbD attacks but also any other types of attacks.

3 Natural Language Processing (NLP) Technique

3.1 Bag-of-Words (BoW)

To calculate various measures to characterize a text, we have to transform the text into a vector. Bag-of-Words (BoW) is a simplifying representation used in NLP. In this model, a sentence is represented as the bag of its words, disregarding grammar and even word order but keeping multiplicity. BoW is commonly used in document classification methods where the frequency of each word is used as a feature for training a classifier. The most common type of features calculated from BoW is a term frequency, namely, the number of times a term appears in the sentence. However, term frequencies are not necessarily the best representation for the sentence. BoW cannot represent grammar, word order and word meaning.

3.2 Word2vec

Word2vec [1] is a model that produces word embedding. Word embedding is the collective name for a set of language modeling and feature learning techniques in NLP where words from the vocabulary are mapped to vectors of real numbers. This model is a shallow, two-layer neural network that is trained to reconstruct linguistic contexts of words. This model takes as its input a large corpus of text and produces a vector space, with each unique word in the corpus being assigned a corresponding vector in the space. Word vectors are positioned in the vector space such that words that share common contexts in the corpus are located in close proximity to each other in the space. Word2vec is based on the distributional hypothesis, which motivates that the meaning of a word can be gauged by its context. Thus, if two words occur in the same position in two sentences, they are very much related either in semantics or syntactic. Word2vec utilizes two algorithms to produce a distributed representation of words. One is Continuous-Bag-of-Words (CBoW), and the other is skip-gram. In the CBoW algorithm, the model predicts the current word from a window of surrounding context words. In the skip-gram algorithm, the model uses the current word to predict the surrounding window of context words. Word2vec enables to calculate the semantic similarity between two words and infer similar words semantically. However, Word2vec is a model that merely produces word embedding. To calculate semantic similarity between two documents, this method has to be extended.

3.3 Paragraph Vector (Doc2vec)

An extension of Word2vec to construct embedding from entire documents has been proposed [24]. This extension is called Doc2vec or Paragraph2vec and has been implemented. Doc2vec is based on the same distributional hypothesis, which motivates that the meaning of a sentence can be gauged by its context. Thus, if two sentences occur in the same position in two paragraphs, they are very much related either in semantics or syntactic in the same way. Doc2vec utilizes two algorithms to produce Paragraph Vector a distributed representation of entire documents. One is Distributed-Memory (DM), and the other is Distributed-Bag-of-Words (DBoW). DM is the extension of CBoW, and the only change in this model is adding a document ID as a window of surrounding context words. DBoW is the extension of skip-gram, and the current word was replaced by the current document ID. Doc2vec enables to calculate semantic similarity between two documents and infer similar documents semantically. Some implementations support also inference of document embedding on unseen documents. This function is important to develop a practical system to detect unseen malicious communication. Because, unseen malicious communication might include an unknown word (e.g. newly-changed FQDN, random strings).

4 Proposed Method

4.1 Separating Logs with Spaces

The key idea of this research is processing proxy server logs as a language. In order to put it into practice, proxy server logs have to be separated into words. Figure 1 shows a sample of proxy server logs.

This sample includes date and time at which transaction completed, request line from the client (includes the method, the URL and the user agent), HTTP status code returned to the client and size of the object returned to the client. The client means user's computer which connects to servers over the Internet. A proxy server records the contents on a line in chronological order. The line originates the request from an internal client and is coupled with the response from the server.

[06/Oct/2014:09:45:13 +0000] "" 10.16.23.23 200 "POST
http://www.xxxxx.jp/2008/12/home/index.php&h9hP1ddwZ=6%14%10ED%40X%14%03EF_GE
DC&1gylb7gEm98h=%24&TBONFa=IUC&YVNVY=%3C%2F9 HTTP/1.1" "" "" "" 279 "Mozilla/4.0
(compatible; MSIE 8.0; Windows NT 5.1; SV1; .NET CLR 2.0.50727.42)" "" ""
[06/Oct/2014:09:45:29 +0000] "" 10.16.23.25 200 "POST
http://www.www.yyyyy.jp/info/yougo/book/index.php&kLbqydMMm=%07%25%21tuqi%252tq
nwsur&zMHzOUNc=%03&date=%2BZ%40.4%22%3A%25%3A%23%22%24%25%1DO%7Eu9%5
EDI%1Dh%1DYQY.4%26%24%20%2CY%1Dh%1DSY%40%3C-%3D HTTP/1.1" "" "" "" 334
"Mozilla/4.0 (compatible; MSIE 8.0; Windows NT 5.1; SV1; .NET CLR 2.0.50727.42)" "" ""

Fig. 1. A sample of proxy server logs.

Our method divides proxy server logs into HTTP status code, request line from the client, size of the object returned to the client and user agent. Furthermore, the request line is divided into method, URL and protocol version.

4.2 Separating URLs with Spaces

We believe a URL is the most important element to detect malicious communication. Therefore, our method separates URLs with spaces. Figure 2 shows an example of a URL leaving a space between words.

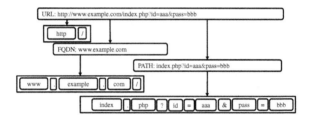

Fig. 2. An example of a URL leaving a space between words.

First, our method divides a URL into scheme, FQDN (Fully Qualified Domain Name) and path which includes query strings. After that, our method separates the FQDN by "dot" (.). Then we can derive top level domain name, sub domain name and so on, which means the country, the organization, the use or the purpose (e.g. www, mail). Our method separates the path by "slash" (/) and "dot" (.), and also separates the query string by "question mark" (?), "equal" (=) and "and" (&). Then, we can derive the directory name, the file name, the extension from the path. We can also derive the variable names and the values from the query string, which are used in the running program on the server. Our method excludes the values used only once from query strings. We decided to leave the delimiters as a word to construct a corpus. Because the delimiters are related to the contiguous word meanings. For instance, some delimiters such as "slash" (/) are closely related to the structure of the URL.

To summarize, our method divides URLs into words by the delimiters which are "dot" (.), "slash" (/), "question mark" (?), "equal" (=) and "and" (&). These words construct a corpus to describe proxy server logs.

4.3   Overview

Figure 3 shows an overview of the proposed method. First, our method constructs a corpus from malicious proxy server logs and benign proxy server logs. Both logs are separated by the previously mentioned method. Then, our method constructs a vector space from the corpus, and converts both proxy server logs into vectors with the labels. The language models which construct a vector space are BoW and Doc2vec. These labeled vectors are training data for classifiers. The classifiers are Support Vector Machine (SVM), Random Forests (RF) and Multi-Layer Perceptron (MLP).

A SVM model is a representation of the training data as points in space, mapped so that the training data of the separate categories are divided by a clear gap that is as wide as possible. Test data are then mapped into that same space and predicted to belong to a category based on which side of the gap they fall. RF are an ensemble learning method that operates by constructing a multitude of decision trees at training time and outputting the class that is the mode of the classes or mean prediction of the individual trees. MLP is a class of feedforward artificial neural network, which consists of at least three layers of nodes. Each node is a neuron that uses a nonlinear activation function. MLP utilizes a supervised learning technique called backpropagation for training.

These are supervised learning models with associated learning algorithms that analyze data used for classification and regression analysis. Given a set of training data, each labeled as belonging to one or the other of two categories, these training algorithms build a model that assigns new examples to one category or the other. After that, we convert unknown proxy server logs into vectors. These unlabeled vectors are test data for the classifiers. Finally, we input these unlabeled vectors to the classifiers, and can obtain a predicted label. The predicted label is either malicious or benign.

4.4   Implementation

Our method was developed by Python-2.7 with open source machine learning libraries, gensim-1.01 [25], scikit-learn-0.18.0 [26] and chainer-1.23 [27].

Gensim is a Python library to realize unsupervised semantic modelling from plain text, and includes a BoW model and a Doc2vec model. Table 1 shows the parameters for the Doc2vec model. We set the dimensionality of the feature vectors 100, and chose DBoW which was the extension of skip-gram. The window is the maximum distance between the predicted word and context words used for prediction within a document.

Scikit-learn is a machine-learning library for Python that provides tools for data mining with a focus on machine learning, and supports SVM and RF. Our method uses a SVC function with a linear kernel for SVM. Our method also uses a RandomForestClassifier function for RF.

Chainer is a flexible Python framework for neural networks, which supports MLP with CUDA computation. We use CUDA 8.0 and cuDNN-6.0. Table 2 shows the parameters for the MLP model. The number of input layer units

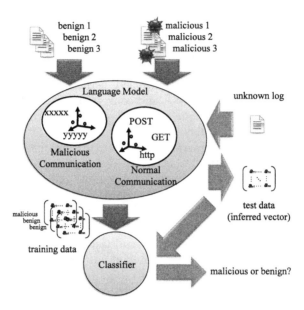

Fig. 3. An overview of the proposed method.

Table 1. The parameters for the Doc2vec model

Dimensionality of the feature vectors	100
Window	15
Number of epochs	30
Training algorithm	DBoW

is the dimensionality of the test data. Thus, the dimensionality is 100 as we mentioned before. The number of labels is 2, namely benign or malicious. ReLU (Rectified Linear Unit) is an activation function defined as follows.

$$f(x) = x^+ = \max(0, x)$$

It is also known as a ramp function and has been used in convolutional networks more effectively than the widely used logistic sigmoid. Adam (Adaptive moment estimation) is an algorithm for first-order gradient-based optimization of stochastic objective functions, based on adaptive estimates of lower-order moments [28]. This method is well suited for problems that are large in terms of data and parameters, and also appropriate for non-stationary objectives and problems with very noisy and sparse gradients.

We use cross entropy as follows to define the loss function in optimization.

$$E = -\sum_{n}^{N}\sum_{i}^{D} t_{ni} \log y_i$$

N is number of the data, and D is number of the output layer units. y means predicted label, and t means true label.

Table 2. The parameters for the MLP model

Number of input layer units	100
Number of hidden layer units	500
Number of labels	2
Activation function	ReLU
Dropout ratio	0
Minibatch size	100
Optimizer	Adam

5 Experiment

5.1 Dataset

To evaluate our method, we use the D3M (Drive-by Download Data by Marionette) dataset, the BOS (Behavior Observable System) dataset and the NCD (Normal Communication Data in MWSCup 2014). These datasets are parts of the MWS datasets [29], and include pcap files. The D3M and the BOS contain malicious communication. Table 3 shows the detail.

Table 3. The detail of the datasets.

D3M		BOS	
Year	Size	Year	Size
2010	130 M	2014	38.9 M
2011	24.8 M	2015	2.25 G
2012	33.2 M	2016	3.48 G
2013	14.6 M	-	-
2014	23.3 M	-	-
2015	334 M	-	-

Both pcap files are malicious. However, the property is different. The D3M is a set of packet traces collected from the web-client, high-interaction honeypot system, which is based on Internet Explorer on Windows OS with several vulnerable plugins, such as Adobe Reader, Flash Player, Java and so on. This data focuses on DbD attacks caused by crawling malicious web sites according to threat transitions from exploiting OS services remotely. The datasets contain packet traces for the two periods; infection and after infection. The D3M is related with exploit kits (e.g. Blackhole Exploit Kit, Elenore, Mpack) which are software kits designed to run on web servers, with the purpose of identifying software vulnerabilities in client machines communicating with them. The BOS comprises some cases of malware samples (e.g. Emdivi, Plug X), packet traces, and a process log collected from a virtual company that is a malware execution environment. The malware that were attached to e-mails are provided as well as the observed attackers activities on the host within the virtual company. The BOS contains recent C&C traffic which uses standard http protocol to imitate normal http communication. Thus, this traffic is difficult to distinguish from normal communication. The NCD is a benign communication pcap file.

Our method aims to detect malicious communication from proxy server logs. Thus, we have to convert these pcap files into pseudo proxy server logs. We extracted http traffic from these pcap files, and coupled the requests and the response. After that, we compounded the malicious logs and the benign logs into datasets at the same rate. We split the datasets into training data and test data to conduct 10-fold cross-validation and timeline analysis. Our method uses only training data to construct a corpus. Because, we presume that the test data is unknown communication. We convert a line into a vector. We also convert a bag of 10 simply consecutive lines into a vector to compare the results. In the timeline analysis, we chose the first half of the dataset as training data, and the rest half is the test data.

5.2   Metrics

Three evaluation metrics are used: precision, recall and f-measure. These metrics are used to performance of every class of communication.

$$Precision = \frac{TP}{TP + FP}$$

$$Recall = \frac{TP}{TP + FN}$$

$$F - measure = \frac{2Recall \times Precision}{Recall + Precision}$$

TP (True Positive), FP (False Positive), TN (True Negative) and FN (False Negative) are defined as shown in Table 4.

TP is the number of instances correctly classified as A, TN is the number of instances correctly classified as Not-A. FP is the number of instances incorrectly classified as A, FN is the number of instances incorrectly classified as Not-A.

Table 4. Confusion matrix for two possible outcomes.

		True label	
		Positive	Negative
Predicted	Positive	*TP*	*FP*
Label	Negative	*FN*	*TN*

5.3   Experimental Environment

Table 5 shows the experiment environment. This method needs only a simple computer, and does not require special equipment.

Table 5. Experiment environment

CPU	Core i7-5820K 3.3 GHz
Memory	DDR4 SDRAM 24 GB
GPU	GeForce GTX980/4G
OS	Windows 8.1

5.4   Result

Tables 6 and 7 show the results of the 10-fold cross-validation. In the D3M dataset, using BoW was not effective. On the contrary, using Doc2vec was highly effective. This is because the words in the D3M are very much related either in semantics or syntactic in the same way. In the BOS dataset, both using BoW and using Doc2vec were effective. BoW cannot represent grammar, word order and word meaning. BoW represents the number of times a term appears in the sentence. Hence, we conclude that the BoW model captured the characteristic that RATs continues to access the same path regularly. To summarize the results of 10-fold cross-validation, our method using Doc2vec could detect malicious communication.

Tables 8 and 9 show the results of the timeline analysis. In the D3M dataset, using BoW was not effective according to expectations. Using Doc2vec was effective even in the unknown proxy server logs. In the BOS dataset, using BoW was effective. This is because the classifier captured the characteristic that RATs continues to access the same path regularly. Referring to Doc2vec, converting multiple lines into a vector is more effective than converting a line into a vector. This is because multiple lines of URLs include the context of DbD attacks. In general, it is difficult to detect malicious URLs from only one line in DbD attacks.

Table 6. The result of the 10-fold cross-validation (D3M).

Log	Model	Classifier	NCD (Benign)			D3M (Malicious)		
			Precision	Recall	F-measure	Precision	Recall	F-measure
1	BoW	SVM	0.57	0.91	0.70	0.75	0.30	0.41
		RF	0.57	0.91	0.70	0.74	0.30	0.41
		MLP	0.59	0.91	0.71	0.77	0.34	0.44
	Doc2vec	SVM	0.92	0.89	0.90	0.90	0.92	0.91
		RF	0.90	0.93	0.91	0.92	0.89	0.90
		MLP	0.94	0.92	0.93	0.92	0.94	0.93
10		SVM	1.00	0.96	0.98	0.96	1.00	0.98
		RF	0.98	0.97	0.97	0.97	0.98	0.98
		MLP	0.99	0.98	0.98	0.98	0.99	0.98

Table 7. The result of the 10-fold cross-validation (BOS).

Log	Model	Classifier	NCD (Benign)			BOS (Malicious)		
			Precision	Recall	F-measure	Precision	Recall	F-measure
1	BoW	SVM	0.94	0.98	0.96	0.98	0.93	0.96
		RF	0.94	0.98	0.96	0.98	0.93	0.96
		MLP	0.94	0.98	0.96	0.98	0.94	0.96
	Doc2vec	SVM	0.94	0.97	0.95	0.97	0.94	0.95
		RF	0.97	1.00	0.98	1.00	0.97	0.98
		MLP	0.98	0.99	0.98	0.99	0.97	0.98
10		SVM	1.00	1.00	1.00	1.00	1.00	1.00
		RF	0.98	1.00	0.99	1.00	0.98	0.99
		MLP	1.00	1.00	1.00	1.00	1.00	1.00

Table 8. The result of the timeline analysis (D3M).

Log	Model	Classifier	NCD (Benign)			D3M (Malicious)		
			Precision	Recall	F-measure	Precision	Recall	F-measure
1	BoW	SVM	0.54	0.91	0.67	0.71	0.22	0.34
		RF	0.53	0.90	0.67	0.70	0.22	0.34
		MLP	0.54	0.90	0.67	0.68	0.22	0.33
	Doc2vec	SVM	0.92	0.84	0.88	0.85	0.92	0.89
		RF	0.92	0.87	0.90	0.89	0.93	0.91
		MLP	0.92	0.87	0.92	0.89	0.97	0.93
10		SVM	1.00	0.96	0.98	0.96	1.00	0.98
		RF	0.97	0.96	0.96	0.96	0.97	0.96
		MLP	0.99	0.99	0.99	0.99	0.99	0.99

Table 9. The result of the timeline analysis (BOS).

Log	Model	Classifier	NCD (Benign)			BOS (Malicious)		
			Precision	Recall	F-measure	Precision	Recall	F-measure
1	BoW	SVM	0.93	0.99	0.96	0.99	0.92	0.95
		RF	0.93	0.99	0.96	0.99	0.92	0.95
		MLP	0.93	0.99	0.96	0.99	0.92	0.95
	Doc2vec	SVM	0.77	0.96	0.86	0.95	0.71	0.81
		RF	0.74	1.00	0.85	1.00	0.64	0.78
		MLP	0.76	0.97	0.85	0.95	0.69	0.80
10		SVM	0.96	1.00	0.98	0.99	0.96	0.98
		RF	0.79	1.00	0.88	1.00	0.69	0.82
		MLP	0.95	1.00	0.98	1.00	0.95	0.98

6   Discussion

6.1   Accuracy

As the results of the experiments, our method using only proxy server logs could detect malicious communication precisely. Above all, using Doc2vec was effective. Our method could even detect malicious communication from only one line in the 10-fold cross-validation. This is because the Doc2vec captured the characteristic of the one line and constructed an optimum vector space to distinguish malicious communication from benign communication. This means that the URLs in DbD attacks have some differences. Our method divides URLs into words by the delimiters, and Doc2vec illustrates the ratio of the co-occurrence probabilities of the two words within the window size. However, BoW merely illustrates the number of times a word appears in the sentence, and is not effective. Hence, we conclude the differences are the words themselves and the structure. Some previous methods use the structure to detect malicious URLs. The structure is, however, devised by a human. Our method learns the structure automatically, even if a human makes no clear indication.

In the timeline analysis, converting a line into a vector is less effective. In particular, the performance in the BOS are remarkable. This means that the URLs in the C&C traffic are slightly similar to benign URLs. For instance, Emdivi uses standard http protocol and a compromised web site as the C&C server in order to imitate normal http communication. However, converting multiple lines into a vector kept the effectiveness. This is because the Doc2vec captured the multiple lines of URLs include the context, and constructed an optimum vector space to distinguish the context. Thus, our method can capture the characteristic of proxy server logs automatically, and can detect malicious communication precisely.

There are some causes of the false positives and false negatives. The primary cause was the sites which provided web APIs (e.g. Authentication, Streaming). A web API is an application programming interface (API) for either a web server or a web browser. A web API produces interactive communication with many parameters to provide a coating high functionality and convenience. This behavior is similar to Exploit Kits or C&C traffic. The attacker needs many parameters to control victim's computer at his will. Thus, Exploit Kits and C&C traffic have to produce interactive communication with many parameters. The other cause was the sites which provided update programs or pattern files (e.g. Anti Virus Scanner). This behavior is similar to downloading malware and malware infections. We can mitigate these false positives with the whitelist. Besides, some benign traffic was mixed in the malicious traffic. In a sense, these impurities are not the cause. We can enhance purity of the malicious traffic to improve the accuracy.

6.2   Adaptability

Our method can detect DbD attacks and C&C traffic as malicious communication in the same method. All we have to do is input malicious and benign proxy server logs. Our method can detect malicious communication regardless of the attack techniques. No prior knowledge of the attack techniques is required for capturing the characteristic. Our method does not use different detection techniques. If attackers change the attack techniques, our methods learn the characteristic automatically. Besides our method does not require to decide the feature vectors. Hence, our method is adaptable to many attack techniques.

6.3   Durability

Our method learns the difference of normal communication and malicious communication automatically with neural networks. In neural networks, it is difficult to specify what feature of an input data a specific feature map captures. This means that an attacker cannot recognize the features either. We tried some experiments to specify the feature. We conducted the same experiments without some elements (e.g. FQDN, User Argent). However, there was no notable change in the performance. This means that our method does not rely on a specific element. Therefore, an attacker has no effective countermeasure to evade this method. The only option is imitating normal communication completely. Thus, our method is effective and durable in the long term.

6.4   Practical Use

Our method requires a few minutes to construct the language model and the classifier. In this experiment, our method took roughly three minutes on average. The greater the pcap files or the log files to construct the models, the longer the required time. However, we can construct the models in advance. Our method can classify unknown logs with these pre-trained models in a few seconds. Thus, our method can analyze network traffic or proxy server logs in real time.

Many previous methods require monitoring all network traffic. Many organizations, however, do not keep all network traffic because the size is too huge.

Actually, we would have to investigate insufficient information such as proxy server logs. Thus, these methods are not practical. Our method does not require monitoring all network traffic, and only uses malicious and benign proxy server logs.

In this paper, we obtained pseudo proxy server logs from pcap files in the MWS datasets. We can obtain these malicious pcap files easily from the websites such as Malware-Traffic-Analysis.net [30], which disclose malicious traffic data. We can also obtain benign pcap files easily from everywhere. Thus, our method has a few constraints in practical use.

6.5   Ethics

In this paper, we used malicious pcap files and benign pcap files. These files might contain privacy sensitive information such as personal information, email addresses and client's IP addresses. Many previous methods require monitoring all network traffic. Therefore, the possibility of accessing the payloads cannot be denied. The payloads might contain personal information and email addresses. However, our method does not require monitoring all network traffic. Moreover, our method does not require client's IP addresses, and does not require even to distinguish the client's sources.

In practical use, our method uses only pre-trained models to detect malicious communication. The models do not include any payload and logs. Therefore, we can share or disclose the pre-trained model without much resistance.

7   Conclusion

In this paper, we described how to construct a corpus from proxy server logs and applied Doc2vec to learn the difference of normal communication and malicious communication automatically. Then, we proposed the generic detection method using supervised learning models to classify normal communication and malicious communication. Moreover, we implemented our method and evaluated the method with the D3M dataset and the BOS dataset contained in the MWS datasets. As the result, our method can detect DbD attacks and C&C traffic as malicious communication in proxy server logs. We also verified that Doc2vec was effective to analyze proxy server logs. Our method does not rely on attack techniques and does not demand devising feature vectors. Furthermore, our method is adaptable, durable and has a few constraints in practical use.

Applying our method to other datasets is a future work. In this paper, we used the datasets which contains DbD attacks and C&C traffic. We believe our method is effective to other attack techniques too. However, the effectiveness to other attacks has to be verified. It is possible that this good accuracy depended on the datasets, and such accuracy might not survive real applications. We should verify the accuracy in other practical condition too. In this time, we presumed proxy server logs were written in a natural language. We can presume any other logs such as IDS alerts, firewall logs, SIEM (Security Information and Event

Management) events are written in a natural language in the same manner. We believe this would enable to classify the detail automatically.

Acknowledgment. This work was supported by JSPS KAKENHI Grant Number 17K06455.

References

1. Mikolov, T., Sutskever, I., Chen, K., Corrado, G.S., Dean, J.: Distributed representations of words and phrases and their compositionality. In: Advances in Neural Information Processing Systems, pp. 3111–3119 (2013)
2. Wang, K., Stolfo, S.J.: Anomalous payload-based network intrusion detection. In: Jonsson, E., Valdes, A., Almgren, M. (eds.) RAID 2004. LNCS, vol. 3224, pp. 203–222. Springer, Heidelberg (2004). https://doi.org/10.1007/978-3-540-30143-1_11
3. Moore, D., Shannon, C., Brown, D.J., Voelker, G.M., Savage, S.: Inferring internet denial-of-service activity. ACM Trans. Comput. Syst. **24**(2), 115–139 (2006)
4. Bailey, M., Oberheide, J., Andersen, J., Mao, Z.M., Jahanian, F., Nazario, J.: Automated classification and analysis of internet malware. In: Kruegel, C., Lippmann, R., Clark, A. (eds.) RAID 2007. LNCS, vol. 4637, pp. 178–197. Springer, Heidelberg (2007). https://doi.org/10.1007/978-3-540-74320-0_10
5. Song, H., Turner, J.: Toward advocacy-free evaluation of packet classification algorithms. IEEE Trans. Comput. **60**(5), 723–733 (2011)
6. Karagiannis, T., Papagiannaki, K., Faloutsos, M.: Blinc: multilevel traffic classification in the dark. In: Proceedings of the 2005 Conference on Applications, Technologies, Architectures, and Protocols for Computer Communications, pp. 229–240 (2005)
7. Erman, J., Arlitt, M., Mahanti, A.: Traffic classification using clustering algorithms. In: Proceedings of the SIGCOMM Workshop on Mining Network Data, pp. 281–286 (2006)
8. Gu, G., Perdisci, R., Zhang, J., Lee, W.: Botminer: clustering analysis of network traffic for protocol and structure independent Botnet detection. In: Proceedings of the USENIX Security Symposium, vol. 5, pp. 139–154 (2008)
9. Bilge, L., Balzarotti, D., Robertson, W., Kirda, E., Kruegel, C.: Disclosure: detecting Botnet command and control servers through large-scale NetFlow analysis. In: Proceedings of the 28th Annual Computer Security Applications Conference, pp. 129–138 (2012)
10. Antonakakis, M., Perdisci, R., Dagon, D., Lee, W., Feamster, N.: Building a dynamic reputation system for DNS. In: Proceedings of the 19th USENIX Security Symposium (2010)
11. Antonakakis, M., Perdisci, R., Lee, W., Vasiloglou II, N., Dagon, D.: Detecting malware domains at the upper DNS hierarchy. In: Proceedings of the 20th USENIX Security Symposium (2011)
12. Antonakakis, M., Perdisci, R., Nadji, Y., Vasiloglou, N., Abu-Nimeh, S., Lee, W., Dagon, D.: From throw-away traffic to bots: detecting the rise of DGA-based malware. In: Proceedings of the 21th USENIX Security Symposium (2012)
13. Rahbarinia, B., Perdisci, R., Antonakakis, M.: Segugio: efficient behavior-based tracking of new malware-control domains in large ISP networks. In: Proceedings of the 2015 IEEE/IFIP International Conference on Dependable Systems and Networks (2015)

14. Kruegel, C., Vigna, G.: Anomaly detection of webbased attacks. In: Proceedings of the 10th ACM Conference on Computer and Communications Security, pp. 251–261 (2003)

15. Choi, H., Zhu, B.B., Lee, H.: Detecting malicious web links and identifying their attack types. In: Proceedings of the 2nd USENIX Conference on Web Application Development, pp. 1–11 (2011)

16. Ma, J., Saul, L.K., Savage, S., Voelker, G.M.: Learning to detect malicious URLs. ACM Trans. Intell. Syst. Technol. **2**(3) (2011). Article 30

17. Huang, H., Qian, L., Wang, Y.: A SVM-based technique to detect phishing URLs. Inf. Technol. J. **11**(7), 921–925 (2012)

18. Zhao, P., Hoi, S.C.: Cost-sensitive online active learning with application to malicious URL detection. In: Proceedings of the 19th ACM SIGKDD International Conference on Knowledge Discovery and Data Mining, pp. 919–927 (2013)

19. Invernizzi, L., Miskovic, S., Torres, R., Saha, S., Lee, S., Mellia, M., Kruegel, C., Vigna, G.: Nazca: detecting malware distribution in large-scale networks. In: Proceedings of the Network and Distributed System Security Symposium (2014)

20. Nelms, T., Perdisci, R., Antonakakis, M., Ahamad, M.: Webwitness: investigating, categorizing, and mitigating malware download paths. In: Proceedings of the 24th USENIX Security Symposium, pp. 1025–1040 (2015)

21. Bartos, K., Sofka. M.: Optimized invariant representation of network traffic for detecting unseen malware variants. In: Proceedings of the 25th USENIX Security Symposium, pp. 806–822 (2016)

22. Mimura, M., Otsubo, Y., Tanaka, H., Tanaka, H.: A practical experiment of the HTTP-based RAT detection method in proxy server logs. In: Proceedings of the 12th Asia Joint Conference on Information Security (2017)

23. Shibahara, T., Yamanishi, K., Takata, Y., Chiba, D., Akiyama, M., Yagi, T. Ohsita, Y., Murata, M.: Malicious URL sequence detection using event de-noising convolutional neural network. In: Proceedings of the IEEE ICC 2017 Communication and Information Systems Security Symposium (2017)

24. Le, Q., Mikolov, T.: Distributed representations of sentences and documents. In: Proceedings of the 31st International Conference on Machine Learning, pp. 1188–1196 (2014)

25. gensim. https://radimrehurek.com/gensim/

26. scikit-learn. http://scikit-learn.org/

27. Chainer. https://chainer.org/

28. Kingma, D.P., Ba, J.: Adam: a method for stochastic optimization. In: Proceedings of the 3rd International Conference on Learning Representations (2015)

29. Hatada, M., Akiyama, M., Matsuki, T.: Empowering anti-malware research in Japan by sharing the MWS datasets. J. Inf. Process. **23**(5), 579–588 (2015). https://www.jstage.jst.go.jp/article/ipsjjip/23/5/23_579/_article

30. Malware-Traffic-Analysis.net. http://www.malware-traffic-analysis.net/

Secure Random Encryption
for Deduplicated Storage

Jay Dave[1(✉)], Shweta Saharan[1], Parvez Faruki[2], Vijay Laxmi[1],
and Manoj Singh Gaur[3]

[1] Malaviya National Institute of Technology, Jaipur, India
jaydaveadms@gmail.com, shweta.17oct@gmail.com, vlgaur@gmail.com
[2] Government MCA College, Ahmedabad, India
parvezfaruki.kg@gmail.com
[3] Indian Institute of Technology, Jammu, India
gaurms@gmail.com

Abstract. In Storage Services, Deduplication is used to reduce the data
size by eliminating storage of duplicate data. Deduplication is an effective data reduction technique to minimize the storage cost as well as
communication cost. However, Deduplication raises significant security
issues. Malicious users and semi-trusted Storage Server tries to learn the
data outsourced by other users. Encrypting the data at user side before
uploading to Storage Server is essential for protecting outsourced data.
However, conventional deterministic encryption techniques are vulnerable to brute-force attacks and dictionary attacks for predictable files. In
this paper, we propose secure random key based encryption technique
for Deduplicated Storage. In our approach, user encrypts the file with a
randomly chosen key. Random key is encrypted by set of hash values generated from plaintext file. In this way, our approach provides protection
against brute-force attack and dictionary attack. We analyze security of
our approach with theoretical proof and experimental analysis.

1 Introduction

As per the report of International Data Corporation, the digital data size is estimated to reach 40 trillion gigabytes by the end of 2020 [1]. To avoid the burden of
maintaining such huge data size, enterprises are outsourcing the data to storage
servers. Deduplication is one of the most widely used strategies to reduce the
storage cost by eliminating duplicate data storage. When a user uploads a file,
Storage Server checks whether the same file already exist or not. Server stores the
file if the copy of file is not present. It leverages the fact that large data sets often
exhibit high redundancy. Deduplication can be categorized by (1) Granularity
of Deduplication, (2) Locality of Deduplication, (3) Intra-Inter user Deduplication. For granularity perspective, it can be either file-level or block-level [2,5]. In
file-level deduplication, storage is scanned file by file to detect an identical file.
If an identical file exists then, Deduplication process avoids storing duplicate
file. In block-level deduplication, storage is scanned block by block. Block-level

R. K. Shyamasundar et al. (Eds.): ICISS 2017, LNCS 10717, pp. 164–176, 2017.
https://doi.org/10.1007/978-3-319-72598-7_10

deduplication can further be categorized as fixed-block size or variable-block size deduplication [3]. On locality basis, it can be either client-side deduplication or server-side deduplication. In client-side deduplication, the hash of the data is computed at the client-side, and sent to the server for deduplicacy check. If no identical hash is found then the user needs to upload the complete data. Otherwise, the server provides the ownership of the existing data to the user. In server-side deduplication, client sends complete data and server verifies the existence of data before storing. At user-level, Deduplication can be viewed as inter-user or intra-user deduplication. In intra-user view, deduplication is performed on individual user's data. In inter-user view, deduplication is performed on among all users' data at Storage Server.

Deduplication, due to its storage space saving to a large extent, plays a vital role in the low cost remote storage services offered by the providers (e.g. Dropbox and Memopal). Client-side deduplication used by these providers saves both storage space and network bandwidth. However, along with various advantages offered, deduplication raises new vulnerabilities and security concerns. For secure data storage, data needs to be encrypted by the user before uploading. However, when the users encrypt data using their own keys, it results in different ciphertexts for the same data. This conflicts with the inter-user deduplication process. For secure Deduplication, Douceur et al. [4] proposed Convergent Encryption (CE) mechanism. In CE, file is encrypted with Convergent key which is hash of file. Hence, the subsequent uploader is able to compute the encryption key and gets access to convergently encrypted file. However, CE is vulnerable to brute force attack and dictionary attack for predictable files. Moreover, Adversary is able to guess the predictable file, encrypt with convergent key and learn the mapping between plaintext file and ciphertext file. To overcome security weaknesses, Bellare et al. [8] proposed random key based convergent encryption. In this approach, file is encrypted with random key and random key is encrypted with convergent key. This approach provides the protection to ciphertext file, but encryption of key is still vulnerable to brute force attack and dictionary attack. Furthermore, some security approaches for Deduplication has also deployed additional key servers to generate the key. These approaches assume that key server is completely secure. However, it is not practically possible in cyber attack era.

To overcome these security challenges, we propose secure random key based encryption mechanism for Deduplicated Storage. Our contributions are as follows.

- We propose a random key based encryption approach for Deduplication. We describe four basic file storage operations of our approach in detail: (1) Upload File, (2) Download File, (3) Delete File and (4) Update File.
- We evaluate the security of our approach using theoretical proofs and experimental analysis. The evaluation parameters are confidentiality of file, security of key, security against poison attack and integrity of data.

The rest of the paper is organized as follows. In Sect. 2, we discuss research problem in detail. We elaborate system model, threat model and security goals of our research. Section 3 describes our proposed approach in detail. We evaluate security of our approach in Sect. 4. Section 5 describes existing research in Deduplication security. And finally, we conclude our paper.

2   Problem Statement

2.1   System Model

Our system model consists three entities (Fig. 1): User, Storage Server and Storage.

1. User: User has limited computation and storage resources. He outsources the data on Storage Server. He permits Deduplication to minimize communication as well as storage cost. For data security, user encrypts his data with a random key before outsourcing.
2. Storage Server: Storage Server provides four basic file storage functionalities. (a) Upload File, (b) Download File, (c) Delete File, and (d) Update File.
   (a) Upload File: User sends Deduplication identity (Hash of the file) to Storage Server. Storage Server checks whether a copy of the file is present on Storage or not. Our approach supports both intra-user and inter user deduplication.

   If a copy of the file is not present, the Storage Server asks User to upload the file. User encrypts the file with random key, also encrypts the random key and uploads encrypted file along with the encrypted key to Storage Server.

Fig. 1. System model

   If a copy the file is present, the Storage Server sends encrypted key. User decrypts it using the file and store it locally.
   (b) Download File: To download a file, User sends Deduplication identity to Storage Server. Storage Server responds with the encrypted file. User decrypts it with the secret key.
   (c) Delete File: User sends Deduplication identity to delete the file. Storage Server verifies ownership of requesting user. If User is an owner of the file, then Storage Server removes entry of the User from file's ownership list.

(d) Update File: In this operation, Storage Server performs "Delete" operation for old file and "Upload" operation for updated file.

3. Storage: This physical storage environment performs (a) Read, (b) Write, (c) Re-write, (d) Erase operations.

2.2 Threat Model

In this paper, we consider two adversaries: semi-trusted Storage Server and malicious User.

– Semi-trusted Storage Server: Storage Server honestly performs file operations requested by User. However, Storage Server tries to learn the information about outsourced files and keys. Storage Server always has access to the encrypted file and encrypted key. Server tries to learn the predictable file and the key by performing dictionary attack. In this attack, server may know some portion of file and tries to guess remaining portion of file.

– Malicious User: Major objective of malicious user is to break the secrecy of encrypted key. He may have knowledge about some portion of file. He use this knowledge to perform dictionary attack for breaking the secrecy of encrypted key/encrypted file.

Secondly, malicious user can perform poison attack by uploading invalid file along with Deduplication identity of valid file. For example, A malicious user Tom uploads ciphertext C_A of invalid file A along with Deduplication identity (Hash(B)) of file B. Notice that, Storage Server is not able to detect such inconsistency, because C_A is encrypted using the key randomly chosen by uploader. When an uploader Bob wants to upload the file B, he sends Hash(B) to Storage Server and he gets access to invalid file C_A.

2.3 Security Goals

Our random key based encryption mechanism achieves the following security goals:

1. Confidentiality: The first security goal of this paper is to provide confidentiality of outsourced files and secret keys. Adversary may have knowledge about some portion of the file. He can perform dictionary attack using such knowledge. Our goal is to prevent such adversary to learn the file or the secret key by performing dictionary attack.

2. Security against poison attack: In our approach, Storage Server is able to detect inconsistency between Deduplication identity and file. In other words, Storage Server is able to differentiate valid and invalid file which are mapped to a particular Deduplication identity. Storage Server gets knowledge about such inconsistency from feedback of file uploaders.

3. Integrity: Data may be accidentally or intentionally modified at Storage or communication network. In our approach, the receiver should be able to detect the unintentional modification in received data and report it to the sender.

3   Proposed Encryption Scheme

In this section, we discuss our approach of random encryption for Deduplicated storage. Our approach provides following basic operations on storage (1) Upload File, (2) Download File, (3) Delete File, and (4) Update File.

1. **Upload File:** Upload operation can be viewed in two categories: (1) First time File Upload, (2) Subsequent File Upload. When a user wants to upload a file, he sends request with hash value of file to Storage Server. In our approach, we use hash of file as Deduplication identity (DedupID). We recommend SHA-512 as hash function. Storage Server verifies the existence of file on storage using this Deduplication identity as discussed in *VerifyDedup* procedure of Algorithm 1.

   - If a duplicate copy of the file is not present on Storage, the Storage Server responds "No" to the requesting user. User as a first time file uploader generates a random key RK and encrypts the file using it. We recommend AES-256 to encrypt the file. User splits file into 512 bits blocks. We consider the file as a matrix of blocks. User extracts n × n sub-matrix from M_{File}, where n is $\sqrt{no.of blocks}$. He computes hash of each row of matrix $B_i = \text{Hash}(M_{File}[i][1] \parallel M_{File}[i][1] \ldots \parallel M_{File}[i][n])$. He encrypts RK with B_is. User sends encrypted file (C_{File}) and encrypted key (C_{RK}) to Storage Server. Storage Server verifies the integrity of received data using hash comparison and stores data to Storage as discussed in Algorithm 1.
   - Otherwise, Storage Server responds with C_{RK} and Hash(C_{File}). User as a subsequent uploader computes B_is and decrypts the encrypted key. To verify the integrity of deduplicated file, User encrypts the file with the key RK, compute the hash value of encrypted file and compare it with received Hash(C_{File}).

Algorithm 1. Upload File

1: **procedure** USER: UPLOAD(File)
2:     DedupID ← Hash(File)
3:     {Blocks} ← Split(File)
4:     n ← $\sqrt{|\{Blocks\}|}$
5:     M_{File} ← $Matrix(\{Blocks\}_{n \times n})$
6:     **for** i=1 to n **do**
7:         B_i ← Hash($M_{File}[i][1] \parallel M_{File}[i][1] ... \parallel M_{File}[i][n]$)
8:     **if** VerifyDedup(DedupID) = TRUE **then**
9:         DecryptKey(C_{RK}, Hash(C_{File}))
10:     **else**
11:         RK $\xleftarrow{\$}$ KeyGen(1^λ)
12:         C_{File} ← Encrypt(RK, File)
13:         C_{RK} ← RK ⊕ B_1 ⊕ B_2 ... ⊕ B_n
14:         SSUpload(C_{File}, C_{RK}, Hash($C_{File} \parallel C_{RK}$))
15: **procedure**   USER: DECRYPTKEY(((C_{RK},   Hash(C_{File})),
        Hash($C_{RK} \parallel$Hash(C_{File}))))
16:     **if** Hash($C_{RK} \parallel$Hash(C_{File}))≠ ReceivedHash **then**
17:         Return "False"
18:     RK ← C_{RK} ⊕ B_1 ⊕ B_2 ... ⊕ B_n
19:     C_{File} ← Encrypt(RK, File)
20:     **if** Hash(C_{File}) ≠ ReceivedHash **then**
21:         Return "False"
22:     **else**
23:         Return "True"
24: **procedure** STORAGE SERVER: SSUPLOAD(C_{File}, C_{RK}, Hash($C_{File} \parallel C_{RK}$))
25:     **if** Hash($C_{File} \parallel C_{RK}$) ≠ ReceivedHash **then**
26:         Return "False"
27:     **else**
28:         Store(C_{File}, C_{RK}, Hash($C_{File} \parallel C_{RK}$))
29: **procedure** STORAGE SERVER: VERIFYDEDUP(DedupID)
30:     **if** DedupID ∈ FileList **then**
31:         Return ((C_{RK}, Hash(C_{File})),Hash($C_{RK} \parallel$Hash(C_{File})))
32:     **else**
33:         Return "No"

2. **Download File:** User sends DedupID for downloading a file. Storage Server verifies ownership of requesting user by checking file's ownership list. If requesting user is not the file owner, then Storage Server responds "False". Otherwise, Storage Server sends C_{File}, Hash(C_{File}) to user. User verifies the integrity of received data by comparing hash value and he decrypt C_{File}.

Algorithm 2. Download File

1: **procedure** USER: DOWNLOAD(File)
2:      C_{File}, Hash(C_{File}) ← SSDownload(DedupID)
3:      **if** Hash(C_{File}) ≠ ReceivedHash **then**
4:          Return "False"
5:      **else**
6:          File ← Decrypt(RK, C_{File})
7: **procedure** STORAGE SERVER: SSDOWNLOAD(DedupID)
8:      **if** User ∈ Ownershiplist(DedupID) **then**
9:          Return (C_{File}, Hash(C_{File}))
10:     **else**
11:         Return "False"

3. **Delete File:** User sends DedupID for deleting a file. Storage Server verifies ownership of requesting user by checking file's ownership list. If requesting user is the file owner, then Storage Server removes his entry from file's ownership list. If file's ownership list is empty, then Storage Server erases C_{File} and C_{RK} from Storage.

Algorithm 3. Delete File

1: **procedure** USER: CDELETE(File)
2:      SSDelete(DedupID)
3: **procedure** STORAGE SERVER: SSDELETE(DedupID)
4:      **if** DedupTag ∈ Ownershiplist(DedupTag) **then**
5:          Ownershiplist(DedupID) = Ownershiplist(DedupID) - Requester
6:          **if** Ownershiplist(DedupID) = ϕ **then**
7:              Erase C_{File}, C_{RK}, $Hash(F)$, $Hash(C_{File})$
8:      **else**
9:          Return "False"

4. **Update File:** Update operation is the combination of Delete and Upload operation. When a user request to update a file, Storage Server performs delete operation (Algorithm 3) for old file and upload operation (Algorithm 1) for updated file.

4   Security Analysis

In this section, we discuss security analysis of our proposed approach. Our security analysis proves Confidentiality, security against Poison attack and Integrity of the proposed approach.

4.1   Confidentiality

Confidentiality of file: In our system model, the Storage Server and Users are not trusted entities. Hence, outsourced files and keys should be kept secret from unauthorized Users as well as from Storage Server.

For confidentiality of file, first time file uploader encrypts the file with a secret random key. Random key based encryption ensures that the ciphertext of two predictable files is indistinguishable. Our encryption mechanism guarantees that outsourced files are secure against dictionary attack. We prove confidentiality of file in our proposed approach in Theorem 1.

Theorem 1. *If file is encrypted with a random key, then file is secure against dictionary attack.*

Proof. We use contrapositive method to prove this theorem. Contrapositive statement of this theorem is as follows:

File is vulnerable to dictionary attack ⇒ File is not encrypted with a

random key.

(1.1)

In dictionary attack, Adversary(Adv) tries to map the ciphertext with plaintext. He guesses the key, encrypts the file and compares with known ciphertext files. Adv may know some portion of plaintext file. He uses this knowledge to compute the key. Adv guesses the unknown portion of file, computes the key, compares generated ciphertext file with known ciphertext files.

It implies that encryption key depends on the file. Adv is able to compute the key using knowledge of plaintext file. Hence, we can say that file is encrypted with a deterministic key which depends on plaintext file. It implies that "File is vulnerable to dictionary attack ⇒ File is not encrypted with a random key".

This contrapositive statement is logically same as "If file is encrypted with a random key, then file is secure against dictionary attack".   □

Confidentiality of Encryption Key: In our threat model, we consider malicious User and malicious Storage Server which attempts to learn the secret key. Secret keys are either encrypted by single hash value or stored at key server in conventional approaches [4,8]. To improve confidentiality level, we encrypt the secret key with multiple hash values, B_1, B_2, ..., B_n computed as described in Algorithm 1. Hence, if a user has complete file, then only he can decrypt the key. Adversary tries to decrypt the key using knowledge about the predictable file.

We assume that the adversary has knowledge about x% of file blocks in file's matrix M_{File}. Hence, Number of unknown blocks = $(100 - x)\% \times M_{File}$. Suppose t attempts are to be performed to guess an unknown block and place it at correct position in M_{File}. If adversary's winning probability is p, then he needs to perform $(1 - p)t$ attempts for successfully guess and place a block.

$$No.\, of\, attempts\, to\, guess\, unknown\, blocks\, = \,\{\frac{(100-x)}{100} \times M_{File}\} \times (1-p)t$$

(2.1)

In conventional MLE-RCE [8], adversary computes single hash value to decrypt the key. Thus, adversary needs to compute the equal number of hash values as number of attempts. In each attempt, adversary computes a hash value and tries to decrypt the key.

In our approach, adversary has to compute n number of hash values (B_1, $B_2, ..., B_n$) to decrypt the key in each attempt. Hence, number of hash operations to get success can be calculated as follows.

$$No.\,of\,hash\,operations\,to\,decrypt\,key = \{\frac{(100-x)}{100} \times M_{File}\} \times (1-p)t \times n \tag{2.2}$$

We analyze MLE-RCE [8] and our scheme with experiments on a range of file sizes as shown in Fig. 2. We assume that 70% of file blocks are known to adversary and he has to guess 30% of blocks. In Fig. 2, we compute adversary's number of attempts to successfully decrypt the file with winning probability 0.5 ($P_{Adv} = 0.5$). We also perform these experiments with $P_{Adv} = 0.6$ and 0.7. From these experimental results, we can say that adversary has to perform significantly large number of attempts for breaking the secrecy of key in our approach as compared to MLE-RCE.

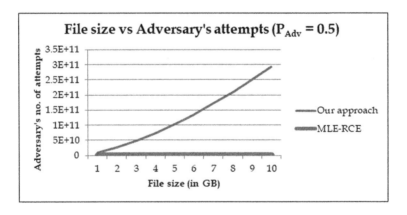

Fig. 2. File size vs Adversary's attempts ($P_{Adv} = 0.5$)

4.2   Security Against Poison Attack

A malicious user can deviate the Deduplication process by performing Poison attack. He upload Deduplication identity of file A (DedupID(A) = Hash(A)) with invalid file C_B. Moreover, Storage Server is not able to map Deduplication ID with randomly encrypted file.

When a subsequent uploader wants to upload file A, he sends DedupID(A) to Storage Server. Storage Server responds with encrypted key C_{RK} and Hash(C_B). Subsequent uploader decrypts C_{RK} and encrypts file A. He finds inconsistency between hash of encrypted file A and received hash value. He reports Storage Server about this inconsistency and request for a new upload. Storage Server allows to upload C_A. Moreover, when a subsequent uploaders requests to upload file A, Storage Server sends C_{RK}, hash of C_A and hash of C_B. Storage server may get knowledge about invalid ciphertext by gathering feedback from subsequent uploaders. In this way, our approach provides security against Poison attack.

4.3   Integrity

Our threat model considers the active attacker who can modify the data at the time of data transfer. Hence, receiving entity may receive tampered data in place of original data. On other hand, data might be accidentally modified during transmission on network.

To detect such unintended data modification, Sender sends hash value Hash(D) along with the data D. Receiver receives D and computes Hash(D). Receiver verifies integrity by comparing computed hash value with received hash value. If computed hash value is not equal to received hash value, the receiver drops the received data.

5   Related Work

For security in Deduplication, Douceur et al. [4] proposed an encryption mechanism "Convergent Encryption" (CE). In CE, file is encrypted with the convergent key which is a hash value of file. Hence, any user who is having the file is able to compute convergent key. However, CE mechanism is vulnerable to dictionary attacks for predictable files [5]. In other words, CE is able to provide security to unpredictable files only. CE has been adopted by many proposed approaches [6,7]. Bellare et al. [8] formalized convergent encryption mechanism. They proposed a random key based message locked encryption (RCE-MLE). In RCE approach, file is encrypted with random key and random key is encrypted with convergent key (hash value of file). In this way, file is secure against dictionary attacks, but encryption of random key is still vulnerable to dictionary attack for predictable files [5]. In [9,10], authors proposed variants of MLE.

Chen et al. [13] proposed Block level Message Locked Encryption (BL-MLE) which allows convergent encryption based block level Deduplication. Xu et al. [14] proposed a mechanism in which file is encrypted with random key and random key is encrypted with file. To improve security level, Puzio et al. [12] employed additional encryption server which re-encrypts each file. In this approach, Deduplication is performed at server side. Li et al. [11] proposed key management mechanism using number of distributed servers.

Liu et al. [15] proposed a scheme which is secure against dictionary attack without any additional servers. However, this approach requires previous uploaders to be online for key exchange. Shah et al. [16] proposed server side Deduplication with the additional key server. The additional key server is appointed to generate the key for a file. User encrypts the file using the key obtained by key server. Zhou et al. [17] proposed blind key exchange between User and Key server. Kaaniche et al. [18] proposed secure deduplication along with strong Proof of Ownership using Merkle Hash Tree. In this approach, User sends complete Merkle Hash Tree as Deduplication identity. However, this approach raises significant communication overhead due to transmission of complete Merkle Hash Tree. Armknecht et al. [19] proposed the Deduplication approach to provide transparency in Deduplication ratio on the Storage server. Hur et al. [20] proposed security against dynamic ownership modification on outsourced files.

To protect the Deduplication system from malicious access, Halevi et al. [21] proposed proof of ownership (PoW) approach for Deduplication. In this approach, Storage Server challenges uploader to prove the ownership of file. These challenges are based on Merkle Hash Tree. Di et al. [22] proposed a PoW approach in which challenges are based on random bits of the file. Li et al. [23] proposed PoW solutions based on Merkle hash tree using third party called Auditor. We can apply secure deduplication on Android malware detection databases [24–28] and Database As A Service model [29].

6 Conclusion and Future Work

In this paper, we discuss security challenges of Deduplicated Storage such as file confidentiality, key security and Poison attack. We observe that deterministic key based encryption mechanism (e.g. CE and MLE) are vulnerable to brute force attack and dictionary attacks for predictable files. We propose secure random key based encryption approach for Deduplicated Storage. We deploy random key based encryption at user side before uploading file. For permitting Deduplication, random key is encrypted by set of hash values computed from the plaintext file. Hence, subsequent uploader of the file is also able to decrypt the random key. Our approach provides confidentiality of file and security of key without any additional key servers. We analyze security of our approach with theoretical proof of file confidentiality and experimental analysis of random key security. As part of future work, we plan to implement the proposed approach with Cloud Storage Servers and study analytical comparison with other security techniques.

References

1. Gantz, J., Reinsel, D.: The digital universe in 2020: Big data, bigger digital shadows, and biggest growth in the far east. IDC iView: IDC Analyze the future 2007, pp. 1–16 (2012)
2. Malhotra, J., Bakal, J.: A survey and comparative study of data deduplication techniques. In: 2015 International Conference on Pervasive Computing (ICPC), pp. 1–5. IEEE, January 2015
3. Nam, Y., Lu, G., Park, N., Xiao, W., Du, D.H.: Chunk fragmentation level: an effective indicator for read performance degradation in deduplication storage. In: 2011 IEEE 13th International Conference on High Performance Computing and Communications (HPCC), pp. 581–586. IEEE, September 2011

4. Douceur, J.R., Adya, A., Bolosky, W.J., Simon, P., Theimer, M.: Reclaiming space from duplicate files in a serverless distributed file system. In: 2002 Proceedings of 22nd International Conference on Distributed Computing Systems, pp. 617–624. IEEE (2002)

5. Harnik, D., Pinkas, B., Shulman-Peleg, A.: Side channels in cloud services: deduplication in cloud storage. IEEE Secur. Priv. **8**(6), 40–47 (2010)

6. Anderson, P., Zhang, L.: Fast and secure laptop backups with encrypted deduplication. In: LISA, December 2010

7. Wilcox-O'Hearn, Z., Warner, B.: Tahoe: the least-authority filesystem. In: Proceedings of the 4th ACM international workshop on Storage security and survivability, pp. 21–26. ACM, October 2008

8. Bellare, M., Keelveedhi, S., Ristenpart, T.: Message-locked encryption and secure deduplication. In: Johansson, T., Nguyen, P.Q. (eds.) EUROCRYPT 2013. LNCS, vol. 7881, pp. 296–312. Springer, Heidelberg (2013). https://doi.org/10.1007/978-3-642-38348-9_18

9. Abadi, M., Boneh, D., Mironov, I., Raghunathan, A., Segev, G.: Message-locked encryption for lock-dependent messages. In: Canetti, R., Garay, J.A. (eds.) CRYPTO 2013. LNCS, vol. 8042, pp. 374–391. Springer, Heidelberg (2013). https://doi.org/10.1007/978-3-642-40041-4_21

10. Stanek, J., Sorniotti, A., Androulaki, E., Kencl, L.: A secure data deduplication scheme for cloud storage. In: Christin, N., Safavi-Naini, R. (eds.) FC 2014. LNCS, vol. 8437, pp. 99–118. Springer, Heidelberg (2014). https://doi.org/10.1007/978-3-662-45472-5_8

11. Li, J., Chen, X., Li, M., Li, J., Lee, P.P., Lou, W.: Secure deduplication with efficient and reliable convergent key management. IEEE Trans. Parallel Distrib. Syst. **25**(6), 1615–1625 (2014)

12. Puzio, P., Molva, R., Onen, M., Loureiro, S.: ClouDedup: Secure deduplication with encrypted data for cloud storage. In: 2013 IEEE 5th International Conference on Cloud Computing Technology and Science (CloudCom), vol. 1, pp. 363–370. IEEE December 2013

13. Chen, R., Mu, Y., Yang, G., Guo, F.: BL-MLE: block-level message-locked encryption for secure large file deduplication. IEEE Trans. Inf. Forensics Secur. **10**(12), 2643–2652 (2015)

14. Xu, J., Chang, E.C., Zhou, J.: Weak leakage-resilient client-side deduplication of encrypted data in cloud storage. In: Proceedings of the 8th ACM SIGSAC Symposium on Information, Computer and Communications Security, pp. 195–206. ACM, May 2013

15. Liu, J., Asokan, N., Pinkas, B.: Secure deduplication of encrypted data without additional independent servers. In: Proceedings of the 22nd ACM SIGSAC Conference on Computer and Communications Security, pp. 874–885. ACM October 2015

16. Shah, P., So, W.: Lamassu: storage-efficient host-side encryption. In: USENIX Annual Technical Conference, pp. 333–345, July 2015

17. Zhou, Y., Feng, D., Xia, W., Fu, M., Huang, F., Zhang, Y., Li, C.: SecDep: a user-aware efficient fine-grained secure deduplication scheme with multi-level key management. In: 2015 31st Symposium on Mass Storage Systems and Technologies (MSST), pp. 1–14. IEEE, May 2015

18. Kaaniche, N., Laurent, M.: A secure client side deduplication scheme in cloud storage environments. In: 2014 6th International Conference on New Technologies, Mobility and Security (NTMS), pp. 1–7. IEEE, March 2014

19. Armknecht, F., Bohli, J.M., Karame, G.O., Youssef, F.: Transparent data dedu-plication in the cloud. In: Proceedings of the 22nd ACM SIGSAC Conference on Computer and Communications Security, pp. 886–900. ACM October 2015

20. Hur, J., Koo, D., Shin, Y., Kang, K.: Secure data deduplication with dynamic ownership management in cloud storage. IEEE Trans. Knowl. Data Eng. **28**(11), 3113–3125 (2016)

21. Halevi, S., Harnik, D., Pinkas, B., Shulman-Peleg, A.: Proofs of ownership in remote storage systems. In: Proceedings of the 18th ACM conference on Computer and communications security, pp. 491–500. ACM, October 2011

22. Di Pietro, R., Sorniotti, A.: Boosting efficiency and security in proof of ownership for deduplication. In: Proceedings of the 7th ACM Symposium on Information, Computer and Communications Security, pp. 81–82. ACM May 2012

23. Li, J., Li, J., Xie, D., Cai, Z.: Secure auditing and deduplicating data in cloud. IEEE Trans. Comput. **65**(8), 2386–2396 (2016)

24. Faruki, P., Bhandari, S., Laxmi, V., Gaur, M., Conti, M.: DroidAnalyst: synergic app framework for static and dynamic app analysis. In: Abielmona, R., Falcon, R., Zincir-Heywood, N., Abbass, H.A. (eds.) Recent Advances in Computational Intelligence in Defense and Security. SCI, vol. 621, pp. 519–552. Springer, Cham (2016). https://doi.org/10.1007/978-3-319-26450-9_20

25. Faruki, P., Laxmi, V., Gaur, M.S., Vinod, P.: Behavioural detection with API call-grams to identify malicious PE files. In: Proceedings of the First International Conference on Security of Internet of Things, pp. 85–91. ACM, August 2012

26. Faruki, P., Laxmi, V., Ganmoor, V., Gaur, M.S., Bharmal, A.: Droidolytics: robust feature signature for repackaged android apps on official and third party android markets. In: 2013 2nd International Conference on Advanced Computing, Network-ing and Security (ADCONS), pp. 247–252. IEEE, December 2013

27. Sinha, L., Bhandari, S., Faruki, P., Gaur, M.S., Laxmi, V., Conti, M.: Flowmine: Android app analysis via data flow. In: 2016 13th IEEE Annual Consumer Com-munications & Networking Conference (CCNC), pp. 435–441. IEEE, January 2016

28. Faruki, P., Kumar, V., B., A., Gaur, M.S., Laxmi, V., Conti, M.: Platform neutral sandbox for analyzing malware and resource hogger apps. In: Tian, J., Jing, J., Srivatsa, M. (eds.) SecureComm 2014. LNICSSITE, vol. 152, pp. 556–560. Springer, Cham (2015). https://doi.org/10.1007/978-3-319-23829-6_43

29. Dave, J., Das, M.L.: Securing SQL with access control for database as a service model. In: Proceedings of the Second International Conference on Information and Communication Technology for Competitive Strategies, p. 104. ACM, March 2016

Security Analysis

On Automated Detection of Multi-Protocol Attacks Using AVISPA

Varun Garg and Anish Mathuria[✉]

DAIICT, Gandhinagar, India
{201301147,anish_mathuria}@daiict.ac.in

Abstract. AVISPA is a well-known automated tool for analysing and verifying security protocols. Many researchers have used AVISPA to find attacks against individual protocols. Multi-protocol attacks use a combination of messages from different protocols to defeat the security objectives of one or more protocols. To our knowledge, multi-protocol analysis using AVISPA has not been investigated before. We describe how to carry out multi-protocol analysis using AVISPA and present several new attacks against combinations of protocols from a previous case study.

Keywords: Security protocols · Automated verification
Protocol attacks

1 Introduction

Security protocols for authentication and key establishment are usually simple to describe, yet notoriously difficult to reason about. Attacks involving combinations of protocols are called multi-protocol attacks. There are many examples of multi-protocol attacks in the literature. Foss [2] demonstrated a multi-protocol attack against a provably secure protocol.

Formal methods have proved quite useful in uncovering flaws in incorrectly designed security protocols. There are many tools available that can analyse and find attacks against protocols, such as AVISPA [3], Scyther [4] and ProVerif [6]. The Scyther tool has the capability of finding multi-protocol attacks [4,5]. To our knowledge, there are no previous studies concerning AVISPA's [3] capability to detect multi-protocol attacks.

In this paper, we carry out analyses of combinations of selected protocols using AVISPA. We demonstrate AVISPA's capabilities and limitations with respect to multi-protocol attacks. As a case study, we target a selected set of protocols against which several multi-protocol attacks were reported earlier [1]. Apart from confirming the known multi-protocol attacks, we found several new multi-protocol attacks using AVISPA.

In order to explain our approach to multi-protocol analysis we modify slightly two example protocols from [7]. In Protocol 1 below, A sends a secret s to B, encrypted using a key K_{AB} known only to A and B.

© Springer International Publishing AG 2017
R. K. Shyamasundar et al. (Eds.): ICISS 2017, LNCS 10717, pp. 179–193, 2017.
https://doi.org/10.1007/978-3-319-72598-7_11

---

1. $A \rightarrow B : \{s\}_{K_{AB}}$

Protocol 1: $\pi 1$

In Protocol 2 below, A sends an encrypted nonce N_A to B. B then sends the decrypted nonce back to A to authenticate itself. We use the notations given in Table 1 throughout this paper.

---

1. $A \rightarrow B : \{N_A\}_{K_{AB}}$
2. $B \rightarrow A : N_A$

Protocol 2: $\pi 2$

Table 1. Notations

Notation	Meaning
X	Identifier for entity X
S	A trusted third party
Spy(X)	An intruder impersonating X
$\{M\}_K$	Message M encrypted with a symmetric key K
N_X	Nonce N generated by X
K_{XY}	Symmetric key shared by X and Y
$N_{X_{\pi i}}$	Nonce N generated by X for use in protocol i
$K_{XY_{\pi i}}$	Symmetric key between X and Y used in protocol i
$\pi i : k, Sj$	Message belonging to step k of session j of protocol i

Attack 1 shows that when the two protocols are used together the attacker can learn the secret s which A believes is shared only with B. The attack relies on the assumption that both the protocols use the same symmetric key K_{AB}.

Note that each of the protocols $\pi 1$ and $\pi 2$ has a vulnerability. An intruder can attack protocol $\pi 1$ by replaying a message from an old run. The protocol $\pi 2$ is susceptible to another form of replay attack, where the intruder in a parallel session sends the message it receives from alice back to alice while impersonating bob. Alice would decrypt the message and return the nonce to the intruder impersonating bob. The intruder can then send the decrypted nonce back to alice and authenticate itself as bob to alice. We emphasize that Attack 1 is orthogonal to the previous attacks and thus it is of independent interest.

The rest of the paper is organized as follows. In Sect. 2, we show how the protocol $\pi 2$ can be formally analysed using AVISPA. In Sect. 3, we demonstrate

$$\pi 1 : 1, S1 : A \rightarrow Spy(B) : \{s\}_{K_{AB}}$$
$$\pi 2 : 1, S1 : Spy(A) \rightarrow B : \{s\}_{K_{AB}}$$
$$\pi 2 : 2, S1 : B \rightarrow Spy(A) : s$$

Attack 1: Multi-protocol attack on $\pi 1$ and $\pi 2$

the multi-protocol attack on $\pi 1$ and $\pi 2$ using AVISPA. Section 4 shows the results of the case study and describes the new multi-protocol attacks discovered using AVISPA. Section 5 concludes the paper.

2 Modeling Example: The Single Protocol Case

In this section, we apply AVISPA to our example protocol π_2. We specify the protocol using HLPSL and demonstrate the effectiveness of AVISPA by finding an attack on the protocol.

```
role alice(A, B : agent,
    Kab : symmetric_key,
    SND, RCV : channel(dy))
played_by A
def=
local State : nat,
    Na : text
    init State := 0
    transition
    1. State = 0 /\ RCV(start) =|>
     State' := 2 /\ Na' := new()
              /\ SND({Na'}_Kab)
    2. State = 2 /\ RCV(Na) =|>
     State' := 4 /\ request(A, B, alice_bob_na, Na)
end role
```

Listing 1.1. Role Alice $\pi 2$

Listing 1.1 shows the HLPSL code for agent A. The role alice contains the steps and events which emulate principal A's behaviour in protocol $\pi 2$. A role is similar to a function and its arguments provide the initial information any role requires to execute the protocol such as pre-established keys. Here, the role alice receives the channel information, its symmetric key with bob and all the principals present in the protocol via arguments. The notations SND and RCV denote the channels for sending and receiving messages respectively. The local variable State is a natural number which is used to keep track of where the protocol execution has reached and which message is to be sent next. The local variable Na is a nonce of type text.

A primed variable indicates that the role is expecting a new value for that variable. Whenever a variable is initialized or a new value for one is received, that variable is primed. In transition 1, when nonce Na receives its initial value via the new() function a primed variable notation is used. The primed notation is also used for the remainder of the transition. In transition 2, the unprimed variable is used as the value of Na is already known and the protocol requires the value of Na to be same in order to successfully authenticate principal B to A.

The code uses two functions, request() and witness(), to specify the authentication goal. The request function means that agent A accepts the value Na and counts on the assurance that agent B (sender of Na) exists and agrees with alice on that value. To complete the authentication goal, it is required for principal B to perform the witness function. There can be many authentication instances in a protocol and each is given its own name as per a basic convention, name of role requesting, name of role witnessing, and name of variable used for authentication. Here alice is requesting authentication and bob is witnessing the same upon variable Na. So the name alice_bob_na is used to identify that particular authentication goal. The code for agent bob is given below.

```
role bob(A, B : agent,
    Kab : symmetric_key,
    SND, RCV : channel(dy))
played_by B
def=
local State : nat,
    Na : text
    init State := 1
    transition
    1. State = 1 /\ RCV({Na'}_Kab) =|>
    State' := 3 /\ SND(Na')
            /\ witness(B, A, alice_bob_na, Na')
end role
```

Listing 1.2. Role Bob $\pi2$

Here agent B is asserting that it wants to be agent A's peer and is sending the value Na for authentication (witness role).

The code to initiate the protocol is specified by the session role. In this role, the channels are declared and all the roles are sent their arguments. A composition means that all the function calls which are specified under it will happen together. So alice and bob receive their required values at the same time. The role containing the event start is where the execution starts.

```
role session(A, B : agent,
    Kab :symmetric_key)
def=
local SA, SB, RA, RB : channel(dy)
composition
alice(A, B, Kab, SA, RA) /\ bob(A, B, Kab, SB, RB)
end role
```

Listing 1.3. Role Session $\pi2$

The role environment is where all the variables and constants are set up and the intruder knowledge is specified. As the channels used are Dolev-Yao channels [8], the intruder has access to all the messages that are exchanged between the honest principals. The intruder's knowledge before the protocol is executed is specified here. A composition of sessions specifies how the protocol is to be executed by AVISPA. For example, one can specify another principal to play the role of the initiator. Here, an additional session has been specified where principal B can play the role of an initiator and A plays the role of a responder.

```
role environment()
def=
const a, b:agent,
    kab : symmetric_key,
    alice_bob_na : protocol_id
    intruder_knowledge={a,b}
    composition
    session(a,b,kab)
   /\session(b,a,kab)
end role
```

Listing 1.4. Role Environment $\pi2$

After the environment role, the goals are specified. In the goal section, the authentication goal is specified. The AVISPA backends try to find attack sequences where these goals are violated.

```
goal
authentication_on alice_bob_na
end goal
```

Listing 1.5. Goals $\pi2$

The protocol $\pi2$ script when analysed by the Cl-AtSE backend shows a replay attack.

```
ATTACK TRACE
 i -> (b,6):   start
 (b,6) -> i:   {n7(Na)}_kab              *

 i -> (a,3):   start
 (a,3) -> i:   {n1(Na)}_kab

 i -> (a,7):   {n1(Na)}_kab
 (a,7) -> i:   n1(Na) & Witness(a,b,alice_bob_na,n1(Na));

 i -> (a,3):   n1(Na)
 (a,3) -> i:   () & Request(a,b,alice_bob_na,n1(Na));
```

Listing 1.6. Attack Trace $\pi2$

In general, redundant messages may be present in the attack traces generated by AVISPA. For example, the starred message shown in listing 1.6 is redundant.

The (agent, number) notations signifies which agent is sending or receiving the message and which session that agent belongs to. In this example, due to the presence of parallel sessions where either agent is the initiator, alice has two numbers. Alice with the numeral 3 is the session where it is the initiator and alice with number 7 is the responder. These numerals are assigned without any ground rules to differentiate between agents belonging to multiple sessions. The attack sequence translated into the Alice-Bob notation is given below. From the above sequence it can be noticed how a replay attack can be used to subvert the protocol $\pi2$. Here, the intruder in a parallel session sends the message it intercepts from alice to alice again while impersonating bob. Then alice returns the decrypted nonce to the intruder. The intruder can then send the decrypted nonce back to alice and therefore is able to authenticate as bob to alice, even though bob is not present on the network.

$\pi2 : 1, S1 \quad A \rightarrow Spy(B) : \{N_A\}_{K_{AB}}$

$\pi2 : 1, S2 \quad Spy(B) \rightarrow A : \{N_A\}_{K_{AB}}$

$\pi2 : 2, S2 \quad A \rightarrow Spy(B) : N_A$

$\pi2 : 2, S1 \quad Spy(B) \rightarrow A : N_A$

Attack 2: Attack on $\pi2$

3   Modeling Example: The Multi-protocol Case

We now write the HLPSL code for the case where protocols $\pi1$ and $\pi2$ are used together. Listing 1.7 shows the code for role alice in protocol $\pi1$.

```
role alice(A, B : agent,
    Kab : symmetric_key,
    SND, RCV : channel(dy))
played_by A
def=
local State : nat,
    S : text
    init State := 0
    transition
    1. State = 0 /\ RCV(start) =|>
      State' := 2 /\ S' := new()
              /\ SND({S'}_Kab)
              /\ secret(S', secretS, {A,B})
end role
```

Listing 1.7. Role Alice $\pi1$

The code uses a function secret() to specify that variable S is a secret between principals A and B.

For the multi-protocol analysis, the scripts of protocols $\pi 1$ and $\pi 2$ are combined into one file. The variables in each script are modified so that each protocol has its own individual copy of local variables such as nonces, state variables, keys or substitutions for unknown strings. In the code for role alice below, there are two state variables State1 and State2. These are used to keep track of protocols $\pi 1$ and $\pi 2$, respectively. As a convention, the state variables have values that belong to different numeral groups to avoid confusion. State1 uses only even numbers and State2 uses only odd numbers.

```
role alice(A, B : agent,
    Kab : symmetric_key,
    SND, RCV : channel(dy))
played_by A
def=
local State1, State2 : nat,
    Na, S: text
    init State1 :=0 /\ State2 := 1
    transition
    1. State1 = 0 /\ RCV(start) =|>
      State1' := 2 /\ S' := new()
              /\ SND({S'}_Kab)
              /\ secret(S', secretS, {A,B})
    2. State2 = 1 /\ RCV(start) =|>
      State2' := 3 /\ Na' := new()
              /\ SND({Na'}_Kab)
    3. State2 = 3 /\ RCV(Na) =|>
      State2' := 5 /\ request(A, B, alice_bob_na, Na)
end role
```

Listing 1.8. Role Alice $\pi 1 + \pi 2$

The role bob is modeled similarly. The role session isn't modified, unless there are additional arguments in either of the protocols.

The environment and goal sections are modified to reflect the name changes (protocol IDs, keys) in the roles alice and bob. The goals of both the protocols are specified together. This ensures that AVISPA looks for an attack sequence that violates any protocol's goal. The multi-protocol code for the roles environment and goals is given below.

```
role environment()
def=
const a, b:agent,
    kab : symmetric_key,
    secretS, alice_bob_na : protocol_id
    intruder_knowledge={a,b}
    composition
    session(a,b,kab)
    /\session(b,a,kab)
end role

goal
secrecy_of secretS
authentication_on alice_bob_na
end goal
```

Listing 1.9. Environment and Goals $\pi 1 + \pi 2$

The multi-protocol script when analysed by backend OFMC shows no attack, however when the same is analysed by Cl-AtSE an attack is found. The output trace obtained from AVISPA is as follows. The trace reveals the same attack that was described in Sect. 1.

```
ATTACK TRACE
i -> (b,6):  start
(b,6) -> i:  {n31(Na)}_kab

i -> (b,6):  start
(b,6) -> i:  {n32(S)}_kab
             & Secret(n32(S),set_66);  Add b to set_66;  Add
    a to set_66;

i -> (a,3):  start
(a,3) -> i:  {n7(Na)}_kab

i -> (a,3):  start
(a,3) -> i:  {n8(S)}_kab
             & Secret(n8(S),set_55);  Add a to set_55;  Add
    b to set_55;

i -> (b,4):  {n31(Na)}_kab
(b,4) -> i:  ()

i -> (b,4):  {n8(S)}_kab
(b,4) -> i:  n8(S) & Witness(b,a,alice_bob_na,n8(S));
```

Listing 1.10. Attack Trace $\pi 1 + \pi 2$

3.1   Writing Multi-protocol Scripts

Below we list the steps to carry out a multi-protocol analysis using AVISPA.

1. The protocols should be individually modeled first.
2. While composing the multi-protocol script, care must be taken to ensure every protocol has its own copy of local variables. For example, if two protocol scripts use nonce Na then when combining the scripts the name should be changed so that each protocol has its own nonce.
3. State variables should be named accordingly as well. Also variable substitution for unknown encrypted strings should have different names.
4. Any additional arguments in either of the protocol models should be added to the functions in the multi-protocol model. Arguments can be additional keys or hash functions used. The same changes should be made in the session role.
5. The names of all variables used to specify goals should also be renamed to avoid a clash. These changes should also be made in the environment and goal sections of the code.
6. After all the above steps are completed, the script can be simulated using the protocol simulator present in AVISPA. The protocol simulator runs the protocol from start till end mirroring the steps of the protocol if there are no problems. If both the protocols can individually reach their final message, then the modeling is complete and can be analysed for the presence of attacks.

Table 2. Protocols analysed using AVISPA

Protocol	Goal	Verdict
Denning-Sacco [9]	Key establishment	Safe
Amended Woo-Lam	Authentication	Safe
ISO Five Pass [11]	Key establishment	Safe
Abadi-Needham [12]	Key establishment	Safe
APG 1,2 & 3 (Perrig-Song [13])	Authentication	Safe
APG 4,5 & 6 (Perrig-Song [13])	Key establishment	Safe
ZF 1,2 & 3 (Zhou-Foley [14])	Key establishment	Safe

4   Case Study

This section presents the results of the multi-protocol analysis we carried out using AVISPA on a set of 13 protocols which are listed in Table 2. A manual inspection of these protocols showed that six pairs of protocols are vulnerable to multi-protocol attacks [1]. Using AVISPA, we were able to find attacks against ten pairs of protocols including the previously reported six pairs.

Table 3. Case study results

$\pi 1$	$\pi 2$	Goal violated	Attack
Denning-Sacco	Amended Woo-Lam	Authentication on K_{AB} in $\pi 1$	Existing
ISO Five Pass	Abadi-Needham	Authentication on K_{AB} in $\pi 1$	Existing
APG 1	APG 2	Authentication on N_B in $\pi 1$	Existing
APG 4	APG 6	Secrecy of N_B in $\pi 2$	Existing
ZF 1	ZF 2	Secrecy of K_{AB} in $\pi 2$	Existing
ZF 3	APG 2	Authentication on K_{AB} in $\pi 1$	Existing
APG 3	ZF 3	Secrecy of K_{AB} in $\pi 2$	New
ZF 1	ZF 3	Secrecy of K_{AB} in $\pi 2$	New
APG 6	ZF 3	Secrecy of K_{AB} in $\pi 1$	New
ZF 3	APG 4	Secrecy of K_{AB} in $\pi 2$	New

4.1   Protocols

The following six protocols here have either key establishment or authentication as their goals. These goals are modeled using the secrecy_of and authentication_on goals in AVISPA. The secrecy_of goal is used to denote a value as a secret among a list of principals. For example, a key established in APG 4 would be a secret among the principals A, B and S. The authentication_of goal is used to specify a particular value as the means of authentication between two principals. The protocol APG 3 uses both nonces N_A and N_B as a means to authenticate A to B and B to A. This authentication goal is specified using two functions, witness and request.

APG 3. This is a mutual authentication protocol between A and B. The authentication goal is specified using the authentication_on clause on nonces N_A and N_B.

---

1. $A \rightarrow B : N_A,\ A$
2. $B \rightarrow S : \{A,\ N_A,\ N_B\}_{K_{BS}},\ B$
3. $S \rightarrow A : \{N_A,\ N_B,\ B\}_{K_{AS}}$
4. $A \rightarrow B : N_B$

Protocol 3: APG 3

APG 4 and 6. These two key establishment protocols use a mutually trusted entity S to generate a session key for use by principals A and B. The goals of the protocols are modeled by making the key K_{AB} a secret among A, B and S and by using N_B and K_{AB} for authentication.

1. $A \rightarrow B : N_A,\ A$
2. $B \rightarrow S : \{N_A,\ N_B,\ A\}_{K_{BS}},\ B$
3. $S \rightarrow A : \{K_{AB}\}_{K_{BS}},\ \{K_{AB},\ N_A,\ N_B,\ B\}_{K_{AS}}$
4. $A \rightarrow B : \{N_B\}_{K_{AB}},\ \{K_{AB}\}_{K_{BS}}$

Protocol 4: APG 4

1. $A \rightarrow B : N_A,\ A$
2. $B \rightarrow S : \{N_A,\ N_B,\ A\}_{K_{BS}},\ B$
3. $S \rightarrow A : \{K_{AB},\ N_B\}_{K_{BS}},\ \{K_{AB},\ N_A,\ N_B,\ B\}_{K_{AS}}$
4. $A \rightarrow B : N_B,\ \{K_{AB},\ N_B\}_{K_{BS}}$

Protocol 5: APG 6

Zhou-Foley Protocols. We consider three key establishment protocols synthesized by Zhou and Foley [14].

1. $A \rightarrow B : A,\ N_A$
2. $B \rightarrow S : B,\ \{A,\ N_A,\ N_B\}_{K_{BS}}$
3. $S \rightarrow A : N_B,\ \{N_B,\ K_{AB}\}_{K_{BS}},\ \{B,\ N_A,\ K_{AB}\}_{K_{AS}}$
4. $A \rightarrow B : \{N_B\}_{K_{AB}},\ \{N_B,\ K_{AB}\}_{K_{BS}}$

Protocol 6: ZF 1

1. $A \rightarrow B : A,\ N_A$
2. $B \rightarrow S : B,\ N_B,\ \{A,\ N_A\}_{K_{BS}}$
3. $S \rightarrow A : N_B,\ \{A,\ B,\ N_B,\ K_{AB}\}_{K_{BS}},\ \{B,\ N_A,\ K_{AB}\}_{K_{AS}}$
4. $A \rightarrow B : \{N_B\}_{K_{AB}},\ \{A,\ B,\ N_B,\ K_{AB}\}_{K_{BS}}$

Protocol 7: ZF 2

1. $A \rightarrow B : A,\ N_A$
2. $B \rightarrow S : A,\ B,\ N_A,\ N_B$
3. $S \rightarrow B : \{A,\ N_B,\ K_{AB}\}_{K_{BS}},\ \{N_A,\ N_B,\ K_{AB},\ B\}_{K_{AS}}$
4. $B \rightarrow A : \{N_A,\ N_B,\ K_{AB},\ B\}_{K_{AS}},\ \{N_A\}_{K_{AB}}$
5. $A \rightarrow B : \{N_B\}_{K_{AB}}$

Protocol 8: ZF 3

We modeled each of the above protocols in HLPSL. AVISPA found no attacks against the individual protocols. However, it proved useful in finding several new multi-protocol attacks on combinations of these protocols.

4.2   New Multi-protocol Attacks

The attack sequences of the newly found attacks are presented below. These attacks were found using the Cl-AtSE backend. The reason for this is that all the attacks below are type-flaw attacks and Cl-AtSE is a backend capable of verifying such attacks. This backend also has options for the type of search used for the attack sequence.

APG 3 - ZF 3. In Attack 3, A runs both the protocols APG 3 and ZF 3, as initiator. In both these runs, the Spy assumes the role of B. The attack trace shows that A successfully completes the APG 3 run, even though B did not participate in any run. Notice that the Spy also learns the session key $K_{AB_{\pi 2}}$ which was generated by S in the ZF 3 run. We can manually extend this trace to Attack 4, enabling the Spy to impersonate B to A in the ZF 3 run. The outcome of the attack is that A accepts $K_{AB_{\pi 2}}$ as a key with B in the ZF 3 run, although it is known to the Spy.

---

1. $\pi 1 : 1, S1 : A \rightarrow Spy(B) : N_{A_{\pi 1}}, A$
2. $\pi 2 : 1, S1 : A \rightarrow Spy(B) : A, N_{A_{\pi 2}}$
3. $\pi 2 : 2, S1 : Spy(B) \rightarrow S : A, B, N_{A_{\pi 2}}, N_{A_{\pi 1}}$
4. $\pi 2 : 3, S1 : S \rightarrow Spy(B) : \{A, N_{A_{\pi 1}}, K_{AB_{\pi 2}}\}_{K_{BS}}, \{N_{A_{\pi 2}}, N_{A_{\pi 1}}, K_{AB_{\pi 2}}, B\}_{K_{AS}}$
5. $\pi 1 : 2, S1 : Spy(B) \rightarrow S : \{A, N_{A_{\pi 1}}, K_{AB_{\pi 2}}\}_{K_{BS}}, B$
6. $\pi 1 : 3, S1 : S \rightarrow Spy(A) : \{N_{A_{\pi 1}}, K_{AB_{\pi 2}}, B\}_{K_{AS}}$
7. $\pi 1 : 3, S1 : Spy(S) \rightarrow A : \{N_{A_{\pi 1}}, K_{AB_{\pi 2}}, B\}_{K_{AS}}$
8. $\pi 1 : 4, S1 : A \rightarrow Spy(B) : K_{AB_{\pi 2}}$

Attack 3: APG 3 - ZF 3

---

9. $\pi 2 : 4, S1 : Spy(B) \rightarrow A : \{N_{A_{\pi 2}}, N_{A_{\pi 1}}, K_{AB_{\pi 2}}, B\}_{K_{AS}}, \{N_{A_{\pi 2}}\}_{K_{AB_{\pi 2}}}$
10. $\pi 2 : 5, S1 : A \rightarrow Spy(B) : \{N_{A_{\pi 1}}\}_{K_{AB_{\pi 2}}}$

Attack 4: APG 3 - ZF 3 (Contd.)

ZF 1 - ZF 3. In Attack 5, A runs both the protocols ZF 1 and ZF 3, as initiator. In both these runs, the Spy assumes the role of B. The attack trace shows that the Spy learns the session key $K_{AB_{\pi 2}}$ which was generated by S in the ZF 3 run. This trace falls short of an attack, as the honest party A has not successfully completed any run. We can manually extend this trace to Attack 6, enabling the Spy to impersonate B to A in the ZF 3 run. The outcome of the attack is that A accepts $K_{AB_{\pi 2}}$ as a key with B in the ZF 3 run, although it is known to the Spy.

1. $\pi 1 : 1, S1 : A \to Spy(B) : \ A, \ N_{A_{\pi 1}}$
2. $\pi 2 : 1, S1 : A \to Spy(B) : \ A, \ N_{A_{\pi 2}}$
3. $\pi 2 : 2, S1 : Spy(B) \to S : \ A, \ B, \ N_{A_{\pi 2}}, \ N_{B_{\pi 2}}$
4. $\pi 2 : 3, S1 : S \to Spy(B) : \ \{A, \ N_{B_{\pi 2}}, \ K_{AB_{\pi 2}}\}_{K_{BS}}, \ \{N_{A_{\pi 2}}, \ N_{B_{\pi 2}}, \ K_{AB_{\pi 2}}, \ B\}_{K_{AS}}$
5. $\pi 1 : 2, S1 : Spy(B) \to S : \ B, \ \{A, \ N_{B_{\pi 2}}, \ K_{AB_{\pi 2}}\}_{K_{BS}}$
6. $\pi 1 : 3, S1 : S \to Spy(A) : \ K_{AB_{\pi 2}}, \ \{K_{AB_{\pi 2}}, \ K_{AB_{\pi 1}}\}_{K_{BS}}, \ \{B, \ N_{B_{\pi 2}}, \ K_{AB_{\pi 1}}\}_{K_{AS}}$

Attack 5: ZF 1 - ZF 3

7. $\pi 2 : 3, S1 : Spy(B) \to A : \ \{N_{A_{\pi 2}}, \ N_{B_{\pi 2}}, \ K_{AB_{\pi 2}}, \ B\}_{K_{AS}}, \ \{N_{A_{\pi 2}}\}_{K_{AB_{\pi 2}}}$
8. $\pi 2 : 3, S1 : A \to Spy(B) : \ \{N_{B_{\pi 2}}\}_{K_{AB_{\pi 2}}}$

Attack 6: ZF 1 - ZF 3 (Contd.)

APG 6 - ZF 3. In Attack 7, A runs both the protocols APG 6 and ZF 3, as initiator. In both these runs, the Spy assumes the role of B. The attack trace shows that A accepts $K_{AB_{\pi 1}}$ as a key with B in the APG 6 run, although it is known to the Spy. In the attack trace, Y is a random string.

1. $\pi 2 : 1, S1 : A \to Spy(B) : \ A, \ N_{A_{\pi 2}}$
2. $\pi 1 : 1, S1 : A \to Spy(B) : \ N_{A_{\pi 1}}, \ A$
3. $\pi 2 : 2, S1 : Spy(B) \to S : \ A, \ B, \ K_{AB_{\pi 1}}, \ N_{A_{\pi 1}}$
4. $\pi 2 : 3, S1 : S \to Spy(B) : \ \{A, \ N_{A_{\pi 1}}, \ K_{AB_{\pi 2}}\}_{K_{BS}}, \ \{K_{AB_{\pi 1}}, \ N_{A_{\pi 1}}, \ K_{AB_{\pi 2}}, \ B\}_{K_{AS}}$
5. $\pi 1 : 3, S1 : Spy(S) \to A : \ Y, \ \{K_{AB_{\pi 1}}, \ N_{A_{\pi 1}}, \ K_{AB_{\pi 2}}, \ B\}_{K_{AS}}$
6. $\pi 1 : 4, S1 : A \to Spy(B) : \ K_{AB_{\pi 2}}, \ Y$

Attack 7: APG 6 - ZF 3

ZF 3 - APG 4. In Attack 8, A runs both the protocols ZF 3 and APG 4, as initiator. In both these runs, the Spy assumes the role of B. The attack trace shows that A accepts $K_{AB_{\pi 2}}$ as a key with B in the APG 4 run, although it is known to the Spy. In the attack trace, Y is a random string.

1. $\pi 1 : 1, S1 : A \rightarrow Spy(B) : \quad A, \; N_{A_{\pi 1}}$
2. $\pi 2 : 1, S1 : A \rightarrow Spy(B) : \quad N_{A_{\pi 2}}, \; A$
3. $\pi 1 : 2, S1 : Spy(B) \rightarrow S : \quad A, \; B, \; K_{AB_{\pi 2}}, \; N_{A_{\pi 2}}$
4. $\pi 1 : 3, S1 : S \rightarrow Spy(B) : \quad \{A, \; N_{A_{\pi 2}}, \; K_{AB_{\pi 1}}\}_{K_{BS}}, \; \{K_{AB_{\pi 2}}, N_{A_{\pi 2}}, \; K_{AB_{\pi 1}}, \; B\}_{K_{AS}}$
5. $\pi 2 : 3, S1 : Spy(S) \rightarrow A : \quad Y, \; \{K_{AB_{\pi 2}}, \; N_{A_{\pi 2}}, \; K_{AB_{\pi 1}}, \; B\}_{K_{AS}}$
6. $\pi 2 : 4, S1 : A \rightarrow Spy(B) : \quad \{K_{AB_{\pi 1}}\}_{K_{AB_{\pi 2}}}, \; Y$

Attack 8: ZF 3 - APG 4

5   Conclusions

From the results of the case study, we can see that AVISPA is able to detect certain types of multi-protocol attacks. As HLPSL does not support timestamps as a data type, AVISPA cannot find multi-protocol attacks against protocols which use timestamps to maintain freshness of messages, for example the Denning-Sacco protocol. Attack 9 shows a multi-protocol attack that breaks the Denning-Sacco protocol using ZF 2.

1. $\pi 2 : 2, S1 : Spy(B) \rightarrow S : \quad B, \; T, \{A, \; N_{A_{\pi 2}}\}_{K_{BS}}$
2. $\pi 2 : 3, S1 : S \rightarrow Spy(A) : \quad T, \; \{A, \; B, \; T, \; K_{AB_{\pi 2}}\}_{K_{BS}}, \; \{B, \; T, \; K_{AB_{\pi 2}}\}_{K_{AS}}$
3. $\pi 1 : 1, S1 : B \rightarrow Spy(S) : \quad B, \; A$
4. $\pi 1 : 2, S1 : Spy(S) \rightarrow B : \{A, \; B, \; T, \; K_{AB_{\pi 2}}\}_{K_{BS}}$
5. $\pi 1 : 3, S1 : B \rightarrow Spy(A) : K_{AB_{\pi 2}}$

Attack 9: Denning Sacco - ZF 2

In the above attack, the intruder is able to make the honest principal bob accept the identifier B as the shared key with A even though A may not be present on the network. The encrypted message sequence with the agent and nonce in step 1 is one from an earlier run.

In several cases AVISPA produced only a partial attack sequence. This limitation is because AVISPA terminates the search immediately when one of the goals is violated. An example of this is the attack on ZF 1 - ZF 3 given before. Moreover, in some cases the attack traces contain spurious messages that have no contribution to the attack.

Acknowledgements. We thank the anonymous referees for their helpful comments on a draft of this paper. The second author was supported by a grant from Indo-French (DST-Inria-CNRS) collaborative research program.

References

1. Mathuria, A., Singh, A.R., Shravan, P.V., Kirtankar, R.: Some new multi-protocol attacks. In: 15th International Conference on Advanced Computing and Communications (ADCOM 2007), pp. 465–471 (2007)
2. Alves-Foss, J.: Provably insecure mutual authentication protocols: the two-party symmetric-encryption case. In: 22nd National Information Systems Security Conference, October 1999
3. http://www.avispa-project.org
4. https://www.cs.ox.ac.uk/people/cas.cremers/scyther/
5. Cremers, C.: Feasibility of multi-protocol attacks. In: ARES, pp. 287–294 (2006)
6. http://prosecco.gforge.inria.fr/personal/bblanche/proverif/
7. Kojovic, I.: An automatic protocol composition checker. Master's thesis, Technical University of Denmark (2012)
8. Cervesato, I.: The Dolev-Yao intruder is the most powerful attacker. In: 16th Annual Symposium on Logic in Computer Science, LICS 2001, pp. 16–19 (2001)
9. Denning, D.E., Sacco, G.M.: Timestamps in key distribution protocols. Commun. ACM **24**(8), 533–536 (1981)
10. Woo, T.Y., Lam, S.S.: Authentication for distributed systems. Computer **25**(1), 39–2 (1992)
11. Clark, J.A., Jacob, J.L.: A survey of authentication protocol literature. Technical Report 1.0 (1997)
12. Abadi, M., Needham, R.: Prudent engineering practice for cryptographic protocols. IEEE Trans. Softw. Eng. **22**(1), 6–15 (1996)
13. Perrig, A., Song, D.X.: Looking for diamonds in the desert: extending automatic protocol generation to three-party authentication and key agreement protocols. In: 13th IEEE Computer Security Foundations Workshop, pp. 64–76, July 2000
14. Zhou, H., Foley, S.N.: Fast automatic synthesis of security protocols using backward search. In: ACM workshop on Formal methods in security engineering (FMSE), pp. 1–10 (2003)

Malicious Application Detection on Android Smartphones with Enhanced Static-Dynamic Analysis

Sandeep Rai, Rushang Dhanesha[✉], Sreyans Nahata, and Bernard Menezes

Indian Institute of Technology Bombay, Mumbai, India
rushangdhanesha@gmail.com

Abstract. Given the widespread use of the Android OS on cellphones and the fact that Android applications can be downloaded from third party sources, it is crucially important to be able to accurately detect which of these may be malicious. In this paper we incorporate several new features related to resource utilization and introduce multi-valued (as opposed to binary) features. We study the impact of these augmentations on accuracy of malware detection. We compare various feature selection algorithms including Extra Tree and Recursive Feature Elimination. We also employ and compare a variety of classification algorithms ranging from Neural Network to Random Forest and XGBoost. Our experiments targeting over 3000 applications show that the enhanced static-dynamic analysis reduces the false positive rate by 25% and the false negative rate by 20%.

Keyword: Android security, Malware detection, Machine learning

1 Introduction

The market base and popularity of the Android operating system together with the number of applications available to the users has increased exponentially. Around 75% of the world's smartphone users use Android. Android provides a substantial number of features to its users. This has also made Android a target of 92% of the world's malware attacks. In contrast to other mobile operating systems, applications for Android can be downloaded from any third-party source. These applications can be easily bundled and distributed with malware. 750,000 new malware apps have been found in the first quarter of 2017 and this number is estimated to hit 3.5 million by the end of the year [1].

Malware detection often uses static and/or dynamic analysis. Static analysis is performed utilizing the contents of the app's source code. Features like permissions, suspicious API calls, etc. are used in static analysis. Many of the malwares are able to mimic the behaviour of benign applications and so evade detection if analyzed using only static features. Dynamic analysis takes into account features like data leaks, network usage, etc. which overcome the drawbacks of static

© Springer International Publishing AG 2017
R. K. Shyamasundar et al. (Eds.): ICISS 2017, LNCS 10717, pp. 194–208, 2017.
https://doi.org/10.1007/978-3-319-72598-7_12

analysis. On analyzing the apps, we introduce new features that help in improving the detection accuracy. These features are related to CPU usage, memory utilization and network utilization. There are some features that are used by both the malicious and benign apps, but their frequency of usage creates a distinction between malicious and benign apps. We assign integer features rather than binary values so they are better able to discriminate between benign and malicious apps. We also compare various feature selection algorithms and classification algorithms to be applied to these features. Lastly, we introduce a simple feature selection metric which helps explain why certain apps are misclassified.

This paper is organized as follows. Section 2 contains background of the terms and machine learning artifacts used in this paper. Section 3 contains a summary of related work. In Sect. 4, we describe the experiments performed and their results. We present results comparing various feature selection and malware classification algorithms used on our dataset. In Sect. 5, we study the effect of our enhanced feature set on a combined static/dynamic approach.

2   Background

Android Package Kit (APK) is the package file format used to install mobile apps in Android operating system. Installing apps from APK files of untrusted origin could introduce malware in the system. Our approach for detecting these malwares involves (a) Feature extraction from APK file, (b) Selection of a subset of all the extracted features and (c) Classification of the app based on these features.

Feature Extraction involves reverse engineering an APK file to get Android-Manifest.xml file and classes.dex file. The former file holds meta information about the application. It has information about the permission that the application requires, hardware components used, etc. classes.dex file contains compiled Java code of the application. i.e. the complete bytecode to be interpreted by the machine. Features can also be extracted from the logs generated by running the app on a device.

In feature selection, we attempt to select only those features which improve classification accuracy. Feature selection techniques include Variance-based Approach [3], Chi-Squared (χ^2) [2], Recursive Feature Elimination (RFE) [4] and Extra Tree (ET) [6]. The Variance-based approach basically removes all features whose variance does not meet some threshold. Chi-Squared technique ranks the features on the basis of dependence of the occurrence of a feature and occurrence of the class. High-ranked features are selected for classification. RFE recursively removes a feature from the set, builds a new model based on the new set and, if the model improves, it eliminates that feature otherwise that feature is retained. Extra Tree feature selection method uses an ensemble of decision trees. It tries to reduce variance at the expense of increasing bias.

The best possible subset of all the features is used for classification. Classification is done with various machine learning models. Naive Bayes is the simplest classification model based on the maximum probability of features that belong to a particular class. It assumes that a particular feature in a class has no relation to the presence of any other feature. It is a strong assumption which does not hold in most real world datasets. An improvement over the naive Bayes, a Support Vector Classifier (SVC) [5] works by constructing a hyperplane separating the classes. Data is mapped to n-dimensional vector space, where n is the total number of features in a dataset.

In a Decision Tree [7], each node tests an attribute and creates branches based on the value of that feature. A multi-level tree is created based on the information gains from a feature. Leaf nodes represent classes. Random Forest [9] improves accuracy by creating an ensemble of decision trees and not just training a single tree. In random forest, each tree is trained based on a random subset of features.

A neural network [8] is made up of many layers of neurons. A weight is associated with each pair of neurons in two adjacent layers. This network is trained by supervised learning which adjusts the weights and biases of each neuron. These trained models are used for classification. To further improve accuracy XGBoost [10] is used. It is an ensemble learning technique which takes multiple models to correct any misclassification by a model.

3   Related Work

Signature-based detection: Currently the most widely used method of malware detection is the signature-based approach. Desnos and Gueguen [19] proposed a technique to create signatures for Android permissions used in applications. They constructed a control flow graph using collected contents of applications. Another signature based system is DroidAnalytics [17] in which signature generation and malware association is based on a similarity score. Instead of assigning scores, RiskRanker [18] detects high and mid level threats on the basis of some features of the app like presence of exploit codes, dynamic code loading and leakage of sensitive information. However, these signature-based methods are often unable to catch malwares that use sophisticated techniques like code loading to evade detection [12]. Also, these techniques cannot detect any new piece of malicious code and hence cannot prevent a zero-day attack. [11] shows that Android malwares are able to circumvent signature-based detection and thus there is need for a next-generation detection mechanism that is difficult to evade. In view of this situation machine learning-based methods seems a viable option.

Detection based on Static Features: Assigning a risk score on the basis of static feature analysis was first proposed by Peng et al. [31]. It scored apps purely on the basis of the permissions requested by the apps. Along the same lines, Liu et al. [21] investigated specific types of malware based on requested permissions and hardware components as features for classification. Chan and Song [22] proposed a feature set containing the permissions and the API calls for Android malware detection. Permissions used from AndroidManifest.xml and API calls from classes.dex are extracted and based on information they identified

19 relevant API calls. The authors concluded that accuracy was increased using permissions and API combined. Like Chan, Drebin [20] extracts huge number of different static features from an application's manifest file (permissions, components, intents) and dex code (restricted API calls, used permissions, network addresses). They demonstrated that malware detection is scalable and can run on Android devices. Its execution time is a few seconds and it outperformed 90% of the anti-virus scanners.

Detection based on Dynamic Features: The main problem in mobile devices is the availability of resources. So, ParanoidAndroid [26] employs dynamic analysis and detects malicious activities using a dedicated server that runs a virtual clone of the mobile device in parallel and synchronized with the device activities. TaintDroid [27] provided an efficient, system-wide dynamic taint tracking and analysis system capable of simultaneously tracking multiple sources of sensitive data. Crowdroid [24] is behavior-based malware detection system for Android. It is based on system calls used by applications embedded as feature vectors which are further used by machine learning algorithms for classification.

A comparison of different feature selection and machine learning approaches was made by Mas'ud et al. [25]. A tool called strace was used to monitor calls of an application. DroidScribe [23] focused on classifying Android malware into families using runtime behavior derived from system calls observed during dynamic analysis. It generates features at different levels, including pure system calls, decoded Binder communication and abstracted behavioral patterns and then feeds this extracted data into a Support Vector Machine for classification.

A Combination of Static and Dynamic Features: DroidDetector [20] used both static features such as requested permissions, API calls and dynamic features from sandbox logs. Hybrid analysis has been shown to be better than pure static or dynamic analysis. DroidDetector used deep learning for classification and explained features exploited by the deep learning engine. MARVIN [29] used a system that combines static with dynamic analysis to assess the risk associated with unknown Android apps in the form of a malice score. Authors developed an end user app into which users submit their app and a score is received as an indicator of how malicious the application content is. MADAM [28] monitored the device actions, its interaction with the user and the running applications. MADAM employed multi-level behaviour analysis on five groups of features at four different levels of abstraction which has shown good results.

4   Experiments and Results

This section describes the steps in detecting of malicious Android apps. We first collect thousands of Android apps from different sources. These include, both malicious and benign apps. We extract hundreds of features that could potentially distinguish between malicious and benign apps and then use feature selection algorithms to identify the most appropriate ones. Based on the reduced feature set, we employ various classification algorithms to detect malicious apps.

4.1   App Collection

In both, the training and testing phases, we require a mix of benign and malicious Android applications. A total of 1522 applications were downloaded from the Google Playstore. We assume that these applications are benign since they have been scanned by various available antivirus software offline and online [16] and downloaded by millions of customers. To maximize diversity, the applications were drawn from various categories such as music, games, videos, communication, education, etc. We also collected 1524 malicious applications. Of these, 500 are from ContagioDump [34], a software repository that offers a platform to share mobile malware samples among security researchers. M0droid [30], in addition to ContagioDump, was a major source of malware samples. Finally, we used the Drebin Dataset which contains samples from 179 different malware families. We used 502 malware samples from the Drebin [20] dataset and the rest from M0droid which also contains recently introduced malware families.

4.2   Feature Extraction

An app is classified as benign or malicious based on its characteristics. To characterize an app, we extract features from the available APK file.

Our feature set is derived from, both, static and dynamic analysis. Static features include permissions requested by the app, API calls, hardware components, etc. Dynamic analysis deals with features obtained by running the application such as network traffic, files accessed, cryptographic usage, etc. The different tools used for analysis and the information provided by them is summarized in Fig. 1.

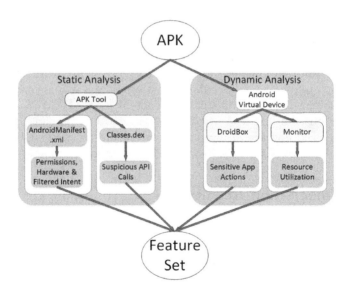

Fig. 1. Feature extraction

Table 1. Different categories of features

Analysis	Feature	Number of features	Type of feature
Static	Permissions	138	Binary
	Hardware components	55	Binary
	Filtered intent	122	Binary
	Suspicious APIs	17	Positive integer
Dynamic	Sensitive app actions	11	Positive integer
	Resource utilization	7	Positive integer

Static Analysis. In static analysis, the features are extracted from the APK file without executing the application. ApkTool is used to reverse engineer an APK file to get AndroidManifest.xml and classes.dex file.

Table 1 shows the categories of features extracted by us and the number of features in each category. Requested permissions, hardware components used and filtered intents are obtained from AndroidManifest.xml. ApkTool converts bytcode to produce a typical folder hierarchy containing assembly language code which can be easily parsed to obtain disassembled code. This code is scanned for suspicious APIs (Table 2) which are usually employed by malicious applications. In previous works [20,21,31], only binary values were considered for API calls. This restricted the ability to distinguish between benign and malicious app using API calls that are contained in both. Instead, we have introduced integer values to count the number of times an API call is present in the code resulting in improvements in the accuracy of classification.

Table 2. Suspicious APIs

API functions	Description
getDeviceId(), getSubscriberId()	API calls for accessing sensitive data
examplesetWifiEnabled(), execHttpRequest()	This API call is required for communicating over the network
sendTextMessage()	API calls for sending and receiving SMS messages
Runtime.exec()	This API is used for execution of external commands
getActiveNetworkInfo(), isConnected()	Used to check whether a network connection is available
Cipher.getInstance()	This API call is frequently used for obfuscation
createSpeechRecognizer()	It allows access to the speech recognizer
getLineNumber, getSimSerialNumber	To read phone state and user information

Dynamic Analysis. In dynamic analysis, various heuristics are used to capture and analyze dynamic behaviour of an application such as monitoring file changes, network activity, cryptographic operations etc. DroidBox tool [32] is used for dynamic analysis. DroidBox provides information about the application such as file read and write operations, cryptographic operations performed using Android API, etc. DoridBox generates activity logs while the app is running on the device. As shown in Table 1, we identified 11 features related to sensitive app actions. We also collected information related to the resources utilized by the application while it is running on the Android Virtual Device (AVD). The resource utilization features include CPU usage, memory consumption and amount of data transferred over the network. Further details about these features are discussed in Sect. 5.1

4.3   Feature Selection

Feature selection discards redundant and irrelevant features while retaining those features and dimensions that are most likely to help us classify accurately. We experimented with the following feature selection algorithms to find the most appropriate algorithm for this application. In particular, we consider all combinations of feature selection algorithms and classification techniques (addressed in Sect. 4.4)

Variance-based Approach: With this approach, the highest accuracy is obtained with threshold value of 0.0475. This leaves us with 91 features and yields an accuracy of 94.5% with the best classification algorithm (reported in the next section).

Chi-Squared Test (Chi2): The best accuracy obtained by this test is obtained by considering the 108 top-ranked features. The measured accuracy is 95.8%.

Recursive Feature Elimination (RFE): Selecting only 110 features provides best accuracy of 96.1%.

Extra Tree (ET): 74 features are selected using this approach and the corresponding classification accuracy is 97.41.%.

Out of the total set of 377 features, we selected the top 70 features ranked by each of the Chi2 test, RFE and Extra Tree. We then computed the pairwise intersection of these feature sets and also the intersection of all three sets. As shown in Fig. 2, 28 features are common across the top 70 features ranked by the three feature selection algorithms. These include SEND_SMS, USS and to_loopback. Using only these features in the classification algorithms, we achieved a classification accuracy of approximately 90% (using the top three classification algorithms discussed in the next section).

In addition to checking the consistency of high-ranked features across feature selection algorithms, we also investigate whether the reduced feature set is stable across datasets. For this purpose, we partitioned the entire set of apps into four disjoint subsets A, B, C, D, each containing the same ratio of malicious to benign apps. We create the four subset S1, S2, S3, S4 as follows:

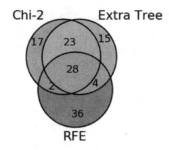

Fig. 2. Intersection of Features among Extra Tree, RFE and Chi2

$$S1 = A \cup B$$
$$S2 = C \cup D$$
$$S3 = A \cup C$$
$$S4 = B \cup D$$

We then ran Extra Tree, RFE and Chi2 feature selection algorithms on each of S1, S2, S3 and S4 and selected the top 70 ranked features from each combination of selection algorithm and dataset.

Table 3 shows the cardinalities of the pairwise intersection of the top 70 features obtained from S1, S2, S3 and S4 using each feature selection algorithm. As can be seen from Table 3, the features selected by Extra Tree and Chi-Squared are more consistent across all datasets,compared with those of RFE. While this experiment is somewhat limited in scope, it suggests that RFE should be used with some caution on a set of completely new Android apps.

Table 3. Common features across dataset

(a) Extra Tree

	S1	S2	S3	S4
S1	70	60	60	64
S2		70	61	59
S3			70	60
S4				70

(b) RFE

	S1	S2	S3	S4
S1	70	39	46	41
S2		70	38	41
S3			70	42
S4				70

(c) Chi-Squared

	S1	S2	S3	S4
S1	70	62	64	67
S2		70	64	63
S3			70	63
S4				70

4.4 Classification

Obtaining a reduced feature set is only the first goal. Our next task is to classify apps as benign or malicious based on the value of each feature in the reduced feature set. We experiment with various classification algorithms and identify the most appropriate one for this task. The dataset collected in Sect. 4.1 is divided into training and testing sets, containing 70% and 30% of the samples respectively. Both the training and the testing sets have an equal number of benign and malware applications. The classifiers used are: Naive Bayes, Support Vector Classifier, Neural Network, Decision Tree, Random Forest and XGBoost.

The accuracy of naive Bayes classifier, is 82.9%. The measured accuracy for support vector classifier with radial basis function kernel is 94.2%, while it is 95.7% for single hidden layered neural network containing 20 neurons. With just 3046 apps available in the dataset, neural network could not be trained enough to improve the accuracy beyond 95.7%.

Using decision trees with tuned parameters, we were able to achieve accuracy of 93%. However, we obtained accuracy of 97% using random forest with 100 decision trees. The random forest algorithm helped in separating the subsets of important features by training an ensemble of different decision trees and combining their outputs to make a final decision. While random forest trains all trees independently, XGBoost trains new trees based on the information from previously trained trees. So XGBoost was further able to improve the accuracy to 97.41%. Figure 3 summarizes the performance of various classifiers.

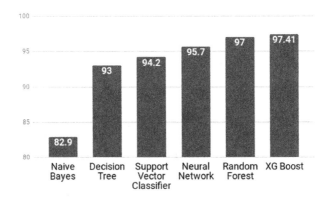

Fig. 3. Percentage accuracy of machine learning models

5   Discussion

In this section, we explain and study effect of the enhanced features on accuracy of malware detection. We also introduce a naive metric for feature selection and use it to explain why certain apps were misclassified.

5.1   Effect of Enhancements to Feature Set

A total of seven resource utilization features are introduced for classification. These seven features are divided into three categories - CPU utilization, memory utilization and network utilization. CPU utilization is the percentage of processing power utilized by the application. Next, the two memory utilization features are USS and PSS. Unique Set Size (USS) specifies the amount of primary memory allocated to the app, that is not shared with any other process. Proportional Set Size (PSS) is the amount of primary memory shared by the concerned app with one or more processes. The remaining four features, from_loopback, to_loopback, from_external and to_external are part of network utilization features. Volume of data exchanged with any external IP are measured and stored in from_external (for downloads) and to_external (for uploads).

Table 4. Top 10 features selected by Extra Tree

Rank	Feature name	Type
1	from_loopback	Resource utilization
2	VIEW	Filtered intent
3	GET_ACCOUNTS	Permissions
4	to_loopback	Resource utilization
5	READ_PHONE_STATE	Permissions
6	ACCESS_NETWORK_STATE	Permissions
7	SEND_SMS	Permissions
8	enfperm	Sensitive app action
9	BOOT_COMPLETED	Filtered intent
10	PSS	Resource utilization

Of these seven features, two from network traffic and two from memory consumption are selected by all feature selection algorithms. As can be seen from Table 4, three of the resource utilization features are ranked among top 10 features by Extra Tree. Also, as seen from Table 5, introduction of these features leads to increase in accuracy.

It is clear from Table 6 that network traffic of malicious applications has low interaction with loopback address as compared to benign application [33]. We have also observed that often the benign apps have high memory requirements as compared to malicious apps and thus have high value for USS and PSS.

Table 5. Classification report

		Precision	Recall	F1-score
Static	Malicious	0.96	0.95	0.96
	Benign	0.95	0.96	0.96
Dynamic only, without resource utilization	Malicious	0.79	0.92	0.85
	Benign	0.90	0.76	0.83
Dynamic with resource utilization features	Malicious	0.93	0.93	0.93
	Benign	0.93	0.93	0.93
All features	Malicious	0.98	0.97	0.97
	Benign	0.97	0.98	0.97

Table 6. Network traffic from and to loopback

(a) From Loopback

Traffic (Bytes)	Malicious	Benign	Total
0-1.5k	1114	63	1177
1.5k-2.5k	159	62	221
2.5k-5k	150	247	397
5k-12k	74	491	565
12k or more	27	659	686

(b) To Loopback

Traffic (Bytes)	Malicious	Benign	Total
0-275	999	97	1096
275-300	71	43	114
300-400	210	311	521
400-500	79	319	398
500 or more	165	752	917

We introduced integer-valued features for API calls and other dynamic features. For example, a suspicious API call feature will count the number of times that API function has been called instead of just assigning True/False as the value for the feature. Also the resource utilization features have integer values.

As concrete examples, consider two dynamic features, fdaccess (number of times read/ write from/to a file) and recvsaction (number of times signal received on occurrence of different events). It is noticed that the number of benign and malicious apps testing positive on these features are comparable. So no decisive action can be taken on the basis of these features if they were binary-valued. As shown in Fig. 4, by using integer-valued features we were able to distinguish between malware and benign apps, judging from their peak concentration at particular values.

Integer-valued dynamic features are selected by all feature selection algorithms. The classification accuracy with only dynamic analysis, after incorporating integer values for these features, increased from 83.87% to 87.8%. Features obtained from API calls (integer-valued) are ranked high by all feature selection algorithms. The classification accuracy for static analysis increased from 95% to 95.5% by using integer values for suspicious API calls instead of binary values.

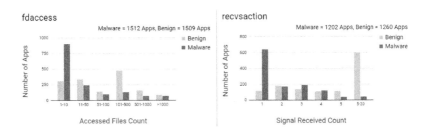

Fig. 4. App distribution for fdaccess and recvsaction

5.2 Misclassification Insights from Naive Feature Selection

In addition to using the standard feature selection algorithms in Sect. 4.3, we introduce a simple, intuitive measure **M1**, that captures the discriminating capability of a feature. For a given mix of malicious and benign applications, **M1** of any feature is computed as:

Fraction of Malicious Applications that have the Feature
+
Fraction of Benign Applications that do NOT have the Feature

Features that have the highest values of **M1** and also those that have the lowest values are naturally expected to be good at distinguishing between malicious and benign applications.

Let **F** be the set of features with the top 35 and bottom 35 **M1** scores. We computed the intersection of **F** with the the top 70 features thrown up respectively by ET, RFE and Chi2 feature selection algorithms. These computations were performed on each of the four application datasets S1, S2, S3 and S4. The cardinalities of the intersecting sets are shown in Table 7. Extra Tree has the maximum intersection between its top 70 features and **F** while RFE has the least. The intersection between top 35 of **F** and features selected by Chi2 is quite low while the intersection between the bottom 35 of **F** and features selected by Chi2 is the highest.

Features with the top 35 **M1** scores could collectively be considered the signature of a malicious application. Such a signature is agnostic with respect to different malware families and their variants and could constitute the first line of defense against Android malware. Features in this set include the more obvious ones like *SEND_SMS*, *BOOT_COMPLETED*, *INSTALL_PACKAGES*, etc. The bottom 35 features by **M1** score include few obvious ones like *TOUCH-SCREEN*, *VIBRATE*, etc. but they are dominated by many such as *getDeviceId*, *WAKE_LOCK*, etc. that could escape the casual analyst. Nevertheless, they play a crucial role in detecting malicious applications.

Table 7. Feature comparison of signature algorithm with the rest

(a) Top 35 of **M1** v/s 70 of Rest

	ET	RFE	Chi2
S1	26	13	19
S2	26	13	19
S3	24	14	16
S4	25	12	19

(b) Bottom 35 of **M1** v/s 70 of Rest

	ET	RFE	Chi2
S1	26	13	32
S2	29	10	30
S3	24	14	16
S4	32	12	31

Based on this, we investigate applications that are misclassified by the machine learning classification models. The applications reported as false positive and false negative are checked with top 35 and bottom 35 features ranked based on **M1** score. The top 35 features characterize malicious behaviour whereas the presence of bottom 35 features suggest benign behaviour. Each row in Table 8 represents a misclassified app and the presence of the top 35 and bottom 35 features. It is clear that malicious applications that are misclassified as false negative show more similarity to benign applications. Similarly benign applications that are misclassified as false positive show comparatively more similarity towards malicious applications.

Table 8. Misclassification analysis

(a) False Negatives		(b) False Positives	
Number of features present in Top 35	Number of features present in Bottom 35	Number of features present in Top 35	Number of features present in Bottom 35
7	29	9	4
6	22	9	5
4	26	7	3
10	27	5	1
0	7	6	4

6   Conclusion

In pursuit of our main goal of detecting malicious Android apps, we collected a total of 3046 apps, of which 1526 apps are malicious and 1522 are benign. This dataset consists of 377 features. We compared different feature selection algorithms to reduce from 377 features to a compact dataset of 70 features. To check the robustness of these techniques, we divided the dataset into four overlapping subsets and compared the features selected with each. We conclude that Extra Tree exhibited consistent behaviour across datasets. We experimented with different classification algorithms including Random Forest, Neural Network and XGBoost. We observed that random forest and XGBoost performed best in conjunction with the Extra Tree feature selection algorithm.

We studied the effect of an enhanced feature set on the accuracy of malware detection. The enhancements include the introduction of resource utilization features and conversion of some binary features to integer-valued. Using just dynamic analysis, the accuracy of malware detection increased from 83.87% to 88.8% with the enhanced features. Pure static analysis yields an accuracy of 95%. However, combined static and dynamic analysis with the enhanced feature set results in an accuracy of 97.41%. Finally, we introduced a naive feature selection metric and attempted to explain why some apps were misclassified.

References

1. The Next Web: Android malware spreads like wildfire: 350 new malicious apps every hour. https://thenextweb.com/apps/2017/05/04/android-350-malware-apps-hour/#.tnw_744We84m. Accessed 7 Aug 2017
2. Chi2 Feature Selection. https://nlp.stanford.edu/IR-book/html/htmledition/feature-selectionchi2-feature-selection-1.html. Accessed 7 Aug 2017
3. Yin, S., Jiang, Z.: A variance-mean based feature selection in text classification. In: First International Workshop on Education Technology and Computer Science, Wuhan, Hubei, pp. 519–522 (2009)

4. Peng, S., Liu, X., Yu, J., Wan, Z., Peng, X.: A new implementation of recursive feature elimination algorithm for gene selection from microarray data. In: WRI World Congress on Computer Science and Information Engineering, Los Angeles, CA, pp. 665–669 (2009)

5. Vapnik, V.: The support vector method of function estimation. In: Nonlinear Modeling: Advanced Black-Box Techniques, pp. 55–86 (1998)

6. Geurts, P., Ernst, D., Wehenkel, L.: Extremely randomized trees. Mach. Learn. **63**(1), 3–42 (2006)

7. Quinlan, J.R.: Decision trees and decision-making. IEEE Trans. Syst. Man Cybern. **20**(2), 339–346 (1990)

8. Haykin, S.: Neural Networks: A Comprehensive Foundation (1998)

9. Breiman, L.: Random forests. Mach. Learn. **45**(1), 5–32 (2001)

10. Chen, T., Guestrin, C.: XGBoost: A Scalable Tree Boosting System, CoRR (2016)

11. Zhou, Y., Jiang, X.: Dissecting android malware: characterization and evolution. In: IEEE Symposium on Security and Privacy, San Francisco, CA, pp. 95–109 (2012)

12. Grace, M.C., Zhou, W., Jiang, X., Sadeghi, A.-R.: Unsafe exposure analysis of mobile in-app advertisements. In: Proceedings of the Fifth ACM Conference on Security and Privacy in Wireless and Mobile Networks, pp. 101–112 (2012)

13. Fereidooni, H., Conti, M., Yao, D., Sperduti, A.: ANASTASIA: ANdroid mAlware detection using STatic analySIs of Applications. In: 8th IFIP International Conference on New Technologies, Mobility and Security (NTMS), Larnaca, pp. 1–5 (2016)

14. Unuchek, R., Chebyshev, V.: Mobile Malware Evolution. AO Kapersky Lab (2015)

15. Zhou, Y., Wang, Z., Zhou, W., Jiang, X.: Hey, you, get off of my market: detecting malicious apps in official and alternative android markets. In: NDSS 2012, vol. 25, no. 4, pp. 50–52 (2012)

16. Virustotal.com: VirusTotal - Free Online Virus, Malware and URL Scanner. https://www.virustotal.com/en/. Accessed 7 Aug 2017

17. Zheng, M., Sun, M., Lui, J.C.: DroidAnalytics: a signature based analytic system to collect, extract, analyze and associate android malware. In: 12th IEEE International Conference on Trust, Security and Privacy in Computing and Communications, Melbourne, VIC, pp. 163–171 (2013)

18. Grace, M., Zhou, Y., Zhang, Q., Zou, S., Jiang, X.: RiskRanker: scalable and accurate zero-day android malware detection. In: Proceedings of the 10th International Conference on Mobile Systems, Applications, and Services, pp. 281–294. ACM (2012)

19. Desnos, A., Gueguen, G.: Android: from reversing to decompilation. In: Proceedings of Black Hat, Abu Dhabi, pp. 77–101 (2011)

20. Arp, D., Spreitzenbarth, M., Hubner, M., Gascon, H., Rieck, K., CERT Siemens: DREBIN: effective and explainable detection of android malware in your pocket. In: NDSS (2014)

21. Lu, Y., Zulie, P., Jingju, L., Yi, S.: Android malware detection technology based on improved Bayesian classification. In: Third International Conference on Instrumentation, Measurement, Computer, Communication and Control, Shenyang, pp. 1338–1341 (2013)

22. Chan, P.P., Song, W.K.: Static detection of Android malware by using permissions and API calls. In: International Conference on Machine Learning and Cybernetics, Lanzhou, pp. 82–87 (2014)

23. Dash, S.K., Suarez-Tangil, G., Khan, S., Tam, K., Ahmadi, M., Kinder, J., Cavallaro, L.: DroidScribe: classifying android malware based on runtime behavior. In: IEEE Security and Privacy Workshops (SPW), San Jose, CA, pp. 252–261 (2016)
24. Burguera, I., Zurutuza, U., Nadjm-Tehrani, S.: Crowdroid: behavior-based malware detection system for Android. In: Proceedings of the 1st ACM Workshop on Security and Privacy in Smartphones and Mobile Devices, pp. 15–26 (2011)
25. Mas'ud, M.Z., Sahib, S., Abdollah, M.F., Selamat, S.R., Yusof, R.: Analysis of features selection and machine learning classifier in android malware detection. In: International Conference on Information Science and Applications (ICISA), Seoul, pp. 1–5 (2014)
26. Portokalidis, G., Homburg, P., Anagnostakis, K., Bos, H.: Paranoid Android: versatile protection for smartphones. In: Proceedings of the 26th Annual Computer Security Applications Conference, pp. 347–356 (2010)
27. Enck, W., Gilbert, P., Han, S., Tendulkar, V., Chun, B.G., Cox, L.P., Jung, J., McDaniel, P., Sheth, A.N.: TaintDroid: an information-flow tracking system for realtime privacy monitoring on smartphones. ACM Trans. Comput. Syst. (TOCS) **32**(2), 5:1–5:29 (2014)
28. Saracino, A., Sgandurra, D., Dini, G., Martinelli, F.: MADAM: effective and efficient behavior-based android malware detection and prevention. IEEE Trans. Dependable Secure Comput. (2016)
29. Lindorfer, M., Neugschwandtner, M., Platzer, C.: MARVIN: efficient and comprehensive mobile app classification through static and dynamic analysis. In: IEEE 39th Annual Computer Software and Applications Conference, Taichung, pp. 422–433 (2015)
30. Damshenas, M., Dehghantanha, A., Choo, K.K.R., Mahmud, R.: M0droid: an android behavioral-based malware detection model. J. Inf. Priv. Secur. **11**(3), 141–157 (2015)
31. Peng, H., Gates, C., Sarma, B., Li, N., Qi, Y., Potharaju, R., Nita-Rotaru, C., Molloy, I.: Using probabilistic generative models for ranking risks of android apps. In: Proceedings of the 2012 ACM Conference on Computer and Communications Security, pp. 241–252 (2012)
32. GitHub. pjlantz/droidbox. https://github.com/pjlantz/droidbox. Accessed 7 Aug 2017
33. Arora, A., Peddoju, S. K.: Minimizing network traffic features for Android mobile malware detection. In: Proceedings of the 18th International Conference on Distributed Computing and Networking, p. 32. ACM (2017)
34. ContagioDump. http://contagiodump.blogspot.com. Accessed 5 Aug 2017

Human-on-the-Loop Automation for Detecting Software Side-Channel Vulnerabilities

Ganesh Ram Santhanam[1]([⊠]), Benjamin Holland[1], Suresh Kothari[1],
and Nikhil Ranade[2]

[1] Iowa State University, Ames, IA 50011, USA
{gsanthan,bholland,kothari}@iastate.edu
[2] Ensoft Corp., Ames, IA 50010, USA
nikhil@ensoftcorp.com

Abstract. Software side-channel vulnerabilities (SSCVs) allow an attacker to gather secrets by observing the differential in the time or space required for executing the program for different inputs. Detecting SSCVs is like searching for a needle in the haystack, not knowing what the needle looks like. Detecting SSCVs requires automation that supports systematic exploration to identify vulnerable code, formulation of plausible side-channel hypotheses, and gathering evidence to prove or refute each hypothesis. This paper describes human-on-the-loop automation to empower analysts to detect SSCVs. The proposed automation is founded on novel ideas for canonical side channel patterns, program artifact filters, and parameterized program graph models for efficient, accurate, and interactive program analyses. The detection process is exemplified through a case study. The paper also presents metrics that bring out the complexity of detecting SSCVs.

1 Introduction

Smartcards and satellite TV have been compromised by side channel attacks [21]. Hackers used a timing attack against a secret key stored in the Xbox360 CPU to forge an authenticator and load their own code [20]. Intelligence agencies have often relied on side-channel attacks to monitor their foes. Side-channel attacks have become a powerful threat to cryptography. One of the first papers on side channel attacks showed how to recover an RSA private key merely by timing how long it took to decrypt a message [18].

This material is based on research sponsored by DARPA under agreement numbers FA8750-15-2-0080 and FA8750-12-2-0126. The U.S. Government is authorized to reproduce and distribute reprints for Governmental purposes notwithstanding any copyright notation thereon. The views and conclusions contained herein are those of the authors and should not be interpreted as necessarily representing the official policies or endorsements, either expressed or implied, of DARPA or the U.S. Government.

© Springer International Publishing AG 2017
R. K. Shyamasundar et al. (Eds.): ICISS 2017, LNCS 10717, pp. 209–230, 2017.
https://doi.org/10.1007/978-3-319-72598-7_13

The possibilities are open-ended for the ways various program artifacts may be used to create side channels. Attackers exploit SSCVs by presenting a set of inputs and observing the space or time behaviors to construe the secret. The input could vary from HTTP requests to multiple log-in attempts depending on the application. The observable differential behaviors could be execution time, memory space, network traffic, or some output patterns of application-specific significance.

Since SSCVs are open-ended, the proposed approach is that of human-on-the-loop [10] automation. It incorporates: application-agnostic automation to determine hotspots, interactive automation to hypothesize SSCVs, and dynamic analysis for validating SSCVs. The automation uses static and dynamic analyses with program graphs as abstractions. We have developed tools that can handle Java source code or Java bytecode. The analyses are integrated and equipped with an interactive and compact visualization so that the analyst can experiment with and gain understanding of the program structure and behavior and apply that understanding to detect SSCVs. The SSCV toolbox is built using the Atlas platform [11].

The major research contributions are:

- A novel human-on-the-loop automation to detect SSCVs: It synthesizes a combination of non-trivial program analyses with program graphs as the enabling abstraction.
- Interactive automation: An interactive automation enabled by software visualization and querying capability to assist with hypothesizing and gathering evidence for side channels.
- Case study and complexity metrics: The case study brings out the significance of the proposed automation and how it can be used in practice. The metrics provide insights into the complexity of analyzing software for SSCVs and serve as a starting point for searching SSCV hot-spots in a given software.

Organization. The paper is organized as: Sect. 2 describes a motivating example, Sect. 3 describes the overarching SSCV patterns and a detection process, Sect. 4 describes fundamental challenges, Sect. 5 describes application-agnostic and application-specific automation, Sect. 6 describes parameterized graph models for interactive application-specific automation, Sect. 7 presents experimental results, Sect. 8 presents a case study of detecting an SSCV, Sect. 9 describes related work, and Sect. 10 concludes the paper.

2   Motivating Example

Consider a login application with valid user names as the *secret*, and the following side channel: by observing the result (login success or failure) of multiple login attempts and the corresponding response time, an attacker can deduce the secret.

As illustrated in Fig. 1, the example has two control flow paths, one of which includes a loop to verify the password. Since the loop path is taken only if the user name is valid, observing the longer time it takes for this path creates the side chan-

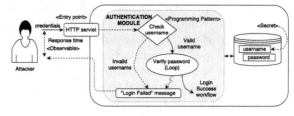

Fig. 1. Side channel in login application

nel. The programming pattern that creates the side channel in time includes: (a) the differential time on two control flow paths, (b) the loop that creates the differential, and (c) the branch condition (we will refer to it as differential branch) which governs the differential paths is tied to the secret. This example illustrates one of the overarching SSCV patterns proposed later (Sect. 3.2). This is an example of side channel in time. This example may also contain a side channel in space, if the application returns responses of different sizes to the client when the user name is valid and when the user name is invalid.

3   SSCV Detection Process

Detecting SSCVs is a nascent field of research. We are not aware of any literature that describes a systematic process for detecting SSCVs. We describe such a process as a starting point for developing the required automation.

Let us start by defining a three dimensional variability spectrum shown in Fig. 2 corresponding to fundamental SSCV attributes: entry points, potential secrets, and programming constructs or artifacts causing differential behavior. Adversaries use *entry points* to provide inputs to induce differential behaviors, *secret types* are the broad categories of secrets that adversaries target, and *observables* are the space or time behaviors produced by program executions.

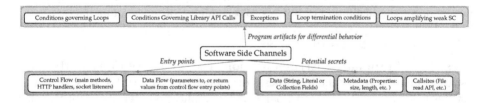

Fig. 2. Three variability dimensions of SSCVs

3.1   Human-on-the-Loop Detection

Detecting SSCVs requires the following: (1) narrow down the possibility of SSCVs to a set of relevant program artifacts, (2) scrutinize these relevant artifacts to hypothesize plausible side channel exploits, and (3) employ dynamic analysis to confirm or reject the exploit hypotheses.

Phase I - Application-agnostic Analysis: Phase I is to pre-compute relevant program artifacts that serve as the foundation for the rest of the analysis. The challenge is to characterize relevant program artifacts. As discussed later, we have developed program artifact characterizations relevant to SSCVs. This automation is application-agnostic and it includes important program artifacts such as entry points, potential secrets, loops and branches, along with attributes relevant to SSCVs. For example, we use the DLI algorithm [29] to identify all loops in the bytecode, and characterize each loop based on attributes such as which library APIs it invokes (e.g., file, network, collection, etc.). The outcome of Phase I is a catalog of relevant program artifacts. The supporting application-agnostic automation is described in Sect. 5.2.

Phase I can reveal suspicious artifacts such as highly complex loops for operations that are often performed in practice by using library routines (e.g. a complex sorting loop). We call such artifacts smells and produce them as a part of Phase I.

Phase II - Application-specific Interactive Analysis: The challenge is to apply application-specific knowledge to develop hypotheses about SSCVs. The applications are often very large and the analyst is not expected to be intimately familiar with the code or the internals of the app. The analyst is expected to explore the app systematically to come up with SSCV hypotheses.

This is achieved in two steps:

1. Select a subset of program artifacts likely to lead to SSCVs.
2. Scrutinize selected program artifacts for the possibility of SSCVs to hypothesize how they could be exploited.

To facilitate the first step, we have automated filters based on the attributes in the program artifact catalog. The analyst can select program artifacts from the catalog that satisfy a combination of attributes. For example, if the analyst identifies that a collection in the app is the secret, he can select all loops (1) whose termination depends on the size of a collection, and (2) that perform file writes (contain callsites to file write APIs). The purpose of the filtering is to narrow down the likelihood of SSCVs to a small set of program artifacts.

To facilitate the second step, we have interactive automation using parameterized graph models, described in Sect. 6.

Phase III - Automatic Instrumentation: The challenge is to enable the analyst to validate or refute the hypotheses developed in Phase II. For this, the analyst needs to instrument relevant parts of the application, perform experiments to record observable events, and then analyze the results to conclude whether the hypothesized differential behavior is actually observable. The automation for this phase is not addressed in this paper. The techniques and tools for statically-informed dynamic analysis (SID) [17] can be used for Phase III.

3.2   Overarching SSCV Patterns

We propose overarching SSCV patterns as guideposts to analysts. We have designed the detection process and the supporting automation to facilitate analysis using these guideposts. The patterns are formulated around: (a) program artifacts that create space or time behaviors (loops or library calls), (b) program artifacts such as branches or exception handling mechanisms that create differential paths.

The five overarching patterns presented here are derived from our study of about 40 DARPA apps and also the reported crypto side-channel attacks [8, 9, 25] which amount to SSCVs. The example in Sect. 2 illustrates the first pattern.

1. *Differential behaviors caused by loops and governing branch condition:* The differential behavior is due to the presence of a loop in one path (as illustrated in the motivating example), or loops with different observable resource consumption in two different paths. In either case, the paths are governed by a branch condition predicated on the input and/or secret.

2. *Differential behaviors caused by Library APIs and governing branch condition:* The differential behavior here is due a branch condition predicated on the input/secret governing a path involving a call to a library API that can cause significant resource consumption (e.g., large array allocation) or produce some other distinct observable behavior (e.g., send a network packet or file I/O) that is absent in the other path governed by the branch condition.

3. *Differential behaviors caused by exceptions:* As exceptions trigger runtime control flow jumps, exception handlers for operations on the input/secret involving resource consuming loops or library calls can cause differential behavior.

4. *Differential behaviors caused by loop termination branch conditions:* When the secret is related to the number of iterations of a loop, the loop's termination branch condition itself serves as the governing branch condition for differential behavior. For example, if the size of a collection is the secret, a loop iterating the collection can consume time or memory proportional to the secret.

5. *Differential behaviors caused by weak side channels inside loops:* The differential behavior may be caused by a weak side channel, wherein the attacker may miss observables due to environmental noise. For example, in the second pattern above, a network packet sent by the app in one path (governed by a branch condition related to the secret) can be lost. However, if the governing branch condition is present within a loop, the weak side channel is amplified and can reveal the secret.

We have made available a repository [4] of example programs extracted from the vulnerable DARPA apps containing SSCVs related to the above patterns.

4 Fundamental Challenges of Detecting SSCV

Let us summarize the fundamental challenges that make detection of side channels quite difficult.

4.1 Path Sensitive Analysis

The challenge is to perform accurate analysis to account for individual behaviors along each of the control flow paths. The exponential growth of the number of paths makes the analysis difficult. The analysis must do the following: (a) account for the execution behavior along each CFG path, and (b) exclude the execution behavior along an infeasible path. Because of its high computational complexity, path-sensitive analysis is avoided in practice by aggregating the execution behaviors [1,2]. This aggregation is the major cause of the large number of false positives and negatives in static analyses.

4.2 Characterization of Program Artifacts

The challenge is to characterize relevant program artifacts that can cause SSCVs. Relevant program artifacts include application entry points, potential secrets, and control flow constructs in the code such as loops, branches and exceptions. It is important to characterize relevant program artifacts and their specific attributes that define how the artifacts relate to the secret, how they create observable space/time behaviors, or how they create differential behaviors.

4.3 Incorporating Application-Specific Knowledge

The challenge is to develop analyses that can account for the variability of application-specific notions of secrets and how they are revealed. The program artifacts obtained through application-agnostic analysis can be too many and they have to be narrowed down to correspond to secrets and side channel mechanisms that are application-specific.

5 Human-on-the-Loop Automation

Figure 3 gives an overview of the automation we have designed for detecting SSCVs. We employ static analysis as a funneling process to narrow down the set of program artifacts. The funneling process incorporates application-agnostic automation and application-specific automation. These correspond to Phase I and II of the detection process described earlier.

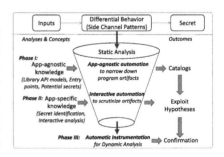

Fig. 3. SSCV detection overview

5.1 Relevant Program Artifacts

In this subsection, we discuss the specific analyses to characterize program artifacts with respect to the variability dimensions discussed in Sect. 3.

Entry Points: Application entry points are computed as starting points for auditing an application for SSCVs. Entry points identify the interfaces through which an attacker can supply input to induce differential behavior in the application. They also identify the part of the code that is reachable, thus helping the analyst to restrict his search for SSCVs to a subset of program artifacts.

Entry points are relevant with respect to the control flow and data flow. There are three kinds of control flow entry points corresponding to whether the application is standalone, web application, or peer-to-peer. These are Java main methods, HTTP request handlers defined in the application, and socket listeners respectively. Analogously for the data flow aspect, the parameters of the Java main methods, the parameters of the HTTP request handlers, the return values of the callsites that read from the sockets are of interest because it is through these interfaces that the attacker can provide inputs to induce differential behavior in the application. The possibility of SSCVs can be restricted to the subset of the artifacts tainted by the data flow entry points. For example, if the analyst suspects that a web application has a side channel pattern involving a loop (i.e., overarching SSCV patterns 1, 4, or 5), then it would suffice to audit only loops that receive data flow from the parameters to the HTTP request handler, namely the `javax.servlet.http.HttpServletRequest` objects.

Potential Secrets: An application can have several side channels but only side channels that reveal a secret are of relevance to the analyst. Identification of the secret in an application is therefore a critical step for the analyst to prune the search for SSCVs. It is one of the first steps the analyst performs using application-specific knowledge.

Secrets can be classified as *data* or *metadata*. Data secrets usually represent contents of variables. Examples of data secrets include primitive values (e.g., integer representing the maximum number of allowed login attempts with invalid password) and Strings (e.g., password or email address of administrator) defined in the app, as well as contents of collections. Examples of metadata secrets include the size of a String (e.g., the number of characters in the username or password) or a collection (e.g., the number of nodes or edges in a graph). Secrets can alternatively be classified as *simple* or *complex*. Secrets that can be deduced by knowing the contents of a single variable in the application are *simple* secrets. Secrets that are a function of multiple variables in the application are *complex*. An example of a complex secret is whether a graph is strongly connected or not. The secret here is a function of the nodes and edges in a graph that may be individual collections. Secrets may not always be present in the code. They can also reside in configuration files read by the application. In such cases, all returns from callsites to the file read APIs in the JDK and the libraries used by the application can be considered potential secrets. For example, in a login authentication application, if the set of valid usernames is the secret and it is read from a file or database, then artifacts corresponding to the returns of callsites that read from files or the database query result are the potential secrets.

Differential Behavior Artifacts: Analysis of relevant loops and branch conditions is key to detecting the presence of SSCV patterns in an application. A loop or branch is relevant to detecting an SSCV pattern if its behavior depends on the secret, i.e., *predicated on the secret*. For example, in the login authentication example, the loop used to verify the password is executed if the branch predicated on the username evaluates to true, and not otherwise. Therefore, the branch governing the loop for verifying password is relevant as it is predicated on the secret (username). A loop or branch is also relevant to detecting an SSCV pattern if it governs events that can be observed by the attacker such as file I/O, network operations, etc. Such a loop or branch is also relevant as they identify events that enable differential behavior to be observed by the attacker.

Therefore, two kinds of loops are important to reason about SSCV patterns in an application: (a) Loops whose termination branch conditions are predicated on secrets (SSCV Pattern 4); (b) Loops whose body contains callsites to certain library APIs (SSCV Pattern 1, 4, 5). Similarly, two kinds of branch conditions are important: (a) Branch conditions predicated on secrets (SSCV Pattern 1, 2, 5); (b) Branch conditions governing certain library API calls (SSCV Pattern 2).

5.2   Application-Agnostic Automation

This automation uses techniques based on classical static analyses (control flow, data flow, loop detection, taint analyses, etc.) to generate three catalogs, one each for: entry points in the application, potential secrets, and programming constructs causing differential behavior in the application. The catalogs include all entry points, potential secrets, and loops and branches relevant to detecting SSCV patterns in the application as classified in the preceding subsections. The loop and branch catalogs identify loops and branches that specifically govern events related to file I/O and network operations, which are common observables in the applications we have encountered as part of our empirical study (Sect. 7). This can however be extended to include loops and branches that govern other events.

The catalog is saved within the Atlas platform as attributes of the program artifacts in Atlas. The branches and loops that match an SSCV pattern are tagged so the analyst can quickly select results from the catalog that match certain tags. The analyst can also export this information as a CSV file to facilitate spreadsheet-style filtering of the artifacts based on their attributes.

5.3   Application-Specific Interactive Automation

We propose two broad categories for interactive analysis: (a) applying selective filters to narrow down the program artifacts, (b) using graph models to detect differential behaviors. The use of interactive analysis is brought out later through the case study presented in Sect. 8.

Selective Filtering of Program Artifacts: The filters are designed to narrow down the loops or the APIs that produce the observable space or time behaviors. The filters place one or more constraints to select a subset of program artifacts.

In order to enable filtering, each loop in the application is characterized with respect to the following properties: (1) nesting depth within the method containing the loop; (2) whether the loop's termination matches a common programming pattern (e.g., loop iterates over a collection using the   `Iterator`'s   `hasNext` API); (3) whether the loop is monotonic (variables controlling the loop's termination are either exclusively incremented or exclusively decremented within the loop); (4) categories of APIs (also called *subsystems*) invoked within the loop's body that indicate the kinds of observable events emitted by the loop's execution (e.g., network operations, file I/O, randomization, etc.); (5) the sizes of control flow and data flow graphs (numbers of nodes and edges) for the loop's body; (6) the number of callsites in the loop; (7) the number of paths within the loop that contain and do not contain callsites. The analyst can create custom filters with constraints on any subset of the above attributes to narrow down loops. We describe one of the commonly applied filters, namely *subsystem interactions filter* that selects loops based on the categories of APIs they invoke.

Subsystem Interactions Filter (SIF): The purpose of this filter is to enable analysts to narrow down the set of loops to loops that interact with a set of APIs. SIF has two configurable parameters: (a) an initial set of loops, and (b) a set of APIs. The analyst configures these parameters and invokes SIF. SIF selects loops that invoke the selected APIs directly or indirectly via function calls.

The resulting loops can be the ones that produce observable behaviors relevant to SSCVs. For example, if the analyst knows that the attacker could observe updates to the log files, he can configure SIF with the logging APIs to get loops which include logging. The case study in Sect. 8 uses SIF to narrow down to loops involving network operations as a crucial step towards detecting an SSCV.

6   Interactive Automation: Parameterized Graph Models

Interactive automation is critically important for human-on-the-loop detection of SSCVs. The analyst must improvise and customize the analysis because of the open-ended possibilities for SSCVs. To be effective at it, the analyst needs to explore the software and gain insights with the help of interactive automation. We employ parameterized graph models as powerful abstractions for interactive automation. The generically defined graph models such as the call graph or the control flow graph are not customizable to solve specific problems. By not being able to focus on only the semantics relevant for a problem, their size explodes and they are no longer effective models to gain insights from. We employ novel graph models that can be parameterized to be problem-specific. The goal is to provide compact representations of software behaviors and structures relevant to SSCVs. These graph models have been developed through our ongoing research on graph models tailored to specific classes of cybersecurity and software safety problems [17, 27].

Table 1 lists our current graph models, their input parameters, their outputs, and how they help the analyst in Phase II of the SSCV detection process to either *select* (narrow down) program artifacts, or to *scrutinize* narrowed down artifacts to hypothesize the presence of SSCV Patterns (Sect. 3.2).

We describe interactive automation using two examples of parameterized graph models: *projected control graph* (PCG) for intra-procedural exploration and the *loop call graph* (LCG) for inter-procedural exploration.

6.1   Intra-procedural Interactive Automation

This subsection describes an intra-procedural interactive automation using the *projected control graph* (PCG) [27] as a parameterized model. As noted in Sect. 4, path sensitive analysis is a fundamental challenge for detecting SSCVs. SSCVs are rooted in differential behaviors. Analyzing each path is computationally

Table 1. Interactive graph models and their use in Phase II of SSCV detection

Parameterized graph models	Input	Output	Phase II activity supported
Loop call graph	Method	Reachable methods containing loops	Select loops w.r.t. entry point
Loop reachability	Dataflow artifact	Loops reached via dataflow	Select loops w.r.t secret
Taint	Source, sink (dataflow)	Taint graph from source to sink	Select loops, branches w.r.t secret
Subsystem interaction	Loops/Methods, APIs	Loops interacting with APIs	Select loops, methods w.r.t APIs
Projected control	Method, events	Reachability preserving CFG reduction	Scrutinize SSCV pattern 1, 2, 5
Exceptional control flow	Control flow artifact	CFG with exceptional flow semantics	Scrutinize SSCV pattern 3
Termination dependence	Loop header	Slice w.r.t. loop's termination condition	Scrutinize SSCV pattern 4

impractical because the number of control flow paths grows exponentially as 2^n for n non-nested 2-way branch nodes. The PCG provides an efficient and accurate model to counter the path explosion issue by focusing on problem-specific distinct behaviors as opposed to distinct paths. As brought out by the study [27], it is an effective solution because the number of problem-specific behaviors do not grow exponentially.

The PCG is parameterized by the set of events relevant to a problem. Events correspond to the nodes of the control flow graph. The behavior along a control flow path is the *event trace*, the sequence of events along that path. The paper [27] formally defines the *event trace*, and an efficient algorithm to compute the PCG.

To create the PCG, two interactive modes are desirable in practice: (a) the analyst selects the events interactively, or (b) the analyst invokes an automated analyzer to create the set of events. We exemplify the two modes. Instead of SSCVs, we use a relatively simple example of *division-by-zero* vulnerability to bring out the gist of interactive automation with the PCG.

In the first interactive mode, the analyst selects the events interactively by clicking on the control flow graph (CFG). In the second interactive mode, the analyst invokes an analyzer to gather the relevant events. For this vulnerability, the analyst invokes the *backward slice analyzer*. Let us describe the first mode in detail. Figure 4 shows a code snippet with an instance of *division-by-zero* vulnerability on line 23. The four selected nodes are tick marked, they correspond to code lines 5, 17, 21, and 23. Instead of clicking on the CFG nodes, the analyst could also click on these lines of code.

Figure 4 shows how the PCG gets refined as the analyst selects the events by clicking on the CFG:

Interaction 1: Analyst clicks on two CFG nodes for statements 17 and 23. That generates the first PCG with two branch nodes and two marked event nodes (colored yellow).

Interaction 2: Analyst clicks on the third CFG node for statement 5. It generates the second PCG as a refinement.

Interaction 3: Analyst clicks on the fourth CFG node corresponding to statement 21. It generates the final PCG for the given vulnerability.

Let us now discuss the significance of the final PCG. Unlike 6 paths in the CFG, the PCG has only 3 paths corresponding to 3 distinct behaviors relevant to the given vulnerability. The relevant behaviors (event traces) are: (a) 5, 17, 23; (b) 5, 23; and (c) 5, 21, 23. The behavior (a) leads to the *division-by-zero* vulnerability. The governing branch condition for these two paths is $C2 = TRUE$ and $C3 = FALSE$. Note that the *path feasibility* analysis is simplified. The governing branch condition must be satisfied for the vulnerability to occur.

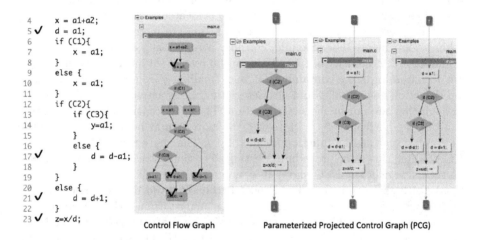

```
4        x = a1+a2;
5  ✔     d = a1;
6        if (C1){
7            x = a1;
8        }
9        else {
10           x = a1;
11       }
12       if (C2){
13           if (C3){
14               y=a1;
15           }
16           else {
17  ✔            d = d-a1;
18           }
19       }
20       else {
21  ✔        d = d+1;
22       }
23  ✔   z=x/d;
```

Control Flow Graph   Parameterized Projected Control Graph (PCG)

Fig. 4. Interactive automation with Projected Control Graph (Color figure online)

PCG use case in detecting SSCVs: Let us describe an use case of PCG for detecting SSCVs. Suppose that an analyst has selected a loop L for scrutiny. Specifically, the analyst would like to know which branch conditions in the application govern the execution of L. This requires the analyst to examine control flow paths from the entry point of the application to L. Using the CFG for this task would involve aggregating the CFGs over all methods in the call graph from the entry point to the method containing L. As shown later using an empirical study in Sect. 7, such inter-procedural CFG are typically very large and prohibitively expensive to analyze. Instead, the analyst can construct a PCG starting with entry point method and prescribing the loop L as the relevant event. The resulting PCGs would retain only the relevant paths from the entry point that lead to L, and elide all other inter-procedural control flow. The graph size reduction from CFGs to PCGs for this use case is a good metric of the PCG's usefulness for SSCV detection. We show by experiments in Sect. 7 that the graph size reduction from CFGs to PCGs is significant.

6.2 Inter-procedural Interactive Automation

This subsection describes an inter-procedural interactive automation using the*Loop Call Graph* (LCG) [17] as a parameterized model. The LCG is a subgraph of the call graph that succinctly represents how loops are distributed across methods in the application. The LCG contains two types of nodes: (a) methods containing loops and (b) methods from which other methods containing loops can be reached via the call graph. A node is colored blue if it contains loops, and grey otherwise. There is an edge from method m_1 to method m_2 in the LCG if m_1 calls m_2. The LCG captures two important pieces of information crucial to analyzing side channels.

Inter-procedural Nesting: First, the LCG captures information about how loops are inter-procedurally nested by using visual (color) attributes for edges. An edge is colored yellow if the callsite of m_2 is located within a loop in m_1 (and black otherwise). This indicates that loops in m_2 are inter-procedurally nested within a loop in m_1. For example, consider a function f containing two loops $L1$ and $L2$, $L2$ nested within $L1$. This can be refactored into two methods f, g, with f containing $L1$, g containing $L2$, and f calling g from inside $L1$. A simple loop detection algorithm would not detect that $L2$ is actually nested within $L1$ although they are not in the same function. The LCG captures this information via a yellow edge from f to g. Moreover, the loop $L2$ may be further down in the call graph – such as in a function h called by g. The analyst can directly use the LCG to infer this inter-procedural nesting. The analyst can infer the presence of a recursive call; the LCG shows it as a cycle with a yellow edge.

Reachability: Second, the LCG is useful to understand how a particular loop can be reached from a selected entry point. An analyst can use this information to restrict the scope of SSCVs to the subset of the application reached by the LCG. For example, a web application could have several HTTP Servlets (Java server side component for handling HTTP requests). To find whether the application has a side channel by which an attacker can deduce a valid username, it may suffice for the analyst to analyze only loops reachable from the Authentication Servlet. The LCG with the Authentication Servlet's HTTP handler method selected shows only methods containing loops reachable from this entry point.

7 Empirical Evaluation with Challenge Apps

We study how the application-agnostic and application-specific automation described in Sects. 5.2 and 5.3 help address the three fundamental challenges (Sect. 4). We present experimental results and evaluation of our tooling with respect to the first two challenges. We illustrate how our process and tooling help address the third challenge using a case study in Sect. 8.

Data Set. This empirical study covers a total of 40 challenge apps provided by DARPA, which have been specifically engineered to include software side channel vulnerabilities involving a broad range of entry points, secrets and programming constructs covering the overarching SSCV patterns discussed in Sect. 3.2. Overall, the data set includes 7,788 loops and 44,542 branch conditions.

7.1 Application-Agnostic Characterization of Program Artifacts: Usefulness of Catalogs

Table 2 shows the distribution of loops across apps. The rows group the apps based on the number of loops they contain (buckets increment by 100 loops). The column $L1$ is the average fraction of loops (across apps in each row) whose termination is predicated on a potential secret (the length of a `String` or size of a `Collection`). The column $L2$ is the average fraction of loops (across apps in each row) that govern observable events (file I/O or network operations).

That a large fraction of loops is identified by $L1$ shows that without using application-specific knowledge about the secret, there may be too many loops to scrutinize for the possibility of SSCVs. Therefore, identification of secret is a key first step that the analyst should perform as part of application-specific reasoning in Phase II. In contrast, the fraction of loops identified by $L2$ narrows the

Table 2. Distribution of loops relevant to SSCV patterns

# Loops	# Apps	L1	L2
0–100	10	94.3%	14.5%
100–200	20	97.2%	14.3%
200–300	5	90.6%	8.2%
>300	5	98.7%	5.3%

search for the possibility of SSCVs effectively even without applying application-specific knowledge. Note that the current $L2$ fraction shown in Table 2 only considers loops governing file I/O and network operations, whereas for certain applications there may be additional events of interest such as call to a specific library (which may in turn emit observable events) or recursion (which may be observable through the growth of stack size). Nevertheless, such special events can be expected to be limited to a small subset of loops, and the loops identified by $L2$ may be used by the analyst to proceed to Phase II.

Table 3 shows the distribution of branch conditions across apps. The rows group the apps based on the number of branches they contain. $B1$ is the average fraction of branches predicated on a potential secret (the length of a `String` or size of a `Collection`). $B2$ is the average fraction of branches that govern observable events (file I/O or network operations). Both $B1$ and

Table 3. Distribution of branches relevant to SSCV patterns

# Branches	# Apps	B1	B2
0–500	17	3.2%	17.0%
500–1000	5	4.0%	10.6%
1000–2000	12	1.7%	6.9%
>2000	6	2.7%	5.2%

$B2$ identify a small fraction of branches in the applications as relevant to detection of SSCVs This shows the usefulness of the branch catalog generated in Phase I - that the possibility of SSCVs due to branches can be narrowed down significantly even prior to applying application-specific knowledge.

7.2 Usefulness of Parameterized Graph Models

Once the analyst has identified a set of loops or branches in the application using the catalog, in Phase II his objective is to develop a hypothesis about how these program artifacts may be exploited to reveal the secret. For this, the analyst has to understand whether the set of paths they induce cause observable differential behavior. Section 6 described two parameterized graph models: LCG and PCG, and how they can be composed to help the analyst understand the equivalence classes of paths from the entry points to a given loop L in the program.

We perform the following experiment using the graph models. For each loop L, we compute the LCG from the entry points to the method containing the loop L, and measure the aggregated number of nodes and edges in the CFGs of all methods in that LCG. We also construct PCGs with entry point and loop L as event, as described in the PCG use case for detecting SSCVs (Sect. 6.1).

Figure 5 shows the comparison of the number of nodes in the CFG versus the PCG (a, b respectively) and the number of edges in the CFG versus the PCG (c, d respectively). The results are presented as histograms with three bins designed to represent small, medium and large instances of the graphs (CFG or PCG). The bin sizes are set to 60 for nodes and 200 for edges, so that the small, medium and large instances correspond to easy, moderate and hard instances for an analyst to comprehend

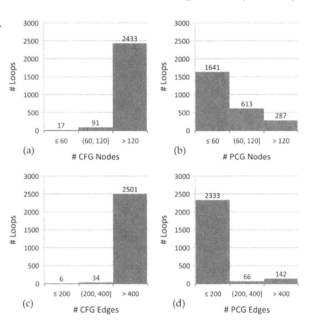

Fig. 5. Distribution of loops w.r.t. size of the CFG and PCG from the entry points to loops

the instance (reachability of the loop from entry point). For example, a loop whose reachability from entry point according to this experiment involves 50 nodes and 150 edges is considered relatively easy. The set of inter-procedurally reachable paths was prohibitively expensive to compute for all the loops. Therefore, the histograms show results for 2542 loops from our data set.

Our results show that, compared to the CFG, the PCG significantly reduces the graph sizes while retaining the SSCVs relevant behaviors. The number of nodes and edges in the PCG was only 13.5% and 2.57% of those in the CFG, which is a drastic reduction. Furthermore, we uniformly observe across the histograms that when using the CFGs, most instances are hard (last bin) and very few are easy (first bin). Whereas the use of PCG reverses the trend: most instances fall in the easy (first) bin, and very few fall in the hard (third) bin.

8 Case Study: SSCV Detection

This section is a study using a challenge application from the DARPA STAC program.

Challenge application. The Law Enforcement Employment Database Server (LEEDS) is a network service application that provides access to records about law enforcement personnel. Employee information is referenced with a unique employee ID number. The database contains restricted and unrestricted employee information. The ID numbers of law enforcement personnel working on clandestine activities is restricted information. The database supports the following functionality: (1) *Search* - search law enforcement personnel by a range of employee ID numbers; (2) *Insert* - create a new employee ID number. Users can search, view, add unrestricted employee IDs and associated information. If a user makes a query for a range of IDs that contains one or more restricted IDs, the restricted IDs will not be included in the returned data.

Side channel question. Consider the following question the analyst has to answer: *Is there a side channel in time in LEEDS that allows an attacker to determine whether the range of values he searches contains a restricted ID?*

Phase I. Our application-agnostic automation generates catalogs for entry points, potential secrets, loops and branches in the application. The analyst observes that there are 8 entry points (7 are main methods and one UDP request handler) and 130 potential secrets (76 fields and 34 callsite returns). The loop catalog reports 106 loops, of which 100 terminate based on Strings or collections, and 17 of the 106 involve events such as network or file I/O. The branch catalog reports 225 branches, of which 75 govern loops or network or file I/O events. The analyst observes that the 17 loops involving network or file I/O could be a good starting point for his Phase II activity of narrowing down program artifacts.

Phase II. In Phase II, the analyst first uses the application's description to identify an entry point and the secret.
Entry Point Identification. LEEDS is a network database server, so the analyst identifies a UDP Request handler as the relevant entry point (other entry points are main methods inaccessible to the clients) for starting his audit.
Secret Identification. To identify the secret, the analyst again leverages knowledge from the application description – that there could be multiple restricted IDs in the LEEDS database, so the secret is likely to be a collection rather than a primitive or a String. Thus, the analyst inspects only the 13 (of the 130) potential secrets that are collections. By manual inspection of the 13 collections, the analyst identifies the field `ids` of type `ArrayList` in the app as the secret (restricted IDs).
Narrow Down Program Artifacts. The analyst decides to explore two strategies to narrow down program artifacts: (1) Use LCG to find reachable loops from

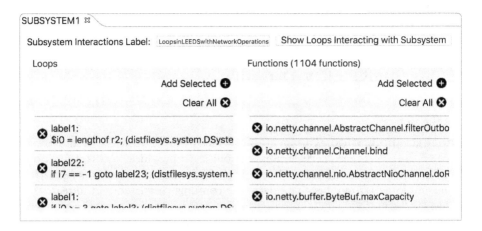

Fig. 6. Subsystems interactions filter UI configured with loops and network APIs used in the LEEDS application

the `UDPServerHandler.channelRead0` entry point; (2) Since the description says that LEEDS is a network database server, and the question is to find a side channel in time rather than space, use subsystem interactions to select loops (time consuming program artifacts) that govern network operations. The LCG from the entry point of interest (`UDPServerHandler`) selects 99 loops (of the 106 loops in the application), which does not provide sufficient reduction of program artifacts to hypothesize SSCVs. Switching to second strategy, the analyst invokes the Subsystem Interactions Filter and configures it with the 106 loops and 1104 network APIs as input (Fig. 6). This results in 14 loops, a significant reduction.

The analyst observes that 8 of the 14 loops, namely $L_1, \ldots L_8$ are present in the entry point method. The analyst further confirms from the loop and branch catalog (generated in Phase I) that the app has a branch condition (b) governing a network write operation as well. At this point, the analyst has narrowed down the program artifacts, and proceeds to scrutinize b, $L_1 \ldots L_8$.

Hypothesizing SSCV Patterns. Observing that b, $L_1 \ldots L_8$ occur in the same method `UDPServerHandler.channelRead0`, the analyst considers plausible SSCV patterns that may be present in the application. Specifically, the analyst has the following questions.

1. Does the branch b create differential paths with and without network operations, indicating the plausibility of SSCV pattern 2?
2. How is branch b related to loop L_i, $i \in \{1 \ldots 8\}$; specifically, do b and any of the L_i's combine to induce differential behavior according to SSCV patterns 1 or 5?
3. Is the branch b predicated on the secret?

Interactive Analysis using PCG. The CFG for `UDPServerHandler`'S `channelRead0` method has 194 nodes and 324 edges, which is difficult to comprehend. To view only the behaviors with respect to network interactions, the analyst decides to inspect the method using a PCG with selected network write operations as events. The analyst uses the following parameters to construct the PCG with respect to L_i : the CFG for the loop L_i's body and the contained network write events. The analyst observes that the resulting PCG with network operation events for one of the loops, say L_1, contains the branch b, so the analyst further scrutinizes the relationship between b, L_1 and network events.

Before proceeding further, the analyst uses an independent taint analysis to confirm that (a) b is predicated on the secret (i.e., there exists a taint from the secret `ids` to the branch condition b), and (b) the loop L_1 iterates for every ID in the database within the search range provided as input. Now the analyst is ready to make a hypothesis.

Figure 7 shows the PCG generated using L_1's loop body and network write event. The top ($\top$) and bottom ($\bot$) nodes in the PCG correspond to the entry and exit for the control flow used to construct the PCG. The cyan node is L_1's loop header, and the yellow node is the selected event (network write operation). The solid and dotted edges from the branch condition nodes (diamonds) correspond to the paths taken when the branch condition evaluates to true and false respectively. For example, loop L_1's header is also its termination branch condition, so when it evaluates to false, L_1 terminates (indicated by dotted edge from loop header to $\bot$).

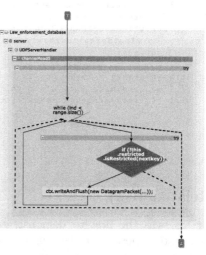

Fig. 7. PCG showing the differential behavior in the LEEDS application (Color figure online)

The PCG clearly identifies b (red diamond) as a branch condition governing differential behavior with respect to two paths: the true path contains a network write operation (call to `writeAndFlush`), while the false path does not. Inspecting the code (Listing 1.1), the analyst finds that the other path b (line 6) governs, has another loop L' (lines 13–15). Since b is already within loop L_1, the analyst hypothesizes that b, L_1 and L' combine to induce differential behavior that has traits of three SSCV patterns 1, 2 and 5 (Sect. 3.2). Specifically, the hypothesis is that L_1 iterates for every ID in the input range, and if it is not a restricted ID (secret), b induces a network event, otherwise b induces a resource consuming operation (loop).

Phase III. Finally, in Phase III the analyst performs dynamic analysis to confirm his hypothesis. The analyst records the timings when searching for a range of IDs including the restricted ID. The analyst confirms that when the range includes a restricted ID, network packets are received for every ID in the database within the range except the restricted ID. The attacker can deduce that a restricted ID is contained in the input range whenever he observes a longer interval between 2 consecutive network packets received from the server. This confirms the analyst's hypothesis.

Listing 1.1. `UDPServer.channelRead0:` code snippet

```
1   int ind = 0;
2   // Loop L1
3   while (ind < range.size()) {
4       Integer nextkey = range.get(ind); ...
5       // Differential branch condition b
6       if (!this.restricted.isRestricted(nextkey)) { ...
7           // Network write event on the true path from b
8           ctx.writeAndFlush((Object)new DatagramPacket(bos,
                (InetSocketAddress)packet.sender())); ...
9           continue;
10      } ...
11      Integer getkey = range.get(ind);
12      // Time consuming loop L' on false path from b
13      while (this.restricted.isRestricted(getkey) && ind < range.size()) {
            ...
14          getkey = range.get(ind);
15      }
16  }
```

9   Related Work

Kocher [18] was the first to demonstrate a side channel attack using timing information to expose secret keys used in RSA, Diffie-hellman, Digital Signature Standard, and other cryptosystems. Subsequently, several side channel exploits against cryptographic algorithms on security hardware and cache architectures have been demonstrated [5, 14–16, 21–23, 30].

In their seminal paper, Brumley and Boneh [8] showed that such side channel attacks also apply to general software systems, and demonstrated a timing side channel attack that could extract private keys from an OpenSSL-based remote web server. Since then, several other side channel attacks have been demonstrated on remote servers and software [6, 7, 20, 24–26, 28]. Software side channel vulnerabilities (SSCVs) are particularly difficult to detect [3, 9]. We discuss related work on the complexity of detecting SSCVs.

Demme et al. introduced Side-Channel Vulnerability Factor (SVF) [12] as a measure of the correlation between execution traces of a microprocessor and an attacker's observation traces. Zhang et al. proposed Cache Side-channel Vulnerability (CSV) [32] as an improvement over SVF specifically to measure cache based side channel vulnerabilities. Köpf et al. [19] model the amount of information about the secret leaked by an application using information-theoretic entropy measures. Doychev et al. [13] perform static analysis to provide a quantitative upper bound on the amount of information contained in various side channel observables such as timing and events corresponding to cache accesses.

The research as noted above pertains to metrics that are specific to certain types of secrets (private keys of cryptosystems), and involve a limited range of observables (e.g., cache access timing, cache hit or miss events, time spent on certain operations on the CPU). In contrast, as we have described, SSCVs admit much wider variability in terms of the secret and observables. As an example, in our case study (Sect. 8), the secret was a globally declared collection in the application and the observable was timing of network packets received from the victim.

Sidebuster [31] analyzes Java web applications to detect and quantify potential side channels. Sidebuster requires the developers or analysts to label program artifacts as sensitive, and uses taint analysis to identify branch conditions tainted by them. The taint analysis based detection performed by Sidebuster is subsumed by the analyses supported by our tooling (see Sects. 5.2 and 5.3).

As far as we know, the open-ended SSCVs and a systematic human-on-the-loop automation for detecting them is being described for the first time with this paper.

10 Conclusion

Software side channel vulnerabilities (SSCVs) pose a serious threat to cybersecurity. They have challenged modern cryptographic algorithms and have enabled attackers to compromise remote servers and web applications. The possibilities for SSCVs are open-ended, beyond the well-studied cryptographic SSCVs. With that in mind, the US defense research agency DARPA created the STAC program [3] to create an innovative technology to address the threat of SSCV attacks. We as STAC participants involved in developing a such technology are challenged with a mixture of benign and vulnerable software to evaluate how well the human-on-the-loop automation works in practice on large software. This paper presents the research for developing such automation.

Our approach tries to bound the open-ended SSCVs by classifying them with overarching patterns. At the current stage of research we have five overarching patterns. We have created a public repository [4] of representative SSCVs based on these patterns. This repository is meant to serve as valuable examples for other researchers interested in pursuing research on SSCVs. We present application-agnostic automation, one that works across all the overarching patterns, to derive and catalog relevant program artifacts and their attributes. The results of application-agnostic automation feed into the subsequent application-specific interactive automation to hypothesize potential SSCVs and gather evidence to prove their existence with targeted dynamic analysis. We present novel interactive automation using parameterized program graph models.

We present a case study to demonstrate how the proposed human-on-the-loop automation can be used in practice. We bring out its significance by an experimental evaluation using metrics to measure the complexity of detecting SSCVs. An interesting and important area for future research is to scan the open-source software to look for potential SSCVs based on the overarching patterns. It involves difficult challenges of minimizing the human effort while maintaining the accuracy of detecting SSCVs.

Acknowledgements. We thank our colleagues from Iowa State University and EnSoft for their help with this paper. Dr. Kothari is the founder President and a financial stakeholder in EnSoft.

References

1. Klocwork source code analysis (2001). http://www.klocwork.com
2. Coverity static analysis (2002). http://www.coverity.com
3. Space/time analysis for cybersecurity (2015). http://www.darpa.mil/program/space-time-analysis-for-cybersecurity. Accessed Mar 2016
4. Software side channel vulnerabilities repository (2017). https://github.com/kcsl/SSCV/. Accessed 18 Aug 2017
5. Benger, N., van de Pol, J., Smart, N.P., Yarom, Y.: "Ooh aah... just a little bit": a small amount of side channel can go a long way. In: Batina, L., Robshaw, M. (eds.) CHES 2014. LNCS, vol. 8731, pp. 75–92. Springer, Heidelberg (2014). https://doi.org/10.1007/978-3-662-44709-3_5
6. Black, J., Urtubia, H.: Side-channel attacks on symmetric encryption schemes: the case for authenticated encryption. In: Proceedings of the 11th USENIX Security Symposium, pp. 327–338 (2002)
7. Bosman, E., Razavi, K., Bos, H., Giuffrida, C.: Dedup Est Machina: memory deduplication as an advanced exploitation vector. In: 2016 IEEE Symposium on Security and Privacy (SP), pp. 987–1004 (2016)
8. Brumley, D., Boneh, D.: Remote timing attacks are practical. Comput. Netw. **48**(5), 701–716 (2005)
9. Chen, S., Zhang, K., Wang, R., Wang, X.: Side-channel leaks in web applications: a reality today, a challenge tomorrow. In: 2010 IEEE Symposium on Security and Privacy (SP), pp. 191–206 (2010)
10. Cummings, M.: Supervising automation: humans on the loop (2008). http://web.mit.edu/aeroastro/news/magazine/aeroastro5/cummings.html. Accessed 10 May 2017
11. Deering, T., Kothari, S., Sauceda, J., Mathews, J.: Atlas: a new way to explore software, build analysis tools. In: Proceedings of International Conference on Software Engineering, pp. 588–591. ACM (2014)
12. Demme, J., Martin, R., Waksman, A., Sethumadhavan, S.: Side-channel vulnerability factor: a metric for measuring information leakage. SIGARCH Comput. Archit. News **40**(3), 106–117 (2012)
13. Doychev, G., Köpf, B., Mauborgne, L., Reineke, J.: CacheAudit: a tool for the static analysis of cache side channels. ACM Trans. Inf. Syst. Secur. **18**(1), 4:1–4:32 (2015)
14. Ge, Q., Yarom, Y., Cock, D., et al.: J. Cryptogr. Eng. (2016). https://doi.org/10.1007/s13389-016-0141-6
15. Gras, B., Razavi, K., Bosman, E., Bos, H., Giuffrida, C.: ASLR on the line: practical cache attacks on the MMU (2017)

16. Gullasch, D., Bangerter, E., Krenn, S.: Cache games-bringing access-based cache attacks on AES to practice. In: Proceedings of the 2011 IEEE Symposium on Security and Privacy, pp. 490–505. IEEE Computer Society (2011)
17. Holland, B., Santhanam, G.R., Awadhutkar, P., Kothari, S.: Statically-informed dynamic analysis tools to detect algorithmic complexity vulnerabilities. In: 2016 IEEE 16th International Working Conference on Source Code Analysis and Manipulation (SCAM), pp. 79–84 (2016)
18. Kocher, P.C.: Timing attacks on implementations of Diffie-Hellman, RSA, DSS, and other systems. In: Koblitz, N. (ed.) CRYPTO 1996. LNCS, vol. 1109, pp. 104–113. Springer, Heidelberg (1996). https://doi.org/10.1007/3-540-68697-5_9
19. Köpf, B., Basin, D.: An information-theoretic model for adaptive side-channel attacks. In: Proceedings of the 14th ACM Conference on Computer and Communications Security, CCS 2007, pp. 286–296. ACM (2007)
20. Lawson, N.: Side-channel attacks on cryptographic software. IEEE Secur. Priv. **7**(6), 65–68 (2009)
21. Matthews, A.: Side-channel attacks on smartcards. Netw. Secur. **2006**(12), 18–20 (2006)
22. Messerges, T.S., Dabbish, E.A., Sloan, R.H.: Investigations of power analysis attacks on smartcards. In: Proceedings of the USENIX Workshop on Smartcard Technology on USENIX Workshop on Smartcard Technology, p. 17. USENIX Association (1999)
23. Oren, Y., Kemerlis, V.P., Sethumadhavan, S., Keromytis, A.D.: The spy in the sandbox: practical cache attacks in JavaScript and their implications. In: Proceedings of the 22nd ACM SIGSAC Conference on Computer and Communications Security, pp. 1406–1418. ACM (2015)
24. Polakis, I., Argyros, G., Petsios, T., Sivakorn, S., Keromytis, A.D.: Where's wally?: precise user discovery attacks in location proximity services. In: Proceedings of the 22nd ACM SIGSAC Conference on Computer and Communications Security, pp. 817–828. ACM (2015)
25. Saura, D., Futoransky, A., Waissbein, A.: Timing attacks for recovering private entries from database engines. Black Hat USA (2007). https://www.blackhat.com/presentations/bh-usa-07/Waissbein_Futoransky_and_Saura/Presentation/bh-usa-07-waissbein_futoransky_and_saura.pdf
26. Song, D.X., Wagner, D., Tian, X.: Timing analysis of keystrokes and timing attacks on SSH. In: Proceedings of the 10th Conference on USENIX Security Symposium, vol. 10 (2001)
27. Tamrawi, A., Kothari, S.: Projected control graph for accurate and efficient analysis of safety and security vulnerabilities. In: Asia-Pacific Software Engineering Conference (APSEC), pp. 113–120, December 2016
28. Vila, P., Köpf, B.: Loophole: timing attacks on shared event loops in chrome. arXiv preprint arXiv:1702.06764 (2017)
29. Wei, T., Mao, J., Zou, W., Chen, Y.: A new algorithm for identifying loops in decompilation. In: Nielson, H.R., Filé, G. (eds.) SAS 2007. LNCS, vol. 4634, pp. 170–183. Springer, Heidelberg (2007). https://doi.org/10.1007/978-3-540-74061-2_11
30. Yarom, Y., Falkner, K.: Flush+reload: a high resolution, low noise, l3 cache side-channel attack. In: Proceedings of the 23rd USENIX Conference on Security Symposium, pp. 719–732. USENIX Association, Berkeley, CA, USA (2014)

31. Zhang, K., Li, Z., Wang, R., Wang, X., Chen, S.: Sidebuster: automated detection and quantification of side-channel leaks in web application development. In: Proceedings of the 17th ACM Conference on Computer and Communications Security, pp. 595–606. ACM (2010)
32. Zhang, T., Liu, F., Chen, S., Lee, R.B.: Side channel vulnerability metrics: the promise and the pitfalls. In: Proceedings of the 2nd International Workshop on Hardware and Architectural Support for Security and Privacy, pp. 2:1–2:8. ACM (2013)

MalDetec: A Non-root Approach for Dynamic Malware Detection in Android

Nachiket Trivedi and Manik Lal Das[✉]

DA-IICT, Gandhinagar, India
nachiket5197@gmail.com, maniklal_das@daiict.ac.in

Abstract. We present a malware detection technique for android using network traffic analysis. The proposed malware detection tool, termed as MalDetec, uses a non-root approach to notify the user in real-time about any malicious URL (Uniform Resource Locator) requests by any malware. MalDetec parses the packet dump file and merges it with the output of our network traffic analysis to generate App-URL pairing in real-time. This is later scanned by Virustotal databases and the user gets notified of suspicious URL requests. In addition, MalDetec maintains a local database containing results of previous scans for quick look-up during future scans. The experimental results show that MalDetec successfully detects the applications accessing malicious URLs, in real-time without having root privileges.

Keywords: Android · Malware detection · Virustotal
Network traffic analysis

1 Introduction

Android dominates the smartphone market by a large margin. According to Gartner [1], off all the phones sold in the last quarter of 2016, android accounted for 81.7%. With such a vast user base and fewer restrictions, security threat on phone device as well as applications is a growing concern. A recent survey by Nokia [2] states that during the second half of 2016, the increase in smartphone infections was 83% following on the heels of a 96% increase during the first half of the year, of which more than 80% was targeted for android.

Malware [3] is an executable code that has malicious intent to a computer, application or system. These malicious programs can perform a variety of functions, including stealing, encrypting or deleting sensitive data, hijacking core computing functions and monitoring users' activity without their permission. Many people save their private information like bank details, photos, passwords etc. on their smart phones, making all these information prone to such malware.

In this paper, we present a malware detection tool using network analysis in real-time. Many android malware contacts malicious servers and our aim is to detect such behaviors in real-time. We develop an application, MalDetec, which can successfully detect malicious URL requests using network traffic analysis [4].

© Springer International Publishing AG 2017
R. K. Shyamasundar et al. (Eds.): ICISS 2017, LNCS 10717, pp. 231–240, 2017.
https://doi.org/10.1007/978-3-319-72598-7_14

MalDetec works in real time, getting URL scan results while the application runs in background, and does not require root privileges. Considering the fact that most of the android users do not root their phones, we made MalDetec completely independent of the device's root status. MalDetec works on the principle of capturing all the URLs accessed by different applications, scanning them for potential malicious content and notifying the user accordingly. We provide the complete working principles of MalDetec along with the experimental results.

The remainder of the paper is organized as follows. Section 2 describes related work. Section 3 presents the proposed MalDetec tool. Section 4 provides analysis and experimental results. We conclude the work in Sect. 5.

2   Related Work

Malware [3,5] detection methods can be broadly classified into two parts: static and dynamic [6]. Static analysis or code analysis means the process of detecting malware when the malicious application is not being executed. This commonly includes segregating the different resources of the binary file without executing it and studying each component. Many smart malware obfuscate the malicious code and therefore, prove difficult to detect using normal static analysis. Dynamic analysis or behavioral analysis means studying the behavior of any application when it is actually running on a host system. Thus, the result of analysis can be obtained at the same instant the application is running. A popular method called sandboxing is used, which executes the malicious software in a virtual environment and thus, not having any adverse effects on the machine [7]. Many advanced malware can exhibit various evasive techniques specifically designed to defeat dynamic analysis including testing for virtual environments or active debuggers, delaying execution of malicious payloads, or requiring some form of interactive user input. Rastogi et al. [8] demonstrated this obfuscation method by using their tool DroidChamelon, which obfuscates malware and successfully evades known commercial anti-malware. There exists a few static and dynamic analysis detection methods in the literature. Song and Hengartner [9] proposed PrivacyGuard, a VPN based platform to dynamically detect information leakage on android devices. Chandramohan and Tan [10] demonstrated a wide variety of detection methods using both the approaches and explained them briefly. Isohara et al. [11] proposed a kernel based dynamic analysis method for malware Detection. Zaman et al. [13] proposed a static analysis method for malware detection in android based on network traffic analysis. Many a time, an application accesses a blacklisted URL while executing. For this, Zaman et al. suggested a method where the network packet data is collected from the android device for a particular time range and later analyzed on the computer. The URLs obtained are then scanned remotely by using the service provided by Virustotal and hence the scanned result is obtained. However, there are two shortcomings with Zaman et al.'s approach. First, the method captures the data from the device and analyses it later on an external computer, which can potentially infect the device before getting detected. It would be better if the tool analyzes the packets dynamically and then, give the scanned results of the URLs as soon as the application accesses it. Second, the method used by them works only for a rooted device, which is risky, as one needs to give device's root privilege to the application.

3   MalDetec: The Proposed Malware Detection Tool

The proposed MalDetec tool analyses the network packets dynamically, scans the accessed URL for blacklist status without having the root privileges of the device, and reports the result to the user for suspicious actions of applications. Whenever an application sends an HTTP request, MalDetec forms a source port to timestamp to url mapping, which is done by continuous parsing of packet dump file (.pcap file) produced by a third party application named tPacket-Capture. The other process gets the timestamp to port to app mapping and by merging the outcomes of the above two processes, we get the App-URL table. MalDetec also maintains a local database- hotdata, containing previous virusto-tal scan results. MalDetec first looks into the hotdata and if found, it reports the user if any blacklisted URL is accessed. If any app accesses a URL whose data is not present in the hotdata, a virustotal scan will take place and subsequently the hotdata will be updated. We also developed another application called Tester for testing purpose.

3.1   System Model

The participating entities in the whole process are android OS, the tPacketCap-ture [12] app, MalDetec, the uid-app database of MalDetec, the hotdata database of MalDetec, and various other applications which are opened and used by the user. Basically, whenever any application is opened and prompted to access any URL, it interacts with android OS to send HTTP request. Meanwhile, tPacket-Capture interacts with android and by using its VPNService [14] it collects the packet dump. MalDetec runs synchronously and interacts with tPacketCapture to use the pcap file generated by it. Later on in the process, MalDetec interacts with its databases and also with android for its own network analysis and URL scanning.

3.2   Prerequisites and Assumptions

There are certain prerequisites for proper functioning of MalDetec. First and foremost, the tPacketCapture application should be installed and running before MalDetec is initiated. This is because MalDetec depends on tPacketCapture for packet dump generation. Another thing that is important but not necessary is to make a database of uid-app mapping, which is also considered in MalDetec. Excluding this step will not affect the working of MalDetec, but the application name will not be displayed when notifying the user. We also made an assumption that each application communicates with external servers via HTTP. Unless any application communicates via a protocol(s) other than HTTP, MalDetec can successfully detect it. Furthermore, MalDetec depends on the services provided by Virustotal for examining the malevolent nature of any URL.

3.3 The Working Principles of MalDetec

We break the whole working of MalDetec in 5 parts as follows:

1. Design of MalDetec.
2. Capturing of packet dump and parsing .pcap file to get the time-port-URL mapping in real time.
3. Capturing the network statistics data and parsing it to get the time-port-App mapping in real time.
4. Merging the outcomes of steps (2) and (3) to get the App-URL table, followed by checking the URL in hotdata for scanned results.
5. Scan the URLs that are present in the for-later-scan database by using the virustotal API, notify the user as well as update the hotdata.

Design of MalDetec. We develop MalDetec using the Kivy framework [16] which is an open source project allowing developers to make android apps in python. It is based on the project python-for-android. We used python to make MalDetec instead of java because of various libraries provided by python for network analysis and parsing packet dump files, in addition to efficient and feasible file management. Another important reason of using Kivy framework was that the code just needs a slight modification to be compatible with iOS, which can be incorporated in the future. Before starting MalDetec, tPacketCapture app needs to be started for packet capturing. Once the main process is started, the working of the app is described in detail in Fig. 1.

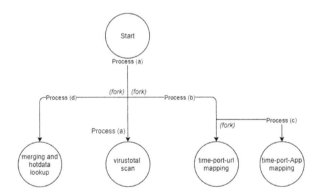

Fig. 1. Processes running concurrently in MalDetec

As shown in the Fig. 1, pressing the start button initiates the process-(a). This process is later forked into a child process-(b). This child process-(b) parses the packet dump file generated by tPacketCapture and forks again to form another child process-(c) which generates netdump files to get time-port-app mapping. The initial parent process-(a) again forks to make another child process-(d) which is responsible for dynamic merging of the outcomes of process-(b) and process-(c) to make the App-URL table. Finally, the initial main process-(a) goes on to do a virustotal scan of the URLs that are generated from process-(d). All these processes are described in following sub sections.

Capturing of packet dump and parsing it to get the time-port-URL mapping. This phase involves continuous parsing of the packet-dump (.pcap) file which is produced by the tPacketCapture app. tPacketCapture is a third party application that captures all the network packets by using VPNService, a service provided by android, where it makes a vpn server for itself to capture network traffic. It makes a single .pcap file which contains all the network packet details and the process-(b) of Fig. 1 parses it. Here, we open the .pcap file to read and parse it in a continuous loop. This is done because tPacketCapture runs continuously in the background, and hence the packetdump file (.pcap file) gets updated constantly. As the .pcap file is opened and closed continuously, we made sure that the already parsed data of any previous iteration is not re-written in our final parsed file, thus saving the CPU time. For parsing the .pcap file, we used the dpkt framework [15] of python. The logic used in capturing of packet dump and parsing it to get the time-port-URL mapping is represented in Algorithm 1.

Algorithm 1. Parsing Packet Dump

1: **while** True **do**
2:     f = open(*File,to read*)
3:     pcap = dpkt.pcap.Reader(f)
4:     **for** ts,buf in pcap **do**
5:         eth = dpkt.ethernet.Ethernet(buf)
6:         ip=eth.data
7:         tcp=ip.data
8:         **if** tcp.dport=80 and len(tcp.data) > 0 **then**
9:             http = dpkt.http.Request(tcp.data)

First, we obtain the pcap object from the pcap file. By iterating through the pcap object, we derived the timestamp and the whole packet buffer for each packet. From the packet buffer, we got the Ethernet, IP and subsequently the TCP objects. The HTTP request data was obtained from the TCP object by dpkt only when TCP destination port was 80. Eventually, by parsing the HTTP object, we got the timestamp, URL, and port which was stored dynamically in a file. This process repeats itself till the user deliberately closes the app. The final file, in which the time-port-URL mapping is stored, should not be made from scratch in each iteration, and thus only the new packet data is parsed and appended to it in every iteration, thereby saving CPU time. Therefore, we get a dynamically generated file having the time-port-URL mapping from this step.

Capturing the network statistics data and parsing it to get the time-port-App mapping. With this phase, MalDetec maps the applications with the ports they were using at any particular time. To fulfill this task Zaman et al. [13] used the netstat command combined with busybox tool which enforced the user to have a rooted device. To overcome this problem, we used the /proc/net/ interface that does the job but does not require a rooted device. We used the proc interfaces [17] /proc/net/tcp and /proc/net/tcp6, which provide details of currently active TCP connections and are implemented by tcp4_seq_show() in net/ipv4/tcp_ipv4.c and tcp6_seq_show() in net/ipv6/tcp_ipv6.c, respectively. It first lists all listening TCP sockets, and next lists all established TCP connections. For using TCP protocol on IPv6 and IPv4, we used the tcp6 and tcp with the /proc/net interfaces. Therefore, by running the following command, a file was made which contains the command's output for a particular timestamp.

```
cat /proc/net/tcp6 >> /storage/emulated/0/MalDetec/files/dump/netdump\$i.txt
```

Now we execute this same command continuously after each second and hence derive a set of files, each containing the network statistics for a particular timestamp. When the above process keeps running, another process for merging these files runs concurrently. The process-(c) mentioned before in Fig. 1 is expanded as shown in Fig. 2.

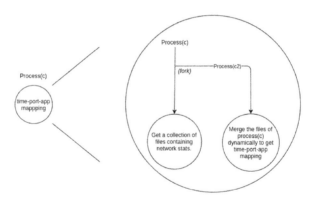

Fig. 2. A flowchart indicating the process-(c)

The other child process-(c2) that runs concurrently, merges all the files produced by the parent process-(c) into a single final file dynamically such that the contents of this file are the time-port-App mappings. Every second a new network statistics file is created as shown here. Thus, as soon as any new file is made, (c2) immediately parses it for the UID (a unique id is provided to each android application at the time of installation) of the app that was accessing a particular port at a particular time. The UID remains unchanged until the app is manually uninstalled (unlike the ProcessID). By getting the app package name from the UID, the time-port-App mapping is obtained and written in the final file of this step. A major hindrance in this step was getting the app package name from the UID. A conventional way to do this task is to use the dumpsys tool [18] by the adb command.

```
adb shell "dumpsys package | grep -A1 'userId=%s' "
```

This option works for a rooted device, as it needs access to application details for all apps on the device and it is present in /data/system/packages.list file, which is inaccessible without root permissions. To overcome this, we connected the phone with a computer and created an adb server. We ran this adb command for all the applications installed on the device and saved in the MalDetec app folder in the device, thus getting the UID-app package name mapping. This was done before MalDetec was started and is required to be done only one time per device. Therefore, while MalDetec is executing, during process-(c2), we extracted the app package name from its corresponding UID by grepping our local database. This way at the end, in the final file of this step, we obtain the time-port-app_package_name mapping dynamically.

App-URL table in real-time and scrutinizing the Hotdata. As the initial parent process-(a) forks into child process-(b) for network analysis, after some time period, another child process is created from the process-(a), depicted as process-(d) in the Fig. 1. The main function of this process is to dynamically merge the files created by process-(b) and process-(c) to get the final App-URL table and notify the user about the scan results of the URL if its data is present in the hotdata. Hotdata is a file that contains the URL scan results and details of previously scanned URLs. As virustotal only allows 4 requests per minute by using their public API, it becomes a very slow and inefficient method to scan every time. To overcome this we used hotdata which is a local database on the device that contains the details of previous scans. Therefore, in this step, after merging, every new URL in the merged file is concurrently searched for in the hotdata first. If found, the user is notified immediately of the details. If not found, the URL and the app name are written in another file for later virustotal scan explained below. Thus the use of hotdata increased performance efficiency of MalDetec.

URLs scanning process. The aforementioned process makes a file for all the App-URL mappings whose details are not present in the hotdata. This file is for later virustotal scan. Every t *minutes*, another process is invoked which scans these URLs by using the API provided by virustotal. Virustotal [19] is a service provided by Google, which uses about 64 URL scanners to scan any file/URLs. It provides developers an API key to use their public API to scan URLs or files, with a limitation of 4 requests per minute. The chosen format for the API is HTTP POST requests with JSON object responses. Therefore, as process-(d) dynamically updates the file *for-later-scan*, every t *minutes*, the new entries to that file is scanned by using virustotal API for potentially malicious content. It takes about 15 s to get the result of a particular request which is later notified to the user. The hotdata is also updated concurrently. The pseudo-code for this process is described in Algorithm 2.

The Request method sends a request to virustotal for the scan of the URL which is here encoded in the data parameter. The response from the virustotal is read by and the JSON file is extracted from it. From the JSON file we obtain a dictionary response_dict containing all the scan result details of the specified URL. All the information like positives, report link, scan date, total scanners can be obtained from this dictionary. The relevant information like the positives is right away notified to the user by a notification. These details are also updated in the hotdata. In the end, we obtain dynamic notifications for any malicious URLs accessed by any of the installed applications.

Algorithm 2. URLs scanning using Virustotal

1: **while** True **do**
2:      f=open(*for later scan file* , *to read*)
3:      hdata=open(*hotdata file* , *to append*)
4:      **for** lines in f.readlines() **do**
5:          Api_Key = *the api key*
6:          words=lines.split()
7:          **if** len(words) = 2 **then**
8:              app=words[0]
9:              get_link=words[1] #*url to scan*
10:             url = 'https://www.virustotal.com/vtapi/v2/url/report'
11:             parameters = 'resource': get_link , 'apikey': Api_Key , 'scan':1
12:             data = urllib.urlencode(parameters)
13:             req = urllib2.Request(url,data)
14:             response = urllib2.URLopen(req)
15:             json = response.read()
16:             response_dict = simplejson.loads(json)

---

4   Experimental Results

We first opened the tPacketCapture application and started to capture the packets. Then we started MalDetec and clicked start to initiate the process. As tPacketCapture and MalDetec were running in the background, we opened a series of applications having the potential to send a network request, one after another. In the background, tPacketCapture was collecting packetdump data into a .pcap file. MalDetec opens this .pcap file, parses it, and does its own network analysis to get the App-URL table and looks first in the hotdata. As soon the app amazon was opened, it downloaded a bunch of .png files whose report was present in our hotdata. Thus, a notification was sent to the user showing the details of the scan report as shown in the Fig. 3c.

For malware testing, we made another application, named Tester. Tester continuously accesses a bunch of URLs via HTTP some of which are known to have malicious data. Therefore, as soon as the Tester app started functioning, it began to send HTTP requests for those URLs in the background. MalDetec, being executed concurrently, catches the URLs and checks the hotdata first. Some of those were not present in the hotdata and hence were placed in the for-later-scan file. As soon as the scan function was invoked after t *minutes*, a complete virustotal scan of the URLs present in the for-later-scan file took place. One such URL accessed by Tester was present in our hotdata. It was caught and scanned as positive by virustotal. Immediately the user was notified as shown below. Some malicious URLs were accessed after a while by the Tester app which were not present in our hotdata. In the notification, as depicted in Fig. 4, the user is notified that whether the URL accessed was present in hotdata (depicted as HData) or not (depicted as Vtotal). The user is even notified the number of positives a particular URL has according to virustotal and also the application name which accessed the URL. If at least one positive was detected according to virustotal, a notification with warning is sent to the user.

(a) tPacketCap-
ture app starting
page

(b)   MalDetec:
initiated by start
button

(c) URLs from
hotdata notified
as HData

Fig. 3. Experimental screenshots

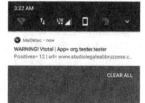

Fig. 4. Malicious URLs notified with warning along with the number of positives

5   Conclusions

We discussed a malware detection technique to dynamically detect any malicious URL access for any android device regardless of its root status. We proposed a tool- MalDetec which used network analysis to get the App-URL mapping in real time, scanned those URLs on the local database hotdata and notified the user accordingly. Whenever any URL which was already present in our hotdata was accessed, we were instantly notified. But, when the URL was not present, it took a while for us to get the notification. This happened because MalDetec undertook a virustotal scan for those URLs and as virustotal only allowed 4 requests/minute, we got delayed results. Therefore, with a locally managed database, the user is notified in real-time of almost all the URL requests. We also demonstrated the experimental results of MalDetec. The limitation of MalDetec is that it cannot detect malware if the app accesses a URL via any protocol(s) other than HTTP, which is a potential future scope of MalDetec to extend its features further.

References

1. Gartner report 2017. http://www.gartner.com/newsroom/id/3609817
2. Nokia Threat Intelligence Report. Mobile infection rates rose steadily in 2016
3. Honig, A., Sikorski, M.: Practical Malware Analysis: The Hands-On Guide to Dissecting Malicious Software. No Starch Press, San Francisco (2012)
4. Arora, A., Garg, S., Peddoju, S.K.: Malware detection using network traffic analysis in Android based mobile devices. In: Proceedings of International Conference on Next Generation Mobile Apps, Services and Technologies, pp. 66–71(2014)
5. Qian, Q., Cai, J., Xie, M., Zhang, R.: Malicious behavior analysis for Android applications. Int. J. Netw Secur. **18**(1), 182–192 (2016)
6. Distler, D.: Malware Analysis: An introduction. SANS Institute InfoSec, Reading (2007)
7. CWSandbox Automates Malware Analysis. http://www.securitypronews.com/cwsandbox-automates-malware-analysis-2006-10. Accessed July 2016
8. Rastogi, V., Chen, Y., Jiang, X.: DroidChameleon: evaluating android anti-malware against transformation attacks. In: Proceedings of ACM SIGSAC Symposium on Information, Computer and Communications Security, pp. 329–334 (2013)
9. Song, Y., Hengartner, U.: PrivacyGuard: a VPN-based platform to detect information leakage on Android devices. In: Proceedings of ACM CCS Workshop on Security and Privacy in Smartphones and Mobile Devices, pp. 15–26 (2015)
10. Chandramohan, M., Tan, H.: Detection of mobile malware in the wild. IEEE J. Comput. **45**(9), 65–71 (2012)
11. Isohara, T., Takemori, K., Kubota, A.: Kernel-based behavior analysis for Android malware detection. In: Proceedings of International Conference on Computational Intelligence and Security, pp. 1011–1015 (2011)
12. tPacketCapture. http://www.taosoftware.co.jp/en/android/packetcapture/
13. Zaman, M., Siddiqui, T., Amin, M.R., Hossain, S.M.: Malware detection in Android by network traffic analysis. In: Proceedings of International Conference on Networking Systems and Security (2015)
14. VpnService. https://developer.android.com/reference/android/net/VpnService.html
15. J Oberheide. Parsing a PCAP file. https://jon.oberheide.org/blog/2008/10/15/dpkt-tutorial-2-parsing-a-pcap-file/. Accessed Jan 2017
16. Kivy - Open source Python library. https://kivy.org/. Accessed Jan 2017
17. /proc/net/tcp documentation. https://goo.gl/2TVZNp. Accessed Jan 2017
18. DUMPSYS: Tool to get system services details by ADB. https://developer.android.com/studio/command-line/dumpsys.html
19. VirusTotal. https://www.virustotal.com

Identity Management and Access Control

DIscovery and REgistration Protocol
For Device and Person Identity Management in IoT

Marco Lobe Kome[1,2(✉)], Mariem Graa[2], Nora Cuppens-Boulahia[2],
Frédéric Cuppens[2], and Vincent Frey[1]

[1] Orange Labs, 4 rue du Clos Courtel, 35510 Cesson-Sévigné, France
{marco.lobekome,vincent.frey}@orange.com
[2] IMT Atlantique Bretagne-Pays dela Loire,
2 rue de la Châtaigneraie, 35576 Cesson-Sévigné, France
{mariem.graa,nora.cuppens,frederic.cuppens}@imt-atlantique.fr

Abstract. With connected things, one service can be used with more than one device, all sharing the same user identity. In this context, the need to figure out whether the service is being used through a desktop computer, a smartphone, or a more constrained device is essential in order to better manage user identity. Given that constrained devices are less tamper resistant, they are more vulnerable to attacks than other appliances. We identified two challenges which make it difficult to apply robusts security mechanisms: the limited resources available on devices and the sharing of a user's identity with the device. To address these challenges, we propose, a DIscovery and REgistration (DIRE) protocol that ensures secure device and person identities management. Our protocol has been formally proven and implemented. The runtime of the whole protocol is short and the code the device must embed is lightweight. As a result of our experiment, we produced a command line client for a user, a device firmware and a server handling the filiation of a user and its devices.

Keywords: IoT · MQTT · OAuth · Identity management · Security

1 Introduction

The Internet of Things (IoT) constitutes a set of objects such as sensors, actuators, smart devices that communicate through the Internet to form a collection of identifiable smart entities [1]. The number and variety of devices that are used to collect data have increased at an accelerated rate in recent years. According to a Cisco study [2], the number of Internet-connected devices exceeded the human population in 2010. This number is expected to reach 50 billion in 2020.

In current architectures of the IoT, users share their credentials with connected objects to have access to services. But, the limited processing, memory and power resources of these objects make it difficult to apply security mechanisms such as high strength encryption and signature algorithms. As a matter of fact, the

© Springer International Publishing AG 2017
R. K. Shyamasundar et al. (Eds.): ICISS 2017, LNCS 10717, pp. 243–262, 2017.
https://doi.org/10.1007/978-3-319-72598-7_15

current authentication mechanisms of internet-connected objects can easily be bypassed and those devices can be infected by a malware such as Mirai [3], making them a botnet in large-scale network attacks [4,5]. Therefore, balancing the utility of running internet-connected objects and the privacy risks is a critical challenge for the IoT.

On the other hand, when the connected object and the user have the same identity, the behavior of the device can be changed by the manufacturer without asking the user. As a real example, Fitbit users are unwittingly sharing details of their sex lives with the world because the manufacturer makes this sexual activity public by default [6].

Based on the two previously identified challenges: the limited resources available on devices and the sharing of a user identity with its devices, the important question that arises is the following: how can we securely bind devices' and persons' identities? In this paper, we propose an original protocol that ensures secure device and person identities management. Our proposed protocol allows to discover and register smart devices into an Identity Provider in a seamless and user-friendly way. We take our inspiration in discovery mechanisms like mDNS [7] and in OAuth2.0 [8] for the registration process. Our contribution is twofold: the protocol adapts OAuth2.0 mechanisms to the IoT context and establishes solid foundations to ease access control policy management. In fact, managing device identity as easily as human identity is a strong base to dynamically adjust access control policy. Our protocol has been formally proven and implemented. As a result of our experiment, we produced a command line client for a user based on a zeroconf browser, a device firmware built with Arduino and a Python server handling the filiation of a user and its devices.

The rest of the paper is organized as follows: Sect. 2 introduces the background knowledge on which we base our approach. Section 3 introduces the protocol by defining prerequisites and depicting discovery and registration processes. In Sect. 4, we deliver a formal verification that the protocol binds human and device identities in compliance with security requirements needed in the smart object networking context. In Sect. 5, we present an implementation of our protocol based on a scenario and we discuss about the attacks detected by the protocol and the remaining work to prevent more. Finally, in Sect. 6 we provide a comparison with the related works before concluding this paper in Sect. 7.

2   Background

2.1   ACE Architecture

Our work is inspired by the security architecture provided by Authentication and Authorization for Constrained Environments (ACE) working group. They are proposing an architecture for authorization in constrained environments [9]. We take from this architecture the actors and redefine interactions between them. There are two reasons why the proposed protocol is based on ACE architecture:

First of all, it takes into account the constraints on code size, state memory, processing capabilities, user interface, power and communication bandwidth of some nodes. Secondly, the entity managing the device is also taken into account unlike other architectures.

Integrating those nodes in the IoT requires a definition of those main actors:

- The **Constrained Device** or **Thing (T).** This actor is complex enough to embed a client and a server both limited by the device resources. The constrained client attempts to access one user's resources while the server is able to produce data related to a user.
- The **Manufacturer (M).** Known by ACE as Requesting Party (RqP). This actor is in charge of the device's identity management. We grant the manufacturer all ACE Client Authorisation Server (CAS) attributes. Identity data collection is part of their business model so manufacturers are maintaining a strong link with their devices.
- The **Resource Owner (RO)** or **User (U).** This actor is in charge of the resource management. It defines the access control policy of the resource server through a less constrained device like a smartphone or a desktop computer.
- The **Identity Provider (IDP).** The IDP can embed a lot of functionalities, in this architecture this actor is in charge of the authentication and authorization of clients capable of having access to owner resources. It is seen as Authorization Server (AS). In many implementations, it also hosts owner resources so it is also considered as Resource Server (RS).

2.2   OAuth2.0

The Open Authorization framework (OAuth) [8] is built on top of the HTTP protocol. It enables a third-party application to obtain limited access to a service on behalf of a resource owner by orchestrating an approval interaction between the resource owner and the service. It is implemented by the most used identity providers (Facebook, Twitter, Google).

OAuth defines:

- A **resource owner**
- A **client** as the application requesting authorization from the resource owner
- An **authorization server** which delivers authorization grants representing the resource owner's authorization
- And a **resource server** hosting owner's resources.

One of the challenges we are addressing in this paper is to allow the constrained device to use owner's resources on its behalf. So we delegate authorizations from owner to device using OAuth framework.

In our proposed DIscovery and Registration (DIRE) protocol, we adapt OAuth2.0 to the context of IoT as there are two different user-agents in the process, a consideration not taken into account in the implementation of the OAuth framework.

2.3   The Things Description Document (TDD)

We define device identity in the DIRE protocol based on the model proposed by the Simurgh framework [10]. It is a framework whose goal is to make an effective discovery, programming and integration of services exposed in IoT. The framework introduces the *Things Description Document (TDD)*. It is a file responding to the JSON format with two main objects:

- **Entity properties** dedicated to describe properties of the entity with a name, location and last modified date. This information is mandatory.
- **Entity services** dedicated to the description of services the entity is exposing through RESTFul routes.

In the proposed protocol, the devices are declining their identity as if they are responding to the questions: *what am I capable of?* And *what do I need to achieve that?* The TDD must then inevitably contain the following items, organized as the JSON file 2.3 illustrates:

- A **thing_id:** a unique identifier for the device. It could be a MAC address for example.
- **capabilities:** an array of strings representing the list of what the device is capable of. An example could be: [temperature, gyroscope, gps]
- **intents:** an array of strings representing the list of what the device intends to do with the data. An example could be: [send-mail, read-mail, social-network-broadcast]
- **scopes:** an array of strings representing the list of R.O's data the device needs to fulfill the intent. An example could be: [email, contact, user-info]

Example of TDD

```
1  {
2  "properties": {
3      "thing_id":"5E:FF:56:A2:AF:15",
4      "name":"Connected flower pot",
5      "description":"This is the description of the connected pot",
6      "last-modified":"2016-07-20",
7      "capabilities":[
8          "temperature",
9          "moisture",
10         "luminosity"
11     ]
12 },
13 "services":[
14     "api":"connected_flower.raml",
15     "intents":[
16         "send-mail",
17         "social-network-broadcast",
18     ],
19     "scopes":[
```

```
20        "profile",
21        "contact"
22     ]
23 ]
24 }
```

Properties and *Services* objects can be filled with additional information for a richer discovery and registration experience.

2.4   Message Queue Telemetry Transport (MQTT)

The MQTT [11] is a standardized protocol designed to have a very low message overhead in order to ease constrained networks. It contributes to the growing interest in the IoT networks as it has been shown to use a significantly less battery power than HTTP polling for similar scenarios [12,13].

MQTT protocol is also very interesting for our implementation because it is based around a publish/subscribe (pub/sub) model [14]. This model is also very useful to make our downstream messages, from server to client. The pub/-sub model works as following: clients can connect to one or more central servers (brokers) where they may publish information or subscribe to receive information, or both. Publishers and subscribers are decoupled from knowing about each other. They are also decoupled in time as interactions are asynchronous.

3   The Approach: Description of the Protocol

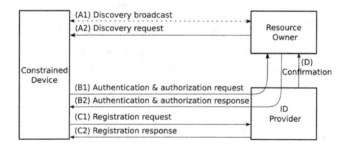

Fig. 1. Discovery and Registration protocol flow

The proposed approach consists in discovering then registering a new connected device into the user's favorite identity provider. In order to achieve that, we use two important paradigms, both are presented in the literature.

The first paradigm relies on the idea that each user and connected device has an identity. If we have an idea of what the user identity looks like, we must define a device identity with the TDD, prior to depicting the protocol. The second paradigm is based on the idea that the user and the device do not trust each other, therefore, each actor must show proof of their respective identity. We use OAuth2.0 to achieve that.

We built the DIRE protocol depicted in Fig. 1, based on the two paradigms listed above.

The Resource Owner uses its user-agent to manage the whole process. It triggers the discovery (A) then the device uses the manufacturer priviledges to ask the resource owner to authenticate itself to the ID Provider (B). The same request is used to ask for authorization to access resources. Once this mutual authentication is perfomed, the device requests for its registration to the ID Provider (C). Finally, the ID Provider sends to the Resource Owner a message about the registration process (D).

3.1   Discovery

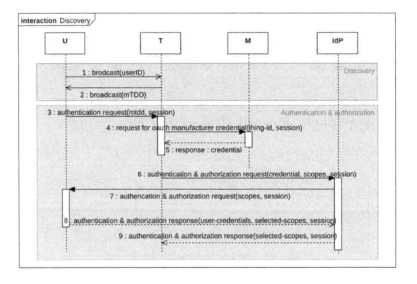

Fig. 2. Discovery sequence diagram

The discovery phase depicted in the sequence diagram in Fig. 2, aims at being aware of all available devices' identity within a network. It is always triggered by a user (resource owner) through its user-agent by broadcasting its *user_id*.
For confidentiality purposes, both the user and devices will disclose public information until they are verified. While the user broadcasts its *user_id*, the device broadcasts a minimal version of the TDD (mTDD) which is a TDD without private information such as MAC address, API resource link.

The principle of mutual authentication relies on the following assertion: *If the user receives an authentication request from its ID Provider - triggered by the device chosen to be registered - then, the device's identity is verified. And if the user correctly responds this request, then its identity is also verified.* At the end of the discovery process, the device will have authenticated the user and vice-versa.

The only role of the manufacturer at this stage is to disclose secrets, like OAuth client_id, to the requesting devices. The OAuth authentication request from the ID Provider to the user contains a list of services (scopes). So that, the user will be aware of the resources the device wants to access. The user can modify the scopes list before sending the OAuth authentication response.

Once the mutual authentication has been perfomed, the device triggers the second phase of the protocol.

3.2   Registration

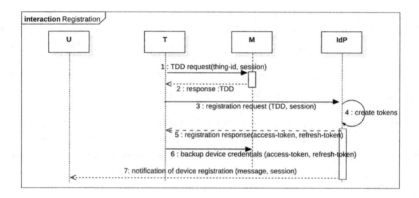

Fig. 3. Registration sequence diagram

The registration phase depicted in sequence diagram Fig. 3, aims at binding user's and device's identities. It starts when the device requests for its TDD to the manufacturer.

The principle of registration stands in the following assertion: *the user's ID Provider must grant credentials to the device the user is introducing.* The user introduced the device in the discovery phase by disclosing its ID. Once the authorization grant is received, the device requests for its registration with its TDD as a parameter. The ID Provider responds with the tokens (Access and refresh token) corresponding to the scopes the user validated. The tokens issued by the ID Provider are manufactured and meant to be used only by the device. That means that those tokens are associated to a TDD and a user in the ID Provider database.

At this stage, the manufacturer has two roles. The first role is to save device's credentials (tokens) in a much more secure database. Thanks to its priviledges the device will be able to fetch them when needed. The second role is to reconfigure the device server and client according to authorizations granted by the user.

At the end of this stage, the device is bound to the user and its actions have been set according to the rights granted by the user. The device can then act on behalf of the user with a separate identity.

A formal analysis of the DIRE protocol shows that our protocol reaches its goals while respecting the required security properties.

4   Formalisation

We present in the following, Event-B [15,16] that we use to formally specify and analyse our approach and we describe the formal specification of the protocol.

4.1   Event-B

Event-B is a formal method for system modelling and analysis based on B method and associated to Rodin Platform [15]. It is an Eclipse-based IDE for Event-B that provides effective support for refinement and mathematical proof. Unlike other formal verification tools like ProVerif [17] or Avispa [18], Event-B provides a very expressive notation rooted in predicate logic, arithmetic and set theory. Models in Event-B are described in terms of contexts and machines.

– **Contexts** contain carrier sets, constants, axioms, and theorems of a model. Axioms are statements assumed to be true in the rest of the model. They describe properties that cannot be derived from other axioms. Theorems present properties that are expected to be able to be derived from the axioms.
– **Machines** define dynamic behaviour. Machines contain the variables, invariants, theorems, and events of a model. Invariants allow defining interaction and security properties. We use them to define security properties of our protocol. A machine event represents a transition. It is composed of guards (the necessary condition for the event to be enabled) and actions (the way the variables of the corresponding machine are modified).

4.2   Formal Specification of the Protocol

We define two machines: the discovery and the registration machines. Both machines are working with the same context. We define the following sets in the Event-B context to formally specify our protocol.

Sets and Constants:

– USR, THG, MAN, IDP, as sets of, respectively, users, things (constrained devices), manufacturers and identity providers.

- MODE as the set of different phases of the system: INIT, DISCOVERY, AUTHENTICATION, REGISTRATION, EXIT.
- MSG as a set of messages exchanged between actors.
- PUBLIC_INFO and SECRET_INFO as sets of, respectively, public and secret information shared between the actors. Table 1 presents public and secret information.
- KEYS as a set of keys used to encrypt information.
- NONCE as a set of nonce.

Table 1. Info classification

Actors	PUBLIC_INFO	SECRET_INFO
USR	id, user agent	credentials (pwd)
THG	id, capabilities, scopes	api
MAN	scopes	tdd, AT
IDP	id(domain)	AT, client_secret, client_id

Variables and Invariants: We use the following variables and invariants to specify events and to formally define security properties. The cartesian product $S \times T$ denotes the set of pairs where the first element is a member of S and second element is a member of T. A partial function $\nrightarrow$ from S to T is a relation that maps an element of S to at most one element of T. If r is a relation between the sets S and T, the domain dom(r) is the set of the elements of S that are related to at least one element of T by r. Similarly, the range ran(r) is the set of element that are related to at least one element of S by r.

- ut_req, mi_vreq, tm_vreq, iu_auth_res, ui_reg_req present the type of messages that has been sent and received by actors in the discovery and the registration machines
  - $ut\_req \in ((USR \times PUBLIC\_INFO) \times NONCE) \nrightarrow MSG$
  - $mi\_vreq \in ((USR \times PUBLIC\_INFO) \times (THG \times PUBLIC\_INFO) \times (MAN \times SECRET\_INFO) \times NONCE) \nrightarrow MSG$
  - $tm\_vreq \in ((THG \times PUBLIC\_INFO) \times NONCE) \nrightarrow MSG$
  - $iu\_auth\_res \in ((USR \times SECRET\_INFO) \times (THG \times PUBLIC\_INFO) \times NONCE) \nrightarrow MSG$
  - $ui\_reg\_req \in ((USR \times SECRET\_INFO) \times (THG \times SECRET\_INFO) \times NONCE) \nrightarrow MSG$
- $umininfo$, $usecinfo$, $tmininfo$, $tsecinfo$, $mansecinfo$, $manmininfo$, $imininfo$ associate public and secret information to each actors
  - $umininfo \in user \nrightarrow PUBLIC\_INFO$
  - $usecinfo \in user \nrightarrow SECRET\_INFO$
  - $tmininfo \in thing \nrightarrow PUBLIC\_INFO$
  - $tsecinfo \in thing \nrightarrow SECRET\_INFO$
  - $mansecinfo \in man \nrightarrow SECRET\_INFO$
  - $manmininfo \in man \nrightarrow PUBLIC\_INFO$
  - $imininfo \in idp \nrightarrow PUBLIC\_INFO$

– *keyuser, keyth, keyman, keyidp* attribute a key to each actor
  - $keyuser \in user \nrightarrow KEY$
  - $keyth \in thing \nrightarrow KEY$
  - $keyman \in man \nrightarrow KEY$
  - $keyidp \in idp \nrightarrow KEY$
– *knownnonce* contains nonce that are already used in the session: $knownnonce \subseteq NONCE$
– *known_user_thing, known_user_man, known_user_IDP* to indicate that the user is known by the other actors
  - $known\_user\_thing \in (user \times thing) \nrightarrow BOOL$
  - $known\_user\_man \in (user \times MAN) \nrightarrow BOOL$
  - $known\_user\_IDP \in (user \times IDP) \nrightarrow BOOL$

Events: We use events to describe messages exchanged between two actors. There is one event for each message. We describe the necessary conditions for the message to be enabled in the guards. If these conditions are verified, we modify the message content. Let's consider for example the event where the device sends a message to the manufacturer, in order to trigger the user authentication. That corresponds to the arrow 4 in Fig. 2. We have to make sure that the previous operation (arrow 3) was realized with the following assertion: $((u \mapsto umininfo(u)) \mapsto n) \in dom(ut\_req)$. We also have to make sure the user is not known by the device $(known\_user\_thing(u \mapsto t) = FALSE)$ and that the nonce is already existing. Afterwards, the message is modified to contain user public information, device public information and a nonce. In addition, the message is encrypted before beeing sent.

> **manufacturer_creds_request** $\widehat{=}$ **ANY** u, t, n **WHERE** $u \in user \wedge t \in thing \wedge n \in NONCE \wedge n \in knownnonce \wedge ((u \mapsto umininfo(u)) \mapsto n)) \in dom(ut\_req) \wedge known\_user\_thing(u \mapsto t) = FALSE \wedge mode = AUTHENTICATION$ **THEN** $msg := tm\_vreq((t \mapsto tmininfo(t)) \mapsto n)$
> $e\_msg := enc(keyth(t) \mapsto msg)$
> **END**

We use events also to describe the phases transition in the protocol. At the beginning of the protocol, we set the variable *mode* to INIT. The only condition to satisfy to switch from INIT to DISCOVERY is formally expressed in the following guard of the *discovery_request* event (arrow 1 in Fig. 2):

grd: $mode = INIT \wedge u \in user \wedge u \in dom(umininfo) \wedge (u \mapsto umininfo(u)) \in dom(ut\_req)$

We can switch from DISCOVERY to AUTHENTICATION mode when the user is not known by the device and received the mTDD beforehand. This condition is formally expressed in the following guard of the *discovery_response_unknown* event (arrow 2 in Fig. 2):

grd: $mode = DISCOVERY \wedge known\_user\_thing(u \mapsto t) = FALSE \wedge (u \mapsto umininfo(u)) \in dom(ut\_req)$

There are two conditions to satisfy the switch from discovery to registration phase. Both are expressed in the guard of the *authentication_response* event. The first condition is that the device must have received the TDD and the authentication and authorization response comming from the IdP. The formal expression of that condition is the following:

grd: $\forall m, msg \cdot (m \in MODE \wedge msg \in MSG \wedge m = AUTHENCATION \wedge$
$msg \in ran(ut\_res)) \wedge ran(iu\_auth\_res) \notin \varnothing \Rightarrow mode := REGISTRATION$

The second condition is that the previous message must have been encrypted with the manufacturer key and must come from the manufacturer. The formal expression of that condition is as following:

grd: $msg \in ran(dec) \wedge m \in dom(keyman) \wedge msg = dec(keyman(m) \mapsto e\_msg) \wedge$
$(t \mapsto tsecinfo(t)) \in dom(tm\_vres)$

Intruder Model: We use the Dolev-Yao intruder model [19]. We assume that the intruder can overhear, intercept, and modify any message exchanged between the actors. In addition, we suppose that the adversary is only limited by the constraints of the cryptographic methods used. So, the adversary can try to know the devices attached to the user in order to extract user information provided by devices. In addition, the intruder can launch man-in-the middle attack to relay and possibly alter the communication between two actors. So, he/she can intercept and use the user public or secret information. Also, the adversary can initiate a replay attack to know devices attached to the user. Finally, the intruder can try to use the actor cryptographic key.

Security Properties: We define security requirements as invariants that hold before events are triggered.

1. **Integrity (Uniqueness of keys).** Each actor (user, thing, manufacturer and ID Provider) must have one and only one key. In both machines, uniqueness of keys is presented by the following invariants. We don't want the intruder to be able to use any actor cryptographic key. Therefore, we can detect the man in the middle attack because she/he cannot use the same key as another actor.
   - $\forall u, v, k, k1 \cdot ((u \in user) \wedge (v \in user) \wedge (k \in KEY) \wedge (k1 \in KEY) \wedge$ $u \in dom(keyuser) \wedge v \in dom(keyuser) \wedge (k = keyuser(u)) \wedge (k1 = keyuser(v)) \wedge (k = k1) \Rightarrow (u = v))$
   - $\forall u, v, k, k1 \cdot ((u \in thing) \wedge (v \in thing) \wedge (k \in KEY) \wedge (k1 \in KEY) \wedge u \in dom(keyth) \wedge v \in dom(keyth) \wedge (k = keyth(u)) \wedge (k1 = keyth(v)) \wedge (k = k1) \Rightarrow (u = v))$
   - $\forall u, v, k, k1 \cdot ((u \in man) \wedge (v \in man) \wedge (k \in KEY) \wedge (k1 \in KEY) \wedge$ $u \in dom(keyman) \wedge v \in dom(keyman) \wedge (k = keyman(u)) \wedge (k1 = keyman(v)) \wedge (k = k1) \Rightarrow (u = v))$

- $\forall u, v, k, k1 \cdot ((u \in idp) \wedge (v \in idp) \wedge (k \in KEY) \wedge (k1 \in KEY) \wedge u \in dom(keyidp) \wedge v \in dom(keyidp) \wedge (k = keyidp(u)) \wedge (k1 = keyidp(v)) \wedge (k = k1) \Rightarrow (u = v))$

2. **Anonymity.** We define the anonymity property to detect the intruders that try to know devices attached to the user in order to extract user information provided by devices. To define anonymity property we verify that messages containing both user and thing information cannot be intercepted by the intruder. When nonce is used in the previous session of communication, this implies that the actor that sends the message is an intruder. In addition, we can detect the replay attack using anonymity property.

   In the discovery machine we have:

   - $\forall u, t, m, n \cdot ((u \in user) \wedge (t \in thing) \wedge (m \in man) \wedge (n \in NONCE) \wedge (n \notin knownnonce) \wedge u \in dom(umininfo) \wedge t \in dom(tmininfo) \wedge m \in dom(mansecinfo) \Rightarrow ((u \mapsto umininfo(u)) \mapsto (t \mapsto tmininfo(t)) \mapsto (m \mapsto mansecinfo(m)) \mapsto n) \in dom(mi\_vreq) \wedge (knownnonce = knownnonce \cup \{n\}))$

   - $\forall u, t, n \cdot ((u \in user) \wedge (t \in thing) \wedge (n \in NONCE) \wedge (n \notin knownnonce) \wedge u \in dom(umininfo) \wedge t \in dom(tmininfo) \Rightarrow ((u \mapsto umininfo(u)) \mapsto (t \mapsto tmininfo(t)) \mapsto n) \in dom(tm\_vreq) \wedge (knownnonce = knownnonce \cup \{n\}))$

   - $\forall u, t, n \cdot ((u \in user) \wedge (t \in thing) \wedge (n \in NONCE) \wedge n \notin knownnonce \wedge u \in dom(usecinfo) \wedge t \in dom(tmininfo) \Rightarrow ((u \mapsto usecinfo(u)) \mapsto (t \mapsto tmininfo(t)) \mapsto n) \in dom(iu\_auth\_res) \wedge (knownnonce = knownnonce \cup \{n\}))$

   In the registration machine there is only one relevant message:

   $\forall u, t, n \cdot ((u \in user) \wedge (t \in thing) \wedge (n \in NONCE) \wedge n \notin knownnonce \wedge t \in dom(tsecinfo) \wedge u \in dom(usecinfo) \Rightarrow ((u \mapsto usecinfo(u)) \mapsto (t \mapsto tsecinfo(t)) \mapsto n) \in dom(ui\_reg\_req) \wedge (knownnonce = knownnonce \cup \{n\}))$

3. **Confidentiality.** We define the confidentiality property to detect intruder that tries to intercept and use secret information of user. We attribute secret information to user only if she/he is know by all other actors.

   In the discovery machine we have:

   $\forall u, t, m, idpro \cdot ((u \in user \wedge t \in thing \wedge m \in man \wedge idpro \in idp \wedge ((u \mapsto t) \in dom(known\_user\_thing)) \wedge ((u \mapsto m) \in dom(known\_user\_man)) \wedge ((u \mapsto idpro) \in dom(known\_user\_IDP))) \Rightarrow$
   $\exists secretinfo1, secretinfo2 \cdot (secretinfo1 \in secret\_info \wedge secretinfo2 \in secret\_info \wedge u \in dom(usecinfo) \wedge secretinfo1 = usecinfo(u) \wedge t \in dom(tsecinfo) \wedge secretinfo2 = tsecinfo(t)))$

   And in the registration machine we have:

   $\forall u, t, idpro \cdot ((u \in user \wedge t \in thing \wedge idpro \in idp \wedge ((u \mapsto t) \in dom(known\_user\_thing)) \wedge ((u \mapsto idpro) \in dom(known\_user\_IDP))) \Rightarrow$
   $\exists secretinfo1, secretinfo2 \cdot (secretinfo1 \in secret_info \wedge secretinfo2 \in secret\_info \wedge u \in dom(usecinfo) \wedge secretinfo1 = usecinfo(u) \wedge t \in dom(tsecinfo) \wedge secretinfo2 = tsecinfo(t)))$

Based on proof obligations (PO) generated by Rodin and that we have proved, all of the security properties modelled in the invariant were respected in the events and preserved by the protocol. Therefore, our protocol ensures uniqueness of keys, anonymity and confidentiality to all actors.

5 Implementation: Application of the Protocol

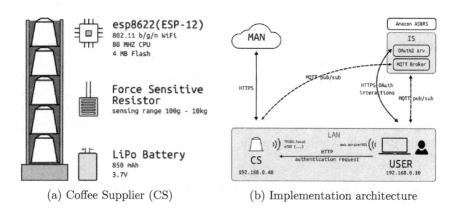

(a) Coffee Supplier (CS)   (b) Implementation architecture

Fig. 4. Auto refill example

In order to illustrate our approach, we consider the case of automatic refills. The owner resources at stake here is its wallet. The use-case consists in never running out of coffee by automatically purchasing coffee capsules on Amazon, each time there is only one capsule remaining. The architecture in Fig. 4b shows the actors involved in the scenario.

We use MQTT in a majority of exchange messages to take advantage of asynchronous interactions. It is very suitable to use because there are a lot libraries available in various languages and platforms implementing the last version of the protocol. For microcontroller-based systems, we use Arduino Client for MQTT [20]. On the server side, we use eclipse paho-mqtt-python [21], as well as for the user application in command line. We secure communication channels using of TLS.

We use Flask-OAuthlib [22] to implement the OAuth server. It provides a convenient framework to deal with OAuth interactions, tokens and errors.

As the originality of this protocol resides on the OAuth authentication with two different user-agents, our implementation focuses, on one hand, on interactions between the device and the user's client. On the other hand, we focus on interactions between the user's client and the Identity Provider.

5.1   User's Client - Device Interactions: Zeroconf Discovery

Applying this protocol requires having total access of the constrained device resources and of the device - manufacturer architecture. We then made a custom connected device we called: Coffee Supplier (CS). It is made of components depicted in Fig. 4a. The device firmware is made of:

- an mDNS server where the device hostname and the mTDD are configured.
- an MQTT client for asynchronous interactions.
- an HTTP client. We use this client for non-asynchronous interactions. Those are exclusively for communication with its manufacturer.

What we implemented on the user's client to run the discovery is the following: the user's client looks for available devices, in the Local Area Network (LAN), with a mTDD object set in the mDNS service properties. The user chooses in the available devices, the one to register, which triggers the authentication request as illustrated in Listing 1.1. We are using the following formalism for the user_ID: $\langle IDP \rangle$_$\langle userName \rangle$_$\langle nonce \rangle$, which communicates the device registration IDP to the device itself. The nonce is the session ID used for the whole process session.

Listing 1.1. Discovery interactions between the TPS and the user's client

```
 1 Starting ...
 2 Looking for available devices ...
 3 Available devices (1) :
 4 1.  Name: CS | Description : Coffee Supplier | Update : 2016-07-20
 5     Capacities: pression
 6     Authorizations: user-profile, payment
 7     Actions: purchase
 8
 9 Select the device you want to register: 1
10 You want to register the device : coffeesupplier.local
11 starting authentication ...
12 Successfully connected to broker : localhost
13 Subscribed to topic : /authN/usr01/azerty123
14 Starting authentication...
15 *   Trying 192.168.1.31...
16 * Connected to coffeesupplier.local (192.168.1.31) port 80 (#0)
17 > GET /authentication/aws_usr01_azerty123 HTTP/1.1
18 > Host: coffeesupplier.local
19 > User-Agent: curl/7.47.0
20 > Accept: */*
21 >
22 < HTTP/1.1 200 OK
23 * no chunk, no close, no size. Assume close to signal end
24 <
25 * Closing connection 0
```

5.2   User's Client - Identity Provider Interactions: Authentication and Registration

As Amazon does not support this architecture we implemented what we call an Identity Server (IS) which has the role of handling filiation by forging a derivative access and refresh token for each device bound to the user. The server makes the filiation after having authenticated the user and getting his consent to grant the rights expressed in the scopes. Tokens to derive are delivered by Amazon Authorization Server (AS) and are forged for the manufacturer.

As depicted in Fig. 4b, the IS is made of:

- an MQTT broker to handle asynchronous messages.
- an OAuth2 server to make OAuth interactions.

The client wants to access Amazon owner's resources and it needs an Access Token (AT) for that. This AT is issued by Amazon AS if the client requests for it with a valid client_id. The only way to get a client_id is to be registered on Amazon AS, as the OAuth specification requires. The problem here is that the constrained device, by definition, is not resourceful enough to securely store client_id, client_secret, AT and Refresh Token (RT). Our solution, described in Fig. 6, is the following:

In the DIRE authentication phase, the device wants to authenticate and ask for the consent of the resource owner at the same time. To do this, the device needs an AT, which it can acquire by using a manufacturer secret: its client_id. After having proceeded to the authorization request, the IS receives the AT and RT, manufactures a thing_AT and thing_RT with the formalism $\langle thing\_id \rangle . \langle AT \rangle$ and $\langle thing\_id \rangle . \langle RT \rangle$. These derived tokens are sent to the device in exchange of the TDD. The device then securely store them on its manufacturer database.

The DIRE registration phase consists in getting the complete identity of the device: the TDD, and appends the device to the list of user devices. The user's client is notified at the end of the process so that it can destroy the nonce. Figure 5 explains the architecture of the implemented IS.

There are two steps out of the scope of this implementation. Firstly, the manufacturer have delivered the connected device a *thing_id* and a *thing_secret* for the device to authenticate to the manufacturer. Secondly, the manufacturer have registered itself on Amazon AS as a constrained client. It then gets a client_id and a client_secret.

5.3   Results

Overall, the system works as intended and shows the following aspects:

- We can keep track of the use of the Amazon API for coffee replishment as the IS clearly identifies which device did what.
- The system is deterministic. Each error message is notified to the owner. There is no blocking state as the formal verification demonstrates.
- Discovering and registering a new device takes less than 30 s. The owner has 2 attempts to rightfully authenticate itself.

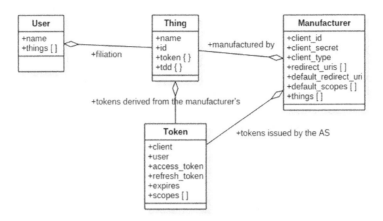

Fig. 5. Class diagram of the IS implementation

- Messages can't be replayed as each session key is generated randomly and the user's client and the IS are keeping a track of used session keys.
- The firmware uses 2046 kB of flash. Which leaves a good amount of memory to build more complex connected device.

Meanwhile, the implementation can be further enhanced.

5.4   Discussion

We identified two ways to enhance the protocol implementation.

Enhance the discovery. The device have to embed two clients: an HTTP and an MQTT one. Because there is a need for a direct relationship between the manufacturer and its devices in the protocol, HTTP would be preferred. In fact, it doesn't require a third party (broker) such as MQTT does.

Enhance OAuth implementation. In the implementation depicted in Fig. 6, we can see that the authentication and authorization request of the DIRE protocol requires two interactions. In fact, we send an MQTT message to the user's client which then requests for authentication using an http client. We did it this way because OAuth2 with MQTT is not adopted yet by IDPs.

We propose, to tacle both issues, to implement the DIRE with another efficient protocol for IoT like the Constrained Application Protocol (CoAP) [23]. In fact, CoAP is able to deal with both synchronous and asynchronous messages, that also may be the reason that motivates the ACE group to define a specification for Authentication and Authorization for Constrained Environments using OAuth 2.0 and CoAP [24].

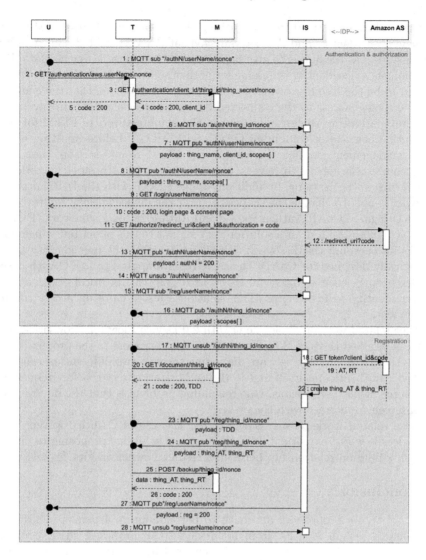

Fig. 6. Sequence diagram of the implementation

6   Related Works

There are a lot of solutions addressing the challenges the DIRE protocol is dealing with. One of those solutions is the OAuth 2.0 Internet of Things (IoT) Client Credentials Grant [25]. This paper proposes to trade https for CoAP and DTLS [26–28] to avoid communication latency due to the use of https. But building an effective encrypted channel only helps to cope with some node resource limitations. In fact, the case where the resource owner and the constrained device are using two different user-agents is not taken into account. In addition, the notion of device identity is missing.

Other solutions derived from OAuth are User Managed Access (UMA) [29] and Federated Identity and Access Management (FIAM) for IoT [30]. UMA is really inspiring as the aim is to give back the end-user control over his data. But the notion of device identity is missing for both of solutions. Each device is always assumed to be the resource owner. Furthermore, it is assumed that the end-user has an exclusive access to the connected device whereas she/he is involved in a tripartite relationship with the device and the manufacturer. In FIAM for IoT, the solution consists of combining OAuth with MQTT before injecting access control management. As it is depicted in the FIAM results section, their approach requires the device to have a user interface with a browser in order to renew device authorizations. In addition, unlike FIAM, with the DIRE protocol the owner is able to change the scopes to grant the device specific rights.

The Delegated CoAP Authentication and Authorization Framework (DCAF) [31] depicts in an IETF draft a solution very similar to this paper but which does not take into account the discovery, there is no link with the user identity and it is specifically designed for CoAP. The same remark applies to IoT OAuth based Authorization Service architecture (IoT-OAS) [32], this protocol does not link the user identity to his devices. This solution stresses more on access control management.

Other related works include the OAuth 2.0 Device Flow for Browserless and Input Constrained Devices [33]. This draft is also very close to the proposed protocol as the device and the user are discussing through two different user-agents. The device authenticates itself first to the authorization server before requesting for resource owner permissions. One remaining problem is that the device must have a screen to interact with the owner.

These related works clearly suggest that the use of OAuth together with IoT devices is worth exploring. Still, there are no solutions proposing to clearly establish a filiation relationship between a resource owner and its devices.

7   Conclusion

In this paper, we propose an approach to better manage a person identity by decoupling a person identity from its devices. The proposed DIRE protocol allows a connected object to act on its owner's behalf. It also allows Manufacturers to build more trusty and interoperable devices. We have proved that our protocol respects the integrity, anonymity and confidentiality properties.
As a result of our experiment, we clearly identified and implemented the element each IDP needs to add in order to solve identity problems in IoT: the IS. We also showed that constrained devices have enough resources to operate the protocol. This experiment shows encouraging results. We propose, as a recommendation, to standardize that approach because it is a solid foundation for identity management in IoT. For futur research emerging from this work, we wish to investigate the management of access control policies in the context of IoT. We also propose to enhance the implementation of this use-case with CoAP, based on ACE recommandation for OAuth2 integration into CoAP.

References

1. Gubbi, J., Buyya, R., Marusic, S., Palaniswami, M.: Internet of Things (IoT): a vision, architectural elements, and future directions. Future Gener. Comput. Syst. **29**(7), 1645–1660 (2013). Including special sections: cyber-enabled distributed computing for ubiquitous cloud and network services & cloud computing and scientific applications – Big Data, scalable analytics, and beyond
2. Evans, D.: "The Internet of Things": how the next evolution of the internet is changing everything. Whitepaper, Cisco Internet Business Solutions Group (IBSG) (2011)
3. Mirai (malware): April 2017. Page version ID: 775046665
4. Hunt, S.T.E.: Cyber attack: hackers 'weaponised' everyday devices with malware. The Guardian, October 2016
5. Attacks on IoT devices more than doubled in 2015, study shows - HOT for Security
6. thenextweb: Fitbit users are unwittingly sharing details of their sex lives with the world (2013)
7. Cheshire, S., Krochmal, M.: DNS-based service discovery. Technical report (2013)
8. Hardt, D.: The OAuth 2.0 Authorization Framework (2012)
9. Gerdes, S., Seitz, L., Selander, G., Bormann, D.C.: An architecture for authorization in constrained environments. Internet-Draft draft-ietf-ace-actors-03, Internet Engineering Task Force, Work in Progress, March 2016
10. Khodadadi, F., Dastjerdi, A.V., Buyya, R.: Simurgh: a framework for effective discovery, programming, and integration of services exposed in IoT. In: 2015 International Conference on Recent Advances in Internet of Things (RIoT), pp. 1–6. IEEE (2015)
11. MQTT Version 3.1.1
12. Messaging: Power Profiling: HTTPS Long Polling vs. MQTT with SSL, on Android (MQdev Blog)
13. stephendnicholas.com
14. Eugster, P.T., Felber, P.A., Guerraoui, R., Kermarrec, A.-M.: The many faces of publish/subscribe. ACM Comput. Surv. (CSUR) **35**(2), 114–131 (2003)
15. Event-B.org
16. Butler, M., Yadav, D.: An incremental development of the Mondex system in Event-B. Formal Aspects Comput. **20**(1), 61–77 (2008)
17. Kobeissi, N., Bhargavan, K., Blanchet, B.: Automated verification for secure messaging protocols and their implementations: a symbolic and computational approach. In: 2nd IEEE European Symposium on Security and Privacy (EuroS&P2017), Paris, France, pp. 435–450. IEEE, April 2017
18. The AVISPA Project
19. Cervesato, I.: The Dolev-Yao intruder is the most powerful attacker. In: 16th Annual Symposium on Logic in Computer Science–LICS, vol. 1. Citeseer (2001)
20. Arduino Client for MQTT
21. eclipse/paho.mqtt.python
22. Flask-OAuthlib – Flask-OAuthlib 0.9.3 documentation
23. Raza, S., Shafagh, H., Hewage, K., Hummen, R., Voigt, T.: Lithe: lightweight secure CoAP for the internet of things. IEEE Sens. J. **13**(10), 3711–3720 (2013)
24. ACE Working Group: Authentication and authorization for constrained environments (ACE) (2017)
25. Tschofenig, H.: The OAuth 2.0 Internet of Things (IoT) Client Credentials Grant

26. Raza, S., Trabalza, D., Voigt, T.: 6LoWPAN compressed DTLS for CoAP. In: 2012 IEEE 8th International Conference on Distributed Computing in Sensor Systems, pp. 287–289. IEEE (2012)
27. Erdtman, S.: Certificate credentials for ACE framework. Internet-Draft draft-erdtman-ace-certificate-credential-00, Internet Engineering Task Force, Work in Progress, April 2016
28. Kothmayr, T., Schmitt, C., Hu, W., Brünig, M., Carle, G.: DTLS based security and two-way authentication for the Internet of Things. Ad Hoc Netw. **11**(8), 2710–2723 (2013)
29. User Managed Access - Kantara Initiative
30. Fremantle, P., Aziz, B., Kopecky, J., Scott, P.: Federated identity and access management for the Internet of Things. In: 2014 International Workshop on Secure Internet of Things (SIoT), pp. 10–17. IEEE (2014)
31. Gerdes, S., Bergmann, O., Bormann, C.: Delegated CoAP Authentication and Authorization Framework (DCAF)
32. Cirani, S., Picone, M., Gonizzi, P., Veltri, L., Ferrari, G.: IoT-OAS: an OAuth-based authorization service architecture for secure services in IoT scenarios. IEEE Sens. J. **15**(2), 1224–1234 (2015)
33. Bradley, J., Denniss, W., Tschofenig, H., Jones, M.: OAuth 2.0 Device Flow for Browserless and Input Constrained Devices

Modelling and Mitigation of Cross-Origin Request Attacks on Federated Identity Management Using Cross Origin Request Policy

Akash Agrawall, Shubh Maheshwari, Projit Bandyopadhyay,
and Venkatesh Choppella$^{(\boxtimes)}$

IIIT Hyderabad, Hyderabad, India
venkatesh.choppella@iiit.ac.in

Abstract. Cross origin request attacks (CORA) such as Cross site request forgery (CSRF), cross site timing, etc. continue to pose a threat on the modern day web. Current browser security policies inadequately mitigate these attacks. Additionally, third party authentication services are now the preferred way to carry out identity management between multiple enterprises and web applications. This scenario, called Federated Identity Management (FIM) separates the problem of identity management from the core functionality of an application.

In this paper, we construct formally checkable models and design laboratory simulations to show that FIM is susceptible to cross origin attacks. Further, we employ the Cross Origin Request Policy (CORP) to mitigate such attacks.

Keywords: Federated Identity Management (FIM)
Cross-origin request attacks · CSRF attacks · Security · Web browser
World Wide Web · Alloy · Modelling · Mitigation

1 Introduction

This paper addresses browser-based cyber attacks. Cyber crime has been around even before the internet [2]. Forbes online estimates that cyber attacks will cost USD 2 trillion globally by 2019 [44]. Notably, costs quadrupled between 2013 and 2015. Newer attack vectors e.g., the browser and IOT devices are adding to the already large set of vulnerabilities.

The World Wide Web began as a way to share marked up (HTML) documents [48]. WWW was created to support the idea of hyperlinks, which initiated a new web (HTTP) transaction to fetch other web documents when explicitly requested by the user (often via a mouse click). Soon however, tags were introduced into the HTML language to support *automatic content inclusion*. Tags like img, introduced in 1993, caused additional, i.e., *cascaded* HTTP transactions without explicit user interaction. The addition of such tags were key to enhancing user web experience. The browser itself, via multiple tabs and windows, allowed multiple, concurrent web sessions. These sessions shared crucial

© Springer International Publishing AG 2017
R. K. Shyamasundar et al. (Eds.): ICISS 2017, LNCS 10717, pp. 263–282, 2017.
https://doi.org/10.1007/978-3-319-72598-7_16

browser data structures, like cookies. The confluence of these factors opened up the web to a new variety of malicious attacks with the browser acting as a vector.

Depending on whether the origin of the request is the same as that of the cascading request, the request is either a same origin or a cross origin request. Attacks exploiting vulnerabilities that fail to distinguish the origins of requests are known as *Cross Origin Request Attacks*. Cross origin attacks like *CSRF* are a very popular as well as serious threat to many web services and even feature in the Owasp top ten [4]. They have the ability to tamper with user data and even cause a denial of service. An example of denial of service, was when Github was affected for three days due to a browser based DDoS attack, a type of infiltration attack [15,46].

Same Origin Policy (SOP) [49], the core security policy driving today's web platform, was designed at a time when the web had static pages connected by hyperlinks. SOP does not address the attacks generated due to content inclusion. Previously, several policies have been proposed to fix the loopholes in SOP and mitigate malicious web based attacks. These proposals have made a significant addition in addressing cross-origin resource inclusion, script inclusion and data exfiltration attacks.

Cross Origin Request Policy (CORP), a browser security policy, was proposed [46] to cover the limitation due to cross-origin resource inclusion. CORP enables a server to control cross-origin interactions initiated by a browser. A CORP compliant browser intercepts the cross-origin requests and blocks the unwanted requests by the server. Our previous work shows the structure and use of CORP in mitigating a certain classes of attacks [46].

As the web is increasingly being used as a communication platform for applications, we are faced with new protocols of user authentication and authorization. *Federated Identity Management (FIM)* [24] was introduced to remove the current gap present in authentication. FIM is a partnership between enterprises where one enterprise (*Service Provider, SP*) trusts another enterprise (*Identity Provider, IdP*) for authentication, thus preventing the overhead of having *authentication credentials* and ensures authentication from an enterprise having better authentication protocol. FIM is an example of a complex cross-origin transaction [13,42].

Over the years, researchers have used formal modelling to analyse the security of network protocols. Modelling is a method which helps make necessary abstractions with the aim of finding out how a system works on the whole. Telikicherla et al. [45] proposed a model demonstrating cross-origin request attacks and its mitigation using CORP. In a similar vein, we create Alloy models (*Pre-CORP* and *Post-CORP*) to include the user authentication flow in FIM systems and demonstrate cross-origin attacks along with their mitigation using CORP. The *Pre-CORP* model captures the current state of the web platform, where we model user authentication via FIM and cross-origin request attacks. The *Post-CORP* model extends this by adding additional signatures, facts and predicates to describe CORP and the constraints it enforces on cross-origin request attacks and shows that no instance of a malicious cross-origin request transaction can occur in the presence of CORP.

Thereon, we conducted experiments in a lab environment, where we made malicious cross-origin request attacks to websites, targeting the login and logout state of the user. We then demonstrate that CORP can be used to mitigate these attacks successfully. Since CORP has a client side dependency, we used a chromium extension to carry out the experiments.

The paper has two main contributions. First, the paper analyses FIM protocols [24] from a security point of view. FIM systems are still vulnerable to cross origin attacks. The paper provides evidence of this phenomena via controlled experimentation with popular sites. Also we verified that these types of cross origin attacks can be mitigated using CORP, as CORP addresses this limitation of current browsers.

The second main contribution of the paper is the modelling of FIM, without and with the presence of CORP. The formal models allowed greater insight on the workflow of FIM protocols and show that the FIM flow is still susceptible to CORA. Further they prove the correctness of CORP by showing that the vulnerabilities can be mitigated in its presence.

The rest of the sections in this paper are organized as follows: Sect. 5 describes other mitigation and modelling techniques against this class of attacks and their limitations. Section 2 gives a background overview of FIM and CORP. Section 3 explains the model of FIM protocol SAML and a cross-origin attack on the protocol after the user is authenticated. In this, we also show the mitigation of this attack using CORP. Section 4 describes the experiments we carried out to show cross-site timing and auto-logout attacks as well as their successful mitigation using CORP, and Sect. 6 concludes with a discussion of future work.

2   Background - CORP and FIM

2.1   CORP (Cross-Origin Request Policy)

Telikicherla et al. proposed *CORP* (Cross Origin Request Policy) to mitigate cross-origin request attacks such as Cross-Site Request Forgery (CSRF) [1], click-jacking [41], and cross-site timing attacks [22]. *CORP* can be seen as a policy that controls *who*, i.e., which site or origin, can access *what*, i.e., which resources on a cross-origin server (e.g. /img/*, /img/xyz.jpg, etc.), and *how*, i.e., through which browser event (e.g. <img>, <script> or other tags). *CORP* is declarative, thus it can be added as an HTTP response header of the website. A web browser enforcing *CORP* would receive the policy in the response header of the website. The browser would store the *CORP* in memory accessible to all tabs in the browser such that when any cross-origin request goes to this website, the browser will intercept it and allow it only if it complies with the *CORP* of the website.

Figure 1 shows the model of a browser which supports *CORP*. It shows the difference between exfiltration and infiltration attacks, thereby explaining how *CORP* differs from CSP. The figure shows a genuine server *G*, with origin http://G.com, an attacker's server *A*, with origin http://A.com and a browser

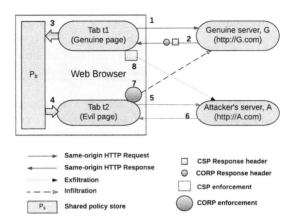

Fig. 1. Browser model showing exfiltration and infiltration and their mitigation by CSP and CORP respectively.

with two tabs - *t1* and *t2*. A general browsing scenario, which is also the sufficient condition for a cross origin attack, where a user logs in at *G.com* in *t1* and then (unwittingly) opens *A.com* in *t2* is depicted in the model.

Once a user requests the genuine site *G.com* by typing its URL in the address bar of *t1*, an HTTP request is sent from *t1* to *G* and in response, along with content, the declarative security headers *CSP* and *CORP* are sent by *G* (shown by arrows 1 and 2 in the figure). The tab *t1* receives these policies, stores *CSP* in its local store (as the current CSP-enabled browsers do) and sends *CORP* to a shared policy store P_s. P_s ensures that *CORP* is available to every tab/instance (arrows 3 and 4 in the figure) of the browser. Now, when a user unintentionally opens a malicious page loaded from *A* in *t2* (arrows 5 and 6 in the figure), every HTTP request initiated by the page in *t2* to *G* will be scrutinized and restrictions in *CORP* will be enforced (location 7 in the figure). Requests from *t2* to *G* will be allowed only if they comply with the configuration in the policy. *CORP* needs to be configured on the server such that when a request is sent to the server, it returns *CORP* in the response header. Complete guidelines on the declaration of *CORP* can be found in [46].

2.2   FIM (Federated Identity Management)

FIM is a partnership between enterprises where trust prevails between the *Service Provider, (SP)* and *Identity Provider, (IdP)* for authentication. The Service provider provides a service to the user while the Identity provider is a third party service which does authentication for it. FIM prevents the overhead of having *user credentials* and ensures authentication from an enterprise having a better user management system. Technologies used for federated identity include *SAML* (Security Assertion Markup Language) [8], *OAuth* [33], *OpenID* [40], *Security tokens*, etc. Single Sign-On (SSO) is a protocol of access control by which a user logs in with their credentials once and enters a federated environment to gain access to various services without having to maintain separate credentials for each [19]. Google is a prime example of this: logging with Google Accounts allows one to use services like Google Drive, Gmail, etc.

We model the FIM protocol - *SAML* since it is a widely used protocol which is extensible, and has strong authentication and authorization systems, thus removing the necessity of having multiple web application passwords. It also allows for single sign-on and single logout. In this, there are three main interacting agents: the service provider, identity provider and the browser. Figure 2 shows a simple transaction workflow of the *SAML* protocol. We divide the transactions involved into 3 parts:

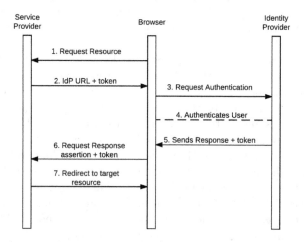

Fig. 2. Transaction flow - Federated Identity Management (FIM)

- **Request resource from SP:** In this transaction (steps *1* and *2*), user types in the *service provider*'s address in *URL address bar*. The service provider sends a response to the user with an *HTML button* to "*Login with IdP*". The service provider also sends a token in the response. Later, this token is sent to the IdP for identifying the partner server SP.
- **Request authentication from IdP:** When user clicks on "*Login with IdP*" button, a request goes from browser to Identity provider (step *3*). The user is then authenticated with the *IdP* (step *4*). After the authentication, IdP sends an encrypted response containing user information and the token (step *5*).
- **Request assertion from SP:** The authentication is done at IdP's end till now. The SP has to verify IdP's response before giving the user access to its resource. A *redirection* request is sent to *service provider* to verify the response sent by IdP (step *6*). The SP verifies the response as well as checks if the token matches the token sent by it in step *2*. We do not model the verification protocol in this model. If the response is successfully verified, then the user is redirected to the target resource (step *7*).

3   Alloy Models of FIM, CORA and Mitigation by CORP

In this section, we propose a model for cross-origin request attacks in a transaction involving FIM. We then extend this model and demonstrate that no instance of malicious cross-origin request attacks can occur in the presence of CORP.

3.1   Salient Features of CORP Alloy Model

This section explains the design considerations of the formal model created in Alloy to validate the soundness of CORP. Alloy[1] is a lightweight, declarative modelling language based on first order relational logic which helps describe the structural properties of a model. Borrowing the basics of the CORP model developed by Telikicherla et al. [45], we created a more modular version specifically for user authentication in FIM systems. Below are the key design considerations of our model:

The model comprises a Browser, Service Provider, Identity Provider and Attacker Server. A *User* uses the *Browser* to interact with various components of the model. First, the User tries to access a *Service Provider (BrowserTab1)*. The User is then redirected to the *Identity Provider*. Upon successful authentication, the User is redirected back to Service Provider. The *attack website (BrowserTab0)*, now becomes active (could have opened at any point of time). A malicious cross-origin request is made from *BrowserTab0* to *BrowserTab1*, thereby affecting the user's state. We model this attack (Pre-CORP model) and mitigate it using *CORP* (Post-CORP model). Thereon, it is assumed that the attacker web page is fetched in another tab. To ensure simplicity, we avoid inclusion of response assertion by the service provider in our model. There are four transactions: the first three are concerned with the authentication via FIM and the fourth is a malicious cross-origin transaction from the *attacker server*, which we mitigate in the *Post-CORP* model.

There are a few essential keywords required to define models in alloy. The *sig* keyword helps define abstract objects in the model. *Fact* is used to enforce invariable constraints while *pred* creates instances of the model following certain conditions.

In this model all the relations between the objects are stored in a dynamic signature called *State* by using the built-in *Ordering* library [6]. The four transactions are shown by instances of the *State* (Listing 1.1).

3.2   Modelling Cross-Origin Request Transaction in FIM (Pre-CORP Model)

In this section, we describe the modelling of cross-origin request transaction along with user authentication via FIM (SAML protocol).

---

[1] http://alloy.mit.edu/.

HTTP Transaction, Browser and Server. To make more realistic model, all the requests and responses are shown using HTTP Transactions (line 7–10 in Listing 1.1). We define multiple objects in Alloy, and their dynamic behaviours are defined in State (explained in Sect. 3.2). The transaction could be of four types *StartAuth*, *IdPAuthentication*, *SPAuthentication* and *CORA*. In the model, *Browser* keyword represents the user's browser. A browser will have multiple *browser tabs*. For the user to interact with multiple servers from the same instance of the Browser at the same time browser tabs are used. There are three different type of servers: *IdentityProvier*, *ServiceProvider* and *AttackerServer*. The *Attacker Server* is the entity which makes a malicious request to the Genuine Servers using the *HTML Elements*. *HTTPEventInitiator* refers to the objects which can trigger an HTML transaction. It can be triggered due to *Redirection* or various other *Elements* (line 5). We classify *Elements* into: *URLAddressBar* and *HTMLElements*. HTML elements can be classified into two types: the elements which cannot trigger HTTP requests are *Passive* HTML elements (e.g. Div, Span, Textbox, etc.) while those which can trigger HTTP requests are *Active* HTML elements (e.g. iframe, script, img, etc.). We do not model passive HTML elements here to keep the model simpler.

State and Status. Listing 1.1 shows the signature where we define *State*. We have defined *Status* such as to map the relationships: *IDP*, *SP*, *authenticationStatus*. *IDP* (line *12*) and *SP* (line *13*) keeps track of the authentication status of *IdentityProvider* and *ServiceProvider* respectively. *authenticationStatus* (line *14*) keeps track of the authentication state of the user and will be *1*, meaning active state, if and only if the states: *IDP* and *SP* are 1.

```
1                    sig State {
2                         transType : HTTPTransaction -> one TransType ,
3                         token : HTTPTransaction -> one Int ,
4
5                         httpeventInit : HTTPEventInitiator one -> lone
                               HTTPTransaction ,
6
7                         req_to : HTTPTransaction -> one Server ,
8                         resp_from : Server -> lone HTTPTransaction ,
9                         resp_to : HTTPTransaction -> one BrowserTab ,
10                        req_from : BrowserTab -> HTTPTransaction ,
11
12                        IDP : Status -> one Int ,
13                        SP : Status -> one Int ,
14                        authenticationStatus : Status -> one Int
15                   }
```

Listing 1.1. State and Status

transType specifies the type of transaction in each transaction. *token* refers to the relay token present in FIM transactions. *httpeventInit* is the *HTTPEventInitiator* which triggers the transaction. A request always originates from *BrowserTab* and goes to *Server*. Similarly, a response originates from *Server* and goes to *BrowserTab*. Hence, the relations: *req_to*, *resp_from*, *resp_to* and *req_from* are defined according to this concept (lines *7–10*). To preserve the ordering of various transactions present in the model, we order the States starting with *s0* to *s3* in the model using the inbuilt library, *ordering*.

3.3   Modelling of FIM and CORA without CORP

To show the various transactions present in the model, we use different instances of *State* ordered from *s0* to *s3*.

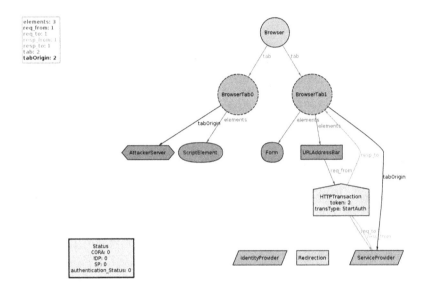

Fig. 3. State - s0: user access the Service Provider

s0 (StartAuth: User accesses SP in BrowserTab1). Figure 3 shows the model projected on the state - *StartAuth*. The request originates from *BrowserTab1* and goes to *ServiceProvider*. The response is received from *ServiceProvider* to *BrowserTab1*. Since the user types in the website's address in the *URLAddressBar*, the *httpeventInit* of the transaction is *URLAddressBar*. The *tabOrigin* of *BrowserTab1* is *ServiceProvider* since the content is fetched from this server. The *ServiceProvider* returns a *token*, in the transaction, with value *2*. Since, no authentication is completed here, the values of *IDP*, *SP* and *authenticationStatus* are *0*.

s1 (IdP Authentication: User logs in with IdP). In this, the user clicks on "*Login with IdP*" and the *browser tab* sends a POST request from the *form* element to the *Identity Provider*. The *response* is then returned from the *Identity Provider* to the *browser tab*.

s2 (SP Authentication: IdP sends conformation of the User authentication to SP). If the *Identity provider* has successfully *authenticated* the user, the browser tab redirects the information in the form of *token* to the *Service Provider*. After authentication and authorization of the user, the *Service Provider* returns the response to the browser tab. Thus, by the end of this state, the user is authenticated by the system.

s3 (Cross Origin Request Attack: Attack triggered by User interaction in BrowserTab0). In this state, the user unwittingly visits an *AttackerServer* which initiates a malicious cross-origin request attack from an *HTML Element* to the *Service Provider*, thus affecting the user even after he or she has successfully been authenticated.

3.4   Modelling the Mitigation of CORA, with CORP (Post-CORP Model)

We extend the previous model to include attributes and predicates, to demonstrate the mitigation of cross-origin request attack using *CORP*.

CORP and RequestPath. In this section we define the CORP object in our model.

– **CORP:** The working of CORP has been explained in Sect. 2.1. In the described model we consider the *Service Provider* to be the *genuine server*. *Browser* stores the *CORP* policy in a shared memory, hence we show CORP as an attribute of the Browser. CORP consists of: *Who* - the source origin of the request, *Where* - the destination path of the request, *How* - the *HTTPEventInitiator* of the request. We have defined the *Who* and *How* in our *Pre-CORP* model (Sect. 3.2). In the Post-CORP model *CORP*'s *origin*, *path*, and *how* are added in the *State*, since the *browser* enforces *CORP* only in the cross-origin transaction. In *Post-CORP*, *RequestPath* is also defined.
– **RequestPath:** There can be *two* types of *RequestPath*: *SensitivePath*, the end-points of websites which are vulnerable to cross-origin request attacks (e.g. */transferMoney*, */delete_user*, etc.), and *NonSensitivePath*, the end-points of websites which are not vulnerable to cross-origin request attacks (e.g. */images*, */videos*, etc.).

We model the cross-origin transaction with the assumption that the content from *Attacker Server* is already fetched in user's browser tab, to keep the model simpler.

Pred - CorpCompliantTransaction. Listing 1.2 filters out the cross-origin transaction with destination as *ServiceProvider*. It takes 3 arguments: *origin (sv)*, *path (pt)*, and *how (ev)*. To make sure that all the cross-origin transactions are complaint, it calls predicate *corpCheck*. *corpCheck* asserts whether the *HTTPEventInitiatior (ev)* of the *Server (sv)* is allowed to make a cross-origin request to the *ServiceProvider*.

```
1                pred corpCompliantTransaction [sv:Server,ev:
                 HTTPEventInitiator, pt: RequestPath] {
2                all s:State |
3                    let sTab= HTTPTransaction.(s.resp_to) | {
4                        sTab.tabOrigin != HTTPTransaction.(s.
                         req_to) &&
5                        HTTPTransaction.(s.req_to) =
                         ServiceProvider
6                    =>
7                        corpCheck[s,sTab,sv,ev,pt]
8                    else
9                        no s.how &&
10                       no s.path &&
11                       no s.http_path &&
12                       no s.origin
13                   }
14               }
```

Listing 1.2. Pred - CorpCompliantTransaction

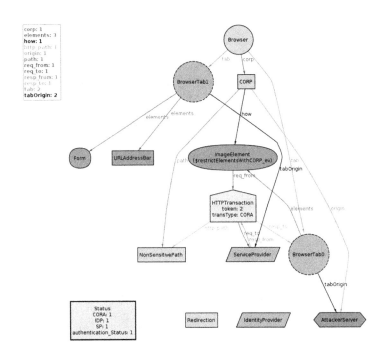

Fig. 4. State - S3 (CORA)

Instances - Post-CORP Model. We generate an instance of Post-CORP model where we add the predicate *restrictElementsWithCORP* in the code. Figure 4 shows the last transaction of the model where *CORP* is enforced on the *HTTPTransaction*. The request is not a malicious cross-origin request since the destination *RequestPath* is a *NonSensitivePath*. *CORP* has white-listed the *AttackerServer*, the origin of the transaction, and *ImageElement*, the *HTTPEventInitiator* of the transaction.

Instance - Malicious Cross-Origin Transaction. Listing 1.3 shows the predicate *maliciousCrossOriginAttackWithImage*, which tells alloy to generate an instance where the destination path of *HTTPTransaction* is *SensitivePath*. We *run* this predicate for at most *20* elements of each object.

Figure 5 shows that there is no such instance generated by alloy, which shows that our model is consistent.

```
1        pred maliciousCrossOriginAttackWithImage {
2             CrossOriginAttack
3             HTTPTransaction.(s3.http_path) = SensitivePath
4        }
```

Listing 1.3. Instance - Malicious Cross-Origin Transaction

Executing "Run maliciousCrossOriginAttackWithImage for 20"
Solver=sat4j Bitwidth=4 MaxSeq=7 SkolemDepth=1 Symmetry=20
158182 vars. 13473 primary vars. 296501 clauses. 493ms.
No instance found. Predicate may be inconsistent. 84ms.

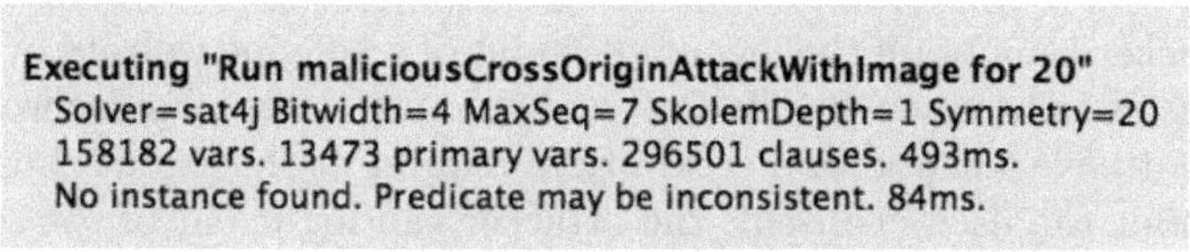

Fig. 5. No instance of malicious CORA generated

4 Experimentation

In this section, we describe the experimentation done to show the vulnerabilities present in the authentication endpoints: *Login* and *Logout*, and mitigate the risks using CORP.

4.1 Mitigating Auto-logout Attack - CSRF Attack

In this attack, an attacker page makes a cross-origin request to the logout endpoint, without the user's consent. Logout CSRF is a known vulnerability, and attacks have been demonstrated by various attackers[2].

Though Google services (which use SSO[3]) are vulnerable to this attack, Google claims that "it cannot be reliably addressed on the modern web" [10].

---

[2] http://superlogout.com/, http://superlogout.github.io/.

[3] https://accounts.google.com.

However, we argue that this attack can pose substantial risks to modern websites as it can be extended to a denial of service to the user - while the malicious page is open, the user would continuously be logged out of some services. Malicious network administrators or those with knowledge of a user's activities could conduct the logout attack at crucial points of time which may result in a loss of data. This attack can also be used in conjunction with other techniques to create phishing attacks [14,39]. Some mitigation techniques have been proposed like using POST requests, via a form, to logout users [9], and using csrf cookies [11]. These, however, are application level fixes. The safety of the user's data will be dependent on security measures that were taken by the service provider.

Auto-logout Attack. This attack works by sending a cross-origin request, on behalf of the user, to the logout endpoint of a server thereby logging out the user. To achieve this, the attacker injects an *img* attribute into an HTML page using the malicious code mentioned in Listing 1.4.

```
1        var img = document.createElement("img");
2        img.src = https://www.genuine.com/logout;
```

Listing 1.4. CSRF attack - Logout endpoint

The attacker can obtain the logout endpoint of a genuine website by using the network console in browsers like firefox[4] and chrome[5]. Even popular websites like Google do not have a check for a cross-origin request at the logout endpoint [10]. Hence, without the user's consent, the attacker can log it out of the service.

1. The Attack   2. User Logged Out

Fig. 6. Logout CSRF attack simulation on Google

Reproducing the Attack. Figure 6 shows the steps we followed to reproduce the attack on *Google*. A user first logs in at https://accounts.google.com and then visits an attacker website, containing the code as described in Listing 1.4, in a separate browser tab. The steps involved are:

---

[4] https://developer.mozilla.org/en-US/docs/Tools/Network_Monitor.
[5] https://developer.chrome.com/devtools.

- **Step 1:** Shows the malicious cross-origin request attack from *Network* tab of Chromium developer tools.
- **Step 2:** Shows that user is logged-out as a result.

As described in Sect. 2.2, Google uses SSO for user authentication. Hence, if the user is logged-out from https://accounts.google.com, it is logged-out of all *Google* websites, e.g. *Google drvie*, *Gmail*, etc.

Logout endpoints of a site can be found by observing the *network activity* from the browser console.

Fig. 7. Mitigation of Logout CSRF attack on Google

Mitigation Using CORP. In this, we show that the attack can be successfully mitigated using *CORP*. Figure 7 shows the steps we follow to mitigate the attack. The following points describe the steps mentioned in the figure:

```
1    CORP-Origins:  http://localhost:3000
2    CORP-Resources:  img
3    CORP-Paths:  /logout
4    CORP-Allow-Or-Deny:  DENY
```

Listing 1.5. CORP Rule - Mitigating Logout CSRF attacks

- **Step 1:** We have used the *Modify headers* extension [3] for google chromium to inject response headers in the HTTP response received from *Google*, since we don't have access to its webserver. Listing 1.6 shows the CORP headers used in this example to mitigate the attack. It shows that the *Origin* http://localhost:3000 cannot send cross-origin request to https://accounts.google.com via *img* tag to */logout* path.
- **Step 2:** We reload the url https://accounts.google.com for the CORP headers to be injected. The browser receives the response and stores it in a shared memory store.
- **Step 3:** It shows that no malicious cross-origin request is sent to https://accounts.google.com.

4.2 Mitigating User Login Detection Attack - Cross-Site Timing Attack

Cross-site timing attacks enable an attacker to receive information from a user's view of a victim site [22]. In our attack, we obtain information about a user's current state: logged in or not. Though this vulnerability has been known for quite a while [47] now, most companies neglect it [34]. To execute this attack, resources which are only accessible upon authentication are found and requested for by the attacker site. Some mitigations methods exist like hosting such resources on a separate CDN server [12]. However, vulnerabilities still exist, as shown by the attack.

Knowledge of whether a user is logged in or not is crucial to the success of many other attacks like phishing [31], deanonymization attacks [16], clickjacking [41], and profilejacking [5]. This kind of attack can also be used to gather user data: if a person is logged into sites like *Facebook*, *Twitter*, etc. then they are a socially active person.

User Login Detection Attack. The vulnerability exploited in this attack is the redirection present in the login endpoint. Redirection information is provided to the login page as a query string, for example: https://www.genuine.com/login.php?next=https:%2F%2Fwww.genuine.com%2Fmyprofile.php

This kind of URL directs the user to the profile page if logged in, and to the login page if the user is logged out. Due to Same Origin Policy, cross-origin ajax requests to genuine server would not be entertained. Cross-origin requests for content inclusion (via *img*, *script*, etc. tags) however would be allowed. Most servers host resources (images, scripts, videos, etc.) to be shared on a CDN (Content Delivery Network). One resource that is not hosted on the CDN and is found in most web servers is the *favicon.ico*.

The login url will look like this after setting up with favicon parameter: https://www.genuine.com/login.php?next=https%3A%2F%2Fwww.genuine.com%2Ffavicon.ico

The above URL will return *favicon* if user is already logged in, otherwise it will return html of login page. Hence, this URL can be used in <img> tag in the website: <img src=https://www.genuine.com/login.php?next=https%3A%2F%2Fwww.genuine.com%2Ffavicon.ico>. The behaviour of <img> tag will be as follows:

- If the user is already logged in, the image will be loaded.
- If the user is logged out, then the request will receive the HTML page of the login screen. This will not be loaded as an image. Hence, it will trigger the *onError* callback

The final exploit will be:

<img onload = "alert('logged in to genuine website')" onerror = "alert('not logged in to genuine website')" src = "https://www.genuine.com/login.php?next=https %2F%2Fwww.genuine.com%2Ffavicon.ico" >

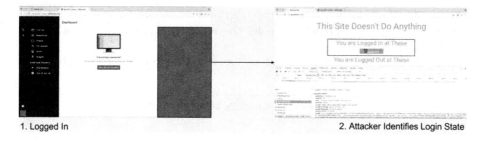

| 1. Logged In | 2. Attacker Identifies Login State |

Fig. 8. Login detection attack - cross site timing attack (simulation on Bitbucket)

Reproducing the Attack. Figure 8 shows the steps we followed to reproduce the attack on *BitBucket*. The following points describe the steps specified in the figure:

- **Step 1:** Shows a logged-in user on https://bitbucket.org/.
- **Step 2:** Shows the attacker website which detects that user is logged-in at *BitBucket*. The network console of Chrome developer tools shows the malicious cross-origin request reaching *BitBucket*.

  BitBucket uses *Google* as its *IdentityProvider* for authentication and is still vulnerable to cross-site timing attack. This shows that even after using FIM, a website can still be vulnerable to cross-origin request attack.

| 1. CORP Headers Added | 3. Malicious Request Not Sent |

Fig. 9. Login detection Mitigation - Cross Site timing attack (Simulation on Bitbucket)

Mitigation Using CORP. In this, we show that the attack can be successfully mitigated using *CORP*. Figure 9 shows the steps we follow to mitigate the attack. The following points describe the steps mentioned in the figure:

- **Step 1:** We have used *Modify headers* extension [3] for google chromium to inject response header in HTTP response received from *BitBucket*, since we don't have access to it's webserver. Listing 1.6 shows the CORP headers used in this example to mitigate the attack. It means that the *Origin* http://localhost:3000 cannot send cross-origin request to https://bitbucket.org/ via *img* tag to /* path.

– **Step 2:** We reload the url https://bitbucket.org/ for the CORP headers to be injected. The browser receives the response and stores it in a shared memory store.
– **Step 3:** It shows that no malicious cross-origin request is sent to https://bitbucket.org/.

```
1              CORP-Origins: http://localhost:3000
2              CORP-Resources: img
3              CORP-Paths: /*
4              CORP-Allow-Or-Deny: DENY
```

Listing 1.6. CORP Rule - Mitigating Logout CSRF attacks

5   Related Work

In this section, we discuss the explorations of various security researchers in modelling web security protocols and in mitigating cross-origin request attacks.

5.1   Modelling

Usage of formal verification to analyse the security of network protocols is not a new concept. Akhawe et al. [17] created a formal model of web security based on an abstraction of the web platform which includes essential details about the browser, servers, cookies, HTTP protocol and discussed different scenarios apropos attacks initiated by various types of potential attackers. Similarly, Ryck et al. modelled CSRF attacks to demonstrate how their proposed method can be used to mitigate the attack using Alloy [30]. Chen et al. proposed App isolation in a single browser to increase the security of many browsers [26]. Alloy was used to model a web browser and verify the proposed method. Cao et al. has used Alloy to model their proposed Configurable Origin Policy (COP) and test it [23]. There have been many such initiatives undertaken to validate web security services by modelling [18,21,28,29,32]. Telikicherla et al. [45] proposed an alloy model demonstrating cross-origin request attacks and its mitigation using CORP. We extend this model to include authentication flow of user via FIM and show cross-origin attacks along with their mitigation using CORP.

5.2   Existing Browser Security Policies

Same Origin Policy (SOP) [49] was designed to prevent scripts from accessing the DOM (Document Object Model), network and storage data belonging to other web origins. The earlier problem of cross-origin requests through automatic form submissions or content inclusion was, however, left unanswered by SOP. Content Security Policy (CSP), introduced in *2010* [27] improves on SOP in mitigating the exfiltration attack (as shown in Fig. 1) by disabling inline scripts and restricting the sources of external scripts. CSP allows a website to instruct the browser to load resources from specific sources. However, CSP can only prevent exfiltration attacks, such as cross-site scripting (XSS) [43], and not cross-origin request attacks via content inclusion (as shown in Fig. 1).

5.3   Other Mitigation Measures

Some other mitigation measures are: Same-site cookie, CSRF Guard [25], CSRFx [25], NoForge [20], SOMA [38], RequestRodeo [35], Browser Enforced Authenticity Protection (BEAP) [37], etc. *Same-site cookies* prevent the browser from sending authentication cookies with cross-origin requests [7]. However, it cannot prevent a server from being flooded with malicious cross-origin requests, thereby leading to a browser-based DDoS attack. This is a type of DDoS attack where *users* and *browsers* are used as vectors to send continuous malicious cross-origin request attacks to a genuine server. *CORP* can mitigate this class of attacks as well [15]. *CSRF Guard* and *CSRFx* are techniques which use tokens generated by the server which are sent to the browser tab to prevent malicious requests from being served from a separate tab which has the attacker's website open. These tokens can, however, be stolen by the attacker via phishing [31] or social engineering techniques [36]. *NoForge* is a server side proxy which implements token validation by adding a secret token to the HTTP response. However, HTML dynamically generated from user's webpage can still launch a malicious cross-origin attack on the website since no token would have been inserted in it. *BEAP* is a browser based solution, which infers whether a request is malicious or not by analysing real-world application, and removes the authentication cookies. However, it strips the authentication cookies of several genuine cross-origin requests, which are common on the web.

6   Conclusion and Future Work

As shown by our experiments, current browser security policies are yet to implement measures to protect against all types of content inclusion cross-origin request attacks. We have investigated a particular scenario that involves FIM (Federated Identity Management) and its susceptibility to cross-origin request attacks. We have built formal models in Alloy of cross-origin request attacks affecting FIM and showed that they can be mitigation using CORP. To validate this hypothesis, we simulated *auto-logout attack* (CSRF attack) and *login detection attack* (cross-site timing attack) on popular sites and mitigated them using CORP in a lab environment. The generic model introduced in this paper subsumes many specific cross-origin attacks, such as CSRF, clickjacking, cross-site timing attack, login detection, and validates the soundness of CORP in mitigating these attacks.

We have implemented CORP in the Chromium browser and are carring out experiments to test CORP's feasibility. In the future, we plan to perform extensive testing of CORP on other platforms of Chromium (Android, iOS etc.) and propose CORP as a standard to the Chromium community. We invite the research community to help integrate CORP with other open-source browsers (like *Firefox*, *Opera* etc.) and verify its utility. On successfully integration, a compelling step would be to propose CORP as a web standard to the W3C community[6].

---

[6] https://www.w3.org/.

References

1. Cross-Site Request Forgery (CSRF). https://www.owasp.org/index.php/Cross-Site_Request_Forgery_(CSRF)
2. Cybercrime time-line. http://www.symantec.com/region/sg/homecomputing/library/cybercrime.html
3. Modify headers for Google Chrome. https://chrome.google.com/webstore/detail/modify-headers-for-google/innpjfdalfhpcoinfnehdnbkglpmogdi
4. OWASP top 10 application security risks - 2017. https://www.owasp.org/index.php/Top_10_2017-Top_10
5. ProfileJacking - legal tricks to detect user profile. Blog, https://sakurity.com/blog/2015/03/10/Profilejacking.html
6. Rivery crossing. http://alloy.mit.edu/alloy/tutorials/online/frame-RC-1.html
7. Same site cookie. https://www.owasp.org/index.php/SameSite
8. Security assertion markup language. Article, https://en.wikipedia.org/wiki/Security_Assertion_Markup_Language
9. User logout is vulnerable to CSRF. https://www.drupal.org/node/144538
10. XSRF in the logout handler. https://sites.google.com/site/bughunteruniversity/nonvuln/logout-xsrf
11. Yii 1.1: Logout CSRF protection. http://www.yiiframework.com/wiki/190/logout-csrf-protection/
12. Your social media fingerprint. https://robinlinus.github.io/socialmedia-leak/
13. Federated SSO primer, April 2015. https://developer.pingidentity.com/en/resources/federated-sso-overview.html
14. Login/logout CSRF: Time to reconsider? Article, March 2017, https://labs.detectify.com/2017/03/15/loginlogout-csrf-time-to-reconsider/
15. Agrawall, A., Chaitanya, K., Agrawal, A.K., Choppella, V.: Mitigating browser-based DDoS attacks using CORP. In: Proceedings of the 10th Innovations in Software Engineering Conference, pp. 137–146. ACM (2017)
16. Elsobky, A.: Novel techniques for user deanonymization attacks. https://0xsobky.github.io/novel-deanonymization-techniques/
17. Akhawe, D., Barth, A., Lam, P.E., Mitchell, J., Song, D.: Towards a formal foundation of web security. In: 2010 23rd IEEE Computer Security Foundations Symposium (CSF), pp. 290–304. IEEE (2010)
18. Armando, A., Basin, D., Boichut, Y., Chevalier, Y., Compagna, L., Cuellar, J., Drielsma, P.H., Heám, P.C., Kouchnarenko, O., Mantovani, J., Mödersheim, S., von Oheimb, D., Rusinowitch, M., Santiago, J., Turuani, M., Viganò, L., Vigneron, L.: The AVISPA tool for the automated validation of internet security protocols and applications. In: Etessami, K., Rajamani, S.K. (eds.) CAV 2005. LNCS, vol. 3576, pp. 281–285. Springer, Heidelberg (2005). https://doi.org/10.1007/11513988_27
19. Armando, A., Carbone, R., Compagna, L., Cuellar, J., Tobarra, L.: Formal analysis of SAML 2.0 web browser single sign-on: breaking the SAML-based single sign-on for Google apps. In: Proceedings of the 6th ACM Workshop on Formal Methods in Security Engineering, pp. 1–10. ACM (2008)
20. Barth, A., Jackson, C., Mitchell, J.C.: Robust defenses for cross-site request forgery. In: Proceedings of the 15th ACM Conference on Computer and Communications Security, pp. 75–88. ACM (2008)
21. Bhargavan, K., Fournet, C., Gordon, A.D.: Verified reference implementations of WS-security protocols. In: Bravetti, M., Núñez, M., Zavattaro, G. (eds.) WS-FM 2006. LNCS, vol. 4184, pp. 88–106. Springer, Heidelberg (2006). https://doi.org/10.1007/11841197_6

22. Bortz, A., Boneh, D.: Exposing private information by timing web applications. In: Proceedings of the 16th international Conference on World Wide Web, pp. 621–628. ACM (2007)
23. Cao, Y., Rastogi, V., Li, Z., Chen, Y., Moshchuk, A.: Redefining web browser principals with a configurable origin policy. In: 2013 43rd Annual IEEE/IFIP International Conference on Dependable Systems and Networks (DSN), pp. 1–12. IEEE (2013)
24. Chadwick, D.W.: Federated identity management. In: Aldini, A., Barthe, G., Gorrieri, R. (eds.) FOSAD 2007-2009. LNCS, vol. 5705, pp. 96–120. Springer, Heidelberg (2009). https://doi.org/10.1007/978-3-642-03829-7_3
25. Chen, B., Zavarsky, P., Ruhl, R., Lindskog, D.: A study of the effectiveness of CSRF guard. In: 2011 IEEE Third International Conference on Privacy, Security, Risk and Trust (PASSAT) and 2011 IEEE Third Inernational Conference on Social Computing (SocialCom), pp. 1269–1272. IEEE (2011)
26. Chen, E.Y., Bau, J., Reis, C., Barth, A., Jackson, C.: App isolation: get the security of multiple browsers with just one. In: Proceedings of the 18th ACM Conference on Computer and Communications Security, pp. 227–238. ACM (2011)
27. Chu, Y.-H., Feigenbaum, J., LaMacchia, B., Resnick, P., Strauss, M.: REFEREE: trust management for web applications. Comput. Netw. ISDN Syst. **29**(8), 953–964 (1997)
28. Clarke, E.M., Jha, S., Marrero, W.: Verifying security protocols with Brutus. ACM Trans. Softw. Eng. Methodol. (TOSEM) **9**(4), 443–487 (2000)
29. Cremers, C.J.F.: The Scyther tool: verification, falsification, and analysis of security protocols. In: Gupta, A., Malik, S. (eds.) CAV 2008. LNCS, vol. 5123, pp. 414–418. Springer, Heidelberg (2008). https://doi.org/10.1007/978-3-540-70545-1_38
30. De Ryck, P., Desmet, L., Joosen, W., Piessens, F.: Automatic and precise client-side protection against CSRF attacks. In: Atluri, V., Diaz, C. (eds.) ESORICS 2011. LNCS, vol. 6879, pp. 100–116. Springer, Heidelberg (2011). https://doi.org/10.1007/978-3-642-23822-2_6
31. Dhamija, R., Tygar, J.D., Hearst, M.: Why phishing works. In: Proceedings of the SIGCHI Conference on Human Factors in Computing Systems, pp. 581–590. ACM (2006)
32. Gordon, A.D., Pucella, R.: Validating a web service security abstraction by typing. Formal Aspects Comput. **17**(3), 277–318 (2005)
33. Hardt, D.: The OAuth 2.0 authorization framework (2012)
34. Grossman, J.: Login detection, whose problem is it? March 2008. http://blog.jeremiahgrossman.com/2008/03/login-detection-whose-problem-is-it.html
35. Johns, M., Winter, J.: RequestRodeo: client side protection against session riding. In: Proceedings of the OWASP Europe 2006 Conference (2006)
36. Krombholz, K., Hobel, H., Huber, M., Weippl, E.: Advanced social engineering attacks. J. Inf. Secur. Appl. **22**, 113–122 (2015)
37. Mao, Z., Li, N., Molloy, I.: Defeating cross-site request forgery attacks with browser-enforced authenticity protection. In: Dingledine, R., Golle, P. (eds.) FC 2009. LNCS, vol. 5628, pp. 238–255. Springer, Heidelberg (2009). https://doi.org/10.1007/978-3-642-03549-4_15
38. Oda, T., Wurster, G., van Oorschot, P.C., Somayaji, A.: SOMA: mutual approval for included content in web pages. In: Proceedings of the 15th ACM Conference on Computer and Communications Security, pp. 89–98. ACM (2008)
39. Wagenseil, P.: LastPass can be spoofed in devastating phishing attacks. Article, January 2016. www.tomsguide.com/us/lastpass-phishing-attacks,news-22139.html

40. Recordon, D., Reed, D.: OpenID 2.0: a platform for user-centric identity management. In: Proceedings of the Second ACM Workshop on Digital Identity Management, pp. 11–16. ACM (2006)
41. Hansen, R., Grossman, J.: Clickjacking. Blog, December 2008, http://www.sectheory.com/clickjacking.htm
42. Ruddy, M.: Decision point for federated identity and cross-domain single sign-on. Article, April 2015, https://www.gartner.com/doc/3029229/decision-point-federated-identity-crossdomain
43. Spett, K.: Cross-site scripting. SPI Labs **1**, 1–20 (2005)
44. Morgan, S.: Cyber crime costs projected to reach 2 trillion by 2019. Article, January 2016. https://www.forbes.com/sites/stevemorgan/2016/01/17/cyber-crime-costs-projected-to-reach-2-trillion-by-2019/#3c5ecbfe3a91
45. Telikicherla, K.C., Agrawall, A., Choppella, V.: A formal model of web security showing malicious cross origin requests and its mitigation using CORP. In: Proceedings of the 3rd International Conference on Information Systems Security and Privacy, ICISSP 2017, Porto, Portugal, 19–21 February 2017, pp. 516–523 (2017). https://doi.org/10.5220/0006261105160523
46. Telikicherla, K.C., Choppella, V., Bezawada, B.: CORP: a browser policy to mitigate web infiltration attacks. In: Prakash, A., Shyamasundar, R. (eds.) ICISS 2014. LNCS, vol. 8880, pp. 277–297. Springer, Cham (2014). https://doi.org/10.1007/978-3-319-13841-1_16
47. Tom, A.: Detect if visitors are logged into Twitter, Facebook or Google+, February 2012. http://www.tomanthony.co.uk/blog/detect-visitor-social-networks/
48. W3C: History of the World Wide Web. Technical report (1989). http://www.w3.org/Consortium/facts#history
49. Zalewski, M.: Browser Security Handbook. Technical report (2011), https://code.google.com/p/browsersec/wiki/Part2#Same-origin_policy

Towards a More Secure Aadhaar

Ajinkya Rajput$^{(\boxtimes)}$ and K. Gopinath

Indian Institute of Science, Bangalore, India
{ajinkya,gopi}@iisc.ac.in

Abstract. Aadhaar is the national identities project of Government of India. The main benefit of Aadhaar is expected to be better decision making using modern analytics as citizens use such an identity to avail services from various government as well as private service providers; this necessarily involves building a huge store with necessary information on citizens such as mapping of ids to biometrics. Such stores raise many security and privacy concerns and therefore should be designed and analyzed very carefully. The threat model for such systems should address both internal and external attackers. Previous writings and research work [12] in this area have discussed problems such as illegal profiling and tracking of individuals, authentication without consent, collusion of multiple service providers leading to correlation of user data, and use of fake biometrics. While some analyses have focussed on cryptography to provide a solution, a comprehensive and workable solution for, say, illegal profiling, is still lacking, and there are also many problems from a systems perspective that need to be addressed such as access control models to constrain the access to sensitive data as well as integrity of its metadata. In this paper, we discuss solutions to such problems, esp illegal profiling.

Keywords: National identities · Privacy preserving identities · Aadhaar

1 Introduction

The national identities in India are provided by the central government under THE AADHAAR (TARGETED DELIVERY OF FINANCIAL AND OTHER SUBSIDIES, BENEFITS AND SERVICES) ACT, 2016 [6]. Under this act, the government has established the Unique Identification Authority of India (UIDIAI), which takes care of the operation of the Aadhaar system. Aadhaar is now possibly the world's largest biometric database with 115+ crore identities stored along with biometric information [14]. During enrollment process under Aadhaar, citizens of India submit their demographic information including name, address, gender and year of birth along with their biometric information including fingerprints, iris scans, and a photograph. Each citizen is then issued a unique 12 digit Aadhaar number which ties all this information together.

© Springer International Publishing AG 2017
R. K. Shyamasundar et al. (Eds.): ICISS 2017, LNCS 10717, pp. 283–300, 2017.
https://doi.org/10.1007/978-3-319-72598-7_17

1.1   Pros of Aadhaar

The central government and many states in India are using the Aadhaar number for direct transfer of various subsidies to citizens and this has reportedly reduced fraud [11] on a large scale. The Aadhaar number can be used to maintain and link census, immunization records, etc. and thus may empower a government to use modern data mining and analytics techniques to make informed policy decisions. Likewise, Aadhaar may also help criminal investigations across the country. In cases of natural disasters or mishaps like train accidents, the Aadhaar system may help in identifying victims for immediate care.

Private sector service providers like banks, telecommunication companies etc. also need to verify the identification information provided by their clients; the Aadhaar system provides this infrastructure. Aadhaar also provides an eKYC API, by which service providers can get identification data directly from Aadhaar database for any Aadhaar number. This is subject to authentication from the client using OTP/Biometrics. This greatly reduces time and effort required to avail services.

1.2   Challenges with Aadhaar

However, there are huge risks involved with maintaining a large store of bio-metric information of all the citizens. A huge centralized database in itself is a problem as a compromise would lead to leakage of data of a large number of citizens. There have been many reported cases, for instance, when hackers allegedly compromised the national identities database of Turkey and stole about fifty million fingerprints [4]. This data can be used for many malicious purposes such as identity theft, financial frauds, tracking of individuals etc. The Aadhaar project has been and is being seriously debated due to privacy and security concerns. One major concern is that of mass surveillance, as government agencies can use Aadhaar system to track or profile individuals without proper warrants. Note that the problem is not trivial as an Internet-wide PKI system. Internet-wide PKI is a much simpler system (it "only" maps users to public keys and does not use biometrics) but even such a system has not been easy to provision or use due to revocations, failures, and disconnections.

Aadhaar numbers have been linked with bank accounts (for example, in UPI applications). Income Tax department of India uses Permanent Account Number (PAN) to identify each tax paying entity. The government of India has made it mandatory to link Aadhaar number and PAN. This makes the security of the whole system more critical since now the finance sector can be targeted by malicious parties. Identity thefts using Aadhaar can now be used in tax frauds.

Also, there have been at least three instances where the ill-designed websites of state government schemes have leaked millions of aadhaar identities [2] with one of them leaking 130M of them. These leaked data can be used in a range of malicious activities. In current practice, Aadhaar ids are collected by all the service providers as a part of "Know Your Customer" requirement. Multiple service providers can collude together or with employees of UIDAI to profile customers and then can abuse/sell this information for profit. This is clearly unethical and the UIDAI should have safeguards in place to prevent such practices.

The Aadhaar act mentions that the system should be secure but does not mention any technical specifications for security and privacy for the system. UIDAI on its website does mention the security measures it has taken but its effectiveness is not clear. Published information indicates that end-to-end encryption is used for security and therefore sufficient. But this is clearly not enough as neither privacy issues can be handled by this nor can one be sure that there are no other ways to attack the system (for example, compromise through HTTPS interception). Another example of the inadequacy of the measures taken by UIDAI is the use of Hardware Security Modules to handle keys. But HSMs under same administrative control as the database is not effective. Although the government of India has made provisions for strict penalties in the Act for fraudulent activities of any kind but these are just legal provisions which have effect only if the breach is known and the violator apprehended.

The government plans on linking health sector and voter identification cards with Aadhaar numbers in near future [16]. Linking of health records to Aadhaar risks public safety. A huge amount of infrastructure and operations are going to be dependent on Aadhaar when usage of Aadhaar is expanded in these areas. The issues mentioned above highlight importance of secure system design and careful analysis of Aadhaar. The system design should be, as far as possible "provably" secure with privacy guarantees as necessary for a system as sensitive as Aadhaar.

1.3   Our Contributions

With all the challenges stated in the previous paragraph, the Aadhaar system needs to be analyzed very carefully and thoroughly from a comprehensive systems perspective. Although there have been many careful analyses of Aadhaar system (for example, by Shweta Agarwal et al. [12] from a cryptographic perspective), such analyses still do not have well worked out models for protecting privacy when aadhar numbers are used across multiple consumer services; neither do they take into account sufficiently the systems perspective. For example, many of the observations in Shweta Agarwal's paper require an access control model and this is not discussed though it is a critical part of the security of the system.

In this paper, we discuss the security aspects of the Aadhaar system and highlight some concerns in the current system such as replay attacks using biometrics, and profiling and tracking of individuals. We put forward our analysis of these problems and propose solutions.

The paper is organized as follows. First, we give a brief outline of the Aadhaar system in Sect. 2. Next, we give an analysis of the current problems in the Aadhaar system and their solutions in Sect. 3. In Sects. 4 and 5, we present our access control based model of Aadhaar. We present our conclusions in Sect. 6.

2   The Aadhaar Architecture

Figure 1 denotes current architecture of Aadhaar system. Following five entities are part currently part of Aadhaar system.

- **CIDR:** Central Identities Data Repositories (CIDR) is the central database in which all the electronic records are stored. It is managed by UIDAI and responds to verification request with a Yes/No response.
- **AUA:** Authentication User Agencies (AUAs) are third party service providers who require their clients to be authenticated by the Aadhaar system using the Aadhaar numbers of clients. They in turn submit the verification request.
- **ASA:** Authentication Service Agencies (ASAs) are connected with CIDR through leased lines and forward authentication requests to CIDR on behalf of one or more AUAs.
- **Aadhaar User:** Aadhaar users are the citizens of the country who are issued Aadhaar numbers. Their biometric information is stored in the CIDR.
- **Authentication Devices:** Authentication devices are the devices which are used to read biometrics from the users for authentication.
- **Enrollment Agencies:** Aadhaar users need to go to enrollment agencies to register their biometric information in the CIDR. Enrollment agencies are hired by UIDAI to perform these duties. (These are not shown in the diagram.)
- **eKYC API:** Third-party service providers can get an electronic copy of Aadhaar card of the user by invoking this API. This API returns the user data only if the request is authenticated by the user through biometrics or by OTP on registered mobile number. This API is gaining popularity as the service provider has to take only a minimum amount of data from the user such as just the Aadhaar number and biometric authentication.

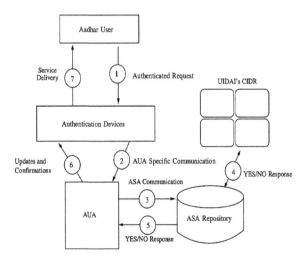

Fig. 1. Architecture of current Aadhaar system

Given the large numbers of actors involved in running the system, a fine grain access control policy is imperative and this is discussed in Sect. 4.

3 Some Serious Problems in Current Aadhaar System and Their Resolution

Some of the concerns raised by researchers (eg. Shweta Agarwal et al. in [12]) in a system like aadhaar are as follows:

- Confusion with respect to basic design goals such as Identification vs. Authentication.
- Identification of individuals without consent using the global Aadhaar number.
- Identification and authentication without consent using demographic and biometric data.
- Surveillance, tracking or profiling of people beyond legal sanctions using the centralized database, either through external hacks or through insider leaks and collusion.
- Lack of a formal model of access control for various actors in the system based on roles and attributes, and the integrity of the attribute metadata.
- lack of analysis from a software engineering perspective on a good design architecture.

Next, we analyze each problem and propose our solutions.

3.1 Identification vs. Authentication

UIDAI seems confused between identification and authentication; note that identification is just verification of a mapping between different attributes of users, while authentication requires some kind of secret or token. For example, we need identity verification for opening a bank account while we need authentication to make a transaction.

In the Aadhaar Act 2016 [6], "authentication means the process by which the Aadhaar number along with demographic information or biometric information of an individual is submitted to the Central Identities Data Repository for its verification and such Repository verifies the correctness, or the lack thereof, on the basis of information available with it". It considers identity verification as authentication. This confusion leads to problems in the design downstream.

3.2 Identification Without Consent

Another major issue with Aadhaar system is that the biometric data used for authentication is considered to be private, which may not be appropriate. Fingerprints of individuals can be easily lifted from the objects once touched or can be forged easily and printed on prosthetic fingers [17]. Iris scans can be extracted from high resolution photographs even from a distance of six feet [10]. This leads to authentication without consent and larger problems like identity thefts. Hence biometric data without liveness detection techniques should not be used for authentication. Another attack vector on the system is by replaying the authentication message by service providers. Such cases are reported and UIDAI has already taken action against involved service providers [13].

Liveness detection checks if the current biometric modality being read is from a live human being. There are various hardware based and software based techniques for liveness detection. The hardware based techniques require extra hardware with the biometric reader. They use different parameters like electrical conductivity, perspiration etc. While software based solutions use signal processing and machine learning algorithms, these algorithms use features like ridge frequency, ridge height and other biometric parameters for liveness detection. These parameters usually change when fingerprint are forged on materials used to spoof fingerprints. This change of fundamental parameters can help software solutions to determine liveness of a fingerprint. Software based solutions are cheaper and non-invasive. Hardware based liveness detection prevent replay attacks.

UIDAI does not mandate liveness detection; In the specifications of the UIDAI for fingerprint scanners [15], liveness detection is "recommended but is not compulsory". This still leaves the issues of non-compliance by the AUAs due to the non-use of a liveness detection enabled fingerprint scanner. Ideally, UIDAI should implement software liveness detection at CIDR along with making liveness detection mandatory for fingerprint scanners used by AUAs.

3.3   Preventing Correlation and Illegal Tracking

The Problem and Its Implications. Aadhaar number is an unique id provided to each individual. This number is consistent across all the domains and is needed to be given to service providers to avail services. Now, these service providers can collude and track and or profile an individual. They can use this information maliciously or sell this information. If an employee of CIDR colludes with the service providers the severity of problem increases multifold as the data available to the malicious party is much more. There are legal provisions in the Aadhaar Act but by definition, these provisions kick in only after the crime is already committed whereas a system design should be robust and secure enough to prevent such practices as far as possible.

The Solution. UIDAI has identified this problem and has proposed a solution. The UIDAI solution is a recommendation to all the service providers to use local ids and maintain a mapping from global Aadhaar ids to local ids. This solution does not solve the problem as the service provides still have access to Aadhaar numbers and can still track/profile users.

This shortcoming is identified by Shweta Agarwal et al. in [12] but is not addressed adequately. Their solution is to maintain a unidirectional reverse linking from local ids to global Aadhaar numbers. If this linking is stored with service providers, this solution is no better than UIDAI's as service providers still have access to Aadhaar numbers. They refer to a solution provided in [3] which involves generating multiple cryptographically embedded local ids, and storing these in the smart cards of the users. This is not feasible with Aadhaar system as Aadhaar users do not have smart cards. We propose a solution based on Crypto-book [9] which solves the problem of preventing profiling and correlation across multiple applications for applications using a single sign-on. Note that the assumptions made for in the Crypto-book solution are reasonable (for example, the feasibility of a secure channel) and we assume the same. A brief summary of the Crypto-book protocol is provided in the appendix.

In single sign-on system, an online service like Facebook or Google provide identities to users. Users can use these identities for accessing third party applications. The same problem arises here: multiple third party applications can correlate their data and profile/track users. The solution proposed in Crypto-book [9] is for third party applications not get the actual identities of the users but get pseudonyms. They achieve this by adding two more layers between the identity provider and third party application (multiple credential producers and credential consumers) and the use of cryptographic blind signatures. Credential producers generate cryptographic, unlinkable but accountable credentials. Credential consumers use these cryptographic credentials to create pseudonyms which are then provided to the third party application. These credential producers and consumers are servers run by unbiased anonymous authorities who ideally should be independent of UIDAI; if collocated there can be possibilities of collusion.

Crypto-book proposes a solution referred as "at-large" which allows a user to share limited information with third party applications using blind signatures. An instance of "at-large" provides a solution to our problem: this can be used to hide Aadhaar number and other unique data and to provide only nonunique data like name, address etc. The client mentioned in the following discussion is the device that performs authentication which is controlled by a service provider (AUA). In Crypto-book, Application-embedded consumer is a type of a credential consumer which is embedded in application itself. We choose this type of credential consumer [9].

Application of Crypto-book. Crypto-book works in a web environment but this is not the case with Aadhaar. We need a different access method for Aadhaar while ensuring that the authentication process should be initiated by the user. We apply Crypto-book algorithm for eKYC API as securing eKYC API also implies securing YES/NO mode because eKYC API gives out more information. The description of actors in our system are

- User: The citizen of India who wants to avail services from AUA (service provider). Citizens use Aadhaar infrastructure to verify their identity to AUAs.
- Client: Client is the device which initiates the verification of identity of user.

– Credential Producer: Is the entity which allows an user to be verified to the AUA without disclosing Aadhaar number to Client.

We propose the use of mobile phones for initiating the authentication process with the authentication flow as follows:

An user will have to follow following steps for Aadhaar authentication:

1. The user communicates the Aadhaar number to a cluster of Credential Producers via an independent channel like SMS or a call to IVRS. This step opens a request and an identifier $tempId$ is generated randomly and returned to the user. This identifier is temporary and can be reused after a certain period of time.
2. The user provides $tempId$ and all the required information along with a fingerprint or iris scan to the client.

After the user completes his part, the steps involved in the identity verification are as follows:

1. The client generates a random number $localID$. This $localID$ is the local identifier of a user for that client.
2. The client sends
   – a hash $h = H(localID, clientID)$ where $localID$ is a random number and $clientID$ is a identifier for client
   – a biometric scan
   – the demographic information that client wants to be verified
   – $tempId$
   to k different credential producers.
3. The Credential Producers find Aadhaar number previously received using $tempId$ and get the data corresponding to the Aadhaar number using the biometric information and eKYC API.
4. If demographic information is verified, the Credential Producer p_i signs h to produce blind signature s_{p_i}. Along with signature, it sends the non-unique data from the aadhaar data that it fetched from CIDR to the client.
5. The client verifies the signatures sent by producers. If at least one of the signature is verified, client considers the authentication to be successful and accepts the data sent by the credential producer.
   Figure 2 gives the summary of our adaptation of Crypto-book for Aadhaar.

3.4   Proof of Privacy of Aadhaar Number

Client Side: The client has access to following data only

1. $localID$, generated by client itself
2. Biometric data
3. Demographic Information
4. $tempId$

- The client cannot infer Aadhaar number from *tempId* because that mapping is only present with Credential Producer.
- Other two data items are unrelated to Aadhaar Number.

Therefore, client cannot infer Aadhaar number of the user. Also, *localID* is considered to be the local identifier for the particular user in the given AUA. This number is randomly chosen by every AUA during authentication of each user. Therefore every AUA will have different local identifier for a particular user. Hence there is no chance of profiling a user across multiple clients.

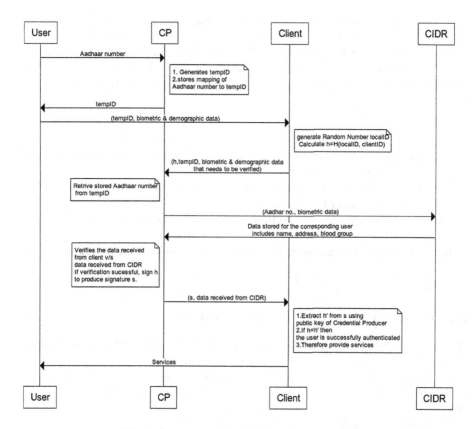

Fig. 2. Summary of authentication sequence
Legend

1. **tempID:** Temporary Identifier randomly generated by Credential Producer for a request generated by the User
2. **Biometric data:** This is the biometric data provided by User.
3. **Demographic data:** This data is the data that the clients needs to verify before providing services.
4. **clientID:** This is identification of client.
5. **h:** is the hash generated with inputs clientID and localID.

Credential Producer: The credential producer only verifies the biometric and demographic data and signs the message m only if it verifies the data. Credential Producer does not have access to $localID$. It signs h blindly without knowing $localID$. This signifies that the Credential Producer cannot infer the client who is trying to authenticate the given user and the $localID$ used by that client. Hence Credential Producer cannot profile the user or track the user from use of Aadhaar number.

Further, we prove the privacy of Aadhaar number using ProVerif protocol verification tool [5]. Our setup is as follows.

- We setup 3 processes named **User** representing the user, **Client** representing the client in our protocol and **CP** representing the credential producer.
- We declare 2 channels: **Internet** which is vulnerable to an external attacker and **Cellular**, an encrypted private channel between User and CP. This channel is used when the client registers a request with Credential Producer.

We prove the privacy of the Aadhaar number as follows

1. We run the whole protocol 2 times with different Aadhaar numbers.
2. ProVerif proves that these two runs are observationally equivalent with respect to an external attacker.
3. Client has only 1 extra piece of data compared to attacker which is $localID$. This $localID$ is generated by client itself.
4. Therefore, the two runs of the protocol are observationally equivalent to the client also.
5. Hence the client cannot infer the Aadhaar number under this protocol.

We have uploaded our ProVerif Files at [1].

3.5 Proof of Correctness of Authentication

We prove correctness of authentication using ProVerif. ProVerif provides a notion of **events** and **queries**. The **events** track various actions taken in the protocol while **queries** can be used to prove certain properties. One use of queries is to prove that if an event e_1 has occurred then it implies that some event e_2 has occurred.

Our setup is as follows

- We setup 3 processes named **User** representing the user, **Client** representing the client in our protocol and **CP** representing the credential producer.
- We declare 2 channels, **Internet** and **Cellular**; we assume the channels are secured with end to end encryption and use of digital signatures to avoid masquerading attacks.
- We declare 4 events
  1. $clientConsidersVerified(tempID)$: This event is recorded when client considers some user who provided $tempID$ verified.

2. $cpActuallyVerified(tempID, data)$: This event is recorded when Credential Producer actually verifies the $data$ corresponding to Aadhaar number corresponding to $tempID$.

3. $cpGeneratedId(Aadhaar\_number, tempID)$: This event is recorded when Credential Producer generates a $tempID$ for a particular Aadhaar number.

4. $dataSubmittedToCP(Aadhaar\_number)$: This event is recorded when a user submits a particular Aadhaar Number to a Credential Producer.

With help of ProVerif we prove that following correspondence of events hold.

1. If an event $clientConsidersVerified(tempID)$ occurred, then it implies event $cpActuallyVerified(tempID, data)$ occurred

2. If event $cpActuallyVerified(tempID, data)$ has occurred, then it implies event $cpGeneratedId(tempID, Aadhaar\_number)$ occurred.

3. If event $cpGeneratedId(Aadhaar\_number, tempID)$ occurred, then it implies event $dataSubmittedToCP(Aadhaar\_number)$ occurred.

Note that the arguments to the events ensure that the events correspond to only one set of $Aadhaar\_number$ $data$ and $tempId$. This correspondence implies that when a person is verified by the protocol, the person is actually who he claims to be.

3.6   Other Considerations

We assume that all users have a mobile phone. A case when the user does not have a mobile phone can be handled with the web interface at service provider and authentication by the user using passwords. This solution solves our problem because the process is initiated by the user and not by the AUA. Thus AUA never gets to see the Aadhaar number of the user and hence cannot correlate the number with other service providers. Also, as stated before, $localID$ becomes a local identifier for the user at that service provider. The credential producer does not have access to $localID$. This scheme also provides accountability in case of abuse by a user. The credential producers should maintain a mapping of Aadhaar numbers to h. This can be used by authorities to identify user's Aadhaar number from the local identifier.

Our integrated solution handles all the above in a single process. For example, the identification vs. authentication issue is moot as we require user initiated authentication as well as a live "OTP"-based solution. The surveillance issue is handled through a system that uses blind signatures.

For this new system to work, some existing practices need to be abolished such as

1. Collection of copies of Aadhaar id cards should be stopped as it gives service providers access to human readable Aadhaar number;

2. Awareness about proper use of Aadhaar number should be disseminated among citizens; specifically, citizens should not provide their Aadhaar numbers to service providers.

As the Aadhaar systems is already operational, there is indeed a significant problem as of now. However, the problem is still not that serious as it has been in light use for just a few years with the expected heavy use only in the immediate future. Hence, using Aadhaar system itself, it may be possible to assign safely a new Aadhaar number for each citizen and use the new Aadhaar number in the future but with privacy guarantees. Maybe one can even advise users to use the old Aadhaar for certain applications such as for emergency/disaster situations where informed consent etc. are not really meaningful and use the new ones for almost all else.

Anonymous Data for Analytics. Data analytics is a powerful tool. But there is a risk of unauthorized correlation of data while applying data analytics on Aadhaar data. The risk factors can be removed from the system by using credentials producers and credential consumers. Credential consumers can generate suitably anonymous data for data analytics applications. The system just has to make sure that the application uses pseudonyms generated by the credential consumer.

3.7   Systems Design Architecture Issues

One can view the Aadhaar system also as a concentric set of layers; the innermost being the core UIDAI functionality of providing Y/N responses ("microkernel"), a middle layer that is the backend of applications that use UIDAI ("kernel") and an outermost layer for the front end of the applications ("apps"). If such is the design, going by core software engineering principles, the question to be posed is what kinds of data can be safely exchanged across these layers.

If raw biometric data is sent across to the innermost layer, an important question is whether we can "validate the inputs"? As biometric data can be complex data objects with a big application suite (50MB is not uncommon) required for its use, any zero-day attacks in the suite can be problematic. Note that malware in jpeg or other image files has been used to get access by attackers. Hence, processing the biometric data in a less critical area is advisable but this means that only a (text) summary is provided to the innermost core. However, replay attacks/DoS may now be possible as only text needs to be generated! Hence, we need again a liveness detection system.

4   Access Control Models

Since the Aadhaar system is a complex one with many actors, the internal processes in UIDAI may be required to follow an access control architecture; we provide such a solution below modeling Aadhaar using a Trust and Role Based Access Control Model (TDBAC). While we also need to ensure the integrity of the attributes used in the access control model, which can be implemented using PKI-like system, we do not discuss it in this paper due to reasons of space.

Furthermore, there are many access control requirements on a system that guarantees security and privacy; this requires a careful process based approach but we take only a few examples.

4.1 Trust and Role Based Access Control Model

Trust and Role Based Access Control Model (TDBAC) [7] is an extension of traditional role-based access control model that uses attributes to determine trust. The roles and the attributes are together called factors of authorization. The factors of authentication decide whether a particular request is to be allowed or not. Many factors don't change frequently and these factors can be embedded in the permissions assigned to roles. But many factors like type of request, time of request, environmental factors, authorization from another entity, special tokens could also be considered to decide on the authorization of a request. Attributes present different conditions under which the roles are granted certain permissions. The values of these attribute, subject to constraints specified at design of the system, also account in successful validation. The attributes give a finer and more constrained role based access control; properly chosen set of attributes also give an excellent way to argue about the information flow of the data.

To summarize in our model,

$$U \to R \to A \to P$$

where U is the user, which maps to roles (R), which maps to relevant attribute checks(A), on passing which the access request is allowed or disallowed. A user creates a session with the required resources and activates one or more roles at any given time in the given session.

5 Instantiation of Access Control Model

5.1 Set of Roles (R)

R = {CIDR-Operator, CIDR-SysAd, CIDR-Service, ASA-Operator, ASA-Service, AUA-POS, AUA-Service, AUA-SysAd, User, Govt-Agency-X, Enrollment-Agency, Auditor}

5.2 Description of Roles

1. **CIDR-Operator:** Employee working at CIDR data center with access to the systems at data center.
2. **CIDR-SysAd:** CIDR employee who sets the rights of people working at CIDR.
3. **CIDR-Service:** The actual process which serves authentication services.
4. **ASA-Operator:** The employee working at ASA, who has access to computers at ASA.
5. **ASA-Service:** The process that handles the authentication requests.

6. **AUA-POS:** The Point of Sale device used by the AUA.
7. **AUA-Service:** The AUA process that sends out the authentication requests. D
8. **User:** is the end user who avails the identification services provided by UIDAI to get the services from the AUAs.
9. **Govt-Agency-X:** is the government agency X that requires Aadhaar data for various reasons like formulation of welfare schemes etc.
10. **Enrollment-Agency:** The agency appointed by government to collect data from citizens.
11. **Auditor:** is the third party who acts as key holder for various encryption keys and also which is responsible for authorization of various internal audits, inspections, and health of the programs running on the CIDR servers.

5.3 Attributes

The set of attributes A is defined as follows.

A = {AUA-ASA-Auth-Token, IP address, Request-Time, Device-Auth-Token, Warrant-X-Y, Disaster-X, Inspection, User-Token Sanctioned-Z}

5.4 Description of Attributes

Obvious ones elided.

1. **AUA-ASA-Auth-Token:** The authentication token should be obtained during the initial authentication of AUA to CIDR.
2. **Device-Auth-Token:** The authentication token that the POS device is legitimate and verifiable; use of trusted devices is one possibility.
3. **Warrant-X-Y:** Warrant issued by the organization X for person Y. This attribute is a token like one issued in Kerberos. It should also be signed by the organization X.
4. **Disaster-X:** This attribute is present when the request is for disclosing the data object X from the database in case of the disaster/emergency issued to government agency X. This token should be signed by the issuing organization.
5. **Inspection:** This attribute denotes that the request is for the inspection. This attribute should be signed by the auditor, which is the third party mentioned in the paper.
6. **User-Token:** This attribute is the user token submitted for authorization. Its values can be Demographic, Bio metric-Fingerprint, Bio-metric-Iris, OTP. This is to ensure that authentication is never attempted without consent. One way to implement this is to use the Crypto-book ("zero knowledge") authentication between AUA and CIDR as discussed earlier.
7. **Sanctioned-Z:** This is the attribute when an analysis task of the Govt-Agency-Z is sanctioned by the Auditor.

5.5   Permissions

Data Objects. To identify the permissions required for this model we identified the data objects which are present in the interactions. The set of data objects D = {Req, Reply, Name, Address, DOB, Nationality, Biometric-Fingerprint, Biometric-Iris, Blood-Group, Aadhaar-Number, Phone-Number, Email, Aadhaar-Local-Linking, Logs, CIDR-UR-Assignment, ASA-UR-Assignment}

Description of Data Objects. Obvious ones elided.

1. **Req:** This is the request received at CIDR. Examples of this request are identification request from AUA or data request from various govt agencies.
2. **Reply:** This is the reply that the CIDR responds to the request. It is Yes/No for authorization request or data for the data request from various agencies.
3. **Aadhaar-Local-Linking:** This is mapping between Aadhaar number and local identifier used by different organizations as recommended by UIDAI.
4. **Logs:** These are the access logs.
5. **CIDR-UR-Assignment:** The assignment of users to roles at CIDR.
6. **ASA-UR-Assignment:** The assignment of users to roles at ASA.

Operations. The authorizations are to be granted on the operations to be performed on the above objects; these are the set O = {Add, Read, Modify, Store, Read-Anonymity, }. Permissions are given by the set P defined as follows:

$$P = D \times O$$

Access Control Checks. As an example, we give 4 rules that need to be checked out of the many (for example, at least 17 such "rules" can be picked out from the English descriptions in Shweta Agarwal's paper [12]) but due to lack of space we do not provide further details):

1. **Rule:** Identification/Authentication of individuals using the global Aadhaar number should not be possible without consent.
   This rule can be enforced by following encoding of roles, attributes and permissions. For all roles for performing read operations to Aadhaar number of a particular user, User token attribute should be present and valid.
2. **Rule:** Employees of UIDAI should not be able to access the user data.
   For role of CIDR-SysAd, read permission should be absent for all user data under all relevant tokens to role of CIDR-SysAd.
3. **Rule:** Identification and authentication should not be possible without consent using public data such as demographic and biometric data.
   Read permission for any role on demographic data should only be granted if user token is present and Valid.
4. **Rule:** Co relation of Aadhaar Number should not be possible.
   This rule can be enforced by not allowing read permissions on Aadhaar number data object for role of AUA.

6   Conclusions

In this paper, we have pointed out some flaws in the current Aadhaar system design such as the lack of distinction between authentication and identification which leads to confusions and insecure design. Also, some important loopholes in security exist such as lack of liveness detection through which it is possible to attack the system using replayed biometrics. These attacks can be used for identity thefts to avail services for e.g. acquiring a telecom service on a stolen identity. It is possible to profile or track individuals in the current system whereas in a citizen centric architecture identification and authentication without users consent must never be possible. This, in turn, solves the problem of illegitimate tracking and profiling. We have provided solutions to each of these problems but these need to be thoroughly evaluated in a realistic context. Furthermore, the internal processes in UIDAI may be required to follow an access control architecture; we have provided such a solution modeling Aadhaar as TDBAC.

A   Crypto-book Algorithm

The architecture of Crypto-book is shown in Fig. 3. The description of the 4 entities in Crypto-book are as follows:

1. **The federated identities producer(F):** like UIDAI, Facebook, Google who provide identities and provide single sign on service
2. **Credential Producer(CP):** who verifies federated identities and provides partially blind credentials to consumer

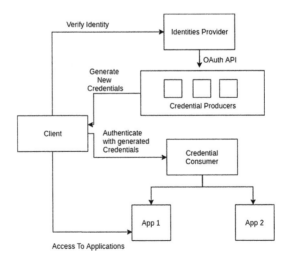

Fig. 3. Architecture of Crypto-book places in

3. **Credential Consumer (CC):** who takes as input the credentials produced by credential producer to produce pseudonyms that are presented to third party applications
4. **Third party applications (A):** These applications use the identities provided by **F**, after authentication by the user at interface provided by **F**.

Crypto-book uses blind signatures to produce pseudonyms which are presented to third party applications. Blind signatures are cryptographic primitive in which a requester can request a signer to sign a message where signer does not learn the content of the signed message. For blind signature, requester first obscures the message m with some secret to produce m' which is then signed by the signer to produce blinded signature s'; Because requester knows the secret he can remove the blinding factor and send m and unblinded signature s to the receiver. A verifier can then verify the signature using public key of the signer [8]. The following are important steps in Crypto-book; here, the client is the user, credential producer is the signer and credential consumer is the verifier.

A.1   Producing Credentials

To obtain a t "at-large" credential for use with consumer with identity idc, a client first generates a random value r which identifies the credential. The client hashes this value r with the identity of the consumer to produce message $m = H(r, idc)$. The client then contacts at least t of the n credential producers with signature requests, uniquely blinding the message m to produce m' for each request. Before signing the message, each credential producer verifies the client's federated identity and, if successful, returns blinded signature s'_i to the client. The client unblinds the signatures from each of the credential producers to obtain a vector of unblinded signatures $s_1, s_2, ...s_t$ which serves at the at-large credential for anonymous identity r with credential consumer c.

A.2   Consuming Credentials

To authenticate with a credential consumer requiring a threshold t at-large credential, a client must provide the credential consumer with the value r defining their anonymous identity along with a vector $s_1, s_2, ...s_t$ of signatures from at least t unique credential producers. The consumer first hashes this value with its own identity to produce message $m = H(r, idc)$. The consumer, using the public keys of the credential producers, then verifies that each signature is, in fact, valid for message m and, if successful, authenticates the client as anonymous identity r.

References

1. Rajput, A., Gopinath, K.: ProVerif files (2017). https://github.com/the-elves/ICISS-codes

2. Sinha, S.K.A.: Information security practices of Aadhaar (or lack thereof). Technical report, The Center for Internet and Society. https://cis-india.org/internet-governance/information-security-practices-of-aadhaar-or-lack-thereof/at_download/file

3. Angell, I.: The identity project an assessment of the UK identity cards bill and its implications. Technical report, London School of Economics (2005). http://www.lse.ac.uk/management/research/identityproject/identityreport.pdf

4. BBC: Turkish authorities 'probing huge ID data leak' (2016). http://www.bbc.com/news/technology-35978216

5. Blanchet, B., Cheval, V., Allamigeon, X., Smyth, B.: Proverif: cryptographic protocol verifier in the formal model (2010). http://prosecco.gforge.inria.fr/personal/bblanche/proverif

6. GoI: The Aadhaar (targeted delivery of financial and other subsidies, benefits and services) act, 2016. Act in Govt. of India, by Ministry of Law and Justice (2016)

7. Jemel, M., Azzouna, N.B., Ghedira, K.: Towards a dynamic access control model for e-government web services. In: 2010 IEEE Asia-Pacific Services Computing Conference (APSCC), pp. 433–440. IEEE (2010)

8. Maheswaran, J.: Building privacy-preserving cryptographic credentials from federated online identities. Ph.D. thesis, Yale University (2015)

9. Maheswaran, J., Jackowitz, D., Zhai, E., Wolinsky, D.I., Ford, B.: Building privacy-preserving cryptographic credentials from federated online identities. In: Proceedings of the Sixth ACM Conference on Data and Application Security and Privacy (2016)

10. Meyer, R.: Long-range iris scanning is here (2015). https://www.theatlantic.com/technology/archive/2015/05/long-range-iris-scanning-is-here/393065/

11. Sharma, A.: Direct benefit transfer leads to Rs. 50,000-crore savings for government in 3 years (2016). http://economictimes.indiatimes.com/news/economy/finance/direct-benefit-transfer-leads-to-rs-50000-crore-savings-for-government-in-3-years/articleshow/57240387.cms, The Economic Times

12. Agrawal, S., Banerjee, S., Sharma, S.: Privacy and security of Aadhaar: a computer science perspective. http://www.cse.iitm.ac.in/~shwetaag/papers/aadhaar.pdf

13. The-Economic-Times: UIDAI lodges FIR against Axis Bank and two more firms for tampering with Aadhaar biometrics (2017). http://economictimes.indiatimes.com/articleshow/57325951.cms

14. The-Guardian: India goes from village to village to compile worlds biggest ID database (2016). https://www.theguardian.com/world/2016/jun/28/india-village-compile-worlds-biggest-id-database-aadhaar

15. UIDAI (2016). http://www.licindia.in/getattachment/Bottom-Links/Tenders/RFP-for-Two-Factor-Authentication-and-Aadhaar-enab/STQC-UIDAI-BDCS-03-08-UIDAI-Biometric-Device-Specifications-_Authentication_1.pdf.aspx

16. UIDAI: The rule of thumb in identity (2016). https://uidai.gov.in/images/news/rule_of_Thumb_in_identity_13042017.pdf

17. Akhtar, Z., Micheloni, C., Foresti, G.L.: Biometric liveness detection: challenges and research opportunities. IEEE Secur. Priv. **13**(5), 63–72 (2015)

Security Attacks and Detection

Parallelized Common Factor Attack on RSA

Vineet Kumar[1], Aneek Roy[1], Sourya Sengupta[1], and Sourav Sen Gupta[2(✉)]

[1] Jadavpur University, Kolkata, India
vntkumar8@gmail.com, aneek.roy5@gmail.com, souryasengupta11@gmail.com
[2] Indian Statistical Institute, Kolkata, India
sg.sourav@gmail.com

Abstract. In this paper, we present a parallel approach to *common factor attack* on RSA moduli obtained by mining TLS and SSH certificates from the Internet. Our work generalizes that of Heninger et al. (2012) for a resource constrained environment, where the memory may not be sufficient to create the *product tree* required for batch-wise GCD computation on the entire dataset. We propose a data-parallel routine to efficiently exploit the batch-wise GCD algorithm in a resource constrained setting, and mount the common factor attack on TLS and SSH certificates to obtain the set of vulnerable RSA moduli with reasonable accuracy.

Keywords: Digital certificates · RSA · Common factor attack
Batch-wise GCD · Data parallelization · Distributed algorithm

1 Introduction

RSA [1], invented in 1978 by Rivest, Shamir and Adleman, is the most widely used public key cryptographic primitive to date. RSA is used as a trapdoor permutation to build encryption schemes as well as digital signatures. The strength of RSA depends upon the intractability of factoring its modulus N, which is a product of two randomly chosen *large* primes p and q. According to SSL Pulse [2], all the sites surveyed in the recent past use 2048-bit RSA moduli or higher, with about 93% of them using 2048-bit RSA moduli. Although PKCS#1 standard for RSA does not mandate primes of the same bit-size, the primes are generally chosen to be of equal bit-size in practical implementations. Thus, the sites recently surveyed by SSL Pulse most commonly use 1024-bit primes p and q.

The best known classical algorithm for factoring the two-prime RSA modulus is the General Number Field Sieve (GNFS), with a computational complexity

$$\exp\left(\left(\sqrt[3]{\frac{64}{9}} + o(1)\right)(\ln N)^{\frac{1}{3}}(\ln \ln N)^{\frac{2}{3}}\right) = L_N\left[\frac{1}{3}, \sqrt[3]{\frac{64}{9}}\right]$$

for an RSA modulus $N = pq$ (one may refer to [3] for details). This means that the computational strength of a 2048-bit RSA is approximately 116 bits (112 bits as per NIST) and that of a 1024-bit RSA is approximately 86 bits

© Springer International Publishing AG 2017
R. K. Shyamasundar et al. (Eds.): ICISS 2017, LNCS 10717, pp. 303–312, 2017.
https://doi.org/10.1007/978-3-319-72598-7_18

(80 bits as per NIST). This claimed strength of RSA (or factoring) against GNFS is valid if the primes composing the RSA modulus are chosen uniformly at random from a full entropy distribution. For example, in case of a 1024-bit RSA, it is expected that the primes p and q are chosen independently and uniformly at random from all possible 512-bit primes, satisfying $p \neq q$.

According to the Prime Number Theorem, there are of the order of 2^{502} primes of bit-size 512. Thus, if two primes p and q are chosen independently and uniformly at random from all possible 512-bit primes, then the chance of getting the same prime twice (with probability 0.5) is approximately 2^{-256} (birthday collision probability). This intuitively obvious idea is challenged by the recent *common factor attacks* on RSA. The reader may refer to [4–6] in this direction.

1.1   Common Factor Attack on RSA

In 2012, Heninger et al. [4] and Lenstra et al. [5] introduced this idea. They performed an Internet wide survey, mined all TLS and SSH certificates, and performed an exhaustive pairwise-GCD computation including every RSA modulus thus obtained. It is intuitively expected that two 1024-bit RSA moduli $N_1 = p_1 q_1$ and $N_2 = p_2 q_2$ will be co-prime with probability close to 1, and $\gcd(N_1, N_2)$ will reveal one of the primes with probability close to 2^{-256}, as is the case with prime collision. However, Heninger et al. [4] found an overwhelming number of primes revealed through the mass GCD computation. They obtained the primes and private keys for about 0.50% of TLS hosts and about 0.03% of SSH hosts, as their RSA moduli shared common primes with that of the other hosts. This was an alarming demonstration of an unnatural vulnerability in RSA usage across the Internet, primarily caused by low-entropy randomness extraction.

Heninger et al. [4] traced the cause of this vulnerability to *sloppy* implementations of RSA in embedded systems, especially in routers, firewalls, and other network devices. In case of random prime generation, RSA implementations tend to use pseudo-random number generators (PRNGs) seeded by fresh randomness each time. However, as the smaller network devices try to generate the primes at boot, quite often they lack a full-entropy source for extracting the random seeds, and hence the primes they generate eventually have a much higher probability of collision. This low-entropy phenomenon is more pronounced in case of devices manufactured by the same vendor, or in devices produced in the same batch, as the prime generation routine in such devices operate identically.

In practice, Heninger et al. [4] found that 0.75% of TLS certificates shared RSA primes, and conjectured that another 1.70% were susceptible to similar compromise due to sloppy implementations. Lenstra et al. [5] reported similar results in the same year. Later in 2013, Bernstein et al. [6] demonstrated that the RSA public keys embedded in the smart cards of Taiwan's national "Citizen Digital Certificate" database can also be compromised due to similar vulnerabilities. Bernstein et al. [6] used batch-wise GCD computation, batch-wise trial division, as well as more sophisticated tools such as Coppersmith-type partial-key-recovery attacks, to compromise a significant number of these RSA moduli.

Although the vendors of security systems have become aware of this issue, the vulnerability still plagues several TLS and SSH hosts across the Internet [7].

1.2   Motivation for Our Work

The recent trend in computing is to move from traditional single-core processing units to massive multi-core computing architectures, primarily targeted at more processing power harnessed through efficient parallelization and pipelining. This trend has seen the rise of GPUs, multi-core CPUs, and hybrid architectures around the globe. In case of *data parallel computation*, the process is parallelized by distributing the data between the compute nodes, in contrast with *task parallel computation*, where the distribution of the computation task is emphasized over the distribution of data. Single instruction, multiple data (SIMD) framework is ideal for data parallel computation, where multiple processors perform same instruction on different pieces of data, as in a distributed file system.

Heninger et al. [4] performed the pairwise-GCD computation of the scanned RSA moduli using the *"batch-wise GCD"* approach of Bernstein [8], which performs the required pairwise GCD computation by building product and remainder trees (as in Fig. 1a). The main idea of [4] is to compute the product of all the accumulated RSA moduli, $P = \prod N_i$, using an binary tree of partial products (called the *product tree*), and then to compute $z_i = P \bmod N_i^2$ for every moduli using successive computation of partial remainders through a binary tree (called the *remainder tree*). The final step is to compute $\gcd(N_i, z_i/N_i)$ for every accumulated RSA moduli and extract prime factors of the vulnerable ones. Given the complexity of multiplication and modular reduction on n-bit integers $O(n \log n \log \log n)$ and that of computing GCDs $O(n(\log n)^2 \log \log n)$, this approach requires an asymptotic runtime of $O(mn \log m \log(mn) \log \log(mn))$ for constructing the binary trees, and $O(mn(\log n)^2 \log \log n)$ to finally compute the GCDs, where m is the number of n-bit RSA moduli in the dataset [4]. Thus, for a large dataset comprising of more than 4 to 5 Million RSA moduli, it requires almost 32 GB of memory and around 60 to 70 GB of storage for scratch calculations [4]. This is the worst computational bottleneck of the approach in [4].

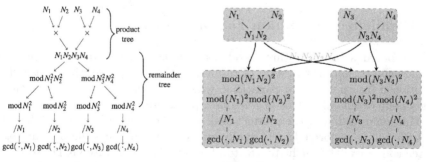

(a) Batch-GCD computation [4]   (b) Parallel batch-GCD computation [7]

Fig. 1. Efficient pairwise GCD computation techniques used by Heninger et al. [4] and Hastings et al. [7], following the *"batch-wise GCD"* approach of Bernstein [8].

In 2016, Hastings et al. [7] proposed a partially parallel implementation of batch-wise GCD, where the dataset is partitioned in subsets and the product tree for computing $P = \prod N_i$ is constructed individually for each subset. While this provides potentially full parallelization in the first phase of the algorithm, the remainder tree is still constructed considering all subset products produced by the product trees (as in Fig. 1b). This acts as a computational bottleneck.

In contrast with [4,7], we choose a data parallelization approach for both the product tree and the remainder tree constructions, thereby parallelizing the complete batch-wise GCD algorithm to remove the computational bottlenecks.

1.3   Contribution of Our Work

In this paper, we propose an alternative approach to achieve similar results as Heninger et al. [4] and Hastings et al. [7], using less computational resources. With the progress from serial to parallel computing frameworks, we choose to adopt the *data parallelization* approach in order to reduce the memory and storage complexity of the batch-wise GCD algorithm in practice.

Consider the master dataset D comprising of several RSA moduli scanned from the Internet. Suppose that the size of D is large enough so that in a regular resource constrained node, one cannot run batch-wise GCD on D. Suppose that a single node can handle a dataset of size at most m, where $m \ll |D|$. The solution that we provide splits the dataset D into $p \sim |D|/m$ partitions, so that each node may operate on the partitions in parallel, and then takes a union of results obtained from several such *random* splits of the data to identify the final set of vulnerable RSA moduli. We prove a bound on the fraction of vulnerable moduli identified by this approach, and show that one may probabilistically extract almost all vulnerable RSA moduli quite efficiently in practice.

The paper is organized as follows. Section 2 summarizes the proposed *parallelized common factor attack* – including the modified batch-wise GCD algorithm (Algorithm 1), the proof for the accuracy of our algorithm (Theorem 1), and the experimental results (Sect. 2.2) to support our claim. Finally, Sect. 3 concludes the paper, illustrating a few scopes and directions for future investigation.

2   Parallelized Common Factor Attack

The proposed attack has three modules – partitioning of data, computation on the subsets, and aggregation of results. In the first phase, the dataset D is partitioned into $p \sim |D|/m$ partitions, where m is the largest data-size that a single node can handle. This m remains a parameter for the user to choose.

The computation of the product and remainder trees to identify vulnerable RSA moduli is performed individually on each subset, using the free and open source code (available at http://factorable.net) for batch-wise GCD. Note that this method does not recover all vulnerable moduli present in D, as there may be several pairs of moduli with common factor split into different subsets. Thus, we require a mechanism to aggregate the results obtained from each subset. We take the union of the sets of vulnerable moduli obtained from each subset of the data D, thus eliminating duplicates, if any. To recover all vulnerable moduli in the master dataset D, we repeat this process over a number of iterations k.

Later in this section, we prove a probabilistic lower bound on the fraction of recovered moduli as a function of the number of partitions (p) and the number of iterations (k). This helps us to choose the optimal number of iterations (k) in our attack, based on the number of partitions (p), size of each partition (m), and the desired level of accuracy (ϵ). The desired level of accuracy (ϵ) acts as another user-defined parameter, and we discuss this in more details in Sect. 2.1.

Proposed Technique — Algorithm 1 presents the parallelized common factor attack, and Fig. 2 illustrates one complete iteration of our proposed algorithm, distributed over the three modules – partitioning, computation and aggregation.

Input   : Set of moduli D, constraint m, accuracy ϵ
Output: V — set of vulnerable moduli in D

1 $p \leftarrow \texttt{ceiling}(|D|/m)$;
2 $k \leftarrow \texttt{chooseIteration}(m, p, \epsilon)$;
3 **for** $i \leftarrow 1$ **to** k **do**
4     $\{d_1, d_2, \ldots, d_p\} \leftarrow \texttt{randomPartition}(D, p)$;
5     $\{v_1, v_2, \ldots, v_p\} \leftarrow \texttt{batchGCD}(\{d_1, d_2, \ldots, d_p\})$;
6     $V_i \leftarrow \texttt{setUnion}(\{v_1, v_2, \ldots, v_p\})$;
7 **end**
8 $V \leftarrow \texttt{setUnion}(\{V_1, V_2, \ldots, V_k\})$;

Algorithm 1: Parallelized Common Factor Attack

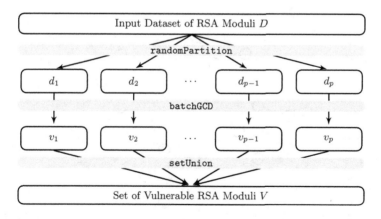

Fig. 2. One complete iteration of the proposed parallelized algorithm.

2.1   Accuracy of the Algorithm

Claim: Algorithm 1, with a *proper* choice of k in subroutine `chooseIteration`, recovers approximately ϵX vulnerable RSA moduli, where X is the total number of vulnerable moduli in the input dataset D, and ϵ is the user-defined accuracy parameter. The *proper* choice of k is proposed and justified in Theorem 1.

Theorem 1. *Suppose there exist X vulnerable RSA moduli in input dataset D. Then Algorithm 1 recovers an expected number of ϵX vulnerable moduli if we set*

$$k \approx \frac{\log{(1 - \epsilon)}}{\log m + \log{(p - 1)} - \log{(mp - 1)}},$$

where ϵ is the user-defined accuracy parameter, m is the user-defined constraint of the individual computing nodes, and $p \sim |D|/m$ is the number of partitions.

Proof. Let us define an undirected graph G_D on input dataset D, with the RSA moduli N_i as vertices, and edges present between vertices $\{N_i, N_j\}$ if and only if $\gcd(N_i, N_j) > 1$. Thus, finding the set of vulnerable RSA moduli in D amounts to finding all the edges of the graph G_D, and this is precisely the output of the `batchGCD` algorithm (as in http://factorable.net) executed on D.

Note that p random partitions $\{d_1, d_2, \ldots, d_p\}$ of the input dataset D partitions the graph G_D into mutually exclusive subgraphs $\{g_1, g_2, \ldots, g_p\}$ (as illustrated in Fig. 3), each with approximately $m \sim |D|/p$ vertices. If we execute `batchGCD` in parallel on each subset in $\{d_1, d_2, \ldots, d_p\}$, we will obtain all edges within each subgraph in $\{g_1, g_2, \ldots, g_p\}$ (illustrated as solid edges in Fig. 3), but will miss the edges $e_{(N_i, N_j)}$ in G_D where N_i and N_j belong to two different subgraphs in $\{g_1, g_2, \ldots, g_p\}$ (illustrated as dotted edges in Fig. 3).

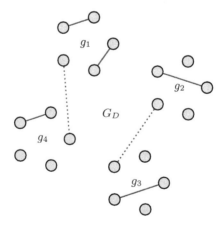

Fig. 3. Illustrative partition of graph G_D into subgraphs $\{g_1, g_2, \ldots, g_p\}$.

Given that the subroutine `randomPartition` randomly partitions the input dataset D into p approximately equal subsets $\{d_1, d_2, \ldots, d_p\}$, and assuming that the edges in the graph G_D appear uniformly at random, depending on the existence of common factors between the moduli (vertices), it is logical to infer that edges in G_D fall within the subgraphs (or outside) proportional to all possible edges in the supergraph of $\{g_1, g_2, \ldots, g_p\}$ (or outside). Thus, the probability that we will miss a specific edge $e_{(N_i, N_j)}$ in G_D after one execution of the parallel `batchGCD` algorithm on $\{d_1, d_2, \ldots, d_p\}$ can be computed as

$$
\begin{aligned}
P_{i=1} &= 1 - \frac{\text{total number of edges in } \{g_1, g_2, \ldots, g_p\}}{\text{total number of edges in } G_D} \\
&\approx 1 - \frac{\text{edges in complete supergraph of } \{g_1, g_2, \ldots, g_p\}}{\text{edges in complete supergraph of } G_D} \\
&\approx 1 - \frac{p \times \binom{m}{2}}{\binom{mp}{2}} = 1 - \frac{m-1}{mp-1} = \frac{m(p-1)}{mp-1}.
\end{aligned}
$$

In turn, the probability that we will miss a specific edge $e_{(N_i, N_j)}$ in G_D after k independent executions of the parallel `batchGCD` algorithm on k independent random partitions $\{d_1, d_2, \ldots, d_p\}$ of D is

$$
P_{i=k} = (P_{i=1})^k \approx \left(\frac{m(p-1)}{mp-1} \right)^k.
$$

Therefore, the fraction of edges recovered after k iterations is $\epsilon \approx 1 - \left(\frac{m(p-1)}{mp-1} \right)^k$. Hence the choice for k prescribed in the theorem.   □

Note that given the input dataset D and with $mp \sim |D|$, as per Algorithm 1, one may also interpret the values of ϵ and k from Theorem 1 as

$$
\epsilon \approx 1 - \left(\frac{|D| - |D|/p}{|D| - 1} \right)^k, \quad \text{that is,}
$$

$$
k \approx \frac{\log(1 - \epsilon)}{\log(|D| - |D|/p) - \log(|D| - 1)},
$$

so that the choice of k in the subroutine `chooseIteration` depends directly on the input dataset D. However, the two interpretations of ϵ and k are identical, and thus one may write the subroutine `chooseIteration` in either way. One may also note the empirical relationship between k, the desired level of accuracy ϵ, and the number of partitions p, from the following experimental results.

2.2   Experimental Results

We downloaded the set of TLS certificates of secured websites from the Internet-wide scan data repository available at https://www.scans.io [9]. The dataset contained around 27 million 1024-bit RSA moduli ($\sim$ 7 GB in size) and around

15 million 2048-bit RSA moduli (~ 6 GB in size). To perform a proof-of-concept validation of our proposed parallelized algorithm, we chose a random 500 MB set of 1024-bit RSA moduli as our input dataset D. The choice of 500 MB dataset D was based on our constraints of computational resources, as the machine used for the experiments (Intel Core i5 4210U CPU, 4 GB RAM) could only process 500 MB of RSA moduli at a time, using the naive `batchGCD` [4] algorithm.

To check the accuracy of our proposed algorithm, we executed naive `batchGCD` on the 500 MB dataset D to know the exact number (X) of vulnerable moduli, and then executed our proposed algorithm on D with various choices of p (2 to 32, in powers of 2) and k (1 to 9) to obtain the experimental values of ϵX. Running this experiment multiple times on our 500 MB random dataset D provided us with a conditional distribution of the accuracy factor ϵ, given the parameters p and k. The experimental distribution of ϵ, given the parameters p and k, is recorded in Table 1, and the expected empirical relationship of the mean of percentage accuracy ϵ with the parameters p and k is illustrated in Fig. 4.

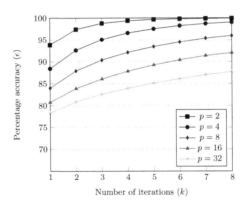

Fig. 4. Relationship between ϵ, p and k from experimental data.

The experimental results clearly indicate that the proposed parallelized common factor attack is capable of recovering more than 90% of the vulnerable RSA moduli from a given dataset D even when the dataset has been partitioned into $p = 16$ parts, provided that we allow multiple iterations; for example, $k = 8$ iterations in case of $p = 16$ seems to suffice. For a fixed number of partitions p, there is a clear monotonic relationship between ϵ and k, indicating the possibility of recovering *almost all* vulnerable RSA moduli from a given dataset, by executing our proposed algorithm for a suitable number of iterations.

Table 1. Experimental results for ϵ given the parameters p and k.

k	Percentage accuracy (ϵ) for $p = 2$									Mean ϵ	Std. dev
1	93.87	93.87	93.71	93.83	93.91	93.72	93.75	93.85	93.85	93.82	0.07
2	97.54	97.35	97.45	97.45	97.30	97.34	97.54	97.43	97.17	97.40	0.12
3	98.79	98.80	98.88	98.73	98.74	98.90	98.77	98.81	98.75	98.80	0.06
4	99.40	99.41	99.35	99.28	99.46	99.39	99.41	99.35	99.31	99.37	0.06
5	99.72	99.64	99.62	99.70	99.69	99.67	99.61	99.76	99.73	99.68	0.05
6	99.81	99.81	99.83	99.86	99.76	99.81	99.83	99.79	99.80	99.81	0.03
7	99.88	99.89	99.92	99.87	99.89	99.87	99.89	99.93	99.90	99.89	0.02
8	99.93	99.94	99.92	99.96	99.93	99.96	99.94	99.90	99.93	99.93	0.02
k	Percentage accuracy (ϵ) for $p = 4$									Mean ϵ	Std. dev.
1	88.19	88.44	88.51	88.56	88.34	88.32	88.74	88.33	88.32	88.42	0.16
2	92.77	92.61	92.77	92.45	92.60	92.72	92.50	92.50	92.66	92.62	0.12
3	95.13	95.30	94.94	95.09	95.16	95.00	95.04	95.12	94.87	95.07	0.13
4	96.69	96.48	96.61	96.65	96.37	96.49	96.55	96.66	96.78	96.59	0.13
5	97.51	97.68	97.69	97.47	97.57	97.60	97.58	97.26	97.41	97.53	0.14
6	98.30	98.31	98.04	98.17	98.38	98.22	98.29	98.19	98.33	98.25	0.10
7	98.85	98.66	98.75	98.62	98.79	98.73	98.83	98.64	98.63	98.72	0.09
8	99.05	99.18	98.97	98.99	99.08	99.14	99.07	98.74	99.05	99.03	0.13
k	Percentage accuracy (ϵ) for $p = 8$									Mean ϵ	Std. dev.
1	84.05	84.05	84.23	83.66	83.85	84.08	84.13	84.01	83.82	83.99	0.18
2	87.95	87.93	87.77	87.90	87.97	88.06	88.01	87.89	87.71	87.91	0.11
3	90.28	90.35	90.48	90.47	90.51	90.51	90.37	90.27	90.36	90.40	0.10
4	92.01	92.09	92.10	92.17	92.13	92.12	92.19	92.17	92.17	92.13	0.06
5	93.37	93.40	93.45	93.47	93.42	93.45	93.47	93.49	93.51	93.45	0.05
6	94.46	94.45	94.51	94.49	94.54	94.56	94.49	94.57	94.52	94.51	0.04
7	95.31	95.38	95.33	95.38	95.32	95.43	95.37	95.48	95.44	95.38	0.06
8	96.07	95.99	96.10	96.11	96.17	96.10	95.87	95.21	96.07	95.96	0.29
k	Percentage accuracy (ϵ) for $p = 16$									Mean ϵ	Std. dev.
1	80.69	80.62	81.08	80.75	80.55	80.89	80.60	80.72	80.74	80.74	0.16
2	83.77	84.25	83.89	83.72	84.13	83.68	83.82	83.92	83.82	83.89	0.19
3	86.26	85.96	85.87	86.20	85.80	85.95	86.06	86.38	86.29	86.08	0.20
4	87.94	87.81	88.13	87.79	87.95	88.04	87.55	87.88	87.50	87.84	0.21
5	89.21	89.48	89.14	89.30	89.35	89.25	89.06	89.19	89.25	89.25	0.12
6	90.43	90.20	90.35	90.39	90.46	90.58	90.69	90.32	90.34	90.42	0.15
7	91.26	91.40	91.45	91.21	91.23	91.44	91.50	91.61	91.31	91.38	0.14
8	92.14	92.17	92.07	92.19	92.05	92.25	92.03	91.17	92.14	92.02	0.33
k	Percentage accuracy (ϵ) for $p = 32$									Mean ϵ	Std. dev.
1	78.54	78.28	78.32	78.01	78.29	78.22	78.33	78.08	78.46	78.28	0.17
2	80.96	80.88	80.67	80.94	80.82	80.91	80.76	81.07	80.94	80.88	0.12
3	82.57	82.44	82.73	82.59	82.69	82.55	82.82	82.45	82.65	82.61	0.13
4	83.84	84.02	83.97	84.02	83.86	84.09	83.95	83.80	83.83	83.93	0.10
5	85.10	85.03	85.05	85.00	85.13	85.20	85.21	85.10	85.26	85.12	0.09
6	86.13	86.13	86.09	86.18	86.02	85.99	86.13	86.04	86.15	86.10	0.06
7	86.98	86.96	87.07	87.01	87.08	86.89	86.99	87.01	87.06	87.01	0.06
8	87.75	87.83	87.91	87.91	87.87	87.83	87.76	86.85	87.75	87.72	0.33

3   Conclusion

In this paper, we generalize the naive `batchGCD` algorithm utilized by Heninger et al. [4] towards a parallelized common factor attack on RSA moduli. Our proposal is naturally scalable over arbitrary sized datasets of a similar nature, and one may consider implementing the same over inherently parallel data processing and computing frameworks like GPU clusters or Hadoop map-reduce platforms.

As a follow up of our work, one may consider extending our proposal to include the partially parallel approach of Hastings et al. [7] as well, keeping the product tree inherently parallel, as it is, and applying our approach towards an iterative parallel computation of the remainder tree. Another interesting line of future work may be to extend our proposal to include the sophisticated approaches of finding vulnerable RSA moduli (using Coppersmith-type lattice based attacks), in lines with the work of Bernstein et al. [6].

Acknowledgement. The authors would like to thank the anonymous reviewers of ICISS 2017 for their constructive criticism, remarks and suggestions, which helped in substantially improving the technical and editorial quality of the paper.

References

1. Rivest, R.L., Shamir, A., Adleman, L.M.: A method for obtaining digital signatures and public-key cryptosystems. Commun. ACM **21**(2), 120–126 (1978)
2. SSL Labs: Trustworthy internet movement - SSL pulse (2017). Accessed 4 Oct 2017
3. Pomerance, C.: A tale of two sieves. Not. Am. Math. Soc. **43**, 1473–1485 (1996)
4. Heninger, N., Durumeric, Z., Wustrow, E., Halderman, J.A.: Mining your Ps and Qs: detection of widespread weak keys in network devices. In Kohno, T. (ed.) Proceedings of the 21th USENIX Security Symposium, Bellevue, WA, USA, 8–10 August 2012, pp. 205–220. USENIX Association (2012)
5. Lenstra, A.K., Hughes, J.P., Augier, M., Bos, J.W., Kleinjung, T., Wachter, C.: Ron was wrong, Whit is right. IACR Cryptology ePrint Archive **2012**, 64 (2012)
6. Bernstein, D.J., Chang, Y.-A., Cheng, C.-M., Chou, L.-P., Heninger, N., Lange, T., van Someren, N.: Factoring RSA keys from certified smart cards: Coppersmith in the wild. In: Sako, K., Sarkar, P. (eds.) ASIACRYPT 2013. LNCS, vol. 8270, pp. 341–360. Springer, Heidelberg (2013). https://doi.org/10.1007/978-3-642-42045-0_18
7. Hastings, M., Fried, J., Heninger, N.: Weak keys remain widespread in network devices. In: Gill, P., Heidemann, J.S., Byers, J.W., Govindan, R. (eds.) Proceedings of the 2016 ACM on Internet Measurement Conference, IMC 2016, Santa Monica, CA, USA, 14–16 November 2016, pp. 49–63. ACM (2016)
8. Bernstein, D.J.: How to find smooth parts of integers (2004)
9. Censys Team, University of Michigan: Internet-wide scan data repository (2016). Accessed 15 Oct 2016

Performance Attacks on Branch Predictors in Embedded Processors with SMT Support

Moumita Das[1], Ansuman Banerjee[1(✉)], Nitesh K. Singh[2], and Bhaskar Sardar[3]

[1] Indian Statistical Institute, Kolkata, India
ansuman@isical.ac.in
[2] Institute of Engineering and Management, Kolkata, India
[3] Jadavpur University, Kolkata, India

Abstract. Designing efficient branch predictors has always been one of the top priority research tasks in computer architecture. In an embedded processor with support for multi-threaded execution, with multiple different applications executing in different threads, and managed by a single predictor, significant inter-application interference due to sharing of predictor data structures has been acknowledged to be a serious concern. In this paper, we show an attack methodology which exploits these shared structures for performance attacks on a benign application. In particular, we propose a methodology for creating a variant of a benign application, which when dispatched in a concurrently executing thread, can definitively slow down the performance of the benign one. We report the effect of such attacks with experiments on the Siemens software benchmarks.

1 Introduction

Branch predictors play an important role in improving the performance and energy consumption of pipelined processors. Branch prediction allows a processor to predict and fetch the successor statement of a branch in advance, often before the branch condition code is decoded, thereby saving processor cycles. A mis-prediction, however, leads to wastage of effort and loss of costly compute cycles, since the entire pipeline has to be flushed and new instructions need to be brought in. For the P4 and P4E processors, as many as 24 clock cycles and around 45 micro-operations are wasted as mis-prediction penalty [8]. An inefficient predictor can thus in turn lead to performance degradation as well.

Dynamic branch predictors which are part of any modern processor today, maintain and manipulate efficient prediction policies at run-time when the program is in actual execution. Dynamic predictors use history information about the branch under consideration for its current prediction and often take into account the direction histories of the preceding branches in addition to the present one while making a prediction for a specific branch. Evidently, the history information has to be stored and manipulated inside a processor, thereby motivating researchers to look at energy and space efficient designs for these predictor tables. The objective of this paper is to explore attacks on these prediction tables in a multi-threaded execution context.

© Springer International Publishing AG 2017
R. K. Shyamasundar et al. (Eds.): ICISS 2017, LNCS 10717, pp. 313–322, 2017.
https://doi.org/10.1007/978-3-319-72598-7_19

In modern processor architectures, Simultaneous Multi-Threading (SMT) [6] is used to improve overall performance of program execution. It allows multiple threads of execution working simultaneously on a processor to better utilize the processor resources. The operating system scheduler and the hardware thread dispatcher underneath seamlessly manage the multiple threads of execution with context switches between the threads at runtime. Indeed, most modern processors today utilize the benefits of SMT with multiple threads working together using separate tables for individual threads to avoid inter-thread interference [11]. However, in a resource constrained embedded environment (e.g. a mobile processor), managing separate predictor tables is often infeasible, and a single shared table [7] turns out to be the only realistic choice to mitigate concerns on high resource usage and energy dissipation.

The setup we consider in this paper is an embedded processor with SMT support, and we study performance attacks on these shared predictor tables. The main motivation behind our attack exploitation was the observation that most embedded processors with shared structures suffer significantly in terms of accuracy of prediction, and in turn, performance slowdown due to the resulting pipeline activity that has to be performed as a mis-prediction penalty. Our analysis of context switching performance for SMT execution on the popular Siemens software benchmarks [9], with multiple independent applications running in different threads mapped to a single core implemented with shared predictor tables, revealed an interesting finding – there is usually a decrease in branch prediction accuracy (and increase in misprediction) in concurrent execution, in comparison to the accuracy achieved when the applications are run in isolation. While pollution effects on the shared cache in multi-threaded execution have been studied in literature [13], effects on branch prediction have been relatively less examined [7,11], to the best of our knowledge. In our setup, our findings revealed that the expected overall performance gain in program execution is reduced as well, due to the extra overhead of handling branch mis-predictions, often leading to a performance slowdown. An in-depth analysis revealed that this was a result of extensive interference on the shared prediction data structures (more specifically, the predictor tables and registers) on which the branch predictors operate, resulting out of the frequent switching between the different applications running in multiple threads, leading to performance slowdown. For branch prediction, a predictor typically uses shared registers and tables to extract the predicted branch direction and updates these with the actual branch outcomes after a branch gets resolved. It may so happen that the prediction information of one application running in one thread stored in some shared data structure is used and overwritten by another application running in a different thread, once context switches during execution. This often leads to a negative interference among the threads, thereby leading to an incorrect direction for prediction, and therefore, accuracy degradation and slowdown.

In this paper, we exploit the negative interference between threads in a shared-table SMT single-core processor to slow down the performance of a benign application. We propose an attack methodology that can automatically create variants of a benign application, which when dispatched in a concurrently running thread, can definitively induce negative interference on the benign one. Our methodology exploits the control flow structure of a given benign application to create the variant. Section 3 presents the details of the attack methodology.

We perform experiments on the Siemens benchmarks [5] to demonstrate the effect of such performance attacks. Experimental results show that the prediction accuracy degrades, leading to performance slowdowns with our proposed attack policy. We further show that a solution that controls this interference by splitting the predictor table for different applications such that no program can share or modify the data stored for the other programs, does not improve performance as well due to excessive intra-thread interference. In this case, the predictor table is partitioned into smaller isolated compartments and each compartment is allocated to an executing thread. However, this adds intra interference cost and also compromises the benefit of positive interference between threads.

The rest of the paper is organized as follows: Sect. 2 presents the background of the branch predictor we use and an overview of the interference phenomenon that may occur for such a predictor in SMT mode. Section 3 elaborates our method of attack construction for negative interference. In Sect. 4, we show the performance effects that result due to such attacks, while the next section mentions some related literature. Section 6 concludes the paper.

2   Predictor Table Interference in SMT

In this section, we first present an architectural overview of the bimodal predictor [10], which we use to illustrate our attack methodology. We choose this predictor for simplicity of illustration and ease of demonstration, attacks with other predictors can similarly be worked out. A bimodal predictor is a simple dynamic predictor that maintains a two bit saturating counter for every branch of a program for prediction. The main data structure of this predictor is a prediction table that stores the two-bit counter state for each branch, as shown in Fig. 1. The counter maintains four different states 00 (strongly not-taken), 01 (weakly not-taken), 10 (weakly taken) and 11 (strongly taken) defined by the 2 bits of it, as shown in Fig. 1. The counter transitions from one state to another in response to a taken (T) or not-taken (NT) outcome resulting from the execution of one or more branch instructions. Each bit of the two-bit counter plays a different role. The most significant bit, called the direction bit is used to track the direction of branches. If the counter is in states 01 or 00, the branch is predicted as NT. When it is in states 10 and 11, the prediction is T. The least significant bit provides a hysteresis which prevents the direction bit from immediately changing when a mis-prediction occurs. When a branch instruction is encountered during program execution, its address is used to index into the appropriate location in the predictor table, and the state of the 2-bit counter is used for predicting the direction of the branch. We now explain the working of this predictor in the context of SMT execution, and the interference generated.

We consider two programs of the Siemens software benchmarks, *printokens* and *tcas*. Consider a situation where *branch n* of *printokens* comes with an

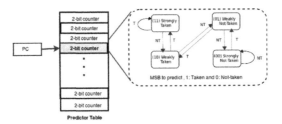

Fig. 1. Bimodal branch predictor

address *101010101* (i.e. the program counter PC value), and a predictor table entry X is accessed with the five bits of it from LSB (10101) (shown with a dotted line in Fig. 2). X gives the final prediction according to the current state of the two-bit counter stored in it and updates the state with the actual outcome after the branch actually gets resolved.

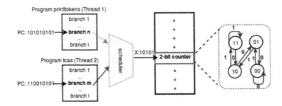

Fig. 2. Predictor table interference of two programs

Consider the present state of the two bit counter stored in X is 10, hence it predicts the branch direction as *taken* since the most significant bit (MSB) is 1. If the actual outcome of *branch n* is 1, its state changes to 11 to give the predicted direction as *taken*, otherwise it changes to 01 to give the predicted direction as *not-taken*. Consider the actual outcome as 0, which implies that the current state of this two bit counter becomes 01, and when this table entry is accessed in future, it provides the prediction as *not-taken*. Now, due to SMT, *branch m* from the *tcas* program is selected with the current PC value as 110010101. If we take the same least significant five bits from it to index the table, we point to the same X entry for this different program counter (shown with a solid line). Hence, the predicted direction for *branch m* is *not-taken*, since the current state of the two bit counter is 01. Now, the actual outcome of this *branch m*, which is 1 changes the counter state to 10 to give the prediction as *taken*. Hence, the branch behavior stored for *printtokens* for a specific pattern is incorrectly interfered and updated by *tcas* for another branch. Now, when the same branch of *printtokens* is encountered again in future, then the same PHT entry X is accessed again for prediction. It predicts the branch direction as *taken* - which is incorrect and cannot give the expected result, since a *not-taken* direction was stored for that pattern, when *branch n* of *printtokens* was processed, but overwritten when *branch m* of *tcas* was processed.

Context switching between threads generates significant negative interference that ultimately has an impact on overall prediction accuracy as well as overall performance, since increase in mis-prediction rate has an adverse effect on energy consumption due to increase in the number of wrong path executions. This phenomenon of negative interference is what we utilise to attack a benign application by creating a carefully crafted variant, as explained in the following.

3   Attack Methodology

In this section, we present the details of our proposed attack creation and execution. Our proposal is based on some assumptions on the underlying architecture model, as outlined below.

3.1   Assumptions

We consider a very simple execution model with disabled Address space layout randomization (ASLR). We assume that the two programs (benign and malicious) execute in the system in SMT mode one after another. We assume that the programs are co-located on the same core and this assumption is needed to ensure that the branch predictor unit is shared. In this work, our assumed branch predictor uses a shared configuration that shares the predictor tables and Branch History Register (BHR) among all the running threads [11]. For the shared configuration, we consider a bimodal predictor that takes only the Program Counter (PC) to index the branch predictor table. We now explain how our attack methodology works on the assumed execution model.

Program P(actual program)	Program P'(clone program)

1: static int next_state(state,ch)
2: int state;
3: char ch;
{
4:    if(state < 0)   //branch 1
5:      return(state);
 	
6: if(base[state]+ch >= 0)   { //branch 2
7:      if(check[base[state]+ch] == state)
                          //branch 3
8:          return(next[base[state]+ch]);
9:     else
10   return(next_state(default1[state],ch));
    }
11: else
12:     return(next_state(default1[state],ch));
}
	1:static int next_state(state,ch)
	2:int state;
	3:char ch;
	{
	4: if(!(state < 0)){} //branch 1
	5: else
	6: return(state);
	7: if(!(base[state]+ch >= 0)) { //branch 2
	8: return(next_state(default1[state],ch));
	    }
	9: else{
	10: if(!(check[base[state]+ch] == state))
	                          //branch 3
	11: return(next_state(default1[state],ch));
	12: else
	13: return(next[base[state]+ch]);
	    }
	}

Fig. 3. Program fragment of printokens and its variant

3.2   Attack Creation

For a program P, we create a variant P' (we also call it a *clone*) that is dispatched in a concurrent thread to spoil the prediction information kept by the predictor for P. This variant program is a replica of the actual one except that all the corresponding branch conditions are flipped. In the illustration below, only conditional branches are considered. The variant creation process has three major steps, as shown in Algorithm 1. We illustrate each step using the printtokens program fragment, shown in Fig. 3.

- **MakeClone:** It is the main method. It takes the benign program P and for each statement of P, creates the variant P' by calling the following functions.
- **CopyOnClone:** This method takes every statement of P and checks if it is a conditional statement. For any statement other than a branch, it simply copies it into program P'. Hence, statements 1, 2 and 3 of program P are just copied into the variant program P'(corresponding statements 1, 2 and 3 are created), as shown in Fig. 3. For every branch statement, it calls the function *IfInversion* to generate a corresponding branch with the condition flipped and inserts it into P'.
- **IfInversion:** This is the most important function of this variant creation process. It flips the condition of every branch of P and writes it into P'. Since we do not want to change the control flow of the actual program in P', we interchange the *if* block with the *else* block of each branch of P in P'. Figure 3 shows the interchange of the *if* and *else* blocks of branch 2 of program P (statement 6) in program P' (branch 2, statement 7). This interchange also happens for branch 3 of program P and it can be seen that statement 8 which is within the *if* block of this branch in P is copied into the else block (statement 13) of the same branch in P'. For every branch of P that has no *else* block, it creates a dummy else block in P' and copies all the statements within the *if* block in P into the corresponding dummy else block in P'. Figure 3 shows the *else* created for branch 1 (statement 4) of program P in P' (statement 5). Statement 5 of P, that is within the *if* block of this branch is copied into this newly created dummy *else* block in P' (statement 6).

The above algorithm recursively goes inside *if* and *else* blocks and creates the corresponding statements, with the conditions flipped and the statement blocks interchanged. We now explain how this program P', when dispatched as a concurrent thread, can definitely spoil the prediction information for P when both are running on the same input. In SMT mode, the two programs P and P' are made to run with a round robin scheduler context switching between the two threads. Since the programs are almost identical to each other except in the branch conditions (flipped in the clone program), the same address value (program counter PC) will be generated for both the programs. Note that PC is a virtual address and the same is used for indexing the predictor tables.

We now illustrate how our clone program causes negative interference for every branch of the benign program for this branch predictor configuration. In this configuration, the branch predictor table and the branch history register are

Algorithm 1. CloneCreation

```
Input: Program P
Output: Clone program P'
Method MakeClone()
begin
    for each statement S in application P do
        CopyOnClone(S)
end
Method CopyOnClone(S)
begin
    if S contains a branch then
        IfInversion(S)
    else
        Copy S onto variant
end
Method IfInversion(S)
begin
    flip the condition of S and write it on P'
    if else block of S is present in P then
        for each statement S₁ in the true path of S do
            call CopyOnClone(S₁) on the corresponding else block of P'

        for each statement S₂ in the else path of S do
            call CopyOnClone(S₂) on the corresponding if block of P'

    else

    Create else block of S in P'
    for each statement S' of S do
        call CopyOnClone(S') on the created else block
end
```

shared by the running threads. The bimodal predictor uses only the PC value to index the predictor table entry for prediction. The prediction information stored by the actual program is flipped in the clone program since the branch condition of the two programs are opposite to each other. Thus, when the two programs are made to run on the same input, the outcome in P will be opposite to the one in P'. Figure 4 shows that for the branch at line 2 of program P, PHT entry PHT_1 is accessed (step 1) and the current state of the two bit counter that is stored in that entry gives the prediction (2). If the current state is 10, the prediction is *taken*. Now, this state is modified according to the actual outcome of the branch. Consider the actual outcome is *not-taken* and the current state becomes 01 to give the prediction as *not-taken*. In future, for the same branch, this state is stored in that entry (3). Now in SMT mode, for the same branch (branch 2) of our variant program P', this entry is accessed since the PC value for both are same. As before, its current state is used for prediction and after that, this state is modified and stored according to the actual outcome (steps are marked as 1', 2' and 3'). The outcome of this branch is *taken* for program P' (as opposite to P) and so the state of the counter is changed to 10. Hence, mis-prediction occurs for branch 2 of program P in future since its prediction information is destructively modified by its variant.

4   Experimental Setup and Evaluation

We carried out our experiment on the gem5 architectural simulator [2]. Multiple user specific programs can run simultaneously in simultaneous multi-threading (SMT) mode where each program is provided a unique thread id with round-robin scheduler as the default scheduler. After execution it generates statistics

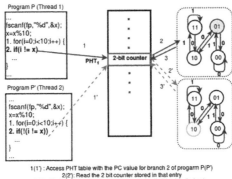

Fig. 4. Negative interference caused by the variant on a benign application

that records data on branch prediction accuracy, energy expenditure, time taken etc. We modified the source code of this simulator to support SMT mode for two programs where same predictor table is shared by them for prediction.

Table 1. Benchmark Detail

Programs	Line of code	Number of branches
replace	565	94
schedule	415	30
schedule2	311	41
totinfo	407	45
printtokens	727	40
printtokens2	564	78

We now report our experience in using our methods on the Siemens benchmark programs. Table 1 present the benchmark details. Third column of this table presents the number of branches that are flipped in our clone program. Figure 5 presents the misprediction rate of each benchmark program when it is run in single mode and run with our created clone program. It is seen that the presence of the clone program increases the misprediction rate. Although the accuracy degradation shown in Fig. 5 is not so high, around 2%, however 1 mis-prediction can increase a significant amount of processor cycles as well as extra instruction fetch. Figure 5 also presents the mis-prediction rate achieved in split predictor table configuration of the bimodal predictor and compares the mis-prediction rates of the benchmark program when run (a) in single mode, (b) with clone program in SMT mode and (c) with clone program in SPIT table configuration. It is observed that SPLIT table cannot improve the mis-prediction rate significantly. The reason behind this is the fact that - though it reduces the

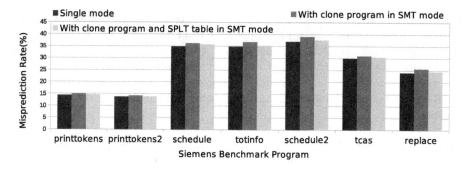

Fig. 5. Mis-prediction rate of Siemens benchmark programs

inter thread interferences, it increases the chances of intra-thread interference since the table size is reduced by this splitting mechanism.

5   Related Work

In this section, we present an overview of related research to address the problem of finding different hardware resources that are sensitive to an attack and different types of attacks that can be performed on them. In recent times, several researchers have proposed side-channel attacks for extracting information from electronic devices [12]. These attacks are typically performed by unauthorized parties in order to access secret information stored within the devices. These attacks have targeted the branch prediction buffer as well [1]. Previous research [3] showed that branch predictors are vulnerable to an attack and can cause serious impacts on processor performance in terms of energy consumption increase. In that work, they chose different predictor components as targets of random attacks and observed the effects on processor performance. Vulnerability of hybrid branch predictors also has been studied [4]. This work performs random attacks on the profile data that are used to select the appropriate predictor for every branch and studies the resulting performance variation. Mitigation of covert channel through branch predictor has also been studied in [7]. In this paper, we have proposed an attack methodology to affect the integrity of data that are needed for branch prediction and shown how it effects on overall system performance. Here, we have shown a systematic method to create a clone of a program that will affect the data needed by that program for branch prediction when both are running in simultaneous multi threading mode. To the best of our knowledge, this is the first study that addresses this theme on branch prediction.

6   Conclusion

In this paper, we observe how predictor table interference affects the performance of a branch predictor in SMT mode. We propose an attack method that jeopardises the prediction accuracy by polluting the predictor tables stored for a benign application using a malicious variant. Examining the results generated using our proposed attack method as well as the extent of performance compromise, we can conclude that our approach can effectively slow down the performance promise expected from a SMT processor. We are currently working on architectural simulations to quantify the effect of the damage on a wider set of benchmarks.

Acknowledgement. This work was partially funded by a research grant from Defence Research and Development Organization, Government of India awarded to Indian Statistical Institute. The authors would like to thank Prof. Sandeep Shukla and Prof. Mainak Chaudhuri of IIT Kanpur for their suggestions on this work.

References

1. Acıiçmez, O., et al.: New branch prediction vulnerabilities in OpenSSL and necessary software countermeasures. In: IMA, pp. 185–203 (2007)
2. Binkert, N., et al.: The gem5 simulator. ACM SIGARCH Comput. Architect. News **39**(2), 1–7 (2011)
3. Das, M., Sardar, B., Banerjee, A.: Attacks on branch predictors: an empirical exploration. In: Jajodia, S., Mazumdar, C. (eds.) ICISS 2015. LNCS, vol. 9478, pp. 511–520. Springer, Cham (2015). https://doi.org/10.1007/978-3-319-26961-0_30
4. Das, M., et al.: Attacks on hybrid branch predictors: an empirical exploration. In: CCSN, pp. 139–140 (2016)
5. Do, H., et al.: Supporting controlled experimentation with testing techniques: an infrastructure and its potential impact. Empir. Softw. Engg. **10**(4), 405–435 (2005)
6. Eggers, S.J., et al.: Simultaneous multithreading: a platform for next-generation processors. IEEE micro **17**(5), 12–19 (1997)
7. Evtyushkin, D., et al.: Understanding and mitigating covert channels through branch predictors. TACO **13**(1), 10 (2016)
8. Fog, A.: The microarchitecture of Intel, AMD and VIA CPUs. An Optimization Guide for Assembly Programmers and Compiler Makers. Copenhagen University College of Engineering (2011)
9. Henning, J.L.: SPEC CPU2006 benchmark descriptions. ACM SIGARCH Comput Architect. News **34**(4), 1–17 (2006)
10. McFarling, S.: Combining Branch Predictors. Technical Report, TN-36 (1993)
11. Ramsay, M., et al.: Exploring efficient SMT branch predictor design. In: ISCA, vol. 26 (2003)
12. Tasher, N., et al.: Protection against side-channel attacks on non-volatile memory. U.S. Patent 9,343,162, 17 May 2016
13. Tullsen, D.M., et al.: Simultaneous multithreading: maximizing on-chip parallelism. In: ACM SIGARCH Computer Architecture News, vol. 23, pp. 392–403. ACM (1995)

An Enhanced Blacklist Method to Detect Phishing Websites

Routhu Srinivasa Rao$^{(\boxtimes)}$ and Alwyn Roshan Pais

Information Security and Research Lab,
Department of Computer Science and Engineering,
National Institute of Technology, Surathkal, Karnataka, India
routh.srinivas@gmail.com, alwyn.pais@gmail.com

Abstract. Existing anti-phishing techniques like whitelist or blacklist detect the phishing sites based on the database of approved and unapproved URLs. Most of the current phishing attacks are actually replicas or variations of other attacks in the database. In this paper, we propose an enhanced blacklist method which uses key discriminate features extracted from the source code of the website for the detection of phishing websites. The main focus of our work is to detect the phishing sites which are replicas of existing websites with manipulated content. Each phishing website is identified with a unique fingerprint which is generated from the set of proposed features. We used Simhash algorithm to generate fingerprint for each website. The features used for calculating fingerprint are filenames of the request URLs (js, img, CSS, favicon), pathnames of request URLs (CSS, scripts, img, anchor links), and attribute values of tags (H1, H2, div, body, form). Our experimentation detected 84.36% of phishing sites as replicas of other phishing websites with manipulated content while maintaining zero false positive rate. The proposed method is similar to that of traditional blacklist with an advantage that it can detect replicated and manipulated phishing sites efficiently.

Keywords: Phishing · Anti-phishing · Document object model
Hyperlinks · Blacklists

1 Introduction

Phishing is one of the cyber-attack which attempts to gain access to sensitive information of online user. Attackers choose phishing because it is lucrative and is easy to perform due to the existence of phishing tool kits. Phishing is a growing threat and is hard to defend against it. It has become highly prevalent problem because distributing millions of fake emails is a trivial task and even a less success rate is significantly profitable to the attackers. According to the latest APWG 2016 fourth quarter report [2], 1,220,523 number of phishing attacks were recorded in 2016 and has been confirmed to be the highest than in any year since it began monitoring in 2004. It indicates there has been an increase

© Springer International Publishing AG 2017
R. K. Shyamasundar et al. (Eds.): ICISS 2017, LNCS 10717, pp. 323–333, 2017.
https://doi.org/10.1007/978-3-319-72598-7_20

of 5,753% of attacks in over 12 years. These figures reveal that phishing attacks increased year after year accounting to billions of dollars in loss.

Attackers use phishing kits to distribute the phishing websites [3,8]. These kits are zip files which contain the files and directory structure (folders) used for developing a phishing site. This observation gives us a hint that there might be manipulation in domain but not in the path of file or anchor links.

Attackers bypass the techniques either by manipulating the domain of the external anchor links or misspelling or skipping the brand name in title, keywords, metadata, copyright or body of the webpage. The techniques which depend on textual content [11,14,15] fail to detect phishing due to the mismatch of brand names with their whitelist. Attackers also bypass the techniques which rely on HTML tags or DOM structure of website either by skipping some tags or add extra tags or empty tags. This manipulation of DOM structure results in less detection rate in identifying phishing site.

The techniques which depend on whitelist may not give effective results when encountered with various forms of phishing sites which target the same whitelisted website. It is because, the anti-phishing techniques mostly maintain a single version of legitimate sites for the detection process and fails to detect which falls out of the list.

To overcome the above limitations in detecting phishing websites, we propose an enhanced blacklist technique which detects phishing sites based on the similarity of proposed features (attribute values of tags, paths of anchor links, scripts, img, CSS, filenames of urls). We also aim at detecting phishing websites with reasonable true positive rate while maintaining the zero false positive rate. We focus on fast identification of near duplicate phishing sites as our method involves simple string comparison. In this paper, we propose a method to identify the replicas or variations of blacklisted phishing sites automatically so that it can be used by industry to reduce or speed up the manual verification of received suspicious websites.

The paper is organized as follows. In Sect. 2, we provide some of the existing anti-phishing techniques in the area of our research. The Proposed work is explained in Sect. 3. Experimentation and results are given in Sect. 4. Limitations are discussed in Sect. 5. We conclude the paper in Sect. 6.

2   Related Work

There exists many techniques in the literature which rely on either whitelist or blacklist information. These techniques use whitelist or blacklist information of websites for the calculation of similarity score between suspicious and target website. The whitelist information is extracted from URL, images, layout, styles, digital certificates etc. Some of the techniques are listed below.

Kirda et al. [10] proposed a layout similarity approach where layout of suspicious site is compared with whitelist of all trusted layouts for the calculation of similarity score. If the score is greater than a threshold then it is classified as phishing else legitimate. BaitAlarm [7] compares the styles of suspicious and whitelisted styles for identifying the status of website. If the similarity score is above the threshold then the site is classified as phishing. Visual similarity based techniques [5,13] maintain list of whitelisted images and the suspicious website image is compared with the database. If the similarity is above the threshold then it is classified as phishing.

The Blacklist information is extracted from URL, text and DOM tags. Some of the techniques which use blacklist information are listed below.

Phishnet [9] detects variants of existing phishing sites based on the URL of phishing site. Authors generated new phishing URLs by interchanging top level domain (TLD), IP address, directory structure, query and brand name of known phishing URLs. The method fails when encountered with a unique URL having the same content of known phishing site. Britt et al. [3] proposed a clustering based phishing detection using DeepMD5 for calculating common file similarity between the suspicious and exisiting phishing kits. The technique provides clusters of phishing websites with the same brand. This method fails when the phishing site contains less number of files compared to the phishing kits. Wardman and Warner [12] proposed an automatic phishing classification system which downloads the files (CSS, img, js) from the visited website and their hash values are used for calculating the similarity between the suspicious and blacklist database.

Exisiting techniques either consider HTML plaintext, tags or layouts, images for the extraction of characteristics of website. Our work differs from the above as we rely on the noisy part of HTML rather than content of the website. We consider attribute values of HTML elements and filenames of request URLs. These features are used for generating blacklist of fingerprints using Simhash algorithm. Due to the property of Simhash algorithm, the fingerprints of near duplicate documents would differ with a small number of bits. Hence, it is fast and robust to manipulation. Our technique can also be employed in whitelist based methods.

3   Proposed Work

The basic idea of our work is to identify near duplicate phishing sites which are variations of blacklisted phishing sites. Note that finding an exact copy is easy but finding the websites that are almost identical is more difficult. In this paper, we divide our work into two phases. First phase includes extraction of features which are used in the second phase for the generation of blacklist database. The flow chart of the proposed system is shown in Fig. 1.

3.1   Extraction of Features

Many attackers aggregate all the required files (CSS, js, images) to design a phishing site into a zip file and then host onto a server. Thereby, the zip file is extracted to create a phishing site [3,12]. This zip file is distributed over the Internet such that fresh or unsophisticated attackers can easily design a website.

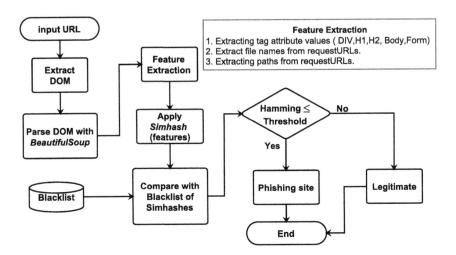

Fig. 1. Flowchart of the proposed system

This hints us that the path of the files in the phishing sites using same phishing tool kits follow the same structure. Sometimes there exists a small change in the path structure of request URLs (CSS, js, images) but not in filenames of the request URLs. Attackers obfuscate the tags by adding empty tags or skipping non important tags in the phishing site. They may also obfuscate the text which reveals the identity of the website (title, meta data, copyright) by skipping or misspelling the text. But, the attribute values of the tags remain same due to the requirement of unavoidable styles, background images and dynamic actions in the website. The attackers must follow the same attributes of legitimate site or start designing the website from scratch to make phishing site visually similar to legitimate site. Based on the above observations, we extracted the following key features which describes unique characteristic of the phishing website. These features include pathnames, attribute values, and filenames based features embedded in the source code of the website.

F1: Attribute Value based Features: On examining various websites, we observed that most of the websites use `div` tag which define a section or divison of the website. It is also used to group the blocks of document to design them with CSS. Hence, this makes the div tag mandatory existence in the website. So we extract the div tag attribute values to define the website. We also observed that most of the websites use brand names or text more related to website in `h1` and `h2` elements. The style of the `body`, `form` of a website is unique and therefore we also considered body tag attribute for feature extraction process. The main attributes involved in performing action to the elements of webpage are `class`, `id`, and `name`. Hence we considered these attributes for all the above HTML tags to generate attribute value based features.

F2: Pathname based Features: Most of the websites consists of request URLs which provides styles, background images and dynamic action to the websites. These request URLs include CSS, Scripts, anchor links, and images. The directory structure of these pathnames are extracted for identifying the uniqueness of the website.

F3: Filename based Features: This feature is similar to F2 but extracts only filenames from the request URLs such as CSS, images and scripts. These filenames also represent unique property of the website. All the features are explained with following simplified paypal phishing source code.

```
<html lang="en"><head>
<script src="js/khawarezmi.js"></script>
<title>Log in~to your paypaI account</title>
<link href="pinto/img/mou.png" link="" rel="shortcut icon" />
<script src="lib/signin.js"></script> </head>
 <header> <div class="paypal-logo"></div></header>
<body class="desktop">
<div role="main" class="main" id="main">
<h1 class="headerText accessAid">Log in~to continue</h1>
<form name="login" method="post" action="checkInfo.php" id="form" class="
    hasErrors">
<div class="fieldWrapper">
<input type="email" placeholder="Email" class="hasHelp validateEmpty"
    name="login_email" id="email" />
</div></div></form>
<footer role="contentinfo" class="footer">
<ul class="footerGroup">
<li><a href="#">Contact Us</a></li>
<li><a href="#">Privacy</a></li> </ul>
<p>Copyright &copy; 1999--2017 PayPaI. All rights reserved.</p>
</footer> </body></html>
```

In the sample source code, attackers intentionally misspelled PayPal to PayPaI at title and copyright. It should also be observed that meta data i.e. description, keywords, and application name etc. are skipped to avoid brand name insertion. This allows the websites to bypass the textual based techniques for phishing detection. Anchor links in phishing sites sometimes point to "#" redirecting to the same login page or point to not-found links or point to its own local files. Similarly images, styles and scripts may be requested from its local files or foreign links. From the above code, it is clear that Attribute value based features include "paypal-logo main headerText accessAid hasErrors fieldWrapper", path name features include "pinto/img/mou.png lib/signin.js js/khawarezmi.js". If there exists presence of non null achor links then their paths are also added to the path name based features. We also extract the filenames of all requested URLs, here js and png file names are appended to the feature string with space delimiter. The filename based features in the above code include "mou.png signin.js khawarezmi.js". All these features are appended to a string and the string is termed as string of features. Note that duplicates of the feature values are removed and also additional spaces are trimmed to form a final string of features. This string is given as input to the Simhash algorithm to generate a fingerprint.

Algorithm 1. Simhash algorithm for generating fingerprint of given website

---

    Input : String of features
    Output: A single fingerprint representing entire website
  1 Tokenize the string into single words by using space delimiter
  2 Initialize size of fingerprint (64 bit)
  3 Initialize an array $V[\ ]$ filled with zeros
  4 For each token in the token-set, calculate hash with any hashing algorithm (MD5, SHA-1, SHA-256)
  5 For each hash, for each bit i in the hash
  6 **if** $i = 1$ **then**
  7      $|V[i] = V[i] + 1$
  8 **else**
  9      $|V[i] = V[i] - 1$
10 **end**
11 For each bit i in the hash
12 **if** $V[i] > 0$ **then**
13      $|i = 1$
14 **else**
15      $|i = 0$
16 **end**
17 print output fingerprint of bits

3.2 Generation of Blacklist Database

We extracted all the features from the source code of the website and converted into string of features. This string is preprocessed before it undergoes hashing process. The preprocessing technique includes conversion of entire text to lowercase, and removal of multiple spaces. This preprocessed string is sent to the hash function to generate a unique fingerprint which distinguishes one website from another. We used Charikars Simhash [4] which generates a fingerprint from a sequence of hashes. The algorithm is proposed by Charikar [4] which generates fingerprints of near duplicate documents that differ with a small number of bits. The Simhash algorithm is presented in Algorithm 1. Manku et al. [6] demonstrated that Simhash algorithm is appropriate for detecting near duplicate websites in real time. Authors experimented the Simhash on a very large data of 2^{32} fingerprints to identify the threshold for similarity between two fingerprints. They observed hamming distance (k) of 3 as appropriate for the experiment. We employed the same algorithm for idenitfying near duplicate phishing websites with the same attributes of [6] (64 bit fingerpint and k = 3). Hence, for each phishing website a fingerprint is generated and stored in the blacklist database. Note that unique fingerprints are stored and any duplicates are ignored.

One of the advantage of using fingerprint is the low dimensional representation of documents. Using the pairwise similarity measure does not fit large scale clustering and hence Simhash fingerprint is used to address the scalability issue.

Detecting Similarity between Webpages: For each suspicious website, discriminative features are extracted followed by fingerprint generation for each website. This fingerprint is compared with blacklist of fingerprints using hamming distance. If the hamming distance is below a threshold it is classified as phishing else legitimate. The threshold is chosen as k = 3 based on the Manku et al. work [6].

4   Experimentation and Results

We used python platform to implement our proposed work for detection of phishing site. BeautifulSoup [1] and LXML are used for parsing and feature extraction from the DOM of the website.

Dataset: We collected legitimate sites from the PhishTank where it contains target websites which are more often targeted. In addition to these legitimate sites, we also collected legitimate sites from Alexa database to test false positive rate of our work. We collected phishing sites from PhishTank database. Prior to the experimentation, we did preprocessing of websites to eliminate the URLs which are unreachable, not-found and which redirect to legitimate sites. The dataset after preprocessing is given in Table 1.

We divided our phishing dataset into two sets. Set 1 (PS1) is used for generating fingerprints of blacklisted URLs. The second set (PS2) is used for testing the number of replicas or variations of phishing sites over the existing database (PS1). We also combined legitimate sites from two sources (part 1 and 2) into single legitimate set (LS).

Table 1. Source of websites

Source	Total instances	Link
Phishing sites (Set 1) for the generation of blacklist	5283	https://www.phishtank.com/developerinfo.php
Phishing sites (Set 2) Testing set	4897	https://www.phishtank.com/developerinfo.php
Legitimate sites (part 1) (from PhishTank)	433	https://www.phishtank.com/developerinfo.php
Legitimate sites (part 2) (from Alexa)	4808	http://www.alexa.com/topsites

Experiment 1: Blacklist URL fingeprint generation

We generated Simhash fingerprints for each website from the proposed features. The fingerprints of near-duplicate websites will have very less hamming distance (HD). Xiang et al. [14] used SHA1 for identifying the replicas of the existing phishing sites. The authors extracted plain text from the website and did preprocessing on the text by removing the space and default values in the HTML input fields. We have implemented the technique of Xiang et al. using PS1 and PS2 as the datasets. The comparison of statistics of near-duplicate phishing websites is given in Table 2.

Table 2. Statistics of near-duplicate websites

Source	Total instances	UniqueHash (Our method)	UniqueHash (Xiang et al.)
PS1	5283	1341 (Single entry-826)	1583 (Single entry- 1038)
LS	5241	5192 (Single entry-5153)	5178 (Single entry-5124)

Both the techniques group all the equal fingerprints into single cluster. In our work, we achieved 1341 unique clusters representing all the phishing websites. Out of these clusters, 826 are single entry clusters and 184 are double entry clusters. We ignored the cluster with single entries for the calculation of percentage of replicated websites in the PS1 dataset. From the experimentation, we detected 84.36% ((5283-826)/5283) of replicated websites in the PS1 dataset. This percentage does not mean a false negative rate of 15.64% because we are only concerned with the detection of replicas but not the case of detecting new phishing sites.

During the clustering process, we observed that Gmail is mostly targeted brand with 202 instances. The top ten targeted brands in the database based on our work and [14] is given in Table 3. From the results, it is also observed that our work has greater number of instances in most of the clusters than the Xiang et al. based clusters. For example, the top cluster Gmail in our work has 202 instances where as Xiang et al. work has only 152 instances. The Xiang et al. achieved poor results due to use of simple obfuscation techniques which varies the content of the website. One of such obfuscation technique is adding date and time to the website resulting in different hash while having same content in both websites. Higher the number of instances within the cluster and less number of total cluster illustrates the efficiency of the clustering method. Our work generated 1341 total clusters with 826 singletons whereas Xiang et al. work generated 1583 total clusters with 1038 singletons. Cluster with more than one entry is actually considered as flagged clusters. Hence total number of flagged clusters (515) generated by our work are significantly lesser than flagged clusters (545) of Xiang et al. work.

To test the false positive rate of our proposed work, we compared the fingerprints of legitimate sites (LS) with the fingerprints of blacklist (PS2) for the number of matchings. The least hamming distance (HD) between the pair

Table 3. Targets of top 10 clusters

Top brands (count) (Our work)	Top brands (count) (Xiang et al.)
Gmail (202)	Gmail (152)
Gmail (155)	Dropbox (118)
Dropbox (118)	Dropbox (99)
Free (108)	Gmail (92)
Dropbox (99)	Free (81)
DHL (85)	Gmail (73)
Alibaba (84)	Dropbox (72)
Generic email (75)	Generic email (72)
Free (74)	Free (70)
Yahoo (72)	Yahoo (69)

of strings is calculated and we got 3 false positives with HD = 0 and 6 false positives with HD $\leq$ 3 out of 5241 legitimate sites. Unfortunately, these false positives are found to be exact replica of original legitimate websites which illustrates how uncommon the phishers directly copy the entire legitimate site for designing their spoof websites. The attackers mostly avoid usage of exact replica of entire content of legitimate sites to bypass most of the anti-phishing filters.

Experiment 2: Detection of Replicated Phishing Websites
We have collected the phishing sites at different time periods for the calculation of percentage of replicas or variations of phishing sites. The dataset PS1 was collected during August 2016 to January 2017 and PS2 was collected during March 2017 to July 2017. We conducted the experiment of testing the PS2 with PS1 for the identification of replicas. With HD = 0, (2853/4897) 58.26% of replicas were found in PS2. Using Manku et al. threshold ($HD \leq 3$) we were able to get (3041/4897) 62.10% of phishing attacks as replicas of earlier phishing attacks.

Overall, our technique is able to detect 84.36% (from Experiment 1) and 62.10% (from Experiment 2) of replicated or variation of phishing sites from phishing sets PS1 and PS2 respectively while maintaining almost zero false positive rate. The reason for choosing the datasets at different times is to illustrate that the phishing sites repeat with same or manipulated content over the time.

5 Limitations

One of the limitation is that the proposed system fails to detect phishing websites which use no tag attributes in their source code of phishing website. But, almost in all the legitimate sites, tag attributes are a must to handle the dynamic actions and visual design of the websites. Hence, if attacker skips all or some of the attributes of tags, online users may identify the difference with respect to legitimate site and get a suspicion on it. The other limitation is, phishing sites which replace entire content of the website with a screenshot of legitimate site might bypass the proposed method. These kind of websites might not include hyperlinks or might contain very few tag attributes leading to the mismatch in the blacklist database.

6   Conclusion

In this paper, we proposed an enhanced blacklist method which detects different variations of existing phishing websites. It is independent of third party services (search engine, page rank and WHOIS etc.) and detects new phishing sites which are replicas or different variations of existing phishing sites. Our method can also be adapted to whitelist based techniques which detects different versions of phishing sites imitating the target website. Our method is fast and robust in detecting manipulated blacklisted phishing sites by maintaining almost zero false positive rate. Hence, our method is adaptable to real world phishing websites.

References

1. Richardson, L.: BeautifulSoup. https://www.crummy.com/software/BeautifulSoup/
2. APWG: Phishing attack trends reports, fourth quarter 2016. http://docs.apwg.org/reports/apwg_trends_report_q4_2016.pdf. Accessed 03 Mar 2017
3. Britt, J., Wardman, B., Sprague, A., Warner, G.: Clustering potential phishing websites using DeepMD5. In: LEET (2012)
4. Charikar, M.S.: Similarity estimation techniques from rounding algorithms. In: Proceedings of the Thiry-Fourth Annual ACM Symposium on Theory of Computing, pp. 380–388. ACM (2002)
5. Hara, M., Yamada, A., Miyake, Y.: Visual similarity-based phishing detection without victim site information. In: IEEE 2009 Symposium on Computational Intelligence in Cyber Security, CICS 2009, pp. 30–36. IEEE (2009)
6. Manku, G.S., Jain, A., Das Sarma, A.: Detecting near-duplicates for web crawling. In: Proceedings of the 16th International Conference on World Wide Web, pp. 141–150. ACM (2007)
7. Mao, J., Li, P., Li, K., Wei, T., Liang, Z.: BaitAlarm: detecting phishing sites using similarity in fundamental visual features. In: 2013 5th International Conference on Intelligent Networking and Collaborative Systems (INCoS), pp. 790–795. IEEE (2013)
8. Rami, M.M., Thabtah, F., McCluskey, L.: Tutorial and critical analysis of phishing websites methods. Comput. Sci. Rev. **17**, 1–24 (2015)
9. Prakash, P., Kumar, M., Kompella, R.R., Gupta, M.: Phishnet: Predictive blacklisting to detect phishing attacks. In: 2010 IEEE Proceedings of INFOCOM, pp. 1–5. IEEE (2010)
10. Rosiello, A.P.E., Kirda, E., Ferrandi, F., et al.: A layout-similarity-based approach for detecting phishing pages. In: 2007 Third International Conference on Security and Privacy in Communications Networks and the Workshops, SecureComm 2007, pp. 454–463. IEEE (2007)

11. Tan, C.L., Chiew, K.L., Wong, K., Sze, S.N.: Phishwho: Phishing webpage detection via identity keywords extraction and target domain name finder. Decis. Support Syst. **88**, 18–27 (2016)
12. Wardman, B., Warner, G.: Automating phishing website identification through Deep MD5 matching. In: 2008 eCrime Researchers Summit, pp. 1–7. IEEE (2008)
13. Wenyin, L., Huang, G., Xiaoyue, L., Min, Z., Deng, X.: Detection of phishing webpages based on visual similarity. In: Special interest tracks and posters of the 14th international conference on World Wide Web, pp. 1060–1061. ACM (2005)
14. Xiang, G., Hong, J., Rose, C.P., Cranor, L.: Cantina+: A feature-rich machine learning framework for detecting phishing web sites. ACM Trans. Inf. Syst. Secur. **14**(2), 21 (2011)
15. Xiang, G., Hong, J.I.: A hybrid phish detection approach by identity discovery and keywords retrieval. In: Proceedings of the 18th International Conference on World Wide Web, pp. 571–580. ACM (2009)

Semi Supervised NLP Based Classification of Malware Documents

Mayukh Rath[1]($\boxtimes$), Shivali Agarwal[2], and R. K. Shyamasundar[1]

[1] Indian Institute of Technology, Mumbai, India
`mayukh.routh@gmail.com`
[2] IBM Research, Bengaluru, India
`shivali.agarwal@gmail.com`

Abstract. Proper classification of the available data into viable Malware classes is very important to analyze the causes, vulnerabilities & intents behind these attacks and to build up systems that are secure from these kinds of attacks. In this paper, we describe an approach that enables us to classify free text documents with good precision and performance. We classify the documents to the malware class that has the highest matching of the characteristics of the document based the ontology model. We have experimented with our integrated approach on a large number of documents and found that it provides a very good classification more precise that than other analysis techniques for documents about malware.

1 Introduction

New Cyber-Threat attacks are being introduced every day at increasingly rapid pace. These attacks are very much complex and involve multiple stages. Referring to the recent trends of attacks, it is noteworthy to mention the Ransomware attack that took place in May 2017 that almost challenged all the security measurements and precautions taken in the windows based systems. It actually required a good amount of time for the security experts to find the loophole and bring back the affected systems to the normal state. So it is very important to gather and understand all the information regarding such attacks available in blogs or social sites etc., to build a system that is secure from such attacks. Analyzing such textual information and classifying them into specific malware classes helps us understand the properties of different such attacks without human intervention. Now the amount of data available is huge, so automated classification of these documents into different malware classes is very useful to further proceed towards necessary steps.

In traditional classification based methods, first, the documents are tokenized followed by *stop* words removal techniques and finally, appropriate filtering is applied to the data. After the process the remaining keywords in the whole document set are used to create tf-idf matrix[1] that is used to learn from a

---

[1] Here, tf represents **term-frequency** & idf stands for **inverse-domain-frequency**.

© Springer International Publishing AG 2017
R. K. Shyamasundar et al. (Eds.): ICISS 2017, LNCS 10717, pp. 334–344, 2017.
https://doi.org/10.1007/978-3-319-72598-7_21

chosen machine learning model. This technique considers only important key-words within the text. However, in our approach, we aim to realize infer patterns/phrases in the text to extract malware related concepts from the text. Understanding inferred malware related information from the text requires natural language Processing techniques that can analyze the text and find out what kind of Malware related information is inferred from the text.

In this paper, we have explored two NLP driven approaches to classify malware related documents:

- **NLP Concept Analyzer with Clustering Technique**:
  Here, documents are represented using a concept vector consisting of pre-decided malware classes as various dimensions. We then classify the documents using the proposed semi-supervised clustering algorithm that starts with initial seeding and progresses based on the document similarity between Malware documents and the centroid of the cluster.
- **NLP Text and Concept Analyzer with Ontology Model**:
  One of the main contributions of our approach has been the design of ontology of malware classes in a hierarchical manner considering characteristics like: Damages, Vulnerabilities, Categories, Removal Techniques etc. Once the ontology is in place, the analysis consists of extracting concepts, entities and keywords from documents using NLP and text analysis tool. We classify a document to the malware class that has the highest matching of the characteristics of the document based the ontology model.

From the application of our approach, we have observed that Ontology-driven NLP based technique can be used to classify documents containing malware related information with a good accuracy.

2   Related Work

In this section, we cover the work in cybersecurity domain from the perspective of text analysis and ontology. We also touch upon the state of the art in document classification techniques.

Most of the text analysis is focused on security vulnerability identification. The work in [4] analyzes the web text to extract information on vulnerabilities and corresponding security exploits. Prior to extracting such an information, it uses supervised classification to identify security related web text. Our approach will aid in such an identification step with little or no training data. In [8], vulnerabilities are detected by mining social networks. Clustering and regex like 'CVE*' is used to identify tweets that speak about vulnerabilities.

Ontology for Cybersecurity domain has received lot of attention. There have been comprehensive efforts to have structured knowledge base for the domain as can be seen in [1,5–7]. We studied these ontologies to arrive at a simplified and relevant ontology for purposes of classification.

There are various machine Learning based techniques that can be applied to the Document Classification problem. Most of them start with tokenizing the document and removing insignificant keywords from the documents. Remaining keywords are used as features for the document classification learning algorithm. Learning a model using these features is the process of assigning weights to the set of features. Once the learning model converges these set of weights can be used for the classification of the training set of documents.

Document Clustering is also another technique that can be used in place of document classification. Here documents with the similar properties clustered into the same bucket. So each of the documents in the same Cluster share similar kinds of properties with each other. So based on whether to classify the documents or cluster the documents, the techniques are broadly divided into two main categories. *Supervised Learning* and *Unsupervised Learning*. Approaches of some of the techniques are briefed in [3,9].

3   Our Aims and Approach

Given a large number of documents that contain malware-related information within it, our aim is to provide the appropriate label to each of the documents based on the malware-related information present in the text. Proper labeling of the documents provides us different sets of documents where each of the set contains documents that infer the same type of malware-related information. We consider only plain text documents, thus transforming the problem to document classification problem with different malware classes as class labels.

3.1   Approach

Our approach consists of integration of the following techniques:

1. NLU API - Automated Concept Extraction.
2. Similarity based classification that has the following techniques: Unsupervised NLU Based Classification, Semisupervised centroid based Clustering, Ontology based Clustering.

These technqiues are decsribed below.

3.2   NLU API - Automated Concept Extraction

Natural Language Understanding (NLU) Api [2] (formerly known as Alchemy API) is a text analyzing software that provides functionalities for inferring important concepts from the plaintext. Each of the functionalities uses NLP based techniques to analyze the plaintext and extract high-level semantic information from the text. In our experiments, we have used Entity Extraction, Keyword Extraction and Concept Extraction APIs only, to extract malware related concepts and features from the text. The output of NLU Api has been used for two purposes:- (1) Create concept vector to represent each document as a vector in multi-dimensional space using NLU Output. Each component of the vector represents different malware classes. The size and format of the concept vector is universal throughout the system implementation. (2) Create three hashmaps of concepts, keywords and entities consisting of the actual terms in the output with the corresponding relevance that is passed through the Ontology Handler for classification.

After representing each document as a multidimensional vector, we apply on these representation, the classification techniques described below. The overall functionality of the system is depicted in Fig. 1.

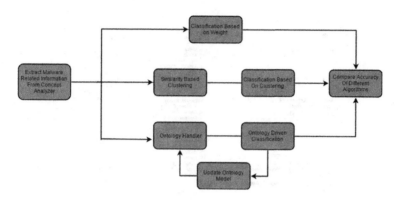

Fig. 1. Workflow_Diagram.

3.3 Similarity Based Classification

Unsupervised NLU Based Classification. This is the simplest technique used to classify the documents. We obtain vector representation of the document using NLU concepts. We now compare each component of the vector to find the class with the largest weight and the document is labeled as that class.

Semisupervised Centroid Based Clustering. In this technique, we train pre-defined clusters with appropriate documents. Then, a clustering algorithm based on cosine similarity measurement between the centroid of a cluster and document vector is applied to new documents. Cosine similarity can be described between two vectors as follows:

$$cos(\theta) = \frac{V \cdot W}{|V| \cdot |W|} = \frac{\sum_{i=1}^{n} v_i w_i}{\sqrt{\sum_{i=1}^{n} v_i^2}\sqrt{\sum_{i=1}^{n} w_i^2}}$$

Ontology Based Classification. NLP tool provides us valuable information extracted from the text as Concepts, Keywords and Entities. But sometimes single Document contains information about multiple malware classes rather than one. Sometimes NLP analyzer fails to assign the largest weight to the malware concept that is most relevant to the document between all the Malware related concepts extracted from the text. To classify the documents accurately into specific malware classes, we create our own ontology model. Ontology model consists of different malware classes, properties, removal techniques etc. in a hierarchical manner. We try to match different characteristics of each of the malware classes to the document with respect to the output of NLP Tool, to figure out the classification of the document.

Before we go further, we describe, our approach to ontology design.

Fig. 2. Spyware_Hierarchy.

3.4   Design of Ontology

Ontology based classification approach requires a suitable ontology in order to get good performance. In this section, we describe the ontology designed for the purpose of classification problem. In our Ontology model, we have tried to represent different malware classes in a hierarchical manner. After going through the recent developments on ontology in cybersecurity domain, we came up with a suitable version for purpose of classification and the same has been described here. The ontology was created manually using keywords and phrases as provided by NLU Api run on wikipedia, textbook chapters and some selected good quality blogs. Malware Characteristics, Attack Intents, vulnerabilities and removal techniques can be captured by our proposed Ontology model. Malware is the top most class in the hierarchy that is divided into different subclasses like Adware, Spyware, Botnet, etc. Now each of the classes is further divided into different subclasses. Example: Malware is further divided into: *Adware, Spyware, Botnet, Virus, Worm, Trojan, Rootkit, Backdoor, Keylogger, Rogue Security Software,*

Ransomware, Browser Hijack, Bitcoin. Now each of the classes are further classified into different subclasses based on Causes, Vulnerabilities, Properties, Types, Removal Techniques.

For example, for Spyware, we create different subclasses like (i) Spyware_causes, (ii) Spyware_Properties, (iii) Spyware_Attacks_Vulnerabilities, (iv) Spyware Types, and (v) Spyware Removal. Each of these classes contain properties that represent characteristics of each of the malware classes in a particular domain. We have shown the ontology created for Spyware class in Fig. 2. Similar ontologies are created for all the remaining malware classes like adware, ransomware etc.

4   Integrated Algorithm for Malware Classification

In this section, we describe the semi-supervised clustering based algorithm and ontology based classification algorithm as highlighted above. We also briefly touch upon a naive algorithm based on simple classification using extracted concepts from documents as well. The first phase in all the cases is NLP analysis of the documents and representing the documents as vectors. For this, the first step was to identify the malware classes that we wanted documents to be classified on. We selected 13 classes after extensive survey. These class labels are: (i) Adware (ii) Spyware (iii) Botnet (iv) Virus (v) Worm (vi) Trojan (vii) Rootkit (viii) Backdoor (ix) Keylogger (x) Rogue_Security_Software (xi) Ransomware (xii) Browser_Hijacking, (xiii) Bitcoins. Each of these classes are a dimension in the vector space. These classes are also referred to as concepts as they form the underlying theme of a document and hence, we say that each document is dedicated to one or more set of concepts. Clustering algorithm is bootstrapped with thirteen clusters such that the centroid of each is the vector denoting the respective concept dimension. Before describing the clustering based classification, we first illustrate how to represent documents as vectors. For instance, if we execute the NLU Api on say, document D and get following concepts: (a) Botnet – x1, (b) Ransomware – x2, (c) Trojan - x3 with other concepts being irrelevant; we represent the document as: Document D - [0,0,x1,0,0,x2, 0,0,0,0, x3, 0, 0]. Each document can be represented in this format. So each document is represented as vector in n-dimensional space.

4.1   Classification Algorithms

We now describe the three algorithms that were developed for classification documents crawled from the internet from security blogs and similar websites.

Unsupervised Concept Based Classification. Extract the main concepts with relevance ranking for a document that is outputted from the NLU API. The concept matching with one of the 13 labels with the highest score is assigned as the class label for the document. This is the most naive method of classification that we started with.

Semi-Supervised Centroid Based Clustering. The naive method is a direct function of the goodness of the NLP engine. Since we did not want to train the NLU APIs with a new dataset, we enhanced the classification algorithm by introduced a small training phase in before carrying out similarity based clustering to assign document to a labeled cluster. The idea behind centroid based clustering and classification is that a document can talk about more than one concepts with varying degree of relevance weights. It is important to capture relationship between these concepts when understanding a concept. This plays an important role in disambiguation implicitly when measuring similarity. The algorithm is described in Algorithm 1 and explained below. The training documents were picked such that some were pure definitions of a malware class while others were a mixture of concepts with one dominant concept. These documents were manually labeled for the dominant concept. We call it semi-supervised since the relations between concepts are partially learned in the training phase and get updated as new documents are seen.

---

    input : CSV file consisting of Training Documents, Test documents
    output: Cluster centroids based on training data, class labels for test
               documents
 1 Initialize:- Choose a Document that belongs to a particular malware concept &
    put it in the corresponding Cluster.
 2 Find the concept vector for all documents in a cluster.
 3 Update each Cluster centroid accordingly by taking an average over the
    document vectors in the cluster.
 4 **for** *every Document D in CSV file* **do**
 5   similarity=0;
 6   cluster= null; **for** *every Cluster Centroid $C_i \in C$* **do**
 7

$$new\_Similarity = \frac{C_i \cdot D}{|C_i| \cdot |D|}$$

 8   **if** *(new_similarity > similarity)* **then**
 9   similarity=new_similarity
10   cluster=c_i
11   **end**
12   **end**
13   **if** *(similarity>0)* **then**
14   Assign Document D to Cluster c_i
15   update the cluster centroid.
16   **end**
17 **end**
18 **for** *every Cluster $C_i \in C$* **do**
19   Print all the Documents in Cluster c_i
20 **end**

Algorithm 1. Semi-supervised centroid based clustering

We assign the document to the cluster with the highest similarity value. For new Documents, compute cosine similarity between each cluster centroid and the document vector. Also, we update the centroid value as the average of all the points inside the cluster. The centroid is updated to capture relations between malware classes. For example, botnet and Trojan horse are found co-occurring in many documents. If we don't update centroid, we miss out on new relations observed in the new documents. Hence, the algorithm learns in unsupervised way in the post-training phase. Formal description of the algorithm is given in Algorithm 1. Each Cluster centroid is represented as a vector, $C_i = <c_1, c_2, c_3, ...c_n >$ and a document D, after analyzing the document via NLU Api is represented as, $D = < d_1, d_2, d_3, ...d_n >$, where n is equal to malware class labels (13 here).

Ontology Based Classification. The design of the Ontology model is described in previous section. Algorithm 2 describes the ontology based classification formally. Ontology Handler takes the output vector generated from NLU Api output, make queries to the Ontology model and matches the properties of Malware classes to the AlchemyApi Output. NLU Api uses a predefined Ontology format in the background to extract **hot phrases** from the plaintext to understand the inferred concept from the text. Based on the NLU Api output, Ontology handler make Queries to the Ontology model to extract properties of specific Malware classes.

Java API has been used to make the query. Extracted set of terms are kept in an ArrayList and further matched to NLU Api output to make the classification. ontology model is upgraded periodically to capture more specific Malware class related properties. **Packages Involved:-** org.semanticweb.owlapi(read the owl file,create owl object,extract information from owl object), org.semanticweb.Hermit packages(Query the .owl file),javax.xml package(Handle NLU Api output)*, org.w3c.dom package.

5 Analysis of the Results: Precision and Performance

The approach described above has been tested on over 250 documents. The precision of classification obtained using different methods is shown in Table 1.

Overall Analysis. There are certain advantages of using Ontology based classification technique over Clustering based classification:-

(1) Ontology Based Classification provides better accuracy than semi-supervised clustering based technique. Both techniques use NLP in the background, but ontology model tries to match the significant patterns present in the text that represents properties of different malware classes. (2) Learning is required in both the models but Ontology model requires less amount of time to merge than similarity based technique. Learning with large number of documents is required in clustering based technique to achieve high accuracy. On the

---

input : Any random Document D (Passed as url)

output: Classification of the Document based on Malware Ontology Model

1 **NLU Api:-** Pass Document Url as argument to NLU Api.

2 Create Vector V of Malware concepts & store it in CSV File.

3 Extract output of NLU Api . Create three Hashmaps of Concepts,Keywords & Entities

4 **for** *every Concept c_i in Vector v* **do**

5   class=null ;

6   **if** *(c_i ¿ 0)* **then**

7   prev_weight = weight ;

8   weight = 0 ;

9   Query Ontology Model of Malware Concept c_i

10   Create list L of all the properties of c_i

11   **for** *every key $K \in Concept.map$ cmap* **do**

12   **for** *every $s \in L$* **do**

13   **if** *isSubString(K,s)* **then**

14   Weight = weight+cmap.getValue(K);

15   **end**

16   **end**

17   **end**

18   **for** *every key $K \in Entity.map$ emap* **do**

19   **for** *every $s \in L$* **do**

20   **if** *isSubString(K,s)* **then**

21   Weight = weight+emap.getValue(K);

22   **end**

23   **end**

24   **end**

25   **for** *every key $K \in Keyword.map$ kmap* **do**

26   **for** *every $s \in L$* **do**

27   **if** *isSubString(K,s)* **then**

28   Weight = weight+kmap.getValue(K);

29   **end**

30   **end**

31   **end**

32   **if** *weight ¿ prev_weight* **then**

33   Class = c_i ;

34   **end**

35   **end**

36 **end**

37 return class

Algorithm 2. Ontology based classification

other hand, Ontology model tends to merge very quickly. (3) Ontology Model provides more richer information about the text. As the Malware classes are structured in hierarchical manner, so each layer provides significant information about the document.

Table 1. Different Malware classification results

Class	Total	Unsupervised			Semisupervised			Ontology		
Label	Doc	Correct	Wrong	Accu	Correct	Wrong	Accu	Correct	Wrong	Accu.
Adware	20	14	6	0.7	18	2	0.9	20	0	1.0
Spy-ware	17	11	6	0.64	12	5	0.7	16	1	0.94
Botnet	50	47	3	0.94	48	2	0.96	50	0	1.0
Virus	20	19	1	0.95	19	1	0.95	18	2	0.9
Worm	17	12	5	0.7	15	2	0.88	17	0	1.0
Trojan	24	16	8	0.66	22	2	0.92	22	2	0.92
Rootkit	45	37	8	0.82	44	1	0.98	44	0	1.0
Back-door	11	7	4	0.63	10	1	0.9	11	0	1.0
Ransomware	20	15	5	0.75	16	4	0.8	20	0	1.0
Rogue S/w	34	24	10	0.7	29	5	0.85	31	3	0.91

6   Conclusions and Future Work

In this paper, we have devised an integrated approach to classify malware related documents based on NLP analysis & ontology matching. Besides classification, our approach also provides other important characteristics like malware removal, vulnerabilities, intents, impact etc. We opine that It will be very helpful for security experts, organizations to classify huge number of malware related documents into appropriate malware classes in a completely automated way. Future work includes optimizing the design of ontology model and devising an algorithm can provide relationship among certain malwares through common characteristics and thus, aid in disambiguation among malware classes.

References

1. Iannacone, M., Bohn, S., Nakamura, G., Gerth, J., Huffer, K., Bridges, R., Ferragut, E., Goodall, J.: Developing an ontology for cyber security knowledge graphs. In: Proceedings of the 10th Annual Cyber and Information Security Research Conference. CISR 2015, pp. 12:1–12:4 (2015)
2. IBM: Watson developer cloud. https://natural-language-understanding-demo. mybluemix.net/
3. Zaki, M.J., Meira Jr., W.: Data Mining and Analysis Fundamental Concepts and Algorithms. Cambridge University Press, Cambridge (2014)
4. Mulwad, V., Li, W., Joshi, A., Finin, T., Viswanathan, K.: Extracting information about security vulnerabilities from web text. In: Proceedings of the 2011 IEEE/WIC/ACM International Conferences on Web Intelligence and Intelligent Agent Technology. WI-IAT 2011, vol. 3, pp. 257–260 (2011)
5. Obrst, L., Chase, P., Markeloff, R.: Developing an Ontology of the Cyber Security Domain (2012)
6. Barnum, S.: Standardizing cyber threat intelligence information with the structured threat information expression. In: MITRE Security (2012). https://stixproject. github.io/

7. Syed, Z., Padia, A., Mathews, M.L., Finin, T., Joshi, A.: UCO: a unified cybersecurity ontology. In: Proceedings of the AAAI Workshop on Artificial Intelligence for Cyber Security. AAAI Press, February 2016
8. Trabelsi, S., Plate, H., Abida, A., Aoun, M.M.B., Zouaoui, A., Missaoui, C., Gharbi, S., Ayari, A.: Monitoring software vulnerabilities through social networks analysis. In: SECRYPT, pp. 236–242 (2015)
9. Trinkle, P.: An Introduction to Unsupervised Document Classification (2009)

Network Security

On De-synchronization of User Pseudonyms
in Mobile Networks

Mohsin Khan[1]([✉]), Kimmo Järvinen[1], Philip Ginzboorg[2,3], and Valtteri Niemi[1]

[1] University of Helsinki, Helsinki, Finland
{mohsin.khan,kimmo.u.jarvinen,valtteri.niemi}@helsinki.fi
[2] Huawei Technologies, Helsinki, Finland
philip.ginzboorg@huawei.com
[3] Aalto University, Espoo, Finland

Abstract. This paper is in the area of pseudonym-based enhancements of user identity privacy in mobile networks. Khan and Mitchell (2017) have found that in recently published pseudonym-based schemes an attacker can desynchronize the pseudonyms' state in the user equipment and in its home network. In this paper, we first show that by exploiting this vulnerability a botnet of mobile devices can kick out of service a large portion of the users of a mobile network. We characterize this novel DDoS attack analytically and confirm our analysis using a simulation. Second, we explain how to modify the pseudonym-based schemes in order to mitigate the DDoS attack. The proposed solution is simpler than that in Khan and Mitchell (2017). We also discuss aspects of pseudonym usage in mobile network from charging and regulatory point of view.

Keywords: 3GPP · IMSI catchers · Pseudonym · Identity · Privacy

1 Introduction

International mobile subscriber identity (IMSI) catchers are threats to the identity privacy of mobile users. Passive IMSI catchers are devices that observe the wireless traffic and store all the IMSIs observed. Active IMSI catchers are malicious devices that can trick a user equipment (UE) to reveal its IMSI. Protection against passive IMSI catchers has been in the cellular networks since the second generation (GSM). However, active IMSI catchers have persisted in all the existing cellular networks, namely, GSM, UMTS and LTE [1–6].

An active IMSI catcher impersonates a legitimate serving network (SN) and asks for the identity of all the UEs in its range. The UEs have no way to differentiate an IMSI catcher from a legitimate SN, and hence reveal their IMSIs to the IMSI catcher.

A potentially simple and backward compatible solution approach is to use frequently-changing temporary identities for mobile users [3, 7–10]. The idea is that, if a UE communicates with an active IMSI catcher, it reveals only its temporary identity. This prevents the IMSI catcher from associating the temporary

© Springer International Publishing AG 2017
R. K. Shyamasundar et al. (Eds.): ICISS 2017, LNCS 10717, pp. 347–366, 2017.
https://doi.org/10.1007/978-3-319-72598-7_22

identity with any user who is previously known. The temporary identities are called pseudonyms. Hence solutions using this approach are called pseudonym based solutions.

Borek et al. [7] and Khan and Mitchell [8] described pseudonym based solutions where the pseudonyms have the same format as IMSIs. From now on we will refer these two schemes as BVR and KM15 schemes. As shown by Khan and Mitchell in [11], these solutions are prone to the loss of synchronization between the pseudonyms in the UE and the home network (HN) of the user. In the worst case, the synchronization is completely lost and there is not even one common pseudonym left in the UE and the HN. Hence all identification and authentication attempts will fail thereafter and the UE will go out of the service. There is a vulnerability in these solutions that can be exploited by an attacker to cause the loss of pseudonym synchronization. The attacker can be a malicious UE or a malicious SN.

In addition to identifying the above vulnerability, Khan and Mitchel [11] also proposed a solution. In the rest of the paper, we will refer to this solution as the KM17 scheme. Careful investigation into this scheme shows that a UE has to use one pseudonym at least twice before it can get a new pseudonym from the network. The authors also argue that their solution may be vulnerable to a pseudonym de-synchronization attack by a malicious SN. To address the issue of malicious SNs, they introduce an identity recovery procedure. But, this procedure adds complexity: the number of temporary identities per user increases from two to six. Moreover, as we will later explain, the recovery mechanism itself can be exploited by an IMSI catcher to track the mobile user.

Our Contribution: We propose a pseudonym based solution that builds on top of the BVR, KM15 and KM17 schemes. The following contributions are made:

1. Identify a DDoS attack against an entire HN when the BVR scheme is used.
2. Design a simpler (than KM17) solution that corrects the identified weaknesses of the pseudonym based schemes (KM15, KM17 and others).
3. Outline some practical concerns of using pseudonyms from billing and regulatory point of view.

2   Preliminaries

Conceptually, a cellular network can be divided into UE, the HN where the mobile user has a subscription, and the SN that is the network to which mobile device connects. The SN and HN are the same when the UE is not roaming. An SN or HN consist of many entities. In this paper we will not discuss those details. However, we need to know some details about the UE. A UE consists of two entities: a mobile equipment (ME) and a subscriber identity module (SIM). The SIM is known as universal subscriber module (USIM) in UMTS. Both SIM and USIM are smart cards which are portable across different MEs. In LTE, the USIM is an application in the universal integrated circuit card (UICC). In this paper, we will refer all of them as SIM for the sake of simplicity.

A user is identified by IMSI. IMSI is a string of 15 decimal digits. An IMSI is a concatenation of mobile country code (MCC), mobile network code (MNC) and mobile subscription identification number (MSIN). MCC is a string of 3 decimal digits. MNC is either 2 or 3 decimal digits and MSIN is 9 or 10. Pseudonyms discussed in this paper are strings of 15 decimal digits that are indistinguishable from IMSIs. In this paper we limit our discussion to only one HN. Consequently, all the IMSIs or pseudonyms we discuss have the same MCC and MNC. When we talk about the IMSI space or the pseudonym space, we actually mean the MSIN space. We denote the size of this space by $\mathcal{M}$ and it is either 10^9 or 10^{10}. We will also use n to denote the total number of users subscribed with the HN.

In the cellular networks, the security is built on a pre-shared master key $\mathcal{K}$ between a user and its HN. The key $\mathcal{K}$ is only known by the HN, and the HN sends the challenge and expected response to the SN. In effect, HN delegates user authentication to the SN. The key $\mathcal{K}$ is only known by the HN. Hence, the HN delegates the SN by sending the challenge and expected response. Pseudonyms are assigned to a user during the authentication. This requires certain changes in the authentication protocol. In UMTS and LTE, the authentication protocols are called UMTS AKA and LTE AKA respectively. Before we discuss the pseudonym based solutions, we present UMTS AKA and LTE AKA briefly.

2.1 UMTS/LTE AKA

We discuss UMTS and LTE AKA only very briefly in order to provide the required background. Details of UMTS AKA can be found in Clause 6.3 of 3GPP TS 33.102 [12] and LTE AKA can be found in Clause 6 of 3GPP TS 33.401 [13].

The UE identifies itself by sending the IMSI to the SN within an attach request or a response to an IMSI inquiry. Upon receiving the IMSI, the SN sends an authentication vector (AV) request to the HN for the IMSI. The HN finds the pre-shared key $\mathcal{K}$, randomly generates a challenge ($RAND$) and computes the expected response ($XRES$), as well as two keys CK and IK as functions of $\mathcal{K}$ and $RAND$. The HN also computes a string called $AUTN$ for the purpose of some cryptographic protections of the authentication protocol. HN forwards $RAND, AUTN, XRES, CK, IK$ to the SN that forwards the $RAND, AUTN$ to the UE. The UE verifies the $AUTN$, computes $SRES, CK, IK$ using the $RAND$ and key $\mathcal{K}$ and forwards $SRES$ to the SN. If $SRES$ and $XRES$ are the same strings, then the authentication is successful. The keys CK and IK are used for confidentiality and integrity protection thereafter, see Fig. 1.

In LTE, upon receiving the AV request, the HN also computes another key K_{ASME}. Contrary to UMTS, the HN forwards $RAND, AUTN, XRES, K_{ASME}$ to the SN. The UE verifies the $AUTN$, computes $SRES, CK, IK, K_{ASME}$ using the $RAND$ and key $\mathcal{K}$ and forwards $SRES$ to the SN. If $SRES$ and $XRES$ are the same strings, then the authentication is successful. The key K_{ASME} is used to generate further keys for confidentiality and integrity protection, see Fig. 1.

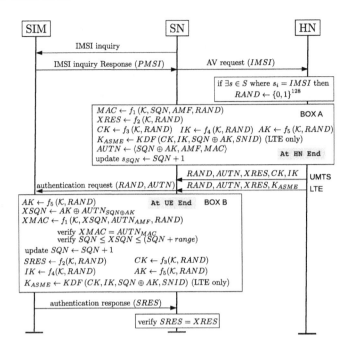

Fig. 1. UMTS/LTE AKA

2.2 Location Update

3GPP TS 23.012 (Sect. 3.6.1.1) [14] specifies that, when a UE registers with a visitor location register (VLR), an entity in the SN, the VLR provides its address to the home location register (HLR), an entity in the HN. When a UE uses an IMSI/pseudonym for the first time, it is considered as a registration in the SN and, consequently the HN is informed with the address of the SN for the IMSI/pseudonym. We will refer to this location update (LU) message sent for IMSI/pseudonym x as LU_x in this paper. We will use these LU messages in our solution.

3   Related Work

The BVR and KM15 schemes describe how pseudonyms can be introduced in the legacy networks. Also other proposals [3,9,10] were published in 2016 and 2017. All these proposals use essentially the same idea of using frequently changing pseudonyms recognized by the HN. The vulnerability identified in [11] is present in all these solutions. We will explain the DDoS attack and our solution in the context of the BVR scheme, nevertheless the principle of the attack applies to all existing pseudonym based solutions.

3.1   BVR Scheme

Along with the shared secret $\mathcal{K}$, every user shares another secret key κ with the HN. The SIM inside the UE stores two pseudonyms at any point of time, $(PMSI, P_{new})$. The SIM uses P_{new} the next time the UE receives an IMSI inquiry and keeps using P_{new} until it receives a new pseudonym. The HN also stores two pseudonyms (p, p') for every user at any point of time. In an ideal situation, $PMSI = p$ and $P_{new} = p'$.

The HN sends the next pseudonym encrypted by the key κ as a part of the random challenge $RAND$ used in AKA. Upon the successful completion of the AKA between the SN and the UE, the next pseudonym can be decrypted by the SIM. The BVR scheme builds on top of the UMTS/LTE AKA. Figure 2 shows the required changes. BOX A and BOX B in the figure refer to those operations in the same boxes in Fig. 1.

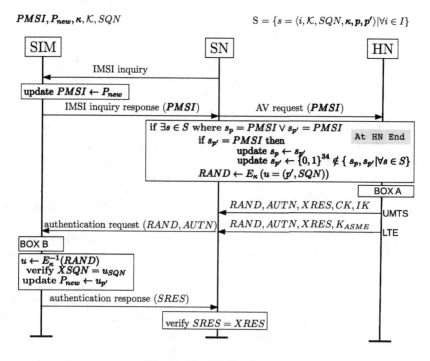

Fig. 2. The BVR scheme

Whenever an AV request arrives for p', the HN forgets p. Forgetting an old pseudonym is important so that it can be reused. However, forgetting a pseudonym before being confirmed that p' has been received by the UE is a vulnerability as pointed in [11]. If a malicious UE identifies itself using a random pseudonym and if, by chance, the random pseudonym is associated with a legitimate UE, then the HN forgets an old pseudonym of this legitimate UE.

In Sect. 4 we will show how this vulnerability can be exploited into a fatal DDoS attack.

3.2   KM17 Scheme

The KM17 scheme uses three pseudonyms at the HN end: $p_{past}, p_{current}$ and p_{future}. It also uses three recovery identities (RID) : RID_{past}, $RID_{current}$ and RID_{future}. The $LU_{p_{future}}$ message sent by an SN to an HN after registration of p_{future} is considered as the confirmation that p_{future}, RID_{future} have been delivered to the UE. Upon receiving $LU_{p_{future}}$, the HN forgets p_{past} and RID_{past} by setting $p_{past} \leftarrow p_{current}, p_{current} \leftarrow p_{future}, p_{future} \leftarrow null$ and after some other verifications sets $RID_{past} \leftarrow RID_{current}, p_{current} \leftarrow RID_{future}, RID_{future} \leftarrow null$. The HN always sends p_{future} as the next pseudonym embedded in the AV. If p_{future} is null, it generates a new one from the pool of unused pseudonyms.

Careful investigation of the KM17 scheme shows that a pseudonym has to be used at least twice before the UE can get a new pseudonym from the HN. The HN forgets p_{past} only when $LU_{p_{future}}$ arrives at HN. $LU_{p_{future}}$ would arrive only if p_{future} was used by the UE already at least once. Notice that $p_{current}$ after the arrival of $LU_{p_{future}}$ is the same as p_{future} before the arrival of $LU_{p_{future}}$. After the arrival of $LU_{p_{future}}$, p_{future} has become null. So, at this point, to get a new pseudonym, the UE has to use $p_{current}$. Consequently, our claim follows. The use of the same pseudonym twice happens because the scheme does not forget p_{past} when $LU_{p_{current}}$ arrives. We take care of this issue in our solution.

The authors argue that the scheme is vulnerable to a malicious SN who tries to attack by sending fake LU messages. As a reactive measure, the authors propose a recovery process that enables a UE and the HN to get back in a synchronized state of pseudonyms. The recovery process uses a temporary recovery identity (RID). The HN sends the RID_{future} as a part of the $RAND$ in a similar way a pseudonym is sent. When a UE gets convinced that the pseudonym synchronization has been lost, the UE sends the RID piggybacked in the reject message $AUTS$. Based on the RID, the process can recover to a synchronized pseudonym state. Detail of the process can be found in [11]. However, an IMSI catcher can convince a UE that the synchronization has been lost and learn the RID of the UE. After learning the RID, the IMSI catcher can track the user using this RID. This is a severe problem because preventing such tracing is the reason for the use of pseudonyms in the first place.

However, one might argue that the RIDs can be changed as frequently as the pseudonyms. Note that forgetting an old RID is also triggered by the same $LU_{p_{future}}$ that triggers forgetting an old pseudonym. Consequently, synchronization of RIDs becomes as vulnerable as synchronization of pseudonyms, when a malicious SN sends fake LU messages. In the analysis of our solution in Sect. 6, we will show that a malicious SN can be detected very quickly and stopped before it can mount a meaningful attack.

4   Attack on BVR Scheme

The attack is mounted by a malicious UE. The attack has two phases.

Phase 1. A malicious UE sends an attach request using a random pseudonym q_1 to a legitimate SN. The legitimate SN sends an AV request for q_1 to the HN. If by chance, $q_1 = p'$ for a user s, the HN forgets p and sets $p \leftarrow p'$. The HN also generates an unused pseudonym p'' and sets $p' \leftarrow p''$. As a result, in the HN, the current pseudonym state for the user s is $(p = P_{new}, p' \notin \{PMSI, P_{new}\})$.

Phase 2. The malicious UE sends another attach request using a random pseudonym q_2 to a legitimate SN. The legitimate SN sends an AV request for q_2 to the HN. If again by chance, $q_2 = p'$, then the HN again forgets p, sets $p \leftarrow p'$. HN also generates an unused pseudonym p''' and sets $p' \leftarrow p'''$. Consequently, the current pseudonym state of the user s is $\{PMSI, P_{new}\} \cap \{p, p'\} = \emptyset$; i.e. the user s and the HN become completely unsynchronized.

The next time the user would need to authenticate itself to a network, the authentication will fail and, hence, the user will be denied of any service. In this attack, it is assumed that the UE has not obtained a new pseudonym via a legitimate SN while the attack was mounted.

4.1   The DDoS Attack Against the BVR Scheme

The DDoS attack is mounted by a botnet of mobile devices. The mobile bots send many attach requests using different pseudonyms to legitimate SNs. The legitimate SNs in turn send AV requests for those pseudonyms to the HN. Let us assume that the total number of pseudonyms sent to the HN is a large integer m. In this case, a user s will be affected by the attack if there exists two integers $0 < x < y \leq m$ such that q_x is equal to p' and q_y is equal to the new p' that is set after $q_x = p'$ was sent.

We have considered two different ways to mount this attack. In one way, the pseudonyms used in the attach requests are chosen randomly with replacement, which means the attack might sent one pseudonym more than once to the HN. In the other way, the pseudonyms are chosen without replacement.

With Replacement: In this case, after sending m pseudonyms to the HN, the expected portion of affected users $E[u_a]$ is

$$E[u_a] = 1 - \left(1 - \frac{1}{M}\right)^m - m\left(\frac{1}{M}\right)\left(1 - \frac{1}{M}\right)^{(m-1)} \tag{1}$$

See the derivation in Appendix A. We have verified the accuracy of the above model via a simulation, see Fig. 3.

Without Replacement: In this case the attacker runs two rounds of the attack. In the first round the attacker sends all the pseudonyms in the IMSI space without replacement, meaning that each pseudonym is sent exactly once. Once the first round is completed, the attacker runs the attack for one more round. After sending m pseudonyms to the HN, the expected portion of affected users $E[u_a]$ is

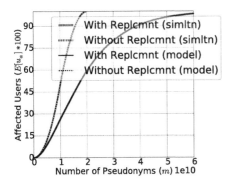
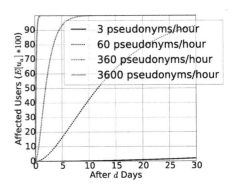

Fig. 3. DDoS Attack. $\mathcal{M} = 10^{10}, n = 10^7$. The model fits so well that it is difficult to distinguish the empirical lines from the model.

Fig. 4. DDoS Attack (with replacement), $\texttt{botnet}_{\texttt{size}} = 10^6$. Different lines represent the success rate as $\texttt{bot}_{\texttt{load}}$ varies.

$$E[u_a] = \begin{cases} \frac{m^2}{2 \cdot \mathcal{M}^2} & \text{if } 0 < m \leq \mathcal{M} \\ \frac{1}{\mathcal{M}}(2m - \mathcal{M} - \frac{m^2}{2\mathcal{M}}) & \text{if } \mathcal{M} < m \leq 2\mathcal{M} \end{cases} \qquad (2)$$

See the derivation in Appendix B. We have verified the accuracy of the above model via a simulation, see Fig. 3. Note that this is an estimation where the without-replacement attack is not a distributed attack. Rather the attack is mounted by only a single malicious UE. In the case of distributed and without replacement attack, the expected percentage of affected users will be less than what is shown in the plot unless the malicious UEs are very well synchronized. However, we believe that, a distributed without replacement attack will have a higher number of affected users than that of a distributed with replacement attack.

4.2 How Fatal Is the DDoS Attack in Practice

The intensity of the attack will depend on the size of the botnet and the number of pseudonyms send by one bot in a unit time. We name these parameters as $\texttt{botnet}_{\texttt{size}}$ and $\texttt{bot}_{\texttt{load}}$ respectively. According to [15], the EPS AKA has the latency of 550 ms. So, the peak value of $\texttt{bot}_{\texttt{load}}$ can safely be considered as 1 pseudonyms/second, i.e., 3600 pseudonyms/hour.

Mobile botnets are on the rise [16–18]. Many mobile botnets have already been observed, e.g., Geinimi [19], Zeus [20], AnserverBot [21], and DreamDroid [22]. A detailed survey of the state of mobile botnets can be found in [23]. In 2011, it was estimated that Dreamdroid was installed on 120,000 mobile devices [22]. In 2014, a mobile botnet of 650,000 mobile phones made an attack to a server [24]. It would not be surprising if we see a mobile botnet consisting tens of millions of mobile bots in the near future. However, for the discussion in this paper, we conservatively set the variable $\texttt{botnet}_{\texttt{size}} = 1$ million (10^6). Figure 4, shows how efficient a botnet of size 10^6 can be for varied values of $\texttt{bot}_{\texttt{load}}$.

This is a severe threat because all the affected users will be locked out of the network permanently. An affected user can rejoin the network only after he or she visits a shop delegated by the HN.

5 Our Solution

In the HN, for a user s, our solution stores the IMSI i and three pseudonyms p, p', p''. In the SIM of the user s, two pseudonyms $PSMI, P_{new}$ are stored. In an ideal situation $PMSI = p, P_{new} = p'$. We build our solution on top of the BVR and KM17 scheme. The pseudonyms p, p', p'' can be compared with $p_{past}, p_{current}, p_{future}$ of KM17 scheme. However, unlike KM17 scheme, our solution uses $LU_{p'}$ to forget p. Let us assume that for a user s an AV request has arrived using the pseudonym p and the HN has responded with an AV by embedding p' in the $RAND$. When an LU for pseudonym p arrives, the HN considers it as a guarantee that pseudonym p' has been delivered to the UE of user s. Figure 5 presents our solution. The bold texts present the changes over UMTS/LTE AKA. BOX A and BOX B in the figure refer to those operations in the same boxes in Fig. 1.

At HN side. Whenever an AV request is received for a user s, using any of its identity, i.e., i, p, p' or p'', the HN responds with an AV that contains the

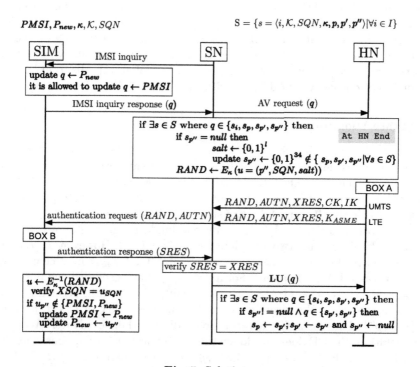

Fig. 5. Solution

pseudonym p'' in the $RAND$. If p'' is *null* then an unused pseudonym is chosen and set as p''. When p'' is not null and LU message $\mathrm{LU}_{p'}$ or $\mathrm{LU}_{p''}$ arrives, the HN forgets p by setting $p \leftarrow p', p' \leftarrow p''$ and $p'' \leftarrow null$.

At UE side. During the AKA, if MAC and $SEQN$ verification is successful, then the UE sends $SRES$ to the SN. Then the UE verifies if u_{SEQN} is the same as $XSEQN$ (see Fig. 5). If this verification is also successful and $u_{p''} \notin \{PMSI, P_{new}\}$, then the UE sets $PMSI \leftarrow P_{new}$ and $P_{new} \leftarrow u_{p''}$. After a successful AKA, the old pseudonym $PMSI$ will still be used (in place of permanent identity IMSI) by the current SN, for example, in paging messages and in subsequent communications between the HN and the SN. The identity P_{new} comes into play in the next SN.

However, it is upon the freedom of the UE to identify itself either with $PMSI$ or P_{new} in an attach request or in response to an IMSI inquiry. If the consequent AKA fails many times after identifying with $PMSI$, the UE would identify itself using P_{new}.

6   Analysis of Our Solution

LU messages may be delayed, lost, or sent multiple times. Also in practice, the LU messages $\mathrm{LU}_p, \mathrm{LU}_{p'}, \mathrm{LU}_{p''}$ might arrive in different order because of the inherent characteristics of IP networks. A malicious or faulty SN might send an LU message even when the corresponding AKA was failed or maybe not even run. To understand how our solution behaves in these unusual but possible situations, we analyze different categories of states a user s can be in the HN or the UE. We do this analysis based on the relevant variables and eventually construct a global state diagram of our solution. Based on the global state diagram, we show how our solution behaves in different situations.

6.1   State Diagrams

We divide all the possible states of a user s in the HN in two categories based on whether p" is null or not. Based on these two categories, we draw a state diagram as presented in Fig. 6 (right side). The notation used below is explained in the lower part of Fig. 6. Note that our solution is not sensitive to LU_i and LU_p. Consequently, only $\mathrm{LU}_{p'}$ and $\mathrm{LU}_{p''}$ are shown in the diagram.

On the other hand, the UE has only one kind of states as shown in Fig. 6 (left side). It always has two pseudonyms $PMSI, P_{new}$. However, $PMSI$ and P_{new} may have different values. The values of $PMSI, P_{new}$ may change only when a successful AKA happens. For a user s, we have excluded the possibility of $\mathrm{AKA}(x, y)$ where $x \notin \{PMSI, P_{new}\}$ because the UE will receive a wrong $RAND$ in that case. We also have excluded the possibility of $\mathrm{AKA}(x, y)$ where $y \notin \{p, p', p''\}$. The reason for this exclusion is discussed in detail later. According to our solution, the UE does not do anything when $\mathrm{AKA}(x, y)$ happens where $y \in \{PMSI, P_{new}\}$. However, even if $\mathrm{AKA}(x, y)$ happens where $y \notin \{PMSI, P_{new}\}$, the UE does not forget $PMSI$ because $PMSI$ would still be used by the SN, e.g., in paging messages. Consequently, only $\text{AKA}(P_{new}, y)$ where $y \notin \{PMSI, P_{new}\}$ is shown in the diagram.

Next we merge the state diagrams of HN and UE into a global state diagram of our solution (Fig. 7). The state of the user's pseudonyms in the system can be described by whether $PMSI$ and P_{new} on the UE side are one of p, p', p'' or not, and by whether in the HN p'' has been allocated for user s or not. Based on this description, there can be $4 \cdot 4 \cdot 2 = 32$ pseudonym-states for a user. However, many of the states are never reachable. For example, it can never happen that $PMSI$ and P_{new} in the UE are the same because a UE forgets $PMSI$ only if the new pseudonym p'' is not in the set $\{PMSI, P_{new}\}$. All the inputs that can cause a transition from one state to another in the state diagrams of HN and UE can also cause a transition from one state to another in the global state diagram (Fig. 7).

In our solution, it is assumed that the initial state of a user in the system is $PMSI = p, P_{new} = p'$ on the UE side, and p'' has been allocated in the HN. Taking into account the possible transitions, we have found out that only 10 out of 32 possible states are reachable from this initial state. Those 10 states are illustrated in Fig. 7. Note that neither the UE nor the HN has the knowledge in which state a user s is in the global diagram. All a UE knows are two pseudonyms $PMSI, P_{new}$ and the HN knows three pseudonyms p, p', p''.

For the limitation of space, we are not going to discuss all the states. Nevertheless, to assist the readers in understanding the diagram, let us take a closer look in a few transitions. Let us consider that the user is currently at State 1. Since, p'' is already allocated, AVR has no impact on this state. Consequently, we do not mention AVR in this state. Since p'' is allocated, it is possible that $\text{AKA}(P_{new}, p'')$ may run. If either one of these two AKAs happen, the UE forgets PMSI. Such an AKA run has no impact in HN until it receives the corresponding LU. Hence, the user moves to State 2 in the solution diagram where $PMSI = p', P_{new} = p'', p'' \neq null$. However, while at State 1, if either one of the LU messages $\text{LU}_{p'}, \text{LU}_{p'}$ arrives in the HN, the HN forgets p. Hence, the user goes to State 4 in the diagram where $PMSI \notin \{p, p', p''\}, P_{new} = p, p'' = null$. The AV request AVR can cause a transition only when $p'' = null$, e.g., State 4.

Observe that the pseudonyms in UE and HN are (i) synchronized in states 1–3; (ii) partially unsynchronized in states 4, 5, 7, 8 and 9; (iii) completely unsynchronized in states 6 and 10, without any possibility of automatic recovery.

6.2   Properties of Our Solution

Behavior of our solution in unusual but possible cases. If an AV request is responded by the HN but the corresponding AKA is failed or not even run, then the UE keep using the pseudonyms $PMSI$ or P_{new} in the upcoming AKA runs until an AKA succeeds. This can happen in global states 1, 5 or 9 (Fig. 7), and in this situation the global state will remain the same.

If an AKA becomes successful but the corresponding LU message is not sent to the HN then the UE will not be able to get any new pseudonym in the successive AKA runs. This can happen in global states 2 or 7 (Fig. 7).

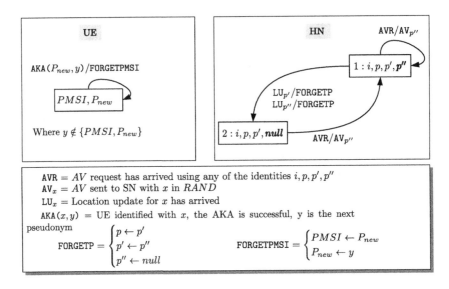

Fig. 6. State diagrams of UE and HN

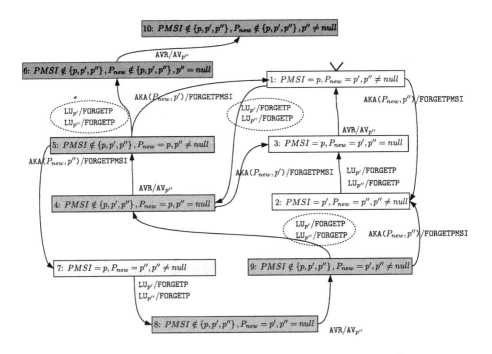

Fig. 7. Global state diagram of our solution for a user $s \in S$.

If the $PMSI$ goes out of synchronization (because of e.g., some internal errors), then the consequent AKA, where the UE is identified by $PMSI$ will fail. However, in this case $\mathtt{AKA}(P_{new}, y)$ may still run where $y \notin \{PMSI, P_{new}\}$. Consequently, the UE forgets $PMSI$ and gets back to synchronization.

If the P_{new} goes out of synchronization (because of e.g., some internal errors), then the consequent AKA, where the UE is identified by P_{new} will fail. However, in this case $\mathtt{AKA}(PMSI, y)$ still may run. Since the UE does not forget $PMSI$ after such an AKA, the UE does not update P_{new} even if $y \notin \{PMSI, P_{new}\}$. Consequently, the UE will not be able to receive any new pseudonym at all. However, a pseudonym ($PMSI$ or P_{new}) going out of synchronization because of some internal errors is an extremely rare event and can be compared with the case of a corrupted SIM. A user can always go to the service center of the HN and get a new SIM. Another remedy of this problem can be to maintain a list of three pseudonyms at the UE end instead of two, i.e., when $\mathtt{AKA}(PMSI, y), y \notin \{PMSI, P_{new}\}$ happens, the UE would store y as the third pseudonym even though it would not forget $PMSI$. We have not analyzed exhaustively what happens when such a third pseudonym is introduced in the solution and that can be considered as a future work.

LU messages can arrive out of order. Receiving $\mathtt{LU}_{p''}$ before receiving $\mathtt{LU}_{p'}$ means the UE could not get a new pseudonym when it identified itself using p'' and ran the consequent AKA.

Receiving the LU messages multiple times for the same pseudonym may lead to the unsynchronized states 6 or 10 (Fig. 7). However, as will be discussed later in this section, the probability of this is small.

Protection Against IMSI Catchers. The pseudonyms are delivered to the UE encrypted by the pre-shared symmetric key κ. Therefore, nobody except the UE can know the next pseudonym the UE will use. Hence an attacker, either active or passive, can not link a pseudonym with a previously known identity. In an ideal situation a UE uses one pseudonym in one successful AKA (notice the transitions State 1 $\rightarrow$ State 2 $\rightarrow$ State 3 $\rightarrow$ State 1 in Fig. 7), which is unlike the KM17 scheme. In KM17 scheme, the UE has to use one pseudonym in two successful AKAs before it can obtain a new pseudonym (see our argument in Sect. 3.2). One pseudonym for one successful AKA essentially prevents an attacker from tracking a UE any longer than the attacker can track a UE using the TMSI or GUTI. However, the MCC and MNC part of the pseudonyms remains the same across all the pseudonyms used by a UE. Consequently, if there are k many users with the same MCC and MNC in the geographical area of the UE, then our solution (similar to BVR and KM17) provides k anonymity of the user. Note that in a roaming situation k may be quite small.

Backward Compatibility. The solution does not require any changes in the legacy SNs since no existing message format has been changed. The only changes are required in the HN and the SIM. Hence, once an HN implements the solution, any user having the upgraded SIM can enjoy the claimed identity privacy. The solution is still operable if the SIM is not updated even after the HN has implemented the solution. This is because, in our solution, the HN keeps accepting the AV requests using the real IMSIs. The effect is that the UE will not be able to extract the new pseudonyms from the $RAND$. Otherwise everything else remains same and operable.

Our solution builds on top of UMTS/LTE AKA without introducing any new messages or changes in any existing messages. Hence, solution provides the claimed privacy in the presence of SNs from UMTS and LTE networks too.

A legacy SN may fetch multiple AVs from the HN for a single pseudonym x. Since $\texttt{AKA}(x,y)$ where $x = PMSI$ does not trigger any pseudonym update, let us consider the cases where $x = P_{new}$, i.e., $\texttt{AKA}(P_{new}, y)$. In such cases, if $y \notin \{PMSI, P_{new}\}$ then the UE forgets $PMSI$ and P_{new} becomes the new $PMSI$. Consequently, if the SN uses the pre-fetched AVs thereafter, it would be the $\texttt{AKA}(PMSI, y)$ cases – this has no impact on the pseudonym states of a user. Hence, our solution works smoothly even when an SN uses pre-fetched AVs for a pseudonym x unless some other user in the same SN is assigned with pseudonym x. Let us assume a user s_1 receives a new pseudonym x from the HN and sets $P_{new} \leftarrow x$. Then user s_1 uses $P_{new} = x$ in an SN where the SN already has a pre-fetched AV for the pseudonym x associated with user s_2 (forgotten by both HN and UE of s_2). In this case, user s_1's AKA will fail. However, this is also very unlikely to happen. If it happens, the user s_1 can still run $\texttt{AKA}(PMSI, y)$. However, such AKAs will not enable the UE to receive a new pseudonym. One remedy of this problem can be that the UE may trigger an SQN resynchronization process if an AKA fails after identifying using P_{new}. By triggering such an SQN resynchronization process, the UE may force the SN to get a fresh AV from the HN.

Protection Against the DDos Attack: The DDoS attack is mounted by a botnet of mobile devices. The objective of the attack is to bring as many mobile users as possible to State 6 of Fig. 7. However, any path in the state diagram (Fig. 7) that leads to State 6 involves at least one LU message. An SN will send an LU message for a pseudonym only if the corresponding AKA was successful. A mobile bot can not participate in a successful AKA with an SN using an arbitrary pseudonym. Hence, the attack does not work without an SN helping the botnet to do so.

Protection Against a Malicious or Faulty SN: In principle, a malicious SN can still attack the HN by sending a fake LU message for pseudonyms p', p'' that are associated with legitimate users. The target of the attacker would be to send a user to state 6 of the state diagram in Fig. 7. We will show that the probability of success for such an attack is very low before the attack is detected and stopped. Besides an SN is in a roaming contract (a business contract) with an HN. The minimal harm the SN can cause to the HN before the attack is detected and stopped is not worth of risking the renewal of the contract.

Notice that all paths that lead to State 6 in Fig. 7 go via State 4. Let us assume that all the users of the HN are currently in State 1 or 9. This is a safe assumption because otherwise the attack would be even less likely to succeed. The malicious SN has to send fake $\texttt{LU}_{p'}$ or $\texttt{LU}_{p''}$ to reach State 4. This implies that the malicious SN needs to know either p' or p'' of a legitimate user s.

The attack can be analyzed for two different situations. In the first situation, the target users are currently not visiting the malicious SN whereas in the second situation, the target users are visiting.

Target Users are not Visiting the Malicious SN: The malicious SN can try to mount a DoS attack against an HN targeting the users who are not even visiting the SN. In that case, the malicious SN guesses $q = p''$ and send a LU for q to the SN. This brings the user to State 4. Then, the malicious SN sends an AV request to the HN using q. This brings the user to State 5. Then, the SN sends another LU for q. This time the user goes to State 6. So, the attack is basically a sequence of an LU message, an AV request, and another LU message using the same guessed pseudonym q. Let us consider that the SN starts from 0 and choose incrementally all the possible pseudonyms across the whole space and send the three messages to the HN using the chosen pseudonym q. In that way after sending m triplets of messages to the HN, the expected number of affected users would be $\frac{nm}{\mathcal{M}}$.

Target Users are Visiting the Malicious SN: If the target users are currently visiting the malicious SN, it is easy to know the users' p' because the UE gives it to the SN. The malicious SN makes IMSI inquiries to all the UEs and hope that most of the UEs will respond with $P_{new} = p'$. Then, the malicious SN sends LU messages for all the pseudonyms received as the response of the IMSI inquiries. This brings many of the users to State 4. Once at State 4, the malicious SN can send an AV request to the HN using p' which will take the user from State 4 to State 5. However, once at State 5, neither the UE nor the malicious SN knows p', p''. So, to reach to State 6, the malicious SN has to guess one of p', p'' exhaustively. Suppose it starts from 0 and incrementally choose all the possible pseudonyms across the pseudonym space and sends LU messages for the chosen pseudonyms to the HN. By doing so, after sending m LU messages to the HN, the expected number of users that will reach State 6 is at most $\frac{2rm}{\mathcal{M}}$, where r is the number of users currently visiting the malicious SN.

To summarize, a malicious SN can attack the users of an HN by sending LU messages to the HN with randomly chosen pseudonyms. But the HN can detect and counter the above attack: In order to desynchronize at least one user of the HN on the average, the malicious SN has to send more than $m \geq \mathcal{M}/n$ LU messages with randomly chosen pseudonyms. (Remember that n is the total number of users having the same MCC, MNC in the HN, and $\mathcal{M}$ is the size of MSIN space, which we assume is 10^{10}.) For example, if $n = 10^8$, then the number of those messages should be at least $10^{10}/10^8$, i.e. 100; and if $n = 10^6$, then the number of those messages should be at least 10^4.

The malicious SN has a large, $1 - n/\mathcal{M}$ chance to guess the pseudonym wrongly in any given LU message. This results in an LU for a pseudonym not belonging to any users of the HN. Even a few such messages should make the HN realize that there is a de-synchronization attack. The HN could then apply countermeasures. For example, in the short term, the HN could temporarily suspend processing any LU messages coming from the SN. This will make the UEs who are visiting the malicious SN more easy to track for the duration of suspension (because they will have to use the same pseudonym), but on the other hand, it will prevent de-synchronization of their pseudonyms. In the long term, the HN may choose not to renew the roaming agreement with the operator of the SN.

Protection Against Replay Attack by an SN: A malicious SN may store an AV that it received from the HN with an intention to use it later in an AKA with a UE. If the SN could do so, then a UE can be tricked to accept an old pseudonym which is already forgotten at the HN. However, an SN can not do that. The pseudonyms that are sent to the UEs are encrypted. No one including the SN knows the pseudonym before it is used by a UE. Consequently, the malicious SN would know a valid AV for a UE identified by the pseudonym p only if the AV was obtained from the HN by making an AV request using the same pseudonym p. The next pseudonym embedded in such an AV can not be forgotten by either the UE or the HN. Hence a malicious SN can not make a replay attack to a targeted UE. However, the malicious SN can use a stored AV to run AKA with all the UEs who are visiting the SN. In that case one user may get affected if the SQN in the AV is still fresh. This may imply that the valid range of SQN has to be small when the UE is roaming.

Charging and LI: The HN has to keep track of the pseudonyms used by a particular user over time. This is needed, first, in order to bill the (right) user. Since the bills are typically settled once per month, the pseudonym usage records have to be retained for at least one month. Second, this is required for lawful surveillance of telecom traffic. The retention period of the records may be different in different countries but, in general, it will be longer than one month. For example, the European Union's Data Retention Directive [25] requires to store call related data for a period of time between six and 24 months. The need of law enforcement agencies to know in real time the true identity of the mobile user can be met by the HN sending that identity to the SN during the connection establishment. However, handling of this identity would be a new feature in a legacy SN. When deploying pseudonym-based enhancements to user identity privacy, some parts in the SN may have to be upgraded to meet law enforcement needs.

Performance Overhead: A random choice of the next pseudonym, and the encryption of the pseudonyms are the additional overheads in generating an AV. This overhead is small. The retention of the history of pseudonyms is also an additional overhead but does not impact the generation of AVs. In the SIM it adds one extra key and one decryption using the key. The SNs would see more users registering in the network because when a UE forgets a pseudonym, it does not inform that to the SN. However, even legacy SNs are familiar with cases where a UE suddenly powers off, and a UE forgetting an old pseudonym would be treated as the UE has powered off.

Parameter Choice: The encryption used in encrypting the pseudonyms will not have forward secrecy since the same key κ is used all the time for encrypting pseudonyms. We have used 34 bits (as the BVR scheme) for the next pseudonym in the $RAND$ instead of 4 bits per digit. This makes sense because the UE can convert it back into the required format. Besides, using less amount of bits for pseudonym encoding leaves room for the length of the *salt*, denoted by l, to be longer. If the cipher used for encrypting $u = (p'', SQN, salt)$ has the block length 128, then embedding the same p'' in the successive $RAND$s can be randomized by the 48-bit long SQN and a 46-bit long *salt*. As the same p'' might be sent in multiple $RAND$s, the cipher used for encrypting u to generate $RAND$ should be immune against related plaintext attack [7]. AES is used in UMTS and LTE network for the implementation of authentication function, and it is immune against related plaintext attack. Hence, it would be enough to use AES for encrypting pseudonym also [7].

7   Conclusion

The need to maintain a synchronized state between the UE and the home networks is one of the key issues in the design and implementation of pseudonym-based enhancements of user identity privacy in mobile networks. In this paper we have proposed a relatively simple design for a layer of pseudonyms between UE and home network that can withstand de-synchronization attacks. This gives hope that pseudonym-based solutions can be applied in commercial cellular networks. Topics for future work include formal verification of our scheme, and its implementation and testing using real UEs and mobile network elements.

Acknowledgement. We thank Markku Antikainen for the useful discussion to characterize the DDoS attack and his help to optimize the code of the simulation of the DDoS attack.

Appendix A

Let us consider $\mathcal{M}$ bins, each labeled with a pseudonym or IMSI. Choosing m random pseudonyms with replacement and sending them in an attach request can be compared with the classic experiment of throwing m balls to $\mathcal{M}$ bins. The number of affected users by sending m attach requests is the same as the number of bins that get two or more balls after throwing m balls to $\mathcal{M}$ bins. The probability that a particular bin gets no balls is $\left(1 - \frac{1}{\mathcal{M}}\right)^m$. The probability that this bin gets exactly one ball is $\binom{m}{1}\frac{1}{\mathcal{M}}\left(1 - \frac{1}{\mathcal{M}}\right)^{m-1}$. Consequently, the probability that the bin will get two or more balls is:

$$Pr[\text{2 or more balls in a fixed bin}] = 1 - \left(1 - \frac{1}{\mathcal{M}}\right)^m - \binom{m}{1}\frac{1}{\mathcal{M}}\left(1 - \frac{1}{\mathcal{M}}\right)^{m-1}$$

If n is the number of users in the HN, then by linearity of expectation, the expected number of affected user would be:

$$E[\text{\#bins with more than 1 balls}] = n\left(1 - \left(1 - \frac{1}{\mathcal{M}}\right)^m - m\frac{1}{\mathcal{M}}\left(1 - \frac{1}{\mathcal{M}}\right)^{m-1}\right)$$

Consequently, the expected portion of affected user would be:

$$E[u_a] = 1 - \left(1 - \frac{1}{M}\right)^m - m\left(\frac{1}{M}\right)\left(1 - \frac{1}{M}\right)^{m-1}$$

Appendix B

In the without replacement attack, the attacker sends all the pseudonyms incrementally starting from 0 across the whole MSIN space. Let us consider that the pseudonym x is the first attack on a user's p'. Once the user's p' is attacked, HN updates $p \leftarrow p'$ and choose a new unused p' randomly. If the attacker sends total m number of pseudonyms to the HN, then the probability that the user's new p' will once again be attacked is: $\frac{m-x}{M}$. If n is the total number of subscribers in the HN and $m \leq M$ (first round) then expected number of subscribers affected after sending m pseudonyms is:

$$\frac{n}{M}\int_0^m \frac{m-x}{M}dx = \frac{n}{M^2}\int_0^m (m-x)\,dx$$

$$= \frac{nm}{M^2}\int_0^m dx - \frac{n}{M^2}\int_0^m x\,dx$$

$$= \frac{nm^2}{M^2} - \frac{nm^2}{2M^2}$$

$$= \frac{nm^2}{2M^2}$$

Consequently, the expected portion of affected users would be $\frac{m^2}{2M^2}$ where $m \leq M$.

Let us now consider the case where $M < m \leq 2M$ (second round). The attacker again sends all the pseudonyms incrementally starting from 0. Choosing a pseudonym x will affect a user (who has not yet been affected) only if x is the pseudonym of a user who was attacked only once in the first round. The probability of that event is: $1 - \frac{x}{M}$. So, after sending $m = M + m'$ number of pseudonyms, the expected number of affected user would be:

$$\frac{nM^2}{2M^2} + \frac{n}{M}\int_0^{m'}\left(1 - \frac{x}{M}\right)dx$$

$$= \frac{n}{2} + \frac{n}{M^2}\int_0^{m'} M\,dx - \frac{n}{M^2}\int_0^{m'} x\,dx$$

$$= \frac{n}{2} + \frac{n(m-M)}{M} - \frac{n}{M^2}\frac{(m-M)^2}{2}\ (\text{since } m = M + m')$$

$$= \frac{n}{M}\left(2m - M - \frac{m^2}{2M}\right)$$

Consequently, the expected portion of affected users would be $\frac{1}{\mathcal{M}}\left(2m - \mathcal{M} - \frac{m^2}{2\mathcal{M}}\right)$ where $\mathcal{M} < m \leq 2\mathcal{M}$.

Even though x in the above derivation is a discrete variable, we have used integration. So, the result we have found here is an approximation since $\mathcal{M}$ is large. We expect it to be a good approximation.

References

1. Samfat, D., Molva, R., Asokan, N.: Untraceability in mobile networks. In: Proceedings of the 1st Annual International Conference on Mobile Computing and Networking, MobiCom 1995, pp. 26–36. ACM, New York (1995)
2. Strobel, D.: IMSI Catcher, July 2007. https://www.emsec.rub.de/media/crypto/attachments/files/2011/04/imsi_catcher.pdf
3. Ginzboorg, P., Niemi, V.: Privacy of the long-term identities in cellular networks. In: Proceedings of the 9th EAI International Conference on Mobile Multimedia Communications, MobiMedia 2016, ICST (2016)
4. Soltani, A., Timberg, C.: Tech firm tries to pull back curtain on surveillance efforts in Washington, September 2014. https://www.washingtonpost.com/world/national-security/researchers-try-to-pull-back-curtain-on-surveillance-efforts-in-washington/2014/09/17/f8c1f590-3e81-11e4-b03f-de718edeb92f_story.html?utm_term=.96e31aa4440b
5. Ney, P., Smith, J., Gabriel, C., Tadayoshi, K.: SeaGlass: enabling city-wide IMSI-catcher detection. In: Proceedings on Privacy Enhancing Technologies, PoPETs (2017)
6. Intelligence, P.E.: 3G UMTS IMSI Catcher. http://www.pki-electronic.com/products/interception-and-monitoring-systems/3g-umts-imsi-catcher/
7. Van den Broek, F., Verdult, R., de Ruiter, J.: Defeating IMSI catchers. In: Proceedings of the 22nd ACM SIGSAC Conference on Computer and Communications Security, CCS 2015. ACM (2015)
8. Khan, M.S.A., Mitchell, C.J.: Improving air interface user privacy in mobile telephony. In: Chen, L., Matsuo, S. (eds.) SSR 2015. LNCS, vol. 9497, pp. 165–184. Springer, Cham (2015). https://doi.org/10.1007/978-3-319-27152-1_9
9. Norrman, K., Näslund, M., Dubrova, E.: Protecting IMSI and user privacy in 5G networks. In: Proceedings of the 9th EAI International Conference on Mobile Multimedia Communications, MobiMedia 2016, ICST (2016)
10. Muthana, A.A., Saeed, M.M.: Analysis of user identity privacy in LTE and proposed solution. Int. J. Comput. Netw. Inf. Secur. (IJCNIS) **1**, 54–63 (2017). MECS Publisher
11. Khan, M., Mitchell, C.: Trashing IMSI catchers in mobile networks. In: Proceedings of the 10th ACM Conference on Security and Privacy in Wireless and Mobile Networks (WiSec 2017), Boston, USA, 18–20 July 2017. Association for Computing Machinery (ACM), United States, May 2017
12. 3GPP: 3GPP TS 33.102 V14.1.0 Security architecture (Release 14), March 2017. https://portal.3gpp.org/desktopmodules/Specifications/SpecificationDetails.aspx?specificationId=2262
13. 3GPP: 3GPP TS 33.401 V15.0.0 Security architecture (Release 15), June 2017. https://portal.3gpp.org/desktopmodules/Specifications/SpecificationDetails.aspx?specificationId=2296

14. 3GPP: 3GPP TS 23.012 V14.0.0 Location management procedures (Release 14), March 2017. https://portal.3gpp.org/desktopmodules/Specifications/SpecificationDetails.aspx?specificationId=735
15. Ahlström, M., Holmberg, S.: Prototype Implementation of a 5G Group-Based Authentication and Key Agreement Protocol (2016). http://lup.lub.lu.se/luur/download?func=downloadFile&recordOId=8895975&fileOId=8895979
16. Traynor, P., Lin, M., Ongtang, M., Rao, V., Jaeger, T., McDaniel, P., La Porta, T.: On cellular botnets: measuring the impact of malicious devices on a cellular network core. In: Proceedings of the 16th ACM Conference on Computer and Communications Security, CCS 2009, pp. 223–234. ACM, New York (2009)
17. Xiang, C., Binxing, F., Lihua, Y., Xiaoyi, L., Tianning, Z.: Andbot: towards advanced mobile botnets. In: Proceedings of the 4th USENIX Conference on Large-scale Exploits and Emergent Threats, LEET 2011, p. 11. USENIX Association, Berkeley (2011)
18. Chen, W., Luo, X., Yin, C., Xiao, B., Au, M.H., Tang, Y.: MUSE: towards robust and stealthy mobile botnets via multiple message push services. In: Liu, J.K.K., Steinfeld, R. (eds.) ACISP 2016. LNCS, vol. 9722, pp. 20–39. Springer, Cham (2016). https://doi.org/10.1007/978-3-319-40253-6_2
19. Linuxbsdos: Geinimi a Sophisticated New Android Trojan Found in Wild (2010). http://linuxbsdos.com/2010/12/29/geinimi-sophisticated-new-android-trojan-found-in-wild/
20. KrebsonSecurity: ZeuS Trojan for Google Android Spotted (2011). https://krebsonsecurity.com/2011/07/zeus-trojan-for-google-android-spotted/
21. Jiang, X.: Security Alert: AnserverBot, New Sophisticated Android Bot Found in Alternative Android Markets (2011). https://www.csc2.ncsu.edu/faculty/xjiang4/AnserverBot/
22. Tung, L.: Android Dreamdroid two: rise of laced apps (2011). https://www.itnews.com.au/news/android-dreamdroid-two-rise-of-lacedapps-259147
23. Karim, A., Shah, S.A.A., Salleh, R.B., Arif, M., Noor, R.M., Shamshirband, S.: Mobile botnet attacks - an emerging threat: classification, review and open issues. KSII Trans. Internet Inf. Syst. 9(4), 1471–1492 (2015)
24. Muncaster, P.: Chinese cops cuff 1,500 in fake base station spam raid, March 2014. https://www.theregister.co.uk/2014/03/26/spam_text_china_clampdown_police/
25. Wikipedia: Data Retention Directive. https://en.wikipedia.org/wiki/Data_Retention_Directive

Leveraging Man-in-the-middle DoS Attack with Internal TCP Retransmissions in Virtual Network

Son Duc Nguyen[(✉)], Mamoru Mimura, and Hidema Tanaka

National Defense Academy of Japan, Yokosuka, Japan
{ed56037,mim,hidema}@nda.ac.jp

Abstract. Denial of service (DoS) attacks recently pose great threat to cloud services since it can be able to cause serious damages to others virtual machines (VM) that are on the same physical server with the victim. This opens a new strategy of DoS attack, which is the attacker attempt to be co-resident with the victim server and execute a cross-VM DoS attack inside the cloud. Among DoS attack techniques, recent studies show that TCP retransmission can be abused for reflective amplification attacks. In a virtual environment, the virtual switch system itself can retransmit TCP packets and therefore it can be abused for amplification attack by an internal attacker. In this paper, we leverage the attack by using both virtual switch's internal TCP retransmission feature and Man-in-the-middle attack model.

Keywords: Virtual network · Amplification attack
TCP retransmission · ACK storm

1 Introduction

1.1 Virtualization and DoS Attack

Recently, virtualization has become a mainstream IT architecture with high abilities in memory, storage and processing power management. It provides the capability to easily move virtual servers between different physical servers to balance demand for resources. This can dramatically reduce the number of physical servers in the data center. Furthermore, virtual machines are much easier to set up and break down. If an application needs a new server, an administrator can provide the resources much faster than setting up a physical server. With these benefits, many companies and institutions are adopting virtual server in their system and deploying all new applications in virtualized environment. Virtualization has opened the gate to cloud computing, in which users and companies can process and store their data in virtual servers of third-party data centers. In 2013, it was reported that cloud computing had become a highly demanded service and a promising business [11].

© Springer International Publishing AG 2017
R. K. Shyamasundar et al. (Eds.): ICISS 2017, LNCS 10717, pp. 367–386, 2017.
https://doi.org/10.1007/978-3-319-72598-7_23

An obvious downside to virtualization is the fact that multiple virtual machines are run on a same physical host machine called a *hypervisor*. This feature, which is called "multi-tenancy", is allowed by many cloud providers. This creates a threat that when the hypervisor falls down, all applications running on virtual machines will become unavailable. In a virtual network, all virtual machines Ethernet connection are managed by virtual network adapters and virtual switch. Virtual network adapters are software constructs that are responsible for receiving and transmitting Ethernet frames into and out of their assigned virtual machine or the management operating system. They are provided by a virtual switch, a software construct, which operates within the active memory of the hypervisor and performs Ethernet frame switching functionality. A virtual switch can use single or multiple physical network adapters to serve as uplinks to a physical switch in order to communicate with other computers on the physical network.

In 2009, Ristenpart, Tromer, Shacham and Savage show an other threat comes from multi-tenancy feature [2]. That is a scenario when the customer's virtual machine is assigned to the same physical server as their adversary. Using Amazon's EC2 as a case study, they prove that an attacker can place and check if the malicious virtual machine is on the same physical machine as that of a target. Furthermore, they show that when the attacker archives that "co-residence" state, some cross-VM attacks due to the sharing of physical resources like side-channel or DoS attack are feasible.

In another work, Somani, Gaur, Sanghi and Conti provides a novel insight into the effect of DDoS attack on cloud computing [1]. Besides the targets' server or network, they show that almost all other components and stakeholders of that cloud architecture are affected by a DDoS attack. In other words, when a virtual machine's resource is overloaded by a DDoS attack, other non-targeted virtual machines, servers and users are also affected. The reason is in the features of cloud computing itself such as auto-scaling, migration, multi-tenancy, resource race, performance interference and isolation. They prove that these features multiply the impact of DDoS in virtualized infrastructure clouds.

In this paper, we show a new threat scenario in which the virtual network is overloaded by making the virtual switch retransmit and amplify TCP packets that come from outside to virtual machines. Therefore, all virtual machines under that switch will be disconnected to the Internet.

1.2 TCP Reflective Amplification Attack

TCP/IP (Transmission Control Protocol/Internet Protocol) protocol suite is a communication rule, which specifies how data should be transmitted. TCP/IP uses a client/server model in which a computer (client) requests and is provided a service from another computer (server) in the network. In order to manage the data transmission, TCP/IP uses two main types of protocol, which are TCP and UDP (User Datagram Protocol). TCP ensures a reliable and ordered delivery of a load of packets from client to server or vice versa, while UDP just sends them to another side of the connection. These features make TCP more reliable than UDP since it manages message acknowledgment and retransmissions in case of packet loss. However, UDP is suitable for applications that need fast transmissions.

Recently, UDP-based public servers such as DNS and NTP are known to be abused for reflective amplification attack. The attacker sends relatively small requests with spoofed source address to the hosts that reflect significantly larger responses to the victim. As a result, it overloads and exhausts the capacity of the victim's network and makes normal client unable to access to the victim's server. This kind of attack is posing a serious problem because of its consequences, which cost the victim a very high cost to remediate the vulnerable systems.

On the other hand, TCP-based public servers are not known to be used for DDoS amplification attacks [6]. However, in 2014 Kührer, Hupperich, Rossow and Holz show that a lot of TCP servers on the Internet can actually allow amplification [4,5]. They labeled those hosts as *amplifiers* and identified three main types of amplification [4].

(a) SYN/ACK packets retransmission
(b) Payload data transmission prior the handshake through PSH packets
(c) Aggressive RST segment storms

This discovery opens a new threat to the Internet security since using TCP for transmitting data is more common in TCP/IP. During the scans, they set not to respond any packets from hosts in order to make it easier to trigger the retransmission due to packet loss. Furthermore, they performed real-world TCP-based amplification attacks using a randomly chosen subset of hosts and gave an overview of countermeasures. In order to mitigate this kind of attack, it is important to identify hosts and devices that have amplification factor beforehand and make changes in their configuration.

Besides the threat coming from outside, cyber attacks can also happen from inside. In fact, IBM has pointed out that 60% of cyber attacks in 2015 were caused by insider threats [7]. As already shown above, in this paper, we consider the threat of TCP-based reflective amplification attack inside a virtual environment, in which the virtual switch system itself can retransmitting TCP packets, that come from external TCP hosts, to virtual machines. An attacker can use this kind of attack to sabotage the entire virtual network or overload the virtual system from inside. Since the incoming packets are generated and come from the target's own virtual switch, this kind of attack is harder to detect than a cross-VM direct flooding attack.

In this paper, we show a fundamental feature of VMWare Workstation Pro 12.0.0 [10] that elaborate the power of this attack. To evaluate the potential of this attack, we assume VMware Workstation Pro 12.0.0 to create a virtual network environment that connects with our physical subnet through a virtual switch system. By our experiments, we observed different retransmitting behaviors of the virtual switch and enumerated any kind of TCP packets retransmitted. In most cases of our experiments, the virtual switch sent up to 300 SYN/ACK packets in an interval time of 30 s. In addition, we also identified that in some cases, the virtual switch retransmitted FIN/SYN/ACK packet, in which did not stop after the retransmission time-out. In order to evaluate the impact of this kind of attack on the virtual network, we did some experiments in which we could control the attack volume. The results show that this kind of attack can easily overload the virtual switch system and poses a new threat to any virtual network that has the same fundamental feature.

1.3   Man-in-the-middle Ack Storm Attack

In 2011, Abramov and Herberg introduced *Ack Storm attack*, a new type of TCP-based amplification attack that creates amplification by exploiting TCP RFC vulnerability [3]. According to RFC 793 [8], when a TCP connection in ESTABLISHED state, and a packet is received with an ACK field number that acknowledges data not yet sent, the client must drop that packet and resend an ACK packet with the old SEQ and ACK number. Therefore, in a scenario when an attacker can eavesdrop the transmission between two TCP hosts, the attacker can spoof one host's IP address then send a packet with wrong ACK number to the other host. This will trigger a loop of sending and receiving empty ACK packet according to the TCP flaw. In summary, their basic method - Two Packets Ack Storm, consists of three main stages:

1. Pick up (at least) one packet from a TCP connection between a client and a server.
2. Generate two packets, each addressed to one party and with spoofed IP address of the other party. The packets contain an ACK field number higher than the actual data sent.
3. Send the packets to the client and the server at the same time.

In this paper, we introduce another method to trigger the ACK storm. The ACK storm is an additional result when we try Man-in-the-middle (MitM) method to trigger the FIN/SYN/ACK retransmission of VMWare from outside. As the result, our attack is leveraged because the virtual switch has to suffer the ACK packets storm while continuously generate TCP retransmission to virtual machines at the same time.

Contributions. This paper has the following contributions:

– Discovery of a new type of TCP retransmission in VMWare Workstation Pro 12.0.0 that can become an advantage for amplification attack.
– Evaluation of the immunity of different operating systems in VMWare environment from this kind of attack, showing Windows OS and macOS on default settings is more vulnerable than Linux Ubuntu.
– Introduction of a method to trigger FIN/SYN/ACK retransmission in the virtual network from outside.
– Discovery of another method to trigger ACK Storm DoS attack.

2 TCP Retransmission from the Virtual Switch

2.1 The TCP RFC Flaw

TCP transmission is defined in RFC793 [8]. Comparing with UDP, the attacker cannot use TCP-based public servers directly for reflective amplification attack due to the three-way-handshake. If the attacker spoofed the IP address, the victim would receive an unknown SYN/ACK packet. Then the three-way-handshake would not complete the connection and the TCP/IP framework does not allow payload data for amplification attack.

However, the attacker can still abuse the TCP retransmission function during the handshake for reflective amplification attack. When the client does not send any responses after received an SYN/ACK packet from the server, the server will consider that the SYN/ACK packet has been lost and will resend the SYN/ACK packet again in an interval of time until it receives any responses. Such resending SYN/ACK can make amplification situation like UDP-based servers. Furthermore, because the TCP connection is not established, the SYN/ACK packets can be reflected to the victim by IP spoofing techniques. In fact, thousands of TCP-based public server which can be abused for amplification attack have been found [4].

2.2 Experimental Environment

First of all, we observe TCP retransmission in the virtual environment. Theoretically, there are nearly no restrictions between the virtual switch system and virtual machines. All the following experiments are performed using VMWare Workstation Pro 12.0.0 [10] with NAT setting for external connection and Linux Ubuntu 15.10 as a virtual machine (Fig. 1).

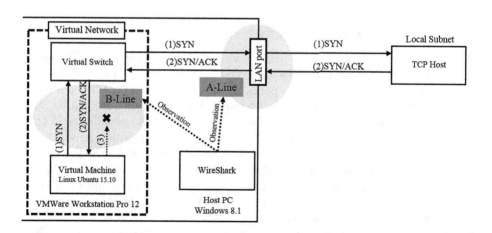

Fig. 1. TCP retransmitting packets capture experiment

In order to make the virtual switch retransmit TCP packets, the internal attacker has to search for external TCP hosts that connect to the virtual network. In this experiment, we use TCP SYN scan on our local subnet to identify connecting TCP hosts. As the result, we found hundreds of open port with 124 types of protocol. In summarize, 579 pairs of ports/devices in our subnet that can be abused for our experimental attack.

In reflective attack, if the victim responds to an unknown SYN/ACK packet with RST segment, the handshake will be canceled and no amplification will be made. However, Kührer shows some conditions for the victim to respond no query. Detailed condition and analysis are shown in [4], we follow their condition to measure the best effectiveness of amplifiers (Fig. 1).

Step-1. From virtual machine, we send a single SYN packet ((1)SYN in Fig. 1) to each open port of TCP hosts in the local subnet.

Step-2. TCP hosts reply by sending SYN/ACK packet ((2)SYN/ACK in Fig. 1).

Step-3. In order to active TCP retransmission in the three-way-handshake, we set that virtual machine does not reply RST to TCP hosts ((3) in Fig. 1).

We observe communication situations in external ("A-line" in Fig. 1) and internal ("B-line" in Fig. 1) of virtual network in Fig. 1 using Wireshark [9] on the host PC. From some experiments, we can find followings:

(a) In A-line, three-way-handshake is established between host PC and TCP hosts on external network. This three-way-handshake is ordinal, therefore no retransmissions are found in this communication.

(b) In B-line, we can observe many retransmitting SYN/ACK packets from virtual switch to virtual machine. This retransmission executes in a time-out interval.

2.3   Analysis of Transmission

Figures 2 and 3 summarizes the virtual switch behaviors that we could observe from the experiment. In A-line, we observed that the virtual switch sent the SYN packet ((1) in Fig. 2) using its own ports. After it received a SYN/ACK packet ((2) in Fig. 2) from the host, it automatically responded with its own ACK packet ((3') in Fig. 2). This procedure finishes three-way-handshake and establishes a TCP connection between the virtual switch and the host. On the other hands, in B-line, the virtual switch redirect this SYN/ACK packet ((2') in Fig. 2) to the virtual machines. However, since the virtual machine did not respond to the SYN/ACK packet ((3) in Fig. 2), the three-way-handshake could not finish and the virtual switch retransmitted the SYN/ACK packet according to the TCP retransmission rule ((α1) in Fig. 2). In most cases, the retransmission stops after 30 s since the first SYN/ACK packet was sent. We deduce that this is VMWare Workstation Pro 12.0.0 retransmission fundamental setting, since layer 2 equipment is not supposed to interfere transport layer protocols. After stopping retransmit SYN/ACK

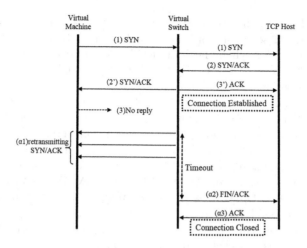

Fig. 2. SYN/ACK retransmitting communication

packet to the virtual machine, we observed in A-line that the virtual switch sent a **FIN/ACK** packet to the hosts in order to end the established TCP connection ((α2) in Fig. 2). 119 out of 124 types of the experimental protocol have been found with this behavior.

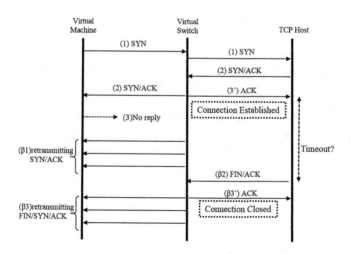

Fig. 3. FIN/SYN/ACK retransmitting communication

We did not find any behavior of payload data transmission before the handshake or **RST** segment storms from the virtual switch. On the other hand, in some cases, we observed that the virtual switch's retransmissions change from **SYN/ACK** packets to **FIN/SYN/ACK** packets. Such **FIN/SYN/ACK** is an abnormal packet. Instead of stopping after 30 s, this kind of retransmission does not stop until we sent an RST segment from the virtual machine to abort the connection. This event only occurs when the host decides to perform an active close and sends a FIN/ACK packet ((β2) in Fig. 3) before the virtual switch ends the TCP connection. The virtual switch subsequently inserts the FIN flag to the retransmitting packet, thus makes a SYN/ACK packet becomes a FIN/SYN/ACK packet ((β3) in Fig. 3). The FIN/SYN/ACK packet retransmission might not be set a timeout interval, which makes it continuously retransmit until receiving respond from the virtual machine. On the other hand, in A-line, the virtual switch responds to the host with an ACK packet ((β3') in Fig. 3) and ends the connection. We deduce that this behavior is also a fundamental feature of VMWare Workstation Pro 12.0.0. We found this behavior when performing experiments on the following ports: 1218, 1947, 3306, 3493 and 60002. Furthermore, some specified pairs of port/device show the same behavior. For example, port 21 and 80 of Canon's Printer send a FIN/ACK packet before the virtual switch.

2.4   Analysis of Data Size

From the analysis of transmission (Sect. 2.2), the total amount of received data by virtual machine in estimated by retransmitting of SYN/ACK ((α1) in Fig. 2 and (β1) in Fig. 3) and of FIN/SYN/ACK ((β3) in Fig. 3). We define the amplification factor (AF) as follows:

$$AF = \frac{SA \times t_1 + FSA \times t_2}{S} \tag{1}$$

where each variable is shown in Table 1. In all cases, SYN packet sizes is fixed to 60 bytes. On the other hand, the sizes of SYN/ACK and FIN/SYN/ACK are various following the protocol. In most cases, 300 times of retransmitting of SYN/ACK packet with 58 bytes is found in our analysis. Already shown above, in some cases, retransmitting of FIN/SYN/ACK is occurred. Since retransmitting FIN/SYN/ACK continues infinite, we observed only within 60 s since the first retransmission in our experiments. Table 2 shows only significant results (13 out of 579 ports/devices).

Table 1. Notations

AF	Amplification factor
S	SYN packet data size [byte]
SA	SYN/ACK packet data size [byte]
FSA	FIN/SYN/ACK packet data size [byte]
t_1	Number of retransmitted SYN/ACK packet ((α1) in Fig. 2, (β1) in Fig. 3)
t_2	Number of retransmitted FIN/SYN/ACK packet ((β3) in Fig. 3)

Table 2. Maximum amplification factor from protocols/hosts in 60 s

Port	Protocol	Device	SA	t_1	FSA	t_2	AF
21	FTP	Printer	137	300	0	0	685.0
22	SSH	Server	101	300	0	0	505.0
23	Telnet	SX-1000U	165	300	0	0	825.0
25	SMTP	PC	156	300	0	0	780.0
80	HTTP	Printer	58	30	248	570	2385.0
515	Printer	Switch	58	1	117	599	1169.0
587	Submission	PC	156	300	0	0	780.0
902	iss-realsecure	PC	58	1	193	599	1927.8
903	iss-console-mgr	PC	193	300	0	0	965.0
912	apex-mesh	PC	160	300	0	0	800.0
3306	mysql	Server	136	92	136	508	1360.0
8080	http-proxy	Router	58	150	426	450	3340.0
9100	Jetdirect	printer	410	300	0	0	2050.0

Because there is a large difference between our experiment (virtual network) and real network, it is obvious that our result is different far from Kuhrer [4]. The differences are summarized as follows:

- An abnormal FIN/SYN/ACK packet retransmission behavior is found.
- Retransmission that endlessly continues without a time-out interval.
- In the real network, the SYN/ACK retransmitting frequency is only 5 packets in 30 s [4]. The virtual network, on the other hand, can have a larger retransmitting frequency depends on their virtual switch's setting. For example, in real network, FTP protocol retransmits with t_1=5 in 30 s [4]. However, in virtual network, it retransmits with t_1=300 (see Table 2).

As the results, we can conclude that, since there are big differences in behavior of retransmitting manner between outside and inside of the virtual switch system, this situation becomes a great vulnerability for virtual machine users.

2.5   Analysis of Different OS Default Response

In previous experiments, we used Linux Ubuntu 15.10 and set it not to reply any TCP packet. In order to use this attack on various virtual machines, we verify the response to TCP packet of different OS in their own default setting. In other words, the virtual machine OS can reply ACK or RST to the retransmitted SYN/ACK packets. We repeat same analysis on default Linux Ubuntu 15.10, Windows 10, 8.1, Server 2016 and macOS 10.12 Sierra.

We found out that, in a virtual environment, Linux Ubuntu 15.10 and macOS Sierra will respond to the incoming SYN/ACK packet and therefore do not create amplification. However, all three kinds of Windows OS did not respond to the SYN/ACK packet. This allows retransmission from the virtual switch, we can evaluate that Windows OS in a virtual network is more vulnerable to TCP amplification attack.

3   Internal TCP Retransmission Attack

3.1   Experimental Model

As mentioned in the first section, virtual machines are easy to set up and break down. Therefore, the hypervisor can terminate the virtual machine that keeps receiving TCP retransmission packets and stop the attack. However, in a situation when the attacker knows other virtual machines' IP addresses, they can spoof the source IP of the SYN packets and make the virtual switch retransmit the responded packets to other machines. This makes the hypervisor more difficult to backup and terminate all of the victim virtual machines.

We estimate the effectiveness of TCP retransmission attack under the virtual network environment with external TCP hosts. We use IP spoofing method and target a Linux Ubuntu 15.10 virtual machine that has no-response to any incoming TCP packet setting. As shown in Fig. 4, we use all of 579 pairs of protocol/host in our local subnet. Our goal is to determine and evaluate how far the virtual switch can be abused for real attacks, in which the attacker repeatedly send SYN packets and trigger the SYN/ACK retransmission. Besides the rise of transmitted data volume and the data bandwidth, we expected that the amplification factor will become lower than our first experiment results, due to the capacity of the virtual switch under overloading situation. First, the attacker sends SYN packets to 579 pairs of protocol/host. In this step, the attacker can send a multiple number of SYN packets using different port number simultaneously. In our first attack simulation, the attacker sends SYN packets from #1234 port to each # of port for TCP host. We define such condition as single-type attack. We expand the single-type attack by increasing the number of sender ports. For example, in 10-SYN-type, the attacker sends 10 SYN packets from ten kinds of port (#1234'#1243) to each TCP host at the same time. In the same way, we also set 50-SYN-type (#1234'#1283) and 100-SYN-type (#1234'#1333) as shown in Fig. 5.

Since the size of SYN packet is 60 bytes, the amount of data E [byte] which is sent from attacker is calculated as follow

$$E = 60 \times 579 \times n \tag{2}$$

where n is number of used source ports from the attacker.

In our attack simulation, we used TCP Hosts in our real subnet. These TCP hosts are actually used for office works and research activity and those management is entrusted to each section. To simulate the realistic attack environment, we did not open our attack experiment to the users of those TCP hosts beforehand. Therefore, we could not make exactly all of TCP hosts respond because some hosts were off-line or were powered off at the experiment time. From these conditions, we observed the following factors in 60 s:

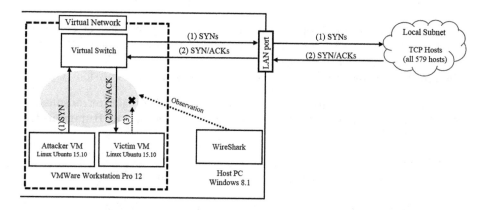

Fig. 4. The adversarial model

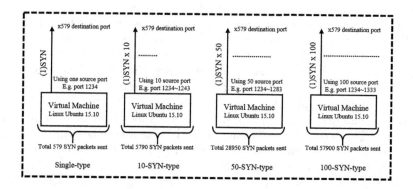

Fig. 5. Four experimental attack settings

– Number of respond TCP Hosts (Responded Port)
– Total amount of Received Data (Received Data)
– Maximum bandwidth of TCP retransmission (Max Bandwidth)

Using these results, we can consider the relation between

Relation-1. Number of SYN packet from attacker and responded TCP Hosts
Relation-2. Number of SYN packet from attacker and total amount of received
data and maximum bandwidth, and
Relation-3. Number of SYN packet from attacker and retransmission type.

In particular, we want to use the characteristic of FIN/SYN/ACK retransmission for more effective attack, the observation and consideration of **Relation-3** is important.

Table 3. The attack experiment results (in 60 s)

SYN sent	Responded ports	Received data	Max bandwidth	AF
Single	540	11.5 MB	364 kbps	346.4
10-SYN	324	51.5 MB	1.91 Mbps	155.1
50-SYN	119	54.2 MB	1.96 Mbps	31.9
100-SYN	125	66.1 MB	2.12 Mbps	19.4

3.2 Results

Table 3 shows attack experiment results. From the viewpoint of Relation-1, the number of responded hosts decrease significantly when sending more SYN packets. We expect that the virtual switch was suffered from overload and it could not respond to every TCP query. On the other hand, on Relation-2, the data volume and bandwidth is increased when increasing the SYN packets. More specifically, the hosts retransmitted 11.5 MB with a maximum bandwidth of 364 kbps in the case of single-type. The attack of 10-SYN-type resulted in 51.5 MB with a maximum bandwidth of 1.91 Mbps, which is 5 times increased comparing to single-type. The retransmitted volume slightly increased when raising the SYN packets to 50 and 100, with 54.2 MB and 66.1 MB respectively. From the viewpoint of Relation-3, *AF* is lower when increasing the number of SYN packet. However, the larger reflected packet size the victim received, the virtual switch suffered more from the effectiveness of DoS and fall into an unstable state, which in some cases we cannot observe the transmission by Wireshark. Furthermore, the FIN/SYN/ACK packets continued to retransmit until the victim responded with RST packets, which slowed down the victim network for a long time. We conclude that our attacks succeeded in term of overloading the entire virtual network.

When receiving 10 or more `SYN` packets, some FTP, SSH, Telnet hosts changed from `SYN/ACK` packet retransmission to `FIN/SYN/ACK` retransmission, as mentioned in Sect. 2.2. In addition, we found new retransmission type using `PSH` packet. In other words, some TCP hosts send `FIN/ACK` ((β2) in Fig. 3) or `PSH` when receiving a lot of `SYN` packet. We did not find these kinds of behavior from those hosts in the single-type attack. As a result, we consider that the hosts' behavior has some relations with the number of `SYN` packet it received. This result benefits attacker when they want to start `FIN/SYN/ACK` retransmission for this kind of attack.

3.3 The Virtual Machine's OS Default Response

In order to observe the capacity of TCP-based reflective amplification attack in a situation that the victim can be able to respond to unknown TCP packets with `RST` segment thus cancel the retransmission, we repeated the single-type and 10-SYN-type `SYN` packets attack on the same experimental model shown in Fig. 4 with victims using Linux Ubuntu 15.10, Windows 10, 8.1, Server 2016 and macOS 10.12 Sierra. Figure 5 shows our experiment model. Table 4 shows received traffic volume with each kind of OS. As the default setting, Linux Ubuntu responds to unknown TCP packets with `RST` segments. However, macOS cannot respond to the `FIN/SYN/ACK` packets and all tested Windows OS continued to receive every reflected TCP packets with no response. Furthermore, in the 10-SYN-type attack, while Linux Ubuntu can still handle all of the reflected packets with `RST` segment, macOS can only response about half of the incoming packets. Therefore, the data volume macOS received is much larger compared to Ubuntu. This indicates the vulnerability of Windows and macOS default settings under this kind of attack. We further test the 100-SYN-type attack on Windows OS victim. As we expected, although all of the virtual machines are still alive, the virtual switch is down and the virtual machines become unable to connect to the external network. In order to recover the virtual switch, we had to restart the virtual environment. As a consequence, all of the running virtual machines are also interrupted and restarted.

Table 4. Received Data on different OS (60 s)

SYN sent	Linux Ubuntu			macOS			Windows OS		
	Responded ports	Received data	AF	Responded ports	Received data	AF	Responded ports	Received data	**AF**
Single	496	31 kB	0.9	325	1.1 MB	33.1	504	10.8 MB	325.3
10-SYN	314	703 kB	2.1	436	23.3 MB	70.1	333	52.9 MB	159.3

4 Man-in-the-middle DoS Attack

As mentioned in the above section, the characteristic of `FIN/SYN/ACK` retransmission is more advantageous for this kind of attack. This kind of retransmission appears when the external TCP host decides to perform an active close and sends a `FIN/ACK` packet before the virtual switch ends the TCP connection. This opens a new scenario that if attacker can monitor the transmission between hypervisor and the TCP host, they can use Man-in-the-middle attack to send a spoofed `FIN/ACK` packet and trigger the `FIN/SYN/ACK` retransmission from outside the virtual network. In this section, we show that this method is practical and analysis of the strengths and the necessary conditions of this attack.

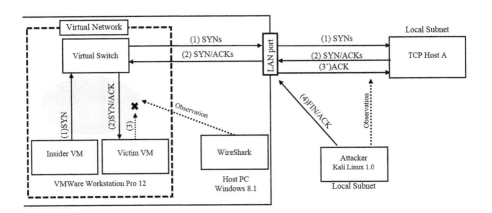

Fig. 6. MitM attack experiment model

4.1 Experimental Model

We extend the experimental model of Sect. 3 by adding one more machine in the same network with the hypervisor and the TCP server (Fig. 6). This machine (called Eve in Fig. 6) is able to observe the transmission from TCP Host and send spoofed packets to the virtual switch. In other words, the adversarial model changed from an insider attacker in Sect. 3 to an outsider attacker that also has an insider VM in the targeted network.

In order to make the virtual switch retransmit `FIN/SYN/ACK` packets, the attacker needs to imitates the situation when the TCP Host decided to perform an active close before the virtual switch ends the TCP connection. Eve needs to know the `SEQ` and `ACK` number of the TCP connection between TCP Host and the virtual switch. Eve also needs to find out which port number the virtual switch used for this connection. These numbers can be revealed by analyzing captured packets from the TCP Host. In summary, our experiment consists of four main steps.

Step-1. From virtual machine, we send a single `SYN` packet ((1)SYN in Fig. 6) to an open port of TCP Host A in the local subnet.

Step-2. TCP Host A reply by sending `SYN/ACK` packet ((2)SYN/ACK in Fig. 6).

Step-3. In order to active TCP retransmission in three-way-handshake, we set that virtual machine does not reply RST to TCP hosts ((3) in Fig. 6). However, the virtual switch still completes the handshake with TCP Host A by sending its own ACK packet ((3')ACK in Fig. 6).

Step-4. Eve generates an IP-spoofed FIN/ACK packet using observed SEQ and ACK number and send it to the corresponding port number of the virtual switch before the connection timeout ((4)FIN/ACK in Fig. 6).

We use the same method of observation in Sect. 2 for external ("A-line" in Fig. 6) and internal ("B-line" in Fig. 6) communication of virtual network. As a result, we can find followings:

(a) In A-line, a specification rule of TCP causes the virtual switch and TCP Host A to be trapped in a loop of sending and receiving empty ACK packet. This loop stops only when one side reaches a timeout and end the connection with RST packet.

(b) In B-line, the SYN/ACK retransmission, as we expected, changes to the infinite FIN/SYN/ACK packets retransmission.

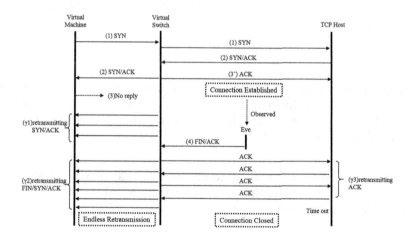

Fig. 7. Transmission behaviors of the virtual switch in the MitM attack

4.2 Analysis

Figure 7 summarizes the transmission behaviors of the virtual switch and TCP Host A that we could observe from the experiment. As we expected, the virtual switch acknowledges the spoofed FIN/ACK packet ((4)in Fig. 7) as it was sent from TCP Host A. In B-line, the virtual switch inserts the FIN flag to the retransmitting packet, thus changes the SYN/ACK retransmission ((γ1) in Fig. 7) to FIN/SYN/ACK retransmission ((γ2) in Fig. 7). On the other hand, in A-line, TCP

Host A receives the ACK packet from the virtual switch that acknowledges the FIN/ACK packet that it has not yet sent. TCP Host A, still in the ESTABLISHED state, must resend an ACK packet with the old SEQ and ACK field number according to the TCP protocol. Despite of having changed to CLOSE-WAIT state, the virtual switch also has to resend its ACK packet when it received the malformed packet from TCP Host A. This behavior triggers the loop again, which creates an ACK packets storm between TCP Host A and the virtual switch ((γ3) in Fig. 7). As we observed, the retransmitted ACK packets from TCP Host A in A-Line does not affect the TCP retransmission in B-line. On the analysis of data size, in 60 s, besides 600 FIN/SYN/ACK packets retransmitted between the virtual switch and targeted VM, the spoofed 60 bytes FIN/ACK packet also causes over 803,000 ACK packets retransmitted between TCP Host A and the virtual switch. As a consequences, with less resources, this MitM attack can overload the victim network more than the previous internal TCP retransmission attack.

5   Threat Scenario

We derive new threat scenarios based on our experimental results. In this section, we show three types of scenario: only insider VM, only outsider MitM and a collaboration of them.

5.1   Attack Using only Insider VM

Conditions. We assume the insider attacker is a user of one virtual machine in the virtual network and his purpose is to sabotage the other virtual machines' activities. The insider attacker has also known other virtual machines' IP address and their running OS (see Sect. 2.5).

Objective. The main goal of the attacker is to sabotage the virtual network by making the virtual switch continuously generates a lot of retransmitting TCP packet and sends to its virtual machines.

Method. The attacker sends SYN packets to TCP Hosts that will redirect retransmitted TCP packets to other virtual machines by IP spoofing. Comparing to direct flooding DoS method, in this attack, the hypervisor can not identify the attacker's identity and can not determine which virtual machine to terminate in order to stop the attack.

5.2   Attack Using only Man-in-the-middle Method

Conditions. We assume the outsider Man-in-the-middle attacker has the ability to observe the communication between the hypervisor and the TCP hosts. The attacker can also generate spoofed IP address packet and send it to the Internet.

Objective. The main goal of the attacker is to sabotage the virtual network by flooding the virtual switch with `ACK` packets. In addition, the attacker can also take down the TCP Host that is connecting with the virtual switch.

Method. Our method is slightly different from the Man-in-the-middle Ack Storm attack mentioned in Sect. 1.3. The attacker observes the virtual server communication with a TCP server and sends a `FIN/ACK` packet to trigger the `ACK` storm and `FIN/SYN/ACK` retransmission inside the virtual network. In order for the attack to succeed, the virtual machine must not react to the retransmitted packet. This can be done if the targeted VM is Window OS, as mentioned in Sect. 2.5. In order to ensure that the attack will work, the attacker can use phishing method to establish a connection between victim's network VM that running Window OS with a TCP server and execute this attack.

5.3 Collaboration Attack Using both Insider VM and MitM Method

Conditions. In this scenario, the two attackers in the above scenarios collaborate with each other.

Objective. The virtual switch is sabotaged by receiving `ACK` packet flood while continuously retransmitting TCP packets to its VM in the same time. The TCP Host that is connecting with the virtual switch is also affected by the attack.

Methods. In this scenario, the attacker use the insider virtual machine to send an IP-spoofed TCP `SYN` packet to an external TCP server. The TCP connection will be established between hypervisor and the TCP servers, in which the attacker can easily capture the packet between hypervisor and those servers. While a `SYN/ACK` retransmission will be done between the hypervisor and targeted VM, the attacker generates a `FIN/ACK` packet with wrong `ACK` field number and send it to the hypervisor using IP address of the TCP server. As the result, an `ACK` packet storm will appear between the hypervisor and the server while the connection between the hypervisor and the targeted VM will enter an infinite `FIN/SYN/ACK` retransmission.

In order to leverage the attack, following three situations can be considered:

(a) The insider VM sends a lot of TCP packet to the external TCP server by using different source port number on each packet (see Sect. 3.1). This method is easy to execute. ((a) in Fig. 8).

(b) The attacker uses a lot of TCP server (botnet) as their external TCP hosts resource ((b) in Fig. 8).

(c) The attacker uses the above two methods at the same time ((c) in Fig. 8).

Furthermore, the attacker can create an environmental risk to the virtual network by using TCP host types that have a high amplification factor (see Sect. 2.4).

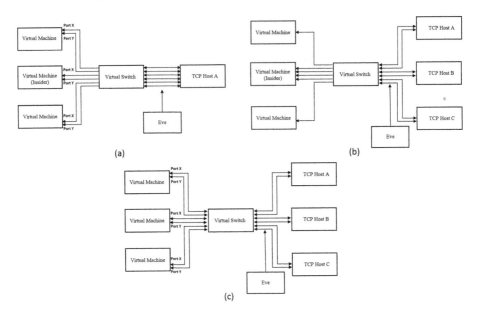

Fig. 8. Three methods to leverage the attack

6   Countermeasures

As mentioned above, the main power of this attack is the fundamental feature in TCP retransmission of VMWare Workstation Pro 12.0.0. Therefore, if the retransmitting frequency is lower down, and the abnormal infinite FIN/SYN/ACK retransmission is limited, the effectiveness of attack will not become so serious. In fact, we have checked the attack effect on recent version of VMWare and found out that the TCP retransmission settings are configured, which make this attack is no longer a threat in term of amplification factor. Therefore, the obvious countermeasure of this attack is to update the newest version of VMWare.

However, default Windows OS under the virtual environment still ignores the unknown TCP packet that retransmitted from the virtual switch. Therefore, in order to completely neutralize the attack, its default setting should be more defensive. For example, if a lot of the same ambiguous packet coming from the virtual server, its should response with RST packets to force the retransmission to end.

7   Conclusions

In this paper, we found a case that the virtual switch itself can retransmit TCP packets and this behavior can be abused for TCP retransmission DoS attack, in particular, VMWare Workstation Pro 12.0.0. The majority of TCP retransmission is SYN/ACK type, which is limited in an interval time-out. Besides that, we also find the FIN/SYN/ACK retransmission type that continues endlessly until the victim responds with RST.packet. We further show that the host's behavior of actively sending FIN/ACK packet also depends on the number of received SYN packets. In addition, we also prove that Windows and macOS virtual machines at default setting are vulnerable to this kind of attack.

Furthermore, we introduce a MitM attack that is able to trigger the infinite FIN/SYN/ACK retransmission of the virtual switch from a third party. Our attack also introduces a new method to trigger the Ack Storm attack. However, existing Ack Storm does not have any direct effect on the virtual switch's retransmitting behavior. This behavior lies in the fundamental feature of VMWare 12.0.0 and it was fixed in the updated version. For any organizations using an old virtual system in their infrastructure (e.g. thin client machine), this kind of attack realistically create an opportunity loss threat. In conclusion, TCP-based retransmission attack poses a threat to any virtual network environment that still has an intense retransmitting behavior.

Acknowledgment. This work was supported by JSPS KAKENHI Grant Number 17K06455.

References

1. Somani, G., Gaur, M.S., Sanghi, D., Conti, M.: DDoS attacks in cloud computing: collateral damage to non-targets. Comput. Netw. **109**, 157–171 (2016). http://www.sciencedirect.com/science/article/pii/S1389128616300901. Accessed 25 July 2017
2. Ristenpart, T., Tromer, E., Shacham, H., Savage, S.: Hey, You, get off of my cloud: exploring information leakage in third-party compute clouds. In: ACM Conference on Computer and Communications Security 2009 (CCS 2009), November 2009. https://cseweb.ucsd.edu/hovav/dist/cloudsec.pdf. Accessed 25 July 2017
3. Abramov, R., Herzberg, A.: TCP ack storm DoS attacks. In: Camenisch, J., Fischer-Hübner, S., Murayama, Y., Portmann, A., Rieder, C. (eds.) SEC 2011. IFIP AICT, vol. 354, pp. 29–40. Springer, Heidelberg (2011). https://doi.org/10. 1007/978-3-642-21424-0_3. Accessed 25 July 2017
4. Kührer, M., Hupperich, T., Rossow, C., Holz, T.: Hell of a handshake: abusing TCP for reflective amplification DDoS attacks. In: 8th USENIX Workshop on Offensive Technologies (WOOT 14), August 2014. https://www.usenix.org/conference/woot14/workshop-program/presentation/kuhrer. Accessed 30 May 2017
5. Kührer, M., Hupperich, T., Rossow, C., Holz, T.: Exit from hell? Reducing the impact of amplification DDoS attacks. In: 23rd USENIX Security Symposium (USENIX Security 14), August 2014. https://www.usenix.org/node/184412. Accessed 30 May 2017
6. Rossow, C.: Amplification hell: revisiting network protocols for DDoS abuse. In: Symposium on Network and Distributed System Security (NDSS), February 2014. https://www.internetsociety.org/sites/default/files/01_5.pdf. Accessed 30 May 2017
7. IBM: Reviewing a year of serious data breaches, major attacks and new vulnerabilities, April 2016. https://www-01.ibm.com/common/ssi/cgi-bin/ssialias?htmlfid=SEP03394USEN. Access 30 May 2017

8. IETF: Transmission Control Protocol, DARPA Internet Program Protocol Specification RFC793 (1981). https://tools.ietf.org/html/rfc793. Accessed 30 May 2017

9. Wireshark: Network protocol analyzer, Wireshark v2.2.6. https://www.wireshark.org/

10. VMWare: Workstation for Windows, VMWare Workstation Pro 12. https://www.vmware.com/products/workstation.html

11. FSN: The economy is flat so why are financials Cloud vendors growing at more than 90 percent per annum? March 2013. http://www.fsn.co.uk/channel_outsourcing/. Accessed 30 May 2017

wIDS: A Multilayer IDS for Wireless-Based SCADA Systems

Lyes Bayou[1(✉)], David Espes[2], Nora Cuppens-Boulahia[1],
and Frédéric Cuppens[1]

[1] IMT Atlantique-LabSTICC, 2 Rue de la Châtaigneraie, Césson Sévigné, France
lyes.bayou@imt-atlantique.fr
[2] University of Western Brittany - LabSTICC, Brest, France

Abstract. The increasing use of wireless sensors networks in Supervisory Control and Data Acquisition systems (SCADA) raises the need of enforcing the security of this promising technology. Indeed, SCADA systems are used to manage critical installations that have hard security, reliability and real-time requirements. Consequently, in order to ensure Wireless Industrial Sensor Networks (WISN) security, Intrusion Detection Systems should be used as a second line of defense, in addition to sensor's embedded security mechanisms. In this paper, we present wIDS a multilayer specification-based Intrusion Detection System specially tailored for WISN. It has a two-level detection architecture and is based on a formal description of node's normal behavior.

1   Introduction

Wireless Industrial Sensor Network (WISN) are now established as a widely used technology in industrial environments. Indeed, comparing to wired technologies, they allow significant decreases in deployment and maintenance costs. In the same time, they increase the system sensing capabilities as wireless sensors can be deployed in hardly reachable and adversarial environments.

In industrial environments, Supervisory Control and Data Acquisition systems (SCADA) are used for monitoring and managing complex installations such as power plants, refineries, railways, etc. These systems rely on sensors deployed over large area to gather in real time information about the industrial process. These informations are sent to a controller that processes them and sent back commands to field devices such as actuators or valves.

Security is an important issue in SCADA systems. Indeed, the disruption of these systems can cause significant damages to critical infrastructures such as electric power distribution, oil and natural gas distribution, water and wastewater treatment, and transportation systems. This can have a serious impact on public health, safety and can lead to large economical losses.

On the other hand, ensuring security in WISN is a challenging task. Indeed, WISN are subject to the same attacks as other wireless networks. Mainly, attackers use wireless communication as a vector to launch their attacks. Furthermore,

© Springer International Publishing AG 2017
R. K. Shyamasundar et al. (Eds.): ICISS 2017, LNCS 10717, pp. 387–404, 2017.
https://doi.org/10.1007/978-3-319-72598-7_24

sensor's limited capabilities in terms of processing power, memory space and energy make hard the implementation of strong security mechanisms.

Thus, in addition to sensor's embedded mechanisms that ensure authentication, confidentiality and availability, Intrusion Detection Systems can be used as a second line of defense for enforcing the overall system security and in particular for detecting unknown attacks.

The exchanged traffic in a SCADA system is highly predictable in terms of amount and frequency. Indeed, it involves limited human interaction and is mainly composed of automated devices that execute defined actions at defined times. Therefore, by modeling the normal expected behavior of wireless nodes, we can detect malicious action as being actions deviating from the established model.

In this paper, we present wIDS, a multilayer specification-based Intrusion Detection System specially tailored for Wireless Industrial Sensor Networks. The proposed IDS checks the compliance of each action performed by a wireless node towards the formal model of the expected normal behavior. To do that, access control rules are used for modeling authorized actions that a wireless node can perform. These rules are mainly built on the base of the specifications of each layer of the communication protocol, node's localization and the industrial process configuration. They also take into consideration the capabilities and limitations of the wireless nodes. Thus, by specifying security policy at an abstract level, we are able to define and manage more accurate and efficient security rules independently from nodes and network characteristics such as sensor natures and density or the network topology. Then, these characteristics are used later when deriving concrete security rules. Also, in addition to alerts that are raised by actions deviating from the normal model, we define additional intrusion rules that aim to detect basic attacker actions such as injecting, deleting, modifying and delaying packets.

The rest of the paper is organized as follows. Section 2 presents previous works done in this field and emphasis their limits. In Sect. 3, we present briefly the protocol WirelessHART that is the use case of this study. We present in Sect. 4, the proposed IDS for Wireless Industrial Sensor Networks. We describe its two-level detection architecture and present the formalism used to build node's normal behavior. Section 5 details security rules defined on the base of WirelessHART specifications. In Sect. 6, we present how detection rules are defined to detect suspicious actions. The performances of the proposed wIDS are presented and discussed in Sect. 7. Finally, Sect. 8 presents the conclusion and future works.

2 Related Work

In the literature, there are only few studies on the security of Wireless Sensor Networks used in industrial environments. Mainly, proposed solutions for SCADA systems focus on applying IDS techniques to wired-based networks [1–3] and neglect those using wireless communications.

More generally, several IDS are proposed for generic WSN [4]. However, proposed solutions are not suitable for WISN. Firstly, WISN have more hard requirements than generic WSN such as real-time and reliable communications. Indeed, dropped or delayed data may lead to physical losses. Secondly, these proposed IDS are mainly restricted to detect specific kinds of attack while WISN must be secured towards a broad spectrum of known and unknown attacks. Nevertheless, these works should be considered in order to propose a solution designed for WISN.

Thus, in [5], Da Sila et al. propose one of the first intrusion detection systems for WSN. They designed a decentralized system in which a set of nodes is designated as *monitor* and is responsible of monitoring their neighbors. The proposed IDS is based on the statistical inference of the network behavior. It only monitors data messages and ignores other kinds of exchanged messages. It includes seven types of rules that aim to detect common attacks.

For its part, Roosta et al. propose in [6] an intrusion detection system for wireless process control systems. The system consists of two components: a central IDS and multiple field IDS that passively monitor communications in their neighborhood. They periodically send collected data to the central IDS that checks their conformity with the security policy. This IDS models normal behavior of the different wireless devices on the base of some network specifications and traffic characteristics inferred statistically. Attacks are detected when there is a deviation from the model. However, it defines a few numbers of rules (8 rules) that do not cover all well-known attacks. Furthermore, as the detection logic is centralized, this solution requires continuous communications with field IDS which can add a significant network overload.

In [7], Coppolino et al. propose an architecture for an intrusion detection system for critical information infrastructures using wireless sensor network. Their solution is a hybrid approach combining misuse and anomaly based techniques. It is composed of a Central Agent and several IDS Local Agents that monitors exchanged messages in their neighborhood. They calculate a statistical model of exchanged traffic and raise a temporary alert when nodes actions deviate from this model. The central agent combines these alerts and confirms them on the base of misuse rules. This IDS focuses on attacks against routing protocols and detects only two kinds of attacks i.e., sinkhole and sleep deprivation attacks.

Shin et al. [8] propose a hierarchical framework for intrusion detection for WISN. It is based on two-level clustering; multihop clusters for data aggregation and one-hop clusters for intrusion detection. This results in a four layer hierarchy: member nodes (MN) are the leaves, cluster heads (CH) manage MNs, gateways (GW) bundle clusters and a base station (BS) is the root of the hierarchy. These different levels implement the same detection logic, however they respond differently. Thus, MN only report to CH while other roles have the ability to react to attacks.

In our study, we aim to propose a solution that is able to detect either known and unknown attacks. Furthermore, such solution should have a multilevel detection architecture to monitor both local and end-to-end communications (generally encrypted) and also in order to provide global coordination. Low detection level should have full detection capabilities in order to avoid overloading the network by additional exchanges and to have quick and accurate detections.

3   Backgrounds on WirelessHART

In our work, we choose to apply our approach to WISN that implements WirelessHART and we will use it as a common thread all along this paper. Indeed, WirelessHART [9] is the first standardized wireless communication protocol specially developed for industrial process management. It is included in version 7 of the HART standard, released in 2007, and was approved as an international standard in 2010 (IEC 62591).

A WirelessHART network, illustrated in Fig. 1, has the following characteristics:

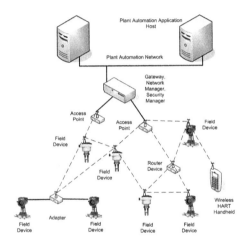

Fig. 1. Example of a WirelessHART network [10]

- A Gateway that connects the wireless network to the plant automation network, allowing data to flow between the two networks. It can also be used to convert data and commands from one protocol to another one;
- A Network Manager that is responsible for the overall management, scheduling, and optimization of the wireless network. It generates and maintains all of the routing information and also allocates communication resources;
- A Security Manager that is responsible for the generation, storage, and management of cryptographic keys;
- Access Points that connect the Gateway to the wireless network through a wired connection;

- Field devices deployed in the plant field and which can be sensors or actuators;
- Routers used for forwarding packets from one network device to another;
- Handheld devices that are portable equipments operated by the plant personnel used in the installation and during the maintenance of network devices.

WirelessHART implements several mechanisms to ensure security in both hop-by-hop and end-to-end communication. In hop-by-hop transmission, security is provided by the Data Link Layer (DLL) using a cryptographic key called "Network Key" shared by all devices composing the wireless network. Each packet is authenticated using a keyed Message Integrity Code (MIC).

The end-to-end security is provided by the Network Layer (NL) using a cryptographic key called "Session Key" known only by the two communicant devices. Packets are both authenticated by a MIC and their payload is also encrypted.

4   Multilayer Specification-Based IDS

In this Section, we present *wIDS* a multilayer specification based IDS for securing Wireless Industrial Sensors Networks. We describe its architecture, its components and its analyzing process.

Specification-based intrusion detection approaches formally define the model of legitimate behavior and raise intrusion alerts when user's actions deviate from the model [3,4]. WISN are composed of nodes that have a predictable behavior and involves few human interactions. Consequently, on the base of the communication protocol specifications, the process configuration and wireless nodes capabilities, we can build an accurate model of the expected nodes's behavior.

We should also note that specification-based intrusion detection system do not require any training step. Therefore, they can be applied and used directly.

In this study, we assume that the aim of the attacker is to disturb the industrial process. This goal can be achieved by dropping some packets, injecting into the network false packets or modifying packets during their transmission. Furthermore, the attacker can also choose to delay the transmission of some important packets (alarms, sensing data, etc.) in order to lead the process to an uncertain state or to hide its malicious actions. Therefore, we consider an attacker that can intercept, modify, forge or delay packets. It can be an insider or an outsider attacker.

4.1   wirelessOrBAC

We propose in this work wirelessOrBAC, an OrBAC [11] extension that we develop in order to efficiently model Wireless Sensor Networks specifications. OrBAC has already been used to specify network security policy, especially in firewall management [12], intrusion detection (IDS) and intrusion prevention systems (IPS) [13]. It allows the definition of a conflict-free security policy and by using the concept of *context*, it makes it possible to define dynamic rules that fit the system's changes. This extension allows using access control rules, modeling authorized actions and the expected behavior of wireless nodes. Then, using this model, we can detect malicious actions by checking the compliance of each node action toward the defined security policy.

Furthermore, wirelessOrBAC allows the definition of both access control rules and intrusion detection rules using the same formalism.

To define a security policy, wirelessOrBAC defines the following concepts:

- wNetwork: It is an abstraction of the considered WSN.
- wRole: It is an abstraction of predefined roles used in WSN such as: wSensor, wSink, wForwarder, wCluster_head.
- wDevice: It is an abstraction of wireless devices. It is composed of one or several wRole.
- wActivity: It is an abstraction of wireless actions that a wDevice can perform such as: sending, receiving, forwarding and aggregating.
- wView: It is an abstraction of messages sent from a wDevice to another one.
- wContext: It is used to model extra conditions that a subject, an action and an object must satisfy to activate a security rule.

Thus, a security rule is defined as follows:

$$wRule(security\_rule, wnet, d, a, v, c) \tag{1}$$

that means that in wNetwork $wnet$, wDevice d is granted $security\_rule$ to perform wActivity a on wView v within wContext c and where $security\_rule$ belongs to {perm, prohib, obl} (Corresponding to: permission, prohibition and obligation).

Finally, concrete security rules are derived as follows:

$$\begin{aligned} &wRule(perm, wnet, wRole, wActivity, wView, c) \\ &\wedge empower(wnet, s, wRole) \wedge consider(wnet, a, wActivity) \\ &\wedge use(wnet, o, wView) \wedge hold(wnet, s, a, o, c) \\ &\rightarrow Is\_Permitted(s, a, o) \end{aligned} \tag{2}$$

where:

- $empower(wnet, s, wRole)$: means that in wNetwork $wnet$, subject s is empowered in $wRole$.
- $consider(wnet, a, wActivity)$: means that in wNetwork $wnet$, action a is considered an implementation of $wActivity$.
- $use(wnet, o, wView)$: means that in wNetwork $wnet$, object o is used in $wView$.
- $hold(wnet, s, a, o, c)$: means that in wNetwork $wnet$, wContext c is active for s, a and o.

4.2   wIDS Architecture

As indicated in Fig. 2, wIDS has a two-level architecture consisting in a central-IDS agent and several IDS-agents.

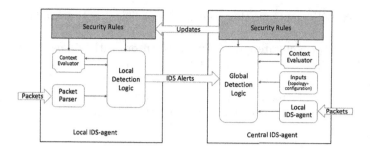

Fig. 2. The Central-IDS and IDS-Agents architecture

– The central-IDS agent: It is implemented in the Network Manager (resp. in the sink) in the case of wirelessHART (resp. in the case of a WISN). In addition of playing the role of an IDS-agent in its neighborhood, it monitors end-to-end communications after they are decrypted. It may check routing tables and transmission scheduling consistency; and performs global coordination between IDS-agents.
– IDS-agents: They are implemented in selected sensor nodes. They are responsible for monitoring local communications of sensor nodes inside their neighborhood. They listen in promiscuous mode to all packets exchanged in their neighborhood. Then, they extract from them, relevant informations in order to check their compliance with the security policy.

The abstract security policy is defined at the central-IDS agent using the wirelessOrBAC formalism. It is also provided with several inputs such as node localizations, industrial process parameters and nodes configuration. The central-IDS agent provisions IDS-agents with security rules and several inputs related to nodes available in their neighborhood (i.e., the list of monitored nodes). It also updates if necessary all these information. Each IDS-agent is in charge of the application of the security policy in its area and alerts the central-IDS agent when policy violation occurs.

4.3 IDS-agents Deployment Scheme

The scheme used for the deployment of IDS-agents, is an important issue. Indeed, as WSN are decentralized systems, the localization of monitoring devices must be chosen carefully otherwise a part of exchanged traffic will not be monitored.

The deployment of IDS-agents is out of the scope of this paper. However, in our study, we use the scheme proposed in [14]. This scheme uses the graph theory concept of *Connected Dominated Set* to ensure the gathering of the whole exchanged traffic. Also, it presents the following characteristics: *(a)* each IDS-agent is able to detect basic attacks occurring in its neighborhood without any cooperation with other IDS-agents; *(b)* it creates a secure and reliable communication channel between each IDS-agent and the central-IDS; *(c)* it requires an acceptable IDS-agents number to ensure an efficient network monitoring and coverage.

In wIDS, IDS-agents are implemented in sensors with enhanced capabilities. These nodes, called *Super-Nodes*, will act as classical sensor nodes by fulfilling sensing tasks and implements in the same time the detection logic. By using the aforementioned deployment scheme, selected *Super-Nodes* represents between 20%–25% of the total network nodes number (Fig. 3).

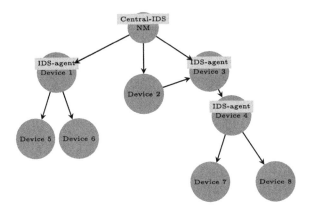

Fig. 3. IDS-agents deployment scheme

5   Expected Behavior Modeling Rules

In this Section, based on WirelessHART specification [9], we define using wire-lessOrBAC rules the expected node's normal behavior. These rules express authorized actions at each protocol layer. We gather them in several categories and present hereafter, examples of each of them.

5.1   Meshed Wireless Network Rules

In a wirelessHART network, all devices have the capability to forward packets of devices that are located several hops away from the Network Manager. That means that a device can send packets to any of its neighbors:

$$wRule(perm, wnet, wDevice, sending, packets, neighbors) \qquad (3)$$

where *neighbors* is a wContext indicating that $s1$ performs action *sending* object *packet* to node $s2$ that is in its neighborhood:

$$Hold(WSN, s1, sending, packet, neighbors)$$
$$\leftarrow is\_dstAddr(packet, s2) \land is\_neighbor(s1, s2) \qquad (4)$$

5.2   Packets Construction Rules

The WirelessHART specifications give guidelines on how packets should be built and the possible values of each field. Thus, the length and value of each field must be checked. Also, fields of the same packet must be consistent with each other.

$$wRule(perm, wnet, wDevice, sending, packet, \_) \atop \leftarrow is\_ValidPacket(packet) \tag{5}$$

where $is\_ValidPacket(packet)$ is a predicate indicating if $packet$ fulfills wirelessHART construction rules. The symbol " _ " indicates that this rule is valid for any wContext.

5.3   Communication Level

WirelessHART defines 5 packet types: *Ack, Advertise, Keep-Alive, Disconnect* and *Data* packets. The first 4 types are generated and processed in the Data Link Layer and are not propagated to the Network Layer or forwarded through the network. This means that these packets are only used in local communication between neighbors.

$$wRule(perm, wnet, wDevice, sending, packet, neighbors) \atop \leftarrow is\_packetType(packet, Ack|Advertise|keepAlive|Disconnect|Data) \tag{6}$$

The Data packet type is the only kind of packet that is transmitted in an end-to-end communication. This means that only data packets can be *forwarded* throughout the network:

$$wRule(perm, wnet, wDevice, forwarding, packet, \_) \atop \leftarrow is\_packetType(packet, Data) \tag{7}$$

On the other hand, data packets are only exchanged between the Network Manager (*wSink*) and wireless sensors (*wSensor*) in both sens. This means that a data packet is never send from a wireless sensor to another wireless sensor. Thus:

$$wRule(perm, wnet, wSensor, sending, packet, \_) \atop \leftarrow is\_packetType(packet, Data) \atop \wedge is\_dstNLAddr(packet, s2.addr) \wedge empower(wnet, s2, wSink) \tag{8}$$

and

$$wRule(perm, wnet, wSink, sending, packet, \_) \atop \leftarrow is\_packetType(packet, Data) \atop \wedge is\_dstNLAddr(packet, s2.addr) \wedge empower(wnet, s2, wSensor) \tag{9}$$

5.4   Communication Scheduling Rules

WirelessHART uses *Time Division Multiple Access* (TDMA) and *Channel hopping* to control the access to the wireless medium. The time is divided in consecutive periods of the same duration called *slots*. Each communication between two devices occurs in one slot of 10 ms.

Typically, two devices are assigned to one time slot (one as the sender and a second as the receiver). Only one packet is transmitted in one slot from the sender to the receiver which has to reply with an acknowledgment packet in the same slot.

In addition, WirelessHART uses channel hopping to provide frequency diversity and avoid interferences. Thus, the 2.4 GHz band is divided into 16 channels numbered from 11 to 26 which provide up to 15 communications in the same slot (Channel 26 is not used). Thus, we have the following rules:

$$wRule(perm, wnet, wDevice, sending, packets, startSlot \land assignedFq) \quad (10)$$

where *startSlot* is a wContext indicating that *s* performs action *sending* object *packet* when a slot time assigned to *s* starts:

$$Hold(WSN, s, sending, packet, startSlot) \\ \leftarrow is\_slotStartTime(s, packet) \quad (11)$$

and *assignedFq* is a wContext indicating that *s* uses its assigned frequency when performing action *sending* object *packet* :

$$Hold(WSN, s, sending, packet, assignedFq) \\ \leftarrow is\_assignedFq(s, packet) \quad (12)$$

For the acknowledgment, we have the following rule:

$$wRule(perm, wnet, wDevice, sending, packet, sendingAck) \quad (13)$$

where *sendingAck* is a wContext indicating that *s1* performs action *sending* object *packet'* when *s1* received *packet* from *s* (at time *t*), and *packet'* is destined to *s* and of type *ack* and *s1* uses the slot and frequency assigned to *s*:

$$Hold(WSN, s1, sending, packet', sendingAck) \\ \leftarrow packet\_received(s1, packet, t) \land is\_srcAddr(packet, s) \\ \land is\_packetType(packet', Ack) \land is\_dstAddr(packet', s) \\ \land is\_assignedFq(s, packet) \land is\_slotStartTime(s, packet) \quad (14)$$

We should note that the Network Manager is responsible of building, managing and updating slots and frequencies planning.

5.5   Packets Transmission Rules

Sensor nodes are configured to send different kind of packets (i.e., sensing data, keep-alive, advertisement) at a defined time. Thus, sensing data must be sent periodically to the Network Manager.

$$wRule(perm, wnet, wDevice, sending, packet, packetPeriodicity)$$
$$\leftarrow is\_packetType(packet, Data) \qquad (15)$$

where *packetPeriodicity* is a temporal context indicating that *s* performs action *sending* object *packet* in the planned sending time:

$$Hold(WSN, s, sending, packet, packetPeriodicity)$$
$$\leftarrow is\_packetPeriodicity(s, packet) \qquad (16)$$

5.6   Packets Forwarding Rules

A wirelessHART network has a meshed topology. Thus, wireless devices that are located several hops from the Network Manager, relay on their neighbors for forwarding their packets to their final destination.

$$wRule(perm, wnet, wDevice, forwarding, packet, ForwardPacket) \qquad (17)$$

where *ForwardPacket* is a provisional context (i.e., based on previous device actions) indicating that subject *s* received object *packet* (at time *t*) and *s* must forward this object:

$$Hold(WSN, s, forwarding, packet, ForwardPacket)$$
$$\leftarrow packet\_received(s, packet, t) \land is\_toBeForwarded(packet)$$
$$\land empower(org, s, forwarder) \qquad (18)$$

5.7   Routing Rules

WirelessHART uses graphs as routing method. A graph consists in a set of directed paths that connect network devices. It is build by the Network manager based on its knowledge of the network topology and connectivity. Every graph has a unique graph identifier that is inserted in the network packet header. Each device receiving this packet, forwards it to the next hop belonging to that graph.

$$wRule(perm, wnet, wDevice, sending, packets, graphNextHop) \qquad (19)$$

where *graphNextHop* is a spatial context indicating that *s* performs *sending* object *packet* to *s2* that is the next hop of *s* following graph *g*:

$$Hold(WSN, s, sending, packet, graphNextHop)$$
$$\leftarrow is\_dstAddr(packet, s2.addr) \land \qquad (20)$$
$$is\_usedGraph(packet, g) \land is\_NextHop(s.addr, g, s2.addr)$$

In graph routing there are two kinds of graphs: an *upstream* graph directed from all devices to the Network Manager and several *downstream* graphs directed from the Network Manager to each device. Thus, sensor nodes use the *upstream* graph for sending packets to the Network Manager:

$$wRule(perm, wnet, wSensor, sending, packet, \_)$$
$$\leftarrow is\_packetType(packet, Data) \qquad (21)$$
$$\wedge is\_usedGraph(packet, g) \wedge is\_upStream(g)$$

and the Network Manager uses *downstream* graphs for sending packets to sensors:

$$wRule(perm, wnet, wSink, sending, packet, \_)$$
$$\leftarrow is\_packetType(packet, Data) \qquad (22)$$
$$\wedge is\_usedGraph(packet, g) \wedge is\_downStream(g)$$

5.8   Cross Layer Consistency Rules

As indicated in Sect. 5.2, packet's fields must complain with the protocol specifications and also be consistent between them. This verification is done according to each layer rules. However, an attacker can bypass this verification giving contradictory information that fulfills each layer rules. Therefore, for some fields a cross layer verification must be applied. For example, in the case of routing information, DLL and NL fields must be consistent:

$$wRule(perm, wnet, wSensor, sending, packet, \_)$$
$$\leftarrow is\_dstAddr(packet, s1.addr) \wedge is\_dstNLAddr(packet, s2.addr) \qquad (23)$$
$$\wedge is\_usedGraph(packet, g) \wedge is\_NextHop(s1.addr, g, s2.addr)$$

6   wIDS Detection Rules

In order to detect malicious actions, wIDS apply a close policy requirement. This means that each action initiated by wireless nodes is compared to the defined security policy and a security alert is raised if the verification failed. Thus, all node's actions must:

1. be explicitly allowed by the security policy;
2. and is compliant with all rules that match the action.

Thus each IDS-agent implements Algorithm 1 in order to check the compliance of actions performed by wireless nodes.

Thus, each time a node s performs an action a on object o, we first build M the set of security rules that matches the tuple {s,a,o}. If the set M is empty this indicates that there is not a security rule that explicitly permits that s performs an action a on object o. Otherwise, the tuple {s,a,o} is compared towards each rule $m \in M$ to check if it is compliant with that rule (see Rule 2). If the tuple {s,a,o} is not compliant with a security rule m, it is considered as a malicious action and an intrusion rule is raised. Else, if the tuple {s,a,o} is compliant with all security rules $m \in M$, it is considered as a legitimate action.

Algorithm 1. Conformity checking algorithm

1: **procedure** ACTIONVALIDATION(s, a, o) ▷ subject s performs action a on o
2:     M=matchingRule(s,a,o);   ▷ Build M the set of rules matching s,a and o
3:     **if** M is empty **then**
4:         **return** $false$;   ▷ s is not permitted to perform action a on o
5:     **end if**
6:     $validAction \leftarrow$ true;
7:     **while** M is not empty $\wedge$ $validAction$ **do**   ▷ repeat until all rules are checked
8:         Select m from the set M;
9:         $M = M - \{m\}$;
10:        $validAction \leftarrow$ checkValidity(s,a,o,m);   ▷ checks if rule m allows that s
            performs a on o
11:    **end while**
12:    **return** $validAction$
13: **end procedure**

6.1   Default IDS Alert

We chose to model IDS alert as *wContexts*. This permits not only the accurate identification of the malicious action but also can allow an automatic reaction by for example the activation or deactivation of some security rules. It also allows the global coordination of alerts in the central-IDS.

To do that, we define *idsAlertCtx* a default context that is activated when an action performed by a wireless node violates a security rule defined in Sect. 5:

$$\forall s \in S, o \in O, a \in A,$$
$$Hold(wnet, s, a, o, idsAlertCtx) \leftarrow \qquad (24)$$
$$Action(s, a, o) \wedge \neg actionValidation(s, a, o)$$

where *Action(s,a,o)* indicates that subject s performed action a on object o and $\neg actionValidation(s, a, o)$ (See Algorithm 1) indicates that $Action(s, a, o)$ do not match any defined security rules.

6.2   Basic Malicious Action IDS Alert

In order to enforce wIDS detection capabilities, we define additional security rules that aim to detect basic actions that an attacker can perform such as intercepting, deleting, modifying, forging or delaying packets.

1. *Packets and fields specification:* According to the communication protocol used by the WSN, exchanged packets must follows some rules in terms of packets size and fields value. Indeed, a malicious node can inject into the network malformed packets in order to lead receiving nodes to unstable state.

$$Hold(wnet, s, sending, packet, not\_valid\_packet)$$
$$\leftarrow \neg is\_ValidPacket(packet) \qquad (25)$$

2. *Forging a fake packet:* In this attack, the subject s forwards a packet o however the context *forwardingPacket* is not active. This means that the packet o is a packet forged by s that pretends forwarding a received packet.

$$Hold(wnet, s, a, o, forged\_packet) \leftarrow$$
$$empower(wnet, s, wForwarder) \wedge consider(wnet, a, sending)$$
$$\wedge use(wnet, o, packets)$$
$$\wedge \neg hold(s, a, o, forwardPacket)$$
(26)

3. *Delaying a packet:* In this attack, the subject s forwards a received packet o after that the maximum forwarding time has expired.

$$Hold(wnet, s, a, o, delayed\_packet) \leftarrow$$
$$empower(wnet, s, wForwarder)$$
$$\wedge consider(wnet, a, sending) \wedge use(wnet, o, packets)$$
$$\wedge packet\_received(s, o, t) \wedge packet\_sent(s, o', t')$$
$$\wedge is\_forwadedVersion(o, o')$$
$$\wedge hold(wnet, s, a, o, ForwardPacket) \wedge (t + \delta) < t'$$
(27)

where δ represents the maximal time a packet must be forwarded within since it is received.

4. *Deleting a packet:* In this attack, the subject s does not forward a received packet o within the defined time δ'.

$$Hold(wnet, s, a, o, deleting\_packet) \leftarrow$$
$$empower(wnet, s, wForwarder)$$
$$\wedge consider(wnet, a, sending) \wedge use(wnet, o, packets)$$
$$\wedge packet\_received(s, o, t) \wedge \neg packet\_sent(s, o, t')$$
$$\wedge is\_forwadedVersion(o, o')$$
$$\wedge hold(s, a, o, ForwardPacket) \wedge (t' < t + \delta')$$
(28)

Thus, a packet is considered as deleted if it has not been forwarded within the time δ' (with $\delta < \delta'$). Between δ and δ' a packet not forwarded is considered as delayed.

5. *Modifying a packet:* In this attack, the subject s forwards a modified version of a received packet o that does not complain with the used communication protocol.

$$Hold(wnet, s, a, o, modified\_packet) \leftarrow$$
$$empower(wnet, s, forwarder) \wedge consider(wnet, a, sending)$$
$$\wedge use(wnet, o, packets)$$
$$\wedge packet\_received(s, o, t) \wedge packet\_sent(s, o', t')$$
$$\wedge is\_forwadedVersion(o, o')$$
$$\wedge hold(wnet, s, a, o, forwardPacket) \wedge is\_ValidPacket(o')$$
(29)

7 Implementation and Evaluations

7.1 Implementation

To evaluate wIDS performances, we use WirelessHART NetSIM [15], a WirelessHART SCADA-based systems simulator. The simulated network is composed of a network manager and 9 wireless sensors. We implement IDS-agents into 3 of them and launched randomly attacks.

7.2 WSN Attacks Implementation

We test the proposed wIDS towards the following well-known attacks on WSN [16]:

- Jamming attack: A malicious node disturbs transmissions of nearby nodes by emitting packets periodically or continuously.
- Denial of Service (DoS) attack: A malicious node overwhelms the targeted node by sending a great amount of packets that will not be able to receive legitimate packets.
- Sinkhole and blackhole attacks: A malicious node misleads routing algorithm by transmitting false information to the base station. Consequently, a part of the traffic will be redirected to the malicious node which can drop the packets partially (wormhole) or totally (blackhole).
- Hello Flood attack: A malicious node with a large transmission range can flood a large part of the network with this kind of packets. Nodes receiving these packets, will assume that the malicious node is in their transmission range and exhaust their battery life by trying to communicate with it.
- Selective forwarding attack: A malicious node chooses selectively to drop some packets and to not forward them to their final destination.
- Forced delay attack: A malicious node delays the forwarding of some packets which can have harmful consequences in WISN where processes are time sensitive.

Furthermore, we test it towards 2 attacks targeting wirelessHART networks:

- Sybil attack [17]: In this attack, a malicious insider node forges a fake *Disconnect* packet (Used by nodes to inform their neighbors that they are leaving the network), puts the targeted node as the packet source address and then authenticates it using the *Network Key* (Shared by all legitimate nodes). As results, receiving nodes erase the target node from their communication planning.
- Broadcast attacks [18]: In this attack, a malicious insider node uses its knowledge of the *Broadcast Session* (A Key used to encipher end-to-end packets broadcasted by the Network Manager to all nodes) for injecting into false commands. This attack is more harmful than the previous one as the attacker pretends to be the Network Manager and can change nodes configuration parameters.

7.3 Experimental Results

As indicated in Table 1, wIDS detects all tested well-known attacks. Each of these attacks, is not compliant with one or several security rules.

Performed tests report 100% correct identification of malicious actions and less than 2% of false positives. Depending on which security rule is violated, false positives is about 0% for sybil or broadcast attacks and about 5% for jamming, DoS or forced delay attacks. Indeed, first cited attacks are composed of actions that are clearly identified as malicious while the second cited attacks can be assimilated to transitory transmission perturbations such as interferences. This rate may be reduced by the use of a threshold.

Table 1. Well-known attacks detection

Attacks	Detection rules
Jamming	Rule (5), Rule (10), Rule (15)
Denial of Service (DoS)	Rule (10), Rule (15)
Sinkhole and blackhole	Rule (3)
Selective forwarding	Rule (17)
Hello Flood	Rule (3)
Forced delay	Rule (17)
Sybil	Rule (3)
Broadcast	Rule (17), Rule (22), Rule (23)

7.4 Discussion

Previous results confirm the correctness of wIDS conception. They show that the normal behavior of wireless nodes can be modelized. As expected, the detection rate is 100% and depends highly of the accuracy of node normal behavior. By combining local and central detection, wIDS can be applied to networks of several sizes both in terms of nodes number and geographical area. Indeed, IDS-agents have the capabilities to detect basic malicious actions without any cooperation between them.

Also, by focusing on the detection of basic malicious actions, wIDS is able to detect known attacks as well as unknown ones and this without requiring any training phase.

8   Conclusion and Future Works

In this paper, we present wIDS an efficient intrusion detection system specially designed for enforcing wireless-based SCADA systems. It builds the normal behavior model of wireless nodes on the base of used protocol specification. Conducted tests confirm that wIDS is able to detect a large number of attacks with a low false-positive rate. These performances rely mainly on the quality of the nodes normal behavior model that depends on expert knowledges.

On the other hand, as tests were conducted in a simulated environments, some physical phenomenons were not considered. Indeed, WISN are expected to be deployed in industrial harsh environment characterized by wide temperature range, vibrations, reflections due to metallic structures, etc. Such an environment can impact communication reliability which can increase the false-positive rate.

References

1. Huitsing, P., Chandia, R., Papa, M., Shenoi, S.: Attack taxonomies for the modbus protocols. IJCIP **1**, 37–44 (2008)
2. Fovino, I.N., Carcano, A., Murel, T.D.L., Trombetta, A., Masera, M.: Modbus/dnp3 state-based intrusion detection system. In: 24th IEEE International Conference on Advanced Information Networking and Applications, AINA, Australia, pp. 729–736. IEEE Computer Society (2010)
3. Mitchell, R., Chen, I.: A survey of intrusion detection techniques for cyber-physical systems. ACM Comput. Surv. **46**(4), 55:1–55:29 (2013)
4. Mitchell, R., Chen, I.: A survey of intrusion detection in wireless network applications. Comput. Commun. **42**, 1–23 (2014)
5. Silva, A.P.R.D., Martins, M.H.T., Rocha, B.P.S., Loureiro, A.A.F., Ruiz, L.B., Wong, H.C.: Decentralized intrusion detection in wireless sensor networks. In: Boukerche, A., de Araujo, R.B. (eds.) Q2SWinet 2005 - Proceedings of the First ACM Workshop on Q2S and Security for Wireless and Mobile Networks, Montreal, Quebec, Canada, 13 October 2005, pp. 16–23. ACM (2005)
6. Roosta, T., Nilsson, D.K., Lindqvist, U., Valdes, A.: An intrusion detection system for wireless process control systems. In: IEEE 5th International Conference on Mobile Adhoc and Sensor Systems, MASS, USA, pp. 866–872. IEEE (2008)
7. Coppolino, L., D'Antonio, S., Romano, L., Spagnuolo, G.: An intrusion detection system for critical information infrastructures using wireless sensor network technologies. In: 2010 5th International Conference on Critical Infrastructure (CRIS), pp. 1–8, September 2010
8. Shin, S., Kwon, T., Jo, G.Y., Park, Y., Rhy, H.: An experimental study of hierarchical intrusion detection for wireless industrial sensor networks. IEEE Trans. Ind. Inform. **6**(4), 744–757 (2010)
9. HART Communication Foundation: WirelessHART. http://www.hartcomm.org
10. Deji, C., Mark, N., Aloysius, M.: WirelessHART^{TM}: Real-Time Mesh Network for Industrial Automation. Springer, New York (2010). https://doi.org/10.1007/978-1-4419-6047-4
11. Kalam, A.A.E., Baida, R.E., Balbiani, P., Benferhat, S., Cuppens, F., Deswarte, Y., Miege, A., Saurel, C., Trouessin, G.: Organization based access control. In: IEEE 4th International Workshop on Policies for Distributed Systems and Networks, Proceedings, POLICY 2003, pp. 120–131, June 2003
12. Cuppens, F., Cuppens-Boulahia, N., Sans, T., Miège, A.: A formal approach to specify and deploy a network security policy. In: Dimitrakos, T., Martinelli, F. (eds.) Formal Aspects in Security and Trust. IIFIP, vol. 173, pp. 203–218. Springer, Boston (2005). https://doi.org/10.1007/0-387-24098-5_15
13. Debar, H., Thomas, Y., Cuppens, F., Cuppens-Boulahia, N.: Enabling automated threat response through the use of a dynamic security policy. J. Comput. Virol. **3**(3), 195–210 (2007)

14. Bayou, L., Cuppens-Boulahia, N., Espes, D., Cuppens, F.: Towards a CDS-based intrusion detection deployment scheme for securing industrial wireless sensor networks. In: 11th International Conference on Availability, Reliability and Security, ARES 2016, Salzburg, Austria, 31 August–2 September 2016, pp. 157–166. IEEE Computer Society (2016)

15. Bayou, L., Espes, D., Cuppens-Boulahia, N., Cuppens, F.: WirelessHART NetSIM: a WirelessHART SCADA-based wireless sensor networks simulator. In: Bécue, A., Cuppens-Boulahia, N., Cuppens, F., Katsikas, S., Lambrinoudakis, C. (eds.) CyberICS/WOS-CPS -2015. LNCS, vol. 9588, pp. 63–78. Springer, Cham (2016). https://doi.org/10.1007/978-3-319-40385-4_5

16. Karlof, C., Wagner, D.: Secure routing in wireless sensor networks: attacks and countermeasures. Ad Hoc Netw. **1**(2–3), 293–315 (2003)

17. Bayou, L., Espes, D., Cuppens-Boulahia, N., Cuppens, F.: Security issue of WirelessHART based SCADA systems. In: Lambrinoudakis, C., Gabillon, A. (eds.) CRiSIS 2015. LNCS, vol. 9572, pp. 225–241. Springer, Cham (2016). https://doi.org/10.1007/978-3-319-31811-0_14

18. Bayou, L., Espes, D., Cuppens-Boulahia, N., Cuppens, F.: Security analysis of WirelessHART communication scheme. In: Cuppens, F., Wang, L., Cuppens-Boulahia, N., Tawbi, N., Garcia-Alfaro, J. (eds.) FPS 2016. LNCS, vol. 10128, pp. 223–238. Springer, Cham (2017). https://doi.org/10.1007/978-3-319-51966-1_15

Dark Domain Name Attack: A New Threat to Domain Name System

Bold Munkhbaatar$^{(\boxtimes)}$, Mamoru Mimura, and Hidema Tanaka

National Defence Academy of Japan, Yokosuka, Japan
{em56038,mim,hidema}@nda.ac.jp

Abstract. There are many domain names which are registered to DNS but unused. We define them as "dark domain name". We show that these dark domain names have serious threat to DNS operating. From our experiments, we found that when query for dark domain names are done, the response time becomes unusually long and huge load is given for retrieval operation in DNS servers. As the result, cashing DNS server, root name server and Authoritative DNS server fall into DoS situation simultaneously, communication receives obstacles intentionally. We discuss the influence of our proposed attack and countermeasure. As the result, we face some dilemmas.

Keywords: Domain Name System · Dark domain name
Denial of Service

1 Introduction

Domain Name System (DNS) is a fundamental system of the Internet [7]. Its function is to solve the associations between domain name and IP address. DNS has a hierarchical structure called domain tree. In general, domain name is presented as a dot-separated string, where each string is called node and the position of node represents its level in the domain tree. The reliability of the connection of the Internet is dependent on DNS. When the answer of DNS is wrong, it can never be connected to requested domain name. And when DNS can not operate normally, many problems occur to connections, and service will become impossible (DoS situation). Therefore DNS tends to be made the attack target. Following attack methods are known.

- DNS cache poisoning attack [6]
- DNS exploit/protocol anomaly [12]

These attacks uses vulnerability of DNS mechanism to generate malicious replies and high technical ability is necessary for attack execution. As the countermeasure, DNSSEC which has cryptographic security is provided [2]. In another way, there are some methods which uses huge deal of communication to DNS. These method is based not on the vulnerability of program but on the weakness of DNS operating or TCP/IP protocols.

© Springer International Publishing AG 2017
R. K. Shyamasundar et al. (Eds.): ICISS 2017, LNCS 10717, pp. 405–414, 2017.
https://doi.org/10.1007/978-3-319-72598-7_25

– DNS amplifier attack [1]
– DNS reflections [4]
– TCP/UDP/ICMP flood to DNS [9]

These attacks uses only communications and do not request high technical ability. Therefore even if beginners can realize serious harmful results easily, they are the big problem which continues from early 1990s.

In our research, domain names that are registered but not used are called "dark domain names". In this paper, we introduce dark domain name attack which has serious effectiveness but easy to execute by even if beginner attackers. We analyze its mechanism using local experimental DNS environment, and show that it is possible to improve the attack effectiveness only by changing the setting of resolver. Our experimental result shows that the response time for normal domain name in about 0.74 s but for dark domain name becomes about 10.88 s. This result shows that it is more effectively giving load to DNS than the existing attack methods. And we discuss the reason that dark domain name is generated. As the results, registration of the domain name which is not used by trademark owners also defends the security for general users as well as a right of trademark owners, but we found the dilemma which causes an attack.

2 DNS Structure

Domain name system (DNS) is a basic system for communication in the Internet [7]. DNS has a hierarchical naming system and associates various information with domain names assigned to each of the participating organizations. Caching DNS servers are operated in each organization or personal, and they store DNS query results for a period time. They reduce DNS query traffic across the Internet, communication request for the root name server and Authoritative DNS server.

Top level domain (TLD) is the highest level in the hierarchical system. They have the information of root zone of name space which is the last label of fully qualified domain name (FQDN). Second level domain (SLD) is below TLD, refers to the organization that registered the domain name. TLD and SLD are managed according to the situation of each country. Authoritative DNS server answers IP addresses asked about names in a zone. This server is the mechanism of substantial DNS. The answers of Authoritative DNS server are stored in caching DNS server as shown above. They are assigned on per-domain base and managed by web hosts. The Internet communication is based on correctness of answers from DNS. Therefore the reliability of operation of DNS is the most important factor in the Internet.

3 Problems of Domain Names

Many problems about domain names are known to public, and especially "The Trademark Dilemma" is famous one [10]. It becomes big problem since late 1990s that the use of trademarks as domain names without the agreement of trademark owner. This problem is also known as "Domain name dispute problem" [11], and "Uniform Domain Name Dispute Resolution Policy (UDRP)" [5] is established by the Internet Corporation for Assigned Names and Numbers (ICANN). There are following damages for trademark owners by this problem.

- Usages which damage an image of the trademark
- Opening cheat site
- Too expensive dealing of specific domain name

To handle this problem, trademark owners register combinations of considerable domain names as much as possible beforehand. And trademark owners use only one domain name which has most effective advertisement and others are unused. As the result, it is possible to stop problems described above, but huge number of domain names which are not used forever are registered. This paper defined such domain names as "dark domain names".

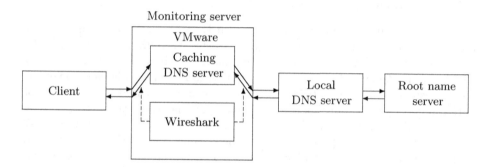

Fig. 1. Experiment environment

4   Dark Domain Name Attack

4.1   Experiment Environment

Figure 1 shows our experiment environment. We regard caching DNS server in this figure as monitoring server. This caching DNS server is set on VMware [13], and its upstream DNS is our local DNS server. We analyze the communication from to caching DNS server by using Wireshark [15]. The upstream of our local DNS server is connect to the root name server directly. Therefore we can regard response time between sending query and receiving answer at client side, as processing time of DNS approximately.

We need huge number of valid domain names for experiments. Therefore we get a list from "Hacker news" site [3]. The list contains 26,068,477 of domain names (file size is 563 MB).

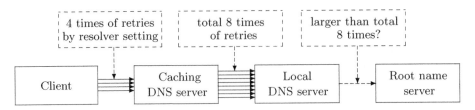

Fig. 2. Communication situation for query of dark domain names

Table 1. Load averages for normal and dark domain names

	CPU (%)	Memory (%)
Normal domain name	3.795	0.466
Dark domain name	13.372	0.229

4.2 Experiments

To analyze the difference in the processing in DNS of normal and dark domain names, we checked domain names in the list using WHOIS [14]. As the results, we pick up each different 100 of normal and dark domain names for experiments. The experiment method measures the response time and calculates the average. As the results, we get about 0.74 s for normal domain name and about 10.88 s for dark domain name. From this result, we can find that retrieval of dark domain names is in abnormal situation from the specification of UDP protocol. We analyzed the communication situation in client using Wireshark. Then we found that DNS queries for dark domain names did Timeout after about 2.0 s and total four times of retries were done. In the same way, we analyzed the communication situation of cashing DNS server on monitoring server. Then we also found that queries from cashing DNS server did Timeout and total two times of retries for each queries were done (total eight times of retries). Figure 2 shows this communication situation. The number of retries by Timeout is depend on each OS settings, it is possible to make the amplifier effect using such mechanism by changing the settings, and give a load the root name server and following servers.

And we measured load average of CPU and memory in caching DNS server. Table 1 shows the results. From this table, we can find that retrieval for normal domain name is less time consuming and load average of CPU is small. And, since the search results are stored in the cache, load average of memory becomes large. On the other hand, the retrieval for dark domain name takes long time consuming and load average of CPU becomes quite large. But, since the search results are nothing, these results are never stored and the load average of memory is small. In addition, we measured same experiment using same normal and dark domain names for 100 times of retrievals. Then we obtained average of about 0.11 s for normal domain name and one of about 10.25 s for dark domain name. Therefore we can confirm that the retrieval results for dark domain names are not stored in caching DNS server, even if many times of search for same name are done. And we can confirm that similar CPU load average are given to root name server and following servers by querying dark domain names.

We can conclude followings for in retrieval of dark domain name.

Since no retrieval result is cached, using only one dark domain name is enough for successful attack.
Since dark domain names are valid, it is difficult to detect queries for them as malicious acts.

Retry by timeout generates amplifier effect.
This characteristic shows that the attack using dark domain names also exhausts bandwidth of communication lines. The local communication traffic is made heavy by this attack, and a typical DoS attack can also be carried out. While our experiments, such local DoS situation were occurred frequently, and we received some complaints.

Since there is no IP address for dark domain name, the load average of CPU for retrieval becomes maximum.
Unfortunately, we could not analyze the root name server, TLD and SLD, this is our expectation. However, the experimental results shown above, can derive this conclusion. Multiple queries for same dark domain name by botnet will be the real threat.

From these facts, we can conclude that the attack against DNS using dark domain names gives attackers absolutely advantageous position.

4.3   Attack Procedure

The procedure of our proposed dark domain name attack is very easy.

Step-1: Select the target dark domain name.
Step-2: Examine DNS query of the target dark domain name.
Step-3: Repeat Step-2 before (Timeout) × (number of retries) [s].

In Step-1, it is necessary to look for the target dark domain name which is recorded in Authoritative DNS server which attacker chooses as the target. It will be easy to obtain by using a list shown in Sect. 4.1. As already described above, only one target dark domain name is enough for attack. If an attacker wants to exhaust any DNS itself, any dark domain name is possible to use.

In Step-2 and Step-3, it is too easy procedures to explain. Any program development is not necessary, so even a beginner attacker can execute this attack method. If a beginner has techniques or knowledge of shell script, he/she will become strong attacker immediately. Following command is an example execution.

$$\$watch \ \text{-n} \ T \ \text{nslookup} \ darkdomainname \tag{1}$$

$$T = (\text{timeout}) \ \times \ (\text{number of retries}) \ [\text{s}] \tag{2}$$

Needless to point out, when attacker uses botnet, DNS falls into the hell state. Obviously, our dark domain name attack does not need open resolvers because the queries are valid and random sub-domain names is not necessary. Therefore the detection of our attack will be difficult and hard to stop beforehand.

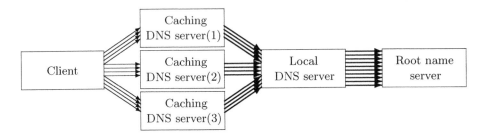

Fig. 3. Outline of amplification using resolver settings in client

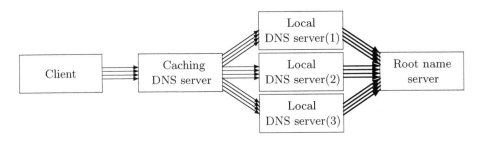

Fig. 4. Outline of amplification using resolver settings in caching DNS server

5   Improvement of Effectiveness of Attack

The effectiveness of dark domain name attack is decided by the following elements.

(E-1) Specification of each DNS servers
(E-2) Communication environment (e.g. TTL, bandwidth)
(E-3) Setting of resolver

For E-1, the higher specification server has, the more higher defensive against the attack. Since it is a given condition to the attacker, it is not possible for him/her to change them for worse situation (convenient for attack). E-2 is also a given condition to the attacker. Since the attack can improve by the setting of Timeout against E-2, it relates to following element E-3. In E-3, resolver is a mandatory program to connect to the Internet, and it is necessary to use DNS. Therefore, all client and servers in the Internet, have each resolver.

This resolver has following parameters which relate to dark domain name attack in particular.

(1) Timeout
(2) Number of retries
(3) List of upstream DNS servers

As already described above, (1) Timeout relates to E-2. It is important to decide the value of T in Eq. (2). If interval time of repeating DNS query is shorter than T, it will be detected as abnormal situation by monitoring system (Note that since query for dark domain names are valid retrievals, the possibility that they are decided as malicious will be low). On the other hand, if the interval is longer than T, it is impossible to give search loads to DNS effectively. It is obvious that (2) Number of retries should be set large value as possible. Table 2 shows some default settings of resolver. Note that we could not confirm the value of Timeout of CentOS. In (3) List of upstream DNS servers, two upstream servers are set as default (primary and secondary), however, many number of upstream DNS servers can be set. Since resolver makes communications with servers in general, number of communications increases following the list.

For example, in the case of client setting with "retry $= 4$" and "number of listed upstream DNS servers $= 3$", the outline of load for DNS is shown in Fig. 3. And as described above, all servers also has each resolver. For example, the case when caching DNS server has the same setting as above client is shown in Fig. 4. In this way, we can conclude that the setting of resolver can have influence on effectiveness of dark domain name attack. And we can also conclude that change in the setting of resolver is serious security risk. Since the setting of resolver is also quite important in countermeasure against DNS amplifier attacks, we can conclude that the importance of existence countermeasure becomes more serious.

Table 2. Default setting of resolvers (limited to OSs we used in the experiments)

OS	Timeout (sec)	Retry (times)
Windows 7 Pro (build 7601)	2.0	2
Windows 8.1 Pro (build 9600)	2.0	4
Windows 10 Home (build 14393)	2.0	4
CentOS 6.5 (build 201311272149)	?	4

6 New Threat and Dilemma

6.1 New Attack Infrastructure

Dark domain name attack needs valid domain names which are registered but unused. It is not so difficult work to find out such dark domain names, but if attackers use a specific one frequently, there will be a possibility to detect attack. Therefore existing of many choice of dark domain names is desirable for attackers. However it is easy to make many such available dark domain names because it is not illegal action to register domain names which is not used. As the result, we can conclude that it is possible to use this operation for preparation dark domain names to attack the specific Authoritative DNS servers. It is sometimes free in registration of domain names, so it is also very convenient for attackers. This is a new threat scenario.

In the attack using botnet, when all malicious client sends different dark domain names as query, it will be difficult to detect and become serious attack. On the other hand, when all malicious client sends same dark domain name, it will be easy to detect but the problem of registration of domain names which are not used, will be open to public. In particular, major trademark owners who have many dark domain names will be blamed, because the cause which permits this attack is made. This is also new threat scenario for trademark owners.

Thus attackers may prepare dark domain names and aim at general-purpose attack scenario and may attack targeted for specific trademark owners using existence dark domain names. We can conclude that today is in the situation favorable to attackers using dark domain names overwhelmingly.

6.2   Right of Trademark Owner or Security

The easy way to solve the threat mentioned above may be to prohibit registration of dark domain names. However it makes trademark owners give up their right. And it will be the result which permits damage to trademark owners described in Sect. 3. It is also the situation favorable to attackers by the different meaning. On the other hand, the serious threat which damages brand image exists as mentioned above even if a right of trademark owners are defended like today.

Whichever way is chosen, the choices of attack scenarios will not be reduced. We can see that DNS and registration of domain names itself has vulnerability. Therefore it is not problem for defense of right of trademark owners or security, it is a problem of DNS mechanism and operations. We consider that it is not technical problem.

6.3   Quality of Service or Security

The easy way to improve of DNS is to make a list of dark domain names. Before executing retrieval of domain names, each server checks the list and stores the result in the cash, we will be able to stop the attack. Such double-check of domain names will improve the security of DNS, however, the cost of DNS operations will become double. Therefore QoS will be reduced. Obviously it will be not a big problem by development of the performance of the computer and the communication environment, however, the cost necessary to DNS infrastructure becomes large certainly.

We consider this double-check scheme as a realistic countermeasure. However, there may be a possibility that a different problem will occur, the detailed analysis and development is our future work.

6.4 Summary of Dilemma

Dark domain name attack shows following dilemmas.

– The mechanism of DNS is in the situation favorable to attackers. The operation to stop this situation will damage the right of valid users in particular trademark owners.
– The protection of right of trademark owners will permit to make the easy situation for attackers, and consequently it will make themselves victims.
– Dark domain names are something troubles for many general users, and they should pay cost for countermeasures. However, since connection to doubtful site is protected by dark domain names, they are also countermeasure and contribute to secure communication.

Dark domain name is not pure evil for the Internet, but on the other hand, the strong attack methods are involved. Even if dark domain name is prohibited, different problems occur and they will be more serious. On the other hand, the usage of IoT is expanding, so dark domain name attack will be more serious problem because the number of clients which need DNS query increases exponentially. We can conclude that the solution of these dilemmas is difficult but threats based on them become serious.

7   Conclusion

The dark domain names is a security countermeasure for trademark owners but also is a countermeasure for general users to stop misleading to illegal or cheat sites. However we found that these dark domain names are useful for attacking DNS and its effectiveness is serious. We discuss threat scenarios by dark domain name attack and analyze influence to DNS mechanism. As the results, we conclude that there are some dilemmas in this attack scenario, and we can find out no effective solution. Our conclusion is that DNS itself is a fundamental mechanism for attack and a new countermeasure will cause a new threat certainly. The Internet usages such as IoT increase greatly, the importance of DNS also rises. We can conclude that the advantage of dark domain name attack will become more serious.

Acknowledgment. This work was supported by JSPS KAKENHI Grant Number 17K06455.

References

1. Anagnostopoulos, M., Kambourakis, G., Kopanos, P., Louloudakis, G., Gritzalis, S.: DNS amplification attack revisited. Comput. Secur. **39**(Part B), 475–485 (2013)
2. Eastlake, D.: Domain Name System Security Extensions, Request for Comments 2535. Internet Engineering Task Force, March 1999
3. Hacker News. https://news.ycombinator.com/
4. Huang, C., Holt, N., Wang, Y.A., Greenberg, A., Li, J., Ross, K.W.: A DNS reflection method for global traffic management. In: USENIXATC 2010 Proceedings of the 2010 USENIX Conference on USENIX Annual Technical Conference, pp. 1–6, June 2010
5. ICANN: Uniform Domain Name Dispute Resolution Policy. https://www.icann.org/resources/pages/help/dndr/udrp-en. Accessed 20 July 2017
6. Kaminsky, D.: Black ops 2008-it's the end of the cache as we know it. In: Presented at BlackHat2008, August 2008
7. Mockapetris, P.: Domain Names - Concepts and Facilities, Request for Comments 1034. Internet Engineering Task Force, November 1987
8. NANOG63 Meeting Presentation, DNS Track, Pseudo Random DNS Query Attacks & Resolver Mitigation Approaches, Moderators D.Wessels (VeriSign), February 2015. https://www.nanog.org/sites/default/files/nanog63-dnstrack-winstead-attacks.pdf. Accessed 20 July 2017
9. Narayan, A., Kumar, U.: A defence mechanism: DNS based DDoS attack. Int. J. Comput. Trends Technol. (IJCTT) **33**(1), 1–8 (2016)
10. National Telecommunications and Information Administration: Statement of Policy on the Management of Internet Names and Addresses, Docket Number: 980212036–8146-02, December 2014
11. National Telecommunications and Information Administration: United States Department of Commerce, Management of Internet Names and Addresses, Docket Number: 980212036–8146-02, February 2015
12. Satam, P., Alipour, H., Al-Nashif, Y., Hariri, S.: Anomaly behavior analysis of DNS protocol. J. Int. Serv. Inf. Secur. (JISIS) **5**(4), 85–97 (2015)
13. VMware Infrastructure Architecture Overview. https://www.vmware.com/
14. WHOIS. https://who.is/
15. Wireshark. https://www.wireshark.org/

Author Index

Printed in the United States
By Bookmasters